THE FORMATION OF HELL

The
FORMATION OF
HELL

Death and Retribution in the Ancient and Early Christian Worlds

ALAN E. BERNSTEIN

CORNELL UNIVERSITY PRESS   ITHACA & LONDON

First published 1993 by Cornell University Press.
First printing, Cornell Paperbacks, 1996.

Library of Congress Cataloging-in-Publication Data

Bernstein, Alan E.
    The formation of hell : death and retribution in the ancient and early
Christian worlds / Alan E. Bernstein.
        p.   cm.
    Includes bibliographical references and index.
    ISBN 0-8014-2893-9 (cloth). — ISBN 0-8014-8131-7 (paper)
    1. Hell—Christianity—History of doctrines—Early church, ca. 30–600.
2. Hell—Comparative studies.   3. Hell—Biblical teaching.
4. Rome—Religion.   5. Judaism—Doctrines—History.   I. Title.
BT836.2.B47   1993
291.2′3—dc20   93-8308

Printed in the United States of America

⊗The paper in this book meets the minimum requirements of the
American National Standard for Information Sciences—Permanence of
Paper for Printed Library Materials, ANSI Z39.48-1984.

For JoAnne

Contents

Preface

Everyone, it seems, has a firm position on hell. Scoffers dismiss it contemptuously as a transparent scare tactic. Others, more moderate, construe it broadly as a symbol of turmoil, despair, or alienation. Yet whether one denies it altogether or interprets it figuratively as an aspect of human psychology, the classic hell of fire and brimstone, outer darkness, weeping and gnashing of teeth maintains a definite presence. The literal hell, too, has many defenders. How did this fearful idea achieve its hold on people? This book explores that question without prior judgment as to hell's existence, its nature, or its value. My goal is neither an attack nor a defense but a history of hell.

Comprehending the rise of hell entails investigating the historical experience and ethical debates recorded in the ancient sources of Egypt, Mesopotamia, Israel, Greece, Rome, and the early Christian community. These peoples shaped the idea of hell as they asserted and denied, accepted and rejected their own and each others' answers to questions concerning death and the dead, justice and evil. This volume, therefore, considers three societies in turn: Greco-Roman antiquity, ancient Judaism, and early Christianity. Parts I and II argue that the cultural traditions of Greco-Roman and Jewish antiquity each display, though largely independently, a tension between two fundamentally different views: neutral death and moral death. In the first, all the dead live on without any distinction between the good and the wicked. In the second, the good are rewarded and the wicked punished. The last two parts of the book treat the early centuries of Christianity. They show how the authors of the New Testament (Part III) and of the church's first centuries (Part IV) developed their particular messages in some measure by choosing between options that these other peoples offered.

Of all the debates that preceded the articulation of a concept of hell and helped to bring it forth, the one that proved most relevant concerns the fate of the wicked dead. What happens to the wicked who die at the height of their wealth and power? Do they ever receive their just deserts? Do they get away with murder? Asserting a measure of justice for those who appear to escape into death, suffering no consequences for an evil life, involves many assumptions about providence and postmortem retribution, implying an order in the universe which corrects the apparent excess of evil.

Focusing on the fate of the wicked dead may seem to detract from the positive message of religion. Yet this approach offers the advantage of a fresh perspective, which, by putting the familiar in a new light, allows greater understanding. The very proclamation of hell indicates that the defenders of religion found it necessary to balance the attraction of its promise with a threat for the "others," who rejected it or failed to meet its tests. This history examines their predictions of the consequences for not measuring up.

A history that seeks to explain how the concept of hell arose can follow no straight line. Though they developed simultaneously, the Greco-Roman and the Jewish cultural traditions were mostly independent. They therefore receive separate chronological treatments here. Further, although written texts constitute the main evidence available, it is the ideas that lie behind and frequently antedate the texts that are the real object of this investigation. For that reason I have given priority to understanding an individual text and the related passages that clarify it, whenever they may have been written, rather than proceeding in strict chronological order. Thus, some parts of the book proceed topically and others chronologically. Chronological order is preferable when possible, but not at the expense of clarity.

These chapters began as an introductory *section* of a single volume on the history of hell in the Middle Ages. Since my training is in the field of medieval history, I never intended to write an independent study of hell in antiquity. Nonetheless, one cannot work on a later period without appreciating its debts to the previous one. That observation applies particularly to a religious subject in the Middle Ages, because medieval authors persistently refer to biblical authority and repeatedly draw on the church fathers, writers of roughly the first four Christian centuries, who themselves accepted and rejected pagan mythology and philosophy only selectively. As I pursued this background material, there came a time when, like a pilot passing a point of no return, I found myself enmeshed in a quantity, richness, and variety of material I could not escape. In order to establish my bearings or, so to say, define my terms, I have unabashedly followed my fascination with these sources to assess the various options from which the tradition's founders chose. As a result, this has become the first installment of a multivolume work on the history of hell from the Bible to Dante.

The academic fields of Classics, Hebrew Bible, New Testament, and Patristics each have specialists of their own, capable of shading or correcting my interpretations. Conscious of these differences in training, I have sought to ground my judgments on close readings of carefully selected texts. Thus I have tried to make my conclusions verifiable and at the same time accessible to a general audience. In principle I have examined every major, extended discussion of what happens to the dead and particularly to the wicked dead within the temporal and geographic limits already mentioned. Naturally, some will spot material I have omitted. My hope is, however, that other texts, had they been treated, would not alter the overall picture.

This book could not have been written without the encouragement of many individuals and institutions. For financial support and the leisure it provides, I wish to thank the Spencer Foundation for a seed money grant, the University of Arizona for a research fellowship under the auspices of the Social and Behavioral Sciences Research Institute, the John Simon Guggenheim Memorial Foundation, and the Institute for Advanced Study, Princeton, New Jersey.

Many individuals over many years have counseled me on all or part of this project. Robert Ackerman, JoAnne Bernstein, Tom Heffernan, Beth Lewis, and Jeffrey Burton Russell have read earlier versions of this work in what was then its entirety. Their reassurance and criticism (only partially answered here) have proved invaluable. Similarly I have benefited from comments made by Glen Bowersock, Dwayne Carpenter, and Elaine Pagels on parts of an earlier draft. Paul Oskar Kristeller helped me with the etymologies of crucial Greek terms. Elizabeth A. R. Brown, Caroline Bynum, Stephan Kuttner, Jacques Le Goff, Hilary Martin, Laurent Mayali, and the late Donald J. Wilcox encouraged me when the project looked a long way from done. Helen Nader gave me key advice at a crucial time. I have been fortunate to have had the help of two research assistants, graduate students at the University of Arizona. My heartfelt thanks go to Andrew Gow and Kathryn Larch for their resourcefulness and dedication. I also thank copy editor Judith Bailey, whose diligence was a stimulus to improvement, and Celeste Newbrough, who made the index with much-appreciated involvement and dexterity.

I particularly wish to acknowledge the encouragement so freely given by JoAnne Bernstein, an unfailing source of insights and suggestions; Dene Bernstein, whose interest in the project heartened me; Beverly Parker, for friendly enthusiasm; Donald Weinstein, Heiko A. Oberman, Richard Eaton, and Jonathan Beck, whose friendship and collegial encouragement sustained me through many dark hours; and Zak Bernstein, who also has a long-term dream.

Alan E. Bernstein

Tucson, Arizona

Note on Translations

Unless otherwise noted, translations of Greek texts are those of the Loeb Classical Library. I cite these works by line of poetry or, for prose, by the standard reference system employed by classical scholars, which generally refers to page and page section of the original Greek editions, not by Loeb's volume and page. All translations from Latin are my own, again, unless otherwise noted. Biblical translations are from the *New Oxford Annotated Bible, Revised Standard Version,* edited by Herbert G. May and Bruce M. Metzger (New York: Oxford University Press, 1973).

THE FORMATION OF HELL

Introduction: Babylonia and Egypt

In the Christian Scriptures the evangelist Matthew reports the words of Jesus responding to a question from his disciples. Relating the events that will bring on the end of time—the Parousia or Second Coming, the Resurrection, and the Last Judgment—Jesus tells how the "Son of man" will come to judge the nations of the world, dividing them as a shepherd divides the sheep from the goats, the docile from the unruly. On the sheep, whom he calls "the blessed of my Father," he bestows "the kingdom prepared for you from the foundation of the world." Then he dismisses those who have not measured up: "Depart from me, you cursed [ones], into the eternal fire prepared for the Devil and his angels" (Matthew 25.31–46). What happens to the wicked is the subject of this book.

How could the idea arise that people could be sentenced to eternal fire? How, particularly, could one offered by his Father to bring eternal life so "that the world might be saved by him" (John 3.16–17) pronounce those words? The answer does not lie in regarding Matthew's passage as exceptional. The evangelist Mark, too, quotes Jesus evoking the threat of Gehenna (hell), "the unquenchable fire," as a warning against succumbing to temptation (9.43–48). The Book of Revelation states of those sent there that "the smoke of their torment goes up for ever and ever" (14.11). Fumes of "fire and sulphur" rise from "a lake of fire," where "they will be tormented day and night for ever and ever" (Revelation 20.10; cf. 20.13–15). Though far more reticent on the subject of damnation than the other evangelists, John agrees that those who do not believe are "condemned already" (John 3.18).

Despite powerful presentations of alternatives to eternal damnation in the intervening centuries, around 425, Augustine, bishop of Hippo on the northeastern coast of present-day Algeria, sternly defended the concept of hell. He ridiculed the tender hearts who thought eternity too long for divine punishment, who thought God's mercy should penetrate hell. Augustine contended that "the fire and the worm" of hell torture the damned physically and that the ability of bodies to withstand this punishment forever is "a miracle of the most omnipotent Creator."[1]

---

1. Augustine, *De civitate Dei*, 21.9.47–48, Corpus Christianorum, Series Latina (Turnhout, Belgium: Brepols, 1955), 2.775. Cf. the translation of Marcus Dods, *The City of God* (New York: Random House, 1950), 778–79.

Neither the evangelists, those earliest biographers of Jesus, nor his later defenders, including Augustine (d. 430), lived in a cultural vaccuum. They knew the Jewish Scriptures, Greek philosophy and mythology (however indirectly), and the practices of the Roman state, its official religion, and the paganism of their neighbors around the Mediterranean. The Hebrew Scriptures had circulated since the third century B.C.E. in a Greek version known as the Septuagint, which constituted "the Bible" for the earliest Christians while the New Testament was being composed; it remains so for Eastern Christians.[2] Terminology used to express such ideas as "Word," "soul," "holy," and, more germane to this investigation, "Hades," "Gehenna," "giants," "Titans," and "demons," which have distinctive connotations in Christian thought, nonetheless carry some older Jewish and pagan echoes simply by the use of Greek. No correct understanding of hell is possible, therefore, without taking into account the conceptual background of the ancient world prior to Christianity. Further, because Christianity arose as one religion among many, one cannot reach a full appreciation of the task of forming the Christian concept of hell unless one also considers the competition.

The study of "background" is complicated, however, by an important factor. The authors of the sources we perceive as background did not foresee the development of the concept of hell. When they addressed the subjects that interest us, they were in fact discussing other matters, however intimately related we feel these may be to the concept that eventually emerged. Their thoughts found expression only in the midst of related ideas that are far more universal: beliefs about death, the dead, the soul, justice, and retribution. To say that this background "anticipated" or "prepared" the concept of hell would be to attribute to these authors a goal they did not have. Homer, Plato, Virgil, Isaiah, the author of Job (to pick a few examples) "anticipate" hell only logically, not purposely. Despite this methodological difficulty, it is possible to consider these prior ideas as contributory to the concept of hell in the sense that they provided options for subsequent authors, within or outside of their own traditions, which could be accepted, modified, or rejected. In that drama lies the excitement of this history.

In order to distinguish the concept of hell from the related issues that helped to shape it, it is necessary to offer a definition. The one I present here is deliberately wordy, its redundancies intended to raise issues that it is not within the province of the historian to resolve. Instead, my purpose is to

2. *The New Jerome Biblical Commentary*, ed. Raymond E. Brown, Joseph A. Fitzmyer, and Roland E. Murphy (Englewood Cliffs, N.J.: Prentice-Hall, 1990), 1091.

provide an outline against which various formulations may be measured, a definition whose refinement will serve as a spur to further investigation.

Hell, then, is a divinely sanctioned place of eternal torment for the wicked. It is "divinely sanctioned" because the God (or, the gods) who established it could have refrained from creating it and could at any time demolish it. Its existence depends on some divinely established purpose. Whether it is a physical place or a psychological state is a matter that must be left open to consideration in the light of each particular source. Although the strictest definition would insist that hell be eternal, some theories have proposed shorter periods. The word "torment" stresses suffering, the idea that the resident of hell experiences a fate contrary to what he or she wills. Using the word "punishment" in this place would stress the justice of one's damnation, but at the expense of suffering. Therefore, to include both suffering and justice, I adopt the somewhat longer formulation, "torment *for the wicked*," which fulfills the requirement that the damned be justly damned— that is, that they deserve their suffering.

This concept of hell arose from an array of approaches to death, the afterlife, and justice long present in the Mediterranean world. Though each community added contributions of its own, we can best understand the process by examining the interplay between the two options that attracted the greatest loyalty and the variations that clustered around them. Written records expressed the first concept, "neutral" death, in Mesopotamia in the middle of the third millennium B.C.E. That view, according to which the dead survive en masse in a pallid half-life without either reward or punishment, later informed classical antiquity through Persia. In the middle of the second millennium the Coffin Texts of Egypt's Middle Kingdom articulated the second concept, "moral" death. That view, according to which the dead are judged by the standard of known criteria and then rewarded or punished, later informed ancient Greece through its colonies in Sicily and through the influence attributed to the mathematician and mystic Pythagoras. No neutral land of the dead, however gloomy, can be hell, since hell must punish.

The range of ideas inspired by these two approaches were available as Jews and Christians shaped their respective views of the afterlife. The most obvious other possibility—that the dead merely die, decompose, and have no existence beyond the grave—seems to have won few adherents. In all the societies under study here, offerings to the dead, burial with grave goods, inscriptions dedicated to them or entreating various divinities for their protection attest to widespread belief that the dead do not simply die. "Mere" death excludes the possibility of hell. Instead, in the valleys of the Tigris and Euphrates in the third millennium B.C.E., the dead were believed to inhabit some distant land; in Egypt a millennium later they were believed to be distributed through the underworld according to what they deserved. It is convenient to consider these two primary conceptions in turn to see what potential they implied for the possibility, or impossibility, of punishing the dead.

The *Epic of Gilgamesh* provides the earliest evidence.[3] The name Gilgamesh corresponds to that of a king of Uruk from the early third millennium, and written fragments survive from the middle of the second millennium. There may have been a gap of a thousand years between the oral circulation of a legend about the hero and its recording on clay tablets. The epic depicts a land of the dead at great remove from the human communities of Babylon. As the story has survived, Gilgamesh first sensed his own mortality at the death of his boon companion Enkidu. "How can I be still? My friend, whom I loved, has turned to clay! Must I, too, like him, lay me down, not to rise again for ever and ever?"[4] Uruk's king then understood that he too would die and determined to seek a remedy. He decided to journey to the land of the dead to consult Utnapishtim, who had lived there since the time of the flood the Babylonian god Enlil had sent to destroy human life. The righteous Utnapishtim (a Babylonian Noah) survived because the god Ea had warned him. Outwitted by Ea, Enlil made Utnapishtim and his wife immortal "like gods," though they were obliged to live among the dead, "at the mouth of the rivers." To find Utnapishtim, Gilgamesh traversed difficult mountains, ranged over all the lands, crossed all the seas—the seas of death—and the land of darkness. Reaching Utnapishtim, Gilgamesh inquired how he had attained eternal life. After telling the story of the flood, Utnapishtim asked Gilgamesh why the gods should grant him a similar privilege: "Who will for thy sake call the gods to Assembly that the life which thou seekest thou mayest find?" (tab. XI, lines 196–97). To show the absurdity of any other mortal's seeking eternal life, Utnapishtim challenged Gilgamesh to remain awake for six days and seven nights. When he failed, Utnapishtim taunted him: "The hero who seeks life cannot resist sleep!" (lines 203–4).

Utnapishtim then disclosed "a hidden thing, . . . a secret of the gods"

3. For an anthology covering many different aspects, see Karl Oberhuber, ed., *Das Gilgamesch-Epos*, Wege der Forschung, 215 (Darmstadt: Wissenschaftliche Buchgesellschaft, 1977). See also Vera Schneider, *Gilgamesch* (Zurich: Origo, 1967); Jeffrey H. Tigay, *The Evolution of the Gilgamesh Epic* (Philadelphia: University of Pennsylvania Press, 1982), with extensive bibliography, 309–33.

4. James B. Pritchard, *Ancient Near Eastern Texts Relating to the Old Testament*, 3d ed. (Princeton: Princeton University Press, 1969), tab. X, Assyrian version, ii, lines 13–16, iii, lines 29–32.

(266–67). A mortal could obtain new life by finding a certain thorny plant at the bottom of the sea. Gilgamesh dived for the root of youth and forced it to shore, but when he left his prize momentarily unattended to wash himself in a spring, a serpent stole the plant and restored it to the depths. Only then did Gilgamesh accept his mortality. He returned to Uruk, his city, where he died.

In the *Epic of Gilgamesh* a great expanse of land and sea divides the living from the land of the dead, characterized as a vast wilderness inaccessible to the living. Only a heroic figure like Gilgamesh can reach this dwelling to obtain the secret of Utnapishtim, who lives on with his wife and knows the cause of mortality.

Further testimony comes from another Babylonian myth, this time concerning a fertility goddess, Inanna, who descended from the heavens to take power from her natural opponent, her sister, Ereshkigal, who ruled the dead. The textual tradition for this myth is extremely complex, and here I simplify it. Basically there is a longer, earlier tradition in Sumerian and a shorter, later tradition in Akkadian. The two differ in detail but retain a similar structure. They agree in their fundamental portrayal of the land of the dead as a sterile country of clay and dust which imprisons its inhabitants, thus preventing any return to life.

The Sumerian (southern Babylonian) version survives in clay tablets datable to the first half of the second millennium.[5] In an effort to obtain Ereshkigal's power over the dead, Inanna, using the pretext of attending a funeral, descended into the netherworld through its entrance, far to the East (81).[6] Evidently her real motive was transparent. As she approached each of the seven gates that guarded access to the fortress of her elder sister, the queen of the dead, the sentry stopped her, refusing to open the gate unless she removed an article of her clothing and silencing her complaints by invoking "the sacred customs of the netherworld" (138–63). Thus, she was progressively stripped of her royal accouterments, which symbolized her divine

---

5. A partial translation can be found in Pritchard, 52–57. Some seventy lines discovered more recently have been incorporated into a full reedition and new translation in the 1974 Johns Hopkins University dissertation by William Sladek, "Inanna's Descent to the Netherworld" (available from University Microfilms International, Ann Arbor, Mich.). Quotations are from Sladek, cited by line number. For a careful analysis, see Manfred Hutter, *Altorientalische Vorstellungen von der Unterwelt*, Orbis biblicus et orientalis, 63 (Freiburg, Switzerland: Universitätsverlag; Göttingen: Vandenhoeck and Ruprecht, 1985), 116–30. Sladek in his abstract gives the date ca. 1900–1600 B.C.E. Pritchard dates it similarly, *Ancient Near Eastern Texts*, 52b.

6. For this resolution of an apparent contradiction, see Sladek, 62–63.

powers. Systematically weakened in this way, she arrived at the inner palace naked and all but dead. Still, when her sister, Ereshkigal, arose, Inanna took her throne. At this, Ereshkigal's counselors or judges, the Anunnaki, sentenced her to death and hung her corpse on a hook.

Cognizant of the danger in her journey, Inanna had previously instructed her messenger Ninshubur what to do if she did not return within three days and three nights, in which case she would effectively be dead. Ninshubur followed her instructions. First, he went to the gods Enlil and Nanna, but they refused to help Inanna, implying that her "death" was just what she deserved for her overweening ambition. The cost of going to the netherworld, they said, is not coming back (190–94, 205–8).[7] Next, Ninshubur sought out Enki, lord of wisdom, who had access to the food and water of life. Enki used the dirt of his fingernails to fashion two fantastic creatures, the *kurgarru* and the *kalaturru,* and he instructed them to carry the food and water of life to Inanna and to revive her with them. When the creatures had succeeded in their mission and Inanna was about to depart, the Anunnaki objected. She could not get away that easily.

> Who has ever risen from the Netherworld? Who has
> ever risen from the netherworld alive?
> If Inanna wants to rise from the netherworld
> Let her furnish a substitute for herself.
>
> (287–89)

Inanna then ascended from the netherworld accompanied by a squad of demons, whose job it was either to obtain a replacement for Inanna or to bring her back. They first approached Ninshubur, but Inanna defended her faithful servant. Similarly, she refused to let them take anyone else they met as long as that person had wept for her during her confinement in the netherworld, when (in appearance at least) she was dead. At length they came upon Dumuzi, her husband, adorned in a splendid robe rather than mourning attire. The result was serious, for Inanna turned him over to the demons. Dumuzi would be her replacement. Using magic to change into a reptile, Dumuzi momentarily escaped and fled to his sister, Gestinanna, who pitied his fate. In the end it was stipulated: "You (Dumuzi will spend) one half of the year and your sister (will spend) one half of the year (in the netherworld)" (407).[8] In the end, "Inanna the pure handed over Dumuzi as her substitute" (410).

---

7. Sladek notes their significance as a corrective to Inanna's lies at 19 and 205.

8. Here I condense radically, but the ambiguity about who makes this declaration is in the original.

It is best to postpone interpretation until we have considered the later, Akkadian variant, which dates from the end of the second millennium.[9] Although the structure of the myth is fundamentally similar, in the later version, the water of life alone replaces the combination of food and water— a change that intensifies the added detail about the underworld itself, an arid waste of clay and dust. In the Akkadian version Inanna is called Ishtar.

When Ishtar descended to the land of the dead, she found it well protected. At the gate she forced her way in with this threat:

> I will raise up the dead and they will consume the living
> And the dead will outnumber the living.
>
> (19–20)

When the gatekeeper notified her of Ishtar's arrival, Ereshkigal was amazed that anyone could covet what she had:

> My condition here is such that I drink water with the Anunnaki
> Instead of bread, I eat clay; instead of beer I drink dirty water.
>
> (32–33)

However surprised, she did not lack the means to defend herself. As Ishtar passed through each of seven gates, guardians removed her regalia, jewelry, and clothing, according to "the sacred customs of the mistress of the netherworld" (44, e.g.). With each loss she became weaker. When she reached her sister's throne, she was nearly dead from the sixty miseries that the queen of the underworld had loosed against her. Simultaneously, a famine struck the surface of the earth: neither people nor animals nor plants could reproduce. The god Ea then sent a eunuch to carry water to Ereshkigal. Distraught, Ereshkigal knew that in return for clean water she would have to free her captive. After cursing the eunuch, she consulted with her infernal counselors, the Anunnaki, who insisted she demand a ransom in the form of a surrogate for Ishtar. On this condition, Ereshkigal ordered the release of Ishtar, who passed back through the seven gates and regained her clothing, jewelry, and crown as she ascended.

Though the Akkadian text does not tell why Ishtar descended, she herself could be ransomed with fresh water, with which, however unwillingly, Ereshkigal sprinkled her heavenly sister. "Life-water" vivifies in this land described in the beginning as a place "where dirt is their food and clay their fare," where "both door and bolt are covered with dirt," where the inmates,

9. For a more accessible translation, see Stephanie Dalley, *Myths from Mesopotamia: Creation, the Flood, Gilgamesh, and Others* (Oxford: Oxford University Press, 1989), 155–62. For the date, see Pritchard, *Ancient Near Eastern Texts*, 107. Sladek gives c. 1100 B.C.E.

like birds, are clothed in feathers and there is no light. Such is the dwelling "which no one who enters ever leaves" (lines 5–11). Only a replacement could provide actual release and then only for a goddess.

The symmetry of the later version is remarkable. The introduction of water dissolves the hold of dirt and clay and opens a possibility of escape from the land of no return. On either side of the introduction of water is the highly ordered, almost ritual stripping and redraping of Ishtar. Ishtar's personal effort, supported by Ea's eunuch envoy bearing life-water, eases Ereshkigal's hold on a land of universal dust and darkness.[10] The sterility of the earth matches Ishtar's own humiliation and apparent impotence. The life-water quickens both. Despite her power over dust and clay, Ereshkigal seems to suffer from her own environment. Water in the underworld compels the chthonic sibling to release her living, heavenly sister and, simultaneously, ends the drought on earth.

This Babylonian underworld is morally neutral. The Babylonians clearly subordinated any moral characterization of the dead to their definitive separation from the living. Ishtar's threat to release them obtained her immediate entry to the stronghold. Neither the *Descent of Inanna/Ishtar* nor the *Epic of Gilgamesh* makes any allusion to the moral quality of the dead. For the Babylonians, keeping them at a safe distance was crucial. Because so much energy was invested in making the underworld contain *all* the dead, their moral character faded into insignificance.[11]

The importance of effectively segregating the dead is emphasized by the contrast between the location of their territory in the Gilgamesh and Inanna/Ishtar stories. The vaguely defined land attained after a spectacular journey by Gilgamesh has acquired a palace and the walled defenses of an ancient Near Eastern city. The fortress or city of the dead, called Ganzir in Sumerian, Kurnugi in Akkadian, has its laws, its monarch, its guardians in their towers, a bureaucracy of judges, and a palace guard of demons. The dead who dwell there are not tormented, but they are imprisoned, kept separate, even from the heavenly gods, and held in an underworld realm resembling that of a Babylonian king.

Thus Isthar's threat to release them is dire indeed, for Ereshkigal's ability to hold all the dead safely separated them from the living. Yet these frontiers

---

10. Hutter discusses the power of the underworld in *Altorientalische Vorstellungen*, 110–12, 122–23.

11. Klaas Spronk, *Beatific Afterlife in Ancient Israel and in the Ancient Near East*, Alter Orient und Altes Testament, 219 (Kevelaer, Germany: Butzon und Bercker; Neukirchen-Vluyn, Germany: Neukirchener Verlag, 1986), 303–5, discusses the irrelevance of character in the disposition of the dead and the insistence on a proper boundary between them and the living.

exist in the imagination. It is the living who tell these myths and participate in their related rituals. Boundaries in the land of the dead imaginatively reinforce distinctions the living require to maintain their own peace of mind. Their myths at once reveal and satisfy their need for security. The farther they make Gilgamesh travel to Utnapishtim, the stronger the gates of Ganzir/Kurnugi, the safer the living are from the return of the dead. That is why the defenses of their underworld fortress so resemble the defenses of their physical cities and storehouses. Penetration of the underworld causes famine as would invasion of the physical territory by enemy troops or an infestation of locusts. As the myths of the *Descent of Innana/Ishtar* make clear, however, no matter how much the living "fortified" the netherworld, its boundaries could be breached: the myths evidence doubts as well as desires.

For that reason, no trespass in the land of the dead could go unpunished. Unlike the *Epic of Gilgamesh,* which makes the hero pay through the length of his journey, the Sumerian/Akkadian *Descent of Inanna/Ishtar* shows that, although it is sufficiently porous to allow a goddess entry, the netherworld does not let her out without a price: water for resuscitation and a substitute for ransom. Nothing could better dramatize the power of the netherworld than this ability to imprison the dead and to impose harsh conditions even upon such divinities as may force their way in with the severest of threats.

Moreover, this segregation of the dead from the living appears to be productive. It guarantees earthly fertility. It seems to allow the living to proceed with their lives, undisturbed by the dead. Ishtar's breach of this boundary between life and death halts the breeding of plants, animals, and humans. What else could happen when a divine force of reproduction goes to the land of death? Conversely, the premature captivity of a living person in the land of the dead has the same effect. The *Descent of Innana/Ishtar* here represents cause and effect ambiguously: Does reproduction cease because Isthar trespasses on the rights of Ereshkigal, queen of the dead, or because Ereshkigal contrives the death of a goddess? Or should the question be put differently: When Inanna/Ishtar "descends" is she a living aggressor brought low for her arrogance and now dead, or does she represent the needed extension of cultivable land, of fertility against scarcity, starvation, and death, whose failure entails drought and famine for the living? There is no answer. Respect of the boundary, the disturbance of equilibrium, counts far more than the identity of the offender.

The opposition between Ishtar's threat to release the life-devouring dead and the famine that follows her captivity represents a fundamental truth. Life can go on only when the living and the dead respect each others' territory. The eunuch sent by Ea and the *kurgarru* and the *kalaturru* formed from Enki's fingernail dirt (not a body part obviously associated with reproductive potency and, strictly speaking, not a body part at all) are able to enter the netherworld and so to rescue Inanna/Ishtar because, being sexually neuter, they are neutral in the confrontation between the reproduction of life and the sterility of death. In this myth, therefore, the division between the living and the dead seems nearly to parallel the division between reproductive power and impotence.

The characteristic segregation of the dead, so fundamental to these Babylonian myths, is shared by other cultures too. The Greek Hades and the Hebrew Sheol, in their own ways, reflect similar concerns on the part of their peoples. The match is not exact between this Babylonian story and the Greek myth of Hades and Persephone. In the Babylonian story there is no rape; Inanna/Ishtar is regarded by the gods as an aggressor, and she trespasses on a female divinity. In both stories, however, the capture of a goddess arrests earthly fertility. Surely the connection between the grave and the granary must be correctly delineated for a society to function properly.

In any event the claims of death cannot be ignored. This moral is driven home by the much more recent tale of another transgressor of Erishkigal's realm, the Assyrian prince Kumma whose account is recorded in a tablet of the mid–seventh century B.C.E.[12] In a dream he penetrated the land of "stillness" and "terror," where monstrous gods stand arrayed as if for battle or execution. Each combined forms of humans and beasts, whether real or legendary. "The evil Utukku had the head of a lion, hands and feet of the Zu-bird; 'Remove-Hastily,' the boatman of the netherworld, had the head of the Zu-bird." At their sides (one cannot say "in their hands") they held weapons and the severed heads of their victims. Confronted with the authorities of the netherworld, Kumma prostrated himself, kissed the feet of Nergal, the consort of Ereshkigal, at first to no avail.[13] Then Ishum, the intercessor, counseled mercy. The interloper was to be released on the condition that he spread the fame of Nergal and his kingdom. "The heart of the all-powerful, the almighty, who vanquishes the evil ones, he soothed like clear water of the well" (110a).

When he awoke, Kumma was terrified, yet purged. The consequences for his personal life are not clear. Terror and relief attached his obligation to his heart as if by a thorn. To avoid further evil and to carry out his bargain he resolved to spread the fame of the underworld throughout the palace: "This

12. Date and translation in Pritchard, *Ancient Near Eastern Texts*, 109–10b, cited by page.

13. On the relationship between Nergal and Ereshkigal, see the observation of W. H. Ph. Römer in C. J. Bleeker and Geo Widengren, eds., *Historia Religionum: Handbook for the History of Religions*, 2 vols. (Leiden: Brill, 1969), 1:136; Römer suggests a parallel between Nergal and the Greek god Pluto.

shall be my expiation" (110b). Like the promise that Hades made to Persephone, that those who deny her honor shall be her prisoners forever, this dream vision contains its own sanctions within it, though here their universal application is only implicit. To avoid death, or at least early death (punishment for his temerity), Kumma must advertise the power of the chthonic gods. He has learned that agreeing to publish the power of death works like water in the land of dust. Accepting the power of Nergal's realm averts death, at least for a while. It is the will of Nergal and the promise of Kumma that all should know.

Facile comparisons between these very different traditions can only be misleading. I propose no direct relationship or literary influence, nor do I invoke the universal structure of the human mind, whereby individual religions necessarily draw from a standard core of archetypes or mythic building blocks. Nonetheless in the arid lands from the Tigris and Euphrates to the Mediterranean, there were a number of environmental and cultural factors shared by many peoples over more than a millennium. These mythic themes, encountered by juxtaposing narratives about the underworld, at least represent options that could be known to neighbors, trading partners, even enemies (few cultural ties are closer than that between victor and vanquished), which could be borrowed or rejected, accented or muted—that is, when they were not spontaneous insights, the brainstorm of a poet, or generated out of local circumstances. For all that, certain common themes stand out. Inanna/Ishtar progresses through the underworld as through a Middle Eastern city, from the town's gates to the palace and ever inward. Hesiod describes the gates of Tartarus within the kingdom of Hades in a similar fashion. A river runs by. How close to the Greek Charon is 'Remove-Hastily,' the boatman of the netherworld encountered by Kumma?[14]

Very different from the tightly sealed Babylonian storehouse of the dead, surrounded like a Bronze Age city by a series of concentric walls, is the distribution of the dead in Egyptian religious texts. Here, the image of the city, while present, is overlaid by the agronomist's grid. Like Egypt itself, the land of the dead, called the Tuat, flanks a great river and, to the left and right, fields and landmarks are inhabited by cultivators of the various gods. They are rewarded or punished depending on how well they chose their divine patrons. Best off are those devoted to the two major gods with author-

14. For Charon, see Ronnie H. Terpening, *Charon and the Crossing: Ancient, Medieval, and Renaissance Transformations of a Myth* (Lewisburg, Pa.: Bucknell University Press, 1985). For Etruscan adaptations, see Franz de Ruyt, *Charun, démon étrusque de la mort*, Etudes de philologie, d'archéologie, et d'histoire anciennes, 1 (Rome: Institut historique belge, 1934).

ity in the Tuat. Worst off are their opponents. Exactly what it meant to oppose the sun, Re, or the resurrected Osiris is not clear. It is possible that opposition in this polytheistic system meant nothing more than neglect of rites sacred to these divinities or devotion to other gods, rather than any wrongdoing in a moral sense. In some texts the Egyptian tradition is explicit about the moral component of its underworld.

As early as the Pyramid Texts of Egypt's Fifth and Sixth Dynasties (2425–2300 B.C.E.), the sun, Amon-Re appears as a chief god. Ruler of the sky, he also had credentials in the underworld, since, as the sun, he traversed it nightly, achieving "rebirth" at dawn. The pharaohs identified themselves with the sun and claimed the same divinity they attributed to him. Just as the sun rose to rule the sky each day, the pharaoh, at death, ascended for an eternal life in the heavens. As a condition to this ascent, however, the king had to take an exculpatory oath, declaring that he had committed no offense. These affirmations are generic in the Pyramid Texts—for example, "He is of those who are not punished and not found guilty of crime."[15] Over the centuries, the pharaohs' identification with the sun god was "democratized" as individual subjects claimed a similar immortality through their participation in the belief system of their rulers. As more ordinary people claimed to live with the sun and their ruler who imitated him, the declarations of innocence came to be more detailed.[16]

Amon-Re had no exclusive claim to rule in the otherworld, however; he had a major competitor in Osiris. An ancient king murdered and dismembered by his brother Seth, Osiris was resurrected by his magician sister Isis, who recomposed his mutilated body, and lying with him, produced a son, Horus. Like the pretensions of pharaohs to identity with Amon-Re, this story had political utility. Living pharaohs identified their fathers with Osiris and thus claimed status as Horus, offspring of divine parents.[17] Having conquered death through his resurrection, Osiris, too, had a claim to jurisdiction, if not outright sovereignty, in the underworld. In his cult, there emerged a positive standard for judgment: not mere exculpation but conformity with justice, rectitude, or truth—a standard called *maat*.[18]

It is the Coffin Texts of the Middle Kingdom (c. 2160–1580) which make clear the democratization of notions applied principally to pharaohs in the Pyramid Texts. In addition to offering immortal life to the pharaoh's sub-

15. S. G. F. Brandon, *The Judgment of the Dead* (New York: Scribner's, 1967), 7.

16. As in Pritchard, *Ancient Near Eastern Texts*, 34–36.

17. Mircea Eliade, *A History of Religious Ideas*, trans. Willard R. Trask, vol. 1: *From the Stone Age to the Eleusinian Mysteries* (Chicago: University of Chicago Press, 1978), 97–99.

18. Brandon, *Judgment of the Dead*, 9.

jects, the Coffin Texts insisted more strictly on the requisite virtue of the person so rewarded. For the first time, illustrations represent the assessment of a life by means of a balance to weigh a person's deeds. Indeed, one text suggests the scale itself became a deity.[19] The image of the balance combined with the notion of *maat* to reflect a clear concern for the reckoning of a life's unfolding.

These systems did not replace each other but coexisted. Thus the exculpatory oath and the weighing of actions came to exist side by side in the famous *Book of the Dead* (New Kingdom, c. 1580–1090). The idea of the papyrus was to serve partly as an amulet, helping to bring about what is depicted, including a successful outcome to the dramatic weighing of deeds.[20] Judgment of the dead stands out clearly in chapters 30 and 125. The latter describes a balance on which the heart, representing conscience or a person's lifetime record, is weighed against a feather, symbol of *maat*. Beside the balance sat an eager Ammit, the crocodile-headed quadruped, ready to devour those who failed this test.[21]

When the heart, called the person's *ka,* or double, stands in at judgment, it is also capable of testifying negatively, accusing its owner. Thus chapter 30, actually a spell to be enclosed in the coffin, intended to aid the person through this ordeal, entreats the heart: "Rise not up as a witness against me."[22] To the extent that simple recitation or possession of a protective formula could avert the consequences of departing from the culture's norms these spells offset the moral force of the innocence declared in the exculpatory oath or the heart's conformity to *maat*.

The spells and the scene of the heart's weighing do not reveal the punishment of souls who fail. Who would commission a scroll showing his or her own future punishment? There are, however, hints of postmortem suffering, and certainly of danger, in chapter 125 of the *Book of the Dead*, which includes two recensions of the declaration of innocence. The shorter, listing forty-two statements, begins each one with an invocation of some allegorical being. The names of these "demonic beings," as S. G. F. Brandon calls them, suggest physical harm, as if for perjury.[23] Taken collectively, they suggest postmortem, though not eternal, torment: Embracer of Fire, Swallower of Shadows, Dangerous of Face, Eyes of Flint, Flamer, Breaker of Bones, Commander of Fire, Dweller in the Pit, White of Teeth, Eater of Blood, Eater of

19. Ibid., 23.
20. Ibid., 31, 41.
21. Ibid., 37.
22. Ibid., 37–38. See Jan Zandee, *Death as an Enemy according to Ancient Egyptian Conceptions* (New York: Arno, 1977), 259–60, for more examples.
23. Brandon, *Judgment of the Dead,* 36–37.

Entrails, Djudju serpent, Wamemti serpent, Wrecker, Mischief-Maker, His-Face-behind-Him, Dark One, Lord of Horns, High-of-Head serpent, and In-af serpent.[24] Though some are not so threatening (Wide of Stride, Lord of Justice (?), Wanderer, Superior of the Nobles, Child, Hot of Leg, Bringer of His Peace, Lord of Faces, Plan Maker, Acting with His Heart, Flowing One, Commander of the People), who would not want to avoid the clutches of these monsters? A clearer idea of what might await the unrighteous lies in other sources.

In Egyptian thought Re, the sun, descended nightly to the Tuat, the land of the dead, not beneath the earth but around it. The river he traveled in his boat flowed through a valley between two ranges of mountains that encircled the earth. He made this circuit in a small boat and ferried with him the god of harvests, so that he might feed the dead, whom he was also able to command, reward, and punish.[25] Great significance attached to the obstacles, aids, and landmarks in the fields to the left or right.

Two illustrated texts recount this voyage. The *Book of Knowledge of What Is in the Other World*, or the *Book Am-Tuat* follows the course of the sun during the hours of the night. Another work, the *Book of Gates*, depicts the sun following a path (rather than a river) through zones separated by twelve gates that also divide the night. It, too, follows the course of the sun, but represents him traveling through a land subject to Osiris.[26] These two works are imprecisely dated to either the Eighteenth Dynasty (1580–1350) or the Nineteenth Dynasty (1350–1200), though the best exemplar is on the tomb of Seti I, and dated around 1375.[27] In each text, the landscape in the zones on either side of the path or river is full of symbolic meaning. Whether in lush fields or lakes of fire, the condition of these figures—overthrown

24. For the complete list, see Pritchard, *Ancient Near Eastern Texts*, 35.

25. Summarized in Francis Bar, *Les routes de l'autre monde* (Paris: PUF, 1946), 15–20.

26. The two books are studied together, summarized, and contrasted by E. A. Wallis Budge, *The Egyptian Heaven and Hell* (1925; rpt. La Salle, Ill.: Open Court, 1974). Although published as a separate volume, this is actually the third volume of a larger work of the same title published once in 1905 and again in 1906 (rpt. New York: AMS, 1976). The third volume has been published separately several times. References lacking a volume are to the Open Court edition of volume 3. References to volumes 1 and 2 are to the AMS edition.

27. Budge, *Egyptian Heaven and Hell*, 85, 93. See Erik Hornung, *Aegyptische Unterweltsbücher*, 2d ed. (Zurich: Artemos, 1984), 17–18, for the nuances of dating. Hornung attributes the inspiration for these books to the transition period between the Old and Middle Kingdoms, with the earliest traces visible on the graves of the followers of Tutmos I (1505–1493).

gods, allies of Osiris or Re, or human devotees of these gods or of their rivals—indicate the disposition of such souls in the otherworld.

An impressive illustration of just reward appears in the sixth division of the *Book of Gates*. Here, after passing through the Hall of Osiris, a chamber where the good and evil deeds of each soul are weighed, in a manner similar to that depicted in the *Book of the Dead,* the boat traverses the land of the blessed. The devotees of Osiris render to him huge ears of wheat, the crop of *maat* that they cultivated during their lives and in the afterlife. The god sustains himself from their offerings, and in turn, he nourishes them with his own substance (Budge 164–65). At the entrance to the land of the blessed, however, is a region where the punishments decreed by Osiris are carried out (Budge 163).

A dramatic example occurs in the fourth division of the *Book of Gates*, where the sun god calls on Horus, requesting the destruction of his enemies. They are dispensed with in four fire-filled pits tended by keepers overseen by a "Master of the Lords of the Pits" (Budge 143). Near the image, a text in hieroglyphics explains: "Horus worketh on behalf of his father Osiris. [He says to him:] 'My heart goeth out to thee, O my father, thou who art avenged on those who would work against thee. . . . Thou hast the mastery, O Osiris, thou hast the sovereignty, O Khenti Anmenti, thou hast what-soever is thine as Governor of the Tuat. . . . The beatified spirits hold thee in fear, and the dead are terrified at thee'" (Budge 2:135). This is the acclamation by which Horus extols his father and lauds his power as governor of the Tuat, ruler over the land of the dead. It also shows that lord accomplishing vengeance over his opponents. Thus Horus instructs the lords of the pits:

> "Smite ye the enemies of my father, and hurl ye them down into your pits because of that deadly evil which they have done against the Great One. . . . That which belongeth to you to do in the Tuat is to guard the pits of fire according as Ra hath commanded, and I set [this] before you so that, behold, ye may do according to what belongeth to you [to do]." This god standeth over (or, by) the pits. (Budge 2:136–38)

Here, then, is the fiery incarceration of opponents of a god who aids souls through death and is himself an example of resurrection.

In the eighth division of the Tuat, according to the *Book of Gates*, to the left of the path is a lake called Serser (which means "blazing fire" [Budge 2:227]), surrounded by human souls who have been sentenced to live there. Twelve *Tchatcha*, or great chiefs, distribute a nightly allotment of food to the souls living by the fiery lake. To the right of the path, twelve enemies of Osiris stand with their arms painfully bound behind them. In front is a huge serpent who breathes fire into their faces. In each of the seven curves of the serpent's body stands a god urged by Horus to aid in the destruction. The book details what happens to these captives, guilty of revealing the god's secrets (Budge, 168–71):

> This scene representeth what Horus doeth for his father Osiris. The enemies who are in this scene have their calamities ordered for them by Horus, who saith unto them: — "Let there be fetters on your arms, O enemies of my father, let your arms be tied up towards your heads, O ye who have no [power], ye shall be fettered [with your arms] behind you, O ye who are hostile to Ra. Ye shall be hacked in pieces, ye shall nevermore have your being, your souls shall be destroyed, and none [of you] shall live because of what ye have done to my father Osiris. . . . O ye shall cease to exist, ye shall come to an end." (Budge 2:234–35)

Horus addresses the serpent Khet:

> [O] my serpent Khet, thou Mighty Fire, from whose mouth cometh forth this flame which is in my Eye, whose undulations are guarded by [my] children, open thy mouth, distend thy jaws, and belch forth thy fires against the enemies of my father, burn thou up their bodies, consume their souls by the fire which issueth from thy mouth, and by the flames which are in thy body. My divine children are against them, they destroy [their] spirits, and those who have come forth from me are against them, and they shall never more exist. The fire which is in this serpent shall come forth, and shall blaze against these enemies whensoever Horus decreeth that it shall do so. (Budge 2:235)

The end of this speech refers to the spells. "Whosoever knoweth how to use words of power [against] this serpent shall be as one who doth not enter upon his fiery path" (Budge 2:235). "Words of power" are, therefore, effective against the serpent, though Khet, as we see, is capable of inflicting severe punishment.

The *Book Am-Tuat* also contains its fiery scenes of torment. In the eleventh hour, Horus presides over the destruction of Re's enemies in pits of fire. The serpent Set-Heh, companion to Horus, stands alongside. A goddess with the head of a lioness vomits fire into the first pit, which consumes those within it. Four more pits contain the bodies, souls, shades, and heads, respectively, of their victims. Goddesses project the fire from their mouths into the pits, and Set-Heh helps provide the fire (Budge 177–78; cf. 1:249–51). A fifth pit of fire called Ant-sekhetu contains bodies immersed upside down. An explanation of this scene reads: "The majesty of this god uttereth the decree, [saying]: —'Hack in pieces and cut asunder the bodies of the enemies and the members of the dead who have been turned upside down, O my father Osiris.'" After a lacuna, Horus seems to provide a rationale of their fate to the sufferers:

My father having [once] been helpless hath smitten you, he hath cut up your bodies, he hath hacked in pieces your spirits and your souls, and hath scattered in pieces your shadows, and hath cut in pieces your heads; ye shall never more exist, ye shall be overthrown, and ye shall be cast down headlong into the pits of fire; and ye shall not escape therefrom, and ye shall not be able to flee from the flames which are in the serpent Set-Heh. (Budge 1:254–55)

The ability of the once-dismembered Osiris to hack apart those who neglect his cult provides an ironic retribution that helps explain why these punishments take place. Despite the inverted posture of the sufferers, there is no suggestion that the god's victims here had any responsibility for his own death. Retribution due a divine victim (though very different) will figure importantly in the system of postmortem justice in Christianity.

Of each fiery pit in which the resurrected Osiris afflicts his victims the text states without a break:

The fire . . . is against you, the flames . . . are against you, the blazing heat . . . is against you [and] stabs at you, and hacks you in pieces, and cuts you up in such wise that ye shall never again see those who are living upon the earth.

As for those who are in this picture in the Tuat, it is the Majesty of Heru-Tuati who giveth the order for their slaughter each day. (Budge 1:255)

However horrible the suffering of these victims, their punishment is not eternal. The dismemberment and burning lead to quick destruction. Each night, Re (or Osiris) consumes the enemies collected the previous day.[28] Moreover, "words of power" can protect the dead from the fire. Jan Zandee has grouped together spells that enable one to pass successfully through the flaming doors described in the *Book of Gates*. Typical is this one: "Oh

28. Budge, *Egyptian Heaven and Hell*, 199: "The beings which were consumed in the pits of fire one day were not the same, though they belonged to the same classes, as those which had been burnt up the day before." Eric Hornung confirms this view in *Aegyptische Unterweltsbücher*, 43–44. Jan Zandee, *Death as an Enemy*, 133–42, confirms Budge and Hornung. At 139, he writes: "Total destruction through death by fire is the punishment of sinners." Note the minority opinions registered by Zandee at 283.

flame, backwards! You that burns there, I shall not be burnt. I wear . . . the white crown."[29] This formula guards the dead from the fire; the crown enhances the protection.

Here is an underworld divided into zones in which supporters and opponents of the particular gods are segregated according to their devotion to or neglect of those gods. Although the punishments are not eternal, polytheism confuses the picture, and spells soften the moral quality of judgment, this scheme was to enjoy a long future and, with the modifications imposed by later developments in Greek, Jewish, and Christian thought, it forms the subject of this book.

Neither the Babylonian nor the Egyptian conception of death lies in a direct causative relationship to these later ideas. It has been important to mention them here by way of introduction because, coming as early as they do in regions that would interact with Greek culture, be subjected to the Romans, and convert at least in part to Christianity and some later to Islam, they represent landmarks in the mental world of the ancient Mediterranean.

Yet dichotomies, such as the one between neutral and moral death presented in this introduction and to be considered in its various guises throughout the book, are potentially dangerous. Too simple a division into opposing conceptions usually distorts by forcing related positions onto the straight line that defines a polarity, whereas it is possible that each of these conceptions was defined without any conscious denial of the other. Further, even granting their direct opposition (which is warranted, given the history of ancient Greek and Jewish religious thought), views related to these key ideas did not conform strictly to their prototypes but rather clustered around and commented on them.

It will become clear how the authors of ancient Greece and of the Hebrew Bible recognized the advantages and disadvantages of each of these concepts for their own religious ideas. For now it is sufficient to conclude that the morally neutral storehouse of the dead and the subdivided, mapped underworld, zoned (at least potentially) according to ethical principles, were options that formed part of the cultural stock, the conceptual repertory, of the ancient world before the first millennium B.C.E.

29. See Zandee, *Death as an Enemy*, 140, for this and other examples.

The Netherworlds of Greece and Rome

Those who do not appease your power with offerings,

. . . shall be punished for evermore.

—Hades to Persephone, *Hymn to Demeter*

If death were a release from everything,

it would be a boon for the wicked.

—Plato, *Phaedo*

Death is nothing to us.

—Lucretius, *On the Nature of Things*

1

Neutral Death

Like their counterparts in the Ancient Near East, the earliest written sources for Greek mythology do not deal directly with hell as defined in the Introduction. Nonetheless they converge to illustrate, in different ways, the ideas of order, fertility, and the survival of personality beyond death. Albeit differently, each bears on the origins, maintenance, and disposition of what the ancient Greeks regarded as the present world order, including the underworld. And each shares with the Babylonian texts a view of death as neutral, embracing all the dead in nearly the same conditions, chiefly marked by strict separation from the living.[1]

Usually dated to the second half of the eighth century B.C.E., the *Odyssey* recounts the hero's voyage to the world of shades, the land of Hades, in order to learn his future from the dead seer Teiresias.[2] The tale incorporates the belief that the soul survives death but that the dead reside at a great remove from the living. It describes the condition of souls after their death. It

1. It is a pleasure to acknowledge the guidance I have received on this chapter and much of Part I from my friend and former student Charles King. He has graciously sent me a draft of his forthcoming article on the Homeric underworld and communicated many acute observations of detail.

2. I take these estimates for the dates from the authoritative monograph of Richard Janko, *Homer, Hesiod, and the Hymns: Diachronic Development in Epic Diction* (Cambridge: Cambridge University Press, 1982), which infers a chronology from the historical development of epic diction. His summary, in table 49 (p. 231), gives the years 750–725 for the *Iliad* and 743–713 for the *Odyssey*.

also exposes a difference between two kinds of dead: first, the human souls of all ranks who wander without punishment but wearied by their memories of life; and second, farther removed from the view of Odysseus, a group of superhuman rebels sentenced to undying exertions for unspecified insubordination against the divine order.

Hesiod's *Theogony* (or *Birth of the Gods*), written circa 700–665, narrates the establishment of that order.[3] It tells how Zeus and his brothers Poseidon and Hades divided among themselves the patrimony they wrested from their father, Kronos (Saturn): Zeus took the heavens, Poseidon the sea, and Hades the earth and its innards.[4] The victors in this rebellion imprisoned the supporters of Kronos, called Titans, in Tartarus, a fearful dungeon, far beneath the earth. The differences between these two aspects of the otherworld—the one a land called Hades for the human dead of all sorts, the other a prison for superhuman rebels—provided crucial ingredients within the cultural background out of which the concept of hell developed.

Fertility, and therefore the maintenance of the divine order, is a major focus of the Homeric *Hymn to Demeter*, which recounts how Hades abducted Persephone to his underworld kingdom and how her mother Demeter vengefully withheld crops from the earth, as if they could be kept underground. This myth, recorded in writing about 678–25, shows how the land of Hades can be at the same time a granary for seed, a place of confinement for Persephone, and a warehouse for the dead.[5] The *Hymn to Demeter* illustrates how carefully storytellers and their audiences wished communication between the dead and the living to be controlled.

3. For the dates, see ibid., table 49, p. 231.

4. For virtually all aspects of Greek mythology the standard reference tool is still Wilhelm Heinrich Roscher, *Ausführliches Lexikon der griechischen und römischen Mythologie*, 6 vols. and 4 supplements (Leipzig: Teubner, 1884–1937). For an encyclopedic tool that covers all classical antiquity, including mythology, see August Friedrich von Pauly, *Paulys Realencyclopädie der classischen Altertumswissenschaft*, new revision begun by Georg Wissowa, Wilhelm Kroll, and Karl Mittelhaus, 34 vols. plus 15 vols. of supplements (Stuttgart: Metzler, 1893–1980). In English, the best starting place is the manual of H. J. Rose, *A Handbook of Greek Mythology* (New York: Dutton, 1959). Robert Graves, *The Greek Myths*, 2 vols. (Baltimore: Penguin, 1955), gives systematic references to the original literature, but his interpretations are frequently idiosyncratic. The otherwise excellent *Oxford Classical Dictionary*, 2d ed., by N. G. L. Hammond and H. H. Scullard (Oxford: Clarendon Press, 1970), is comparatively weak on mythology. There are many useful, though summary, entries in Charlton T. Lewis and Charles Short, eds., *A Latin Dictionary*, rev. ed. (Oxford: Clarendon Press, 1958).

5. The dates, again, are from Janko, *Homer, Hesiod, and the Hymns*, table 49, p. 231.

The view of the netherworld portrayed in these sources did not remain unchallenged. Following suggestions in the *Hymn to Demeter,* some began to speculate about different fates for different folk and to ask whether adherents of esoteric doctrines, practitioners of secret rites, might fare better than the others. The first signs of this greater concern about possible differences in the afterlife appeared in Orphism, the poetry of Pindar, and Aristophanes' *Frogs.*

BOOK 11 OF THE *ODYSSEY*

The most extended discussion of the fate of the dead in Homer's epics occurs in book 11 of the *Odyssey.* Like the first part of book 24, it involves a trip to the otherworld, describes conditions there, and even reports the words of the dead. I shall focus primarily on book 11, but draw as necessary on book 24 and on the *Iliad.*[6]

In the course of his difficult return home from the Trojan War, the goddess Circe told Odysseus he must journey to the land of the dead, which she called the house of Hades (*Odyssey* 10.491), to consult the blind seer Teiresias about his future and to learn why his progress to Ithaca had so far been frustrated. She directed him to cross Ocean, which encircles the inhabited earth like a river, then to find on the far shore the land ruled by Hades, home of the shades.[7] There, the famed four rivers of the underworld come together. From the Styx flows the Cocytus, which joins Pyriphlegethon, the river of fire, and together they come to the Acheron. At the place where the rivers meet on a forested shore sacred to Persephone, is a rock. There, Odysseus must promise the dead, and Teiresias in particular, that he will dedicate sacrifices to them. In between Erebos, from which the shades would

6. The two *nekyai* (or journeys to the underworld) of *Odyssey* 11 and 24 are sometimes taken to be interpolations. Erwin Rohde favors this view in *Psyche: The Cult of Souls and Belief in Immortality among the Greeks* (London: Routledge and Kegan Paul, 1925), chap. 1. Emily Vermeule, *Aspects of Death in Early Greek Art and Poetry* (Berkeley: University of California Press, 1979), 28–29, cites the poetic nature and purpose of the epics and defends the genuineness of these sections against "perfectionists," whom she lists at 218 n. 49. Of the inconsistencies in the Homeric mythology of death, Walter Burkert observes: "Contradictions are freely tolerated." *Greek Religion: Archaic and Classical* (London: Basil Blackwell; Cambridge: Harvard University Press, 1985), 196. How else could the heroes see the dead in the murky gloom of subterranean darkness?

7. The earth was conceived of as a disk, around whose edges ran Ocean. Tributary rivers ran across parts of the disk (the earth) to empty into Ocean, which in turn replenished them.

come when properly summoned, and the riverbank, Odysseus was to dig a pit into which he was to allow the blood of two rams to run (528–30; cf. 491).

Now this crucial area deserves special attention. It figures significantly in three passages concerning the unburied dead. In the *Iliad*, the dead Patroklos, impatient to be buried, appears in a dream to the mourning Achilles, even as his friend supervises the funeral proceedings. Patroklos urges action since until he is buried he cannot "pass through the gates of Hades," for at death one "goes down under the gloom and the darkness" to "the house of the death god" (23.71, 51, 19). While he is unburied, he says, "the souls, the images of dead men, hold me at a distance, and will not let me cross the river and mingle among them, but I wander as I am by Hades' house of the wide gates" (72–74). By contrast, Odysseus's unburied companion Elpenor, who died in a fall from Circe's roof, meets Odysseus right there beside the pit in the plain with no barrier between him and the other spirits. Odysseus talks first to Elpenor, and then, without moving a foot, to Teiresias. In book 24 of the *Odyssey*, Hermes, the god who gathers up the souls of the slain suitors, guides them, "gibbering" like bats, "along down" to the underworld beyond "the Ocean stream" at the meadow of asphodel, "the dwelling place of souls, images of dead men" (24.5–14).[8] There they converse with long-departed heroes. Thus the river was not always a barrier. And which river is it? The tradition that would make it the Styx is not specified here and certainly it is not clear from Circe's directions. The river reinforces Patroklos's appeal to Achilles, who is not only alive but still within human society. Part of Odysseus's heroism consists precisely in crossing the ocean to the meeting point of the rivers, penetrating the grove of Persephone, and finally reaching the meadow that leads to where the shades live, an act that impresses even Achilles (11.474–75). By means of his sacrifices, Odysseus had met his obligations to all the dead of whom he was aware. Therefore he was present among the dead, including Elpenor, whose primary concern is obtaining burial. The message—that the dead must be buried—is the same in these three passages, but the technique of presenting it differs. Absence of burial is a technicality for the slain suitors. It is no responsibility of their enemies, Odysseus and his family, but will be taken care of by their own kin as soon as word of their death is out. Though even here, this obligation is repeated axiomatically (186–90). Having Hermes herd them down reinforces Odysseus's action in slaying them and provides

8. English quotations are from the Richmond Lattimore translations of *The Odyssey* (New York: Harper and Row, 1967) and *The Iliad* (Chicago: University of Chicago Press, 1951).

the delicious spectacle of forcing them to admit to Agamemnon how Penelope outwitted them (24.123–85).

This space, therefore, is not defined with literal precision. In general there seems to be a level expanse between a river and the actual dwelling of the dead. Yet it is not clear in Homer which river it is, or what its function. Similarly, it is uncertain whether Erebos is a synonym for the house of Hades, and both describe the whole region generically, or whether the house of Hades, with its gates, is a particular spot within the underworld. Unlike the banks of the underworld river in ancient Egypt, the otherworld visited by Odysseus has no map.

One thing is sure: the land of the dead is very far away from human habitation. Odysseus objected to Circe that no living person had been there before (10.501–2). Homer, and presumably, his audience, is certainly concerned to separate or, in Erwin Rohde's term, to "banish" the dead.[9] As in the *Epic of Gilgamesh*, the length of the voyage to the land of the dead indicates the extent of the society's desire to maintain a vast separation between the living and the dead. Like Gilgamesh, Odysseus travels not beneath the earth but far to the west, beyond the flow of Ocean, which bounds the land, beyond the sunset, to the land of the Cimerians shrouded in mist and cloud, where the sun never shines (12–19). This emphasis on horizontal passage seems to contradict the many references to the downward path of the dead (*Iliad* 23.51; *Odyssey* 10.560, 11.65, 24.10) to "the gates of Hades, underneath the earth's secret places" (*Odyssey* 24.204). Conversely, after Odysseus makes his offerings, the souls come "up out of Erebos" (*Odyssey* 11.36–7) as if it were a lower pit that extended beneath the surface. It is at once distant and below.[10] Perhaps this ambiguity between depth and distance to the land of souls matches the apparent contradiction between cremation and burial for the disposal of bodies.[11]

In book 11, the poet offers only a loosely structured account of the land of the dead. Odysseus narrates the series of dialogues he conducted with the

9. Rohde, *Psyche*, 171. More recently Robert Garland has explained this phenomenon somewhat differently. He posits "an innate Greek insistence on the preservation of a system of categorization which, in this instance, was designed to keep the world of the living rigidly apart from that of the dead." *The Greek Way of Death* (Ithaca: Cornell University Press, 1985), 121. Walter Burkert, *Greek Religion*, 197, also stresses "the radical separation of the dead from the living."

10. Burkert, *Greek Religion*, 196.

11. For an introduction to the simultaneous practice of cremation and inhumation in antiquity, see "Dead, Disposal of," in the *Oxford Classical Dictionary*, and more particularly, Ian Morris, "Attitudes toward Death in Archaic Greece," *Classical Antiquity* 8 (1989): 316.

shades. Interruptions are frequent, and the narrative itself juxtaposes Odysseus's conversations paratactically. That is, they are simply listed, separated by the temporal adverb "next." The hero (rather than the nature of the place) imposes order with his sword as he prevents the crowd of shades from overwhelming him at the pit of blood which alone can give them the strength to speak. Nor are the dead grouped by any moral categories. Rather, their social status seems to structure the sequence of speakers.[12] When questioned by Odysseus, they relate how they died, not what they endure. Although they suffer from the bleakness of their surroundings, their fate has no punitive quality. As they approach Odysseus in turn, it becomes clear that they suffer from the memory of their life or the shame they experienced in the manner of their death but not from the condition of Hades' kingdom.

The thirst of the shades for the vital juice of the blood is such that Odysseus must stave off the mob with his sword to assure his consultation first with Teiresias, the blind seer, whom he wishes to consult about his future. Nonetheless Elpenor claims precedence, for, as one unburied, he is in an ambiguous, intermediate position: although certainly no longer alive, without decent burial he is not yet welcome among the dead. Odysseus, too, is in a liminal relationship to the dead, as appears from his question to Elpinor. Not only is he still alive, he is a newcomer in their land, and he has to ask how Elpinor managed to arrive before him, for though Odysseus had fast ships, he had to sail through many days of darkness, (57–58). The trip to the realm of Hades is slow only for the living!

The precedence that Homer grants Elpinor also emphasizes the separation of living and dead. Clearing the boundary between life and death is crucial. Perhaps religious scruples dissuade even the poet from proceeding until after his hero has confronted this responsibility, neglected because of "this other errand" (54). Elpinor entreats Odysseus to bury him lest "I might become the gods' curse upon you" (73). The responsibility of the living for the dead must be satisfied before either the poet or the hero can pursue his goal among the shades.

A further interruption appears in the form of Antikleia, Odysseus's mother, of whose death he was ignorant. Although he says kind words to her, he perseveres in his intention to interview Teiresias first. The conversation with Elpinor is directly juxtaposed to the appearance of Antikleia. Separating the two incidents with no more than the adverb "next" underlines the randomness Homer attributes to the crowding of the shades. Brandishing his sword,

---

12. For the importance of status in funerals of the archaic age in Greece, see Ian Morris, *Burial and Ancient Society: The Rise of the Greek City-State*, New Studies in Archaeology (Cambridge: Cambridge University Press, 1987), 46–48.

Odysseus allows only Teiresias to approach the strength-giving blood (84–89).

Addressing Odysseus, the prophet observes that he has left the sunlight to come among the dead, to a "place without pleasure" (94). Only after drinking from the blood (96, 99) is Teiresias able to identify Poseidon, father of Polyphemos, whom Odysseus outwitted and blinded, as the key to his troubles.

After she in turn drinks from the blood, Antiklea questions her son to find out how he could be there while still alive (155–56). Odysseus asks his mother how she died; in "longing," she replies, for his return (202). When Odysseus seeks to embrace his mother, his arms pass through her spirit [psychē] three times as "she fluttered out of my hands like a shadow [skiēi] or a dream [oneirōi]" (205–8). Are you just an image [eidōlon]? No, child, this is not Persephone's doing, for when one dies, "the sinews no longer hold the flesh [sarkas] and the bones [ostea] together"; the funeral pyre consumes them (219–21). "But the soul [psychē] flitters out like a dream [oneiros] and flies away" (222). From her own experience, the hero's mother tells him what happens when people die. The soul survives but is subject to the fog and darkness of a pleasureless world. The soul (psychē) is not "just" an image (eidōlon), for it retains its identity and memory. Achilles had the same experience when Patroklos appeared to him (Iliad 23.97–101). The surviving warrior asked for an embrace and learned something about the soul: it can be seen but not touched. Achilles concluded: "Even in the house of Hades there is left something, a soul [psychē] and an image [eidōlon], but there is no real heart of life in it" (104).

After these three individuals, Odysseus encounters his first group, a female category, as Persephone, the queen of the underworld, acting perhaps as patroness of dead women, sends him those who had been the wives and daughters of princes. This category is defined not by behavior in life but by gender and rank. Wielding the sword, Odysseus forces them to drink only one at a time, so that he can question them individually. He sees Tyro who bore two children to Poseidon (235–65), Alkmene, who bore Zeus's son Herakles, and Megara, wife of Herakles (266–70). These women are known by their divine lovers or male children. The fame of Leda, mother of Kastor and Polydeukes, also comes (in this account) from her sons, who are both dead yet living. Each one is granted life on alternate days, and both are honored as gods for overcoming death in this way. They provide a breach in the boundary between the dead and living which Homer otherwise emphasizes (298–304).

Vengeance provides another link between the living and dead which is more active than a mother's pride in the deeds of son or husband. Epikaste, mother of Oedipus, does not brag of his deeds. Instead, she tells Odysseus how she sent her Furies (Erinyes) from the land of Hades to pursue her son (271–80). Punishment is not always initiated by the mother, as in the case of Iphimedeia's sons, who nurtured rebellion against the Olympians. Apollo killed them before they ever grew beards. Early death as preemptive retribution for, or a precautionary measure against, rebellion threatens to break the boundary that might assure life.

Odysseus's account of the women typifies this treatment of the dead. Although they are introduced as a group, Odysseus narrates their stories separately. There is no apparent reason for the order of his treatment (I have done some regrouping) and the narrative lacks any logical connectives, stating only: "and after her I saw . . ." (e.g., 266, 305). Further, the women are dramatically segregated from the men.

Scattered now by Persephone, the women yield their place to Agamemnon and his troop. Although noticing a sluggishness in the demeanor of his former leader at Troy, Odysseus presumes (or pretends to presume) a valiant end in battle for the king and asks how he died. Agamemnon's anger and shame in admitting death in the house of Aigisthos, the lover whom his "sluttish" (411) wife had accepted while he was before the walls of Troy, create immense suffering for the humiliated general. The pain comes, however, from the continuance of his emotion at the time of death, rather than from the nature of the underworld or the fact of death. Even when he was mortally wounded in the ambush and calling to Klytemnestra, she refused to close his eyes or mouth as he expired, "though I was going to Hades' [house]." As if in return for the undying humiliation he believes she caused him, Agamemnon berates all women for her infidelity.[13] Agamemnon's envy of Odysseus for his faithful wife (praised by Teiresias at 117 and Antikleia at 181) is apparent (447–53). Agamemnon repeats his praise of Penelope in the *nekyia* of book 24 (lines 194–98). Although, like the other shades, Agamemnon tells how he died rather than what he endures in the underworld, it is clear that his pain comes from the manner of his death. The one consolation possible for him would be news about his son Orestes, but Odysseus cannot provide it (457–64). Here the fate of a dead person would be alleviated by knowledge of living kin. Agamemnon suffers from the contrast between himself and Odysseus, either in their fame or in the knowledge the two fathers enjoy of their two sons. Since, as Teiresias explained earlier

13. The legend that Agamemnon had sacrificed his daughter Iphigenia and so given "cause" for Klytemnestra's transfer of fidelity, as related in Euripides' play *Iphigenia in Tauris*, depends on a post-Homeric tradition—or, at least, is passed over by Homer here.

(148), a shade is empowered to tell the truth, Agamemnon prophesies that Odysseus will see his son and enjoy his embrace.

As was the case in moving from woman to woman, Homer has Odysseus turn from Agamemnon to Achilles with no further explanation than "after this." The point of this technical detail is to remark on a lack of articulated progression, plan, or organization such as will be found in other authors narrating similar events. The most that can be said is that here (465–66), as between Elpinor and Teiresias (81–83), there is a one-sentence winding down of the conversation and a sharing of "sad words" before the approach of the next person.

Achilles compliments Odysseus for the "bigger endeavor" (474) of getting live to the underworld, among those "senseless dead men," the "mere imitations of perished mortals" (475–76). Odysseus refers to the near-divine honor paid Achilles in life and implies that he must also rule over the dead men's shades, and thus need not be so pained by death. Achilles answers:

> O shining Odysseus, never try to console me for dying.
> I would rather follow the plow as thrall to another
> man, one with no land allotted him and not much to live on,
> than be a king over all the perished dead.
>
> (488–91)

Even if they existed, no honors after death can compensate the loss of life. Achilles' statement again stresses the distance between life and death, though here the distance is psychological.

Like Agamemnon, Achilles asks for news of his son and father. With a vigor that recalls his life, he states his desire to be whole again so that he might avenge his aged father against his detractors (494–503). Though clearly not grieving in the manner of Agamemnon from a shameful death, Achilles suffers from death itself, from being unable to execute his plans to restore his father's rule. The one possible consolation after death has nothing to do with lordship over the dead or one's reputation in life. When Odysseus tells Achilles of his brave son (507–37), Achilles strides buoyantly off through the meadow of asphodel (538–40).[14] The contrast between Agamemnon and Achilles is as marked in the *Odyssey*'s account of their fates in death as is the *Iliad*'s account of their lives.

After learning of this one measure of comparative happiness, Odysseus summarizes other conversations succinctly: "Now the rest of the souls of the

---

14. A flower associated with the dead because of its gray-yellow color. See *Encyclopaedia Britannica*, Micropaedia, 1:589.

perished dead stood near me grieving, and each one spoke to me and told of his sorrows" (541–42). It is clear that, the fate of Achilles apart—and Achilles is explicit about his resentment of death—death is a time of sorrow but not punishment. The shades of the warriors are tormented by the continuity between life and death: they bear in death the reputation they had at the moment they died.[15] Thus there is no escaping the shame of being cuckolded or of dying ingloriously. The one consolation seems to be knowledge of compensatory glory acquired by one's descendants, particularly sons.

Emphasis on the moment of death is clear, as warriors appear in blood-spattered armor (41). Ajax provides another example of emotional continuity. He still bears a grudge against Odysseus for winning the arms of Achilles. His rebuff of Odysseus confirms the notion that the warrior shades of Homer's underworld are frozen in the emotions they felt at death, for Ajax had committed suicide, still incensed at this reverse (543–66). In this respect like the women, the warriors console themselves, when possible, with the vicarious glory of their offspring.

Odysseus's account closes with another sequence of items he saw: "Then I saw," "and after him," "and I saw." The sequential logic of the narrative, the spare, paratactic listing that stresses the discreteness of each conversation has been important from the beginning of this account. Yet the continuation of this technique is surprising here, because from this point until his encounter with Herakles, Odysseus begins to see completely different sights. Whereas the others with whom he conversed had presented themselves to the bowl of blood and been allowed by Odysseus to drink, the glimpses that conclude this account are disclosed to Odysseus as if he had obtained some new perspective, perhaps a different vantage point from which he could see into the home of the shades or farther around the meadow where they gather. Before, he had conversed with shades who came "up out of Erebos" (11.36–7) to meet him. Now, he seems to see into the place from which they came. In contrast to Dante, who sometimes explains precisely how he placed his feet, Odysseus here simply lists the sights he saw. Perhaps it is enough that the hero could itemize his perceptions. Each is as distinct as a sword stroke. Who but a hero could bring back even these scant impressions from the earth's core's "darkness and gloom"? Nonetheless, the teller's rigorous adherence to a listing of sights comes at the expense of explanation. For Odysseus to be able to take in these punishments, each of which requires

15. Burkert, *Greek Religion*, 196: They "may persist in their activity of life or situation of death: Orion the hunter hunts, Minos the king dispenses justice, and Agamemnon is surrounded by those who were slain with him."

different physical settings and considerable space, his gaze certainly must comprehend far more than just the throng of souls crowding about his sacrificial pit of blood.

However it happens, Odysseus next sees "by the wide-gated house of Hades" King Minos, holding a golden staff, as he deals out justice to the dead clustered around his throne (568–71). This is a view of the daily life of the dead. Litigants array themselves around the seat of a judge within the land of Hades. Odysseus sees his identity and his symbol of office. His report suggests not a judgment *of* the dead according to their lives, but a kind of magistracy within the city of Hades by which Minos acts as a judge *for* the dead (568–71).

"Next," Odysseus sees Orion carrying an unbroken club, rounding up wild animals in the meadow of asphodel (572–75). Orion precedes figures who are suffering punishment, and he may rank among the guilty. In this case his activity seems to reverse the offense he gave when he sought to exterminate the animals on the island of Crete. Earth intervened and sent a scorpion to kill him. He is an example of one condemned to wander in eternal labor or pursuit.[16] An alternative explanation would emphasize his promotion to heavenly status as a constellation, like Herakles, consider him a hero, and view his herd as a trophy he displays before all the dead.

"Next," Odysseus sees Tityos, son of Earth, stretched out over nine acres. Vultures tear at his liver, seat of his desire for Leto, a Titan, mother of Apollo and Artemis, whom he had manhandled (576–81).

"Next," Odysseus sees Tantalus perched between receding sources of water and fruit. As he reaches down for water, it dries up, revealing the barren earth beneath. Similarly, the wind blows fruit-bearing boughs overhead out of his reach (582–92).

"Next," Odysseus sees Sisyphus, pushing his burden up a hill, until the weight once more spins him around and sends the cruel burden bounding to the plain, whence he must start pushing it again (593–600).[17]

"Next," Odysseus encounters Herakles, who speaks to him. This last exchange appears to be of the type that preceded the glimpse of Minos, for Herakles tells of his deeds. Further, Odysseus specifies that he speaks with the image, the *eidōlon* (602), of Herakles. Although Antiklea had said shades are not mere images but souls (213–22), what Odysseus sees of

16. There is an early account of Orion in the pseudo-Hesiodic *Astronomy*, sec. 4, in *Hesiod, the Homeric Hymns, and Homerica*, trans. H. G. Evelyn-White (Cambridge: Harvard University Press, 1982), 71. I thank Charles King for this reference.

17. *Oxford Classical Dictionary*; Rose, *Handbook*, 270, 294, and notes. See also "Thanatos," *Oxford Classical Dictionary*.

Herakles is precisely his image, since the real self of this son of Zeus has been apotheosized and dwells as a constellation among the immortals. In the land of Hades it is his image from whose approach the shades flee (606–7). Odysseus senses the flutter of lesser souls in the darkness of the place.

Addressing Odysseus, Herakles asks whether he too has some evil destiny beyond the reach of the sun. Herakles tells how Hermes and Athena aided him in his theft of Cerberus from the underworld. His story told, the image of Herakles strides back into the house of Hades. The meeting of Odysseus and Heracles returns us to the scene at the pit of blood. In the foreground there seems to be a crowd of souls that have emerged from some opening that permits entrance from below, perhaps a cavern whose mouth is the backdrop for the scene. Herakles' return to that passageway in the rear reorients us. (Although the shades fluttered away from his presence, his approach was not described.)

After the departure of Herakles, fear overcomes the curiosity of Odysseus. He stays in place, he says, hoping to see other heroes emerge (again, the original setting), perhaps even Perithous and Theseus, but then a mob of shades surrounds him giving forth a frightening shout. The sound apparently makes Odysseus conscious of his transience, that he is not yet dead and that he is a puny mortal before the power of death. Homer, incidentally, volunteers no such explanation, connecting the shout to Odysseus's fear with a simple "and" (633).

In this moment of fright, when the need for flight overtakes Odysseus, what he fears to see emerge from that cavern is the snake-haired, evil-eyed Gorgon, whom Persephone might send up against him, who, if their eyes met, might turn him to stone.[18] Odysseus has tarried with death as long as he dares. He whirls and makes for the ship. After rejoining his men, they sail back across Ocean, over the wide sea toward the dawn, into the rays of the sun.

However loosely the details are knit together, however the poet resists explaining the impressions he simply lists, Odysseus's account of his visit to the dead is not without structure. Though the physical setting lacks detail, enough is clear to permit a distinction between the conversations that take place in the meadow near the river and the other incidents nearer the area from which the shades emerge. In the meadow, the shades swarm in a group and endure their deaths without distinction except as permitted to regain strength through drinking from the blood. These souls are equal in death, are barely conscious, and live without either reward or punishment. Only the manner of their deaths, the emotions of that moment, and pride in the

18. See Rose, *Handbook*, 29.

achievements of their offspring tinge their pale existence. By contrast, those farther from the river—Orion, Tityos, Tantalus, and Sisyphus—with whom Odysseus does not speak, pursue their fates persistently, with no need of the sacrificial blood, inexorably driven to repeat their tasks indefinitely. Orion (if he is punished), Tityos, Tantalus, and Sisyphus stand out from the common dead, examples of the worst punishments for the worst offenses. This distinction between punishment and mere existence in death comes, in some sources, to affect the view of death itself. In Homer, however, death for all the purely human shades is morally neutral. Distinctions of social status brought over from life, memories and aspirations, vicarious pride or shame at loss of status characterize the dead, it is true, but these emotions do not affect their basic condition, and as compared to the fact of death, the place itself adds nothing.

HESIOD'S *THEOGONY*

Whereas the *Odyssey* recounts the deeds of humans within a world affected at every turn by the gods, Hesiod's *Theogony* relates the gods' foundation of that world.[19] Key to establishing their divine order is the punishment of the tyrant gods and rebels against the Olympian system. This theme of divine punishment begins with the very origin of the world. From the Void (Chaos) came Earth (Gaia), who created Sky (Uranus) as her mate. Of their children, the first was Ocean, the last and most important was Kronos (Saturn). Beyond the gods and goddesses shaped in the form shared by gods and humans were the gigantic offspring of Earth and Sky, the three Cyclops, who had only one eye in the center of their forehead but were otherwise like the gods. They invented the lightning bolt and later gave it to Zeus. Also monstrous, but still immortal, were Gyes, Cottus, and Briareus, three creatures of terrible strength, being possessed of a hundred arms and fifty heads

19. Robert Lamberton, *Hesiod* (New Haven: Yale University Press, 1988), esp. 38–104, on the *Theogony*. For a review of scholarship on Hesiod, see Ernst Heitsch, *Hesiod*, Wege der Forschung, 44 (Darmstadt: Wissenschaftliche Buchgesellschaft, 1966). Considering the *Theogony* as a text about creation, see Giancarlo Finazzo, *La realtà di mondo nella visione cosmogonica esiodea* (Rome: Atenea, 1971). See also Ewald Rumpf, *Das Muttertrauma in der griechischen Mythologie: Eine psychologische Interpretation der "Theogonia" von Hesiod* (Frankfurt am Main: Peter Lang, 1985). The translation I use is that of Norman O. Brown, *Theogony* (New York: Bobbs-Merrill, 1953). Greek terms are taken from *Hesiod, Homeric Hymns* (Loeb).

apiece, called the Hundred-Arms (lines 116–53).[20] Sky hated and mistreated his children. Their mother, Earth, contrived to punish him by devising a sickle of stone, which she gave to Kronos, who used it to castrate his father (156–82). This rebellion of Kronos was to be followed by his own overthrow at the hands of Zeus.

Earth and Sky had predicted that Kronos would be overcome by his own son. To avert this fate, the youngest son of Sky devoured his children by his sister and consort Rhea as soon as they were born. He confined the Hundred-Arms under the ground. Finally Rhea reacted. When Zeus was born, she confided him to Sky and Earth and delivered to Kronos a stone wrapped in a blanket, which he devoured. Meanwhile Zeus was raised secretly. Earth outwitted Kronos and induced him to vomit up his children, so they could participate in the rebellion (453–506).

Meanwhile Zeus called all the gods together and promised those who held office that if they supported him, they would not lose their privileges and that those who had been excluded by Kronos would receive new honors. Styx, the daughter of Ocean, was the first to pledge support and so she received special rewards: Zeus made Styx the name by which all the gods swear and promised immortality to all her children (383–452).

For ten years, an indecisive battle was waged between the brothers of Kronos, called the Titans, and his sons. Then Rhea advised Zeus to free the Hundred-Arms from beneath the earth and thus obtain their aid. Hesiod presents a dialogue in which the bargaining is explicit. Zeus made clear the terms of the Hundred-Arms's release and characterized their earlier situation as a liberation from bondage, an escape from darkness and gloom (*hupo zophou ēeroentos*) to light (652–53). In the end, the lightning of Zeus and the force of the Hundred-Arms prevailed. The Titans, who supported Kronos, were confined beneath the earth in Tartarus. This action established a new order. With the elder generation under control, the younger gods and their allies, at the suggestion of Earth, appointed Zeus their ruler, and he divided their territories (881–85). Zeus took the heavens, Poseidon received the sea, and Hades the earth (and what is inside).[21]

---

20. Hesiod states that the Hundred-Arms were born of Earth and Sky (147) but names only Earth (139) as parent of the Cyclops. That Sky was their father is mentioned in a fragment of the epic cycle on the War of the Titans. *Hesiod, Homeric Hymns* (Loeb), 481.

21. The actual distribution is not explicitly laid out in the *Theogony* but is clear in the nearly contemporary Homeric Hymn, no. 2, to Demeter, lines 81–84. Even in the *Theogony* 850, Hades is called king of the dead in the underworld. Plato explicitly restates the idea at *Gorgias* 523b and assumes it as common knowledge in *Cratylus* 402–3.

The story traced in the *Theogony* is curiously (or perhaps intentionally) ambiguous, for it sanctions both legitimate monarchy and rebellion against its abuse. The coin produced by these paired images seems brighter on the side of monarchy, perhaps, because it was presumed that Zeus would not rule like his father. Yet Kronos had not learned to avoid the evils of his sire, and so the foundation myth of the world reserves a place for both authoritarian rule and its violent overthrow. Hesiod apparently believed (or hoped) that the Olympian power established by the rebellion of Zeus, his brothers, and his sisters, would assure the stability of the universe (which was vital lest Zeus himself be deposed). To Hesiod it served as a model for countless smaller monarchies in Greece. As he reported, the support of Zeus, conferred through his daughters the Muses, enables men to rule after his example, for "it is the gift of Zeus that makes men kings" (88, 96). The rule of Zeus anticipates and shapes the rule of human kings. Yet, as Hesiod observed in the *Works and Days*, should anyone puff himself up beyond measure, Zeus has already made provision. Hubris brings on another of Zeus's daughters, Dike, punishing justice, his instrument of divine retribution. Famine, plague, defeat, and a cursed progeny await the ruler who neglects justice (213–85).[22]

Confining the Titans was not enough. Power established must also be maintained. The greatest threat apparently came from Atlas, Menoetius, Epimetheus, and Prometheus, the sons of the Titan Iapetus and the river goddess Clymene (daughter of Ocean). Hesiod does not specify the offenses of each. His characterization is presumably self-explanatory. Zeus struck down the "proud-spirited" Menoetius with a thunderbolt "because of his savage insolence and overbearing boldness" and sent him to nether darkness (Erebos) (514–16). He "condemned" the "violent-spirited" Atlas to hold up the sky (517–20).

Hesiod documents the case of Prometheus more completely (520–616). The first offense of this "cunning trickster" occurred at a ceremony sealing peace between the gods and men (there were not yet any women). In distributing the parts of a sacrificial ox, Prometheus tried to give the best portion to the men at the expense of Zeus. Suspicious now of Prometheus's sympathies, the jealous Zeus tried to conceal fire from the race of men. Again Prometheus betrayed him by bringing fire to men. First Zeus punished men for receiving fire by causing a clay woman to be made—a decoy. Hesiod characterizes this as the origin of what he calls "the damnable race of women—a plague

---

22. See the discussion in Konstantinos St. Panagiotou, *Die ideale Form der Polis bei Homer und Hesiod* (Bochum, Germany: Studienverlag Dr. N. Brockmeyer, 1983), 153–54.

which men must live with" (592–93). Zeus, Hesiod explains, dispensed a beautiful curse (woman) to go with a blessing (fire).[23] Prometheus, too, had to suffer. Zeus had him chained to a rock with a stake driven through his middle. Each day the god caused a vulture to devour his liver and each night he caused the organ to be renewed so that in the morning the vulture could attack with renewed appetite (507–22).

Another brother, Epimetheus, is called "the half-wit." He was the first deceived by the clay woman. Zeus condemned him for bringing "bad luck on men who earn their bread by work" (511–14).

Zeus punished all the sons of Iapetus and Clymene directly. It seems that these punishments were originally intended to be without end, but what may be a later interpolation in the text explains how Zeus finally relented and permitted Herakles to slay the vulture that gnawed Prometheus's side in order to exalt the reputation of the hero (523–33).[24] Atlas, of course, still bears the heavens on his shoulders, perhaps because his punishment was too generally useful to remit. That subsequent opinion should provide an end to Prometheus's suffering is important. Later in antiquity there are other examples of a desire to mitigate divine punishment and to allow a hero to soften justice by ending the torments of the victims of divine wrath.

The last step in Zeus's establishment of the cosmic order was his defeat of Typhoeus. In the Olympian system, whose establishment Hesiod celebrates as well as narrates, the gods of all generations had the same outward appearance as human beings except for the Cyclops and the Hundred-Arms. Part of the effect of Zeus's rule was to retain the community between men and gods represented by the common human (divine) form they shared and destroying all else, which was thus defined as monstrous. In this way Zeus established another aspect of his order by means of his victory over Typhoeus, a hideous dragon with a hundred snake heads growing from his neck. The brothers of Zeus tried to exterminate him, but it was Zeus who attacked him in single combat. Their struggle produced tremendous cataclysms felt even to the depths of Tartarus: "Trembling seized Hades, king of the dead in the underworld and the Titans who stood by Cronus and who live at the bottom of Tartarus" (848–53). Finally victorious, Zeus threw Typhoeus into the depths of Tartarus (869). Only after this defeat does Hesiod call the work of the gods done (881).

It is curious that Typhoeus was the son of Tartarus and Earth. The charac-

23. The misogyny of Hesiod's account of the creation of women must be paired with his separating Hestia, Demeter, and Hera, the sisters of Zeus, Poseidon, and Hades from power. We shall consider soon the treatment of Demeter.

24. See Brown, *Theogony,* 68.

ter of Tartarus as a person receives no extensive development, however. Even though he fathered this monster, Tartarus is far more important as a place than as a person. Yet Typhoeus is so mighty that, even confined in Tartarus, his breath provokes the evil winds that trouble human beings on earth (870–80).

Hesiod completes the picture of Zeus's conquests not only by celebrating its pinnacle atop Olympus but also by plumbing its foundations beneath the earth and narrating the establishment of a credible sanction, Tartarus, prison of the Titans and these monsters. Tartarus is "beneath the highways of the earth" as far from the earth's surface as the ground is beneath the sky. It would take ten days for an anvil of bronze to fall that distance (722–25). In addition, Tartarus is surrounded by a bronze wall girded three times by the thickness of night, which encircles it like a necklace (726–28). Poseidon fashioned the wall's bronze gates (732). So deep are its confines that even if a man entered, he would not reach the bottom for a year but would be tossed and wracked by dark storms that terrify even the gods (741–43). Though he does not give it such extended treatment, Homer attributes similar characteristics to Tartarus. In the *Iliad* he tells how Zeus warned that if any god intervened in the Trojan War, he would "dash him down to the murk of Tartaros, far below, where the uttermost depth of the pit lies under earth, where there are gates of iron and a brazen doorstone" (8.13–15).

Hesiod reinforces the strength of the great dungeon with an analysis of its location. He rivets our attention by pointing repeatedly to the same place. "There" [*entha*]) meet the boundaries of Tartarus, earth, sea, and sky" (729, 736–37). "There" live the Hundred-Arms, guardians of the gate that encloses the Titans (734–35). Just in front (*prosthen*), Atlas plants his feet to support the sky (746–48). The same recess conceals the meeting of Night and Day, for Night lives inside, awaiting her time to come out. "There" live the mysterious gods, Sleep and Death, children of Night (758–59). Tartarus, then, occupies a mystical location, where opposites are joined. Here is the beginning and end of every cycle that makes the world go round: where night passes into day, sleep into death, the center into the edge and vice versa (cf. 728–32).

The conjunction of center and periphery is suggested by the presence "there" of the river goddess Styx (775). The River Styx runs from the world-encircling Ocean through the night and past this point at the core of the universe. Because of her importance as the first to pledge allegiance to Zeus against the Titans, the king of the gods decreed that the Olympians should swear their oaths upon the water of this river (cf. 389–403). They must make amends if they perjure themselves, suffering one year in feverish stupor followed by nine years of exile from the company of the gods. Only in the tenth year can the lying god return to Olympus (775–820). No trouble arises from the fact that the course of the Styx runs right through this space "between" Tartarus and the house of Hades. The variable imagery does not weaken the mythical force of this insistent iteration. The residence of the goddess Styx and the god Hades outside the gate of Tartarus and the need for even Gods to contend with the possibility of a punishment rooted here intensifies the awe already focused in this place.

Hesiod has already said that Tartarus lies far below the earth (721–25). Yet now he continues to say "there" (*entha*), but this time adds "in front" or "outside" (*prosthen*), a word that introduces a difference. In this place, then, but outside it, stand the halls of Hades, god of the underworld (767), and his wife Persephone. Guarding the front of their palace is a cruel hound (Cerberus, named at 311), who greets with wagging tail all who arrive, but devours all who would leave (770–73). In this different place in the same location, whether across from or above the gates of Tartarus, is the land of Hades, to which, as appeared in the *Odyssey*, the human dead are sent. Homer provides another detail: Tartarus is as far beneath the house of Hades as the earth is beneath the sky (*Iliad* 8.16). Hesiod's confrontation of Tartarus and the house of Hades, therefore, is mysterious. However uncertain their physical relationship to each other, the difference in their function is clear. The *Odyssey* certainly showed the house of Hades as the residence of human shades and another, unnamed area as the place of punishment for a few, outstanding, superhuman rebels. Hesiod, focusing rather on the prison of the Titans and barely describing Hades, provides another list of criminal demigods. Besides the Titans, he accounts for Atlas, Menoetius, Epimetheus, Prometheus, and Typhoeus. Whereas Odysseus simply devoted a separate part of his narrative to the superhuman criminals he mentioned, Hesiod provides them their own prison, Tartarus, somehow a different place in the same location as the house of Hades. Homer suggests that this difference is in level: Tartarus lies far below, but clarity of physical location is not available in Hesiod's description.

Homer and Hesiod give actual punishment only to a few special persons. Whatever evil brought Tityos or Prometheus to their fates, neither Homer nor Hesiod could conceive of a human deserving anything similar. Although there is no suggestion that the human shades in the house of Hades will ever cease to exist, neither are they punished. The distinction between Tartarus, prison of superhuman miscreants, and Hades, land of all the human dead of whatever character, is a crucial aspect of the cultural environment from which the concept of hell emerged. Later, it would be possible to imagine unending punishment for humans, too.

If the roots of heaven, earth, and sea come together before the gates of

Tartarus, which imprisons the overthrown Titans, then it must be a special place for a goddess revered by both Titans and Zeus (411). It is the goddess Hecate, who, like the Olympians collectively, has rule (424) in the earth, heaven, and sea, for she gives catch (441) on the sea, victory (431) in battle, and flocks (444) on land. So productive a goddess cannot be ignored. Moreover, her path intersects with that of another goddess—this one barely mentioned by Hesiod—although Persephone, to whom I refer, resembles Hecate in that she too functions very significantly in more than one of the realms separated by Zeus. Throughout this book it will be important to note systematically those who permeate or transcend established boundaries, whether physical, like those established by Zeus and his brothers, or categorical, like those to be defined by Plato.

Persephone was the daughter of Zeus and Demeter, who "nourishes all life" (908), one of his many consorts.[25] For reasons that are not stated, Zeus permitted his brother Hades to abduct Persephone and keep her as his wife down in his shadowy realm. A further clue to these associations comes when Hesiod tells how Demeter united once not with Zeus but with the hero Iasion "in a fallow field ploughed three times and bore Pluto (Wealth), who gives prosperity" (969–73).[26] Both Persephone and Pluto, though they have different fathers, are linked through their mother with the earth's fruitfulness. In Hesiod there can be no confusion between Hades and Pluto, yet as time wore on, these figures fused: Hades as lord of the dead became associated with the earth as storehouse of seed; Pluto as a personification of Plenty (that is seed and produce in an agricultural society) took on attributes of rulership.[27] The Homeric *Hymn to Demeter* helps explain this overlap between the underworld as grave (necropolis, city of the dead, catacomb) and granary, the connection between the inner earth and the fertility of its surface, the relationship of Hades/Pluto, Persephone, and Hecate.

HYMN TO DEMETER

The story is told in the Homeric *Hymn to Demeter*. Hades abducted Persephone, the daughter of Zeus and Demeter, with her father's connivance

25. Günther Zuntz, *Persephone: Three Essays on Religion and Thought in Magna Graecia* (Oxford: Clarendon Press, 1971).

26. Rose, *Handbook*, 94, cites this story as an unrelated variant to the myths of Demeter and makes no connection between "Plutos, *i.e.*, Wealth, meaning of course the wealth of the ground, abundant harvests," and Hades.

27. Burkert, *Greek Religion*, 200. Cicero's character Balbus derives Pluto from *plutus*, meaning "plenty," without challenge in *De natura deorum* 2.26.66.

and brought to her live with him in his underground kingdom. Demeter heard her daughter's cries for help but could not locate her for nine days until she met Hecate, carrying a torch, who informed her that she too had heard the screams but did not know who removed the girl (39–58). Demeter learned the abductor's identity from Helios (the Sun), who stressed that Zeus "gave" her to Hades. Helios sought to calm the mother by observing that Hades was certainly a fitting husband for her daughter. The brother of Zeus and of Demeter herself, he had received a third share of the division made by the sons of Kronos and had become lord of the place where he dwells (74–87).

Demeter was infuriated and, in protest, withdrew from the company of the gods. Further, she instituted a terrible plague for humankind: she kept the grain hidden beneath the earth, so that it would not grow (305–8). There it would remain, she threatened, until her daughter was restored. Before allowing Persephone to leave because of pressure from the Olympians, Hades encouraged her to accept her lot with him: "You shall rule all that lives and moves and shall have the greatest rights among the deathless gods" (364–66). He promised that those who deny her the honor to which she is thereby entitled, "those who defraud you and do not appease your power with offerings, . . . shall be punished for evermore" (lines 367–69: "shall do penance everlastingly," says Rohde, *Psyche* 219). To ensure that she could not stay with her mother permanently, he secretly gave her some pomegranate seed, for it was well known that whoever ate while in the underworld could never return entirely to the light (370–74).

Demeter learned in horror that Persephone had accepted food from Hades, and though it is not stated explicitly, she entrusted her daughter to Hecate: "And often did [Hecate] embrace the daughter of holy Demeter: and from that time the lady Hecate was minister and companion to Persephone" (439–41). Zeus then commanded Demeter to rejoin the gods and Persephone to spend a third of the year "in the darkness and gloom" (*hupo zophon ēeroenta* [446; cf. 402]), the same terms Hesiod used to describe the conditions from which the Hundred-Arms sought liberation (*Theogony* 653). Then Demeter restored prosperity to the earth she had made barren. She revealed her mysteries to the people there and explained the performance of her rites (475–76), which would become the Eleusinian Mysteries.[28]

The story told in the *Hymn to Demeter* complements Hesiod's report of the underworld. This narrative helps explain the fusion of Demeter's brother

28. Paul Foucart, *Les mystères d'Eleusis* (Paris: Picard, 1914). See also Karl Kerényi, *Eleusis: Archetypal Image of Mother and Daughter*, trans. Ralph Manheim (New York: Pantheon Books, 1967); George Emmanuel Mylonas, *Eleusis and the Eleusinian Mysteries* (Princeton: Princeton University Press, 1961).

(Hades) and son (Pluto) into one god representing two important aspects of the underworld: its wealth as a storehouse of seed and its darkness as a repository of corpses. Without overlooking the crucial differences I have mentioned, it is not inappropriate to recall the similar associations bound up in the Akkadian treatment of the *Descent of Ishtar,* which also linked violence in the netherworld (though in this case, coming from the female heavenly aggressor) to famine on earth. The complex relationship perceived between the disposal of corpses and the storing and planting of seeds was interpreted and treated differently in different places. The *Hymn to Demeter* shows that from Demeter's point of view, the underworld is a granary. For Persephone, as for Inanna/Ishtar, it nearly became a grave but turned out to be only a place of temporary confinement. For seeds, the underworld is a temporary place of rest, a bed. For souls it is a permanent container except under very carefully regulated conditions.

Knowledge of how this fertile cycle came to be is at the core of the mysteries Demeter established at Eleusis.[29] So vital is the cyclical connection between death and regeneration, between the inside of the earth and fertility, that participation in the rites that commemorate its establishment was believed to affect one's fate in the afterlife: "Happy is he among men upon earth who has seen these mysteries; but he who is not initiated in the rites and who has no part in them, does not share the same good things once he is dead, down in the darkness and gloom [*hupo zophōi ēeroenti*]" (482–84).[30] This passage clearly indicates that humans can experience different fates after death.[31] Rebel gods such as Prometheus, the overthrown Titans, threat-

29. This second myth suggests Hades the person as a source of evil, the underground as a negative force, a cause of barrenness, which can be cajoled or appeased only through performance of certain rites, i.e., the Eleusinian Mysteries. The sense of compulsion is very strong. Note the speech of Hades, where he assures Persephone of the honor in being married to Zeus's brother, of Zeus's complicity in the abduction, and that those who neglect to cultivate her honor will be punished forever. See also Mara Lynn Keller, "The Eleusinian Mysteries of Demeter and Persephone: Fertility, Sexuality, and Rebirth," *Journal of Feminist Studies in Religion* 4 (1988): 27–54.

30. Cf. Charles Boer, trans., *The Homeric Hymns* (Dallas: Spring, 1970), 133. The Eleusinian Mysteries were open to all applicants except murderers. Diogenes the Cynic criticized them by pointing out that according to Eleusinian tenets a thief who had been initiated would have a better fate in the underworld than a hero who had not. Cited by W. K. C. Guthrie, *The Greeks and Their Gods* (Boston: Beacon, 1950), 321.

31. On the possibility of happiness in the other world, see Larry J. Alderink, "Mythical and Cosmological Structure in the Homeric *Hymn to Demeter*," *Numen: International Review for the History of Religion* 29 (1982): 1–16. For the different degrees of initiation, see Ken Dowden, "Grades in the Eleusinian Mysteries," *Revue de l'histoire des religions* 197 (1980): 409–27.

ening monsters such as Typhoeus are all constrained by Zeus's order. These, however, are confined in Tartarus. Hades may dwell at or above the gates of Tartarus, but not all within his realm are punished, as the visit of Odysseus to the land of the dead made clear.

With its introduction of the possibility of more than one fate for humans in the afterlife, the *Hymn to Demeter* activates an important strategy. Crucial to the foundation myth of those rites is Hades' promise to Persephone: she will rule alongside him, and those who refuse to honor her will know suffering every day forever (367–69). This is eternal punishment. Almost nothing is known of the rites themselves, but this sentence, which nearly amounts to a marriage contract between Pluto and his bride (or at least regularizes their relationship, originally founded on violence), spoken in the presence of Hermes (and surely known to Hecate, who had heard the cries of the frightened victim), establishes a postmortem sanction within the story itself. The poet's editorial promise of a happier afterlife for initiates is different in kind from these words spoken directly by the god. The poet, author of the hymn, could be wrong, but the god's promise to his bride must be rooted in a special mythical truth. Hades may be capable of trickery, but perjury was punished even among the Olympians. Consequently, through the poet, we have it from Hades himself that anyone who fails to make offerings to Persephone will be punished forever. Embedded within a text that was presumably recited at or around the performance of the mysteries ordained by its telling, these words enjoin the performance of those very rites in order to avoid the threatened fate. That "embedding" gives the text a self-reflexiveness: Do the deeds commanded here or suffer the consequences threatened here. What authority does a self-reflexive text have over those who give it no credence? They risk finding out in darkness and gloom.

THE ORPHIC FRAMEWORK

The sources presented so far, committed to writing at the end of the archaic age, suggest the existence of two different traditions concerning life after death. Homer sees it as a prolongation of the moment of death for humans. Only superhuman offenders are punished. His view is an inspiration to glory, to deeds that, if interrupted by death, will lead to satisfaction in the reflection upon them which will occupy the shade ever after. The contrast between Agamemnon, who died at the hand of his wife's lover, and Achilles, who died aspiring to restore his father's rule, could hardly be stronger. Yet both shades are equal residents of the land of Hades. Contrasts such as that between opponents and adherents of Osiris and impatience over equality in death such as emerged from reflections on the Hebrew Sheol do not apply here. The mysteries, however, introduced another tradition in which very different conditions awaited the dead. The *Hymn to Demeter* stated that those who have "looked on" those rites would know a better life than those who had not been initiated. Since the hymn related the establishment of the very rites that determined one's fate in the next world, that provision made the hymn self-enforcing. The *Hymn to Demeter*, therefore, provided its own sanction—a sanction built around a profound contrast in people's fates in the afterlife.

The Orphic religion took this contrast even further. The difficulty is that it is virtually impossible to reconstruct Orphism as it existed in the archaic period. The first surviving signs come from just before 500 B.C.E.; a few clues come during the fifth century; and the majority of the information is from the Hellenistic age and later. Indeed, since Orphism was held secret, virtually none of its precepts are stated by adherents of that mystery. Traces of them can be recovered, however, from other sources: the odes of Pindar, the philosophy of Plato, and allusions in even later sources.[32]

The Orphics believed that human nature enclosed a conflict between two elements, the body and the soul. Using the euphony of the Greek words *sōma* (body) and *sēma* (prison), they considered the body a prison confining the soul and preventing it from realizing its proper nature. They supported this theory by reference to a myth that can be reconstructed with difficulty from a series of poems, the *Twenty-Four Rhapsodies*. Although different scholars present varied interpretations, the effective thrust of the narrative (which is obviously influenced by or competes with Hesiod's *Theogony* in its conception and general outline) is to tell the history of the gods and the world.[33]

The chthonic, underworld setting colors the story from the outset. Persephone is the mother of the hero, and the imprisoned Titans are the chief villains. In this myth, Zeus rapes Persephone, who gives birth to Dionysus, who is also called by the non-Greek name Zagreus.[34] The Titans lure the infant into their reach with toys and set upon him. Changing forms ingeniously, Dionysus attempts to escape, but the Titans finally overcome and devour him when he is in the form of a bull. (That is why it is a bull that is

---

32. For an overview on Orphism, see Martin L. West, *The Orphic Poems* (Oxford: Clarendon, 1983). Burkert, *Greek Religion*, 198, confirms the date and radical nature of this change.

33. Burkert, *Greek Religion*, 296, notes the effort to "outdo" Hesiod's *Theogony*. See his discussion, 296–304.

34. There is a prehistory, prior to the birth of the Olympians, which I omit. It is recounted in Aristophanes, *The Birds* 693–702.

sacrificed in Orphic ritual.) Athena, however, saves the heart of Dionysus and gives it to Zeus, who eats the heart of his son by Persephone. This time, coupled with Semele (whom Dionysus would later lead out of Hades), Zeus fathers Dionysus again. To avenge himself upon the Titans, Zeus destroys them, though from their ashes arises the human race, possessed, therefore, of a hybrid nature, part Dionysian, heavenly (Olympian), and good; part Titanic, chthonic, and evil.[35]

The duty of human beings is to cultivate the Dionysian and slough off the Titanic side of their character. It may take several lifetimes, through repeated reincarnations, to attain this goal. Although the soul is freed from the body at death, it experiences an intermediate period of punishment, purification, or reward before being reborn in another body. This cycle may continue indefinitely, or it can be broken, as Orpheus showed, through the worship of Dionysus. "Reincorporation" ends only with redemption and a final reunion with the divine.

As to the origin of these ideas, we are in the dark. Herodotus, who lived from around 484 to 430 or 420 B.C.E.,[36] tells us in his *Histories* (2.81) that certain Egyptian ideas were known to Pythagoras (active c. 530) in the Greek colonies of southern Italy and that they resembled the ideas of the Bacchic and Orphic cultists.[37] Pausanias, the second-century C.E. geographer, credits the first writing of these tales to a seer named Onomakritos, who was favored at the court of the Pisistratid tyrants in Athens (around 540s to 520s B.C.E.).[38] Even this sketch is based on later sources, and any fuller sense of Orphism as a system can only be conjectured.

The Homeric *Hymn to Demeter* states that knowledge of the Eleusinian Mysteries affects one's fate in the afterlife. The Boeotian poet Pindar (518–438) agrees, though he comments in regard to the Orphic mysteries: "Blessed is he who hath seen these things before he goeth beneath the hollow

35. This much, Rohde, *Psyche*, 340–41.

36. *Oxford Classical Dictionary*.

37. For a review of the legends circulating about Pythagoras, see Rohde, *Psyche*, app. X. Isidore Lévy, *La légende de Pythagore de Grèce en Palestine*, Bibliothèque de l'Ecole des hautes études . . . sciences historiques et philologiques, 250 (Paris: Champion, 1927), 79–93, analyzes a putative account of his descent into Hades. Diogenes Laertius refers to this legend in *Lives of Eminent Philosophers*. According to Diogenes Laertius, Pythagoras claimed while in the netherworld to have seen Homer and Hesiod in torment for their lies about the gods (8.21). Unfaithful husbands are also punished there, according to Pythagoras. (Cf. 8.38 and 41.) In *The Cock* Lucian makes fun of the legend.

38. Pausanias, *Description of Greece* 8.37.5. Guthrie, *The Greeks and Their Gods*, 314, notes that she was a woman.

earth; for he understandeth the end of mortal life, and the beginning (of a new life) given of god" (frag. 137). Simple understanding, however, does not ensure salvation. Pindar's Fragment 131 speaks of a rite that releases from toil, a toil generally associated with the cycle of lives: "And while the body of all men is subject to overmastering death, an image of life remaineth alive, for it alone cometh from the gods. But it sleepeth, while the limbs are active; yet, to them that sleep, in many a dream it giveth presage of a decision [krisin] of things delightful or doleful." The "image" is an *eidōlon* (the same term that Odysseus's mother used for the same idea), here said to be of divine origin and to endure for ages (*aiōnos*). Almost epigrammatically, this fragment suggests a future judgment prior to an afterlife of suffering or contentment. Who but a god could judge this heaven-sent *eidōlon*?[39]

After the division of souls, the heroes pass into a sunlit, though subterranean, meadow adorned with flowers and fruit trees. Incense fills the air, and men train on horses, wrestle, quench their thirst, or enjoy music, while fire from the god's altar illumines all their satisfying activities. But "from the other side sluggish streams of darksome night belch forth a boundless gloom" (frags. 129, 130).

Pindar's "Second Olympian Ode," in praise of Theocron of Acragas in Sicily, winner of a chariot race in 476, confirms these impressions gleaned from the fragments. Victory, Pindar says, gives release from hardships, but the greatest boon, "the truest light of man" (55–56), is the knowledge by which life may be guided—that is, knowledge of the judgment at death and the consequences that follow from it. Immediately after death a divine ruler (*Dios archai* [58]: Persephone?)[40] passes judgment. "Lawless spirits" receive a "stern and inevitable sentence," and "the good" are granted a toil-free life where the sun shines forever (*aiei*) in the presence of the gods (58–62). Stating the matter a second way, Pindar contrasts those who rejoiced in keeping their oaths (remember, perjury was punished even among the gods), who will know a tear-free life after death, to "the others [who] endure labour that none can look upon" (one thinks of Sisyphus and of the Belides,

---

39. Pindar speaks of Persephone, who "shall exact the penalty of their pristine woe." This phrase suggests a discretionary role for Persephone, but it is unclear exactly what she is judging or why the penalty must be exacted, especially since this passage refers to the best men, who will become monarchs and heroes. Since the woe is pristine, it would seem to originate with the formation of humans and thus refer to our Titanic nature, which should have been purged away before she "restoreth their souls [*psychas*] to the upper sun-light" (frag. 133). Still, this reference is only to those who deserve remission of punishment, and there is no indication as to the grounds on which it was granted.

40. Zuntz, *Persephone*, 86.

who carry water in sieves) (65–68).[41] Further, Fragment 134 states that "the happiness of the blessed is no fugitive," and it seems clear, though it is not stated, that the labors of the wicked are not easily ended either. The "night" and "gloom" of Fragment 130 refer to them. Sketchily, therefore, Pindar intimates an afterlife about which knowledge is a greater boon than victory because it warns that the good are treated far better than the wicked. Belief in a postmortem judgment that sends souls either to happiness or to pain— that is, the division of the dead—is clearly related to what the concept of hell would be. Thus far, however, no clear criteria for judgment are mentioned.

ARISTOPHANES' FROGS

By the end of the fifth century, reflection on these differences intensified. The more important the contrasts in the afterlife became, and the more they were said to result from deeds in this life, the more important it became to know what the consequences of one's actions might be. Indeed, it seems that the spread of the mysteries occasioned a rise in speculation about the hereafter.[42] By the end of the century, Aristophanes (c. 450–385) could satirize the tendency to exploit fearful images of death for purposes of self-aggrandizement. His play The Frogs, first performed in 405, reviews some of the horrors attributed to the otherworld, while it parodies the abuse of this lore.

The Frogs is typical of a new level of consciousness about the afterlife among the Greeks because it contrasts the fate of the good and the wicked explicitly and at length. Indeed, the play focuses directly on the distinction between those dead who suffer and those who rejoice. It was designed for public performance at state expense during the Athenian festival of Dionysus. It seems clear that it represents a basic minimum of common knowledge about the mysteries and their teachings concerning the land of the dead.

The play concerns a common citizen of Athens named Dionysus. Imitating his divine namesake, who had removed his mother from the underworld, Dionysus the citizen seeks the return of the newly deceased Euripides from

41. A third restatement is ambiguous; it begins with an "if" and speaks of the wise and their rewards but provides no counterpart for the unwise (68–79).

42. Rohde, Psyche, makes this point at 218–19, and especially clearly at 236, but he qualifies it at 239–41, where he insists that these differences in fates in the afterlife came from "mere" initiation, not moral conduct. He regards the notion of postmortem retribution as foreign to the ancient Greeks in general and of interest only to isolated theologians, playwrights, and philosophers.

the land of Hades, since no good poets remain in the city. To prepare for the journey, Dionysus has decided to go with his slave Xanthias to ask advice directly from Herakles, since he has made the journey several times.[43] From Herakles he learns what to expect. Down below, he will see

> weltering seas of filth
> And ever-rippling dung; and plunged therein,
> Whoso has wronged the stranger here on earth,
> Or robbed his boylove [little boy lover] of the promised pay,
> Or swinged [lit. "nailed"?] his mother, or profanely smitten
> His father's cheek, or sworn an oath forsworn.
>
> (145–50)

These are the offenders and this is their fate. Their pool of mire is surrounded by tens of thousands of snakes and savage monsters (141–42).

Dionysus protests: "You can't scare me, I'm still going to go" (143–44). Later, when Xanthias asks where all the monsters are (before they actually appear), Dionysus brags that Herakles was just trying to scare them off (280–82). Here is an early instance of an explicitly reductionist interpretation of traditional beliefs about the underworld. As Dionysus puts it to Xanthias, Herakles used the fear of subterranean monsters to prevent this mission, which, if successful, would diminish his heroic reputation. Herakles might also be taken as a genuine hero warning an impostor about the dire consequences of persisting in a solemn mission with an irreverent attitude. Instead, Dionysus portrays him as manipulating fear of postmortem horrors.

In contrast to the company in the pool of mire, Herakles continues, is the fate of the "happy mystic bands," who wander in the kind of glorious sunshine humans enjoy on earth and who rest in the shade of myrtle groves and clap their hands in triumph to the accompaniment of flutes (154–58). They dwell at Pluto's gate and can tell Dionysus all he wants to know (161–62). Initiation in the mysteries, therefore, provides the knowledge necessary to teach one's fellows how to avoid the hazards of the underworld and enjoy a blissful life after death. Herakles' account coincides with the hints found in the earlier Orphic tradition.

Now the mystics appear as the "lovely youthful chorus" that will go to "the marshy, flowery plain" (351–52). They recite what must be taken as a characterization, if not a caricature, of the Orphic rites. Their prayer gives

---

43. This story seems to ignore the tale that Dionysus successfully led his mother Semele from the underworld to Olympus, perhaps because it would enhance the reputation of Dionysus whose cult is the object of a roasting here.

another set of contrasts between good and evil, sacred and profane, piety and blasphemy. Invoking Iacchus,[44] they seek to avert what is evil and base, to keep away those who are uninitiated in the Dionysian rites and who entertain sordid desires. They separate themselves from anyone who corrupts his office with gifts or bribes, betrays his city or fort or fleet, or deserts to or trades with the enemy. Any who would deface images of Hecate or blaspheme her feasts should keep away (353–71). It is implied that perpetrators of these deeds go to the mire.

The mystics depart for the flower-filled meadows that the Fates reserve only for the blessed (452–53). They explicitly claim that their place in the sun derives from their superior conduct, for they have consistently striven with pure endeavor to guide their steps aright (455–59).

As Dionysus and Xanthias reach Hades' palace, Aeacus, considered a judge of the underworld in other sources,[45] confronts them and invokes all the dark world's threats:

> So close the Styx's inky-hearted rock
> The blood bedabbled peak of Acheron
> Shall hem thee in: the hell hounds of Cocytus
> Prowl round thee; whilst the hundred-headed Asp
> Shall rive thy heart-strings: the Tartesian Lamprey
> Prey on thy lungs, and those Tithrasian Gorgons
> Mangle and tear thy kidneys, mauling them
> Entrails and all, into one bloody mash.
>
> (465–77)

Here then are some of the details of the gruesome punishment. Dire enough are the first threats, but then the eellike delicacy, the *Tartesian* Lamprey—a play on "Tartarean"[46]—probably inflicts only heartburn. The final torments are more amusing than frightening through the contrast between anatomical terms and generic gore. Aristophanes alludes to horrors rumored to exist in Hades' land but dilutes them with humor, just as he demotes Aeacus from judge to concierge.

The chorus of mystics returns and informs the audience about the benefits of their mystery. They appeal to the Muses for redemption from both slavery

44. For Iacchus and his problematic origin and connection with Dionysus, see Rose, *Handbook*, 95; and *Oxford Classical Dictionary*.

45. For example, Plato, *Gorgias* 523e.

46. Rogers's note to line 470, in Aristophanes, *The Frogs*, trans. Benjamin Bickley Rogers, Loeb Classical Library (London: Heinemann, 1924).

and sin.[47] Their allusion to the Four Hundred, who ruled Athens at this time as oligarchs, implicitly compares tactical error in politics to moral error or sin. For this they seek forgiveness (686–92). Redemption, they say, liberates the mystics through religion the way civic ritual grants citizenship to slaves who fight well in the city's wars (698–99). They complain that the citizens with the oldest virtues are treated like dirty old coins and cast aside in favor of new mintings that have not yet proved their value (718–33). This simile heralds the theme of discrimination to be addressed in the poetry contest between Euripides and Aeschylus. The challenge is to recognize substance beneath polish in language, coinage, and conduct.

Although Dionysus had undertaken his descent to win back Euripides, Pluto promises him the poet he deems best for Athens (1415–16). Aeschylus and Euripides then present themselves before Dionysus, who acts as judge. In their debate Aeschylus invokes Demeter, but Euripides refuses (886–89)—a particularly damning error considering Demeter's importance in the history of the place where they now stand. In making his choice, Dionysus weighs differences of substance and style between Aeschylus and Euripides. In the end Dionysus affirms that utility to the city must be the criterion (1420–21).

By having Hades release Aeschylus so that Athens may keep its choral games (1419) and his words may counsel the state (1499–1501), Aristophanes exhorts his audience to cherish the public good. Far more important, however, is the emphasis he places on individual choice. Whatever considerations go into it, whether of public or private good, one's conduct in life determines one's fate after death. By contrasting the fates of the mystics and the frogs, Aristophanes raises the stakes in the game of life, as did the Orphics. The discriminations one makes in life, between impostors and heroes, style and content, private pleasure and public benefit, the crowd pleaser and the craftsman—these will all correspond after death to a more telling judgment that leads to the meadows or the mud. Given the contrasts it matches between good and evil in life, joy and pain in death, *The Frogs* is a crucial document in the history of discrimination in the underworld. It cannot be included in the following chapter, devoted to the concept of the moral afterlife, however, because it is not clear whether Aristophanes advocated this distinction, reported it, or was, through his satire, opposing it—or at least its abuse. Plato provided a less ambiguous appraisal.

47. Remember how Hesiod portrays the Muses as instruments of Zeus who bestow his favor on princes, thus ensuring just rule. *Theogony* 84–90, 96.

Moral Death

Assuming that the date of the *Hymn to Demeter* in the mid–seventh century and the few dates that can be connected with the introduction of Orphism into Greece, sometime before 500, are correct, it appears that the notion of distinction of fates in the Greek afterlife arose later than the concept of neutral death, so apparent in Homer's *nekyai*, or visits to the dead, with their roots in the older, Mesopotamian ideas. This chronological sequence is significant because it suggests that the division of the dead occurs in part as an objection to the older view. As will become clear in Part II, a similar event also occurred in Hebrew thinking about the dead.

Plato certainly knew the main ideas of Orphism, as he showed by referring to the "Titanic nature" to which humans could return through inattention to political order (*Laws* 701c).[1] In the *Cratylus* he attributed to the Orphics

---

1. In quoting Plato I use the translations in *The Collected Dialogues*, ed. Edith Hamilton and Huntington Cairns, Bollingen Series, 71 (Princeton: Princeton University Press, 1961). Plato (c. 429–347 B.C.E.) made his teacher, Socrates (469–399), the protagonist in his dialogues. Since Socrates distrusted the newfangled technique of writing and expressed himself only orally and through his style of life, his ideas are known to us primarily as recorded by Plato in the dialogues. Frequently the dialogue is named after the leader of debate against Socrates. It is impossible to tell when Plato is reporting Socrates' views accurately and when he uses Socrates as a vehicle for his own theories. The same applies to the interlocutors of Socrates, whose positions Plato may be reporting faithfully or inventing as a means of airing his own doubts. Nonetheless, as literary productions, the dialogues have attained a life of their own and Plato must be cited through them.

the belief that the body is the tomb of the soul.[2] He ascribed other important themes to "mystics" whom he did not always identify as Orphic, as in the *Phaedo*, where he has Socrates favorably recount the ideas of "the people who direct the religious initiations." "He who enters the next world uninitiated and unenlightened," they say, "shall lie in the mire, but he who arrives there purified and enlightened shall dwell among the gods" (69c–d).[3] Less sympathetic to this view is Adimantus, a participant in Plato's dialogue the *Republic*, who argues that many do what is just not from a love of justice but only because the gods are reputed to have promised rewards for justice and threatened punishment for injustice. He traces this pernicious doctrine to the Orphics. "Musaeus and his son,"[4] Plato has Adimantus complain, portray the initiates crowned with wreaths and feasting at a banquet, while they picture the others buried in mud and compelled to carry water in a sieve (363d–e). They assert that the living can purify themselves from sins "by means of sacrifice and pleasant sport" (364e). They also maintain, Adimantus continues, that these same rites can be used to alleviate the conditions of the dead in the next world.[5] This remarkable comment suggests that some Orphic adepts claimed ceremonies enacted by the living could benefit not

2. Plato, *Cratylus* 400c: "Probably the Orphic poets were the inventors of the [derivation], and they were under the impression that the soul is suffering the punishment of sin, and that the body is an enclosure or prison in which the soul is incarcerated, kept safe [*sōma, sōzetai* (preserve[d]?)], as the name *sōma* implies, until the penalty is paid." This does it, Socrates observes, without changing a letter! Here the effort is to identify an etymological derivation (though it is not completely clear which term derives from which). Socrates considered these derivations "ridiculous, and yet plausible" (402a).

3. Cf. *Meno* 76e. In the *Laws* 870d–e, Plato referred to "those who occupy themselves with these matters at the Mysteries." Here Plato explains the belief of the mystics without mentioning the mire. They teach, he says, that evildoers suffer in a new incarnation exactly the violence they have inflicted in this one.

4. Identified as Eumolpos by Rohde, *Psyche*, 359 n. 70.

5. "There are also special rites for the defunct, which they call functions, that deliver us from evils in that other world" (365a). Paul Shorey's translation carries into English the play on words in Greek between "defunct" (*teleutēsasin*) and "functions" (*teletas*). The Greek, however, does not use two separate terms for "special rites" and "functions." Shorey is filling in an elliptical expression. A more literal translation would refer back to "the sacrifice and pleasant sport" for the living and then continue: and there are also for the defunct what they call *teletas*. The reason for insisting is that *teletē* is a very usual term for initiation in the mysteries or celebration of the mysteries in general. Thus, when we realize Adimantus is condemning not some obscure rite employed only to relieve the suffering of the dead but the whole practice of initiation in the mysteries, we see how deep is his disdain.

only the person performing the rite but the souls of the departed too. (This aid must exceed that which is afforded simply by burying the dead.) For the moment it is sufficient merely to note this belief that the dead can be helped by the devotion of the living. It will receive fuller treatment later.

Beyond promising boons for the dead, these devotees also threaten those who shun their mysteries. "Terrible things," they say, "await those who have neglected to sacrifice" (364–65a). The thrust of Adimantus's objection is that, through their emphasis on reward and punishment, Orphic beliefs undermine the love of justice necessary for a well-ordered society. His scorn for these ideas does not diminish the correspondence between his characterization and their portrayal by Aristophanes.

PLATO

Plato was fascinated with the notion of postmortem retribution. It is important to observe in advance that Plato does what Adimantus has done—assesses these religious beliefs, at least in part, for their effects upon social organization and political order. Indeed, the *Republic* could be considered an effort to refine and apply the beliefs condemned by Adimantus in such a way as to encourage justice. Plato ends the *Republic* with an elaborate vision, called the myth of Er, which derives from ideas similar to those Adimantus derides, and he concludes by saying that the tale "will save us if we believe it"; it will enable us "to be dear to ourselves and to the gods both during our sojourn here and when we receive our reward" (621c). Plato also encouraged acceptance of postmortem punishment, summarizing his views in a letter: "We must at all times give our unfeigned assent to the ancient and holy doctrines [*hierois logois*] which warn us that our souls are immortal, that they are judged, and that they suffer the severest punishments after our separation from the body. Hence we must also hold it a lesser evil to be victims of great wrongs and crimes than to be doers of them" (*Letters* 7.335a).

For the soul to experience reward or punishment beyond the grave, it must survive the death of the body. If the soul can outlive the body that houses it, we must ask what could ever destroy it. Indeed, Plato maintained that the soul is immortal. He described the moral consequences of the immortality of the soul in the *Phaedrus*. In humans the soul is like the union that exists between a charioteer and his team of steeds.[6] (Because the coursers draw the

6. This extended simile is an example of Plato's use of analogies, which he sometimes calls myths, tales, parables, even, in a famous instance, a falsehood, though he

soul, they have wings.) The two horses, though, are of different nature: one is good, the other is not, making the task of the charioteer very difficult (246a–b). The situation of the gods is different, for both their steeds are docile (246b), and they drive them in bliss over the prospects of the heavens, where alone there is true existence (247b). Mortals can trace this path only to the extent that the worse of the two steeds is properly disciplined (247b) by "reason alone, the soul's pilot" (247c). As the lower steed brings them down, the souls will be planted in bodies in successive incarnations according to their ability to retain the heavenly vision. Only a soul that has seen the truth may enter a human form (249b), since humans need knowledge of the truth to reason with, and this knowledge can come only from the memory of what has been perceived in winging through the heavens (249c). Philosophy is the practice of cultivating reminiscences of that divine truth. Failure to pursue and adhere to these truths brings about a series of deprivations, or lacks, each of which can be seen as a punishment suffered by nonphilosophers. The brevity of one's tour of the heavens itself results from previous failure to discipline the unruly "horse" and thus may be considered the consequence of a previous delinquency. The soul's reduction to the world of matter, its incarnation, is a further punishment. Plato calls it an imprisonment (250c). It appears that the falling souls perceive their loss. Plato dramatically describes the moment when they realize ascent is no longer possible, when their wings begin to give out. Those who are falling collide with others still striving for a better view. There is competition and confusion. Horses out of control break the wings of those ascending, and finally all must descend unsatisfied, deprived of a perception of reality, forced to live once more in the world of appearances (248b–c). The resulting incarnations are graded in nine levels from philosopher to tyrant according to the amount of truth absorbed during the flight through the heavens (248e). One's demotion through the levels of body may proceed, if the descent continues, to the places of punishment under the earth (249a).

It seems both logical and ironic that further detail on these questions should emerge in the *Phaedo*, a dialogue that purportedly relates the last conversations of Socrates with his disciples. Here, in prison awaiting the poison he must drink, the philosopher consoles his friends by reminding them that the real Socrates consists not of his body, which will die, but of his soul, which will not. And since Socrates has conducted his life by the beliefs

---

qualifies it as "noble" or "opportune" (*Republic* 414b). He seems to suggest that his myths are approximations pointing toward a truth accessible only to the blessed and the divine. See *Republic* 521c; *Phaedrus* 246a and 265b.

he outlines for them, he does not fear death but rather considers it the beginning of the career for which he has disciplined his soul. To make his point, Socrates outlines the path followed by the soul at death.

When a person dies, the mortal and immortal parts are separated (107a). Since the soul (*psychē*) survives death, its fate in the next world depends on how well one has prepared it in this world (107c). Here Socrates observes a link between beliefs about the afterlife and conduct in this life which many today would characterize as functionalist: "If death were a release from everything, it would be a boon for the wicked, because by dying they would be released not only from the body, but also from their own wickedness together with the soul" (107c). This observation amounts to maintaining the utility of belief in punishment after death as a deterrent to evil behavior. For Plato, the social utility of an idea is only one measure of its validity. It would not be right if it did not conform to cosmic truth, and if it were true by that standard, correct understanding of it would certainly guide the human pursuit of justice.

Here, then, is what happens after death. In the land of Hades the soul is met by its "guardian spirit" (*hekastou daimōn*) (107d), a personal supernatural guide, which leads it to the place of judgment. A soul that is well disposed follows its guide properly, whereas a soul that excessively loves its body and the visible world lives here as a ghost (81b–d; cf. 108b). That soul must be forcibly removed to the next world by the appointed spirit (108b). When such a soul reaches the place of judgment, the other souls avoid it and refuse it counsel or guidance, so that it wanders aimlessly, until finally it is thrust into the place assigned to its kind, its "proper habitation" (108c). These two types of soul closely resemble the trained and rebellious horses of the *Phaedrus*. And just as the winged souls in the *Phaedrus* reached the appropriate height, so in the *Phaedo* Plato designates a particular destination for each type of soul.

As stated in the *Phaedrus*, souls that are repeatedly demoted eventually receive retribution beneath the earth. Thus a full knowledge of the earth's interior is necessary to understand future punishment. In the *Phaedo*, Plato takes the earth to be a porous, pumicelike sphere with hollows and channels that penetrate it in every direction. The holes are connected by subterranean rivers that carry various fluids into different internal seas. They run with mud, cold and hot water, and fire (111d–e). Penetrating the whole earth, however, is Tartarus, a funnel, drain, or chasm through which all the other rivers flow. For although an oscillating motion of the earth forces each river to the center of the earth, sometimes through serpentine coils, sometimes more directly, they do not flow into each other, and each returns to its place of origin, though each in a different way (112a–e).

Four principal rivers, already mentioned by Homer, run into Tartarus. Ocean flows around the earth in a circle, and in the opposite direction, the Acheron runs through uninhabited regions and then descends underground to the Acherusian Lake. Here most of the dead come for varying amounts of time until they are reborn as living beings. A third river, which Plato calls the Pyriphlegethon (later called, simply, Phlegethon), falls into a region burning with a great fire, where it gathers into a body of boiling, muddy water larger than the Mediterranean Sea. From there it winds to the edge of the Acherusian Lake, but does not mix into it, and finally bores into Tartarus. Cocytus, the fourth river, runs into the Stygian Lake and flows toward the Acherusian Lake from a direction opposite the Pyriphlegethon but similarly mixes with no other body and finally plunges, again from the opposite side, into Tartarus (112e–113c).

The dead populate the interior of this complex, riddled, spongelike earth. They are assigned to different regions at the judgment after their deaths. Four fates are possible: that of the holy, that of those who have lived lives of indeterminate character, that of those guilty of sins that can be expiated (*iasima* = curable), and that of the incurably wicked (*doxōsin aniatōs*).

The morally neutral are sent to the Acheron in vessels provided for the purpose. They dwell at the lake until they are purified, paying penalties for misdeeds and receiving rewards for any (slight) good deeds (113d). The incurable, who have committed great wrongs, many acts of sacrilege, murders, or other such crimes, are cast into Tartarus, whence they never (*oupote*) emerge (113e). That is eternal punishment. Others are judged curable even if they may have violently afflicted their father or mother or perhaps committed manslaughter, provided they performed these deeds in only a momentary passion and they have spent the remainder of their lives in repentance. These too are sent to Tartarus, but annually the oscillations of the earth wash them out. The slayers of humans flow through Cocytus and the offenders of parents through Pyriphlegethon. As they approach the Acheron, they call out from their respective streams for the forgiveness of those whom they wronged. If pardon is granted they come out into the lake and their suffering ends, but if not, the current carries them back again into Tartarus, where they stew for another year until the cycle is repeated (113e–114b). It is important to observe how their fate is in the control of those they offended. In this context, the value of forgiveness is inestimable. Finally, those who are judged to have led holy lives are freed entirely from these cycles within the earth. Having purified themselves by philosophy they move without bodies to the pure regions, where they share the ether with the gods and rise to even more beautiful dwellings (114b–c), presumably with experiences similar to those described in the *Phaedrus*.

This account offers some approximation of the afterlife and the nature of judgment, says Socrates. We should live as if it were true—it is "a belief worth risking" (114d)—for it encourages us to consider everything secondary to the welfare of the soul, and it promotes "self-control, and goodness, and courage, and liberality, and truth" (114e), with which to prepare the soul for its journey, whenever it is called to the next world (115a). Again, Plato assesses certain beliefs according to their utility for the moral life and the social order.

Plato gives a different account of the division of the dead in the *Gorgias*. If, as Plato had Socrates explain in the *Phaedo*, human beings are assigned to places in the afterlife according to how they cultivated their souls, then the appearance of the soul at death is a matter that requires careful study. To explain, Socrates relates a tale concerning the reform Zeus and his brothers instituted when they took over the cosmos.

In the time of Kronos the just were sent to the Isles of the Blessed to live in happiness and the unjust to the "prison of vengeance and punishment" called Tartarus (*Gorgias* 523a). The judges, however, were living humans unduly influenced by the physical appearance, rank, and lineage of the people they examined. When Zeus and his brother took over, Pluto denounced this bias.

Zeus therefore reformed the procedure. Humans would no longer have advance knowledge of their death. They would be tried dead, stripped of all their worldly accouterments. The judges, sons of Zeus, would also be dead, and thus beyond any earthly advantage. From then on Rhadamanthus tried souls from Asia and Aeacus from Europe. They performed this function at the Meadow of the Dividing of the Road, where they separated those going to the Isles of the Blessed from those condemned to Tartarus (524a). Bearing a golden scepter, Minos presided, ready to determine doubtful cases.[7]

This reform, Socrates believes, takes better account of what actually happens when a person dies. For although at death the soul is disconnected from the body, nonetheless, it continues to bear the signs of its life (524d). Thus, the judge, whether Aeacus or Rhadamanthus, sees the naked soul of each person and decides exclusively by the soul's condition. If souls such as those of philosophers indicate a life devoted to "piety and truth," he sends them to the Isles of the Blessed (526c). If a soul shows no signs of health or of ever receiving the nourishment of learning or contemplation of the truth but instead is covered with blemishes, scars, and deformities that result from licence, perjury, and evil deeds, the judge "sends it away in ignominy straight

---

7. This portrayal of Minos differs considerably from that of Homer at *Odyssey* 11.569.

to the prison house, where it is doomed on its arrival to endure the sufferings proper to it" (525a). Since some cases are less severe than others, before he sends them to Tartarus for punishment, the judge labels the "evil" (*poneros*) either "curable" (*iasimos*) or "incurable" (*aniatos*), and upon arrival, they are treated accordingly (526b–c).[8]

Plato's distinction between the curable and incurable directly confronts the issue of eternal punishment. After being purified by their punishment in Tartarus, the curable return to a new life. The incurable never do. Since the incorrigible cannot profit from their pains, they suffer them "throughout eternity" (*pathe paschontas ton aei chronon*: suffer sufferings for all time [525c]). Plato explicitly states that the punishments of the incurable, which last forever, are of no benefit *to them*. Rather, hanging in the infernal dungeons, they serve as examples, a horror and a warning for other evildoers who may arrive periodically, so that they may take fright and amend their lives accordingly. The eternal punishment of the incurable *deters* the curable as they serve their time in Tartarus in the process of renewal. In addition, their own temporary punishment *purifies* the curable, those apt to benefit from it.

Indicative of the social utility of this scheme is the choice of the tyrant Archelaus, the king of Macedon (c. 413–399 B.C.E.), to represent the incorrigible. Archelaus illustrates Socrates' contention that powerful men, rulers, and public administrators with broad freedom of action are much more likely than common citizens to do great wrong. It is rare and praiseworthy when a man free to do whatever injustice he pleases nonetheless lives a just life (526a). Homer agreed, Socrates believes, for he shows the kings and princes Tantalus, Sisyphus, and Tityos enduring "eternal punishment in Hades" (*en Haidou ton aei chronon timoroumenous* [525e]). Thus Plato interprets Homer as testifying to eternal punishment for the incorrigibly evil. This view presents a different angle on the matter, because Plato makes no allowance here for the superhuman character of those in Homer's Tartarus. He seems to place powerful human rulers there alongside the demigods that Homer portrayed as eternally punished. Plato distinguishes sharply between tyrants and notorious rascals such as the impertinent Thersites, who railed at Agamemnon (*Iliad* 2.211–77), who must, as private person, be put in a separate category. People who are merely annoying cannot be considered incurable and will have another chance at life. It is primarily the freedom that comes with power, in Plato's view, which usually generates incorrigible rather than amenable evil and merits eternal rather than cura-

8. It is unclear in the *Gorgias* whether Minos intervenes to decide between Tartarus and the Isles of the Blessed or on the curability or incurability of impure souls.

tive punishment.[9] Here, as in the *Republic*, Plato applies his view of the other world to prevent or restrain the abuse of power.

These themes, then, are certainly clear in Plato: the soul is immortal; it is judged for the character it acquires during its life in the body; it can be rewarded or punished after death. The rewards of the blessed and the punishment of the incurably wicked endure forever.

As the case of the curable makes clear, suffering in the next world can also *benefit* those who experience it. The myth of Er, which concludes the *Republic*, explains the options open to souls returning from their life beyond the grave and how differently they are affected by their experience of hardship or ease. The source for this knowledge is the account of a warrior named Er, who died on the battlefield but whose body, when recovered by his friends, had not decayed. Twelve days after his "death" he revived and related that in the interim he had been in the otherworld, where he was ordered to observe all that went on so that he might return as a messenger to humankind and report what he had seen (614b–d).

According to this account, when a person dies, the soul leaves the body. It comes to a meadow like the one referred to in the *Gorgias*. There it approaches two pairs of openings: one pair conveys those leaving for and returning from the heavens, the other conducts souls leaving for and returning from the interior of the earth. Judges of souls send the unjust downward to the left, scarred by the evidence of all their deeds on their backs. The just are sent upward to the right, marked with a sign of approval. Returning toward the meeting place are the shabby and dusty souls from within the earth and the clean, pure souls from above.

The souls returning to the meadow have just completed an afterlife consisting of ten century-long lives after death for a total of a thousand years. During each century the souls received retribution for their previous life, whether good or evil. The punishments affected anyone who "had been the cause of many deaths or had betrayed cities and armies and reduced them to slavery, or had been a participant in any other iniquity" (615b). The cycle of ten centuries makes it possible for the majority of sins to be compensated by

9. This seems a feeble criterion for differentiating between curable and incurable sins. Does this simply show the absence of a notion of the will or of a distinction between voluntary and involuntary acts? Surely some private persons can commit crimes as heinous as those of despots. Perhaps not, because no private person can, by the distraction from duty consequent upon self-indulgence, deprive so many other citizens of the benefits of a well-ordered community. Even so, the fact that a private person does not cost his or her fellows so much does not make that person responsive to correction through suffering.

ten repetitions of the appropriate punishment. Perhaps some repeated experience of the sin itself—this time as victim[10]—determines the gravity of punishment. Special provisions were made for infants or those who died young, whereas honor paid or denied gods and parents was rewarded (or punished) on a higher scale, though the differences are not specified (615c).

Every thousand years the souls within the earth are tested, as part of their ascent, by passing through a mouthlike opening. If the soul is one of the incurably wicked (*tis tōn houtōs aniatōs echontōn eis ponērian*) or not sufficiently purified (*[tis] mē ikanōs dedōkōs dikēn*), the mouth bellows and the soul is denied return. When the alarm sounds, "savage men of fiery aspect" (615e) seize the souls and flay their skin and card their flesh with thorns while they explain to the other souls passing by why their victims receive this treatment. (We must note the unusual harshness of this punishment and how rarely Plato gives any physical details at all. Perhaps he is conforming here to the genre of the dream vision, which, as will appear, generally portrays more vivid torments.) After the alarm sounds and the torment is completed, the demons fling these sinners back into Tartarus. Among those detained are the incurably wicked, such as the parricide and fratricide Ardiaeus and other despots; but private persons guilty of great crimes are probably also without the possibility of rebirth (615e). That fate would match the sentence of the incurables described in the *Gorgias* (525c–26c), where Archelaus is the prime example. However physical the punishment of the incurable detained at the mouth of Tartarus, those who successfully pass through it, ascending after sufferings within the earth, report that their worst experience was the dread they felt as they approached this point and realized that exit might be refused (615c–16b). Here great fear contributes to purification. Thus Plato dramatizes the difference between temporary and eternal punishment.

Those permitted to ascend from punishment rejoin the souls descending from the heavens at the meadow adjacent to the four openings, whence the returned souls are taken to a pillar of light, around which the spheres of the cosmos turn, as whorls encompass a spindle. Under the supervision of the Fates, who preside in the presence of these mechanisms of Necessity, the returned souls choose lots that give them priority in selecting their next life on earth. Before choosing their new earthly life, they know whether it will involve poverty and virtue or power accompanied by great crimes. They are completely free to chose the life they wish. Once they choose, they will be bound by Necessity to that life.

10. Plato ascribed this belief to devotees of the mysteries (*Laws* 870d–e).

Er relates the choices made by various souls and explains that those returning from the heavens, who had not suffered during their previous term of a thousand years of afterlife and were not disciplined by suffering, chose power as an important part of their new lives. By contrast, those who had returned from under the earth, who knew their own and others' suffering, chose more carefully (619d). Again Plato's conviction that knowledge of certain truths has behavioral consequences is evident. He seeks to correlate correct knowledge with correct behavior, thus leading, as far as possible, to a just society that will respect the pursuit of truth. He constructs his myths to that end.

After each soul has chosen its fate in the next life, Lachesis, a daughter of Necessity, gives to each the genius (*daimona* [620e]) it has chosen, and the genius leads it to drink from the River Lethe, the river of unmindfulness, whose water obliterates all memory. New lives begin with no memory of the past. Whereas in the *Phaedrus* one's position in this world depends on how well one remembers the view of absolute being while on high, in the myth of Er it is awareness of the lessons learned which informs one's choice of a new life, which is then determined—beginning to end—at the beginning. Both accounts, however, stress Plato's conviction that at death only the condition of the soul matters. Therefore we must choose the various aspects of our lives exclusively with regard to their effect upon what makes our soul just or good (618d–19a). In Plato's other dialogues, decisions that effect the soul are made in the course of one's life. The myth of Er dramatically condenses the decisions of a lifetime into one.

It is important to insist that these passages of Plato do more than just leave open the possibility of unending punishment. His theory of the soul renders the punishment of the incurable eternal. In the *Republic*, Socrates argues that the soul always (*aei*) exists (*einai*) and so is immortal (*athanaton*) since it can be destroyed neither by its own faults nor by anything outside itself (610a–11a). Glaucon objects that it is hard to conceive of a thing existing always (*aidion einai*) when, as we know the soul, it comprises so many contradictory impulses (611b). Socrates insists that the immortal soul (*athanatos psychē*) can be inferred by imagining the soul not as we know it in this world but in a purified, abstract state, so that we may see the implications of its attraction "to the divine and the immortal and to eternal being" (*zyggenēs ousa tōi te theiōi kai athanatōi kai tōi aei onti* [611e]). Now the term for "immortal" is *athanaton*, literally, "deathless." Further, though, Plato pairs the term "immortal" with the expression "existing always." The term *aei* (always) carries much force because it is a simple adverb paired with a more technical word, *einai* (to be). The term that Glaucon uses for "immortal," which he considers hard to believe, is *aidion* (611b), which is a shortening of *aeidion*, and means "always-like" (combining the adverb *aei* with the adjectival suffix *-dion*). Thus, in his introduction to the myth of Er, Plato reviews the technical language that can ascribe immortality to the soul. The suggestion is that the cycles of life for those renewed are endless, but Plato's discussion also implies that those such as Ardiaeus, retained below, or those mentioned in the *Gorgias* (Archelaus) as never returning are condemned to Tartarus forever. Nor does this conclusion depend on inference. In the *Phaedo*, the incurable souls cast into Tartarus are said to emerge "no more" (*oupote* [113e]). Further, this was the way Plato interpreted the punishments of Tantalus, Sisyphus, and Tityos, who, he says, suffer everlastingly in the land of Hades.

These discussions of punishment after death occur in the context of Plato's teaching on the nature of the soul. In both the *Phaedo* and the *Republic*, the passages summarized here follow demonstrations of the immortality of the soul. Thus, returning to the *Republic* and specifically to Glaucon's objections, even he concedes, when led on by Socrates and in a slightly different context, that the fact of being unjust will not kill the soul as if injustice were a fatal disease. For if injustice could bring the death of the soul, "that would be a release from all [its] troubles" (610d). Glaucon's desire to see justice done (eventually) is leading him to admit the immortality of the soul. For only an immortal soul, the implication goes, can be eternally punished, as justice demands in the case of the incurably wicked.

Plato makes the same argument in the *Phaedo* (107c–d). A soul that dies cannot pay for the evil it has wrought, and so the mortality of the soul (in addition to being wrong on metaphyscial grounds, as discussed at 105d–106e) would be a boon to the wicked, who would escape with lighter punishments than they deserve. Justice, therefore, demands the immortality of the soul; and the immortality of the soul makes eternal punishment possible. It seems, then, that Plato is the earliest author to state categorically that the fate of the extremely wicked is eternal punishment.

THE DESCENT OF AENEAS

Whereas Odysseus traveled to the gates of the land of the dead and glimpsed the victims of divine torment, and Plato probed the inner earth's anatomy, Aeneas traversed the whole jurisdiction of Pluto. He crossed the Acheron, stared down the gorgonian forms within the cavern's mouth, traversed the dusky plain just within, glimpsed dark Tartarus from a hillside above its gates, strolled through the Elysian Fields with his father, and returned alive to fulfill the paternal prophecy. A refugee from fallen Troy,

Aeneas could not establish the city he was destined to found until he discovered his own identity. After his ordeal in the land of death, he understood the cycles of life and his role in history.

Virgil (70–19 B.C.E.), who tells the story, wrote in close association with the emperor Augustus. Without neglecting the aesthetic qualities of the poem, one may nonetheless truly say that Virgil was providing a genealogy, and hence literary legitimacy, for the principate of his patron. Given the first emperor's ambitions, the Roman past could be portrayed only a certain way. Virgil was the celebrant of that past.

Virgil constructs Aeneas's approach to the underworld in book 6 of the *Aeneid* through a series of contrasts between light and darkness, which symbolize ignorance and truth, fear and confidence. Touching the Cumaean beach marks his transition from sea to land, from fugitive to founder (83–84; cf. 112–13). He continues through the forest to a temple, whose priestess, the Sybil, will guide him on his journey. Praying almost apologetically, he explains that he claims nothing not due him by his destiny (66–67). Despite the darkness, he is attracted by the tenebrous valley leading to a cavern. Examples from the past also beckon: such penetration had been accomplished by Orpheus, Pollux, Theseus, and Herakles (116–23). The Sybil admits that the way in is easy (126–27); getting back to the light is the trial (128–29)! She mentions how the River Cocytus snakes through the forests that hedge the way (131–32), how the lake of Styx must be crossed *twice* (134). Yet Virgil describes her prophecy as "truth cloaked in obscurity" (100).

If, despite the dangers, Aeneas wishes to try his *amor mentis,* the drive of his resolve (133), he must first discover a golden bough, a token of divine approval, his key to the underworld. Guided by doves sent by his mother, Venus, he finds the wreath of gold glistening amid dense vegetation (136). A moral chiaroscuro is in effect here. The contrast of color matches the effect of discovering truth by mastering darkness. Virgil applies this same imagery to his task as a narrator, seeking to link the deeds of Aeneas to their higher significance: "May I be permitted . . . to clarify the meaning submerged beneath the subterranean darkness" (265–67).

Though now prepared, Aeneas delays even his propitiatory offerings when he rejoins his comrades and finds them grieving over the corpse of their fallen shipmate Misenus. Unwilling, in contrast to Odysseus, to allow any errand to distract him from his duty, he immediately presides over the funeral.

In sacrifice, he then conciliates the infernal divinities. The Romans adopted large components of Greek mythology, as the invocations of Aeneas make clear. He offers his prayers to Hades, called the Stygian Jove, and to Proserpina (Latin for Persephone) correspondingly called the "infernal Juno" (138). He does not neglect Hecate, who, as we have seen, functions in heaven and in Erebos, the land of darkness, which the Latins also called Orcus. The Romans, too, called Hades by his other name, Pluto, meaning "the rich one," which, in Latin is Dives. They shortened it to Dis, and with a mixture of affection and respect, called him Dispater, Father Dis, as Lady Dis (397) is Proserpina. Aeneas also invokes Night, the Furies' mother, and Earth, her sister (250). Erebos is the brother of Night.[11]

As Aeneas actually sets foot within the cave, the narrative changes character, becoming less suggestive and more dogmatic. Instead of sensitively organized symbols and allusions balanced to establish the somber tenor of the doings, Virgil deals in categories, with one or two individuals chosen to typify the rest. The shift from evocation of mood to enumeration of persons and categories is marked by the list of allegorical figures who dwell by the gateway to the lower world. Grief, Care, Disease, Age, Fear, Hunger, Poverty, Death, Pain, and War—the remains of life—reside before the jaws of Orcus, the underworld.

An early incident illustrates this combination of precept and example. Immediately inside the gates of the underworld, Aeneas spies hybrid monsters: the Centaurs, Briareus, the Chimera, and Geryon, then the monstrous forms of Gorgons (here plural) and Harpies. He draws his sword, but the priestess tells him they are empty shapes immune to any steel (292–94). The lesson corrects the hero's impulse as a warrior.

As numerous as the leaves that previously concealed the golden bough, the spirits of the dead crowd the shores of the river begging Charon, the boatman, to ferry them across. Without proper burial, souls must wait a hundred years before they can reach their infernal home. As Aeneas considers the throng entreating Charon, the priestess groups many people into one category and says: "This collection, which you see, is the unburied crowd left resourceless" (*Haec omnis, quam cernis, inops inhumataque turba est* [325]). So many words in the singular for so many souls! Categories described by a past participle are crucial to Virgil's view of the dead. Despite his narrative, despite his celebration of the hero's destiny, grouping similar sorts is a major concern of the poet. The laws of his otherworld resemble the laws of his patron's principate.

In the meantime, though, Aeneas's vision focuses upon Palinurus, one of their number, the helmsman unburied because he died when washed ashore

---

11. On these divinities, see Eduard Norden, *P. Vergilius Maro, "Aeneis," Buch VI*, 4th ed. (Stuttgart: Teubner, 1957), 199; and R. G. Austin, *P. Vergili Maronis, "Aeneidos," Liber Sextus: Commentary* (Oxford: Clarendon Press, 1977), 111–12. I have made my translations from Austin's Latin text, 1–29.

after falling overboard. Aeneas asks him how he died. Thus the pattern is set. From a past participle describing a whole category of the dead (the unburied), Virgil picks an individual known to Aeneas, with whom he speaks. Again precept is illustrated by example. Like Odysseus, Aeneas does not ask (as Dante will) what the person suffers, but only how he died. In the case of Palinurus, the question takes on urgency because Aeneas implies that his death is a case of divine betrayal, for the gods had promised that Palinurus would reach the shores of Italy unharmed (345). His tale answers both of Aeneas's questions at once: No, the gods are not deceitful, and this is how I died. Palinurus begs Aeneas to bury him or cause him to be buried. He wishes an end to his wandering so that his life after death, at least, may be peaceful (371). The Sybil intervenes. She reassures him that a shrine will be built over his remains and that the place where he died will bear his name.[12] Yet she also chides the sailor for supposing that the prayers of a shade could affect the decrees of a god.[13] Whereas Plato put a sharp taunt in the mouth of Adimantus, Virgil has the Sybil deny outright the possibility of changing the fate of the dead.

When Aeneas approaches the shore of the lake, Charon confronts him with his suspicions. All the other living souls he has ferried into the underworld have betrayed him. Theseus and Perithous tried to kidnap Persephone; Herakles stole Cerberus. When the Sybil declares they have no such intent and shows the golden bough, token of the journey's divine approval, Charon allows Aeneas aboard. The substance of his still-living human body causes the stern to dip: Aeneas is no wraith. The living have weighty bodies; shades do not. At the distant shore Cerberus awaits, but the Sybil quiets him with drugged food and the two enter a cave farther up the bank.

Within the cavern, Aeneas encounters the first five groups of the dead. Here, what is effectively a catalog rather than a narrative takes over. The groups are separated by adverbs of place: "just at the boundary" (*in limine primo* [427]), "nearby" (*iuxta* [430]), "at the next place" (*proxima . . . loca* [434]).[14] Virgil characterizes each group either with a quick sentence or by engaging Aeneas in dialogue with its exemplary members. These souls have their premature death in common. They were unfortunate rather than blameworthy, in contrast to others Aeneas will encounter later, after a crucial fork in the road, who either led evil lives and will be sent to Tartarus or

---

12. Misenus was granted the same boon at 234–35.

13. Literally, "cease to hope that prayer may deflect the god from his decree" (376).

14. "Deinde" is added to "proxima loca."

led pure lives and will be sent to Elysium. Thus these first five groups consist of the morally neutral: those who died in infancy (428–29), those executed for crimes they did not commit (430), and suicides (434–38) are followed slightly farther on, in an area called the Mourning Fields, by those who died of love, whether of another person or of country, and those distinguished by feats of arms.

Death does not diminish the cares of those in the last two groups (444). Thus among those who died of love, Aeneas finds himself opposite Dido, who cannot address him and turns away when he seeks to explain the compulsion of destiny that took him from her (450–76). Though it was love of Aeneas that caused her death, she now turns away in hatred. Struck by her undeserved fate, Aeneas feels pity and gazes after her retreating form for a long time, in spite of his tears (475–76).

Similarly, the same passions that motivated their lives still drives the warriors. As Aeneas passes among the shades of famous soldiers, the Trojan dead crowd around to speak with him, but the Greeks begin to flee (as in life they had taken to their ships). The continuity of emotion suffered in life and death is indicated visibly by the presence of physical marks. Though a shade, Dido's form reveals the self-inflicted wound of her knife, and the scars of Deiphobus, the Trojan prince who married Helen of Troy after the death of Paris, expose the betrayal that caused his mutilation. On their wedding night Helen had revealed his hiding place to Menelaus and Ulysses, the Greek commanders who, concealed in the Trojan horse, had entered his city by stealth. These signs remind us of Homer's blood-spattered warriors and the souls scarred by misdeeds who present themselves for judgment in Plato's *Gorgias*. Even without punishment, wearing the signs of one's life (or having victims wear those one inflicted), makes the Mourning Fields an encouragement to virtue.

Virgil contrasts the infants to the suicides. Infants he considered without guilt (*insontes* [435]). They hardly knew life at all (427). The suicides regret their fate. Although they are not blamed for taking their own lives, they regret their action. However unhappy they had been in life, they now know its advantages over death and would return to the light, were it not prohibited by divine law (*fas obstat* [438]).

The clarity with which these categories are delineated clouds over with the one I have saved for last: "Next to those [who died in infancy] were those falsely condemned for a capital crime.[15] But these places are not assigned

---

15. Plato reports that Socrates imagined a category of the unjustly accused with whom he might compare notes in the afterlife (*Apology* 41a).

without a lot, without a judge. Minos, as *quaesitor*, shakes the urn. He solicits the counsel of the silent and ascertains lives and crimes" (430–43). This account contains several ambiguities: who are "the silent"; what places does Minos assign, and to whom? Put another way, is it correct to conclude that places are assigned in this area to those whose lives and crimes Minos, with the help of his jury (chosen by lot), has reviewed and accepted? Of the possible answers no one is fully satisfactory; each has drawbacks. It is best, however, to ask who serves on the jury before deciding to whom the places are assigned.

Minos is characterized as a judge; yet neither the infants, the suicides, nor those in the Mourning Fields seem to be involved.[16] Only the wrongly accused might benefit from a judgment that rectifies the absence of a valid trial in life. That is the first possibility. Because Minos's function is analyzed within verses describing a place devoted only to the unjustly executed, it might be tempting to conclude that it is only their lives that are reviewed and that they alone constitute the pool for the jury. Thus, some critics have assumed that the court of Minos rectifies the situation of these souls by providing an honest trial.[17] That assumption neglects Virgil's statement that the jury is drawn by lot from among "the silent," which seems to cover all five of these groups. Also, the reference to "places" (in the plural) means that not even emphasizing the proximate demonstrative pronoun (*hae* as opposed to *illae*) can restrict attention to the cluster of the unjustly executed. Moreover, although Virgil's expression is typically elliptical, and one must frequently fill in to complete his meaning, the word "theirs" does not occur in the text. Minos ascertains lives and crimes, but the poem does not say whose. The innocence of the falsely executed souls is clear by definition, and a new, postmortem trial would be redundant. These souls and the places they assign must have some other function. It is therefore not possible that Minos and his jury simply give the falsely executed their day in court.

A second possibility would stress the role of "the silent." Perhaps liability

16. On the function of Minos, Norden, 245–46, cites parallels with institutions from ancient societies.

17. That is the position of Austin, 156. Norden, 245–46, stresses the legal character of the terminology but says nothing to suggest expanding its jurisdiction beyond the "falso damnati." S. G. F. Brandon ignores the role of Minos in Virgil entirely. *Judgment of the Dead*, 92. In *The Divine Verdict: A Study of Divine Judgement in the Ancient Religions*, Studies in the History of Religions, Supplements to *Numen*, 52 (Leiden: Brill, 1991), 294–97, J. Gwyn Griffiths cites Minos (together with Rhadamanthus) as indicative of Egyptian influence on Greece via Crete in the matter of posthumous judgement and dwells little on the question of his actual jurisdiction, whether in Homer, Plato, or Virgil.

to jury duty pertains to all the prematurely dead. Since they are neither in Elysium nor in Tartarus, are they a group of morally neutral souls who can help Minos judge all the others since they can recognize those that are better than themselves and worse? The drawback to that hypothesis is that it would include the infants, who have had no experience of life, among the jury. Another disadvantage, though less severe, is that it it would include the suicides, who, sometimes for reasons considered honorable in antiquity, did not fully learn the consequences of their actions. Further, it would give great responsibility to those consumed by love. The burden would not necessarily be too great for those who died for love of country or through heroism in war, except that Virgil portrays them as partial: the Greeks hate, fear, and run from Aeneas; the Trojans flock to him in adulation. That behavior hardly portends dispassionate analysis. Dido, too, is a poor representative of a potential jury. That leaves only the unjustly executed able to serve. Of all the groups who could make up the jury of Minos, these are most qualified to counsel the quaesitor. Themselves victims of sham trials, they can be counted on to value justice more than any others.

The return, by the process of elimination, to the unjustly executed brings up the second part of the question. If they are the pool from which the jury is chosen by lot, which souls fall under their jurisdiction and what "places" may be assigned to them? It is already clear that the unjustly executed do not merely certify newly arrived souls for membership in their own group. Possibly, though, they review all the prematurely dead prior to admitting them to the area of the threshold reserved to the morally neutral. But with the jury's guidance, Minos learns not only people's lives but also their crimes (*vitasque et crimina discit* [433]).[18] Hence those possibly guilty of crimes must also come under their jurisdiction. Thus the places to which the people they judge may be sent must include Tartarus. The "places," then, must be the neutral antechamber, Tartarus, and Elysium. Why have a court if all those to be heard are innocent?

This consideration leads to the best solution: the unjustly executed help judge all the dead. Every soul must ride on Charon's barge, must pass

---

18. Austin, 157, insists on translating *crimina* as "charges," not "crimes." But if Minos and his jury hear the lives of and charges against those falsely condemned to death, the charges must have been for capital crimes. If they were all falsely condemned then, by definition, no new trial is necessary. If some were indeed guilty of capital offenses, then not all the cases heard by Minos and his counselors end up in these places. In the translation that precedes his commentary (75–77), Norden regards the function of Minos as verifying the earthly sentence (cf. p. 246), but these are falsely executed.

Cerberus, and all the dead must pass over this threshold before coming to the crossing that separates Tartarus from Elysium. Why should all the dead not be reviewed by those most qualified to hear their cases? Minos is quaesitor; his jury is chosen by lot from among the falsely executed, and employing their counsel, he assigns the dead their places.

One danger with this solution is anachronism, reading back into Virgil the same role that Dante gives Minos or the universal eschatology of Christian theology. Ancient precedent averts that danger: Plato, the Orphics, and in some regards, the Egyptians also proposed a strict judgment after death.

The biggest remaining drawback is the jurisdiction of Rhadamanthus over Tartarus (566–69). Why would he need to hear, chastise, and constrain the wicked to confess (567) if their cases had already been heard by Minos? Minos did not need confession. He could damn on the testimony of others. Perhaps, as Plato suggested, he could see their souls. Virgil makes ample use of visible signs on his shades. The problem of overlap in jurisdiction is not insuperable, however. There is sequential difference. Minos clearly had jurisdiction over the neutral, those at the threshold. With his jury chosen by lot from among the unjustly executed, he conducts a preliminary screening, sending the wicked to Tartarus, where they come under the jurisdiction of Rhadamanthus, and the virtuous to the Elysian Fields, where there are no fixed residences (673). All three districts are under the supervision of Pluto, who resides in a castle beyond the entrance area, just at the crossroads that leads either to Tartarus or Elysium (541).

That intersection marks a distinction. The land of the first five groups, just inside the threshold, corresponds to a neutral, gray land characterized by consciousness of being dead, longing for life, and eternally reliving life's unresolved passions, but without blame. After the fork in the road, each soul is destined either for Elysium or Tartarus. The souls in Tartarus committed actual misdeeds that produce active punishment. The souls in Elysium are granted their freedom and experience positive joy. Thus Virgil's underworld resembles Plato's: both contain an area of judgment distinct from Elysium and Tartarus.

The road divides in two. To the right stands the fortress of Dis (Pluto, Hades). Beneath its wall, the right road leads on to Elysium, where Aeneas is going to meet his father. "The leftward way leads to unholy Tartarus and exacts punishment from the wicked" (542–43). The words *mali* (the wicked) and *poenae* (punishments) have not been used before. They reinforce the image of the two "ways"—right and left, right and wrong, Elysium and Tartarus—as in the myth of Er.

From his vantage point, Aeneas can see Phlegethon's rushing, fiery current, which churns the white-hot boulders in the moat. The Fury Tisiphone, wearing a bloody mantle, guards the unyielding gate from atop an iron tower. The sounds of dragging chains, grating iron, and savage lashings do not drown out the groans and cries of the prisoners beyond the fortress's three rings of walls. Aeneas will not be permitted inside, for no one who is pure may penetrate the castle's stronghold. Instead, the Sybil says that when Hecate gave her authority over Avernus, they toured the place together and the goddess explained the divine punishments (565). Rhadamanthus of Cnossus (considered the brother of Minos) rules there. He hears and punishes the crimes of each one sent to him, but more particularly he causes each to confess the deceitful acts of their lives which they had concealed complacently but foolishly, delaying atonement beyond death, when it was too late (566–69). These then are turned over to Tisiphone who, with her sister Furies, drives them along with scourges and frightening snakes (572).

So much the Sybil explains to the accompaniment of screams and the grating of instruments of torture. So much can Aeneas learn through his ears. Now he sees. The gate (573–74) suspended between the adamantine columns (552) grinds open, permitting the Sybil to point out what kind of monster guards the entrance (*limina* [575]), and inside (*intus* [577]) sits the Hydra with fifty gaping jaws, "and finally, Tartarus itself stretches back headlong beneath the darkness" a void twice as deep from there as Olympus is in the other direction (577–79). Guided by the Sybil, the gaze of Aeneas penetrates as far as the eye can see into the earth's interior.

Here are punished the superhuman rebels against the gods. The Titans, sons of Earth, overthrown when Jupiter and his brothers took over the cosmos, lie in the deepest depths. So do Otus and Ephialtes, the twin sons of Aloeus.[19] Salmoneus brandished a fire of his own creation and, challenging Jupiter, hawked it around the world seeking human adoration. Tityos, who had tried the virtue of a goddess (Leto in the *Odyssey*), is stretched over a nine-league field, his "immortal" (598) liver exposed to the incessant pecking of a vulture. "Nor is he given any rest," since his liver is constantly reborn (600). Passing over the stories of Ixion, Perithous, and the Lapiths, the Sybil describes how they tremble beneath a rock that seems always ready to fall and crush them. If these are tormented by a punishment that always

19. These overthrown rebels are also mentioned in the *Odyssey* 11.305–7 as sons of Iphimedeia. They occupy the conceptual position of Hesiod's Titans, their offspring, or monsters such as Typhoeus—threats to the new order established by Zeus/Jupiter.

threatens, there are others who, imitating the fate of Tantalus, suffer in view of relief they can never attain, as the most savage Fury wards their hands from a table whose fare would sate their hunger (601–7).

From the superhuman offenders, the Sybil passes to humans, though these are not mentioned by name, only by category. These are those who hated brothers, struck their fathers, defrauded clients, refused to share the benefits of newfound wealth with their families, took up arms for a false lord or failed to follow a just one, or those slain on account of adultery (608–13). But the variety of crimes and their matching punishments is too great to recount. Confined here, these offenders await chastisement (614). The punishment may not have started, but it is not clear when or whether it will end. The concept of continual, eternal punishment is present, especially in the case of Tityos, but it does not apply to all humans. The variety of punishments exhausts the Sybil: Aeneas is not to ask about them. She gives a few examples. Some roll boulders; others are stretched across wheels. Theseus sits unhappy and so will sit forever (*aeternum* [617]). Phlegyas, in extreme misery, calls forth through the shadows the lesson to be learned: "Now that you have been warned, learn to do justice and not to scorn the gods" (620). With this moral capping what appears to be a systematic account of Tartarus's torments, the Sybil points out a few of the more notorious offenders: "Here is one who sold his country for money and set a tyrant over it; another who established and annulled laws for a price; another who invaded the chamber of his daughter and imposed a forbidden bond upon her. Monstrously, all dared what was forbidden and attained what they dared" (621–24). As if in despair at the extent of evil, the Sybil protests: "Even if I had a hundred mouths, a hundred tongues, and a voice of iron I still would not be able to tally all the forms of evil nor figure all the punishments" (625–27).

However diverse the crimes, none escapes punishment. But only the superhumans, Tityos, Ixion, Perithous, and Salmoneus, are named. The punished are types, not individuals. Even so, the punishment is not fitted to the sin. If the liver is the seat of concupiscence, Tityos would be an exception, but he is of the Titan generation. Among humans, "divine law" or "justice" prevents (*fas obstat* [438]) the suicides' return to life after they have purposely departed from it (cf. 435). Rarely, however, can this type of symmetry be reconstructed.

Even in the land of the blessed, there is no clear indication of what particular virtue earned any special aspect of the light, open, airy, meadowlike space. The whole region is encircled by a wall made by the Cyclops, at whose gate Aeneas deposits the golden bough as if it were a ticket of admission (630–36). This gate is the last boundary other than returning to life itself. No Minos or Rhadamanthus rules; the spirits enjoy freedom to dance, sing hymns of praise, or meditate, accompanied by Orpheus playing his lyre. The theme of death as a continuation of life, established in the Mourning Fields and in Homer, is repeated here, as the valiant Trojans exercise beside the weapons and armor that had previously assured their glory (653–55). Groups of various blessed souls can be identified. Some still bear wounds endured in defending their countries; some were perfect priests or seers; some improved the lives of their fellows by human inventions; others were distinguished for outstanding service. Musaeus, the legendary poet and disciple of Orpheus, proclaims the freedom of the place and guides Aeneas and the priestess to Anchises (673–75).

The father of Aeneas is meditating on the future of his progeny, his own descendants and theirs, though not yet born to his son. As father and son spy each other, they approach and three times seek to embrace, but as Homer had dramatized before, there can be no physical contact between a body and a shade, an image (*imago*), which passes quickly, like a breeze or a moment in a dream (700–702). Aeneas observes clusters of people rushing toward the banks of the Lethe and asks his father to explain (703–12). In reply, Anchises expounds a metaphysical system that legitimates Rome's claim to rule by emphasizing the heavenly descent of its founders (724–51).

His account restates what appear to have been the main tenets of Orphism. To begin with, all that exists, even the Titanic sun (725) is mixed with spirit (*spiritus* [726]) and mind (*mens* [727]). When these elements depart at death, the body's influence continues to stain them (736–77). "Therefore they are disciplined by punishment and pay with suffering for deep-seated evils" (739–40). Some souls are exposed helpless to the winds, others submerged in whirlpools or plunged into fire, but "each of us suffers his own personal demon" (743).

The process continues even in Elysium, where, as a result, there are three kinds of souls. All have been purified in their own way. There are the perfect, some few who have attained its broad fields never to leave again, always to converse with Musaeus and the other followers of Orpheus, whose lyre strains accompany all their activities. Others can complete their purification by the experiences of Elysium itself, that is, by philosophical discourse, musing in the glens and woods, or in military or gymnastic exercises.

The third group in Elysium needs the further purification of other physical lives, and these require a magical draught from the Lethe to lose all memory of previous life (713–14, 748–51). Even before their purification, they were not merely neutral, like those at the exit of the cave, but good. Destined to be reborn, they rank just under the perfect and the perfectible. As one of the perfected, Anchises can foretell the destiny of his descendants, drawn from this group, the highest moral class from which anyone can still come back into the world (752–886). Such will be the founders of Rome. It is important to note that, although they are less than perfect, reincarnation is no punishment here. Immune from the Platonic scorn of bodies, these souls are eager for their new lives. As Roman conquerors, they have work to do!

Thus Aeneas learns in detail how correct he was when, early in book 6, while still barely able to pray in the Sybil's cave, he stated that he sought no more than what destiny had assigned him (66–67). He now proclaims his newfound confidence with the rhetorical question: How can we, knowing this, hesitate to act with courage and settle these lands (806–7)? What he has learned inflames "his soul with the love of the fame that is to come" (889).

To exit from Elysium, Aeneas and the Sybil do not, as she had stated earlier (133–34), retrace their steps and reemerge from the cave. Instead, Anchises ushers them to the matching gates of horn and ivory; they must leave through the ivory gates since only "true shades" may use the horn gates. The Manes, or spirits of the dead, send false dreams (*falsa . . . insomnia* [896]) through the gates of ivory. Thus book 6 ends with a considerable mystery.[20] The words of the Sybil prove false, and the hero exits through a notorious way—the way of dreams—not to be trusted by the living. Yet one may ask when Aeneas fell asleep. Was he not conscious through all that he experienced in the Sybil's company? What pall is cast over the prophecy of Anchises? Perhaps the lessons Aeneas has learned can be applied to life only in the manner of a dream, and that is the obscurity in which the Sybil's truth was cloaked (cf. line 100).

Whatever epistemological puzzle is posed by the gates, it is necessary to consider how Virgil has revised the tale of Odysseus's voyage to the dead. Two major differences stand out.

The first is less directly relevant. It concerns the character of Aeneas's mission. Whereas Odysseus's quest is personal, and his return home the goal of an individual, the destiny of Aeneas is not his alone but that of a people. Whatever pride ancient Greeks may have taken in the cunning or perseverence of Odysseus, his travels did not transplant a state. In contrast, the destiny of Aeneas far transcends its bearer—or its instrument. Though Odysseus and Aeneas both leave the underworld with an enhanced understanding of their futures, the founder of Rome also possesses a blueprint for history.

Second, and more important, Virgil's netherworld is not neutral but moral. He has adjusted it in the sense suggested by Orphism and the philosophy

20. For one interpretation, see R. J. Tarrant, "Aeneas and the Gates of Sleep," *Classical Philology* 77 (1982): 51–55.

of Plato. Though free to wander, the souls in Elysium follow laws of metempsychosis derived from the myth of Er, complete with Lethe's water. None of the wicked escape here! Like Plato's souls, Aeneas encounters the neutral, the curable, the blessed, and the incurably evil. Plato's moral categories are charted on Virgil's underworld landscape. (Here is a mapping faintly reminiscent of the Egyptian *Book of Gates*, whose doctrine is also played out along the traveled path.) Though it is not explicitly stated, there seems no escape—ever—for the inmates of Tartarus. Lacking either purity or the purification available in Elysium, the prisoners of Tartarus seem eternally confined. These are those who thought they would escape their evils when they died, against whom Socrates protested in the *Phaedo*. In Virgil it requires the torture of Rhadamanthus to force them to acknowledge their sins and commence an atonement postponed till after death, when it lasts indefinitely (566–69). Here the punishment of the dead is firmly established.

PLUTARCH ON THE DELAY OF VENGEANCE

Book 6 of Virgil's *Aeneid* draws in different ways on traditions that go back in epic poetry to Homer, in philosophy to Plato, and in religion, if that is the correct term, to Orphism. Looking in the other direction, this pagan tradition continued strong even as Christianity appeared and began to spread. If Virgil celebrated the political destiny of Augustus Caesar, in whose reign Jesus was born, another gifted writer's career almost matches the period when the New Testament was being written. Although not as recent as Lucian, who will be considered later, Plutarch of Chaeronaea deserves a place in this survey for his use of Plato's themes and his skillful adaptation of a near-death experience like Er's to an extended investigation of divine justice and punishment after death.

Plutarch was born in Chaeronaea before 50 C.E. and left the last trace we have of him after 120. From about 90, he was a priest of Apollo's oracle at Delphi, where this dialogue is set. An ancient list catalogs 227 separate works by him, though not all have survived. The most famous are his *Lives*. The others are grouped into a collection called the *Moralia* or *Ethical Works*, of which *On the Delays of the Divine Vengeance* is one.

In this dialogue the question is whether punishment after death works. Several speakers, whom Plutarch will later refute, object that delaying justice indicates an absence of divine supervision. If the gods punish the dead, do they not thereby spare the wicked who are alive and active? When punishment comes so late, people doubt its existence and are less deterred from evil. Clearly these questions reflect a concern like that dealt with (as we shall see) in the Book of Job, that the prosperity of the wicked implies a lack of justice. These speakers prefer a system of retribution akin to Hesiod's punishing justice, Dike, the daughter of Zeus who effects the dramatic downfall of oppressors inflated with hubris. With Dike at work, says Hesiod, the wicked suffer swiftly and visibly for the evil they do (*Works and Days* 213–85). Plutarch's opponents approve of this kind of justice. When victims and righteous people see the disgrace of oppressors, they are edified by the spectacle, as by a public execution, which deters evil and restores equilibrium to the community (1–3, 19 [561c]). To assert the superiority of punishment after death, Plutarch must establish that it is superior to visible justice in the world and that it is a sign not of divine indifference but rather of the gods' providential care.

Plutarch's ally in the dialogue, Timon, argues that delay allows for persons of mixed character to reform (6). Further, the deity can allow the wicked (tyrants, for example) to persist in evil, thus punishing large populations.[21] Plutarch enters the debate arguing that vice is its own punishment, that evildoers spend their lives dreading their comeuppance, which is sometimes announced to them by oracles, the ghosts of their victims, or in dreams (8–9). Anxiety makes ill-gotten gains into empty, passing pleasures, whereas the guilt from evildoing endures, even beyond the grave (11).

Although Timon had previously spoken of the advantages of divine delay, he now introduces his gravest doubt. One aspect that the interlocutors regard as corollary with punishment after death, and whose justice Timon questions, is the matter of the gods' punishing descendants for the crimes of their predecessors. This position also comes from the *Works and Days*, where Hesiod says the wicked are punished through their offspring, who inherit a taint for their forebears' offenses.[22] Whereas the previous speakers had criticized the system for being too soft on criminals, Timon objects that in this regard it is misdirected, affecting not the criminals but their heirs for generations. In this case, he objects, late punishment afflicts the innocent. "For what reason should the wrath of the gods at first sink out of sight, like certain rivers, only to resurge later against others, leading in the end to the direst calamities?" (12 [557e]).

Plutarch answers with a contrast. Whereas postmortem punishments are not known on earth, the penalties inflicted on the offspring of wicked par-

---

21. This is the principle used by Paul in Romans 13 and by Augustine in the *City of God*.

22. Hesiod reports that the good are rewarded with children who resemble their fathers; thus, the unjust are implicitly threatened with the contrary (*Works and Days* 235). Hesiod evokes suffering for the descendants of the unjust (284).

ents are visible and act as a deterrent. In the army, the punishment of one man in ten, by way of example, inspires dread in the whole corps to the benefit of all (16). The same is true of civilians: "The reason for making a public spectacle of the punishment of evildoers . . . is to restrain some men by punishing others" (19 [561d]).

It makes sense that this should work in families too, since, he says, the family is a particularly effective channel for the transmission of vice and evil character. Plutarch claims that it is through inherited psychological proclivities that the force of postmortem punishment makes its effect felt on the heirs of evildoers. Just as a hero is comemmorated for generations to the glory of his kin, so the progeny of the wicked should be tainted with shame (13 [558a–b]; cf. 15). Just as we would warn children of parents with a hereditary disease of the dangers they face, similarly their suffering in life for the evil of their parents is also a salutary warning, he says (16; cf. 19 [561f]). Humans can conceal their vices from others until the moment when they exercise them. Thus God punishes sufferers to remove those vices before they get the opportunity to affect those in whom they reside (20). Allowance is made for individuals free from the characteristics of the group. Nonetheless, in general, "if a man's disorder reproduces the traits of a vicious ancestry, it is surely fitting that he should succeed to the punishment of that viciousness as to the debts of an estate" (21 [562f]). Thus Plutarch answers Timon's objection about the submerged river: "The first generations often conceal traits and passions of the soul, while later, and in the persons of others, the family nature breaks out and restores the inherited bent for vice or virtue" (21 [563b]).

What one might call Plutarch's "moral genetics" provides an account of a different mechanism held to assure that the consequences on earth of punishment after death be realized and discoverable to rational investigation. The temporal purging of inherited vice complements the mechanism of metempsychosis in Plato's *Republic* and *Phaedrus*. Here, in philosophical language, Plutarch expresses the desire to punish descendants of the unscrupulous rich who gloat over the crimes of ancestors whose wealth they enjoy. Ostensibly devised to deter tyrants and other powerful figures from abusing their advantage, it could also, horribly, be used to explain the servitude of subject peoples.

In Plutarch's theory, both the malefactors and their descendants are punished together. "No punishment," he says, "is more shameful or galling than to see one's progeny suffer on one's own account" (18 [516b]). The dead know the fate of their family on earth, and so, he says: "The soul of an impious and lawless man who should behold after death not statues or honours subverted, but children or friends or his own kindred involved in terrible calamities through his own fault and paying the price, could never be induced, for all the honours rendered to Zeus, once more to become unjust and licentious" (18 [561b]). Thus providence works, Plutarch is saying, by a double mechanism. Persons who inherited innate evils are purified in life by a suffering brought on by their forebears. At the same time, those forebears experience punishment after death which consists, in part, of knowing the suffering of their progeny. This knowledge helps deter them from further evil in a subsequent life. By the combination of these two devices, Plutarch implies, providence uses evil in both this world and the next to educate, to purify, and to deter. It would seem that evil so well targeted is self-regulating and consequently a proof of providence.[23]

If there were any doubt, Plutarch confirms his account in a vision of the otherworld obtained by a man whose fall brought him near death. Upon his recovery the man, Aridaeus, related his experience to a friend from whom Plutarch heard it. This otherworld exists in the heavens. As Aridaeus lay near death, his intelligence, not his soul, traveled upward where the composition of the spheres, particularly the influence of the moon, was evident. The layout of this supernal region recalls the *Phaedrus* and the myth of Er, where Plato, too, displays the consistency of his cosmology, his psychology, and his theory of justice.

Like the *Phaedo*, this vision begins by recounting the place where souls meet. In a heightened state of consciousness—his intelligence sees through his soul on all sides at once, as from a single eye—Aridaeus perceives the haphazard motion of toplike spirits, whirling confusedly in various arcs. After a long time, the spinning souls grow barely steady and assemble in groups sharing a sympathetic motion. The well-ordered souls cluster higher than, and separate from, those gyrating wildly (23).

One of the higher souls recognizes Aridaeus but greets him as Thespesius, the name of a kinsman who had died when Aridaeus was a child. This soul then serves as guide. He reveals that Aridaeus's real name is Thespesius, that he is not dead but present there in his intelligence, "having left the rest of your soul, like an anchor, behind in your body" (24 [564c]). Souls of the dead do not cast a shadow or blink their eyes, he tells Thespesius, who then realizes that a faint shadow is following him, whereas the others give off different amounts of light. Resembling moons and symbolizing their various levels of virtue, they appear as clear beams, mottled with spots or just barely speckled (24 [564d]).

---

23. J. Gwyn Griffiths, *The Divine Verdict*, 83–85, gives similar emphasis to Plutarch's concept of providence.

Perceiving his own shadow confirms Thespesius's confidence in the reliability of his guide, who now tells him about the division of authority in this region. In a manner that recalls the categories of Plato, Plutarch puts a different figure in charge of each. Similarly Virgil had given a separate jurisdiction to Minos and Rhadamanthus under the overlordship of Pluto and had claimed the blessed roam free.

Adrasteia, daughter of Necessity and Zeus, a figure known primarily from this passage, has jurisdiction over all crimes. She is helped by three personified avenging deities modeled on the Furies, who exact different punishments. First is Poine (Punishment), who punishes in the body and through it. Her method, Plutarch says, is comparatively gentle, for it passes over many of the faults requiring correction. Her punishment is exercised in life and is basically superficial, affecting the body and external possessions only, not the root viciousness itself. Poine affects opinion and the senses (25 [564e–f]).

Poine corresponds to the classical notion of nemesis or Hesiod's Dike, which personifies swift, visible, external retribution. Plutarch's negative portrayal of Poine, suggesting that she causes only regret but not change of character, helps establish his argument in favor of the sterner justice that he believes can exist only through providence and after death. The attackers of punishment after death have argued that Poine alone is more effective. Plutarch, however, uses the vision of Thespesius to show the further duties of these agents of Adrasteia, herself a personification of punishment or vengeance.

More vicious than those subjected to Poine are those delivered after death to Dike (Justice) (25 [564f]). Since Plutarch is refuting conventional wisdom here, he uses Poine to replace Hesiod's Dike, and makes his Dike, as if to say *true* Justice, operate at a much deeper level. Plutarch's Dike takes those who have not been purged or punished in the world. These souls arrive before her naked and exposed, unable to conceal any of their baseness. She shames them by parading them before their good parents and ancestors, if there are any, as being unworthy of them. Or if their progenitors are wicked, the newly dead are made to see the shame that has gone before, and the predecessors see how it endures in their progeny (26 [565b]). Here the vision confirms the principle of moral genetics, where the opinion that one relative holds of another, one's reputation within the clan, is taken to be a severe sanction.

Shame, however, does not suffice. The prisoners of Dike also undergo prolonged punishment, "each of [their] passions being removed with pains and torments that in magnitude and intensity as far transcend those that pass through the flesh as the reality would be more vivid than a dream" (26 [565b]). The different passions are reflected by different colors whose intensity varies according to the depth of the passion's roots. Gradually the colors of the respective passions yield until the purified soul begins to glow in purity. This color coding illustrates Plutarch's tendency to group like with like and punish each type similarly.

Because the image of old passions remains in the soul, it may relapse by consenting to them. When this happens, the passion may be driven out by renewed punishment, and the soul returned to its bright, glowing state. Others who have fallen back into their old passions, are again inserted into the bodies of living things (here seen as a punishment, as in Plato), while a third group, although still longing to reexperience past physical pleasures, suffers not through rebirth but from continual frustration of their desire to reattain physicality (26 [565b–66a]).[24]

To recapitulate, there are three possibilities: (1) the soul lapses, but the passion is beat out by renewed punishment, though the relationship of the punishment to the passion is not specified; (2) the soul lapses by "the violence of ignorance and the image of the love of pleasure" and is sent to another body; and (3) the soul continues in the very same desire for pleasure, but reincarnation is denied. In this case, the soul continues to experience the same unrealized desire, presumably until this passion is spent. In this case the punishment is to suffer the desire itself.

It is the function of Dike that is being tested in this dialogue. The attackers of punishment after death have argued that Poine alone is more effective.

The third agent of Adrasteia is Erinys (Fury), who takes the incurable rejected by Dike and destroys them. The suggestion of annihilation is a significant departure from Plato and Virgil, one that will come up again in connection with the New Testament. Although obviously differing from Plato and Virgil, however, Plutarch seems not to be suggesting that the incurable are annihilated. Rather his expression implies confinement to oblivion. The process is clearly painful; yet it ends in a place where nothing can be known about either the "physical" condition or the state of consciousness of those confined there. Erinys "makes away with them," each differently but "all piteously and cruelly, imprisoning them in the Nameless and Unseen" (25 [564f]).

So far the vision of Thespesius has viewed only one spot in the other world, where he hears one exposition of the administration of divine justice. When his guide takes him farther he sees where these functions are carried out. Significantly, there is no further mention of the incurable in oblivion.

---

24. It is unclear whether the last phrase of this sentence sketches a third option (as I take it) or is a parenthetical explanation of why it is that the second group should want to rejoin their bodies.

Thespesius travels an immense distance over rays of light to the verge of a great chasm "extending all the way down," from which an extraordinarily pleasant aroma arises. Thespesius wishes to linger with the other souls in a trancelike revelry around it, but his guide forces him away, explaining that "the intelligent part of the soul is dissolved by pleasure, while the irrational and carnal part is fed by its flow and puts on flesh and thus undergoes memory of the body; and that from such memory arises a yearning and desire that draws the souls toward birth"—an earthward, downward inclination (27). This incident illustrates Plutarch's ethical principle that pleasure opposes intelligence, applicable to the second type of Dike's punishment: the love of pleasure resulting in a new birth.

Traveling another long way, about the same distance, Thespesius sees a chasm with variously colored streams pouring into it. As he approaches, the crater takes on a whiteness and the other colors fade. He sees there three demons who blend the streams in different proportions. This is the source of dreams (28).

Nearby is the oracle of Apollo, but the intelligence of Thespesius is prevented from advancing so high while still attached to its body. What the guide endeavors to show him is invisible to Thespesius because of its brightness. Still, he dimly discerns the voice of a Sibyl prophesying the future, but because of the motion of the moon to which the Sibyl is attached, he makes out only a little. The implication of this interesting analogy is that prophetic authority is linked to heavenly bodies as our souls are to our bodies. This concept should give prophecy through oracles very high credibility. Through this chasm in the heavens, then, the otherworld is accessible to humankind through dreams, prophecy, and oracles such as the one at Delphi, where Plutarch was a priest (29).

From the brink of this same chasm, perhaps the one through which Plutarch was able to ascertain by reason the principles he has expounded, Thespesius and his guide turn and see the punishments. At first Thespesius distinguishes only a series of severe and lamentable afflictions, but then he begins to recognize respected friends, acquaintances, and relatives, who, contrary to his expectations, undergo grievous and degrading punishment and, sobbing, beg for his pity.[25] One man emerges from a chasm and ex-

25. The physical quality of the punishments to be described calls for some note. In a detailed consideration of *On Late Punishment* and the vision of Thespesius, Roger Miller Jones in *The Platonism of Plutarch and Selected Papers* (Menasha, Wis.: Banta, 1916; rpt. New York: Garland, 1980), 42, considers these in the context of Plato's ideas. He remarks that Plato rarely describes his punishments and traces Plutarch's doctrines to the *Republic* 615e–16a—the carding of those denied exit

tends his hands toward Thespesius. His arms are covered with scars and open wounds. Examining him further, Thespesius recognizes his father, who, forced by those in charge, confesses to his son that he had secretly poisoned his wealthy guests for their gold. These crimes escaped detection on earth, but in the other world he has been judged guilty and has so far achieved only partial expiation. Before Thespesius can recover from his surprise, the demons in charge of the place force him away from the area. Frightened by their appearance, Thespesius turns to look for his guide, who is not there. This moment of abandonment, horribly frightening for the visionary, is a staple component of otherworldly visits. Forcing the living guest to confront what is ultimately a personal responsibility and his potential liability to precisely these conditions is a crucial element in the vision's didactic purpose.

The appearance of Thespesius's father drives home the contrast between the justice of Poine and that of Dike. Thespesius sees that the shades of wicked people recognized as such on earth, who therefore had suffered at least in their reputations here, were not mistreated as harshly or in the same way as those who, like his father, had escaped from life scot-free. For those who had already been punished on earth it is only the irrational and passionate part of their soul that is afflicted in the beyond, since they have already expiated in their bodies the crimes for which they had been caught. Only the tendency to evil still must be eradicated (30).

But the fate of people such as Thespesius's father supports the argument in favor of punishment after death, because only then can crimes for which the perpetrator escaped punishment be requited. Thus other tormentors surround those who, under the cover of an assumed external virtue, had passed their lives without being suspected. These tormentors painfully turn some of these souls inside out. They strip the skin off others to display their souls, all mottled with bruises bearing the marks of vice right up to its reasoning and superior part. Such is the punishment for a life of hypocrisy. In death the true inner self is forcibly exposed by either stripping away the false exterior or covering it with matter drawn from the inside. By this inversion Plutarch dramatizes the contrast between Poine's purely superficial chastizing by re-

---

from Tartarus in the myth of Er. Pointing precisely to the more evident and more vivid descriptions of punishments, Albrecht Dieterich, *Nekyia: Beiträge zur Erklärung der neuentdeckten Petrusapokalypse* (Leipzig: Teubner, 1893), 147, believes Plutarch's sources to go back beyond Plato, to the Orphics. Jean Hani, *La religion égyptienne dans la pensée de Plutarque* (Paris: Belles Lettres, 1976), points in another direction. In that sense, see also J. Gwyn Griffiths's edition of Plutarch, *De Iside et Osiride*, with an introduction, translation, and commentary (Cardiff: University of Wales Press, 1970).

moving external goods in the world and Dike's radical transformation of the inner person.

Other souls are interlaced like vipers, in groups of two or three or more, devouring one another in anger or despair under pressure of the memory of the evil they did or suffered in the course of their life. Are these souls that had acted illicitly in concert and now turned against each other? The rationale for this punishment is not clear.

Still near the second chasm are ponds placed side by side: one of boiling gold, another of frozen lead, a third of surging, molten iron. Like black-smiths, demons equipped with tongs move souls from one lake to the other. These had sinned by cupidity or ambition. After the heat of the gold makes them begin to glow and become transparent, the demons throw them into the pond of lead. Then, once they are frozen and hardened like hailstones, they put them into the pond of iron. There, they become frightfully black and so stiff that they burst. Even though each turn through the three ponds costs them a thousand tortures, the demons force the souls through the cycle over and over again (30).

These physical-seeming punishments inflicted on the souls are now com-plemented with more shame, but shame that almost approaches the physi-cal. The worst punishment of all occurs just as the appropriate one of the three previous penalties has been paid and the victim souls think themselves acquitted of punishment. These are those elders whose evil deeds have caused suffering for their children and their descendants. The afflicted mem-bers of younger generations attack their forebears like hordes of bees or bats. Hurling insults and reproaches, they force their evil parents back before Dike demanding a renewal of the torments. The parents groan because they know in advance the horrors that await them (31).

Since these souls subjected to alternating pain and shame are not confined in oblivion, they cannot be among the incurable. Eventually then, they will be reincarnated. Thespesius sees this procedure too. The souls destined for a new birth are forcibly bent into the shape of all sorts of animals as the workers change their form by beating them with their tools, stuffing certain parts, twisting and polishing others, or sticking them perfectly so as to adapt them to new behaviors and new lives (32).

Among these souls Thespesius sees that of the emperor Nero, already in terrible shape and pierced all over with glowing spikes. The workers have shaped him into the form of a viper, and in this body he is obliged to live again so as to devour his mother. But suddenly a great light flashes, and from this light emerges a voice that ordains changing him instead into an animal that sings on swamps and ponds. He has paid for his crimes; indeed, he has a right to the favor of the gods because he had given freedom to the Greeks, the best and most pious of all the people subjected to his empire. Thus Plutarch dramatizes the effect of one good deed, even among many seriously evil ones, which counts in a person's favor as the divine powers evaluate the appropriate afterlife or, in this case, new life. This device, applied here to the supremely wicked Nero (32), would be applied to Judas centuries later in "The Voyage of St. Brendan."[26]

In addition to the moment when his guide abandons him, Thespesius knows one other shiver of dread. A woman of great height approaches him with a glowing stick such as painters use and announces her intention somehow to engrave these memories on him, but another, kindlier woman prevents her. Suddenly Thespesius is sucked away back into his body and finds himself beside his tomb (33).

Plutarch, then, defends the idea of punishment after death—though not eternal punishment—against those who would prefer a quicker, visible retribution. Such retribution, he says, would satisfy only the resentful victims, would merely cause regret in the perpetrators of wrongs but not change their character. Through three techniques—punishment in the afterlife, demotion of the soul into another body, and denial of reincarnation and enforced frustration until the passion is spent—Dike can achieve radical purification by uprooting unjust passions, as opposed to "merely" reversing fortune and inspiring regret as Poine does. The incurable are in the control of Erinys, who casts them into oblivion. It is impossible to say whether this punishment is conceived of as eternal because, by definition, we know nothing more about those who endure it.

Plutarch strongly emphasizes shame. He contrives dramatic confrontations between suffering offspring and their responsible ancestors. It is not chance but justice that brings the father of Thespesius face to face with his son and forces him to acknowledge his hidden crimes. This technique, too, is curative. In Platonic fashion Plutarch insists that the punishments of crimes undetected and unrequited are more severe than those expiated in life.

Beyond Plato's confidence in reincarnation to achieve expiation through repeated lives, Plutarch added the refinement of souls *between* lives through a series of tortures distinguished by graphic physical images, which emphasize their painfulness and diversity. Starting with the degrees of spotting, he moves

---

26. I refer to the mitigation of the punishment of Judas Iscariot in "The Voyage of St. Brendan" edited by W. W. Heist, *Vitae sanctorum Hiberniae*, Subsidia hagiographica, 28 (Brussels: Société des bollandistes, 1965), 56–78 at 72–73, and translated in Eileen Gardiner, *Visions of Heaven and Hell before Dante* (New York: Italica Press, 1989), 117–20.

to the wildly gyrating tops and progresses to the flaying of skin to reveal the soul, turning bodies inside out, immersing them in vats of molten metals. He finds groups of interlaced bodies devouring one another and the smithy for reshaping souls. These are associated with a large component of shame and a system of color coding indicative of guilt, together with a chronological dimension that accounts for the relationship between the generations: the guilt of parents stains their children, and the progeny express their resentment. Similarly, metempsychosis itself is both a punishment and a means of purification.

In the end, purification is Plutarch's primary concern. Since those in oblivion are of no further interest, and those punished by Poine in this life—if there were only this life—are merely battered and regretful, Plutarch focuses on Dike's long term. Although it may require a complicated series of near-industrial procedures, generations of chastisement by descendants, and even a long sequence of rebirths, postmortem punishment is superior because it extirpates the wickedness that causes harm.

The moral afterlife in Plato, Virgil, and Plutarch is dynamic. It judges, divides, processes, rewards, and punishes. To perform these functions it needs its categories: only the good can be rewarded; only the wicked punished. If purification is a possibility, procedures are needed that cannot be applied at random. Method, analysis, intelligence—indeed, what Plutarch himself considered divine guidance or providence—are at the core of this conception. Conception, however, is not the right word, because this afterlife *works*. It operates, it is a system. The *Book of Gates* charts regions through which the god and his devotees progress. Virgil funnels his dead through a cavernous opening, across a threshold, by a magistrate's chambers, then to a fork in the road which separates good from evil. Even his Elysium sorts out its inhabitants: some require purification by further torment, others by living new lives, while a third group deserves to stay in blessedness forever. Like the oscillating rivers of Plato's *Phaedo*, Plutarch's deferred judgment turns out to function like a flow chart. Souls arise, spinning, and find their own level like hydrometers. They are then channeled to the appropriate space above the suitable chasm. Beams of light, openings, and whirlpools wring base passions from suffering souls. A workshop fits souls into new bodies. Everything happens by design and toward an end. Is the history of punishment after death, then, the review of steadily improving systematizations of how souls are sorted and treated? The next chapter considers some of the countervailing tendencies that restricted ordered views of death like these to the level of pious hopes for a few systematic thinkers.

Porous Death

The concern for proper burial was fundamental to the ancients.[1] Elpinor's entreaties to Odysseus, like those of Palinurus to Aeneas, reflect a stage in the belief in Hades (or Orcus) when the underworld was thought to contain or manage the dead. This hope (of the living) was only partially realized, as we shall see. Nonetheless, the belief that Charon would deny the unburied passage to the land of the dead, where they could be effectively confined, sanctioned the obligation to inter the dead. Yet, although this duty was firmly in place by Homer's time, the underworld was no sealed vessel. On the contrary, both Greece and Rome devised escapes from death and exceptions for their heroes. Moreover, the landscape itself provided numerous passageways on which the intrepid might pass back and forth between the earth and its innards. Beyond these physical apertures, dreams and near mortal weakness, as in disease or the battle wounds of Er, were avenues through which the living might glimpse the future world. Conversely, the dead themselves were sometimes thought to return.

1. Morris, "Attitudes toward Death," interprets the introduction of burial as a solidification of boundaries between gods, humans, and the dead symptomatic of similar consolidation in the social order. In *Burial and Ancient Society*, 32–33, Morris emphasizes the stages of the gradual separation of the living from the dead in ancient Greece. In Homer, they are almost fully removed. Robert Garland similarly emphasizes the Greek design "to keep the world of the living rigidly apart from that of the dead." *The Greek Way of Death*, 121.

This chapter, therefore, is devoted to avoiding the trap of accepting the systems of the ancients at face value. Perhaps the best introduction to these "exceptions" is through the work of Lucian of Samosata (c. 120–c. 200 C.E.), famous for irreverent satirical dialogues that poke holes in the Greek conceptions of the afterlife. Lucian adopted the Cynic perspective, or at least made Diogenes of Sinope (c. 400–c. 325 B.C.E.), the founder of that school, and Menippus of Gedara (first half of the third century B.C.E.) his favorite protagonists in works that deal with the underworld.[2] The Cynics advocated no formal philosophy but espoused an ethical code that emphasized simplicity in life, acceptance of one's lot, and systematic doubt in matters of belief. Lucian particularly relished their delight in exposing sham. All may cheer the death of a tyrant, but stony silence greets the death of Menippus, who always told the truth in plain language (*Dialogues of the Dead* 20 [373, 375]). For all his explicit links to the Cynics, Lucian shared themes with other philosophical schools of antiquity too. He drew on Plato's ideas of judging the dead and agreed with the Stoics that pleasure is no boon and death no evil.[3]

In an important group of works concerning death, Lucian's protagonists are either Cynics or gods of the underworld who interact with his heroes, false philosophers, and other knaves. Although they don't call themselves philosophers, leaving the title to "impostors" (*Dialogues of the Dead* 13 [393], 20 [368], 21 [379]), it is only the Cynics such as Diogenes and Menippus, who, as true philosophers, have made their lives a preparation for death. "If [people] had realized at the very beginning that they were mortal, and that after this brief sojourn in the world they would go away as from a dream, taking leave of everything above ground, they would live more sanely and would be less unhappy after death," says Charon after a tour of the earth's surface (*Charon; or, The Inspectors* 17). Reconciling people to death is the core of philosophy, according to Lucian.[4] Those who look for any other reality, those who construct great rational systems, are only deluding themselves. Property and happiness are false goods. Wisdom, frankness, and truth, in which there is more grandeur and majesty than in the Persian Empire and which form the "wealth" of the Cynics, are the only valid

2. Marcel Caster, *Lucien et la pensée religieuse de son temps* (1973; rpt. New York: Garland, 1987), 68–84, offers a nuanced appraisal of Lucian's view of the Cynics, with a special place for the satirist Menippus.

3. For the Stoics, see Marcia L. Colish, *The Stoic Tradition from Antiquity to the Early Middle Ages*, Studies in the History of Christian Thought, 34–35 (Leiden: Brill, 1985).

4. The classic study of Lucian is Rudolf Helm, *Lucian und Menipp* (Leipzig, 1906; rpt. Hildesheim: Olms, 1967).

currency in the land of Hades (*Dialogues of the Dead* 21 [378–79]). Apparently confining himself to frank speech, Lucian subtly shifts his perspective to the land of the dead, a vantage point from which he can jab at the follies of mortals, who pretend that they will never arrive there. This "death's-eye view" accomplishes the goal to which Plato dedicated the near-death experience of Er—to make the living imagine themselves dead and to question, with an eye to the grave, the importance of their lives' goals. Lucian's ability to view both worlds at once reveals the porosity of the boundary that nominally isolates the dead.

Lucian employs no single model in depicting death. The *Dialogues of the Dead* mostly portray a land of Hades that brings no more suffering than life itself, except that it lacks life's pleasures. In this vast democratic grave, even Alexander the Great turns out to be mortal (12, 13), and all are reduced to skeletal equality (18). In *Menippus; or, The Descent into Hades* (17), they occupy only the space of a foot. Sometimes, as we shall see, Lucian attributes a true punitive effectiveness to the netherworld.

In contrast to the democratic model are scenes where the kingship of Hades is apparent, where special cases are heard, privileges are sought and granted. One story makes this other model clear. Married on the day of battle, Protesilaus was the first Greek to die in the Trojan War. Despite the bonds that confine him in death, he yearns for the touch of his bride. Now he seeks permission from King Pluto and Queen Persephone to return to life to consummate his marriage. Pluto asks why he has not drunk from the waters of Lethe to forget his earthly longings. His love is stronger than Lethe water, he replies. Protesilaus argues his case by observing how porous the boundary is. Others have conquered death for love, the soldier-groom reminds the king. Orpheus won back Euridice and Herakles Alcestis. You, yourself, he tells Pluto, have ascended for love. Pluto counters: But you, Protesilaus, are a skeleton; you would disgust your bride! Here Persephone intervenes and urges Pluto to restore Protesilaus to his former appearance. The royal couple accords him, under the guidance of Hermes, one day on earth to consummate his marriage (*Dialogues of the Dead* 28 [427–28]).[5] Here Lucian makes one more breach in the division between life and death.

What Persephone grants the dead Protesilaus for love, she must have granted the dead philosophers of Greece for truth. After a certain scrivener

5. Two complementary stories concern Laodameia, the bride. In one, she dies in the arms of the shade who returns. In another version, she herself fashions an image of her husband with which she consoles her grief. Her sister-in-law throws the statue onto a pyre, whereupon Laodameia throws her on too, to burn with the image. Ernesto Curotto, *Dizionario della mitologia universale* (Turin: Internazionale, 1958), 269.

named Lucian ridiculed the founders of all the philosophical schools in a satirical piece called *Philosophies for Sale*, the great thinkers obtained permission to return to earth and bring action against him in the court of Athens. In *Charon*, the Stygian ferryman wins leave to investigate the earth to see what these pleasures are that mortals renounce with such difficulty. In *Menippus*, Lucian's favorite subject, while still alive, follows his magus guide on a path trod by Odysseus, Orpheus, and Herakles, who also visited the land of death while living. Imitating these three heroes at once, and thus surpassing Aristophanes' citizen Dionysus, Menippus and his guide seek out the dead Teiresias. They sail to the end of a lake at the other side of the Euphrates, dig a pit, and put in sacrificial blood. As a chasm opens, they descend. Menippus calms Cerberus with a stroke upon his lyre. Seeing the cynic dressed in his lion skin, Charon clears a seat for him on the bark. Scintillating in its layers of satire, *Menippus* nonetheless indicates the depth of familiarity a second-century audience could be expected to have with the many tales of descent into the underworld. Thus, it is not only Lucian who proposes this porosity in the boundary between life and death; he assumed his audience would understand it too. Rigid categories are for theorists and philosophers. The public welcomed greater flexibility.

Lucian exploits the porosity of the boundary between life and death. With the poet's eye he sees the dead arrive at Charon's ferry, or he interviews Cerberus. These settings are overt acts of imagination. Others, though, presuppose the penetration of life's boundary by either a dead person such as Protesilaus or an underworld god such as Charon. In *Menippus* a living person accomplishes yet another descent into the underworld. Nor is Lucian's mischievousness the only reason for this interpenetration of the living and the dead.

In an era when each city-state had its own divine patrons and its own heroes, it was common for similar achievements to be claimed as the deeds of different protectors. Thus Thebes claimed to be the birthplace of Herakles, at the expense of Argos on the Peloponnesus,[6] and Athens molded Theseus into its own local Herakles. It sometimes seems that every town had its own Herakles. Cicero ridiculed the inventive facility of the Greeks by pointing to the imaginary people of Alibanda, who worshipped their town's founder, Alibandus, with the quip "Let the wrath of Alibandus fall on me and that of Hercules on you."[7]

The rise of Athens after the Persian Wars produced some standardization

---

6. *Oxford Classical Dictionary*, 498.

7. Cicero, *De natura deorum* 3.19.50, trans. Harris Rackham, Loeb Classical Library (Cambridge: Harvard University Press, 1979).

in the view of the Olympian gods, as did the Olympian Games, the Delphic Oracle, the Festival of Dionysus, and the Eleusinian Mysteries, but regional variations remained extremely strong. It may even be that the generations of the gods recounted in Hesiod's *Theogony* distantly reflect a shift of political influence from one group or region to another. The "defeat" of Pythos by Apollo at Delphi seems a good example of one cult replacing another, and this religious switch probably also accompanied a change in political dominance.[8] As compared to the replacement of Kronos by Zeus, the overlap of jurisdiction between Hecate and Persephone may reflect cultic and political shifts that were less clearly defined.

The decentralized pattern of Greek religion may help account for the many successful raids on the netherworld. The figurative conquest of death symbolized by a return from the land of the dead was claimed for Dionysus, whose tales link him to Thrace; for Orpheus, the Hellene who preached Apollonian moderation among Dionysus's followers; and for Theseus and Herakles.[9]

Indeed, living heroes invaded the land of the dead so often that they nearly lost their mythic overtones. Diodorus of Sicily (c. 60–c. 30 B.C.E.) catalogs them almost routinely. Narrating Herakles' theft of Cerberus, Diodorus explains that he went to Athens to participate in the Eleusinian Mysteries, where Musaeus, the son of Orpheus, presided. Mention of Orpheus reminds Diodorus to provide a brief biography, which includes his voyage to retrieve Eurydice. Then parenthetically, and with no appreciation for the mythic resonance of the deed, Diodorus observes: "In this exploit [Orpheus resembled] Dionysus; for the myths relate that Dionysus brought up his mother Semele from Hades." Returning to Herakles' quest for Cerberus, he notes that Persephone welcomed him like a brother (as they were both offspring of Zeus), he released Theseus and Perithous back to the upperworld, and finally, with Persephone's permission, he carried off the hound of Hades in his chains (4.25.1–26.1).

The presence of Theseus and Perithous in Hades' land shows how intertwined these stories became as a broader Hellenic culture overlay the regional observances. After the death of his wife, Perithous visited Theseus in Athens and learned that Theseus's wife had committed suicide. They decided to kidnap the young Helen (before her adventure with Paris led to the Trojan War) and agreed that whoever married her would help the other find a wife. Theseus was to win the young girl but had to abandon the plan. Nonetheless

8. Rohde, *Psyche*, 97.

9. *Oxford Classical Dictionary*, 352; Guthrie, *The Greeks and Their Gods*, 315. See the informative note under Orpheus in Graves 28.4 (1:115).

Perithous insisted that Theseus aid him in obtaining Persephone for a wife. Together they made their way to the land of darkness, where Hades learned their plan and confined them in chains (4.63). Although earlier (4.26) Diodorus said that Herakles obtained freedom for both of them, here he gives another version according to which Herakles could free only Theseus. As the ringleader in their prior conniving, Perithous must remain behind and endure eternal punishment (*timōrias aiōniou* [4.63.4]). Yet other versions state that the would-be kidnappers were not chained but glued to their chairs. When Herakles drew Perithous up by the hands, the earth shook and he abandoned the effort. He was able to free Theseus, though not without the sacrifice of a layer from his posterior.[10] Like the heroes who regularly (it seems) raid his territory, humor too can penetrate the realm of Hades.

These stories derive from older oral traditions potentially of considerable import. As the teller's tremor of awe for heroic deeds faded and the settings for their repetition were lost, they became mere literary relics. Further, they frequently contradict one another, for the reasons already noted. Nonetheless, they provide details useful for interpreting yet other stories. When compiled in encyclopedias, whether ancient or modern, these variations risk losing their force. Cataloging stills the resonance of each tale for each locality, each hero's hometown, or for the devotees of shrines in the places mentioned.

The multiplicity of places associated with departure and return from the underworld shows two aspects of cataloging: first, that many towns desired their own special access and, second, that such points lost their mythic power as they proliferated. Frequently considered the boundary between the living and the dead, the River Styx, for example, is also personified as a river goddess, a daughter of Ocean, and an early ally of Zeus. Further, Styx was the name of an actual river near Pheneüs in Arcadia, whose water was said to corrode metal, shatter glass, and poison humans (Pausanias, *Description of Greece* 8.17.6–19.3). The Acheron, too, is both a person and a place. As a person, Acheron is the father (with Gorgyra or Orphne) of Askalaphus who saw Persephone eat the pomegranate seed and said so, thus necessitating her annual stay in the house of Hades (Apollodorus 1.33; Ovid, *Metamorphoses* 5.539–48).[11] But Acheron can also be matched with a headland beneath the cape of Acherusias facing the Bithynian Sea (northwest Asia Minor). Below the cliffs is a Cave of Hades from which an icy breath comes up in the morning, and through it a path leads to Hades' realm (Apollonius 2.728, 251–55).

10. Graves, *The Greek Myths*, 103d (1:364).
11. Cited in Rose, *Handbook*, 100 n. 62.

Nor was this the only opening through which heroes could pass on their way to or from the underworld. Apollodorus tells us that when Herakles descended in quest of Cerberus, he used the Laconian Taenarum, and he ascended through Troezen (2.5.12). Erwin Rohde catalogs these entrances in a rich note. The number of such passageways he considers evidence for the breakdown of the Homeric conception of death, which "banished" the dead beyond the encircling river, Ocean. A new conception pulled the dead in closer to the communities of the living, and the passages called *ploutōnia*, which lead down to the underworld, and *psychopompeia*, through which dead souls can come out, proliferated. The Areopagus of Athens contained a fissure in which underworld beings lived. At Ermione, near the same Troezen up through which Herakles brought Cerberus, ran another River Acheron that made the local residents so confident of their proximity to the underworld that they thought it superfluous to include the coin of passage in the mouths of their dead.[12] According to the fifth-century historian Herodotus, there was an oracle of the dead on the Acheron (5.92).

It is not my desire to sacrifice local difference to standardization. As was apparent even to the Hellenistic encyclopedists, the mythical background of Greco-Roman culture was not tidy. Diodorus of Sicily, Apollonius of Rhodes, and Pausanias all devised strategies to deal with inconsistencies in the myths and the overlapping claims of rival shrines.

Even when an author seeks to show the overall pattern that informs religion, he exposes himself to ridicule, such as occurs in Cicero's dialogue *On the Nature of the Gods.* Balbus, the interlocutor most inclined to preserve the relevance of the gods, regards them as a cultural inheritance of the Romans from the Greeks, false, though still valuable because they express certain truths about the nature of the physical world.

Basing himself on Hesiod, Balbus traces the genealogy of the Greek gods and supplies their Latin names. Thus, when Saturn was overthrown, the cosmos was divided among Jupiter or Jove, Neptune, and Dis (*De natura deorum* 2.26.66). The name Dis is a shortened form of Dives, which translates not Hades but Pluto (Plouton) and means "wealthy" because he obtained all that is earth and within the earth. Thus he is rich because everything originates from and returns to the earth (2.26.66).

The Greeks further allegorized the functions of nature, Balbus says, by specifying that Proserpina represents the corn seed. Thus they "propound the fiction" (*fingunt*) that she was hidden away. Her seedlike quality, they imply, accounts for details in the story that make her appearance on earth seasonal. That she dwells within the earth makes her the consort to Dis, and

12. Rohde, *Psyche,* 186–87 n. 23, 171, 162.

the Greek name of her mother Demeter is a corruption of *gē mētēr* (Greek for "mother earth"), just as in Latin Ceres is a corruption of *Geres*, from *gero*, because she "bears" the crops (2.36.66–67).[13] Thus, using etymological acrobatics, the Greeks make the names of these gods approximate the names for the cycles of nature. Although he concedes that the myths must be considered "impious fables," Balbus maintains that they encode a not inelegant explanation of the physical universe (2.24.63).

Balbus's sympathetic interpretation draws only scorn from the doubter Cotta, who classifies the underworld divinities among the false gods. If the Romans grant divinity to Orcus (a personification of the underworld and hence another name of Dis/Pluto) because he is a brother of Jupiter and Neptune, why exclude Cerberus and Charon? (3.16.43–44). It is clear that the whole pantheon stands or falls with the personnel of the underworld. "If the latter monsters do not withstand scrutiny, neither do the [gods] mentioned first" (3.17.45; cf. 3.20.52).

Cotta was not the only one to see absurdity in the myths. Varro, too, in a book that no longer survives, tried to dispense with the embarrassing gods. He declared that one could not trace every aspect of life to a different divinity. It was wrong to have not just a god of love but a male and a female god to preside over the male and female sex organs. Christian apologists such as Augustine of Hippo, devoted to extirpating ancient paganism, delighted in exposing what seemed obvious excesses (*De civitate Dei* 6.9). Two interesting phenomena combined to make Greek mythology peculiarly heterogeneous. First, complications arose from intense localization of cults, whether of gods, heroes, or geographical landmarks, which fragmented the picture from the very beginning. Second, it proved impossible, despite the efforts of ancient encyclopedists and mythographers and the delight of scoffers, to make these localized loyalties mutually consistent.

There was another obstacle to consistency beyond the variety of accounts of the exploits of mythic figures: no one explanation for death encompassed the whole Greco-Roman cultural ambience. Comprehending death may be a universal aspiration, but it presents two problems. For one thing, death in its many dimensions—scientific, medical, religious, emotional—eludes our mental constructs. Anthropology suggests that every known culture offers its own formulation. Second, each effort to provide a system for comprehending death asserts only norms. Like a blanket too short to cover both the shoulders and the toes, it necessarily leaves something bare. A good example exists in the *Phaedo* (108c), where Plato tells how the souls gather for distribution after death. He says that those who lag behind near their bodies

13. Rackham's translation is indispensable for this passage.

must be forcibly (*anagkēs*) drawn along by the appointed guardian spirit and put in their "proper habitation" (*prepousan oikēsin*), in "the place which is proper to [them]" *topon prosēkonta*). Plato's need to provide for this eventuality suggests that ghosts were suspiciously and inconveniently independent. For his view of the afterlife to work, they had to be forced into place.

Since these signs of recalcitrance are unlikely to be the actions of the dead, it must be the living who persist in moving these ideas, desires, or fantasies through their imaginations.[14] Though these symbols, phantasms, or images are imaginary, the act of inventing them takes on a historical dimension, particularly when they are shared by large numbers of people over long periods of time and when they differ from the ideas expressed in epic poetry or the explanations articulated in philosophy. In the minds of these noncon-formists live those of the dead who, thanks to the inventive efforts of the living, become "outlaws" resisting their banishment, free spirits independent of the otherworld. Thus, the evidence on ghosts appears in no official continuous record, and their survival must be inferred from the traces left even though authorities declared them under control.

By considering a wide variety of literary genres, from philosophy to fantasy to history to rhetoric, from the fifth century B.C.E. to the second century C.E., it is possible to show a persistent series of ephemeral themes indicating a continuing interest in the deeds of the dead on earth, the relationship of the living to revenants (spirits who return), and a tendency on the part of the living to use this belief to manipulate others.

Grouping the dead into ancestral clans like those in which the Greeks and Romans lived (though of course the history of the family in these cultures differed from each other and varied over time) ordered the dead in imitation of society. In parallel fashion, those who discussed the hereafter from Homer on, moved rulers or magistrates from this world to the next. Homer established Minos alone; Plato appointed Aeacus and Rhadamanthus. Eventually writers established a whole bureaucracy of specialized officials from Hermes to Charon to administer the dead. Linking them to ancestors and regulating their coming and going were effective ways to manage them. Outside these confines, they were threatening.

---

14. For this formulation—"to move a figure through one's imagination," thus making it a positive action rather than "merely" imaginary—I am indebted to Juana Armanda Alegría, *Sicología de las Mexicanas* (Tlacoquemécatl, Mexico: Diana, 1978), 120–21, cited by José E. Limón, "*La Llorona*, the Third Legend of Greater Mexico: Cultural Symbols, Women, and the Political Unconscious," *Renato Rosaldo Lecture Series* 2 (1984–85): 74.

Belief in the existence and powers of ghosts vexed many writers. Cicero debated the matter in his dialogue *On Divination*, where he assigned the defense of the belief to his brother Quintus and claimed the attack for himself, Marcus. Pliny the Younger used an apparently sincere question about the existence of ghosts to open the letter in which he told the story of Athenodorus (7.27). Lucian delivered a scathing diatribe against superstition in *Philopseudes; or, The Lover of Lies*. Provoked by his neighbors' uncritical acceptance of stories he considered farfetched, he wrote them down and so provided excellent evidence for the belief in ghosts. The topic was a lively one in antiquity. The genre flourished, questions abounded, and many disseminated the tales, motivated either by their own belief in ghosts or to debunk the beliefs of many others.[15]

Ghosts are shades on earth. Persons encountered by heroes in Hades' kingdom are not ghosts, since burial has removed them from the earth's surface, they have crossed the Styx, and only under exceptional circumstances can they return. To be sure, they share some of the characteristics of ghosts. They are separated from their bodies; they retain their features and the motivations they died with, that is, their personalities; and thus, in most accounts, they are recognizable. Yet, because they were properly buried, they have been disposed of as influences on human life. How fortunate for his enemies that Homer's pale Achilles was unable to return to help establish his father's rule!

Burial worked in two ways. It provided access to the underworld for the dead, but also, in principle at least, it safely isolated them from human habitation. But not all accounts of death confined the dead as confidently as Homer's. Odysseus had to conjure up the dead so that he could consult them. For many, the problem was precisely the reverse: how to dispose of them permanently. Thus, poets portrayed the spirits of the unburied, impatiently awaiting Charon on the bank of the Styx, as suffering in comparison

15. For the subject of ancient ghosts in general, see the classic discussion of Franz Cumont, *Lux perpetua* (Paris: Geuthner, 1949), 78–108; and more recently, R. C. Finucane, *Appearances of the Dead: A Cultural History of Ghosts* (London: Junction Books, 1982), chap. 1. For a popularized telling of the stories themselves, see Lacy Collison-Morley, *Greek and Roman Ghost Stories* (1912; rpt. Chicago: Argonaut, 1968). Orientation in a broader context is available in the articles "Soul," "State of the Dead," and "Demons and Spirits," in James Hastings, ed., *Encyclopaedia of Religion and Ethics*, 13 vols. (Edinburgh: T. and T. Clark; New York: Scribner's, 1908–27), 11:725–55, 817–54, 4:565–636; and the articles "Geist," "Geisterschlacht-kampf," and "Gespenst," in *Handwörterbuch des deutschen Aberglaubens*, ed. Eduard Hoffman-Krayer and Hanns Bächtold-Stäubli (Berlin: de Gruyter, 1930–31), 3: cols. 472–510, 546–49, and 766–71.

to the shades who had crossed and attained their destiny. Some haunted the earth before reporting to the river, and some came back across.

Lack of burial could motivate a soul's return to haunt the living. Patroklos is the most famous case, but there are other examples. Pliny the Younger (d. 112 C.E.), the adviser of Trajan, wonders how seriously to take them. In a letter he queries Licinias Sura about just such a tale (7.27.5). The philosopher Athenodorus, Pliny relates, was attracted to a house in Athens because of its low rent, the result of eerie noises heard there in the dark. During his first night in the house, a spirit summoned him and revealed his remains unburied in the courtyard. Athenodorus notified the local authorities, and when they disposed of the body properly, the haunting ceased. Lucian relates a similar story (*Philopseudes* 30–31), though he is repelled by the credulity of those who told it to him. Suetonius, the chronicler of the emperors and their households, who lived until after about 121 C.E., blends accounts of ghosts into historical narratives. He tells how Caligula haunted the Lamian gardens until his sisters returned from exile to supervise his proper burial (*Gaius* 59).

Even criminals could demand proper burial. At Tecmessa, according to Pausanias, one of Odysseus's sailors got drunk and raped a virgin, for which act he was stoned to death by the townspeople. Because they disapproved of his crime, Odysseus and his men abandoned him unburied. But then he returned as a ghost and continued murdering and raping the citizens until they agreed to sacrifice a virgin to him once a year. Years later Euthymus, the boxer of heroic stature, defeated the ghost in combat, drove him into the sea, liberated the town, and married the virgin who had been selected as that year's sacrifice (6.6.7).

Others came back to request corrections in burial procedures imperfectly carried out. Herodotus (*Histories* 5.92) tells how the tyrant Periander of Corinth, who ruled from 625 to 585 B.C.E., summoned the spirit of his wife, Melissa, to consult her about "a deposit that a friend had left." She refused to give the information she had, however, because she had been improperly buried. The drapery in which Periander had buried her had never been burned, she said; thus, she lacked its protection in Hades and consequently lived cold and naked in the gloom. To make amends, the tyrant invited all the women of Corinth to the temple of Hera. Expecting a festival, they appeared in their finest clothes. Periander commanded his troops to strip the women and burn their clothes in a pit while he made imprecations to the spirit of his wife. The ghost of Melissa signaled her appreciation by indicating the location of the deposit.

Centuries later the theme was still alive. In Lucian's *Philopseudes* (27) a man's wife returned twenty days after her funeral to advise her husband that he had neglected to include one of her slippers in the funeral pyre. She revealed where it had fallen and asked him to burn it too. Lucian tells the story to ridicule it and stories like it, which apparently were widely accepted.

The motif of the lost receipt recurs even under the pen of Saint Augustine. In his essay dedicated to Paulinus of Nola around 421–23, *The Care to Be Taken for the Dead*, the bishop of Hippo alludes to the type of story in which dead persons appear to the living to indicate their remains and request burial. He explicitly rejects dreams as an explanation, maintaining that even apparitions in dreams can be accurate because these things have happened to the faithful and living persons testify to this occurrence. When he himself was living in Milan, he heard of a son whose father had settled a debt but failed to obtain the released note before he died. The creditor then fraudulently pressed the son for (a second) payment, whereupon the dead man appeared while the son was sleeping and told him where to find the receipt.[16]

Greeks and Romans were less inclined to dismiss dreams as deceptive than they were to see the affinity of sleep with death.[17] Consequently, storytellers could advance their plots by means of dreams or apparitions that occurred to sleepers, knowing that their audience would understand these phenomena as part of the wondrous past or an aspect of the elevated consciousness that surrounds epic, drama, and storytelling in general. Homer used this device to permit the appearance of Patroklos (*Iliad* 23.65–107). In the second century C.E. Apuleius, in *The Golden Ass* (8.4) tells how Thrasyllus appeared to his wife (Apuleius does not give her name) in her sleep to denounce his friend Tlepolemus as his murderer and warn her of his designs upon the widow.

Ghosts punish offenders. Suetonius tells us how the emperor Otho reestablished some of the officials and artworks set up by Nero which Galba had purged. Galba's ghost then appeared to him in a frightening nightmare. The next day, when Otho attempted to perform the auspices, a strong wind knocked him off his feet (*Otho* 7). Folklore frequently associates the activities of ghosts with the wind. Plutarch relates a belief held "among the Britons" that the death of "great souls . . . fosters tempests and storms and often infects the air with pestilential properties" (*The Obsolescence of Oracles* 18 [419f]).

---

16. "The Care to Be Taken for the Dead," trans. John A. Lacy, in *Saint Augustine: Treatises on Marriage and Other Subjects*, ed. Roy J. Deferrari, The Fathers of the Church, 27 (New York: Fathers of the Church, 1955), 366–70. See the account in Jacques Le Goff, *The Birth of Purgatory*, trans. Arthur Goldhammer (Chicago: University of Chicago Press, 1984), 79–82.

17. For example, see Cicero, *De divinatione* 1.29.60, citing Plato, *Republic*, bk. 9.

Ghosts seek vengeance. Antiquity knew cases of ghosts who revealed themselves to complain they had been murdered and sometimes, like Hamlet's father, to demand vengeance. Apuleius tells two such stories in *The Golden Ass*. In a third tale a corpse reanimated by a wizard announces that his wife had killed him. Yet here it is necessary to distinguish necromancy, in which the dead are called back to life by living experts—such as the witch of Endor—from an autonomous appearance in which the dead person takes the initiative.

Plutarch relates how the ghost of a young girl, Cleonice, achieved vengeance on her own. Pausanius, the tyrannical Spartan general, abused his powers over Athens by demanding Cleonice from her parents. Disconsolate at the prospect of his attentions, she intended to kill him but stumbled in the dark over furniture in his room. Fearing himself under attack, Pausanias stabbed the girl without knowing who it was. Thereafter her spirit drove him to distraction by appearing nightly in his sleep, repeating, "Go to the doom which pride and lust prepare" (*On the Delays of the Divine Vengeance* 10 [555c]). Discredited for this and other overbearing behavior that embarassed the Spartans and for treason too, Pausanias was driven from Athens (*Lives*, "Aristides," 23.1–6). In desperation he consulted the oracle of the dead at Heracleia (a *psychopompeia* at work) and called up the spirit of Cleonice. She rose and assured him with some irony that he would be delivered from his troubles once he reached Sparta. Thucydides completes the story, saying that, when Pausanias returned, the Spartans, whom he had embarrassed with his high-handed behavior, placed him in solitary confinement and starved him to death (*History of the Peloponnesian War* 1.128–34).

Aelian tells how a traveler was murdered by an innkeeper of Megara for his gold. The victim immediately appeared to a townsman and revealed where the murderer was even then hiding his body. The corpse was discovered where the ghost had indicated, and the murderer was punished (frag. 82).[18] Cicero also tells this story, identical in its essential components, in *On Divination* (1.27.57). In his essay on divine vengeance, Plutarch took for granted the role of ghost victims in making the wicked fear their comeuppance.

Ghosts return favors. A class of stories relates how ghosts of persons buried out of kindness come back to aid their benefactors. Cicero tells of a merchant named Simonides who once charitably paused to bury the body of a stranger. Some time later a ghost revealed himself as the spirit of that corpse. The grateful shade warned his former helper not to sail on a certain ship. Ultimately Simonides heard that the vessel had sunk.[19]

18. Quoted in Collison-Morley, 62.

19. Collison-Morley, 59, cites Cicero, *De divinatione* 1.27.56, and calls it the

Ghosts return for love. Phlegon of Tralles, a freed slave of the second-century emperor Hadrian and author of a collection of marvels titled *Mirabilia*, related how Philinnion had been married by her parents to Alexander the Great's general Craterus, although she loved Machates, a foreign friend of her father's.[20] She died six months after the marriage. Six months after that she returned from the dead to visit Machates for several nights. The couple was discovered by a servant woman who told the parents. Charito, the mother, wrung the story out of Machates, who promised to show the daughter to the mother should she reappear. The next time Philinnion rose, Machates summoned the parents, but Philinnion resented their cruelty in preventing her postmortem liaison, which "brought harm to no one." Spitefully, she made them pay for their meddling by dying all over again. An investigation of her grave, with civic officials present, revealed it to be empty, because the body was still on the bedroom floor. The local diviner advised reconsecrating the town's temples and burying Philinnion outside the city. Machates committed suicide.[21]

Ghosts seeking love did not always return for sexual encounters. One arose out of filial devotion. In his tenth declamation, Quintilian, a rhetorician of the first century C.E., challenges the student orator to prosecute a father for criminal cruelty in an imaginary case. A recently deceased son

---

basis of Chaucer's "Nun's Priest's Tale." Cf. Valerius Maximus 1.7; Libanius 4.1101. There is a Jewish version too. Collison-Morley relates it from Gordon Hall Gerould, *The Grateful Dead: The History of a Folk Story,* Publications of the Folk-lore Society, 60 (Nendeln, Liechtenstein: Kraus Reprint, 1967), 27: "The son of a rich merchant of Jerusalem sets off after his father's death to see the world. At Stamboul he finds hanging in chains the body of a Jew, which the Sultan has commanded to be left there till his coreligionists shall have repaid the sum that the man is suspected of having stolen from his royal master. The hero pays this sum, and has the corpse buried. Later, during a storm at sea he is saved by a stone, on which he is brought to land, whence he is carried by an eagle back to Jerusalem. There a white-clad man appears to him, explaining that he is the ghost of the dead [man], and that he has already appeared as stone and eagle. The spirit further promises the hero a reward for his good deed in the present and in the future life." For further analysis, see Sven Liljeblad, *Die Tobiasgeschichte und andere Märchen von toten Helfern,* diss. (Lund: P. Lindstedts Univ.-Bokhandel, 1927), cited by Finucane, *Appearances of the Dead,* 28 n. 27.

20. Although the beginning of the story is missing, we may assume they forced her to marry the general. Erwin Rohde, "Zu den Mirabilia des Phlegon," *Rheinisches Museum für Philologie* 32 (1877): 329–39.

21. Collison-Morley tells this story, 66–71. There is a Latin version in *De mirabilibus and longaeuis libellus,* translated from the Greek by Guilielmus Xylandrus in Antoninus Liberalis, *Transformationum congeries* (Basel: Thomas Guarinus, 1568), 69–74.

visits his bereaved mother to comfort her, whereupon she urges him to pay the same attentions to his father. The father resists such a visit from the dead to the extent that he consults a sorcerer to help him confine the son's spirit within the grave by means of spells and even iron bands around the tomb. Though its purpose was to train advocates in defending the interests of the father against the mother and vice versa, this story illustrates considerable ambivalence about the dead in ancient Rome. The dead were neither as fully dead nor as fully alive as the living might wish. As fantastic as the plots of some of his declamations may be, Quintillian clearly assumed that lawyers in training would benefit from arguing the cases, however imaginary. Presumably it served no one's purpose to argue that the mother had no case because dead sons do not visit their mothers, and fantasies have no standing in court.

Death itself was no absolute boundary. Indeed, gravestones frequently bore an inscription expressing the desire of the living to alleviate the suffering of deceased persons, who were obviously conceived of as possessing some form of consciousness: "May the earth lie light upon you."[22] The premise behind this widespread plea emerges from matters ranging beyond mere burial. When she returned as a spirit, Melissa, the dead wife of the tyrant Periander of Corinth, proved that she spoke the truth about her deprivation in Hades by using language that only Periander could understand. She referred through double entendre to the sexual use he had made of her cadaver. The story assumes that the spirit knows what happens to the corpse (Herodotus, *Histories* 5.92).

Ghosts await new bodies. In an earlier passage of the *Phaedo* (81d) than the one considered before, Plato explains the appearance of ghosts. These are souls so "beguiled by the body," so "permeated by the corporeal," that they are "weighed down and dragged back into the visible world," hovering about tombs and graveyards. Their affinity for the physical so affects the soul that in the interval between incarnations, they are faintly visible, "which is why they can be seen." These wicked souls are "compelled" to haunt their bodies (for that is what they do in graveyards and near tombs) "as punishment for their bad conduct in the past." Their continued desire for the physical "unceasingly pursues them" until they are imprisoned once more in a body, where they are cursed with the same desires that led them astray in

22. Iiro Kajanto, *Classical and Christian: Studies in the Latin Epitaphs of Medieval and Renaissance Rome*, Annales Academiae Scientiarum Fennicae, series B, vol. 203 (Helsinki: Suomalainen Tiedeakatemia, 1980), 77: "In the pagan epigraphy of Rome, words of leave-taking, *vale, valeas,* together with the wish for well-being in the grave, *sit tibi terra levis,* were the commonest acclamations." Rohde cites the equivalent for ancient Greece, *Psyche,* 540 and 570 n. 120. Cumont finds the same parallel, *Lux Perpetua,* 393.

their previous life. Plato allies his theory of ghosts to his philosophy of justice, but he does not preface this interpretation with any disclaimer as he does with his myths. He seems to acknowledge ghosts as an exception to the views he expounds elsewhere, categorizing the dead according to their moral qualities and postmortem fates.

Ghosts announce the future. Cicero reports in *On Divination* that Gaius Gracchus told many that his brother Tiberius appeared to him in a dream saying he must die the same death as his brother (1.26.56). And Quintus chides Marcus, that is, Cicero himself, for deriding divination, when he had previously related with pride how auspicious it was that the famous tribune and consul Marius appeared to Cicero during his banishment and directed him to his own temple for safety. When the Senate voted Cicero's recall, they did so in the Temple of Marius (1.28.59). Pliny says that Nero appeared to the historian Fannius to read the manuscript he was working on concerning the evil deeds of this emperor. When the spirit vanished after reading the first three books, Fannius inferred that he would not live to complete another, which was indeed the case (*Letters* 5.5).

Ghosts return in groups. Whole troops of ghosts were said to haunt the battlefields where they died. According to Philostratus in the *Heroica*, the heroes of the Homeric battles still haunt the fields around Troy and protect the farmers of the region who honor them. After Attila and the Huns besieged Rome, the clash of arms was heard as opposing armies fought in the sky for three days and three nights (Damaskios, *Vita Isidori* 63).[23]

It is not merely these anecdotal, fanciful literary accounts—ghost stories—that show how deeply ingrained was the belief in ghosts and how strongly felt was the need to manage them, for the rites that dealt with the dead were incorporated into the pantheon and the calendar of the state in ancient Rome. Later authors, such as Cicero or Ovid (43 B.C.E.–17 C.E.), who sought to explain the origin of these customs, were no eyewitnesses to the events they describe. Macrobius, the grammarian and antiquarian of circa 400 C.E., was even farther removed. Indeed, he lived in a world in which these customs were severely challenged. Nonetheless, a series of disparate texts discloses a continuous concern for these subjects. I assume here that writing about custom is not pure invention, that an author supposed a probability of recognition on the part of his audience, and that if the origins of the Latin language or calendar concern one person, they also concern others.

These disparate authors, then, in discussing the origins and meanings of

23. Philostratus and Damaskios are cited in Collison-Morley, 25, 24, with no further reference.

the customs they examine, make it clear that Roman cities strictly regulated access to the underworld. The remarkable institution of the *mundus* is an excellent example. Each municipality formed a sacred space marked by its *pomerium* or boundary.[24] At a certain place on the *pomerium* the Romans created a lined pit called the *mundus*, capped by a single stone, considered the entrance to the underworld for the city's ancestors, the *manes*. Each year on August 24, October 5, and November 8, the stone was removed, the dead were allowed free passage, and offerings were thrown in to appease them.[25]

More than just the residence of the city's dead, the *mundus* was also a source of its fecundity. Ovid in the *Fasti* (4.820–24) and Plutarch in his *Life of Romulus* (11) tell how the *mundus* was established at the birth of the city. In order to consolidate the new populations from the neighboring lands he had conquered, Romulus caused each of the defeated Etruscan leaders to cast a clod of earth from his home territory and an offering of first fruits from the new settlement into the pit. According to this founding myth and the ritual that commemorated it, the city's ancestors thus provided the *mundus* with the stock from which the new community's produce and progeny derived. Each subsequent Roman city was said to have its own *mundus*, which, in principle, would exercise the same power for its locality.[26] Thus, the *mundus* (of which no trace, incidentally, has ever been found) was a localized underworld.[27]

The sources do not tell why it was considered desirable to open the *mundus*. That it was done suggests some recognition that the two worlds needed to communicate. The dead had attained nearly divine status and they were ruled by gods of the underworld. Festus says it was "an occult and secret religion of the divine manes" (4.144). Macrobius (*Saturnalia* 1.16.17) says that each of these days when the underworld is open is "a time sacred to Father Dis and to Proserpine."[28] Macrobius communicates Varro's greater sense of dread by quoting: "When the *mundus* lies open, the nether realm of the gloomy gods lies open like a gateway." Thus, it is a bad time to commence battle, raise troops, and set out for war; weigh anchor; or marry for the sake of raising children—all enterprises in which the risk of death is

24. For the *mundus;* see Macrobius, *Saturnalia* 1.16.16. For the *pomerium*, see Varro, *On the Latin Language* 5.143; and Livy, *From the Founding of the City* 1.44.4–5.

25. Cumont, *Lux perpetua*, 59–60.

26. Ibid., 59.

27. Dario Sabbatucci, *La religione di Roma antica, dal calendario festivo all'ordine cosmico* (Milano: Mondadori, 1988), 290.

28. Quoted ibid., 291.

great. It is better to campaign when Pluto's jaws are shut.[29] Battle was considered illicit on other occasions, too, but out of respect for peace rather than fear of death.

Two Roman festivals, the Parentalia and the Lemuria, further illustrate the sacred character of the dead. Erwin Rohde likens them to the Greek Genesia and Anthesteria, though it is difficult to draw parallels. The Genesia were the birthdays of the departed, an occasion when their survivors brought small offerings to their graves. Beyond these individual anniversaries, there was also a common public Genesia festival celebrated on the fifth day of the month Boëdromion, at which time the citizens commemorated all their dead together.[30]

Contrast this attention to the dead, who are close by and need to be both supported and propitiated, with those who are "banished" beyond Ocean in the Odyssey.[31] Homer's was a newer system, but it never eliminated the previous one. History is not that simple. The ghosts remained. They, or those who respected them, were the free spirits resisting reform, or at least they remained independent of reform and systematization, theology, and philosophy, and they would remain so down through the ages.

During the Roman Parentalia of February 13–21, the living would go during the day to the tombs of the dead, offer token sacrifices, and acclaim their deceased kin with the venerable term of *parentes*, ancestors.[32] Once, Ovid tells us in the *Fasti*, because of a war, the Romans omitted this commemoration, and far more dangerous armies of specters demanding the due observances afflicted the Roman community with plagues, prodigies, and deaths (2.533). Only performance of the overdue cermonies restored calm.[33] Dario Sabbatucci specifies that "ancestors" are only certain of the dead and that not all dead qualify as ancestors (48). These, however, as founders of patrician dynasties (here on the model of a monarchy, but at the level of the Roman *gens*, or clan), when properly venerated—or appeased?—are patrons of their descendants, but when neglected, they become spiteful opponents.

This latter aspect of the dead becomes clear in the Lemuria, on odd-numbered nights of March between the nones and the ides, when the living

29. I translate from the edition of Jacob Willis, Bibliotheca Teubneriana (Leipzig: Teubner, 1963). Sabbatucci, 293, emphasizes the commemoration of peace over fear of Orcus.

30. Rohde, *Psyche*, 167–68, 197 n. 91, 166.

31. Ibid., 171.

32. On the Paternalia, see Pauly, *Real-encyclopädie*, supplement vol. 12, pp. 979–82.

33. Cumont, *Lux perpetua*, 83.

would protect themselves from the dead by ritually sweeping them out of the house and making a token offering of beans.[34] Whether the *lemures* are a separate group of the dead or the meaner aspect of insufficiently appeased ancestors is not entirely clear. According to Pomponius Porphyrion, the lemures are "wandering shadows of men dead prematurely whom we should therefore fear," and hence they are a separate class altogether.[35] According to Ovid, at the end of the Lemuria, the paterfamilias would command, "Paternal spirits depart!" (and at the similar Greek festival: "Begone, ye Keres; Anthesteria is over!"), suggesting that lemures are the ancestors (*manes paterni*) under another aspect.[36] Yet in order to derive the names of the feasts from the names of the related spirits (Parentalia from *parentes* and Lemuria from *lemures*), Ovid may have overdrawn the contrast between the lemures and the parentes. To further his theory, he also contrasted Remus and Romulus. As Romulus killed Remus and went on to found the city of Rome, so the spirit of Remus—the first *lemur,* according to Ovid—is to be feared as a haunting presence and that of Romulus—the first *parens*—venerated as a guiding ancestor, father of the state.[37] Thus, manes would be protectors and guides, forebears who return to their survivors, ancestors to be honored at the tomb. Lemures, however, would be ghosts, specters, which invade the house and must be repelled.[38] Whatever the term for the spirits, it seems legitimate to distinguish between two feasts that consider the dead under two aspects, one protective, the other threatening. Whether one must fear the prematurely dead or the scorned ancestors, it is clear that in Roman society piety and safety depended on proper respect for the dead.

In the spectrum of supernatural powers, a city's ancestors ranked very high. They were only barely distinguished from divinities. In Rome, in fact, the city's founder, Romulus, became the god Quirinus. Further, the Romans perceived these dead as such a powerful source of strength for the cities they protected, that they sought to deprive their enemies of this support prior to attacking them. To this end they developed a ceremony called "evocation." Only the highest commanders could officiate (Macrobius, *Saturnalia* 3.9). They invoked Veiovis, an old Italic god of the shadows, opposed to Jupiter

34. Sabbatucci, 164.
35. Quoted ibid.
36. Rohde, *Psyche,* 168, 198 n. 100.
37. Ovid, *Fasti,* 5.479; Sabbatucci, 165–66. Cf. Cumont, *Lux perpetua,* 397–98.
38. Older literature uses the word *larvae* to distinguish unwelcome spirits from manes. *Lemures,* first found in Varro (116–27 B.C.), seems to have been coined after the name of the festival. See article "Lemuria," in Pauly, *Real-encyclopädie,* 24th half vol., cols. 1931–33.

but, like him, possessing a temple on the Capitoline, to whom they added Dis (that is Hades), and the *manes*, their departed ancestors.[39] By invoking both gods they blended together the chthonic powers with authority over the dead from different stages of Roman religion. By means of "evocation," the Roman commander aimed to cut the enemy city off not only from its gods but from its ancestral roots too. Another frightening aspect of evocation depends on the belief that the manes, the beneficent ancestors, would welcome their progeny to the underworld.[40] If the enemy city had lost its manes, then that city's troops and, in the worst case, its whole population would face death without any possibility of finding sympathetic guides through the earth's inner recesses—a fearful prospect indeed.

In the Italic wars of the city's early history, when Rome's opponents were neighboring cities in Latium, they shared the same blend of Etruscan religion overlaid with Hellenic beliefs from Magna Graecia, the Greek colonies that dotted the Mediterranean shore. Thus the expectation that the neighboring city would share these beliefs would be high. According to Macrobius, however, the Romans used evocation not only against their own neighbors, who might be presumed to share similar ideas, but also against Carthage and Corinth and in Gaul, Spain, and North Africa. It seems the Romans considered the belief to be widespread.

One famous instance, related to evocation, and indicative of its power, is the theft of the Palladium. Roman authors, again shaping their own history by reimagining the Trojan War, talk of a statue of Pallas Athena (hence, Palladium) which the Trojans regarded as a divine gift and a talisman ensuring the city's invulnerability since it had descended to them from heaven. Exploiting their enemy's confidence in this token of divine favor, Diomede and Odysseus sneaked into the city and stole the statue; Trojan alarm at this disappearance should have facilitated the task of the Greeks.[41] Evocation would have a similar effect, at least for Roman troops, without similar risk to its greatest leaders.

In evocation, therefore, the officiating Roman commander would seek to attract the opposing city's gods, including those of the underworld, to Rome's protection by asking these gods and nearly divine spirits to rededi-

---

39. Cumont, *Lux perpetua*, 57–58.
40. Ibid., 59.
41. Silius Italicus, *Punica* 13.36–50; and Ovid, *Fasti* 6.433–54, cited in "Palladium," *Oxford Classical Dictionary*. Another version, also related by Silius (13.79–81), has Aeneas save the statue from the burning Troy and bring it to Rome where it would guarantee the safety of its new home. Both versions involve the transfer of supernatural protection, much as the evocation intended.

cate themselves to the Romans.[42] By deserting (*desero*), abandoning (*relinquo*), and exiting (*abeo*) the enemy city, these divinities put upon it fear (*metus*), dread (*formido*), and oblivion (*oblivio*)—emotions associated with death—and transferred their loyalty to Rome, in return for temples and games. Then, prior to launching an attack, the commander would offer a sacrifice and examine an animal's entrails for a sign that the ceremony had been effective (Macrobius, *Saturnalia* 3.9.8).

No wonder Balbus thought attention to auguries was crucial to the military advancement of the city! (Cicero, *De natura deorum* 2.3.7–9). It clearly served a commander's purposes to exploit an enemy's beliefs about death or, conversely, enhance his own army's confidence by attributing its anxieties to the enemy and acting as if the enemy were discouraged. Ancient historians recognized that strategy depended on manipulating an enemy's fears in this way. Herodotus regarded the widespread belief that apparitions haunt battlefields as the basis for a successful ruse that the diviner Tellias advised the Phocians to try against the Thessalians. Covering the bodies of six hundred picked men with whitewash, he had them attack at night. The Thessalian sentries "took them for some sort of appalling apparition" and in panic, spread their fear to the rest of the troops, four thousand of whom were easily slaughtered (*Histories* 8.27).[43] Tacitus attributed a similar stratagem to the Harii in the region north of the Carpathian Mountains and at the southern reaches of the Vistula, who, he said, prepared for war by smearing their shields and bodies with black and fighting their enemies at night. "They inspire terror by evoking the dread shadow of an army of the dead, and no enemy can withstand an appearance so unexpected and seemingly infernal" (*Germania* 43). It seems clear that Tacitus believed the Harii were intentionally exploiting their enemies' fear of ghosts.[44] In antiquity, therefore, the porosity of death was so clearly understood that magistrates sought to manage it and strategists to exploit it.

---

42. For the link between a city's citizens and its gods, see "Evocatio," *Oxford Classical Dictionary*.

43. Trans. Aubrey de Selincourt (Harmondsworth: Penguin, 1954), 509–10. See the detailed study by Ludwig Weniger, "A. Feralis exercitus," *Archiv für Religionswissenschaft* 9 (1906): 201–47; "B. Das Weisse Heer der Phoker," ibid., 223–47; and 10 (1907): 61–81 and 229–56.

44. See Hans Plischke, *Die Sage vom wilden Heere im deutschen Volke*, Diss. (Leipzig: Offenhauer, 1914), 21. By the manner of their battle dress "they wished to instill the impression of a ghostly horde, arisen from the realm of the dead. From that it follows that the enemies of the Harii possessed a belief in the existence of such a ghostly horde, before which one experiences a certain anxiety and fear, which the Harii sought to take advantage of precisely by their manner of doing battle."

In conclusion, three subjects have shaped this chapter: Lucian's heroes and gods who shuttled back and forth between earth and Hades, ghosts who permeated the membrane that separated life from death, and communities that sought to govern this communication between the living and the dead. Clearly, Greek and Roman religion, at least as seen in the documents reviewed here, maintained no absolute boundary between this and the other world.

Using fissures in the earth or dramatic rock formations, which seemed perfect passageways for souls, heroes went back and forth between the world of the living and the land of the dead. When a wit like Lucian scrutinized the contradictions between these stories and the myths behind cults or the great philosophical systems, the rifts gaped wider.

The genre of the ghost story shows that one need imagine no actual opening to communicate with the otherworld. The difficulty in pinning down the nature of these stories matches the ephemeral nature of the ghosts themselves. Homer sought to confine all the dead beyond the earth-encircling river, Ocean. Plato, Virgil, and Plutarch mapped out an other-world with separate regions and treatments for each kind of spirit. Yet, more independent, or less systematic, minds insisted the dead were free to wander. Ghosts are the hoboes, the cowboys of the ancient world. By imagining them alive, or at least not yet fully dead, their descendants or loved ones or murderers or benefactors were acting on their behalf, extending to them a partial existence (one cannot call it a life) beyond the grave. It is wrong to call these manifestations "apparitions," since that term implies that the dead do return, do show up, do appear. It is more accurate to say that these fantasies, these visions, these individual or collective acts of imagination defy the system.

Yet others *sought* system. Communities, particularly Rome, aspired to regulate the comings and goings of the dead. It was no simple task. Piety demanded some respect for those who had gone before, founded the site, built the walls and temples, established the city's institutions. Whether they were "simply" parents, venerated ancestors, or heroes either deceased and revered or adored like Romulus/Quirinus as a god, they helped define the identity and mobilize the loyalty of each community. That is why the Romans had recourse to evocation: it seemed to give them the power to undermine these emotional ties in enemy cities. The dead were, or could also be, specters evoking dread, fear, and timorous respect. It is no surprise that Romulus killed Remus precisely for jumping over the boundary of the city. Remus was a system breaker, and Ovid portrayed him as the prototypical *lemur*. The manner of his death weighed on the city too, creating a situation that called for spiritual management. Thus the city's early leaders developed the liturgical calendar of the state religion. They set dates that would ensure the regular opening of the *mundus* and established taboos around it. Similarly, in the Parentalia descendants venerated the dead as possible protectors, and in the Lemuria they averted the unwanted attention of the same or other potentially threatening shades.

Taken together, these data suggest a certain order involving this world with the next. Despite the proclaimed segregation, there were persistent efforts among the living to retain community, and therefore communication, with the dead. Each such act that makes it into the written record is a manifesto representing countless others that were not recorded. The emotion invested in this communication, or the imagining of it, elicited various amplifications and generated different attempts to calm, sublimate, rationalize, ridicule, channel, systematize, ritualize, develop, control, or exploit these emotions. No study of punishment after death can neglect this almost always silent resistance to those who professed jurisdiction—the right to judge, reward, or punish spirits (whether cherished or dreaded), whose memories their kin, soldiers, lovers, and even enemies still tended. The porosity of death, then, forms the penumbra of hell, a background without which its own contours cannot be discerned.

Useful Death

The previous chapters have presented three logically distinct but historically concurrent views of death. The tendency to regard death as neutral reflected an effort to confine the dead in storehouses or at the limits of the world, where they could not disturb humankind. Distancing them from the human community was more important than judging them. By contrast, the moral view, which seems to have followed but not replaced the neutral view of death, accentuated the effects that knowledge about the dead were considered to have on the morale and behavior of the living. This approach elicited attempts to categorize the dead and correlate certain fates after death with behavior in life. Many resisted these efforts at confinement and categorization by imagining ghosts in order to prolong their interaction with the dead. This refusal of categories pierced the boundary of death.

Although I know of no ancient discussion that delineates these three approaches as such, some sources debate the relative advantages of each view. In general, they interpret ideas, including religious beliefs, according to their effect on, or function in, society. Proponents of this method tend to accept or reject ideas more readily depending on whether they estimate that widespread adoption of those beliefs would cause people to live better—that is, obey the gods, honor their parents, serve the state, or rule their baser natures. This is the criterion of utility.

This chapter, therefore, examines some explicit discussions in ancient literature of the relationship between beliefs about death and conduct in life. Hints of this important theme have already emerged. Plato said that death would be an escape for the wicked if there were no future life (*Phaedo* 107c). He also explained the deterrent effect of purified souls returning with knowledge of Tartarus (*Gorgias* 526). Virgil constructed his underworld to inform the future behavior of Aeneas. Now, before moving on to Jewish and Christian ideas of death and punishment after death, it is necessary to consider how the ancients of Greece and Rome analyzed the social and moral utility of their own religious traditions.

I do not mean to portray the ancients as reducing all ideas to their function. Yet the thinkers to be examined in this chapter noted the correlation between certain beliefs about the dead and the corresponding effects (whether beneficial or detrimental) on the society that accepted or rejected them. Another related premise claims that social order should by definition conform to the order of the cosmos: anything else would be chaos. Thus, correct belief about the nature of the world (including what happens after death) would advance the correct arrangement of society and the correct behavior of its members.

Some authors, such as Critias, Polybius, and Livy, state that the founders of their communities purposely devised myths to achieve a more tightly bound society whose members would cooperate more readily and exercise more self-control under the sway of these inventions than without them. Cicero held that correct understanding of the postmortem reward for patriots was part of what allowed the republic's great heroes to excel and, therefore, their descendants should also accept these beliefs. Lucian, too, operated under the assumption that recognizing the leveling effects of death would improve one's perspective in life. The authors discussed in this chapter agree that holding common beliefs about the afterlife binds a society together and enhances its propensity for virtue. Jewish and Christian authors do not make such statements in the period covered by this volume. Indeed, this feature of pagan philosophical self-consciousness usefully contrasts to an important aspect of divine providence in Judaism and Christianity. What the pagans attributed to human devising or themselves knowingly applied, Jews and Christians consider part of the providential working of divine justice.

CRITIAS

Critias was an Athenian politician and playwright who lived from about 460 to 403 B.C.E. He was pro-Spartan and one of the Thirty Tyrants. Close to the Academy, he figured alongside Socrates in some of Plato's dialogues.

He wrote a play called *Sisyphus* of which a surviving fragment contains a theory of the human origins of belief in the gods.

Critias posited two innovations in the transition from anarchy to the development of morals and respect for law. After an initial period of anarchy, men devised laws based on retribution to deter crime, but these checked only open offenses. The law could not control hidden deeds. Finally, "a wise and clever man invented fear (of the gods) for mortals." He devised a concerned and vigilant intelligence who could know whatever is thought or done. Critias's emphasis on fear implies that because no evil can escape these gods' notice, no evil will remain unpunished. Critias thus imagines the psychological effects of belief in such divinities. It was good for society, he suggests, to believe in these immortal, immaterial, knowing, and caring beings, for such "divinities" would deter crimes that no human agency could successfully prevent or prosecute. According to this view, their invention was a milestone in human history.[1]

POLYBIUS

Polybius (c. 200–after 118 B.C.E.), the son of an Achaean statesman, was raised in Greece but sent to Rome where he became attached to Scipio Aemilianus. He served as a Roman diplomat and emissary from Rome to Carthage, whose destruction he witnessed. In his *Histories* he considers Rome's attainment of world domination inevitable, but he also seeks human rather than purely fatal or providential causes for it. Considering the contribution of laws and institutions to the durability of regimes, Polybius notes a correspondence between the harmony of individual character and that of the social order, between the soul and the city. In constitutions "what is desirable . . . makes men's private lives righteous and well ordered and the general character of the state gentle and just, while what is to be avoided has the opposite effect" (6.48.4).

Polybius believed that religions, or at least the beliefs acted out in rituals, could be contrived to serve the state and that the Romans were particularly adept at devising such rites. Thus, he considered the ability of Roman religion to incorporate the funeral rites of the individual *gens*, or kin group, into the larger public reverence for the community's heroic dead as fundamental to the formation of Roman character and the success of Rome's expansion.

1. Critias, fragment of the lost play *Sisyphus*, trans. Kathleen Freeman, in *Ancilla to the Pre-Socratic Philosophers* (Cambridge: Harvard University Press, 1948), 157–58. I thank Charles King for this and the following passage from Polybius.

As an example of how to cultivate both personal and civic loyalty, Polybius singles out the burial practices of military heroes at Rome. In these ceremonies, the great man is laid out at the rostrum and publicly praised in such a way that the loss comes to be shared, he says, not only by the mourners but by the whole community. After interment, the death mask of the deceased is placed prominently in the house and, on public occasions, carried about the city. At a funeral of a descendant, all the death masks of a family's venerable ancestors are brought out, and the funeral speech praises not only the most recently deceased, but the whole lineage, beginning with the most ancient. Each ancestor is represented by an impersonator wearing a toga trimmed according to the level of magistracy attained, and these sit in special ivory chairs in front of the assembly, so that the whole community may commemorate the contributions of the venerable *gens* (6.54). The gallery of heroic "ghosts" arrayed before the community thus reinforces the prestige of the family in question and motivates others to emulate their example. "Who would not be inspired," he wonders, "by the sight of the images of men renowned for their excellence all together and as if alive and breathing?" (6.53.10; cf. 6.52.11, 55.4, 54.3). In this case, commemoration of notable ancestors, not classification of all the dead, is the operative model, whose utility Polybius praises.

Awe for distinguished forebears was not the only aspect of reverence that served the community. The Romans excelled over all other peoples, Polybius thought, in the depth of their religious convictions.[2] Their fear of the gods, which other peoples ridicule as superstition, "maintains the cohesion of the Roman State" (6.56.8). Were the state made up only of wise men, it would not have been necessary to cultivate this belief, but since the multitude does not know what it wants, does not reason, and cannot contain its desires and passions, it must be checked by "invisible terrors and suchlike pageantry" (5.58.11).

The term "superstition" does not take full account of the benefits of these beliefs. It would be rash for his contemporaries to drop them, Polybius warns. Among the Greeks, where "notions concerning the gods and beliefs in the terrors of [Hades (*haidou dialēpseis*)]" are being abandoned, no official can be trusted with the smallest sum of money, though he be forced to find witnesses for every document and surround himself with auditors. Yet Roman magistrates, even those who deal with large sums of money, "maintain correct conduct just because they have pledged their faith by oath" (6.56.14). For Polybius, then, beliefs about gods and ghosts, should be

_____

2. Here is an opinion echoed in Cicero, *De natura deorum* 2.3.9, and made part of Jupiter's (self-serving) prophecy in Virgil, *Aeneid* 12.839–40.

judged not for their intellectual sophistication but for their utility. And as one who knew public life in both Greece and Rome, he thought Roman officials behaved more honestly than their Athenian counterparts because they feared the gods.

LUCRETIUS

The Roman philosopher and poet Titus Lucretius Carus (99–55 B.C.E.) rejected the invisible terrors of future judgment which Critias and Polybius considered crucial to a society's discipline. These tales, he believed, chain the human mind in slavery to superstition; imagination is self-delusion. The correct understanding of how this world is related to the next, what happens after death, will liberate humankind from the crippling fears imposed by religion. There is no future judgment and, in the sense intended by the Orphics, Plato, and (later) Virgil, there is no transmigration of the soul.

In *On the Nature of Things*, he explains why these ideas are misconceptions. For Lucretius, as for his teachers Epicurus and Ennius, nature is a constant flux of material particles he called *semina*, "seeds" (1.59), which come together for a time to constitute a body if the particles are densely packed or a soul if they are rarefied.[3] At death, these combinations end, the particles scatter, and in the constant flux of matter, they form new bonds as each seed is recycled. The former union of body and soul which made up a human being ends. The recycled particles continue to exist, but no conscious person remains (3.847–61). These cycles go on independently of the gods (1.158). Punishment after death, therefore, is impossible. The tales about the underworld, postmortem judgment and punishment, gorgonian monsters, and chained Titans are mere figments of the imagination. Worse, these beliefs, Lucretius claimed, are based on guilt and the fear of death, which emotions are exploited by priests to ensure adherence to their cults, respect for their authority, and patronage of their shrines. This popular religion, what Lucretius calls "the old religions" (6.62), as fostered by priestly conspiracy, breeds fear and oppresses humankind (1.63–65).[4]

Whereas Critias maintained that the notion of postmortem scrutiny was

3. For the place of Lucretius in the Epicurean tradition, see Diskin Clay, *Lucretius and Epicurus* (Ithaca: Cornell University Press, 1983), 197–98; also Dietrich Lemke, *Die Theologie Epikurs* (Munich: Beck, 1973).

4. In *Lucretius on Death and Anxiety: Poetry and Philosophy in "De Rerum Natura"* (Princeton: Princeton University Press, 1990), 14, Charles Segal argues that Lucretius is concerned to combat the terror of nonbeing rather than of the afterlife. Segal further discusses fear of the afterlife at 17–25 and 165.

consciously contrived to improve social behavior, Lucretius argued that belief in the gods arose from the consistency of our dreams, for people dream of strong and beautiful beings. Since the poets have described them the same way for so long and never shown them fearing death, we consider them immortal (5.1169–82). Ever since, humans have made themselves miserable by imagining the gods as causes for what they do not understand (5.1185–87, 1194; cf. 1.151–54). The gods pursue only those who misunderstand them. They do not take vengeance on their victims. They haunt only the credulous souls who imagine them as spirits (6.71–79).

The correct understanding of divine sublimity exalts the gods beyond these petty concerns (such as punishing us for our misdeeds) and values their peace, their sublimity—in a word, their divinity (6.68–71). Lucretius himself invokes "nurturing Venus" as the provider of earth's bounty (1.1–5). In turning to Venus, however, he shuns Demeter, Persephone, and Hecate, the goddesses of fertility in the Eleusynian Mysteries, figures connected to the fear of death, whose exploitation he deplores. The love of Venus exhausts Mars and so brings peace (1.29–40). She offers herself to Mars, however, for her own purposes, unaffected by human prayers, beyond any wrath human beings imagine she might direct against them (44–49).

Who would fear death if people understood that neither their spirits nor their bodies, but only "pallid simulacra," survive to reach the Acheron (1.122)? In fact, what happens in death is analogous to sleep, when we feel no want of ourselves or of consciousness. Why should we feel it in death, when our mind and body will be even further scattered (3.919–30)? Like the body, the mind is mortal (3.831). "Therefore death is nothing to us" (3.830).[5] Even if our particles, after decomposition, were to be recomposed in exactly the same form, the very process of recomposition would preclude any continuity of feeling (3.847–61). Thus, "in death there is nothing for us to fear, nor can anyone be miserable who can not even exist, . . . since immortal death has taken away our mortal life" (3.866–69).

Beyond the fear of simply being dead, Lucretius distinguishes the fear of punishment after death.[6] As the gods arose from our dreams, the fear of punishment after death emerged from our guilt. According to Lucretius, human society developed in orderly fashion until the discovery of gold, which engendered greed and conflict, particularly between the poor and the

5. For this slogan, see Barbara Price-Wallach, *Lucretius and the Diatribe against the Fear of Death: "De Rerum Natura" III 830–1094*, Supplement to *Mnemosyne*, 40 (Leiden: Brill, 1976); and Jean Salem, *La mort n'est rien pour nous: Lucrèce et l'éthique*, Bibliothèque d'histoire de la philosophie (Paris: Vrin, 1990).

6. Paul Eugène Lortie, "Crainte anxieuse des enfers chez Lucrèce: Prolegomènes," *Phoenix* 8 (1954): 47–63.

rich. But then, tired of strife, people framed laws to contain their ambitions. Later, they perceived that their earlier actions had exceeded the limits set down in the laws, and they began to fear punishment. For when one has practiced violence, the injury one has done usually reverts upon its author in the form of a fear of unintended self-betrayal "screaming in a nightmare or in feverish delirium" (5.1151–60; cf. 3.825–29). A combination of residual guilt and anticipated shame produces this emotion. The fear of death, like the dreams that induce us to believe in the gods, is wholly a product of the imagination.

Thus the famous punishments said to be administered in the underworld exist not there but in the living persons who fear them:

> There is no miserable Tantalus cringing beneath the great rock in the air above him and stilled by fruitless fear, as the story goes; rather [that rock] is the vain fear of the gods that afflicts mortals in this life and the fear of future blows with which destiny threatens us. (3.978–83)[7]

Similarly Tityos is laid out *here* before us (3.992). The vulture gnawing his liver represents the anxieties that pierce his being. In passing, Lucretius sarcastically remarks that the bird would never find an eternity's worth of fodder in his victim's liver even if it covered the whole earth, nor would Tityos be able to bear the pain forever (3.984–95). Sisyphus "too is here in this life before our eyes" (3.995). The rock against which he labors is his unrealizable ambition for office and power. The Danaides, maidens cursed with the task of filling perforated urns, represent people unsatisfied by the fruits of life, brought in measure by the seasons. The holes in the urns in which they "carry" water are the gaps in their satisfaction with nature's bounty. "Cerberus, the Furies, the scarcity of light, and Tartarus belching frightening fire from his maw have never existed, nor can they" (3.1011–13).[8]

Where, then, do these fears come from? The answer is the same: from life itself (3.1014). The Roman state has punishments aplenty, rightly to be feared—prison, being cast from the high (Tarpeian) rock, lashings, executioners, pitch, metal plates, torches. But even without these, the mind dwells upon its deeds, applies goads to itself, and tortures itself with lashes, all the while fearing punishment in advance (3.1014–19). Thus, the human soul

7. Lucretius follows a different variant of the Tantalus legend from the one presented in Homer and Virgil.

8. Gian Biagio Conte, "Il trionfo della morte e la galleria dei grandi trapassati in Lucrezio III, 1024–1053," *Studi italiani di filologia classica* 37 (1965): 114–32. See also André Desmouliez, "Cupidité, ambition, et crainte de la mort chez Lucrèce (De R.N. III 59–93)," *Latomus* 17 (1958): 317–23.

punishes itself through obsession not only with the imaginary torments described in myths but also with the real penalties of the judicial system. And in its guilt ("conscious of its own deeds" [3.1018]) it imagines itself, in advance, suffering penalties in death which it has so far escaped in life. There is no question, then, where the punishments come from. What seems remarkable to Lucretius is people's need to imagine themselves liable to such torments forever.

By contrast, Lucretius continues, the penalties of the judicial system will end. Yet adherents of the old religions consider finite punishments insufficient and insist on imagining that after death the punishments will be still worse. "At length the life of fools is made into a hell on earth" (3.1023). Lucretius interprets the popular fear of punishment after death as a correct perception of state-sanctioned penalties confused with torments from the mythical past, internalized by the guilt-ridden out of anxiety about having misdeeds discovered, and finally projected ahead into an afterlife when the gravity of the punishment will be intensified and, worse yet, unending. No effort to postpone it will work, nor will it diminish the time spent dead, for "that eternal death will nonetheless remain" (3.1091). The punishments after death are figments of the imagination; only death itself is eternal. And that is more peaceful than sleep![9]

Lucretius provides a rare opportunity to consider an ancient who denies the existence of any afterlife. For him the torments are allegorized representations of psychological problems. Sisyphus suffers indeed rolling his boulder, but not in the underworld and not in death. By comparing them to dreams, *On The Nature of Things* makes the beliefs promulgated by the regional Mediterranean cults entirely imaginary. The myths linking each shrine to its caretakers, the priests, gained credibility from their resemblance to the actual justice system of Rome and their traditional repetition by generations of poets and bards. Beyond the circulation of cultic myth and folklore were the written versions in Greek literature read by Romans. Yet these sources constitute the limit of their reality. Since in life these torments are confined to the judicial system, dreams, and classical (Greek) literature, they are invalid indicators about the nature of death, which we can understand only through philosophy (*ratio*). Lucretius thought only matter and death were eternal.

For Lucretius therefore, belief in the gods, though supported by some psychological realities and aspects of institutional life, produces a debilitat-

9. See Phillip Mitsis, *Epicurus' Ethical Theory: The Pleasures of Invulnerability*, Cornell Studies in Classical Philology, 48 (Ithaca: Cornell University Press, 1988).

ing subjection to imaginary terrors spawned by poets and fostered by greedy temple attendants. Clearly thinking in terms of cause and effect, Lucretius urged a life unencumbered by the emotional baggage of religion.[10]

CICERO

At first glance, Cicero would also seem to have no patience with the notion of punishment after death, for he is suspicious of all the gods, including those of the underworld.[11] If he disposes of the agents of postmortem retribution, he deprives the dead, or the wicked dead, of their tormentors. Clearly that is the impression he gives in *Pro Cluentio*. There, he calls "transparent fabrications and fables" the belief that "in the underworld there exists a site or a region devoted to the punishment of the wicked" and that a wicked man "would encounter there more persecutors than he left here." "Since all of this is false, as everyone knows," Cicero takes his discourse in another direction (171). He also implies in the fourth speech against Catalina (3.8) that these beliefs were a human invention that had long since lost their currency, typical, as they were, only of olden times.

The first debate in the *Tusculan Disputations* comes to the same conclusion.[12] The philosophical neophyte "A" contends that death is a great evil for humankind. The more experienced "M" undertakes to persuade him of the opposite view. First, however, M must remove any suspicion that A fears death because of the fables associated with a painful or punitive afterlife. You're not afraid of mythical beasts like the three-headed Cerberus, are you, he asks him, or of scrutiny by Greek judges such as Rhadamanthus and Minos, the rivers Styx or Acheron, or the torments of Sisyphus or Tantalus? Even the novice knows better: Do you think I'm crazy? (1.5.9). Again Cicero

10. See the paraphrase in Segal, *Lucretius*, 35–36. Cf. Salem, *La mort*, 116. For Lucretius's direct attack on superstition, see 1.62–79; and M. J. Edwards, "Treading the Aether: Lucretius, *De Rerum Natura* 1.62–79," *Classical Quarterly* 40 (1990): 465–69.

11. See R. J. Goar, *Cicero and the State Religion* (Amsterdam: Hakkert, 1972); also Woldemar Görler, *Untersuchungen zu Ciceros Philosophie*, Bibliothek der klassischen Altertumswissenschaften, 2d ser., vol. 50 (Heidelberg: Winter, 1974).

12. For Cicero's philosophy, see A. J. Kleijwegt, "Philosophischer Gehalt und persönliche Stellungnahme in Tusc. I, 9–81," *Mnemosyne*, 4th ser., 19 (1966): 359–88; Olof Gigon, "Die Erneuerung der Philosophie in der Zeit Ciceros," *Entretiens Fondation Hardt* 3 (1955): 25–59. Paul MacKendrick, *The Philosophical Books of Cicero* (New York: St. Martin's, 1989), offers a summary (149–63) and a brief commentary (163–68).

dismisses the underworld as unworthy of serious consideration by the so-phisticates who frequent his villa. In fact, we are told, the underworld is empty (1.6.11).

Fears of the underworld may be put to rest when one understands how these erroneous beliefs arose. According to M, the mental capabilities of the human race have progressed. Only at the older, primitive stage was any belief in a punitive underworld necessary, and it sprang from reflections on nature, the source of all the knowledge of the ancients. They did not, how-ever, understand the causes and principles behind the physical phenomena they observed. In this state of ignorance, they inferred from nighttime appa-ritions (ghosts coming back in dreams) that those who died and reappeared lived on after death (1.13.29). Moreover, this belief was not confined to the ancient Romans; it was accepted throughout the world. And what all peo-ples agree on should be considered a law of nature. Therefore, it is nature that inspires the belief that the dead live and continue to feel and experience a kind of life (1.13.30). Belief in reward after death for noble exertion in life, then, is the general consensus, and it would not have arisen without some natural basis. We should, therefore, accept it (1.16.35).

Since it is natural that we should believe that souls live on after death, we must learn what this afterlife is like, for ignorance has produced exaggerated fears, which appropriately occasion scorn (1.16.36). Because, in earlier times, people were unable to conceive of souls apart from bodies, they saw them as continuing to live underground, where they were interred, as if the corpses had not been burned before burial. Conceiving of the dead, includ-ing ghosts, as still joined to their bodies was a mental necessity for those who could not imagine an independent soul, and poets have built on this deficiency (1.16.37).

But with learning (*doctrina*) and the application of reason (*ratio*), says M, we can transcend this error. With the superior powers of conceptualization it brings, philosophy has led us away from these primal fears based on primi-tive myths. This realization has been accomplished in stages, with the help of Pherecydes of Syros, then his disciple Pythagoras, and finally by Plato (1.16.38).[13] Whatever its exact nature (1.11.24, cf. 1.17.41), once we can conceive of an immaterial, eternal soul, the whole question of death appears different (1.19.43–1.20.47).

Drawing directly on *Phaedrus* 245 and *Republic* 610–11, M claims that the soul is divine and demonstrably on a par with God, which fact renders the body unimportant (1.23.53–1.27.67). In this sense, as Plato said in the

---

13. Cf. 1.21.49, where Cicero denies that Plato dispelled these errors.

Phaedo (67c), the whole life of the philosopher is a preparation for death. Although they avoid committing suicide, the wise welcome death (*Tusculan Disputations* 1.30.74). Drawing on *Phaedrus* (246–47), M explains that after death, the soul goes either away from or toward the gods (1.30.72). In place of the scars Plato describes as visible on the naked soul in the form of a body (*Gorgias* 524), M imagines chains that permit the body to advance farther or not, depending on the degree to which the soul was liberated from ties to the body. Greater or lesser cultivation of the soul and control of the body, then, determines the length of one's restraints and the ability of one's soul to rise. Although there is no specific punishment for the wicked, this system of graduated reward distinguishes people's fates after death. No matter how high one rises, death frees the soul from the shackles of the body and only then does life truly begin, for "this life is death" (1.31.75.). Death, then, is a liberation—and therefore hardly an evil—since through its portals we either become gods or join the gods (1.31.76).

The debate "reported" by Cicero presents a theory of the growth of knowledge which accounts for the widespread belief, born of a more primitive age, promoted by the poets, and still accepted among the common people, which fosters fear of death and particularly the possibility of punishment in the earth, where Hades (or in his Roman form, Pluto or Dis) rules. In contrast, the philosphical view distinguishes body and soul in life and death. The fate of the soul has no relation to the fate of the body. The underworld, based on an assimilation with the grave, is not relevant. It is empty of souls (*Tusculan Disputations* 1.19.43–1.20.47). For those who care, the body experiences nothing, as Lucretius had already taught.[14]

Cicero devotes the remainder of the first dialogue to considering the alternative possibility, that the soul does not survive the body. Using Lucretius, he shows how, in that case, there would be no sensation (since the body can have no consciousness without the soul, and both are dead). The only afterlife this view affords the dead is in their reputation on earth (1.45.109). It is in fact intolerable to believe that the dead actually experience the pains of the underworld of which the crowd is convinced (1.46.111). This conclusion again reflects how Cicero's analysis builds on the distinction between the learned few and the gullible populace. The learned understand the principles of nature and have no need of myth; the ordinary people perceive nature

14. In this passage (1.21.48–49), Cicero pretends independence of Lucretius and Plato, though it is clear from preceding passages that they are the cornerstones of his argument: Plato, for the idea that the soul has a fate separate from the body (*Phaedrus* 245–47); Lucretius, for the idea that the body experiences nothing after death (*De rerum natura* 3.830–977).

directly, without the benefit of learning (*doctrina*), and hence remain prey to the poets' tales (or myths), which exploit their fears of the underworld.

Even though the underworld of torments is empty, heaven teems with heroes—but heroes of a special sort. It is the distinguished servants of their country who live on in glory. In his dialogue *On the Nature of the Gods*, Cicero again builds on his view that religious belief begins with the perceptions of the uneducated embellished by the bards.[15] As in the *Tusculan Disputations*, one important basis for the reverence we owe the gods comes from the respect universally accorded them, which derives in turn from their harmonious relationship with natural forces. The existence of the gods derives from the observation of nature by all and so must be accepted (*De natura deorum* 1.16.43; cf. 2.24.63). The question is not whether they exist but what they are like (2.5.13).

Whatever we eventually determine on this question, says Balbus, one of the disputants, it should be observed that religion, which he defines as "respect for the gods" (*cultus deorum* [2.3.9]), is good for social order and the expansion of the state, for conquest is linked to *pietas* and respect for the auguries. He reports that generals who neglected the auguries failed, which shows that "those who submitted to the principles of religion extended the state by their command" (2.3.7–8). However the Romans measure up against other peoples in other areas of culture, Balbus says, they excel in one crucial regard: in their religion. Since most of the subject peoples in 44 B.C.E. might have thought it was in military organization, territorial expansion, and command that Rome excelled, Balbus here is firmly, though implicitly, connecting piety with military success (2.3.9).

The strict connection Balbus claimed between Rome's ancient religious devotion and its military success exemplifies the ancient technique of assessing ideas for their social utility, which is the subject of this chapter. Although the true cognoscenti do not take religious myths literally (indeed, he distinguishes between religion and superstition [2.28.72]), Balbus finds that reason can draw beneficial and useful principles from the observation of nature (2.28.70). Although the tales about the gods are false, conformity to the rituals that recognize the power of forces acknowledged the world over is not only beneficial but indispensible to the success of the noble order, the stability of the republic, and its military expansion.[16]

---

15. On this work, see Martin van den Bruwaene, *La théologie de Cicéron* (Louvain: Bureaux de recueil, Bibliothèque de l'université, 1937).

16. Goar, *Cicero*, 117, observes that Cotta, the other disputant, also insists on upholding the traditional Roman rituals, even as he attacks much else that Balbus tried to salvage.

Selecting an example, Balbus—and Cotta does not challenge him on this point—blames the negligence of the noblity (2.3.9) for the public's loss of respect for the auguries, which it is their responsibility to maintain. According to Balbus, the ceremony's history in the republic's early days links traditional respect for the supernatural to the caste charged with administering its rites.

Whether it conforms to Cicero's private opinion or not, the theory outlined by Balbus evaluates religion in terms of its utility to the state. In his view, those political communities advance which conform in their ritual and social structure to the natural forces that govern the universe as these are understood by reason and enshrined in religion, though, where religion is concerned, the philosopher will distinguish true principles from the embroidery of popular proverbs, the myths of poets, and indiscriminate superstition. Nonetheless, because we can see certain physical truths through these principles, and because of the respect we owe tradition—remember the social utility of the auguries, mentioned at 2.3.9—it is our duty to uphold and venerate them (2.28.71). Balbus sharply distinguishes this grudging acceptance of religion from superstition. Whereas superstition accepts all these fables, religion is critical and selective (2.28.72).

We have seen in the previous chapter how Cotta attacked Balbus's conciliatory exposition by insinuating that the existence of Zeus, indeed of all the Olympians, depends on the likes of Cerberus. But Cotta disavows any intention of debunking the gods, for it would hardly be suitable for a philosopher to remove all belief in them (3.17.44). More important, as he did in the first of the *Tusculan Disputations*, Cicero makes his most critical disputant allow a crucial exception within the ranks of the divine—patriots: "We should declare against those who say that these gods whom we all honor piously and reverently were transferred from the human race into heaven not in fact but only in the opinions of men" (3.21.53). This is a theory dear to Cicero. He includes it in his summary discussion of death in *On Old Age* (21, 23) and with even greater clarity in that part of *On the Republic* (book 6), known as the *Dream of Scipio*, where it constitutes a veritable civic theology.[17] The deceased grandfather of Scipio Africanus appears to him in a dream and reveals the nature of the world in order that he might defend his country more steadfastly. Further, nothing pleases the gods more than those communities that rule themselves by the convocations and deliberations of men under the law, which are called states. It therefore follows (*certum est*)

17. On this work, see Pierre Boyancé, *Etudes sur le "Songe de Scipion"* (1936; rpt. New York: Garland, 1987), 121–46; and Karl Büchner, *"Somnium Scipionis": Quellen-Gestalt-Sinn* (Wiesbaden: Steiner, 1976), 73–81.

that the gods make special provisions for those who dedicate themselves to the well-being of these communities: "For all who defend, aid, and expand the fatherland, there is a specific place set aside in heaven, where the blessed will enjoy an unending age of happiness" (*De republica* 6.13).

Scipio's dream contains a revelation not touched on in the *Tusculan Disputations*. There, Cicero's disputant M observes that the country's ancient heroes lived in a purer age and perceived nature more directly than we do. Given that advantage, they behaved as if they (that is their souls) would enjoy future reward for service to the fatherland, and we should draw the appropriate conclusion by imitating their example: "And if we judge that the souls of those who excel either by inventiveness or virtue, since they are the best by nature, and since they are also those who have served posterity best, and are most likely to be the best able to perceive the forces of nature, and since they have acted as if there is some consciousness after death, [we should too]" (1.16.35). But in *Scipio's Dream* Cicero makes his informant reveal the basis of their foresight: they have seen that future. That is how they were able to know that the soul lives on and that it is rewarded for devotion to the country's welfare. Heaven is not only the reward they attain; it is also the source from which they come—much like the orbiting souls of Plato's *Phaedrus*. As Cicero had the Elder Scipio say it: "Their governors and defenders come from that place [i.e., the heavens] and return there" (13). Although this shuttling back and forth between heaven and the country they serve no doubt diminishes their enjoyment of the "sempiternal" happiness, it explains their clearsightedness in advising posterity.[18]

The elder Scipio's revelation concerns more than the structure of the heavens. Clearly Cicero believes certain kinds of knowledge or belief will have behavioral consequences for those who share it. Thus the younger Scipio should know these things because, when they are known, even noble youths imbued with the traditions of their heroic forebears will dedicate themselves to these goals "with greater alacrity" (13). In the fictional dream, this link between belief and conduct motivated Scipio the Elder's communication of these truths to his grandson.

The contrast between his philosophical writings and his oratory, aimed at a wider audience, highlights the utility Cicero attributed to the link between belief and conduct. In his philosophical works, written in retirement, before his imprisonment and execution, Cicero denied the existence of punishment after death. There are no gods in the underworld. Nor do the dead experience the fate of their bodies. Thus, there is neither tormentor nor victim

---

18. Goar observes, *Cicero*, 122, that the *Dream* provides an afterlife only for statesmen; nothing is said of the other souls.

beneath the earth. However empty the earth's innards, heroes crowd the heavens. Those who devote themselves to the service of their country and imitate the ancestors of the Romans will attain unending glory after death. If they do not actually become gods, they will live with them (*Tusculan Disputations* 1.31.76). In expounding the apotheosis of patriots Cicero denies a systematic mapping of the otherworld. He denies any space to the wicked, thus, as Plutarch would do later, consigning them to oblivion. In allowing Cotta to destroy the Olympian gods along with their chthonic counterparts, Cicero invents a heaven populated only by the gods of his choosing: outstanding servants of the (Roman) state. It would seem, therefore, that in Cicero's view, only one destiny is possible after death: everlasting life for patriots. Such, at least, is the conclusion he reaches in his philosophical works.

Yet in the *Philippics*, whose purpose was to mold senatorial opinion against Mark Antony, he alludes clearly to the idea of divine retribution. Indeed, that fate already threatens Mark Antony as an enemy of the state. Men and gods work together for the preservation of the state, Cicero reminds the less philosophically sophisticated senators. Thus, public consensus must indicate the will of the gods. Although he feigns uncertainty about the reliability of the signs he sees, Cicero nonetheless affirms the state's safety and Antony's impending punishment (4.4.10).

Cicero is less roundabout describing the fate of Antony's troops. The orator assures the senators that, as warriors who died achieving victory for the fatherland, the dead men of his own side will dwell with the pious. Then, likening his opponents in a civil war to parricides for their offense against the fatherland, he guarantees the Senate that its enemies will pay for their crime with infernal punishment. Affecting to address the warriors slain in defense of the republic, he concludes: "Therefore, those impious ones whom you have killed will pay the punishments for their parricide in the underworld [*ad inferos*], but you, who have expended your last breath in victory, have attained the condition and the abode of the pious" (*Philippica* 14.12.32).[19] It is therefore clear that although in his philosophical works he found the idea of punishment after death distasteful and suited only to the incredulous, in his oratory he used it for political ends.

Now we understand why Cicero made Cotta hesitate. Divinities are not to be eliminated entirely, for their existence provides a reward for patriotic heroes. In philosophy leaders of the state may scorn the beliefs of the crowd and call them superstition, but as the situation with the augurs illustrates, they should set a limit to their disrespect. Statesmen do not want a multitude

19. I wish to thank Lee Williams for calling my attention to this passage.

that believes in nothing. Then the people would lose respect for tradition and the authority claimed by the men who minister to it.

LIVY

Livy, too, had a keen sense of the utility of religion for the state. A native of Padua born in 59 B.C.E., Livy came to Rome, where he devoted himself to his historical writing and died in 17 C.E. He gave public readings of his work, became friends with Augustus, and formed part of the literary circle that included Virgil, Horace, and until his exile, Ovid. His major work is a history of the Roman republic in 142 books collected into groups of ten, called "decades."[20] This work begins with the earliest legends "from the foundation of the city," a technique of organization that gives the work its title, *Ab urbe condita*. Immediately following his account of the establishment of a unified monarchy on the site by Romulus, Livy begins with his successor, Numa, and turns the subject from military consolidation to civilian foundation.

Inheriting a unified monarchy, Numa the legislator decided to instill a fear of the gods in the minds of the Romans in order to provide discipline that would hold the community together despite the lack of an external military threat. Since he knew he would gain no acceptance for his institutions without some little wonder (*miraculum*), he let it be known that he met nightly with the goddess Egeria, who advised him as to what ceremonies would most please the gods and how to dedicate a priest for each one (1.19.1). Livy built his theory of the function of religion into his historical account. Looking back from his vantage point, Livy imagined that Numa's stratagem served its purpose: the Roman state had been successful (from his perspective). Clearly, this fiction had called forth no retributive disaster from vengeful gods; rather, it had encouraged virtue among the citizens from the earliest days of Rome. Nor did Numa limit himself to the heavenly powers, Livy says; he also arranged to appease the chthonic forces, establishing ceremonies to placate the departed spirits of the dead (1.20.7).

More important than the historical nature of a decision Livy attributed to a legendary king is the readiness he must have assumed on the part of his audience to see the effectiveness of the innovation. Livy expected his readers to see a likely correlation among conscious reflection, founding myths, belief in supernatural sanctions by the common people and a moral order consistent with military readiness in peacetime.

20. For an introduction to this work, see T. J. Luce, *Livy: The Composition of His History* (Princeton: Princeton University Press, 1977).

The scheme worked extremely well, Livy says. Concern for the gods (*cura deorum*) became so ingrained that the people perceived a heavenly spirit residing among them and they came to direct their affairs out of respect for promises and trust in one another rather than fear of the punishments stipulated by the laws (1.21.1).

Livy, then, assumes as plausible a notion that human reason can, by means of myth, instill a code of ethics that will regulate a voluntary association of citizens. He does not explain why the myth (or *miraculum*, as he calls it), "the little source of awe," should be necessary rather than the laws themselves or some philosophy of justice. He says only that the populace was uneducated (*rudis*) and inexperienced (*imperita*) in the arts of peace (1.19.4). Nonetheless, as Plato had before him, Livy attributed to the founders of the Roman monarchy, replaced by the republic, a fond concern for the stories that inspire right conduct. These, he suggested, lay at the basis of the Roman community. In his tale of Numa, Livy uses a theory of religion's social utility closely akin to that of Critias.

UTILITY IN LUCIAN

Much of Lucian's art, as we have seen, consists in locating his audience in the underworld, so that it may appreciate the vanity of life from the perspective of the dead. Yet the viewpoint of the deceased must be imagined, and it is very clear that Lucian composes his shade's view of life from his own particular perspective. What is clearer from the underworld than from the surface is the value of the Cynic's outlook. However otherworldly Lucian's dialogues, whether in setting or perspective, both the writer and the audience are focused on earth. Lucian's model of the hereafter is not so much an otherworldly doctrine as a setting from which to "observe and prescribe for the sins of man" (*Downward Journey* 7). Because he advocates spreading a certain idea of the afterlife to change the beliefs and therefore the behavior of the living, Lucian forms part of the pragmatic tradition that considers religion useful.

In the *Dialogues of the Dead*, renowned underworld personalities attest that only Cynics face death calmly. Cerberus himself informs Menippus that Socrates' death scene was only for show: he was as frightened as the others on the bark across the Styx. The same authority assures Menippus that he alone confronted the passage into death with equanimity (4 [422]).[21] The crossing of the Styx in Charon's bark is a moment of truth. Lucian revels in

21. Menippus hanged himself according to M. D. MacLeod in the Loeb edition of Lucian (7:117), citing Diogenes Laertius, *Lives of Eminent Philosophers* 6.100.

the shrieks of hypocrites who reveal themselves as they part with their "possessions" to lighten the load for the crossing and enter the equality of death. The tyrant gives up his diadem and robes. The warrior lays down his arms. The philosopher relinquishes his quarrelsomeness and hair splitting; the rhetorician, his antitheses, balances, and periods (20 [366–74]). There is no wealth, no ancestral title, no rank, no epitaph, and, as Diogenes forces Mausolus himself to admit, no mausoleum among the dead (29 [431]). Lucian's lesson, therefore, is that these things are pointless in life too. He uses the poverty of death to teach simplicity in life.

Menippus sums it up: "In Hades all are equal, and all alike" (30 [433]). Socrates, famous for his snub nose and bald head, is unrecognizable, just a skull (6 [417]). Helen of Troy's beauty exists no more; she's all bone (5 [408–9]). Teiresias does not stand out as blind, because *none* of the skulls have eyes (9 [445]). Nireus and Thersites ask Menippus to determine which of them is better looking. He says he can't tell them apart. Then what of how we were? Menippus insists on seeing them as they are, as he would claim he did in life too (30 [433]).

To change the lives of his audience, Lucian draws freely on belief in judgment and punishment after death. In *Menippus*, the Cynic tours the underworld in the company of a Zoroastrian magus. They come to the court of Minos where the Poenae, Avengers, and Erinyes stand as assessors. The dead are brought in chains: procurers, publicans, sycophants, informers. The rich wear heavy, spiked collars. In a detail that comes from Zoroastrian literature, fitting for the guide in this dialogue, the dead are accused by their own shadows (11).[22] Yet, although Dion accuses him of many crimes and his shadow confirms the charges, Aristippus of Cyrene intervenes on behalf of

22. The Zoroastrian text is *The Book of Arda Viraf* or, in a recent publication, *Arda Wiraz Namag: The Iranian "Divina Commedia,"* trans. Fereydun Vahman, Scandinavian Institute of Asian Studies Monograph Series, 53 (London: Curzon Press, 1986). Here a virtuous soul sees "his own religion and his own good deeds in the form of a [beautiful] girl" (194), and a wicked person sees "his own religion and deeds ⟨in the form of⟩ a naked whore" so tainted with spots she resembles "a reptile, most filthy and most stinking" (201). For an older translation see *The Ardai Viraf Nameh; or, The Revelations of Ardai Viraf,* trans. J. A. Pope (London: printed for Black, Parbury, and Allen, 1816), 52–101. In this version the demon that personifies the soul's evil deeds and thus afflicts it, is not a hag covered with blotches but "a form of the most demoniacal appearance; it had teeth like an elephant, and the nails of its hands and feet were like the talons of an eagle; his eyes were like blood, and out of his mouth issued volumes of pestilential vapour that mixed with the wind" (55). When questioned as to his identity, the demon answers: "I am your genius, and have become thus deformed by your crimes (whilst you were innocent I was handsome)" (56).

Dionysius of Syracuse for his patronage of literature! (13). This, again, is the self-promotional aspect of Lucian's work. He favors the Cynics, and yet—for all he says about the rich—their generosity to authors weighs heavily in their favor.

Menippus and the magus come to the place of punishment: whips snap, fires burn, the rack creaks. Victims on the gibbet and the wheel moan and cry. Cerberus and the Chimera feast on the others. As he encounters dead men he knew, Menippus reminds them with gusto how wealthy they had been. The rich were often criticized for arrogant displays before the poor who stood outside the gates of private estates awaiting alms. Thus, Menippus chides the recently deceased rich for scornfully ordering their servants to close the gates to the many or, when they were in a good mood, appearing splendidly attired before the gathered hoi polloi and offering a hand or breast to be kissed (12).

What principles of punishment are at work here? Lucian presents his contrasts in graduated order. The guilty poor are chastised half as severely as the rich, being allowed periods of rest equal to their terms of punishment (14). Mausolus is given the same single square foot of space allowed any plebeian, but the man after whom imposing burial monuments derive their name must also bear the weight of his tomb (17). His earthly folly distinguishes him in death. In other cases, Lucian presents true reversal in the sense that the victims become the tormentors of those who persecuted them in life. Kings and their officers are reduced to poverty, and like the meanest of slaves, they are subject to blows from passersby. Xerxes, Darius, Polycrates, and other former rulers now are begging, reduced to dependency on their former subjects or people like them (17).

The simplicity and uniformity that death imposes on all has political consequences. The system according to which the poor as a class reverse dominance with the rich as a class, is endorsed by a plebiscite. Ruling now by force of numbers, the former poor imitate the *boulē* of the democratic city-states. The popular assembly approves a new law proposed by a certain Skull, son of Skeleton, of the deme Corpse and the tribe Anatomy. They provide that henceforth the rich should have their bodies sent below to be punished like those of other malefactors, but their souls should be forced to live in donkeys, transmigrating from ass to ass, bearing burdens under the "tender mercies" of the poor for a quarter million years, and only then being allowed to die (20). In this mode of justice one class exchanges its position with another so that victims come to dominate (20).

Whereas *Menippus* presents a reversal of classes, *The Downward Journey* offers a nearly direct confrontation of opposed individuals. The first of its two parts contrasts the deaths of its protagonists. The Cynic philosopher Cyniscus helps Hermes bring the tyrant Megapenthes down to the land of Hades.

Poisoned by one of his cronies, Megapenthes is far too busy with all his schemes to be ready to die. He tries to escape from Hermes, who gathers up the dead, and must be brought down in fetters (3). Even at the shore of the Styx he tries to bargain with Clotho, one of the Fates, and then to bribe her for extra time. In the conversation, she reveals his great crimes (8–9). Cyniscus rebukes and threatens Megapenthes with his club as Hermes finally forces the tyrant on board Charon's boat (13). In life, annoyed because of the philosopher's frankness in denouncing his evil, Megapenthes had "come within an ace" of tying Cyniscus to a cross. Now Cyniscus takes satisfaction in seeing Megapenthes tied to the mast for the crossing of the Styx (13). Here is a near reversal of fates.

A cobbler named Micyllus, who had been working at his leather when summoned, accepts death much better. The cobbler had nothing on earth worth longing for, and now the prospect of death, where all are equal and justice is unbiased, looks good to him. "The tables are turned, for we paupers laugh while the rich are distressed and lament" (15). The cobbler had been the tyrant's neighbor, had seen all that went on in his house, and had counted him fortunate until the awful row he created at his death exposed the truth (16–17). The bark is full and Micyllus is not yet on board. Hermes offers him a ride on the shoulders of Megapenthes, which would create a dramatic inversion of their relationship in life, but Micyllus must pull an oar since he has not even a single obol with which to pay for the crossing. Urged by Hermes to lament his past life, he ironically bemoans the loss of hungry days and cold winters in tattered rags (20). The opening section, therefore, contrasts Megapenthes first to Cyniscus, notable for his right understanding, and then to Micyllus, remarkable for his simple life and his ability to learn from Megapenthes' negative example—exactly as Lucian's readers should!

In the second section, the setting is that of Plato's *Gorgias*. The three shades appear together before Rhadamanthus, who presides. Cyniscus insists on denouncing Megapenthes. The tyrant admits his public crimes but denies his more refined private vices. At the suggestion of Cyniscus, his bed and his lamp are summoned to testify, and these personal accouterments condemn him. Then, according to the reform of judgment procedures which Plato attributed to Zeus, the tyrant is stripped, and the testimony of bed and lamp is confirmed by blotches on his soul, which, as in Plato, signify his many vices. The punishment is that he should never get a drink of Lethe water, so that he must remember all he misses forever. As he must long for what he can never attain, he is sentenced to a place next to Tantalus (26–28). Under similar inspection, the soul of Cyniscus reveals some old, very faint scars that have been nearly eradicated by the practice of philosophy (24). The soul of Micyllus is entirely clear. Rhadamanthus sends Micyllus and Cyniscus to the Isles of the Blessed (24–25).

This Micyllus appears in another dialogue called *The Dream; or, The Cock*. Awakened from a dream of possessing the gold of his oppressive neighbor Eucrates by the crowing of his rooster, Micyllus rails at the bird, which, surprisingly, answers his scolding. The cock is Pythagoras in one of his many reincarnations, who instructs Micyllus about the folly of trusting in wealth. In the dialogue, however, Micyllus conveys his resentment of the ostentatious Eucrates and Simon, who hoard their own goods, steal from Mycillus, and extract extravagant displays of deference. Unlike *The Downward Journey*, *The Dream* provides no reversal of fortune. Mycillus simply sees how hollow are the "advantages" of the rich. When, in *The Downward Journey*, Rhadamanthus sends Mycillus to the Isles of the Blessed, he rewards a victim who has learned to live simply in his modest condition. A similarity has been noted between this Micyllus and the Lazarus so conspicuously neglected by the rich man in one of the parables of Jesus retold by the evangelist Luke.[23] In *The Downward Journey*, however, Mycillus "converts" after he dies and takes in the scene created by Megapenthes, and in *The Dream*, although his outlook is changed in life, Lucian does not portray his end. For this comparison to work well, one must combine the early conversion of Micyllus in *The Dream* with the sentence rendered in *The Downward Journey*.

Lucian, however, was no systematizer. His underworld is too porous. It is both a monarchy and a democracy. His shades can be tortured or punished or shamed or simply unhappy. No single, consistent vision rules. Lucian himself appears to warn interpreters against putting too rigid a construction on his dialogues. Proof comes in a dramatic judgment scene in the *Dialogues of the Dead* (24), which opens with Minos assigning punishments to the wicked and the Elysian Fields to the good. The pirate Sostratus objects to his sentence. Using reason, he forces Minos to admit that the Fates compelled him to live his life as he did. Since he was not responsible for his actions, he cannot be punished for them. Minos agrees, suspends his punishments, entreats him not to spread the word, and admits it is not the only contradiction he will find among the dead.

23. For a careful study of these parallels, drawing particularly on *The Dream* and *The Downward Journey*, see Ronald F. Hock, "Lazarus and Micyllus: Greco-Roman Backgrounds to Luke 16:19–31," *Journal of Biblical Literature* 106 (1987): 455.

Whether because of punishment or simple confrontation with the reality of death, in Hades the dead now understand and lament their follies. They realize the worthlessness of possessions, the vanity of worldly ambitions. Lucian excoriates the schemers who hoped to inherit from aged, wealthy, childless benefactors who outlive the sycophants who courted them (14–19). Varying the theme of Tantalus, Lucian makes their deaths resemble their lives, as they come to Hades with their "open-mouthed greed," as if their thirst for wealth were about to be slaked (15 [345]). The only money allowed them in death is the penny they will surrender to the ferryman (21 [379]).

Not property but the consciousness of death should be the guiding principle of life, according to Lucian (3 [337]). He emphasizes this moral in the last line of *Charon* (24): "How silly are the ways of unhappy mankind, with their kings, golden ingots, funeral rites and battles—but never a thought of Charon!" (that is, of death). As Antilochus confides to Achilles, who is just as restless in Lucian's underworld as in Homer's, the key to life after death serves also for life: remain silent, "bear and endure it all," or else "become a laughing-stock" (*Dialogues of the Dead* 26 [401]). Or as Menippus tells Chiron the Centaur, who preferred life in the underworld to the boringly predictable sequence of seasons, night and day: One should do what "a sensible man is reputed to do—be content and satisfied with one's lot and think no part of it intolerable" (8 [436]). However bleak his prescription for happiness, Lucian still proclaims the superiority of life over death. Though Lucian has Diogenes chide him for it, an aged, crippled, deathly sick, and nearly blind man arrives at Charon's bark admitting that death frightens him and that he longs for the light (22).

As much as Lucian enjoys satirizing the beliefs of the many, he subordinates his scorn for superstition to his didactic strategy. He portrays death to shape behavior and to teach moderation in conduct, frankness in speech, awareness of death, and the fundamental equality of all mortals.

The existence of this utilitarian approach to the afterlife in Greek and Roman antiquity is of the utmost importance, because it shows that this technique of analysis was available in the ancient world. Thus its absence from Jewish and Christian literature assumes all the more importance. Although they share with Greek and Roman philosophers the idea that humans should govern themselves according to the laws of the cosmos, Jewish and Christian writers regard their God as the creator of that universe and thus represent their ideas about the afterlife as a revelation of the truth by which their divinity rules the world. In the Jewish and Christian literature of antiquity, the principles of human government derive not from considerations of utility but from divine provision. In contrast, the Greek and Roman authors studied here present the elements of their world view as human discoveries, inventions, or in the worst cases, delusions. They accepted the notion that beliefs about the afterlife affect behavior. They actively participated in shaping those beliefs and sought thereby to improve the lives of the people around them.

The Afterlife in Ancient Judaism

If you obey the commandments of the Lord your God, . . . then you shall live and multiply. . . . But if your heart turns away, I declare to you . . . that you shall perish.

—Deuteronomy 30.16–18

There is an evil in all that is done under the sun, that one fate comes to all.

—Ecclesiastes 9.3

Shall not the Judge of all the earth do right?

—Genesis 18.25

And many of those who sleep in the dust of the earth shall awake, some to everlasting life, and some to shame and everlasting contempt.

—Daniel 12.2

Spirits of the Dead

There now exists a broad consensus as to the evolution of the biblical text as it has come down to us, although individual scholars differ widely on matters of detail.[1] As distinct from the oral traditions upon which it is based and which, in some cases, may be centuries older than the surviving text, the Hebrew Bible was composed approximately 900–165 B.C.E. Stages of composition can be distinguished using differences in terminology, institutional bias, explicit references to outside events, and implicit influences from politics and social conditions. Some parts of the Bible relating events that are logically or historically prior to others were in fact written later. For example, parts of Genesis, particularly verses 1.1–2.4 (which relate the earliest possible events), were in fact written after parts of Exodus

---

1. That consensus has shifted considerably over time and continues to do so. Confessional polemics are not the only problem. New techniques of historical, formal, and linguistic analysis permit new insights. Newly discovered texts and newly unearthed artifacts continually change the way even the most specialized scholars understand the Bible. Similarly, innovations in fields outside biblical studies proper also affect approaches to the Bible. A well-rounded recent survey of these changes is by Alexa Suelzer and John S. Kselman, "Modern Old Testament Criticism," in the *New Jerome Biblical Commentary* (Englewood Cliffs, N.J.: Prentice-Hall, 1990), 1113–29. The work of biblical scholarship began even in biblical times, as compilers of the text commented on and emended the work of their predecessors. See Michael Fishbane, *Biblical Interpretation in Ancient Israel* (Oxford: Clarendon Press; New York: Oxford University Press, 1985).

and many other books. Except for the oldest fragments in the writings of the prophets, virtually no text of the Bible is contemporary with the events it describes. Further, any part of the Bible written early was subject to revision by writers working later.[2]

The canon of the Hebrew Bible, then, was formed of these diverse writings composed by many men or women over a long period of time, under many different circumstances, and in the light of shifting patterns of religious belief and practice.[3] Consequently, discussion of divine punishment in the Hebrew Bible must not assume that concepts "evolved"—in the sense of gradually becoming more sophisticated or approaching perfection—over time. Instead, it is best to proceed by means of topical, rather than chronological units. The very difficulty of dating the books of the Bible virtually dictates this procedure, and more important, the Jewish community was too diverse, the concerns of its writers too varied, the circumstances that provoked reflection too changeable to propose a single, straight line of development. Indeed, the questions under investigation in this book concerning the end of an individual's life, the nature of death, the possibility of divine judgment, and the resultant reward or punishment—questions that come under the heading of eschatology (from the Greek *eschaton*, meaning "end")—are simply too crucial to have attracted a single solution unanimously accepted over the near millennium of biblical composition. To find a focus in this variety of

2. For a general introduction to these and related matters, see J. Alberto Soggin, *Introduction to the Old Testament: From Its Origins to the Closing of the Alexandrian Canon*, 3d ed. (Louisville, Ky.: Westminster, John Knox Press, 1989); R. J. Coggins, *Introducing the Old Testament* (Oxford: Oxford University Press, 1989); J. A. Bewer, *The Literature of the Old Testament*, 3d ed. rev. by E. G. Kraeling (New York: Columbia University Press, 1962); Otto Eissfeldt, *The Old Testament, an Introduction: The History of the Formation of the Old Testament.* (Oxford: Blackwell, 1962); Walther Eichrodt, *Theology of the Old Testament*, 2 vols. (Philadelphia: Westminster, 1967); Jacob Weingreen, *Introduction to the Critical Study of the Text of the Hebrew Bible* (Oxford: Oxford University Press, 1982).

3. The term "Hebrew Bible" is preferable to "Old Testament," which is an exclusively Christian way of referring to these writings. Jews believe that the testament, or covenant, revealed to them is still in effect. "New Testament" carries the implication that Christianity superseded Judaism, which, while it is a matter of faith for Christians, carries negative connotations for Jews. Nonetheless "New Testament"—unlike "Christian Scriptures," which is more neutral—in addition to being the term Christians prefer to name their revelation, avoids ambiguity, inasmuch as the Hebrew Bible is also part of Christian Scriptures. Hence, when describing matters of Christian belief, I shall use the term New Testament. When I use the term Bible, it will be clear from the context whose scriptures are in question.

eschatological concerns, I shall concentrate on one central question: What happens to the wicked?

JUDAISM AND DIVINE PUNISHMENT

The Jewish people were formed by a series of covenants with God. God assured Noah that he would never again destroy the earth. He promised prosperity to Abraham in return for accepting the mark of circumcision. He gave the law to Moses and pledged to defend his followers and descendants in return for observance of those ordinances. These covenants, however, carried with them a terrible corollary. The God capable of great rewards was also capable of terrible punishments.

One method of punishment was by sheer destruction. God annihilated Pharaoh's troops beneath the waters of the Red Sea. At the time of Noah, God sent a flood to cleanse the earth of the depredations of wicked giants who had corrupted humankind. He destroyed Sodom and Gomorrah with a storm of fire and sulfur. In the Book of Jonah, too, God would have destroyed Nineveh had its people not turned from their evil ways.

Still, God would make provision for the righteous. He saved Noah and his family from the flood and Lot from Sodom, and he granted the land of Canaan to the slaves escaped from Egypt. Indeed, his representatives could argue, as Abraham did, over what actually constitutes a wicked city. To forestall a possibly hasty vengeance, Abraham asked, "Wilt thou indeed destroy the righteous with the wicked?" and "Shall not the Judge of all the earth do right?" (Genesis 18.23, 25). When the moment came, however, God would destroy his enemies, whether oppressors of the Jewish community or malefactors within it.

Besides destruction, the Bible offers another method of divine punishment: long-term suffering. The most prominent example is the consequence of disobedience in Eden. Thenceforth, women must bear children in pain and be subject to their husbands; men must earn their livelihood by working the ground. Both men and women are barred from the tree of life, and in death they "return to the ground" as dust to dust (Genesis 3.19). These effects will last as long as humanity itself.[4] Similarly, when Ham pointed out

---

4. Cain provides another example. After Cain murdered Abel, God made farming impossible for him and compelled him to make his way as "a fugitive and a wanderer on the earth" (Genesis 4.14). Cain's first reaction was to fear being killed by someone who would take advantage of his being a stranger. So God put a mark on Cain in

to his brothers the nakedness of Noah, their father, he was punished through his son Canaan, who, with all his descendants, was sentenced to slavery under Shem and Japheth (Genesis 9.18–27). The descendants of Ham and Canaan were to serve the descendants of Shem and Japheth as slaves for the indefinite future. The Tower of Babel, too, provoked long-lasting punishment. When the men said, "Let us build ourselves a city and a tower with its top in the heavens and let us make a name for ourselves, lest we be scattered abroad upon the face of the whole earth," God "scattered them abroad from there over the face of all the earth" (Genesis 11.4, 8, 9). Their punishment was to experience exactly what they sought to avert. Moreover, no end was set to it. The confusion of language and the dispersion of peoples will last as long as the human race. Whether the arrogance of the tower builders was a greater sin than the wickedness of the giants who brought about the Flood, the contrast between the two types of punishment is clear: the Flood is destruction; the scattering of peoples is long-term impairment. It is possible that placing the Babel story in the middle of two different accounts of Shem's progeny (10.21–32 and 11.10–32) represents an editorial comment on the flood as a model for punishment, an objection, actually, suggesting the substitution of long-term suffering for destruction. Such a protest would be strategically placed between two accounts of the repopulation that followed the flood.

As long as divine punishment consists of destruction, there is no possibility of punishment after death, which can only grow out of the view of punishment as long-term suffering. These variations in belief about God's disciplinary practices emerged as a consequence of the association of a number of themes that arose for very different reasons. These varied Jewish beliefs, when they were all present, could be synthesized in some circles as a belief in punishment after death.

BELIEF THAT DEAD SPIRITS LIVE

It is frequently maintained that there is no belief in life after death in Judaism, but that statement is not universally true. It is clear from biblical texts that in the process of conquering Canaan and intermingling with the

order that people would know not to kill him and threatened anyone who killed him with a sevenfold punishment. Cain was to experience a lifelong exile. Other interpretations are possible: perhaps Cain was penitent, and so his life was spared. Nonetheless, even if the death sentence that one might expect was lightened, Cain must be considered the recipient of lifelong ostracism.

vanquished, some of the Jewish people adopted from them certain practices that, if they do not quite form a cult of the dead, at least constitute a reverence for or dedication to the dead that is very hard to delineate now but that the authors of the Bible were at pains to extinguish.[5] These are among the customs that 2 Kings 16.3 calls "the abominable practices of the nations whom the Lord drove out before the people of Israel" (cf. Deuteronomy 18.9). Archeological evidence includes the remains of sacrifices made to propitiate the spirits of dead family members and vessels placed in tombs, presumably to supply their needs.[6] Biblical prohibitions against communicating with the dead would make no sense unless some people propitiated, consulted, or venerated deceased family members. Leviticus 19.31 and 20.6 forbid consulting mediums; Deuteronomy 18.11 prohibits the practices of divination and necromancy.[7] Deuteronomy 26.14 enjoins that a person state to the officiating priest that none of the matter being offered in a sacrifice had been offered to the dead. Psalm 106.28 mentions prior wrongs committed by the Jewish people. In addition to occasionally worshiping "the Baal of Peor," they also "ate sacrifices offered to the dead." In a telling critique of the practice, Isaiah associated the dead with false gods. "Should not a people seek unto their God? On behalf of the living should they seek unto the dead?" (8.19). These practices and the opposition they provoked reflect belief in a range of beings at once less than human—that is, merely shades (unless they were the shades of kings and therefore more potent)—and more than human (because of the demands they could make) but less than divine. Initially, at least, these beings inspired reverence among the Hebrews who settled the land of Canaan.[8]

5. Klaas Spronk, *Beatific Afterlife in Ancient Israel and in the Ancient Near East*, Alter Orient und Altes Testament, 219 (Kevelaer, Germany: Butzon und Bercker, 1986), 345; George C. Heider, *The Cult of Molek: A Reassessment*, Supplement to *Journal for the Study of the Old Testament*, 43 (Sheffield, England: JSOT, 1985), 383–94, esp. 391.

6. Victor Maag, "Tod und Jenseits nach dem Alten Testament," *Schweizerische theologische Umschau* 34 (1964): 21 nn. 26, 27; Eichrodt, *Theology of the Old Testament* 2.210–20. The archeological evidence shows that "the inhabitants of Palestine believed in some form of continued existence of the deceased." Spronk, *Beatific Afterlife*, 37.

7. Maag, "Tod und Jenseits," 22.

8. Even without considering them rival divinities, attributing any numinous quality to them at all could be seen to undermine reverence for God. Conversely, not all reverence for the dead amounts to worship of them. Heider, *Cult of Molek*, 387, makes this commonsense distinction. Comparative evidence from the Canaanite town of Ugarit (now Ras Shamra), discovered in 1929, points to a belief in similar

In dispositions clearly meant to be exemplary for their descendants, Genesis describes the arrangements Abraham made for Sarah and relates his own burial in the same cave east of Mamre (23.1–20, 25.7–11). Isaac died at Mamre "and was gathered to his people" (35.29). Rebekah was buried there (49.31). Jacob buried his wife Leah there and ordered that he also be buried at Mamre (49.29–32). He too was "gathered to his people" (49.33). The expression applied to Isaac and Jacob, but not to Abraham, connotes more than proximity in a family lot. Rather, it suggests some localized drawing power by which deceased elders attract their descendants. It is significant that Abraham, who left his father's home, was not so "gathered."[9]

The most dramatic case of contact with the dead concerns the distraught King Saul, who faced an impending battle with the Philistines. Saul lacked confidence after the death of Samuel, who had previously guided him. Although the king himself had banned access to mediums who would summon the dead, he broke his own prohibition by going in disguise to ask a woman necromancer at Endor to call Samuel back from death. When the spirit arose, the seeress said she saw elohim, "gods" ("a god" in the Revised Standard Version, that is, not *the* God)—strong indication of the supernatural, though not necessarily fully divine powers attributed to the specter (1 Samuel 28.13).[10] Further, the risen figure was clearly Samuel. Possessed of Samuel's memory, it was able to remind Saul of the disobedience that cost him God's favor and cast him into confusion. The spirit of Samuel also had the power to see the future, and "he" accurately predicted Saul's death in the upcoming battle.

This part of the story of Saul and the witch of Endor reflects the lingering practice of consulting the dead. But another aspect of the dramatic event shows elements of what would come to be the common belief for centuries.

---

beings called *rp'm* in Ugaritic, who also attracted awe among Israel's neighbors. See Conrad L'Heureux, "The Ugaritic and Biblical Rephaim," *Harvard Theological Review* 67 (1974): 265–74.

9. See O. Loretz, "Vom kanaanitischen Totenkult zur judäischen Patriarchen- und Elternehrung," *Jahrbuch für Anthropologie und Religionsgeschichte* 3 (1978): 149–204.

10. The form of "elohim" is plural, though the context indicates that only Samuel arose. Perhaps he is one (of the) elohim. Friedrich Nötscher, *Altorientalischer und alttestamentlicher Auferstehungsglauben* (1926; rpt., Darmstadt: Wissenschaftliche Buchgesellschaft, 1980), 209 n. 1, interprets this term to mean an otherworldly or transcendental being, rather than a god ("ein jenseitiges, transzendentales Wesen"). See also Gerhard von Rad, *Old Testament Theology*, 2 vols. (New York: Harper and Row, 1962), 1:276.

Samuel comes *up* from the earth *below*.[11] Saul's summons has "disturbed" Samuel (1 Samuel 28.15). Must we infer that Samuel had been below in a place where he was at rest? If so, that place is probably Sheol, the grave.

Before analyzing Sheol in detail, the most important point to note is that it contains all the dead, good and evil alike. When Samuel prophesies Saul's death, he says: "Tomorrow you and your sons shall be with me" (1 Samuel 28.19). Thus, the disobedient Saul and his progeny will join Samuel below, in the world of the dead. From the very beginning, then, Sheol combines the righteous and the wicked. Like the Babylonian fortress of the netherworld, like the kingdom of Hades, it is morally neutral. So close were these conceptions that the earliest translators of the Bible into Greek, whose work of the third and second centuries B.C.E. formed a compilation known as the Septuagint, translated Sheol as Hades. The New Testament would also employ this translation, thus blending the Jewish and ancient Greek traditions. In his translations, Jerome rendered Sheol as *infernus* or *inferus* and Hades as *infernus* (except in Matthew 16.18, when it is *inferus*). The Revised Standard Version retains Sheol and Hades.

Beyond its glimpse of the world of the dead, the story of Samuel suggests yet other considerations. If the late king is referred to as one of the "elohim," a term also used to name the divinity, then there was uncertainty about a range of minor gods, supernatural spirits, ghosts who could be considered competition for the one God. Any veneration of the dead, whether recently deceased immediate family members or revered ancestors, could constitute a throwback to something akin to polytheism, or at least a distraction from the more focused, centralized, urban, Jerusalem-based institutions of monarchy and Temple.[12] The centralizing efforts of the regime would clearly be enhanced if these clan-based elohim could be moved from the burial places of prominent families into a collective grave inhabited by all and ruled by the one God preached from Jerusalem.[13] Thus the kings and the governing elite around them came to assert the claims of Sheol to all Israel's dead. It fit the

11. Nicholas J. Tromp, *Primitive Conceptions of Death and the Nether World in the Old Testament* (Rome: Pontifical Biblical Institute, 1969), 27.

12. See von Rad, *Old Testament Theology* 1:42–49, for the institutional measures of David and Solomon and 1:275–79 for a "radical . . . desacralising of death." That is, according to von Rad, the dead were to be excluded from any participation in the spiritual community of Israel. Maag, "Tod und Jenseits," 19, concurs.

13. See W. O. E. Oesterley and Theodore H. Robinson, *Hebrew Religion: Its Origins and Development*, 2d ed. (London: Society for Promoting Christian Knowledge, 1930), 358–59, on measures taken to bring the ancient Hebrews' ideas about the afterlife into line with the cult of Yahweh. Eichrodt, *Theology of the Old Testament*, 221–22.

unifying tendency of the monarchy to have an underworld where, as they had been subject in life to one king, the dead would be subject to one God. In this, Israel would conform to the pattern of other Near Eastern kingdoms, which also had unified and morally neutral netherworlds.

SHEOL BELOW

The word for this vast collective sepulcher, Sheol, literally means "the grave." Unlike *qever*, which also denotes the grave, Sheol took on a wide variety of meanings. It sometimes indicated a specific place with definable physical attributes; sometimes it represented the innards of the earth; and sometimes it simply served as a synonym for death.[14] A few quotations will indicate the spectrum of connotations associated with Sheol. Jacob fears the possible loss of his favorite son, Joseph, believing that it "would bring down my gray hairs to Sheol" (Genesis 42.38, 44.29, 44.31). In this expression Sheol is a synonym for death. When Jacob is shown the bloodstained coat of many colors and told that Joseph was killed, he loses all desire to live and moans: "I shall go down to Sheol to my son, mourning" (37.35). Preferring the company of his son to life itself, Jacob ponders going to the land of the dead. In David's charge to Solomon, he cautions him against letting Joab escape unpunished in these terms: "Do not let his gray head go down to Sheol in peace" (1 Kings 2.6). As for Shimei, Solomon should "bring his gray head down with blood to Sheol" (1 Kings 2.9). In these passages, Sheol is simply the destination of the dead, said to be downward, presumably beneath the earth, like a grave.

Sometimes, as in Psalm 31, one might desire the calm that would result from one's enemies' departure for that destination:

> Let me not be put to shame, O Lord,
>> for I call on thee;
> Let the wicked be put to shame,
>> let them go dumbfounded to Sheol.
> Let the lying lips be dumb,
>> which speak insolently against the righteous
>> in pride and contempt.
>
>> (17–18)

14. On the concept of Sheol, see Georg Beer, "Der biblische Hades," *Festschrift Holtzmann* (Tübingen: J.C.B. Mohr, 1902), 1–29; Adolphe Lods, *La croyance à la vie future et le culte des morts dans l'antiquité israélite* (Paris: Fischbacher, 1906); Christoph F. Barth, *Die Errettung vom Tode in den individuellen Klage- und Dankliedern des Alten Testaments* (Zollikon, Switzerland: Evangelischer Verlag, 1947); H. H. Rowley, *The Faith of Israel: Aspects of Old Testament Thought* (Philadelphia: Westminster, 1956), esp. chap. 6; Tromp, *Primitive Conceptions.*

As will be explained in more detail later, Job momentarily desires the peace of death as a refuge (Job 3.11–22) and Sheol as a hiding place from the wrath of God (14.13). Most, however, thank God for preserving them from death, often called Sheol. The author of Psalm 116 describes his experience:

> The snares of death encompassed me;
>> the pangs of Sheol laid hold on me;
>> I suffered distress and anguish.
> Then I called on the name of the Lord:
>> "O Lord, I beseech thee, save my life!"
>
> (3–4)

The snares of death and the pangs of Sheol are synonymous, and they are the opposite of life. But sometimes Sheol is used figuratively to mean not death itself but a precarious situation that threatens death. Thus, when Jonah survives his experience in the whale, he tells how he feared for his life and prayed to God "from the belly of Sheol" (Jonah 2.2). David, too, celebrates his release from danger by comparing his plight to death: "For the waves of death encompassed me, the torrents of perdition assailed me; the cords of Sheol entangled me, the snares of death confronted me" (2 Samuel 22.5–6; cf. Psalm 18.4–5). Death (*maveth*) and perdition (*b'liya-ah*) are both synonyms of Sheol here, each somehow equipped to entrap David. By associating these synonyms with the concept of Sheol, poets made their view of the underworld richer and more complex.

Now if Sheol has waves, torrents, and snares that can sweep the living in and retain them, then it can also have other physical characteristics that make escape difficult. An idiomatic expression, "go down to the pit" (*yor'day bor*) actually means "to die."[15] One word translated "pit" is *bor*, which means a hole dug in the ground as for a well, a cistern, or a dungeon.[16] Using this term to refer to the grave and hence the land of the dead is a simple figurative extension. It occurs in Psalm 30: "O Lord, thou hast brought up my soul from Sheol, restored me to life from among those gone down to the Pit [*bor*]" (3). The psalmist is thanking God not for resurrecting him but for preventing him from dying. This passage shows, further, that the part of the person which descends into Sheol at death is the *nephesh*, or "soul." When the person is rescued from the brink of death, it is the *nephesh* that comes back to reanimate him. Further, as will become clear, once one is dead and

15. See Ps. 28.1, 30.3, 88.4, 143.7; Prov. 1.12; Isa. 38.18; and examples from Ezekiel in the following note.

16. Nötscher, *Altorientalischer*, 210: *bor* (pit, cistern) and *sheol* were used interchangeably, indeed "promiscuously" (Isa. 14.15; Ezek. 32.18, 21, 23, 27, 29; Ps. 30.3, 88.3, 4; Prov. 1.12).

makes up part of the population of Sheol, one forms part of the *rephaim*, or the "shades," who dwell down below.

Psalm 16 relates another recovery, though the poet uses a different word to describe the grave. *Shachath* means "corruption" and alludes to the decomposition of the body in the grave.[17] It is translated as "pit" because of the clear association with the grave, a precise type of corruption in a space that can also be called a *bor*. In Psalm 16, then, the poet gives thanks after a close call with death and, through metaphor, compares death to the grave somewhat more exactly:

> Therefore my heart is glad, and my soul [*nephesh*] rejoices;
> > my body also dwells secure
> For thou dost not give me up to Sheol,
> > or let thy godly one see the Pit [*shachath*].
> Thou dost show me the path of life.
>
> > > > > > > > > > (9–11)

A similar use of *shachath* occurs in Psalm 49, which refers to men who think they will "continue to live on forever, and never see the Pit" (9). In Job 33, the pit sounds even more like a grave as the poet describes mortal sickness: "His flesh is so wasted away that it cannot be seen; and his bones which were not seen stick out. His soul draws near the Pit [*shachath*] and his life to those who bring death" (21–22).

Equating the grave with a pit emphasizes the impossibility of escape because of its depth. In Psalm 86, when the psalmist says, "Thou has delivered my soul from the depths of Sheol" (13), he is thanking God for sparing his life. Therefore, "the depths of Sheol" functions by synecdoche, referring to the whole through a part, and so is only a synonym for Sheol itself. Although the term "depths" (*tachtyoth*) may be a synonym for Sheol, like the pit, it can also identify the lowest part, the bottom, a separate space within it.[18]

Before proceeding to that aspect of history of the underworld, it is important to note how firm the concept of Sheol became. Whereas at a certain stage in Jewish history the spirits of ancestors might have competed for loyalty with God, there came to be a danger that the spirits in Sheol might

17. Tromp, *Primitive Conceptions*, 69–71. On page 70, Tromp argues that in this passage (Ps. 16.10), *shachath* "serves as a local name," i.e., denotes a place, perhaps the "place of corruption." The Qumran evidence for the existence of *sht* (= corruption) in Hebrew suggests that the Hebrew Bible might have known this meaning as well (ibid.).

18. Samuel J. Fox, *Hell in Jewish Literature* (Northbrook, Ill.: Whitehall, 1972), 36.

constitute a world of their own, independent of divine power.[19] Perhaps God can bring back a sick person from the brink of Sheol, but does his writ run down below? Perhaps it is a separate area, where God's rule does not reach.

Tending in that direction are some passages that draw on the spirit of Abraham's argument with God over Sodom. They resemble dialogues in which men close to death try to convince God that he should not let them die, because they could not praise him from Sheol. In Psalm 6, the poet, believing death to be near, prays for his life and reminds God that "in death there is no remembrance of thee, in Sheol who shall give thee thanks?" (5).

In Isaiah 38, the context is equally explicit. When Hezekiah, king of Judah, learned from the prophet that he was about to die, he appealed in prayer directly to God. Much like Job, he argued that he had acted faithfully and done good with a whole heart all his life. God answered through Isaiah that he would add fifteen years to his life. In his poem of thanksgiving, Hezekiah commends God for holding him back from "the pit of destruction" (shachath b'lee)—another synonym for Sheol rather than a particular part of it (17). Then he reasons that God would have made a big mistake to let him die, because "Sheol cannot thank thee, death cannot praise thee; those who go down to the pit [bor], cannot hope for thy faithfulness" (18). Only the living can thank you, says Hezekiah, as I do this day (19).[20]

The passage cited to illustrate the figurative use of the term bor (pit) expresses a similar sentiment. Remember that the psalmist has had a close brush with death, but God has called him back from the bor. Then, in retelling the story, he asks, "What profit is there in my death, if I go down to the Pit [shachath]? Will the dust praise thee? Will it tell of thy faithfulness?" (Psalm 30.9).

Psalm 88 illustrates this reasoning too. The poet declares his nearness to death. "Let my prayer come before thee. . . . For . . . my life draws near to Sheol. I am reckoned among those who go down to the Pit" (yor'day bor) (2–4). Even though the poet may have justly provoked God's wrath (7, 16), in his prayer he asks God to consider the cost of punishing him with death:

> Dost thou work wonders for the dead [methim]?
> Do the shades [rephaim] rise up to praise thee?
> Is thy steadfast love declared in the grave,
>   or thy faithfulness in Abaddon?

19. Lods, La croyance, 225.

20. For more on this line of thought, see Nötscher, Altorientalischer, 212. See also Josef Scharbert, Nachtrag zum Neudruck (Afterword to the reprinted edition of Nötscher [1980]), 349–97, esp. 387–96, for an extensive bibliography on Sheol as well as resurrection, covering scholarship published between 1926 and 1970.

> Are thy wonders known in the darkness,
>> or thy saving help in the land of forgetfulness?

(10–11)

All these terms function synonymously here: the grave, Abaddon, darkness, the land of forgetfulness and, from just above, the pit, destruction. All are parallel to Sheol, which was already (in verse 3) declared the poet's destination should he die.

These parallel expressions add clarity to the concept of the world beyond the grave. Moreover, this passage provides a name for the dead. These shades called *rephaim*, used in parallel with *methim* for "the dead," provide a population of the underworld consisting of more ordinary folk than the elohim represented by Samuel. Proverbs 9.18 also locates the rephaim below: "But he does not know that the [*rephaim*] are there, that her guests are in the depths of Sheol." Isaiah, too, names the dead. In declaring loyalty to God, the prophet concedes that Israel has known other rulers but that the righteous acknowledge only him as Lord. Of those others he says, "They are dead [*methim*], they will not live; they are shades [*rephaim*], they will not arise. To that end, thou hast visited them with destruction and wiped out all remembrance of them" (26.14). Since these are enemy kings or perhaps wicked kings of Judah, Isaiah desires the separation. What matters in this context, however, is the terms used to describe inhabitants of the land from which they will not return.[21]

Thus, the separation of Sheol from either human awareness or God's consideration might be desired or not. Yet no question could remain as to whether the dead are free of God's power.[22] The prophet Amos reports the Lord's warning to the wicked of Israel: "Not one of them shall escape. Though they dig into Sheol, from there shall my hand take them; though they climb up to heaven, from there I will bring them down. Though they hide themselves on the top of [Mount] Carmel, from there I will search out and take them; and though they hide from my sight at the bottom of the sea, there I will command the serpent, and it shall bite them" (9.1a–3). This God rules the heavens and the earth, from the top of the mountain to the depths of the sea, and even below the surface, where one must dig. The author of Psalm 139 internalizes this same perspective. Such a God knows his wor-

---

21. There are two principal meanings of the term *rephaim*—the one given here, i.e., shades of the departed, and the race of giants who inhabited the land of Canaan before the Hebrews. See Eichrodt, *Theology of the Old Testament* 2:214 n. 1. For an update including new evidence from Ugaritic texts, see the material Spronk sums up, *Beatific Afterlife*, 195–96, 227–29.

22. Nötscher, *Altorientalischer*, 211–15.

shipers, inside and out, in word and deed, even before thoughts arise. Therefore, "Whither shall I go from thy Spirit? Or whither shall I flee from thy presence? If I ascend to heaven, thou art there! If I make my bed in Sheol, thou art there!" (7–8)

The notion that God rules the universe from its farthest limits to its innermost recesses and the suggestion that with God's help one can avoid death or Sheol also carry the implication that his anger can send one there directly. After escaping from the Egyptians through the Red Sea, the Hebrews gave thanks, saying: "Thou didst stretch out thy right hand, the earth swallowed them" (Exodus 15.12). If one ignores Sheol as a metaphor signifying destruction, the question arises, if the earth swallows God's enemies, where do they go?

One answer occurs in the resolution of Korah's rebellion.[23] During the years in the wilderness, Moses announced that only the descendants of Aaron would possess the priesthood (Numbers 3, cf. Leviticus 10.8–15). But Korah, Dathan, and Abiram opposed establishing a monopoly for one clan. They challenged Moses, claiming that all were equally holy. Two hundred fifty heads of household came out with incense in their censers to show that their offerings were also acceptable. So fundamental a conflict about the religious organization of the community had to be resolved. Moses asked the three clan leaders to stand before their tents with their wives and children and asked the others to move away from them. What followed was a warning to any who would challenge the priesthood: "The ground under them split asunder; and the earth opened its mouth and swallowed them up, with their households and all the men that belonged to Korah and all their goods. So they and all that belonged to them went down alive into Sheol; and the earth closed over them, and they perished from the midst of the assembly" (Numbers 16.31–33). Not only the ringleaders and their families were punished: "And fire came forth from the Lord and consumed the two hundred and fifty men offering the incense. [And this happened] . . . so that no one who is not a priest, who is not of the descendants of Aaron, should draw near to burn incense before the Lord, lest he become as Korah and his company" (Numbers 16.35, 40). In addition to explicitly making divine punishment a sanction enforcing adherence to religious authority, this account locates Sheol beneath the earth, where it is entered through a mouth, and associates it with fire.[24] It is a sanction against any challenge to the priests' authority, to the claim that their monopoly is of divine institution.

23. The text that narrates these events seems to combine several versions, but the climax is clear.

24. See Tromp, *Primitive Conceptions*, 26.

How different from the quiet Sheol of darkness and dust! Here Sheol seems the belly of a fire-breathing beast whose mouth devours God's enemies at a signal.

When the prophet Ezekiel predicted Nebuchadnezzar's destruction of Tyre, he portrayed the guilty city's fate in terms that also evoked the underworld.

> For thus says the Lord God: When I make you a city laid waste, like the cities that are not inhabited, when I bring up the deep over you, and the great waters cover you, then I will thrust you down with those who descend into the Pit [bor], to the people of old, and I will make you to dwell in the nether world [eretz tachtyoth], among primeval ruins, with those who go down to the Pit, so that you will not be inhabited or have a place in the land of the living. I will bring you to a dreadful end, and you shall be no more; though you be sought for, you will never be found again, says the Lord God. (Ezekiel 26.19–21)

Sheol and the pit are below, either beneath the waters (e.g., of the Red Sea) or under the earth.[25] Again Ezekiel associates Sheol with the pit and with deep waters: "For they are all given over to death, to the nether world [eretz tachtyoth] among mortal men, with those who go down to the Pit [bor]. Thus says the Lord God: 'When it goes down to Sheol I will make the deep mourn for it, and restrain its rivers, and many waters shall be stopped'" (32.14–15).

It is clear, then, that God can send people down to the depths suddenly or, if he favors them, recall them from the brink. "The Lord kills and brings to life; he brings down to Sheol and raises up" (1 Samuel 2.6). How does he decide? To answer, it is necessary to recall certain characteristics of biblical Judaism.

DEUTERONOMIC PUNISHMENT

In general, Judaism is much less a faith, in the sense of a series of propositions requiring assent, than a law, a holy way of life to be followed. Further, Jewish law was not only a code to govern human society, but also a compact or covenant with God. The Jewish people considered themselves chosen in the sense that they had accepted this additional responsibility, that is, to observe the laws divinely revealed to them. The Ten Commandments are the most famous statement of the code, but in the traditional Jewish view, the Torah in its entirety constitutes that law. In return for observance, God

25. Ibid., 68.

would favor them with long life and prosperity; the price of disobedience would be catastrophe. The terms of the arrangement are these:

> If you obey the commandments of the Lord your God . . . by loving the Lord your God, by walking in his ways, and by keeping his commandments and his statutes and his ordinances, then you shall live and multiply, and the Lord your God will bless you in the land which you are entering to take possession of. . . . But if your heart turns away, and you will not hear, but are drawn away to worship other gods and serve them, I declare to you . . . that you shall perish; you shall not live long in the land which you are going over the Jordan to enter and possess. (Deuteronomy 30.16–18)

This, then, is the Deuteronomic outlook: obey and prosper; turn away and perish. From this perspective it is easy to see how prosperity or hardship, whether collective or individual, could be seen as a merited recompense for adherence to or neglect of the divine precepts.

In Deuteronomy 32 God teaches Moses a song recapitulating his relationship with Israel and complaining that, although he liberated them from Egypt and offered them the covenant, the Israelites have turned to foreign idols and worshiped "what is no god" (32.21). In return God threatens them with foreign invasion, plague, and death. "A fire is kindled by my anger, and it burns to the depths of Sheol, devours the earth and its increase, and sets on fire the foundations of the mountains" (32.22). The fire of his wrath will sweep the unfaithful to death by warfare, strife, and pestilence. "Then he will say, 'Where are their gods. . . . Let them rise up and help you, let them be your protection!'" (32.37–38). According to this view, the calamities that beset Israel and Judah have been brought about by Jewish disobedience.[26]

The Deuteronomic outlook functions on the individual level too. "Men of blood and treachery shall not live out half their days" (Psalm 55.23). "The Lord preserves all who love him but all the wicked he will destroy" (Psalm 145.20). Psalm 34 also says, "Evil shall slay the wicked; and those who hate the righteous shall be condemned" (21).

Individual evildoers can pollute the community, potentially making it liable to collective discipline. Thus, the community has a natural interest

---

26. J. Luyten, "Primeval and Eschatological Overtones in the Song of Moses, Deut. 32.1–43" in *Das Deuteronomium: Entstehung, Gestalt, und Botschaft*, ed. Norbert Lohfink, Bibliotheca ephemeridum theologicarum Lovaniensium, 68 (Leuven: University Press, 1985), 341–47. See also in the same volume (329–40) P.-M. Bogaert, "Les trois rédactions conservées et la forme originale de l'envoi du Cantique de Moïse, Deut. 32.43." Both articles observe that in this song God threatens Israel's enemies more than Israel itself. See Bogaert, 339.

in cleansing itself of individual sin. Deuteronomy prescribes a ceremony whereby the priests can purge the whole community of any taint from an unsolved murder (21.1–9). The need for such a ritual comes from the belief that wrong done by one member or just a few can harm the entire community.[27] Thus, on the Day of Atonement (Yom Kippur), the priests ritually gather the sins of each individual and symbolically transfer them to two sacrificial goats, one dedicated to Yahweh and sacrificed in the priest's tent, the other guided into the desert, where he is released as an offering to Azaz'el, the spirit that dwells there (to be discussed later).[28] The ceremony elicits confession of the people's sins, so that the live goat should "bear all their iniquities upon him" (Leviticus 16.22) and take them away where they can no longer harm the people.[29] These collective rituals establish the link between sins of individuals and the welfare of the community. The Deuteronomic system applies, therefore, whether the evildoers are one or many.

The most thorough catalog of blessings and curses mentioned as sanctions for obedience and disobedience is in chapter 28 of Deuteronomy (cf. Leviticus 26). The conception of reward and punishment is not different from the one previously described and this repetition and overlap betray the hands of editors and revisers. Nonetheless in a study of hell it is important to examine these punishments, which, although they are threatened in life rather than death, are clearly said to be sent from God and to punish people who turn away from his commandments.

First come the rewards for obedience. "If you obey, . . . all these blessings shall come upon you" (Deuteronomy 28.1–2). Persons, cattle, and fields will multiply (3–5, 8). Enemies will be scattered (7). You will lend of your

27. Paul E. Dion, "Deutéronome 21:1–9: Miroir du développement légal et religieux d'Israël," *Studies in Religion/Sciences Religieuses* 11 (1988): 13–22; David P. Wright, "Deuteronomy 21:1–9 as a Rite of Elimination," *Catholic Biblical Quarterly* 49 (1987): 387–403. See also Georg Braulik, "Zur Abfolge der Gesetze in Deuteronomium 16.18–21.23: Weitere Beobachtungen," *Biblica* 69 (1988): 63–92.

28. Walther Eichrodt, *Theology of the Old Testament* 2:224–25, suggests a link between Azaz'el of the desert in Lev. 14 and the fallen angel of *1 Enoch* 10:4–6. Beer derives the name Azaz'el from the word *az* (= goat) and describes the scapegoat as a homeopathic remedy ("homöopathisches Mittel"): the desert demon in the form of a billy goat is kept away by sending a billy goat out into the demon's territory. "Der biblische Hades," 12.

29. L. L. Grabbe, "The Scapegoat Tradition: A Study in Early Jewish Interpretation," *Journal for the Study of Judaism in the Persian, Hellenistic, and Roman Periods* 18 (1987): 152–67.

produce, and the nations will respect you and count you blessed (10, 12, 13). "But if you will not obey the voice of the Lord, . . . then all these curses shall come upon you" (15). One by one, the blessings of verses 3–13 are inverted and turned to hardships. "The Lord will send upon you curses, confusion, and frustration, in all that you undertake to do, until you are destroyed and perish quickly, on account of the evil of your doings, because you have forsaken me" (20). After this recapitulation, the list of curses grows beyond symmetry with the blessings. The people will be afflicted with disease, drought, and defeat (21–25). Instead of feeding the nations, "your dead body shall be food for all birds of the air, and for the beasts of the earth (26)." And they will be punished as God punished Egypt, that is with "boils . . . , ulcers, the scurvy and the itch" (27), with madness, blindness, and confusion (28). The reference to the plagues of Egypt, mentioned again at verse 60, serves partly to remind Israel of the debt it owes the Lord, who had previously liberated them by weakening their enemies with precisely those afflictions. The logic is this: what the Lord has done to your enemies to redeem you, he can also do to punish you.

A series of scenes that evoke the consequences of having no military strength, of complete disorder in the land, follow: "you shall be only oppressed and robbed continually, and there shall be no one to help you" (29). Another man will sleep with your bride, your children will be taken into slavery, your cattle will be stolen, "and there shall be no one to help you" (31). Indeed the country will be occupied by foreign powers who will impose their gods and consume your produce (33, 36).

Verses 36–48 contain another series of hardships that again reverse the blessings of verses 3–13. Foreign invasion is included once more, but this time the author delineates a punishing siege whose horrors he describes in terms as graphic as the most vivid accounts of hell. In the siege, food will become so scarce that parents will eat the flesh of their own children (53). It is worth pausing to observe that children are counted among the blessings conferred by the Lord as part of the covenant. Thus punishment for disobedience could entail depriving parents of the children "whom the Lord your God had given you" (53). Yet this account goes far beyond merely saying that the blessing of children will be removed. Instead, it emphasizes the pain of that loss. In the siege, "the man who is the most tender and delicately bred among you will grudge food to his brother, to the wife of his bosom, and to the last of the children who remain to him; so that he will not give to any of them any of the flesh of his children whom he is eating, because he has nothing left him" (54–55). While men will be driven to commit atrocities using violence, women will commit unspeakable acts in secret.

The most tender and delicately bred woman among you, who would not venture to set the sole of her foot upon the ground because she is so delicate and tender, will grudge to the husband of her bosom, to her son and to her daughter, her afterbirth that comes out from between her feet and her children whom she bears, because she will eat them secretly, for want of all things, in the siege and in the distress with which your enemy shall distress you in your towns. (56–57)

These laws are written, the text continues, "that you may fear this glorious and awful name, the Lord your God" (58). Again, the threat is resumed: "If you are not careful to do all the words of this law which are written in this book," God will bring upon you afflictions, sicknesses, and "all the diseases of Egypt" (58, 60).

Four times the curses have been listed, some with horrible amplification. Yet possibly someone still imagines that the disobedient might be spared some particular horror. On the contrary, no escape is possible: "Every sickness also, and every affliction which is not recorded in the book of this law, the Lord will bring upon you, until you are destroyed" (61). Surely God will be saddened by the failure of his contract with a people. Surely he will punish them only with regret. The reverse is true: "And as the Lord took delight in doing you good and multiplying you, so the Lord will take delight in bringing ruin upon you and destroying you" (63). The Lord will scatter you among the nations, where you will live in the greatest insecurity, always unsure of your survival. Time will pass exceedingly slowly, so that your very life will become a torment, from morning to evening (64–67).[30]

The next suggestion, though it is listed last, may be an alternative idea rather than the next event in a sequence. The Lord will return the disobedient nation to Egypt, where the men and women will be offered for sale as slaves, but they will be so miserable that no one will buy them (68). Clearly, the only end to this excruciating existence will be death, or as the text says in several places, "until you are destroyed" (20, 61, 63). Deuteronomy 28 makes destruction the longed-for culmination of long-term suffering.

However harsh the penalties, they are due for breach of contract. Do not swindle the Lord! Deuteronomy 28 begins with a list of benefits provided,

30. The harshness of this passage is extreme. It is necessary to balance it against the idea of covenant, the promised blessings, and the many expressions of thanks for God's willingness to withhold deserved punishment. In a passage examined above, Hezekiah thanks God for disregarding his sin and granting him further life (Isaiah 38.17b). Psalm 106, in particular, lists all the offenses of Israel and the consequent punishments but shows how each was tempered with mercy.

and the terms are clear. The children to be eaten are reminders of past fertility; so it is not God who has broken his word. Similarly, the threat of affliction with the ten plagues or of return to Egypt calls to mind benefits previously conferred upon a people who owe in return only obedience—an obedience, it should be added, that will further multiply the blessings.

Deuteronomy 28 deals with the Deuteronomic system as it applied to the whole community. It also functioned on the individual level. Within its general framework, however, is a special set of provisions worth particular note. These are sayings that describe the punishment of wickedness by the wicked deed itself. By this mechanism one punishes oneself by one's own wicked action, and the harm one does is harm to oneself. In this view the world is so composed that the perpetrator of evil becomes his or her own victim. Because these statements all show the subject of the verb that describes the action becoming the object of that same action, I call this "reflexive justice."[31]

In Psalm 7, the poet prays that the wicked will fall into the pit they dug with their own hands, that their mischief will return upon their own heads (15, 16).[32] Their own nets should catch the wicked in Psalm 141, verse 10. In Psalm 94, the poet prophesies that God will bring back on the wicked "their iniquity" (23). Reflexive justice also works for whole peoples. Psalm 9 speaks of nations who "sink in the pit which they made; in the net which they hid has their own foot been caught" as "the wicked are snared in the work of their own hands" (15, 16). A similar logic structures Psalm 64. Evildoers aim words like arrows and shoot from ambush at the blameless (3–4). They will be undone "because of their [own] tongue" (7–8). Isaiah looks forward to the time when "the house of Israel will take captive those who were their captors and rule over those who oppressed them" (14.2). Against the deporters, the psalmist yearns: "O daughter of Babylon, you devastator! Happy shall he be who requites you with what you have done to us!" (Psalm 137.8).

31. Mitchell Dahood, *Psalms 100–150*, 3d vol. of *Psalms: Introduction, Translation, and Notes*, in *The Anchor Bible*, vol. 17A (Garden City, N.Y.: Doubleday, 1970), 304, comments, "The law of retribution requires that evil-doers be done in by the same means they used to harm others."

32. See Mitchell Dahood, *Psalms 1–50*, 1st vol. of *Psalms: Introduction, Translation, and Notes*, in *The Anchor Bible*, vol. 16 (Garden City, N.Y.: Doubleday, 1966), 47, concerning the wordplay and puns in Psalm 7, which reinforce the sense of fittingness of this "reflexive justice." See also Robert L. Hubbard, "Dynamistic and Legal Processes in Psalm 7," *Zeitschrift für alttestamentliche Wissenschaft* 94 (1982): 267–79.

The next verse of Psalm 137, however, unites a new theme to that of reflexive justice. Beyond simply hoping to see retribution exacted against offenders by precisely the same evil that they originally inflicted, the prophet foretells another vengeance, this one carried out by a third agent: "Happy shall he be who takes your little ones and dashes them against the rock!" (137.9). Psalm 140, too, moves from reflexive justice to third-party vengeance as the poet prays the Lord not to further the plots of the wicked: First it is their own evil, "the mischief of their lips" (9) that should overwhelm them, but then the punishment should continue: "Let burning coals fall upon them! Let them be cast into pits, no more to rise!. . . . Let evil hunt down the violent man speedily! (10–11). In these two cases, the vengeance is to be wrought on the evildoer not through the deed itself, not by his victim, but by a third, unnamed agent.

It is clear that reflexive justice carries its own rationale within it. When evil circles back on its perpetrators, there is no need to explain why their suffering was just. If, conversely, one seeks a broader vengeance on one's enemies, the supplicant must show why they deserve that fate. In Psalm 139, the psalmist explains that it is because he is pure and loves God, whereas his enemies are God's enemies too.

> O that thou wouldst slay the wicked, O God,
>> And that men of blood would depart from me,
> men who maliciously defy thee,
>> who lift themselves up against thee for evil!
> Do I not hate them that hate thee, O Lord?
>> And do I not loathe them that rise up against thee?
> I hate them with perfect hatred;
>> I count them my enemies.
>
> (19–22)

Why should it be necessary in Psalm 139 to appeal to God to do what he said, in Deuteronomy 28 and many other places, he would do? If God destroys the wicked, how can they survive to provoke these imprecations? What prevents the functioning of reflexive justice, according to which evil punishes itself? Pleas for vengeance such as this one make it clear that the armies of Judah and the administrators of its cities could not cleanse the world of evil on their own. Only a mounting perception of worldly injustice could prompt these biblical authors to write as if it were necessary to remind God of his obligations. These petitions imply that no human efforts, only divine agency, can right these wrongs. For that reason, they give evidence of an understanding that justice cannot be attained by humans but must be postponed until God sees fit to arrange matters properly; justice must be sublimated. The postponement or sublimation of justice, however, does not fit the Deuteronomic scheme. Like that of Hesiod's Dike, Deuteronomic justice is visible. When poets need to trust in a better future, a different model is operating.

Because the Deuteronomic system measures justice according to standards of prosperity and adversity in life, some have argued that biblical Judaism contains no concept of the afterlife and that all its rewards and punishments were confined to this world. Although the Deuteronomic system is the most prominent response to evil in the Hebrew Bible and remains influential to this day, other options were explored and preserved as "minority opinions" within the biblical text.

Other interpretations looked to the future for an escape from persecution. According to one of these forward-looking approaches, Israel was, if not innocent of abuses, at least disciplined by hardship. If the Israelites remained true under these trials, after a time a leader would come, a Messiah, who would establish an invincible and just regime whose law would enlighten the world. Jews still await the coming of that Messiah. Christians regard this as the most fruitful, indeed prophetic, approach to the question of evil because it was realized, they believe, in Jesus of Nazareth.

Messianism, however, is only one of these alternative interpretations of how Israel's suffering and God's promises could be reconciled. Other views necessitated waiting for vindication until after death. The next chapter leaves the Deuteronomic system and messianism aside to explore the Bible's other explanations of retribution for oppression and wickedness.

Dividing the Dead

The central concept of justice in the Torah is set forth in Deuteronomy. It consists of rewards for adherence to, and punishments for neglect of, Israel's covenant with God. These punishments frequently entailed remarkable suffering—famine, plague, defeat, captivity—prior to an early, if not ignominious, death. After death, however, the wicked and the good alike descended to a single, vast receptacle called Sheol, "the grave." In the light of prolonged foreign domination of Judah, the Babylonian Exile (586–538 B.C.E.), and the much-resented prosperity of Jews who flaunted their disregard of the law, it began to appear that God did not visit his wrath as promptly as he promised. Although the Deuteronomic system permeates many portions of the Hebrew Bible and remains influential today, the Bible preserves some passages, and even whole books, in which writers considered other possibilities.

Dissatisfaction with the Deuteronomic view was the first stimulus to the exploration of what would come to be called hell. The seekers of an alternative solution saw too many evildoers who were not cut off from life. Foreign rulers imposed terrible hardships on the whole populace. Within the Jewish community itself the greedy and ambitious suffered no horrible end. Moreover, if their sins were to bring calamity on the whole community—the Deuteronomic view—why should the righteous have to share in the punishment? Could God approve such injustice? Although there are hints of it earlier, discussion of this option took place in portions of the Bible referred to as the Wisdom Literature.[1] It is the subject of this chapter.

THE CALL FOR MORAL DEATH

The prophet Malachi recognized that many in his community were disillusioned with Deuteronomic justice. In their view, as he put it, "It is vain to serve God. What is the good of our keeping his charge or of walking as in mourning before the Lord of hosts? Henceforth we deem the arrogant blessed; evildoers not only prosper but when they put God to the test they escape" (Malachi 3.14–15). The author of Psalm 73 admits that he shared this view, at least for a time, in a crisis of faith. "I was envious of the arrogant when I saw the prosperity of the wicked" (3). Why should one do God's will if he does not prevent the wicked from doing theirs. The wicked scoff at justice and "loftily they threaten oppression" (8). The people are intimidated by the brazenness and blasphemy of the impious, who taunt the believers by claiming that God does not know the difference. "How can God know? Is there knowledge in the Most High?" (11). Despite their arrogance, they are "always at ease, they increase in riches" (12). Do the wicked not enjoy the benefits God promised to those who follow Him? Are the righteous not excluded from prosperity? Why not profit from evil rather than suffer in righteousness? "All in vain have I kept my heart clean and washed my hands in innocence" (13). The psalmist's doubt is resolved in the Deuteronomic manner: he returns to the notion that the wicked are destroyed suddenly and terribly (18–20). In contrast, God will "receive" the psalmist even into "glory" or "honor" (24). Thus, whereas "those who are far from thee shall perish" (27), for the psalmist "it is good to be near God" (28). Although the poet recovers his Deuteronomic faith, the importance of this psalm is how it questions the appearance of injustice, God's waiting too long to destroy his enemies.

These authors were not the only ones to notice this problem. In Ecclesiastes, chapters 8 and 9, the Preacher (also referred to by the Hebrew term Qoheleth or Koheleth) explores the same question. "There is a vanity which takes place on earth, that there are righteous men to whom it happens according to the deeds of the wicked, and there are wicked men to whom it happens according to the deeds of the righteous" (8.14). And the situation is never rectified: "This is an evil in all that is done under the sun, that one fate

1. An early and influential discussion of this theme within ancient Jewish literature, biblical and apocryphal, is O. S. Rankin, *Israel's Wisdom Literature* (1936; rpt. New York: Schocken, 1969).

comes to all. . . . The living know that they will die, but the dead know nothing, and they have no more reward" (9.3, 5). Thus the Bible records doubts about the Deuteronomic system. To many people it seemed that God waited too long to visit ruin on the wicked. "One fate comes to all": neutral death. Since there seemed to be no difference between the good and the evil in life, except that the wicked advance by mocking and persecuting the righteous, perhaps they might know some difference in death. According to the Preacher, even that consolation is denied.[2] Here is a call for moral death.

Whereas the Deuteronomic system can be challenged, however momentarily, by wondering how the evil can prosper, the Book of Job examines how a good man can suffer.[3] The book has several divisions reflecting its various redactions. A preface establishes the plot of the drama that unfolds among the sons of God when the Lord vaunts Job's righteousness. One of the angels (for these are the sons of God) named Satan (literally, "the Satan") challenges the Deuteronomic system by asking whether rewards prove a person's goodness. Remove the rewards, Satan argues, and the apparently righteous person will lose his motivation to do good. God then authorizes Satan to test Job's righteousness by afflicting him with hardships, to see whether he will curse God and abandon his faith. Satan tries Job. He imposes some of the curses named in Deuteronomy 28 by removing his flocks and his children and afflicting him with terrible boils (1.1–2.8). His wife tempts him to curse God, but he will not (2.9–10). Three friends then appear to comfort Job and, until chapter 33, the book consists of Job's dialogue with them. A fourth friend, Elihu (chapters 32–37), must have been added last, for Job never replies to him. In the end God appears to Job to rebuke him for his doubts and also to chastise Job's friends for insisting on his guilt. God concedes Job's innocence, but declares himself above Job's challenge. The theophany was probably added later than Job's debate with the three friends

2. For this interpretation see Anton Schoors, "Koheleth: A Perspective of Life after Death?" *Ephemerides theologicae Lovanienses* 61 (1985): 295–303, who observes that the Preacher's view is more negative than that of the biblical tradition as a whole (303). See also Graham S. Ogden, "Qoheleth IX 1–16," *Vetus testamentum* 32 (1982): 158–69. A. A. DiLella, "The Problem of Retribution in the Wisdom Literature," in *Rediscovery of Scripture: Biblical Theology Today*, Report of the 46th Annual Meeting of the Franciscan Educational Conference, August 8–11, 1965 (Burlington, Wis.: Franciscan Educational Conference, 1967), 109–28. DiLella claims that the Preacher is the first to reject the traditional view explicitly (120).

3. Spronk, *Beatific Afterlife*, 73: "The fact that divine retribution apparently not always comes to the persons involved [the wicked] would have become a problem to the pious Israelite (cf. Job and Koheleth)."

but before Elihu's speech, since God makes no reference to the fourth friend. An epilogue, also a later addition, describes Job's return to prosperity.

The three try to persuade Job that his suffering must be a punishment for sin. He replies to them each in turn. The dialogue can be summarized as a challenge followed by a response. Eliphaz reminds Job that "those who plow iniquity and sow trouble reap the same" (4.8). Yet God's love is such, he says, that these punishments are for the good: "Happy is the man whom God reproves; therefore despise not the chastening of the Almighty. For he wounds, but he binds up; he smites, but his hands heal" (5.17–18). Elihu puts this argument more forcefully. He builds on the theme that the suffering God sends is meant to chasten (33.19), to correct (36.9–11), to draw erring men from the brink of the pit (33.18, 24, 28, 30). He claims that God "delivers the afflicted by their affliction, and opens their ear by adversity" (36.15). Thus, Job's friends advocate the Deuteronomic way. As Elihu sums up God's justice: "For according to the work of a man he will requite him, and according to his ways he will make it befall him" (34.11).

But Job is impatient with the conventional wisdom. "Your maxims are proverbs of ashes," he retorts (13.12). He steadfastly protests his innocence. In chapter 29 Job lists his good deeds (12–17), and in chapter 31 he sets forth the temptations he has avoided, inviting just retribution (5–40). Certainly, however, his current distress is not warranted. Without denying God's majesty, Job still asks who among the birds and beasts and even the plants does not know "that the hand of the Lord has done this?" (12.9). The conclusion is inescapable. If Job is innocent and still suffers, then God sends affliction "without cause" (9.17).

Zophar challenges Job's attempt to understand God: "Can you find out the limit of the Almighty? It is higher than heaven—what can you do? Deeper than Sheol—what can you know?" (11.7–8). Job intends to take his case directly to God, but while he is suffering directly under God's wrath, he cannot (13.18–21). Sheol might provide at least a temporary refuge. "O that thou wouldest hide me in Sheol, that thou wouldest conceal me until thy wrath be past" (14.13). Like a shoot from a stump (14.7), he might appear again to answer before God. "Thou wouldest call, and I would answer thee" (14.15). Job's ambivalence could hardly be more profound. On the one hand, he wishes to hide from his maker in Sheol; on the other hand, he wishes to confront him, to "maintain the right of a man with God, like that of a man with his neighbor" (16.21). Yet such a relationship is hardly possible with the one who made him and can destroy him (10.8; cf. 9.5–12). But if God, who wrongs him, is not just another neighbor, so his neighbor wrongs him if he "make[s] my humiliation an argument against me" (19.5).

Judging a man's virtue by his prosperity, in Job's view, is clearly wrong—and that was Satan's starting point.

Here, then, is the central challenge to the Deuteronomic system: the innocent Job suffers while the wicked prosper. "The earth is given into the hand of the wicked" (9.24). Or again, "Why do the wicked live, reach old age, and grow mighty in power?" (21.7) What evil ever happens to them? "How often is it that the lamp of the wicked is put out?" (21.17). The dying groan deep within the city, and the wounded cry for help; "yet God pays no attention to their prayer" (24.12). Sheol is said to snatch away those who have sinned (24.18, 19); "yet God prolongs the life of the mighty by his power" (24.22). And how can we oppose him, since his power is so great? He rules Sheol and Abaddon (26.5–6).

Envy of the wicked, however, is not Job's problem, nor does he long for their sudden destruction. Job's complaint concerns the nature of death. If death is destruction, there is no justice, for "he destroys both the blameless and the wicked" (9.22). If suffering in life strikes the blameless and passes over the wicked, then adjustments are still due. Like Abraham, Job wants God to spare the innocent. Since Job's experience shows he does not, Job yearns for an answer, for another solution. But there is no evidence of one: "God has cast me into the mire, and I have become like dust and ashes. I cry to thee and thou dost not answer me" (30.19–20). God's silence now is part of the injustice: "Yea, I know that thou wilt bring me to death, And to the house appointed for *all* living" (30.23). The chief injustice is that all the living know the same death, no matter how differently they lived: "One dies in full prosperity, being wholly at ease and secure. . . . Another dies in bitterness of soul, never having tasted of good. They lie down alike in the dust, and the worms cover them" (21.23–26). The same worms cover the wicked and the just! Like the Preacher in Ecclesiastes, Job resents the lack of distinction in death.[4] This is a call for postmortem discrimination. The good and the wicked, Job seems to say, should not know the same grave.[5]

Will death be only a continuation of life? Will the wicked escape to sleep in peace with Samuel? Will the tables never be turned? The Deuteronomic system affirms God's rule over life and his ability to send humans to Sheol. But God rules death too: "The shades [*rephaim*] below tremble, the waters

4. John E. Hartley articulates a similar view of Job in *The Book of Job*, New International Commentary on the Old Testament, ed. R. K. Harrison (Grand Rapids, Mich.: Eerdmans, 1988). DiLella, "The Problem of Retribution," also agrees that Job questions the traditional doctrine of retribution but insists that he finds faith in the end.

5. Neither Hartley nor DiLella, cited in the previous note, suggest that Job's arguments carry this implication.

and their inhabitants. Sheol is naked before God, and Abaddon has no covering" (26.5–6). Surely the ruler of Sheol and Abaddon can redress this wrong. Can matters not be righted in the dwelling of the dead? Job's question continues Abraham's objection that God might destroy the good with the wicked, thus ending their lives at the same time. Job has accepted the hard fact that human beings may not experience justice in life, but he wants the Lord, who can make the underworld quake, to treat them differently in death. Far be it from God, he seems to be paraphrasing Abraham at Genesis 18.25, to let the "righteous fare as the wicked!" Elihu understands the thrust of Job's words. He accuses him of adding "rebellion to his sin" (34.37). If God rules death as he rules life, Job must simply accept whatever comes.

Job gives no answer to Elihu. The dialogue is interrupted by the direct appearance of God, who "answered Job out of the whirlwind" (38.1). The Lord sets forth his credentials as creator and regulator of the world: "Where were you when I laid the foundation of the earth?" (38.4) "Have you commanded the morning since your days began?" (38.12). "Have the gates of death been revealed to you, or have you seen the gates of deep darkness?" (38.17). Can you hunt Behemoth or fish up Leviathan out of the deep? (40.15–41.34). Can a human accuse the Lord? "Will you even put me in the wrong? Will you condemn me that you may be justified?" (40.8). So challenged, Job retreats and declares his repentance (42.6).

Then (without reference to Elihu), God criticizes the three friends, saying, "You have not spoken of me what is right, as my servant Job has" (42.7). As if in further vindication of Job, God agrees to hear his prayer on behalf of his friends and "blesse[s] the latter days of Job more than his beginning" (42.8, 12).

Job's experience, therefore, and his articulate complaint, challenge the belief in the nature of death as it existed when his story was written. This hypothesis may be tested by looking at those passages in which Job considers the world of the grave in its various guises. Given the depth of his anguish, death sometimes looks to him like an escape. Given his respect for a Lord, creator of heaven and earth, before whom Sheol and Abbadon lie exposed, his comments about the underworld are of particular importance.

In his suffering, Job sometimes imagines a gray, almost featureless Sheol, where he might escape: "As the cloud fades and vanishes, so he who goes down to Sheol does not come up" (7.9). At least that retreat, he hopes, will earn him some respite from God, "for now I shall lie in the earth; thou wilt seek me, but I shall not be" (7.21). In the last case, his escape would be into nonexistence. Consequently, he also fears that Sheol will offer no consolation. Therefore, he should find his peace in life:

Are not the days of my life few?
   Let me alone, that I may find a little comfort
before I go whence I shall not return,
      to the land of gloom and deep darkness,
   the land of gloom and chaos,
      where light is as darkness.

                                    (10.20–22)

In one passage, Job confronts the contrast between two views of death: death as peace and death as a continuation of life's injustice. If he had died at birth, he says, "I should have lain down and been quiet; I should have slept; then I should have been at rest" (3.13). But then he thinks of the mixed lot that awaits him even there, among the kings and counselors of the earth, princes with their gold and silver, stillborn infants, the prisoner and the taskmaster, the wicked and the weary (3.14–19). Job's complaint does not come only from the inequities of life. The key to Job's despair is his realization that not even death provides escape from life's injustice. The peace he seeks is tainted by the mixture of good and evil in Sheol. This obstacle to his peace in the grave adds force to his accusation.

Even if I die, he says, my peace will not be restored. What good will it do to take my hope with me to Sheol?

   If I look for Sheol as my house,
      if I spread my couch in darkness,
   If I say to the pit [shachath], "You are my father,"
      and to the worm, "My mother," or "My sister,"
   where then is my hope? Who will see my hope?
   Will it go down to the bars of Sheol?
      Shall we descend together into the dust?

                                    (17.13–16)

This passage could be taken literally to mean that one's hope is extinguished at death, that death is final. If that is Job's meaning, then the injustice remains, for death would not correct the inequities of life. Yet Job has referred to the possibility of sprouting up from death (14.7–15), to the rephaim in Sheol who quake at God's power (26.5), and despite its gloom and darkness, to the quiet to be found there (3.13). If that peace is denied because of the mixture of evil and good, then God's arbitrariness, his tendency to send affliction "without cause," can continue into the grave. Job knows he cannot change the earth. He yearns for a purge of the grave. In sum, Job's experience is made more poignant by his recognition that not even death will improve matters. The story of Job is a call for compensatory discrimination in death. If the righteous must suffer without cause in life, let them at least sleep with the innocent in a peaceful death. Job demands an end to the moral neutrality of the grave.[6] The story of Job, therefore, discloses a major difference in Hebrew views of death. Although he cannot prophesy about the other world, Job hopes that it will not simply continue the injustices of this one. The grave, Sheol, ought to offer some compensation for the innocent who suffered unjustly in life. His plea is a call for moral discrimination in the afterlife, for a moral death. Remember that "moral death" is the term I applied to a similar tendency in Greek thought, which regarded a neutral afterlife as an escape for the wicked and found equilibrium only in reward and punishment after death.

Another echo of the frustration that leads to Job's call for the separation of good and evil in death may be heard in Psalm 49, which provides the solution to the riddle posed in Psalm 73.

> Why should I fear in times of trouble,
>> when the iniquity of my persecutors surrounds me,
> Men who trust in their wealth
>> and boast of the abundance of their riches?
> Truly no man can ransom himself,
>> or give to God the price of his life, . . .
> That he should continue to live on for ever,
>> and never see the Pit.[7]
>
> (5–9)

No matter how wealthy, the wicked cannot buy exemption from death. Only through God can they overcome their natural end (the pit), and their ill-gotten gains will be of no avail in his eyes. Their misguided achievements in life are as nothing against death.

> Their graves are their homes for ever,
>> their dwelling places to all generations. . . .
> Like sheep they are appointed for Sheol;
>> Death shall be their shepherd;
>> Straight to the grave they descend,
>> and their form shall waste away;
>> Sheol shall be their home.
>
> (11, 14)

6. R. Z. Friedman, "Evil and Moral Agency," *International Journal for the Philosophy of Religion* 24 (1989): 3–30.

7. This last line can easily be taken out of context. See Dahood, *Psalms 1–50*, p. 298: "Immortality is offered to all men who are willing to put their confidence in Yahweh and not in riches."

The fate of the psalmist differs: "But God will ransom my soul [*nephesh*] from the power of Sheol, for he will receive me" (15).

The mechanics of this redemption are not clear. The psalmist suggests that he, and presumably any righteous person, will escape Sheol because God will provide what money cannot buy and invite the one to be spared Sheol into the divine presence. Like Psalm 73, Psalm 49 asserts that the righteous will enjoy God's company in the end. Whereas in Psalm 73, verse 18, a fall to ruin separates the wicked from the good, and the righteous trust they will enjoy the presence of God, Psalm 49 proposes a different solution, one that indicates a new departure: the righteous and the wicked are to be separated in death. The author is not troubled by the apparent prosperity of the wicked, because he believes the true difference between the wicked and the good appears not in life but in death. This assertion of two conditions after death answers the complaint that there is only one fate. As in ancient Greece, articulate voices in ancient Israel called for discrimination in death: two separate fates, one for the righteous, one for the wicked.[8]

SEGREGATION IN SHEOL

This great theme of distinction in the afterlife occurs first in the Book of Ezekiel, composed between 598 and 586, in the context of a prophetic announcement to Egypt that Persia will destroy it like the other peoples it has conquered.[9] The prophecy first discusses Egypt and then compares it to the nations that fell previously, which will greet its arrival in the underworld.[10] All these nations experience death differently from their honored

8. Maag, "Tod und Jenseits," 26–27, also regards these Psalms as demarcating a fundamental break.

9. For dating, see Eissfeldt, *Old Testament*, 374–78. This passage is a funeral dirge addressed to the pharaoh which belongs to a series of threats against foreign nations dated from the beginning of the deportation of King Jehoiachin in 598. The date of this particular passage may be in error, since it interrupts the chronological order of the previous threats. Nonetheless this passage would predate the conquest of Jerusalem and the destruction of the temple in 586 B.C.E. The variety of opinions on the genuineness and date for revisions and compositions of pseudepigraphical parts is reviewed by Eissfeldt, 367–72.

10. See John B. Geyer, "Mythology and Culture in the Oracles against the Nations," *Vetus testamentum* 36 (1986): 129–45. Geyer compares Ezek. 25–32 with Amos 1–2, Isa. 13–23, and Jer. 46–51, which, he argues, "share the same form" of oracles against the Gentiles. See also Georg Fohrer and Kurt Galling, *Ezechiel*, Handbuch zum Alten Testament, 13 (Tübingen, Mohr, 1955); Walter Eichrodt, *Ezekiel: A Commentary on the Book of the Prophet Ezekiel*, 2 vols., Hermeneia

ancestors. Ezekiel repeats key phrases that, for the first time in Hebrew Scripture, portray the underworld as more than mere death. His picture blends in shame and adds a discriminatory element that departs from the notion that all the dead share an equal gray fate. If oppressive nations wield their power unjustly and there is not to be a unique grave for both the oppressors and their victims, then some difference in their fate after death must distinguish them. Ezekiel provides the first indications of what those differences might be.

> Son of man, wail over the multitude of Egypt, and send them down, her and the daughters of majestic nations, to the nether world, to those who have gone down to the Pit:
>
>> "Whom do you surpass in beauty?
>> Go down, and be laid with the uncircumcised."
>
> They shall fall amid those who are slain by the sword, and with her shall lie all her multitudes. The mighty chiefs shall speak of them, with their helpers, out of the midst of Sheol: "They have come down, they lie still, the uncircumcised, slain by the sword." (32.18–21)

Egypt is no more beautiful than any other nation and not exempt from overthrow. It too must go down to the pit. The voice of a dispatching agent, or perhaps the prophet, mocking Egypt slightly, pronounces sentence. "Why should you be different?" this voice seems to ask. "Go down to the grave." What follows contrasts markedly to what other texts have shown of Sheol. There seems to be a special section of the underworld for the uncircumcised and, within it, a place for those slain by the sword, and these are separated by nation. Ezekiel imagines the dead kings who have preceded Egypt awaiting its arrival, commenting, as if on some natural occurrence, "Here comes Egypt too."

Egypt will join Assyria and the peoples of Elam, Meshech, and Tubal. Repeated formulas reinforce the notion of separate areas within the pit, and a few details further distinguish its special parts:

> Assyria is there, and all her company, their graves round about her, all of them slain, fallen by the sword; whose graves are set in the uttermost parts of the Pit, and her company is round about her grave; all of them slain, fallen by the sword, who spread terror in the land of the living. Elam is there, and all her multitude about her grave; all of them slain, fallen by the sword, who went down uncircumcised into the nether world, who spread

(Philadelphia: Fortress Press, 1979–83).

terror in the land of the living, and they bear their shame with those who go down to the Pit. They have made her a bed among the slain with all her multitude, their graves round about her, all of them uncircumcised, slain by the sword; for terror of them was spread in the land of the living, and they bear their shame with those who go down to the Pit; they are placed among the slain. Meshech and Tubal are there, and all their multitude, their graves round about them, all of them uncircumcised, slain by the sword; for they spread terror in the land of the living. (32.22–26)

Each of the destroyed nations that opposed Judah is uncircumcised and lies in multitudes. Each has a principal grave bearing the name of the people, around which ("their graves round about her") the slain are buried separately (around, rather than in the central grave), because they died "by the sword," having "spread terror in the land of the living."

In a passage with so many parallels and repetitions, there is a great temptation to apply individual details to all. For example, all but Assyria are called uncircumcised, though surely Assyria was not circumcised. Those of Elam "bear their shame with those who go down to the Pit," and the special graves in Assyrian territory are "set in the uttermost parts of the Pit [yarch'tey bor]" (23). Is it legitimate to ascribe shame and location in the depths of the pit to this whole group of Judah's enemies even though these characteristics are ascribed only to Elam and Assyria respectively?

As if to answer in the affirmative, Ezekiel (or perhaps a later editor) recapitulates the separateness of these ancient enemies: "And they do not lie with the fallen mighty men of old who went down to Sheol with their weapons of war, whose swords were laid under their heads, and whose shields are upon their bones; for the terror of the mighty men was in the land of the living" (32.27). If "the fallen mighty men" are the previous kings or heroes of each of the peoples and being buried "round about" them is the same as "not lying with" them, this verse reinforces the previous six and further suggests that these warriors were denied burial in the place of honor (with their kings) and in the traditional way (with their swords beneath their heads and their shields on their chests). Indeed, the reference to burial "in multitudes" might indicate that these evil warriors were lying about in heaps, unburied (cf. Isaiah 14.19–20; 66.24), but that idea is contradicted by reference to their graves—unless these are mass graves. Although the precise layout of these burial sites is uncertain, it is clear that the bodies of those who "spread terror in the land of the living" are disposed of less honorably than others of their people and, since these circumstances of burial remain unchanged, they describe the netherworld too (32.18, 21). Through the pharaoh, Egypt will know the same fate: "So you shall be broken and lie among the uncircumcised, with those who are slain by the sword" (28), for the same reason, "for he spread terror in the land of the living" (32).

Verses 29 and 30 may also be interpolations, because they interrupt the mention of Egypt in verses 28, 31, and 32, which completes the main thrust of chapter 32's catalog of Egypt's predecessors in the netherworld. Verses 29 and 30 nonetheless complement the preceding discussion by applying these formulas of disgrace to still other peoples, "the princes of the north and all the Sidonians, . . . who . . . bear their shame with those who go down to the Pit" (30). Shame, then, is not restricted to the violent Elamites.

The shame applied to Elam, the princes of the north, and the Sidonians, together with differentiation of the graves of the violent around, rather than in, the central grave of their people and Assyria's confinement in the "uttermost parts," makes it clear that this passage assigns different places in the netherworld to those who abuse military force.[11] That is, Ezekiel 32 applies moral criteria to the arrangement of the netherworld. Sheol is acquiring a map. This combination of shame and segregation is the earliest reference in the Hebrew Bible to what would come to be called hell and the beginning of the Hebrew Bible's answer to Job's complaint (or a complaint that found its archetypal expression in Job), namely, that all the dead are treated equally. When it designates a separate part of Sheol, then, the pit signifies denial of honorable burial. It inflicts no punishment but confines those buried there in a place of shame.

The layout of the otherworld described in Ezekiel 32 recalls the ancient Egyptian mapping, whereby souls of different types are distributed among separate regions of the Tuat. Whereas the Egyptian sources parceled the dead among territories traversed by a river or a road, Ezekiel 32 portrays an underworld burial field dotted with tombs. The tendency, apparent in verse 27, to make difference in the arrangement of corpses for burial carry over into the netherworld, as a feature of death, was developed further in later texts.

In a passage of Isaiah, probably by a continuator called Deutero-Isaiah, in addition to stigmatizing former oppressors, the poet vaunts the contrast in the enemy's fate, from captor to captive. Thus, he imagines a day of retribution against Babylon: "I [the Lord] will put an end to the pride of the arrogant and lay low the haughtiness of the ruthless. . . . And Babylon the glory of kingdoms . . . will be like Sodom and Gomorrah when God overthrew them. . . . And the house of Israel . . . will take captive those who were their captors and rule over those who oppressed them" (13.11, 19; 14.2). What was high will become low; the captives will rule the captors; the

11. Beer, *Biblische Hades*, 21.

world will be turned upside down. Nor will death be an escape: "Sheol beneath is stirred up to meet you when you come, it rouses the shades [*rephaim*] to greet you, all who were leaders of the earth; it raises from their thrones all who were kings of the nations. All of them will speak and say to you: 'You too have become as weak as we! You have become like us!'" (14.9–10). The prophecy develops the reversal in the world's mightiest kingdom exacted by death, the equalizer: "Your pomp is brought down to Sheol. . . . maggots are the bed beneath you, and worms are your covering" (14.11). The taunt continues, now addressing Babylon ironically personified as a heavenly luminary, destined to end beneath the earth. "How far you are fallen from heaven, O Day Star, son of Dawn! How you are cut down to the ground, you who laid the nations low! . . . But you are brought down to Sheol, to the depths of the Pit" (14.12, 15).

"The depths of the Pit." The Hebrew here is *yarch'tey bor*," the same place that Ezekiel assigned to Assyria (32.23) and which the Revised Standard Version translates there as "the uttermost parts of the Pit." The extremities of the pit can mean either its farthest bounds or its depths. It is a separate area reserved for the violent uncircumcised.

Isaiah's challenge does not say only that Babylon will fall, like all evildoers, to be destroyed and subject to death, as Deuteronomy would indicate. Rather, it will be put in a separate part of the netherworld and, in accord with the spirit of Ezekiel 32, it will experience shame. As Isaiah puts it, the other dead will wonder at them, and "Those who see you will stare at you, and ponder over you: 'Is this the man who made the earth tremble, who shook kingdoms, who made the world like a desert and overthrew its cities, who did not let his prisoners go home?'" (14.16–17).

Beyond attracting attention in the world of the dead, the fallen king of Babylon with his officers and army will be separated from his victims in a special part reserved for the unburied, for those who lived, or died, by violence: "All the kings of the nations lie in glory, each in his own tomb; but you are cast out, away from your sepulchre, like a loathed untimely birth, clothed with the slain, those pierced by the sword, who go down to the stones of the Pit, like a dead body trodden under foot. You will not be joined with them in burial, because you have destroyed your land, you have slain your people" (14.18–20). The imagery here recalls that of Deuteronomy 28, but the rationale is different, for here the curse endures after death. The former oppressors suffer the scorn of the other shades. Unlike the other royal dead, they lack a proper tomb. Indeed, throughout the ancient Mediterranean world, improper burial signified great disgrace.[12] Here, neglect of their

12. Tromp, *Primitive Conceptions*, 182.

corpses leaves them strewn about Sheol like carrion, under the bodies of the people they have slain (19). Newcomers to Sheol tread over them, lying about unburied.

Ezekiel 32.24 and Isaiah 14.15–20 agree that there is more than one fate in death. The wicked suffer ignominy in the deepest recesses of the underworld.[13] Shame in death is the beginning of hell.

If this passage of Isaiah is properly dated to the period of anticipation before Cyrus defeated Babylon in 539,[14] or shortly thereafter,[15] it is probably the Hebrew Bible's second earliest expression of belief in segregation after death, for it would precede the story of Job or Psalms 73 and 49. This apparent reverse in chronology indicates a vitally important point: the different approaches to death and punishment after death which occur in the Hebrew Bible do not develop toward some perfect or more sophisticated position. No linear model applies here. It is not the case that the religious writings of each century refine earlier, "primitive" ones. Rather, the different positions expressed simultaneously reflect various sensibilities within the religious community. They suggest a competition within the biblical tradition for the loyalty of reciters, scribes, and editors.

GEHENNA

The separation of good and evil in the afterlife did not grow exclusively from the deepening of Sheol or the naming of areas within it: the uttermost parts of the pit (Ezekiel 32.23), its depths (Isaiah 14.15), or its stones (Isaiah 14.19). Another place simultaneously came to exercise many of the same functions as the dishonoring pit. That place, a gully just outside the walls of Jerusalem, beyond the Potsherd Gate (Jeremiah 19.2), was a ravine called Ge-Hinnom, the Valley of Hinnom or the Valley of the Son of Hinnom (Nehemiah 11.30; cf. Joshua 15.8). The translators of the Hebrew Bible into the Greek Septuagint transliterated this name as Gehenna. Early Greek-speaking Christians used the Septuagint as their Bible and later as the "Old Testament," and so they preserved this term. As they wrote the New Testament, they distinguished Hades from Gehenna.[16] Some English translations

13. Ibid., 181–82.

14. Eissfeldt, *Old Testament*, 97, 320, though he concedes some plausibility to composition in similar circumstances before the fall of Nineveh in 612.

15. Bewer, *Literature of the Old Testament*, 210–12.

16. T. H. Gaster, "Dead, Abode of the," in *The Interpreter's Dictionary of the Bible*, 4 vols. (New York: Abingdon, 1962), 1:787–88; and idem, "Gehenna," ibid.,

of the Bible still preserve the reading Gehenna. The Revised Standard Version translates Gehenna as "hell," but supplies a footnote providing the Greek expression.

In the center of the Valley of Hinnom was a high place called Topheth. Second Kings 16.3 states that when King Ahaz fell under the influence of neighboring peoples to the extent of following their religion, he offered his son as a sacrifice to the god Molech in Ge-Hinnom. Apparently he was not alone in that practice. When Josiah instituted the reforms returning the country to the worship of Yahweh, he defiled the altar on Topheth in Ge-Hinnom to prevent sacrifices of children to Molech (2 Kings 23.10). Forever tainted as a center for the occasional worship of a false god, and possibly the sacrifice of children,[17] Ge-Hinnom was associated with burning, shame, and wickedness.

It is the prophet Jeremiah who seared the memory of these rites into the Jewish imagination. He pointedly and repeatedly reminded the Jewish people of how far they had fallen before. It is no good to protest your innocence, proclaims the prophet. "How can you say 'I am not defiled, I have not gone after the Baals'? Look at your way in the valley; know what you have done" (Jeremiah 2.23). For you have built altars sacred to Baal on the high place of Topheth in the Valley of the Son of Hinnom. You have "profaned that place by burning incense in it to other gods . . . and filled this place with the blood of innocents" (19.4) by "burning [your] sons and [your] daughters in the fire" (7.31) "as burnt offerings to Baal" (19.5). This desecrated ravine, where the bodies of sacrificial victims were disposed of, will become a burial place: "Therefore, behold, the days are coming, says the Lord, when it will no more be called Topheth, or the valley of the son of Hinnom, but the valley of Slaughter: for they will bury in Topheth" (7.32).

2:361–62; Joachim Jeremias, "Hades," in *Theological Dictionary of the New Testament*, ed. Gerhard Kittel and Geoffrey W. Bromiley, 10 vols. (Grand Rapids, Mich.: Eerdmans, 1964), 1:146–49; and idem, "Gehenna," ibid., 1:657–58.

17. For reservations on this score, see "Molech," *Encyclopedia Judaica*, 16 vols. (Jerusalem: Encyclopedia Judaica, 1978). For evidence in the affirmative, see John Day, *Molech: A God of Human Sacrifice in the Old Testament* (Cambridge: Cambridge University Press, 1989); and Heider, *Cult of Molek*. After an exhaustive review of evidence from archaeology, comparative religion, and Scripture, Heider tentatively supports the existence of this cult on an "irregular and voluntary" basis (406). See Morton Smith, "A Note on Burning Babies," *Journal of the American Oriental Society* 95 (1975): 477–79; against Mosche Weinfeld, "The Worship of Molech and of the Queen of Heaven and Its Background," *Ugarit-Forschungen* 4 (1972): 133–54.

Thus, death would always be associated with the spot.[18] The bodies of executed criminals and others lacking proper attention were discarded there. Varying from a place where innocents were sacrificed to a collective grave for executed criminals, this valley was ripe for metaphorical extension into a place of torment, though in two stages, according to Jeremiah. As a result of the evil practices, terrible calamities will befall the country (Jeremiah 19.7–9). But then, once a new covenant has been established, the tainted valley will seem an appropriate destination for evildoers, and "the whole valley of the dead bodies and the ashes . . . shall be sacred to the Lord" (31.40). Because the corruption there resembles Ezekiel's violent multitudes in graves of shame and Isaiah's image of corpses in heaps, the Valley of Hinnom eventually took on the characteristics of the depths of the pit and came also to function as the fate of the wicked. Again, adverse conditions of burial create a stigma that lasts beyond death.

In the meantime, the imagination of biblical writers focused on the character of a more severe punishment than the early death (destruction) that the Deuteronomic system threatened. Like the burning that consumed sacrificial victims on Topheth, the punishment imagined most often for the wicked was that of long-lasting fire. In Psalm 21 a fire devours the Lord's defeated enemies. "Your hand will find out all your enemies; your right hand will find out those who hate you. You will make them as a blazing oven when you appear. The Lord will swallow them up in his wrath; and fire will consume them" (8–9). In the Book of Malachi, when the prophet has condemned those who complain that God's vengeance is slow to come (3.14), he reports that God will finally consume the malcontents: "For behold, the day comes, burning like an oven, when all the arrogant and all evildoers will be stubble; the day that comes shall burn them up says the Lord of hosts, so that it will leave them neither root nor branch" (4.1). The patient who fear God will escape the conflagration. They will go forth healed and will "tread down the wicked, for they will be ashes under the soles of your feet, on the day when I act, says the Lord of hosts" (4.3). This passage reaffirms the Deuteronomic answer that in the end the wicked will be destroyed. Yet, in this case, destruction of the wicked will follow a future judgment: "Once more you shall distinguish between the righteous and the wicked, between one who serves

18. L. R. Bailey, "Gehenna: The Topography of Hell," *Biblical Archeologist* 49 (1986): 187–91. Bailey suggests that even after the altars devoted to foreign gods had been abandoned, the valley "continued to be regarded as the location of an entrance to the underworld over which the sole God was sovereign" (191). That would make it parallel to the *ploutōnia* encountered in ancient Greece. If it is true, it would also help explain how the name of the valley came to be applied to the underworld itself.

God and one who does not serve him" (3.18). The result is the final destruction of the wicked, and a new life for the righteous: "For you who fear my name the sun of righteousness shall rise, with healing in its wings. You shall go forth leaping like calves from the stall" (4.2). With the passage of time, threats of retribution were less isolated and more closely associated with themes invoking a future day of judgment, punishment for the wicked, and for the righteous, reward and renewed life. This cluster of apocalyptic themes became more common in the later books of the Hebrew Bible.

Psalm 11 presents the pattern very concisely. It contrasts the righteous and the wicked. Evildoers will know the punishment of Sodom and Gomorrah, but the righteous will see God.

> The Lord tests the righteous and the wicked,
>> and his soul hates him that loves violence.
> On the wicked he will rain coals of fire and brimstone;
>> a scorching wind shall be the portion of their cup.
> For the Lord is righteous, he loves righteous deeds;
>> The upright shall behold his face.[19]
>
> (5–7)

Similarly, in Psalm 140, verses 1–8, the poet asks God to deliver him from evil men. In imagining how liberation might come about, he employs the pattern of a future manifestation of justice with fiery punishment for the wicked and the presence of God for the righteous.

> Let burning coals fall upon [the wicked]!
>> Let them be cast into pits, no more to rise!
> Let not the slanderer be established in the land;
>> let evil hunt down the violent man speedily!
> I know that the Lord maintains the
>> cause of the afflicted,
>> and executes justice for the needy.
> Surely the righteous shall give thanks to thy name;
>> the upright shall dwell in thy presence.
>
> (10–13)

19. Marina Mannati, "Le Psaume XI," *Vetus testamentum* 29 (1979): 222–27, rehearses the difficult textual history of corrections; verse 6a in her translation reads, "Sur les impies il fera pleuvoir des pièges " (222). Her restoration of this apocalyptic verse from its "corrected" state ("coals of fire" for "snares," "traps") restores the sense of reflexive justice: the wicked are "hunters after souls" ("chasseurs d'âmes") (verse 2). God pays them back in kind, he takes them "in the snares of his wrath" ("aux pièges de sa colère") (225–26). I am indebted to Andrew Gow for this observation.

In these apocalyptic passages the good receive a reward whose end is not specified, whereas the wicked undergo destruction, usually by fire. Yet a new continuator of Isaiah called Trito-Isaiah transfers the interminability of the reward to the punishment when he imagines another fire—one that would not end. The prophet envisions a convocation of all the nations in Jerusalem. There, God will manifest himself in a sign (Isaiah 66.18–20). Whereupon some, presumably those who recognize the sign, will enter the city, where they will be welcomed as priests and Levites (21). "The new heavens and the new earth" will shelter the descendants of this regenerated elect "from new moon to new moon" (22–23). Then, those who had entered will exit the city and see that the others have been felled: "And they shall go forth and look on the dead bodies of the men that have rebelled against me; for their worm shall not die, their fire shall not be quenched, and they shall be an abhorrence to all flesh" (24).

Now Isaiah 66 has almost certainly not survived in its original form. The scene portrayed at verses 18–20, which tells of the peoples' coming together, suggests nothing of the rebellion punished in verse 24. And if "all flesh shall come to worship" before the Lord (23), what need is there to destroy rebels? Perhaps the rebels who have fallen before the city walls come to Jerusalem but fail to see "the sign." Perhaps they refuse to accept the leadership of those who, having been initiated inside, exit to lead the world under "the new heavens and the new earth" (22). Whatever gave cause to the rebels, only one line describes their punishment. Their cadavers are piled outside the walls and, within the heaps of their carrion, the worms will be undying, the fire will not be extinguished, and all who look upon them will be repelled.[20]

The interminability of this fate is of the utmost importance. Whether as rebels or as people unprepared to see "the sign" or as a sample of wicked people generally (by synecdoche), the bodies piled outside Jerusalem will suffer an unending ignominy. The fire recalls the burning of the sacrifices at Topheth in the Valley of Hinnom; the worm recalls the grave. Whatever the precise associations, the condition will not end. The fire will burn and the worms will gnaw those carcasses unceasingly.

It would be an exaggeration to claim this image as a synthesis of the two types of punishment: destruction and long-lasting suffering. The poetic device leaves a paradox that is not explained. The fire and the worm do not destroy, or else the burning and the gnawing would cease. Yet, since these are

20. See Norman H. Snaith, "Isaiah 40–66: A Study of the Teaching of the Second Isaiah and Its Consequences," in *Studies on the Second Part of the Book of Isaiah*, Supplements to *Vetus testamentum*, 14 (Leiden: Brill, 1967), 135–264.

cadavers, the "persons" involved cannot suffer. To interpret this passage further would be to "theologize" and to insist on a more systematic statement than actually exists. Suffice it to say that, in contrast to Psalms 21.8–13, 11.5–7, 140.10–13, and Malachi 4.1–3, but like Jeremiah 8.1–2, Isaiah 66.24 extends the punishment of the wicked beyond their death. Unlike Jeremiah 8.12, Isaiah 66.24 states that the torments applied to the bodies of the dead will not end.

RESURRECTION AND JUDGMENT

The book of Job and related passages indicate a feeling that the equality of the grave is unjust. Apocalyptic literature proclaims a future judgment that will separate the good from the wicked, so that they will no longer share the same soil in the underworld. In this solution, however, a problem arises if at the time the Lord comes to execute his judgment by fire (see Isaiah 66.16) he tries only those alive at that time. In that case, those who have died previously will remain in their undifferentiated state, good and bad in Sheol together. One way to rectify this situation is for the judgment to include a sentence on the dead. If the dead could be awakened, raised, so that they might undergo divine judgment and then be separated, justice could operate retroactively.

Although this line of speculation never became a major current in biblical times, some passages suggest that resurrection would serve the justice that underlay the covenant from the beginning. Indeed, the sequel to the passage from Jeremiah (7.30–32) which describes the abominations at Topheth implies that at least the servants of this altar and those who worshiped there have not been sufficiently punished by simply dying but need to be disinterred for additional humiliation and disgrace, which would serve as further punishment. Their bones should be spread around the ground and exposed to the heavenly bodies that they worshiped, and their punishment should, in effect, give them what they pursued during their evil lives: "They shall be spread before the sun and the moon and all the host of heaven, which they have loved and served, which they have gone after, and which they have sought and worshiped; and they shall not be gathered or buried; they shall be as dung on the surface of the ground" (8.2). In this case, at least, the prophet agrees with Job: the grave is too much like the quiet storehouse of the Middle Eastern netherworld, a place to which kings and priests who participated in human sacrifice could escape. The existence of such a refuge subverts right order in the world.[21] In Jeremiah, these false leaders were not

21. A crucial element of this punishment, described in the next verse (Jer. 8.3), is the humiliation of the descendants, who will, as a consequence, prefer death to life.

to be resurrected, brought back to life, but a further postmortem penalty was nonetheless to be exacted.

Although later Jewish literature would consider the subject in great detail, the Hebrew Scriptures speak very little of resurrection. Further, when the subject is addressed in the Hebrew Bible, it is not always in the context of postmortem judgment. In Ezekiel 37.5–13, it is to enable a restoration of Israel, the establishment of unity and peace to fulfill God's promise. In a vision, Ezekiel sees himself in a valley full of bones, and God orders him to prophesy to the bones in God's name: "I will cause breath to enter you, and you shall live. And I will lay sinews upon you, and will cause flesh to come upon you and cover you with skin, and put breath in you, and you shall live; and you shall know that I am the Lord" (37.5–6). These restored persons will reconstitute the house of Israel. They will have new breath and new spirit: "I will open your graves, and raise you from your graves, O my people; and I will bring you home into the land of Israel. And you shall know that I am the Lord, when I open your graves, and raise you from your graves, O my people" (37.12–13). Here is a messianic prophecy according to which the kingdoms of Israel and Judah will be reunited under King David (22–24). Evildoing will be ended, and there will be peace. In other prophecies, the simple restoration of unity, order, and peace would have been sufficient miracle. Here Ezekiel adds the resurrection of the dead.

Another important allusion to resurrection occurs in Isaiah (26.14–27.1). In this passage the prophet contrasts Judah to nations that do not worship Yahweh. Unbelieving nations are dead and suffer destruction (26.13–14), but Judah remains (15). Yet, under divine discipline the people feel as if they are dead or not yet born (17–18). Still, they have the potential of returning to the right ways. Thus, unlike those of other nations, the dead of Israel "shall live, their bodies shall rise"; the "dwellers in the dust" will awake (19). Bloodstains on the ground will reveal where they lie; the earth will uncover them and give them birth again (21). Then the victims of oppression will be restored to life. They will take shelter (20), while the Lord punishes the others: "For behold, the Lord is coming forth out of his place to punish the inhabitants of the earth for their iniquity and the earth will disclose the blood shed upon her, and will no more cover her slain" (21). Nor is divine discipline limited to humans. God's wrath also scours the earth and the sea. As God told Job that only he can control the monsters of the land and the deep, so he tells Isaiah that he can punish the wickedness of the world symbolized by Leviathan: "In that day the Lord with his hard and great and strong sword will punish Leviathan the fleeing serpent, Leviathan the twisting serpent, and he will slay the dragon that is in the sea" (27.1).

This passage, called the apocalypse of Isaiah, blends images of birth and rebirth.[22] Thus, Israel's "death" is a metaphor for the nation's condition under chastisement. Rebirth describes Israel's return to divine favor. In this view, resurrection will enable the righteous dead to be freed of oppression. The wicked will be punished, but the apocalypse of Isaiah makes no mention of the wicked dead.[23] Here God wreaks his vengeance on the living wicked. Will the wicked dead escape punishment?

The prophet Daniel foretells a resurrection that explicitly includes the wicked—a double resurrection.[24] Daniel sees forward to a time of trouble that would test everyone. Those whose names appeared in God's book would be delivered (Daniel 12.1). The scrutiny would also review the dead: "And many of those who sleep in the dust of the earth shall awake, some to everlasting life, and some to shame and everlasting contempt" (2). It is not clear why only "many" (rather than "all") will be resurrected. Nonetheless, those who are judged will experience contrasting fates of equal consequence. "The wicked shall do wickedly" (10), but the wise "shall shine like the brightness of the firmament" (3). The wise are "those who turn many to righteousness" (3). They "shall purify themselves and . . . be refined . . . [and] understand" (10). In both cases, the final condition will endure everlastingly. Unlike the apocalypse of Isaiah, which foresees a liberation of the innocent from death but says nothing of the wicked, Daniel's vision includes a trial for both the righteous and the wicked dead. Here is an innovation of tremendous moment! Christian writers later seized eagerly on this prophecy. It provided the basis for a Last Judgment of stark simplicity, one foundation of another faith.[25]

There are significant differences between these three prophecies of resurrection. The bones in Ezekiel's field will be resurrected to form a new, united Israel under King David, free from transgression and weakness (37.23–24),

22. Authorship of the apocalypse of Isaiah, chaps. 24–27, is hotly contested. Some attribute it to Trito-Isaiah, others discern the hand of a fourth Isaiah, and some maintain it is by either the first Isaiah or by Deutero-Isaiah. For a beginning, see Paul L. Redditt, "Once Again, the City in Isaiah 24–27," *Hebrew Annual Review* 10 (1986): 317–35.

23. George W. E. Nickelsburg, Jr., *Resurrection, Immortality, and Eternal Life in Intertestamental Judaism*, Harvard Theological Studies, 26 (Cambridge: Harvard University Press, 1972), 18.

24. For this expression, see Nickelsburg, *Resurrection*, 22.

25. See Louis F. Hartman and A. A. DiLella, *The Book of Daniel*, vol. 23 of *The Anchor Bible* (Garden City, N.Y.: Doubleday 1978). They comment on this passage: "The inspired author of 12:1–2 is the first Old Testament writer to affirm unambiguously the truth of eternal life after death for at least some individuals, viz. the righteous Jews" (308–9). See also DiLella, "Problem of Retribution," 109–12.

and implicitly free from oppression. That Israel will be a community of the righteous. Yet this resurrection contains no judgment and no punishment for the wicked. Although it lays the conceptual groundwork for the resurrections seen by Isaiah and Daniel, it does not apply directly to punishment after death.

In Isaiah 26.14–27.1 there are ambiguities. The righteous victims are either born or restored to life, but it is not clear whether the "inhabitants of the earth" (26.21) are like the "dwellers in the dust" (19) and so will be raised, or whether they are the living wicked. Nor is it clear what the fate of the wicked will be. In terms of the complaint about the injustice of a single fate for all, this passage would seem to ensure that if the righteous knew no peace in life, at a suitable time, after God's wrath had passed, they could be resurrected to enjoy life as it should be. The wicked will be punished, but nothing is said of how or for how long.

Daniel's vision presents a remarkable symmetry. The wicked and the righteous are both raised from the dead, separated, and given over to fates that last forever. Daniel's picture, therefore, is the clearest. In fact, he goes beyond the punishment that Isaiah 66.24 proclaimed for the carrion outside Jerusalem, of which it is said that the fire will "not be extinguished" and the worm will "not die." Daniel passes to the affirmative and specifies, with deliberate parallel construction, that the fate, whether good or ill, whether life or contempt, will be "everlasting" (Hebrew, *olam*; Greek, *aiōnion*).

The Book of Daniel, probably composed around 165 B.C.E., was the last to enter the Hebrew Bible. Its symmetrically constructed judgment prophecy matches parallel developments in apocryphal Jewish books, particularly *1 Enoch*, or at least parts of it, which had circulated during many of the centuries when the Hebrew Bible was also being committed to writing. The next chapter will take up the *Book of Enoch* to consider some ramifications of these themes.

Before moving on to Enoch, I want to reiterate that it is not my contention that Jewish thought "developed" toward these apocalyptic speculations or that they constitute a kind of "perfection" of Judaism. I assume no such evolutionary model. In religious literature the end is not necessarily better than the beginning. On the contrary, the Hebrew Bible is composed of many strands, expressions of religious sentiments that vary from person to person and age to age according to individual outlooks and changing circumstances. The advocacy of these tendencies—sublimated vengeance, the Deuteronomic system, messianism, apocalypticism—varied over the course of biblical composition.

The coexistence of these different viewpoints within the Bible testifies to a considerable latitude maintained over several centuries by scribes, editors, compilers, and authors, who, even while inserting their own additions and revisions, retained traditional material representing different convictions. The convergence and submersion of conflicting insights is characteristic of this tradition. Excluding Job from the canon of the Hebrew Bible would have been easy. Deuteronomy and Job (I speak of Job himself, not his friends) represent opposed theories of God's use of evil. Malachi considered impious those who complained about God's delay in avenging evil. It might have seemed expedient to urge references to customs adopted from the wives of kings or to the practices of backsliding kings (veneration of Molech by Ahaz) or even the people at large (veneration of ancestors). By retaining them, the poet of Psalm 106, to mention one example, illustrated God's forebearance.

Whatever else this diversity shows, it should warn us of one thing. There is no one statement that can describe the "position" of the Hebrew Bible on a given subject, certainly not on the question of divine punishment and justice. We cannot define a Jewish position by quoting one line of Scripture, or even a collection of isolated lines. Imagine taking a single statement by one of Job's friends as representing "the" Jewish attitude. Even worse, imagine taking one of Job's declarations!

To be sure, a religious community defines itself to a large extent by selecting its canonical literature. Yet all populations are divided by differing tendencies and preferences, sensibilities and concerns. Thus whereas a large fraction lives on the central plateau of consensus, it is not always a majority, and many minority groups live on the slopes of partial agreement or at the fringes of dissent toward various extremes. This variety was certainly characteristic of ancient Judaism, where the religious community was also a political one that was divided, scattered, and partially regrouped. The texts that both reflect and define the community that produced and reveres them will also reflect this diversity. For these reasons we cannot speak of one biblical tradition or characterize Judaism by any one quotation.

Instead, we need to conceive of the Bible, like any other collection of traditionally revered texts, as a complex whole, strengthened in some places by core elements that analysis can expose as fundamental, but which move in certain tense relationships with one another. Themes within a textual tradition are not static like the pillars of a building but more like the nuclei of cells, capable of movement, division, reproduction, and lending strength to successive organisms. Perhaps they are more like the angles of an optical illusion: the more one focuses on one point, the less clear the others seem; yet, when one focuses on another, even the previous point loses some of its sharpness. Although theologians, judges, and codifiers working within a religious tradition attempt to eliminate this slippage between points, the historian need not, and indeed should not. My purpose is not to support the jurists against the poets or the theologians against the mystics, but rather to identify what moves each one, to understand how each one functions and how they interact.

Eternal Punishment

The vision of Daniel, probably written about 165 B.C.E., prophesied two eternal fates: everlasting life and everlasting contempt. In its symmetrical vision of separate postmortem destinies for the righteous and the wicked, it stands apart from the bulk of biblical opinion. Although it represents a minority point of view within the biblical canon, there is evidence to suggest that during the second and first centuries B.C.E. and during the first century C.E. the population of Jerusalem at least tended more and more to distinguish fates in the afterlife.

The variety in Jewish interpretations of the fate of the soul and the possibility of resurrection was clear to one Jewish observer of the second half of the first century C.E. Flavius Josephus was a prominent member of Jerusalem's priestly aristocracy. Though not an initiator of the Judean revolt against the Romans in 66, he commanded the Jewish forces against the Romans who came to repress it. The Roman offensive under Titus led to the siege of Jerusalem, the destruction of the Temple, and the dispersion of the Jews outside of Roman Palestine in 70. Josephus wrote an account of these campaigns in the *Jewish War* and later he composed the *Jewish Antiquities*, a history of the Jews to that time. A survivor of these campaigns thanks in part to imperial patronage, Josephus had an unusual and highly personal relationship to Greco-Roman culture. His description of Jewish thought gives it more Greek philosophical overtones than it probably had in reality. Nonetheless, his account is indispensable.

In these works Josephus described the loyalties of the Jewish community as divided among what he called three "philosophies," those of the Pharisees, the Sadducees, and the Essenes. Himself a Pharisee and clearly partisan in this account, he portrayed the Sadducees as an outmoded elite unable to govern independently of his own party, which he said enjoyed greater popular support. One aspect of religious belief that aligned the Pharisees with the people, in the opinion of Josephus, was their belief that the soul survives death and receives either the reward of a new life in another body or eternal punishment in the underworld (*Jewish War* 2.14.163; see also *Jewish Antiquities* 18.14). The Sadducees denied both the immortality of the soul and postmortem sanctions (*Jewish War* 2.14.165). Although the Essenes numbered only about four thousand in his estimation, Josephus considered them at greater length than the other sects, describing their way of life as well as their beliefs. He stressed their communal sharing of property and avoidance of marriage and made so much of the latter that he characterized a splinter group within the sect as differing on that count alone (2.13.160–61). Josephus greatly admired the Essenes' bravery in the war, which he attributes in part to their belief in the immortality of the soul, for they shared with the Greeks the idea that after death the souls of the good reside on Isles of the Blessed, whereas the souls of the wicked are tormented forever in a dark, stormy dungeon (2.11.154–5).[1]

THE BOOK OF ENOCH

Josephus does not provide the only evidence for late ancient Jewish belief in punishment after death as preserved outside the Bible. Although the date of its composition cannot be precisely set, the *Book of Enoch* (or at least its Ethiopic version, designated *1 Enoch*) stands out from a great variety of extracanonical sources for its extended treatment of the themes developed in the previous chapter. Whereas the Book of Daniel may have been committed to writing very soon after the events that inspired it, the written version of the *Book of Enoch* seems to be at a much farther remove from the origins of the oral traditions it sets forth.[2]

1. For more on Josephus's account of Judaism, see Steve Mason, *Flavius Josephus on the Pharisees*, Studia post-Biblica, 39 (Leiden: Brill, 1991). For an extensive effort to define the relationship between the parties differently from Josephus, see Roger T. Beckwith, "The Pre-history and Relationships of the Pharisees, Sadducees, and Essenes: A Tentative Reconstruction," *Revue de Qumrân*, no. 41 (1982): 3–46.

2. This is the conclusion of Martha Himmelfarb, *Tours of Hell* (Philadelphia: University of Pennsylvania Press, 1983), 172–73. On Jewish apocalyptic literature in

According to Genesis 5.18, Enoch belongs to the seventh generation of humankind, the sixth generation after Adam. He was the great-grandfather of Noah. In his 365th year, "Enoch walked with God; and he was not, for God took him" (5.24). As this mysterious line of Scripture shows, the belief arose that Enoch did not die but was carried bodily to heaven. (The same was said of Elijah.) Later writers attributed to Enoch revelations of what he saw when raised to the heavens, which have survived in Ethiopic (*1 Enoch*), Slavonic (*2 Enoch*) and Hebrew (*3 Enoch*), with fragments in other languages such as Greek. Only Ethiopic *Enoch* is relevant now, because it is probably the only one written before the coming of Christianity.

Ethiopic *Enoch* (*1 Enoch*) is a compilation of five different versions of the same story. It tells how an initially pure world was polluted by evil angels, how God planned to punish the angels and their offspring and cleanse the world, what the fate of the world would be afterward, and how in the end all would be judged. For this reason, *1 Enoch* logically follows the discussion of apocalyptic in the Hebrew Bible. Although the five versions are by different writers working at different times, its pre-Christian date and Jewish authorship are demonstrable.[3] Hebrew excerpts from many parts of *1 Enoch* were

---

general, see also Richard J. Bauckham, "Early Jewish Visions of Hell," *Journal of Theological Studies* 41 (1990), 355–85; David Syme Russel, *The Old Testament Pseudepigrapha: Patriarchs and Prophets in Early Judaism* (London: SCM, 1987); Marinus de Jonge, comp., *Outside the Old Testament*, Cambridge Commentaries on Writings of the Jewish and Christian World, 200 B.C. to A.D. 200 (Cambridge: Cambridge University Press, 1985); Leonhard Rost, *Judaism outside the Hebrew Canon: An Introduction to the Documents* (Nashville: Abingdon, 1976). The sources are translated and presented with scholarly introductions in James H. Charlesworth, ed., *Old Testament Pseudepigrapha*, 2 vols. (Garden City, N.Y.: Doubleday, 1983). Very useful is Matthew Black's translation with commentary, *The Book of Enoch or I Enoch: A New English Edition*, Studia in Veteris Testamenti pseudepigrapha, 7 (Leiden: Brill, 1985). The old translation is in R. H. Charles, ed., *The Apocrypha and Pseudepigrapha of the Old Testament in English*, 2 vols. (Oxford: Clarendon Press, 1968). See also his classic *The Book of Enoch or 1 Enoch*, 2d ed. (Oxford: Clarendon Press, 1912).

3. Michael E. Stone, "The *Book of Enoch* and Judaism in the Third Century B.C.E.," *Catholic Biblical Quarterly* 40 (1978): 479–92. Stone sums up the scholarly consensus in dating the Book of Watchers and the Astronomical Book to at least the third century B.C.E., which makes them the oldest surviving extrabiblical Jewish religious literature (484). See also George W. E. Nickelsburg, "*1 Enoch* and Qumran Origins: The State of the Question and Some Prospects for Answers," *Society of Biblical Literature Seminar Papers* 25 (1986): 341–60; J. T. Milik, ed., with the collaboration of Matthew Black, *The Books of Enoch: Aramaic Fragments of Qumran Cave 4* (Oxford: Clarendon Press, 1976). For an overview of recent scholarship,

discovered among the Dead Sea Scrolls at the ascetic community (probably related to the Essenes) that existed in Qumran from about 130 to 68 B.C.E.[4] Chapters 37–71, which are called the Book of Similitudes (or Book of Parables) were not represented among the Qumran fragments and hence may be of later date.[5] If one further excepts chapters 1–5 as a late but still pre-Christian addition and the last chapter as a very late addition, the remainder (again excepting chapters 37–71) is dated during the last two centuries B.C.E. What remains, then, is to consider book 1, the Book of the Watchers, chapters 6–36, as the core of the book, to which four other retellings were added. The first of these is the Apocalypse of Weeks from book 5; then there are the Dream Visions that make up book 4, other Dream Visions from book 5, and finally, the problematical book 2, the Book of Similitudes. Book 3, the Astronomical Writings, may be omitted because it is unrelated to the idea of justice. The Book of the Watchers and its four variants differ over whether divine punishment should consist of destruction or long-term suffering after death.

Like the compilers of many apocryphal works, the authors of the *Book of Enoch* attributed their text to an authority of hoary antiquity with a special eminence in their religious tradition. As one who never died but entered heaven directly, Enoch was a perfect candidate for narrator. The author of the Book of the Watchers claims this authority for him: "I Enoch, I saw the vision of the end of everything alone; and none among human beings will see as I have seen" (19.3).[6] Thus the *Book of Enoch* is falsely attributed to Enoch, and so is called pseudepigraphical.

The visions of "Enoch" are set in a time that is ill defined in the Bible. Genesis 6.2 explains the origin of the wickedness that infected the world in the time of Noah and necessitated the Flood. The "sons of God" (same expression as in Job 1.6), whom *1 Enoch* calls the Watcher Angels, became distracted by women on earth and abandoned heaven to mate with them. Genesis 6.4 expands the story and introduces new terminology. In this ver-

---

see Florentino García Martínez and E. J. C. Tigchelaar, "The *Books of Enoch* (*I Enoch*) and the Aramaic Fragments from Qumrân," *Revue de Qumrân* 14 (1989): 131–46, and their bibliography 149–74.

4. The significance of this discovery is set forth in Milik and Black, *Books of Enoch*.

5. See Black, *Book of Enoch or I Enoch*, 187–88, which ascribes this section to Jewish circles between 40 B.C.E. and 70 C.E. Other authorities consider this section a Christian text that may be as late as the second or third century C.E.

6. I quote the translation of Ephraim Isaac from Charlesworth, *Old Testament Pseudepigrapha* 1:13–89.

sion, the Nephilim were already on the earth when "the sons of God came into the daughters of men," and their offspring were "the mighty men [*gibborim*] that were of old, the men of renown." The Septuagint does not distinguish between the Nephilim and their offspring, translating both Nephilim and *gibborim* as "giants" (*gigantes*). It is unclear how many generations were involved and when the name changed from Nephilim (presumably the first to abandon heaven), to the more generic *gibborim*, mighty men or giants. This confusion in terminology may reflect the mixing of two groups, angels and women, which the narrator believed should have remained distinct. God abhorred the ensuing wickedness and determined to destroy the earth with the Flood.[7] These two versions of the same story, each given in just one line of Scripture, provide alternative explanations for the origin of evil in the world.[8]

As a longer version of this story, the Book of the Watchers has the allure of clarifying mysterious aspects of the origins of the human race.[9] The story it tells must be at least as old as the time of the writing down of Genesis 6.2 and 6.4, for if the story contained in the Book of Watchers did not already exist, the author of the Genesis verse would not be likely to refer so succinctly to a tale of the origins of evil.[10] Whatever the age of the legend, as distinct from the surviving text, however, we have only the text for evidence and must content ourselves with that.

In *1 Enoch* the vision or dream appears again as a means of transport to the otherworld to produce the narrator's ensuing appreciation of God's

7. This doubling of the story of Eve, making women responsible for the misdeeds of angels (as if Eve's tempting Adam were not serious enough a charge) should be noted.

8. Despite the parallels with the story of Adam and Eve, however, their story should be distinguished from the Fall of the Angels. See Ida Fröhlich, "Les enseignements des Veilleurs dans la tradition de Qumrân," *Revue de Qumrân* 13 (1988): 177–87. Bernard Teyssèdre, *Le diable et l'enfer au temps de Jésus* (Paris: Albin Michel, 1985), considers *1 Enoch* in depth in his chapter "La naissance de l'enfer," 23–48.

9. See Carol A. Newsom, "The Development of *1 Enoch* 6–19: Cosmology and Judgment," *Catholic Biblical Quarterly* 42 (1980): 310–29; and Neil Forsyth, "Rebellion and Lust: The Watcher Angels in the Aramaic Enoch Books," in Forsyth, *The Old Enemy: Satan and the Combat Myth* (Princeton: Princeton University Press, 1987), 160–81.

10. Matthew Black, *The Book of Enoch*, 124–25 compares the age of the two texts, with evidence on both sides. Paul D. Hanson considers *1 Enoch* 6–11 to be based on Genesis, instead of deriving Genesis from an older, oral version of an Enoch-like myth. See his "Rebellion in Heaven, Azazel, and Euhemeristic Heroes in *1 Enoch* 6–11," *Journal of Biblical Literature* 96 (1977): 195–233.

justice. Another common device in these tales, the guiding angel (psycho-pomp), explains to the narrator-visionary what he sees: the divisions of the underworld, its torments, and the reasons they are applied to sufferers.

The *Book of Enoch* is remarkable for the way it combines elements of the earliest history of the earth with prophecy about its end. Angelic prehistory serves as a cause of the human condition, prophesies about the end of the angels (their eschatology and ours), and thus serves as a warning. Since in the earliest days wicked angels came to earth, humans may be judged for the way they interacted with them, that is, whether a man or a woman accepted their influence or maintained righteousness despite the angels' strength.

Ethiopic *Enoch*'s interest in angels accords with a theme that was very congenial to the ascetic Qumran community, although quite foreign to the Hebrew Bible as a whole. Whereas Scripture frequently urged people to "be fruitful and multiply," *1 Enoch* advocates an angelic model for human behavior. It portrays sex as a corruption of both human nature and angelic purity. Given this sense of pollution and recognizing the imminence of the Noachian flood in the story, one might expect *1 Enoch* to endorse destruction as the preferred form of divine punishment. In fact, that tendency varies from one version to the next. Recognizing what is at stake in stories about angels and humans, let us begin our examination of *1 Enoch* with the Book of the Watchers.

THE BOOK OF THE WATCHERS

Chapters 6–11 of *1 Enoch* represent a first version, retold in expanded form in chapters 12–36. At the suggestion of the angel Semyaz, two hundred "sons of God" (the watcher angels) moved from heaven to earth to unite with the daughters of men (6). Their offspring were the Nephilim or the giants who devoured so much of the earth's produce that men refused to feed them. As a result, the giants began to devour the people themselves and also other animals. Finally, they began to eat one another.

At the same time, they taught their wives the magic of medicine (7.1). Different angels taught humans different skills, crafts, and sins. Azaz'el taught weaponry, Amasras incantation, Baraqiyal astrology, Asder'el deceit, and Semyaz taught them sex (8.3, 9.7–8) until "all their conduct became corrupt" (8.2). The earth "brought an accusation against" its oppressors (7.6). Even the dead were ready to bring suit (9.10).

In heaven, the angels Michael, Surafel, and Gabriel heard this call for judgment and carried it before God (chap. 9). God decided to cleanse the earth by means of a flood, but one flood only he promised. To punish

Azaz'el, he ordered the angel Raphael to bind him and throw him into a hole in the desert to be covered with rocks, "in order that he may not see light and in order that he may be sent into the fire on the great day of judgment" (10.6). He ordered Gabriel to cut the remaining rebels off from life and to ignore their pleas to live, even though, as angels, they expected to live forever (10.10). He ordered Michael to announce to Semyaz and the others guilty of fornicating with women that they would die in filth with their wives. They should be left to engage in mutual destruction and then be bound "for seventy generations underneath the rocks of the ground until the day of their judgment and of their consummation, until the eternal judgment is concluded. In those days they will lead them into the bottom of the fire, —and in torment—in the prison (where) they will be locked up forever" (10.12–13). And those who followed them "will be bound together with them from henceforth unto the end of all generations" (10.14). Thus the earth will be cleansed.[11] In chapters 6–11, which some authorities consider a fragment from a lost *Book of Noah*, joined to the *Book of Enoch* by a compiler, the wicked do indeed suffer punishment rather than "mere" destruction.

Beginning at chapter 12 Enoch introduces himself as one whose whereabouts was unknown to people while he was in fact "with the Watchers and with the holy ones" (12.2). He was therefore ordered as a "scribe of righteousness" (12.4) to notify the Watchers of these orders and to warn the ones who "abandoned the high heaven, the holy eternal place," that there would be neither peace nor forgiveness for them forever (12.4–6). At the same time, from earth the Watchers asked Enoch to intercede on their behalf and to read their petition. Reading it, Enoch fell asleep and had visions that enabled him to understand the fate of the Watchers (13). He reported to them by way of prophecy: "Your prayers will not be heard throughout all the days of eternity; and judgment is passed upon you. From now on you will not be able to ascend into heaven unto all eternity, but you shall remain inside the earth imprisoned, all the days of eternity" (14.4–5). The punished angels will suffer forever.

After this vision in his dream, Enoch was rapt before the divine throne (14.8–25), where God explained that the Watchers had "abandoned" their spiritual, eternal lives, in order to defile themselves with women, with flesh and blood. They had not needed wives in heaven, "for the dwelling of the spiritual beings of heaven is heaven" (15.7). But their offspring were now of

---

11. On the need for special action, see George W. E. Nickelsburg, "Apocalyptic and Myth in *1 Enoch 6–11*," *Journal of Biblical Literature* 96 (1977): 383–405. See also Corrie Molenberg, "A Study of the Roles of Shemihaza and Asael in *1 Enoch 6–11*," *Journal of Jewish Studies* 35 (1984): 136–46.

the earth, and they would live on the earth and in it. From the bodies of the Watchers had come evil spirits (15.8–10), which would oppose the human offspring of the women until the consummation of the age (15.12–16.1). Because they had revealed some of heaven's mysteries to women, the others would be hidden from them and, for their betrayal, they would "have no peace" (16.3).

Different angels then accompanied Enoch to see the boundaries of the universe. At a place where the heavens came together, he saw a pit immeasurably deep and high, "with heavenly fire on its pillars" and no cover over it or bottom beneath (18.10–13). The angel who accompanied him said, "This place is the (ultimate) end of heaven and earth: it is the prison house for the stars and the powers of heaven," for stars that do not keep God's commandments and do not arrive punctually (18.15). This would be the place of punishment for the "spirits of the angels which have united themselves with women" (19.1). In this explanation, the angel compared the fallen stars to fallen angels—a metaphor taken up again by the Christian Book of Revelation.

Enoch then saw another place, chaotic and without limit, a prison for the errant stars, which "are bound in this place until the completion of ten million years, (according) to the number of their sins" (21.6). Thus, the duration of the punishment corresponds to the gravity of the sins.

Next Enoch saw a second place even more terrible than the first: an immense fire, whose boundaries could not be seen but whose surface had a cleft from which pillars of fire poured out as far as the last sea. The angel Ura'el called it "the prison house of the angels," who "are detained here forever" (21.10). Thus the void confined the stars, and the fire surrounded the Watcher angels. This fire divided by the cleft may be Gehenna, translated to cosmic status and transported into the space beyond the earth.

Enoch then saw a third place. Inside a high mountain located to the west he saw a deep and dark space formed by four finished corners. Except that it seems more a constructed tomb than a grave, this space resembles Sheol. It is a place where "the souls of the children of the people" would gather until the day of judgment. Deep within, Enoch heard the voice of Abel calling out for the extermination of Cain's seed from the earth. The encounter with Abel reinforces the notion that this is Sheol, for here is the spirit of the first person to die, still "alive" in this sepulchral twilight.

The angel explained that the tomb is organized into three areas, but then he enumerated four. The divisions were "made in order that the spirits of the dead might be separated" (22.9). The souls of the righteous are placed around a spring of water in a lighted place. The sinners are sequestered when they die and "are buried in the earth and judgment has not been executed on them in their lifetime" (22.10). They await judgment in a place of torment. A third place is set aside for those with accusations to bring against the sinners of olden days (presumably the Watchers or the Nephilim). Then there is a fourth place, which contains "the souls of people who are . . . sinners and perfect criminals, . . . who will not be killed on the day of judgment but will not rise from there" (22.13). "Perfect criminals" probably means "completely wicked." These people would apparently suffer here forever. Learning of this disposition of the dead, Enoch praised the righteousness of God. Enoch's praise of God's justice contrasts with the complaint of Job (and the author of Psalm 49), who longed for an underworld that would separate the righteous from the wicked.

It is impossible to resolve the contradiction over these subdivisions. To posit four groups is to suggest that the righteous are separate from those who will testify against the sinners. Assuming that only the righteous can testify against them, then the accusers do not need a separate place and the three spaces would enclose: (1) the righteous, (2) sinners who did not suffer in life, and (3) the completely wicked (the "perfect criminals"). It would be idle to try to distinguish these places unequivocally, since the text is ambiguous. The primary notion is that the underworld is divided into places set aside for each of three or four separate types. Those who deserve further punishment are simply waiting here. There is an implication that the first group of sinners, those who were not punished in life, are being tested: if they curse, they will be bound there forever, no matter whether their punishment began as early as Semyaz's or Cain's (22.11). Those who do not curse may be released. They will be punished sufficiently in this place and deserve no further penalty after the judgment. The souls of the completely wicked will "not be killed," and they will never leave.

After seeing this storehouse where souls await the great judgment, Enoch saw a valley surrounded by seven mountains that would form the base of God's throne when he comes to perform the great judgment. Then "he shall take vengeance on all and conclude (everything) forever" (25.4). In the valley between the seven mountains was one very beautiful and fragrant tree which was "for the righteous and the pious." From that tree in "the northeast, upon the holy place—in the direction of the house of the Lord, the Eternal King," would come fruit to feed the blessed (25.5).

Then Uriel showed Enoch mountains and valleys irrigated by streams, but to the west was another mountain above a deep, dry, and barren valley (26.4, 5) "This accursed valley," the angel explained, was "for those accursed forever" (27.2). Contrary to expectation, it is said to be not for the Watchers or the Nephilim but for those "accursed ones, those who speak with their mouth unbecoming words against the Lord and utter hard words concerning his glory. Here shall they be gathered together, and here shall be their judgment in the last days" (27.2). Perhaps these are the souls who, when confined until the judgment in the mountain tomb of 22.10, complain against God.

In contrast to the mountain tomb, which held souls until the judgment, this place was for those who would suffer after it. In addition to being confined in a deep, dry, and burning valley, these souls would be visible to the blessed: "There will be upon them the spectacle of the righteous judgment, [for they will be] in the presence of the righteous forever" (27.3). Although the geography is mystical and symbolic, it seems that from their valley the righteous will be able to see the accursed in theirs. Thus the damned will provide an unending display for the pious. The logic of this idea seems related to the exhibition of skeletons prophesied by Jeremiah 7 and 19 for the shame of their descendants. Similarly, it is related to Isaiah 14.9–20 and Ezekiel 32.17–32, in which the taunts of the shades in Sheol add the element of shame to the fate of the wicked dead. Nonetheless, the Book of Watchers in *1 Enoch* is probably the first text in the Jewish tradition to juxtapose and yet distinguish Sheol and Gehenna. The first is a holding place for all the dead until the judgment; the second is a place of eternal punishment for the wicked.

In sum, then, the Book of Watchers offers a variation on the background to the Noachian flood as told in Genesis. Reduced to a mythic simplicity, it relates the fall of the Watchers, evil sons of God who rejected a future in God's company. They corrupted the earth with gigantic offspring (the Nephilim), science, technology, and sex. The separation of these evil beings is not clearly defined. The first fiery valleys mentioned may be for the fallen stars, the Watchers, only. Their offspring, the Nephilim, and their earthly followers will be held in captivity for seventy generations in a mountain-covered, tomblike prison, where they will be confined under trying circumstance, liable to accusation by the innocent (possibly their victims). A final judgment will come, after which some will be annihilated and others held to suffer in the bottom of another valley of fire before the eyes of the righteous forever.

THREE OTHER VERSIONS

The other fragments of *1 Enoch* variously confirm or modify the general import of the Book of Watchers.

The Apocalypse of Weeks is an allegory that retells the history of the world in ten segments, called weeks, followed by an eternity of "weeks without number forever" (91.17).[12] It parallels the Book of Watchers in telling a history in which the world's "first week" was a period of righteousness, followed by a second week (after Enoch), a time of "great and evil things," when "deceit should grow," which would call forth a "first consummation" (93.4) that we know as the Flood. Nonetheless, a man (Noah) would be saved. The history continues with symbolic references to the patriarchs, Moses, the building of the Temple, the time of the prophets, and on until the second century B.C.E. The continuity of Israel is assured by the cultivation of an "eternal plant of righteousness" (93.5), which contains a "clan of the chosen root" (93.8). In the ninth week, the "righteous judgment" will try the whole world (91.14). As a result, "all the deeds of the sinners shall depart from upon the whole earth, and be written off for eternal destruction; and all people shall direct their sight to the path of uprightness" (91.14). In the tenth week, a second assize, the "great" judgment, will renew the heavens (91.15). Then eternity will commence and "sin shall no more be heard of forever" (91.17).[13]

Here, then, with one exception, is a significant confirmation of the Book of Watchers: a period of purity was sullied leading to a purging cataclysm. History will relive these tensions between righteousness and sin until a final judgment that will restore goodness and destroy wickedness and those who practice it. In a crucial distinction the judgment will not lead to the punishment of the wicked as in the Book of the Watchers. Instead, they will be destroyed. The destruction of the wicked shows the influence of Noah's story. The biblical account also shows the Flood eradicating the wicked, cleansing the earth, which the righteous inherit.

Book 4, the Dream Visions, comprising chapters 83–90, also proposes

12. This version may be reconstructed from chapter 93 and 91.1–11, 18–19. They are separated and their order reversed because pages of the best Ethiopic manuscript are no longer in their original position. See Stephen B. Reid, "The Structure of the Ten-Week Apocalypse and the Book of Dream Visions," *Journal for the Study of Judaism in the Persian, Hellenistic, and Roman Periods* 16 (1985): 189–201.

13. If the allegory that animates this fragment is correctly understood, the sequence recounted here ends with no reference to the Maccabean uprising and therefore is dated about 170 B.C.E. Eissfeldt, *Old Testament*, 619. James C. Vanderkam, "Studies in the Apocalypse of Weeks: *1 Enoch* 93:1–10, 91:11–17," *Catholic Biblical Quarterly* 46 (1984): 511–23, contests Milik's dating and sets the date of the Apocalypse of Weeks as 170, or 166–65 B.C.E. if a reference to the Maccabean uprising can be established.

destruction as the end of the wicked in contrast to the punishment advanced in the Book of the Watchers. Book 4 doubles as a parable, retelling the history of Israel using allegorical (animal) figures.[14]

Chapters 83–85 preface what follows as background to Noah. Enoch dreams of the earth falling into an abyss (83). Therefore, he prays to God (84). He acknowledges that "angels of your heavens are now committing sin (upon the earth), and your wrath shall rest upon the flesh of the people until (the arrival of) the great day of judgment" (84.4). But Noah begs God, "Do not destroy all the flesh of the people and empty the earth (so that) there shall be eternal destruction" (84.5). Do destroy the sinners, but sustain the righteous "as a plant of eternal seed" (84.6). This is another Noachian pairing of destruction for the wicked with preservation of the righteous. Further, the expression "eternal destruction" confirms the suspicion that destruction is incompatible with punishment, because the Flood is clearly the example in mind. The victims of the Flood suffer no more after drowning.

Though dressed allegorically, the Book of Dream Visions begins parallel to the Book of Watchers. Stars descended from heaven to mate with snow-white cows, which bore elephants, camels, and donkeys (85). A heavenly messenger overthrew the stars and "bound all of them hand and foot and cast them into the pits of the earth" (88.3). The actions of the messenger are then analyzed more carefully. He conducted a judgment in three stages. First, the stars were condemned and "thrown into an abyss full of fire and flame and full of the pillar of fire" (90.24). Then he condemned the shepherds set over the flocks, whom he cast into the same abyss (90.25). Then the sheep blinded by the shepherds were taken to a second abyss, "full of fire [which] was opened wide in the middle of the ground" (90.26), and they were "cast into this fiery abyss, and they were burned" (90.26) right to the core of their bones (90.27). Then the lord of the sheep built a new house and welcomed the surviving sheep that had remained pure and called back all the other animals that had been scattered under the ample roof of the house (90.28–39). As in the other versions, the beginning of the Book of Dream Visions conforms to the structure of the Book of Watchers, but the fate of the wicked does not. In the allegory of the animals it is unclear whether those cast into the fiery abyss were to be destroyed or to live there forever in torment.

14. The last stage in this history is the triumph of the Maccabees, but it is unclear how many of the Hasmoneans who ruled afterward are included. Thus, it must be dated imprecisely to the period under either John Hyrcanus (134–103) or Alexander Jannaeus (103–76 B.C.E.). Eissfeldt, *Old Testament*, 619. See Reid, "Structure."

Book 5 (Chapters 91–107 excluding the Apocalypse of Weeks) is a patchwork of letters from Enoch to his descendants, explaining the consequences of his earlier visions. Prefatory material describes separate ways for the righteous and the wicked (91.18) and asserts that the Lord will execute judgment. The righteous and the wise will awake. Oppression and deceit will be "thrown into the judgment of fire, and perish in wrath and in the force of the eternal judgment" (91.9). Yet further on Enoch asserts that the wicked will "have no peace" (101.4), that they are "accursed forever" (102.3).

Although it cannot resolve this tension, one passage, reminiscent of Psalms 73 and 49, particularly aptly illustrates the desire turn the tables on oppressors in the afterlife. Enoch instructs his children how to reply to the taunts of the ambitious. At your graves, he says, the sinners gloat that the righteous die before they do. Why should one observe the laws? "Like us they died in grief and in darkness, and what have they more than we? From now on we have become equal" (102.7). But Enoch has seen what is written down in heaven concerning the righteous. Theirs is a bright future, Enoch tells his children; their "lot exceeds even that of the living ones" (103.4). Because their spirits will live on, they need not worry about humiliation now (104.4). This is the first hint of what will become a major theme later in history, the idea that life in this world is nothing compared to what the next life offers the blessed. It is distinctly a minority voice in *I Enoch*.

As for those who humiliate the righteous, Enoch dramatically imagines himself addressing the wicked in Sheol, where, as in the mountain tomb of 22.11, they suffer. "Woe unto you sinners who are dead!" (103.5). The sinners on earth will gloat about the deeds of their predecessors, now in Sheol, but the wicked dead already know that "they shall experience evil and great tribulation—in darkness, nets, and burning flame" (103.7). Here is a call for vengeance. It demands more than "mere" death for the wicked who taunt the righteous. They should suffer for their sins and pay the same price for tempting the righteous of today, Enoch seems to say, as the Watchers paid for corrupting earth's women.

THE BOOK OF SIMILITUDES

To conclude this consideration of *I Enoch*, it is necessary to turn to chapters 37–71, the problematic Book of Similitudes. For reasons that cannot be determined, this section of *I Enoch* is unrepresented among the Hebrew fragments found in Qumran. Thus, it was probably composed later than the Dead Sea Scrolls compiled by the Qumran community, which began about 140 or 130 B.C.E. and was destroyed during the repression of the uprising against the Romans in 68 C.E.[15]

Some of the main ascetic themes of the Book of the Watchers (particularly the angelic model for human purity in chapter 15) are echoed in the Book of Similitudes, and judging by its attitude toward the origin of sin and the fate of the wicked after death, it fits very well with the other segments of *1 Enoch*, whose Jewish authorship is undisputed. Certainly, it contrasts the fates of good and evil persons. The righteous will congregate, and the sinners will be judged and expelled from the earth; kings and rulers will be delivered into the hands of the righteous and annihilated (38).[16] The holy ones will dwell with the holy angels forever (39). Nonetheless, there is considerable evidence to suggest that the Book of Similitudes is the work of a Jewish Christian of the second century C.E., since some of its ideas occur in the latest books of the New Testament, Revelation, and 2 Peter. Certainly there are important parallels between some of its passages and New Testament ideas.[17] God is called by titles he receives nowhere else in *1 Enoch*. Some names for God in the Book of Similitudes seem more appropriate to the Messiah of Christian literature: the Son of Man, the Antecedent of Time, and the Elect One.[18]

The punishment of sinners is described in greater detail than anything encountered so far in Jewish sources. Enoch sees "a deep valley with a wide mouth" prepared to punish the sinners. In here "they shall fulfill the crimi-

---

15. Theodor H. Gaster, trans., *The Dead Sea Scriptures* (Garden City, N.Y.: Doubleday, 1976), 3.

16. Although this expression seems clear enough, there is a puzzling statement at 41.2 which describes the expulsion of sinners which follows the judgment: "And they could not stand still because of the plague which proceeds forth from the Lord of the Spirits." This expression suggests long lasting torment rather than destruction. It contradicts 38.6, but it is an exception in the Book of Similitudes.

17. Gillian Bampfylde dates the Similitudes to 51–50 B.C.E. in her article "The Similitudes of Enoch: Historical Allusions," *Journal for the Study of Judaism in the Persian, Hellenistic, and Roman Periods* 15 (1984): 9–31. The Similitudes are a Jewish text from the first century C.E., not, as Milik suggested, a Christian text of the third century, according to David W. Suter, "Weighed in the Balance: The Similitudes of Enoch in Recent Discussion," *Religious Studies Review* 7 (1981): 218–19.

18. Since they are also found in the Hebrew Bible, these names do not prove any connection with the New Testament, according to Joseph Coppens, "L'élu et les élus dans les Ecritures saintes et les écrits de Qumrân," *Ephemerides theologicae lovanienses* 57 (1981): 120–24. A lively controversy on their significance nonetheless persists. See George W. E. Nickelsburg, Jr., *Resurrection, Immortality, and Eternal Life in Intertestamental Judaism*, Harvard Theological Studies, 26 (Cambridge: Harvard University Press, 1972), esp. 68–78.

nal deeds of their hands and eat all the produce of crime which the sinners toil for" (53.2). They must consume the fruits of their illict desires in disgusting abundance. Despite this detail, however, the whole is summed up as destruction, which is not the fate of the wicked in Revelation. "Sinners shall be destroyed from before the face of the Lord of the Spirits—they shall perish eternally" (53.2).

Some details are remarkably close to their New Testament counterparts. It is said that the Elect One will preside at the resurrection of the flesh, when "Sheol will return all the deposits which she had received and hell [Abaddon][19] will give back all that which it owes" (51). This description fits the account in the Christian Book of Revelation (see 20.13) more than its antecedents in Ezechiel, Isaiah, and Daniel.

In another departure from older passages in *1 Enoch*, the Book of Similitudes, like the Book of Revelation (12.9), names Satan as a principal instigator of evil, though here he is still closely associated with the other sons of God. Chief among his associates is Azaz'el with his army and the powerful of the earth.

Like the other evil angels, Satan must be punished. Enoch sees the "angels of plague" preparing chains for Satan (53.3). He sees more chains prepared for the armies of Azaz'el, to drag them "into the abyss of complete condemnation" (54.5). Four angels will seize them and cast them into the furnace of fire that is burning that day, so that the Lord of the Spirits may take vengeance on them for bearing the message of Satan and leading people astray (54.6). Then those cast into the valley will be flooded by the waters from the heavens (called "masculine") and the waters from underneath the earth (called "feminine") (54.7–10). The word about the Elect One's ability to judge Azaz'el will go out, and the kings and potentates will be warned (55.4). For some, however, it is already too late. Giving the vision explicitly political overtones, Enoch sees kings and potentates being chained and thrown into a deep valley burning with fire (54.1–2). This motif also occurs in the New Testament (Jude 1.6; cf. 2 Peter 2.4–9), where the chaining of the angels or of Satan serves as an example to future evildoers.

Each angel is condemned to punish his followers in a place where the angels, too, will suffer. Thus, they are called "angels of punishment" (56.1). These angels carry nets of iron and bronze with which they will catch their followers and cast them between the cracks in the depths of the accursed valley. "Then the valley shall be filled with their [accursed] elect and beloved ones; and the epoch of their lives, the era of their glory, and the age of their leading (others) astray shall come to an end and shall not henceforth be

19. The term is supplied by Black, *Book of Enoch*, 214.

reckoned" (56.4). Once the "angels of punishment" have been introduced, the Book of Similitudes refers consistently not to destruction but to punishment.

The second vision related in the Book of Similitudes confirms this shift from destruction to punishment. The end of God's forbearance will be announced by startling signs. An earthquake will occur of such magnitude that it will sunder the union of those two monsters, the female Leviathan and the male Behemoth. Leviathan will henceforth dwell in the depths of the ocean, and Behemoth will go into the dry deserts (60.7–10). Then the desert will resurrect those who perished in its wilderness, wild beasts will restore their prey, and the fish of the sea will return those they have eaten (61.5).

Then the Son of Man will try all the powerful of the earth. His identity had been known only to his righteous ones, but now he will avenge those who oppressed them (62.11).[20] The wicked of the earth will plead for mercy. They will complain that they have only "now come to know that we should glorify and bless the Lord of kings" (63.4). "Would that someone had given us a chance so that we should glorify, praise, and have faith before his glory!" (63.5). As in Luke 16.29 and 31, the appeal will be denied, and the angels who led the world astray will be dealt with similarly (64).

God now speaks to Noah and assures him that because of his righteousness he will be the seed of the future and protected from the flood (67.1–3). Yet in the Book of Similitudes, the introduction of Noah does not lead to a shift from punishment to destruction. Indeed, mentioning the elements of the mountains that form the valley of the west and adding turbulent water and the production of sulfur suggest alchemical processes similar to the juxtaposed ponds into which souls were successively immersed in Plutarch's vision of Thespesius.[21] Noah says God showed him the same valleys he had shown Enoch, including "that burning valley" in the west among the mountains of gold, silver, iron, bronze, and tin, and also another valley filled with churning water. And the fire of the valley combined with the bronze of the mountain to produce a smell of sulfur that pervaded the water (67.6). This he called the "valley of the perversive angels," where "those angels who revealed oppression" (67.4) and "who perverted those who dwell upon the earth . . . shall (continue to) burn punitively underneath that ground" (67.7).

Yet it is not only angels who will be confined there but also the powerful of the earth, "kings, rulers, and exalted ones" (67.8). "Lust shall fill their souls

20. This idea parallels the fate of those bearing the mark of the beast in Revelation 13.11–14.11, 19.20.
21. Plutarch, *On the Delays of the Divine Vengeance*, sec. 30.

so that their bodies shall be punished" because their lust will lead them to deny the Lord (67.8). The more their bodies are tormented, the more their spirits will be "transmuted," that is, following the alchemical metaphor, changed through and through (67.9).

Burning, however, is not enough. The hot and cold of the water and the fire will alternate, depending on whether the kings or the angels are being punished (67.11). Following on the idea that those undergoing punishment wish they had known before that these torments existed, the fate of the angels "is itself a testimony to the kings and rulers who control the world" (67.12).[22] Unlike the fire and worm of Isaiah 66.24, these punishments attack not rotting carrion but living flesh. "These waters of judgment are poison to the bodies of the [kings, rulers, and exalted ones] as well as sensational to their flesh; (hence) they will neither see nor believe that these waters become transformed and become *a fire that burns forever*" (67.13, my italics).[23]

The valley of the perversive angels applies unending punishments to angels and kings. It consists of fire, water, and sulfur. Without any mention of the worm, Isaiah 66.24 cannot be its model. Closer, perhaps is the "valley of the dead bodies and the ashes" that will become "sacred to the Lord" (Jeremiah 31.40), namely, Ge-Hinnom. Yet whatever its precise imagery, this passage clearly presents a single valley for the punishment of apostate angels and ungodly human "kings, rulers, and exalted ones." These elements create a central depository in which to punish rebels against God with physical sensation, in an accursed place, with undying fire, forever.

The clear attribution of eternity to these torments impresses the angels too. In heaven, Michael declares his astonishment at the severity of the judgment, which, he observes to Raphael, will be "forever and ever" (68.5). A catalog of the crimes of the fallen angels follows, as if it were necessary to explain what evil called forth these punishments. Enoch identifies the fallen angels. He enumerates the enemy hosts, the centurions, the chiefs over fifties, and the chiefs over tens, as if they were an army (69.3).[24] The misdeeds include tempting the other angels with women, misleading Eve, intro-

22. Again, this theme is similar to that in 2 Peter 2.4–10, where the implication is that if God can discipline angels, he can certainly handle mere princes.

23. The bracketed phrase replaces the word "angels" in the text. Ephraim Isaac is correct to note in the apparatus to 67.13 (in Charlesworth, *Old Testament Pseudepigrapha*, 46) that, despite the unanimity of the manuscripts, "bodies of kings" must be what is meant. Black, *Book of Enoch*, 242–43, also applies this phrase to the kings and powerful of verses 8 and 10.

24. See also the organization of Jewish administration in the wilderness, Exod. 18:21. They were called the army of Azaz'el in *1 Enoch* 54:5.

ducing humans to the sword, to armor, to writing. In addition to these skills, the rebel angels also turned over secret knowledge concerning the creation of the heavens, the earth, the sea, the sun, moon, stars, the winds, thunder and lightning, hail, rain, dew (69.16–25). Their crimes consisted in introducing humans to lower pursuits, "for indeed human beings were not created but to be like angels, permanently to maintain pure and righteous lives" (69.11). These are the "perversive angels" who caused the powerful of the earth to "believe in the debauchery of their bodies and deny the spirit of the Lord" (67.10). Beyond betraying heavenly secrets, these angels are guilty of rejecting their own status and, in their evil, turning humans from the imitation of angels to debauchery, from spirit to bodies.

Here the Book of Similitudes again reinforces this theme from chapter 15 of the Book of the Watchers. The notion of an angelic model for human behavior would have been very attractive in the ascetic community of Qumran. If this text was not included in their Enoch material, it is either because it circulated only where it could not be known in Qumran or, what is more likely, because it was written too late.

The consequences of these angelic misdeeds will call forth the Son of Man, who will never perish. When they see him, the people will rejoice, "but those who have led the world astray shall be bound with chains, and their ruinous congregation shall be imprisoned; all their deeds shall vanish from before the face of the earth," and "thenceforth nothing that is corruptible shall be found" (69.28, 29). This allusion to destruction at the very end seems out of place in the Book of Similitudes, which has presented such graphic descriptions of eternal punishment. Perhaps this sentence refers only to the surface of the earth, which will be purged, and does not apply to the depths of the valleys, where torment will be eternal.

The contradiction between long-lasting (indeed, here, eternal) suffering and destruction should not be neglected. For the competition between these themes appears in many "opposed" passages of the Hebrew Scriptures. *1 Enoch* is no different.

The compiler of *1 Enoch* collected mythic material combining background to Noah with apocalyptic speculation. This he used to frame the cosmological lore in chapters 72–82, which serves to enhance "Enoch's" credentials as a reporter of the world and God's power as the creator of so intricate a universe.[25] The five main segments derive either from one among them or from some other version. For lack of concrete evidence to the contrary, I have assumed that the Book of Watchers is the earliest complete

25. This association of the power to create and the power to punish emerges in chap. 101.

story; yet the brevity of the Apocalypse of Weeks suggests that it might be older than the Book of the Watchers, which, in that case, would have served to elaborate it. Given the main elements of *1 Enoch*, there is no reason to suppose that the juxtaposition of these ideas awaited the actual writing down of any of its five parts; *1 Enoch* comments on more of the biblical tradition than just the background to Noah. Although it provides its own answer to the question Job took from Abraham, its dedication to that debate shows that it draws on issues discussed in other biblical texts long before the Book of the Watchers was committed to writing.[26]

Destruction of the unrighteous stands out as a vivid experience in the early history of God's relationship with humankind. It happened to the generation of Noah's flood, Sodom and Gomorrah, Pharaoh and his armies, Korah, Dathan, and Abiram. God had promised in the covenant that the enemies of Israel would be destroyed. Parallel to these associations with God's ability to cleanse his creation is the tradition of Sheol, a morally neutral underworld. Yet, although Sheol was frequently considered equivalent to destruction because it meant the end of life, a competing, though generally less diffused, tradition distinguished different parts of Sheol and segregated the dead according to the conduct of their lives.

There is a distinct possibility, then, that insisting on a crisp distinction between destruction and punishment is anachronistic. Throughout the Hebrew Bible is the notion, thoroughly consistent with the Deuteronomic tradition, that destruction means death. Yet the dead go down to Sheol, where they live on in a pale half existence. Thus, destruction is no end. If the worst of the living, the oppressors of the righteous, go to the worst part of Sheol to lie unburied and in disgrace (Isaiah 14.19), then that is similar to what happens in Gehennna, according to the prophecy of Jeremiah (chapters 7 and 19). It could be, then, that in *1 Enoch*'s five versions of the Enoch story, Sheol and Gehenna come to be one place. Those who are destroyed are dead, and in death, the wicked suffer.

That conclusion, however, would be exaggerated. It stresses coherence and consistency in religion over latitude and resonance for a diverse community. It violates the history of the Bible's composition and the relationship between oral and written traditions in the ancient world. It is impossible to analyze the Hebrew Bible without speaking of layers of composition and the presence of conflicting traditions. The same applies to the *Book of Enoch*, another compilation. Therefore we must tolerate as much diversity as did the people we study. It would be wrong to attribute to them a demand for

26. Himmelfarb, *Tours of Hell*, 172–73.

consistency that emerged in other times and under other circumstances. For the time being, then, it is best to leave these differences unresolved and leave Sheol and Gehenna in juxtaposition. The ancient Jewish idea of punishment after death was a late concern of a minority, though it was definitely there.

Rather than theological consistency in Scripture, it is better to search instead for the conflicts of opinion that energized religious life and existential feeling about God, oneself, and the world. There was no definitive resolution of the competition between destruction and long-term suffering for the wicked. Instead, these fates may be seen as two incompatible "cores" that attracted different members of the community at different times under different circumstances.

The legends concerning the Nephilim and their heirs provide further evidence that it would be wrong to look for consistency in these matters. According to the Noah stories of both the Bible and *1 Enoch*, only the descendants of Noah would remain after the Flood. Yet the Hebrew Bible has many references to descendants of "the Nephilim and the mighty men that were of old" of Genesis 6.4. At the end of the wandering recounted in Exodus, they appear in the Land of Canaan. When Moses sent leaders from each tribe to explore the Negev around Hebron, some of the scouts were discouraged by the stature of the inhabitants and reported people so large that the Hebrews seemed like grasshoppers beside them. These, they said, were the sons of Anak, who came from the Nephilim (Numbers 13.33). This was a fabrication, meant to exploit the people's fears and encourage a return to Egypt rather than an attack on Canaan. Moses and Aaron and Joshua prevailed, however, and soon *all* the inhabitants of Canaan had to be reckoned with. Listed among them, was a people conspicuous for their height, like the Anakim, who were also called Rephaim (Deuteronomy 2.11, 20). Here the Rephaim came to be confused with the Nephilim, but both served the same function: they were gigantic residents of the land of Canaan, descendants of the offspring of the angels. Eventually the Hebrews conquered King Og of Bashan, the last "remnant of the Rephaim," whose bedstead was so large (nine by four cubits) that the Ammonites preserved it in Rabbah (Deuteronomy 3.11; cf. Joshua 12.4, 13.12). These giants apparently gave their name to the land they occupied, the Valley of the Rephaim (Joshua 15.8).[27] As late as the time of David, the attributes of the ancient giants were ascribed to the Philistines. Gath, the hometown of Goliath, also produced other tall and powerful men, capable of wielding impressive weapons

27. See also Josh. 18.16; 2 Sam. 5.18, 22; 23.13; 1 Chron. 11.15; 14.9; Isa. 17.5.

(2 Samuel 21.16, 18, 22). These men were called descendants of the giants (Rephaim) of whom Sippai was said to be the last (1 Chronicles 20.4, 6, 8).

The lore about giants scattered in the Hebrew Bible should not be the basis for any dogmatic assertions. The connection between the Nephilim and the Rephaim is stronger than it might seem, however, since the Septuagint translates the Nephilim of Genesis 6.4 as *gigantes*, and Rephaim is either transliterated as *Rephaim* or translated as *gigantes* or *Titanes* (giants or Titans). Thus the Jewish scholars of the second or third century B.C.E. who made the Greek translation of the Hebrew Bible saw enough similarity between Nephilim and Rephaim to render them by the same Greek term and associate them with Hesiod's Titans.

Although the case of the giants is an extreme example, the point is that the logic here is not that of theology. The giants of Gath are given six fingers on each hand and six toes on each foot. It is not unusual for writers to see the opponents of their people and their God in monstrous terms. And that is true whether it applies to giants in the antediluvian dawn of time, the early inhabitants of promised lands (Canaanites), or more recent enemies to the north (Philistines).

Similarly, it would be an anachronistic error of "theologizing" to assert a strict identity between the Rephaim "descended" from the Nephilim and the *rephaim* (or shades) who dwell in Sheol. Even if the giants have become extinct and can surely be considered spirits who haunt the underworld, the *rephaim*, the shades, were all the human dead and not only the wicked. Thus the range of *rephaim* forms a corollary to the differences between Sheol and Gehenna. Whereas Gehenna punishes the rebellious angels who abandoned the company of God and corrupted the earth and the Nephilim giants who followed them, Sheol is the neutral resting place of all the dead, only sometimes divided so as to segregate the good from the wicked. The senses of Rephaim can be similarly divided. By means of a gradual demotion, the Nephilim, whom Genesis 6.4 called "mighty men that were of old" and *1 Enoch* 6.2 considered apostate angels and consigned to Gehenna, blurred with foreign enemies of heroic stature and came to be called Rephaim. The Rephaim were in turn demoted from enemy princes to common shades, the residents of the undifferentiated Sheol, as they are in Psalms 88.10, Proverbs 9.18, and Isaiah 26.14. This distinction between the enemy chiefs and the common dead appears in two passages already considered from another point of view. In Isaiah 14.9 all the shades (*rephaim*) taunt the fallen Day Star, but the text specifically registers as present the "leaders of the earth," and "all who were the kings of the nations." In Ezekiel 32.21, from "out of the midst of Sheol," it is "the mighty chiefs" (*gibborim*) who speak and taunt fallen Egypt. These texts explicity separate leaders and kings from the background of the common dead.

A similar range of meaning occurred under the cognate term for Rephaim among the Canaanites, according to scholars who have examined texts from Ugarit. In one text, the *rephaim* are dead kings who return to this world to attend sacred rites, for example, coronations of new kings.[28] Since these are Canaanite leaders from a Hebrew point of view, they fit well with the idea of great men among the enemy. Other Ugaritic evidence suggests that the Canaanite term was a generic name for the dead which can be directly connected with the Hebrew usage.[29]

As in the juxtaposition of Sheol and Gehenna, so there is a range of associations from the Rephaim as high-ranking enemy dead to the *rephaim* as common shades. These differences in the geography and population of the netherworld occurred in ancient Greece too. Homer and Hesiod clearly distinguished between the land of Hades and Tartarus. Homer, too, made Tantalus and Sisyphus suffer in a different place from the rest of the shades, who do not suffer, and among whom the warlords and heroes, their wives and mothers stand out. It is not clear whether the differences proposed in the underworld by the Orphic and Eleusinian mysteries antedated the segration that eventually divided Sheol. Probably, though, Greek writers distinguished Tartarus from the land of Hades earlier than Jewish authors separated Gehenna from Sheol. Long oral traditions preceded the writing of texts in both these cultures, however, so that dating the rise of concepts is very difficult. Further, neither society prescribed dogmatic positions that can be called *the* Greek or *the* Jewish position. There were differences, of course. Judaism delegated no assignments to specialized gods. Nonetheless, both cultures employed reports of differences in the layout of the underworld and the status of its residents to address similar questions.

RECAPITULATION: A JEWISH MODEL

Let us conclude by returning to Jewish developments. The challenge at the beginning of Part II was to understand how a belief in punishment after

28. Baruch A. Levine and Jean-Michel de Tarragon, "Dead Kings and Rephaim: The Patrons of the Ugaritic Dynasty, with Text and English Translation of KTU 1.161)," *Journal of the American Oriental Society* 104 (1984): 649–59. On 656, speaking of Ugaritic evidence, they observe: "Kings and heroes do, ultimately, become rephaim."

29. Speaking of the Ugaritic term, Spronk, *Beatific Afterlife*, 229, says: "Rephaim is in the first place a name of the dead. There is no problem in connecting it with the use of Hebrew (rephaim) as denoting the dead in general."

death could arise among a people frequently said to deny any belief in an afterlife. To be sure, one could simply maintain that there is no clear affirmation of that belief, no genuine building upon the idea in Hebrew Scripture, and so it would be a mistake to exaggerate the importance of the apocryphal *1 Enoch*. The passages upon which rests the argument that a notion of punishment after death did develop in Hebrew Scripture are too isolated to bear the weight of so hardy a contention (Psalm 49; Ezechiel 32.18–28; Daniel 12; Isaiah 66.24; Jeremiah 7 and 19; and others). Nonetheless, the opposite position (denial of any belief in an afterlife) is also too extreme in light of the evidence presented. The idea of punishment after death is there, and it stems from logically prior notions firmly established in the Jewish biblical tradition.

To conclude this chapter, therefore, I want to review in abstract terms the ideas about death and justice which in some quarters amounted to the belief in punishment after death. Each point in this reconstruction has already been identified as an idea expressed in the Hebrew Bible.

Let us imagine that one person feels angry with another, as Cain did with Abel and then God with Cain or Pharaoh with Moses and then God with Pharaoh. The nature of that anger, and particularly its expression, varies according to whether it affects a relationship between equals, unequals, or as an extreme case, between a human being and God. The angry person may wish the other some loss or pain, which would satisfy the angry person alone, because such anger is only personal. The loss that the offended person wishes to see affect the other might last for varying periods of time, even a lifetime, possibly for the lifetime of the offender's children, or for several (or many) generations.

Beyond simple personal satisfaction, there may be some larger purpose to result from the loss inflicted on the other. The angry person may wish to bring about an apology, to make the offender regret the offense (even if only in its consequences—that is, this pain), or it may serve as a deterrent to others. Seeing the fate of one offender will teach others to respect one who can cause regret. An apology, if accepted, would have the benefit of restoring the original relationship between the two parties. In this case, the offender would need to accept responsibility, regret the offense, and admit that the punishment is deserved.

In my example so far, the desire to see another experience pain arises for a merely personal reason, one person's anger, and the offender's pain satisfies only the offended person. Now let us assume that the offender has actually wronged the offended person by some objective standard. Or imagine that the wrong committed was not merely wrong but something the offender had expressly promised never to do, that it is a betrayal, a double cross, a breach of contract. In these cases, the pain the offended person wishes to see inflicted on the offender would satisfy not only the one wronged but also justice.

Suppose, further, that this breach of contract is not the first offense. If there is sufficient repetition of the offense that the ability to adhere to the contract is rendered doubtful, the offender may desire the help of the punisher, may welcome the punishment as a sign that the offended party still cares. If the offender recognizes the justice of the original agreement and the fairness of the punishment and seeks the continued acceptance of the punisher, he or she may feel reassured by punishment.

So far, I have been assuming that the punisher is right, of course, that the offended party has a legitimate right to desire the offender's loss. If not, the loss is absurd.

Now these considerations can be generalized to apply to a community. If the community believes its welfare depends on the right conduct or belief of all its members, then any deviation by an individual would be seen as harmful to the general welfare. One case would be a misdeed that weakens the community against an outside enemy, perhaps a person giving out defense secrets; then, wrongdoing becomes treason. Another case would be a misdeed that weakens the community's internal regulation, for example, falsifying tax records; then, wrongdoing becomes fraud. A third case would be a misdeed that weakens the community in the observance of its obligations to God by, for instance, contravening or neglecting religious law; then, wrongdoing becomes sin.

Now, if the community believes that its prosperity depends on its adherence to a law to which it is bound through agreement with the divinity, then any hardship experienced by the community must be traced to misconduct, assuming, as previously, that the one who inflicts loss does so fairly. But if outside communities seem to prosper at the expense of the home community or people who flout the divine law seem to prosper at the expense of its adherents, the imbalance needs to be rectified. Either hidden evildoers must be discovered, the arrogant must be brought low, or foreign oppressors must be overthrown.

It is possible that the community may take action to accomplish these goals on its own. If it is successful, belief in the order of a world structured through a covenant with the divinity will be reinforced or at least remain intact. But if the community's action is not effective, the injustice will endure, the validity of the covenant may be called into question, and the desire for correction may remain unsatisfied.

When the community or its religiously committed individuals cannot restore justice themselves and when their faith demands rectification, they must either abandon their faith or sublimate the desire for justice. The religiously committed are left with a desire to see vengeance inflicted on the offender by a third party (in this case, God) in order to restore justice to the community or peace to the individual soul.

A deeply felt or long-lasting desire for unrealizable punishment leads to severe strains. At all costs the community, especially the religiously committed within it, wants to avoid the conclusion that it is the divinity who is the source of the evil—the imbalance—or that the covenant is not valid or that the divinity's rule is whimsical or absurd. Excluding these undesirable conclusions, however, leaves only a few options: God's ways are not knowable; questioning is not licit; God will restore justice, but later in this life; God will restore justice, but in the next life.

Belief in future punishment is a manifestation of the sublimated desire for vengeance. Belief in punishment after death becomes necessary when no sign of restoration is visible in life. It includes the possibility, but not the necessity, that through resurrection all wrong will be punished and not just the wrongs committed by evildoers alive at the time of punishment.

I have constructed this abstract model by arranging its component ideas— each of which occurs in Hebrew Scripture—in logical order to show how a belief in punishment after death may arise. Many psalmists and prophets, indeed most of them, stopped short of expressing this belief. Statements concerning punishment after death occur only at the end of the biblical period, and in religion, later is not necessarily better. Although this belief was articulated late, held by only a few, and therefore possessed only shallow roots, we shall see in the rest of this book how carefully the plant was tended and what weighty fruit it bore.

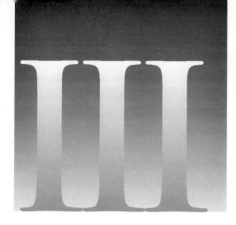

Hell in the New Testament

God sent the Son into the world, not to condemn the world, but that the world might be saved through him.

—John 3.17

Depart from me, you cursed [ones], into the eternal fire prepared for the devil and his angels.

—Matthew 25.41

And the smoke of their torment goes up for ever and ever; and they have no rest, day or night, these worshipers of the beast and its image, and whoever receives the mark of its name.

—Revelation 14.11

8

Destruction

The focus of Christianity is on eternal life, not punishment after death. Christians hold that by his divine sacrifice, Christ made it possible for humanity to imitate his resurrection through the reunion of the soul with a body made spiritual, forming a renewed person who will enjoy eternal bliss in the kingdom of God (John 3.16; 1 Corinthians 15.44). For the Christian, death, the last enemy, is conquered; Hades is overthrown (1 Corinthians 15.26, 55; Revelation 20.14). In the Gospels, Christ raises the dead (Luke 8.40–56; John 11.1–44; Matthew 27.52) and identifies himself with resurrection (John 11.25). A life devoted to this faith and the charitable actions inseparable from it makes death infinitely porous (Romans 1.17; 1 Corinthians 13.2). Yet, in Christianity, as in Judaism, one's life is unique. Developing the implications of the apocalyptic strand of late ancient Judaism, Christianity broke definitively with the Greek notion of cycles and proclaimed linear, teleological time. Chapter 10 will consider this concept more fully, but from the beginning it is essential to understand that the Christian view of history develops along a line from Creation to Redemption to Resurrection. For the individual there is only one life: no reincarnation, no second chance after death. The individual must keep faith and practice charity while alive. Thus death becomes the deadline for conversion and right action. Part III is devoted to examining the New Testament's teachings about those who do not meet the deadline.

There is no certainty concerning the authorship, the dates, or the order of composition of the books of the New Testament. In general, Paul's epistles, which date from the early 50s to the late 50s or early 60s of the first century, are considered the earliest testimony to the shape of Christian belief in the primitive church. Of the Gospels, Mark was first and may barely overlap with the last of Paul's epistles. It was used by the authors of both Matthew and Luke, who wrote in an order that cannot be determined. These three are called the synoptic Gospels because, in addition to the dependence of both Matthew and Luke on Mark, all three probably share a now-lost common source; so they have a "single" point of view and are consequently "synoptic." John was written later than the other three, probably as late as around 95. The Acts of the Apostles may be contemporary with the synoptic Gospels. The most recent of the books in the New Testament canon are held to be Revelation (also called the Apocalypse) and 2 Peter, which may have been written as late as the first or second decade of the second century.

One difficulty in accepting this chronology is a psychological one. It means that Paul's letters are the earliest surviving testimony to the teachings of the primitive church, and Paul was never one of the immediate followers of Jesus. The authors of the Gospels, the evangelists, are not the apostles of the same names, but in reading the quotations they ascribe to Jesus, one has the impression that they were present at the events they describe and heard his words themselves. Although they draw upon an oral tradition that may indeed date back to Jesus, the Gospels are literary compositions that post-date Paul's epistles. In order to follow the chronological development of the concept of hell in the New Testament, therefore, one must consider the Epistles first, then the Gospels, and Revelation last. Other works can be interspersed as necessary, and minor problems can be ironed out as they arise, but the present state of biblical scholarship necessitates this general approach.[1]

The purpose of Part III is to examine what the New Testament teaches concerning those not saved. To understand those teachings, it is necessary to consider how one comes to be saved and how one is judged. Yet the core question concerns the fate of those who do not measure up. The authors of the Christian Bible considered three possibilities.

The first possibility is "mere" death. Those who fall short could simply

---

1. A few introductions to the New Testament are Edwin D. Freed, *The New Testament: A Critical Introduction* (Belmont, Calif.: Wadsworth, 1991); Bruce Manning Metzger, *New Testament Studies: Philological, Versional, and Patristic* (Leiden: Brill, 1980); Norman Perrin and Dennis C. Duling, *The New Testament, an Introduction: Proclamation and Paranesis, Myth and History*, 2d ed. (New York: Harcourt Brace Jovanovich, 1982); Schuyler Brown, *The Origins of Christianity: A Historical Introduction to the New Testament* (Oxford: Oxford University Press, 1984).

remain in their graves, decompose, and pass into nothingness. That would be natural or simple death, or what the New Testament calls destruction. Those left out of the resurrection would not know eternal life or inherit the kingdom of God, but they would not be aware of their loss either.

A second view holds that simple death does not suffice: justice demands retribution.[2] Those who reject the Christian message will also be resurrected, but then they will be sent to a fate separate from, and worse than, that of the blessed. The damned will suffer "wrath" or "evil," either temporarily or unendingly in eternal damnation.

If the postmortem sufferings are temporary, will they simply end or will they gradually reform the offenders and allow them to be returned to God and his company? If punishment is administered under divine jurisdiction, how can it fail to correct? Does the continued existence of a group being punished not imply the ineffectiveness of divine action? Reasoning from such questions as these, other Christians proposed a third possibility: universal salvation (universalism, restoration, reconciliation). Surely God would eventually draw all to himself, even if after punishment.

PAUL

Paul did not have a clear idea of hell. His concern was more intently focused on the positive side of the Christian message. He never used the word "Gehenna," and in the one place where he refers to Hades it is in the context of celebrating the resurrection of the flesh, the defeat of death. "Death [*thanatos*] is swallowed up in victory." "O death [*thanate*], where is thy victory? O death [*Hade*], where is thy sting?" (1 Corinthians 15.54–55). Here Paul is quoting two of the Hebrew prophets, Isaiah (25.8) and Hosea (13.14), who also scoff at death. The prophets use Sheol as a synonym for *maveth* (death), just as Paul is here assimilating *thanatos* (death) to Hades and taunting them both. Paul's idea is that in the resurrection brought about by Jesus, the ancient prophecies are fulfilled, and death is overcome. It will be necessary to return to this famous passage, but for the time being, it is sufficient to note that the point of Paul's only reference to Hades is to celebrate its impotence!

Paul was indeed aware that not everyone accepted this message. Raised a Jew by the name of Saul, Paul had himself, earlier in his life, persecuted the church's early adherents. After his conversion to Christianity, whereupon he

2. See especially Chaim Milikowsky, "Which Gehenna? Retribution and Eschatology in the Synoptic Gospels and in Early Jewish Texts," *New Testament Studies* 34 (1988): 238–49.

took the name Paul, he knew of rivalries not only with Jews but with Christians who wanted to retain the observance of Jewish customs. He also knew how even those Christians whom he had converted could turn from what he saw as the right path. Further, some were duped by the teachings of what he considered to be false apostles or false prophets. Still farther afield were the pagan Greeks and Romans, the Gentiles, whose conversion he regarded as his special mission.

Given Paul's Jewish background, his training under the Pharisee Gamaliel (Acts 22.3), and the task he took upon himself as missionary to the Gentiles, one may assume that he knew the eschatological debates of his own people and of those he sought to convert. Very little of this material makes its way into his discussion of the fate of the wicked, however. Surely Paul knew the passages describing the compartmentalization of Sheol. Surely he knew *1 Enoch* and the apocalyptic tradition.[3] Surely a native of Tarsus, a masterful Greek stylist familiar with Greek philosophical terms such as *pneuma*, *sarx*, and *psychē* knew the mythic and literary traditions about Hades and Tartarus and had considered the scar-bearing souls of Plato's *Gorgias* (523–26).[4] Yet, though there are allusions to these ideas in other passages of the New Testament, Paul seems, by and large, to have turned his back on them. Although he believed in judgment (2 Corinthians 5.10), for Paul, the netherworld was no prison. Far less was it subdivided by deed or misdeed. For Paul (and John, as we shall see), as the kingdom beckoned, Hades faded. It remained, at most, a memory—at least for the saved. What about the rest?

Because Paul was the author of the earliest surviving Christian writings and had formerly opposed the Christian message himself, his views of what might happen to those who reject Jesus are of particular importance. Paul's epistles reveal that although he was extremely attracted to the third option, universal reconciliation, he actually adopted the first, annihilation. His consciousness of the need for a human response to the opportunity offered by redemptive action convinced him that those without faith or guilty of evil action are excluded from eternal life. Although Paul proclaimed that the blessedness of the saved would be eternal, he never applied that term to

3. Among many other works, see W. D. Davies, *Jewish and Pauline Studies* (Philadelphia: Fortress Press, 1984); and idem, *Paul and Rabbinic Judaism*, new ed. (Philadelphia: Fortress Press, 1980); H. J. Schoeps, *Paul: The Theology of the Apostle in the Light of Jewish Religious History*, trans. Harold Knight (Philadelphia: Westminster, 1961).

4. Werner Jaeger, *Early Christianity and Greek Paideia* (Oxford: Oxford University Press, 1969); Wilfred L. Knox, *Some Hellenistic Elements in Primitive Christianity* (London: Published for the British Academy by H. Milford, 1944).

those not saved. It is this difference in outlook that I wish to describe with the term "positive."

In the First Epistle to the Thessalonians, which is generally regarded as the earliest of Paul's letters, this question is not addressed directly.[5] Nonetheless, certain passages reveal attitudes that will reemerge in Paul's more detailed considerations of the problem. He tells, for example, of the persecution of the early Christian communities and of obstacles experienced by Paul himself (2.2, 14–16). Paul finds consolation in the thought that "God's wrath [*orgē*] has come upon [the persecutors] at last" (2.16). Thus, those who oppose the preaching of truth and the purposes of the church will know divine wrath.[6] It is hard to know whether "wrath" implies punishment in this passage. It is clear, though, that God's wrath has ended this oppression.

Persecution from outside was not the only problem calling for supernatural sanctions. Within the church was a group of "enthusiasts," who believed that possession of the Holy Spirit entitled them to freer behavior than that permitted others. Paul combated this temptation to license by saying, "The Lord is an avenger [*ekdikos*] in all these things" (4.6),[7] using a formulation that makes wrath appear more like punishment. If an action calls forth wrath, it is a transgression that entails consequences, for God does not tolerate those who set aside his will. Indeed, he carries out vengeance, punishment, judgment against offenders. Wrath, it appears, has two sides: one is the sudden cutting off of evil by divine intervention; the other is the punishment that follows on wrongdoing.

The ambiguity is continued when Paul declares the suddenness with which divine justice is rendered rather than the harshness of the fate that awaits the guilty. Paul warns his friends in Thessalonica that it will be administered at the time of the Lord's return, on the day of the Lord, which will come upon them in the future, unannounced:

5. For a review of the letter as a whole, see Christopher L. Mearns, "Early Eschatological Development in Paul: The Evidence of I and II Thessalonians," *New Testament Studies* 27 (1981): 137–57. See also Robert H. Gundry, "The Hellenization of Dominical Tradition and Christianization of Jewish Tradition in the Eschatology of 1–2 Thessalonians," *New Testament Studies* 33 (1987): 161–87. A broader perspective can be found in Charles A. Wanamaker, *The Epistles to the Thessalonians: A Commentary on the Greek Text*, New International Greek Testament Commentary (Grand Rapids, Mich.: Eerdmans, 1990).

6. It is not clear in this passage whether Paul believes these offenders have already experienced divine anger or will do so in the future.

7. Wanamaker, *Epistles*, 150–59; Michael McGhee, "A Rejoinder to Two Recent Studies Dealing with 1 Thess. 4:4," *Catholic Biblical Quarterly* 51 (1989): 82–89.

For you yourselves know well that the day of the Lord will come like a thief in the night. When people say, "There is peace and security," then sudden destruction [*olethros*] will come upon them as travail comes upon a woman with child, and there will be no escape. But you are not in darkness, brethren, for that day to surprise you like a thief. For you are all sons of light and sons of the day; we are not of the night or of darkness. (5.2–5)

Paul makes a clear distinction between those likely to be surprised by judgment, who will thus be destroyed, and those who need not fear the judgment whenever it comes.[8] It is important to note in passing how Paul contrasts the sons of light to the sons of darkness. This opposition dramatizes the contrast he feels between the forces of good and evil. His symbolic parallel with light and darkness continues: "But, since we belong to the day, let us be sober. . . . For God has not destined us for wrath [*orgēn*], but to obtain salvation through our Lord Jesus Christ, who died for us so that whether we wake or sleep we might live with him" (5.8–10). Here Paul opposes "wrath," which he called "destruction" in verse 3, to "salvation." "Us" in this passage refers to the Christian community, for no others would acknowledge the expression "our Lord Jesus Christ." Yet it is also possible that "us" refers to all humankind. That possibility is not stated explicitly in 1 Thessalonians, but it receives some support from verse 10, which begins to suggest that Christ's sacrifice was efficacious for *all* humans "whether we wake or sleep," whether (by extension) we are of the darkness or the light.

Thus, already in 1 Thessalonians there are hints suggesting the three possible options. Those who oppose the church's goals, much like the opponents of Israel, will experience divine wrath (although the precise meaning of that term is not clear) or will undergo destruction. The lack of any clear reference to either suffering after death or eternal punishment is characteristic of the positive tradition. If Paul modifies any of the views of divine sanction in the Hebrew Bible, it is in the opposite direction, that is, to emphasize the possibility of eternal blessing, for, Paul writes cryptically, suggesting the third possibility, "we" are destined for salvation "so that whether we wake or sleep we might live with him." Does this statement include the wicked, chastened by God's wrath?

The tension among these three views of the fate of the wicked (that is, destruction, punishment, and reconciliation) is explored at greater length in 1 Corinthians, where, as in 1 Thessalonians, Paul addresses the tendency for some members of the church in Corinth to believe that their acceptance of

8. See Wanamaker, *Epistles*, 176–90, esp. 178–83, for a discussion of this passage in the context of apocalyptic thought.

Christianity had made them "spiritual" and had thus exempted them from observing the law. Paul threatens the enthusiasts or libertines with unpleasant consequences. "Do you not know," he asks, "that the unrighteous will not inherit the kingdom of God? Do not be deceived; neither the immoral, nor idolaters, nor adulterers, nor sexual perverts, nor thieves, nor the greedy, nor drunkards, nor revilers, nor robbers will inherit the kingdom of God" (6.9–10). Twice Paul insists on the punishment for violation of the moral code: exclusion from the kingdom of God. This is a simple formula. Later in his letter Paul considers in more detail how this exclusion might be carried out.

In the chapter 15 of 1 Corinthians, Paul discusses at length the question of the resurrection of the body. Here, he was opposing a belief current in the Greek world that the body dies but the soul is immortal. Paul believed that with the General Resurrection, modeled on that of Jesus, the body too would be reborn. His explanation of how this might be draws on a view of history which it is necessary to describe:

> But in fact Christ has been raised from the dead, the first fruits of those who have fallen asleep. For as by a man came death, by a man has come also the resurrection of the dead. For as in Adam all die, so also in Christ shall all be made alive. But each in his own order: Christ the first fruits, then at his coming those who belong to Christ. Then comes the end, when he delivers the kingdom to God the Father after destroying [*katargēsēi*, annulling] every rule and every authority and power. For he must reign until he has put all his enemies under his feet. The last enemy to be destroyed [*katargeitai*, annulled] is death. . . . When all things are subjected to him, then the Son himself will also be subjected to him who put all things under him, that God may be everything to every one. (15.20– 26, 28)

Here, Paul explains the nature of history by examining its beginning, its middle, and its end. He asserts Christ's resurrection (verse 20), the event that brings the other poles of the time line into focus. Then he describes the first segment of history, from Creation to the Resurrection. He explains how Jesus' rebirth reverses the death brought by Adam's sin (21–22). Verse 22 suggests that *all* will be saved, Christ's passion reversing Adam's action. In verse 23 Paul shifts to the second segment of history, from the Resurrection to the end of time. Paul makes Jesus' resurrection foreshadow that of those who "belong to" him. In that second segment, the first event is the resurrection of Jesus; then, at his return (the Second Coming, the Parousia), the resurrection of "those who belong to Christ" will take place. By stipulating that this resurrection will be for "those who belong to Christ," Paul implies that *not all* will be saved, that resurrection to life will be denied those who do not belong to Christ. Now, focusing on the end of time, Paul predicts that Jesus will deliver "his" people, "the kingdom" to the Father. This delivery depends, however, on two things: first Jesus must defeat every "rule, authority, and power" that might have some other claim on his people; and second, he must free them from death, for many of his people will have died (a problem addressed in 1 Thessalonians).

In the light of the interpretation of history Paul has sketched here, it is possible to address the question of what happens to those who do not "belong" to Christ, to those who, as it says in 1 Corinthians 6.9, will not inherit the kingdom of God. Verses 24 and 26 say that all forces opposed to Christ will be "destroyed." Thus Christ's delivery of his kingdom to the Father will result from his ability to neutralize any other rule, authority, or power to which they might be subject (verse 24)—and that includes the rule of death (verse 26).

Now let us consider what it means to say that God is "everything to every one" or, as other translations put it, "all in all." When can one person be said to be "everything" to another? One possibility might be when the first has the power to determine the second person's fate. Or the first person may be the sole object of the second person's love, as in the colloquial expression "You are everything to me." Let us momentarily assume the second possibility, that the time when God is all in all is a time when he is the sole object of everyone's love.

Now, if there will be a time when God is all in all, what happens to the difference between "those who belong" and the implied group of those who do not belong? Those persons who are excluded, along with "every rule, authority, and power," and death itself would have to be destroyed for God to become "everything to every one." God would then be all in all because nothing that is not part of him would exist anymore. This hypothesis may be confirmed by returning to the idea that when one person is everything to another, that person has absolute control over the second person's fate and so, clearly, has the power to destroy the other. If "those who belong" must be separated from those who do not and the sense of "all in all" can be preserved by destroying those who do not belong, then one may conclude that God will be all in all only when those who do not belong are destroyed. Thus Paul's notion of destruction and annihilation would seem to be gaining over that of punishment (wrath) as a fate for those not saved, because the existence of offenders and the need to punish them continuously would conflict with the harmony of all in all.

Paul's theory of time, then, is both a history and a prophecy. It aligns the future with the past using Christ as the pivot. With Adam came death, but

Christ brought life, which will be the boon of those who follow him. This life was not granted with his resurrection but will be given at the end of time, with his return. Then his followers will receive life; then all rules, authorities, and powers not part of the community ruled by Christ will be destroyed, as, at the very last, will death itself (cf. Revelation 21.4). Therefore, at the end of time, death and all otherness will no longer exist and God will be everything to everyone. Paul does not mean, it seems to me, that the nonmembers will have become members and will be enjoying eternal life with Christ; rather, they will no longer exist and so will be excluded from the experience of having God be everything for them. The potential granted by Christ's passion for all to be saved is not to be realized, for there are some who do not belong to his kingdom. Thus the implications of "all" in verse 22 must be balanced against the implications of "those who belong" in verse 23. Fulfillment of the prophecy that God will be everything for everyone depends on the destruction of those for whom God will not be everything.[9]

But, further on in 1 Corinthians 15, Paul gives greater stress to the universal effectiveness of redemption. Just as in verses 20–28 Paul suggests that resurrection can be the lot of all humans by virtue of the historical progression between the two ages—that of Adam yielding to that of Christ—so a few verses later, even while repeating the Adam/Christ theme, he describes the ultimate victory of life over death, which he equates with the victory of the spiritual over the physical, presented in terms of the biological image of sowing and reaping. The seed must temporarily lie dead in the ground in order to rise again and bear fruit (cf. John 12.24):

> So it is with the resurrection of the dead. What is sown is perishable, what is raised is imperishable. It is sown in dishonor, it is raised in glory. It is sown in weakness, it is raised in power. It is sown a physical body, it is raised a spiritual body. If there is a physical body, there is also a spiritual body. Thus it is written, "The first man Adam became a living being"; the last Adam became a life-giving spirit. But it is not the spiritual which is first but the physical, and then the spiritual. (15.42–46)

9. Jan Lambrecht, "Paul's Christological Use of Scripture in 1 Cor. 15:20–28," *New Testament Studies* 28 (1982): 502–27. Lambrecht argues that Paul is thinking of the resurrection of only Christians in v. 24 (505) and does not address the fate of nonbelievers. See also C. E. Hill, "Paul's Understanding of Christ's Kingdom in I Corinthians 15:20–28," *Novum Testamentum* 30 (1988): 297–330. For Hill the impenitent are resurrected, but their fate is not redemption. For an extended treatment, see L. Joseph Kreitzer, *Jesus and God in Paul's Eschatology*, Supplement to *Journal for the Study of the New Testament*, 19 (Sheffield: Sheffield Academic, 1987), esp. 149–64. Charles H. Talbert, *Reading Corinthians* (New York: Crossroads, 1987), 96–104.

Paul constructs a complex analogy here. The spiritual body will succeed the physical one just as the plant succeeds the seed, just as Christ succeeded Adam, as power succeeds weakness, and the imperishable the perishable. The same idea is reiterated through the contrast of the man of dust and the man of heaven:

> The first man [Adam] was from the earth, a man of dust; the second man [Christ] is from heaven. As was the man of dust, so are those who are of the dust; and as is the man of heaven, so are those who are of heaven. Just as we have borne the image of the man of dust, we shall also bear the image of the man of heaven. I tell you this, brethren: flesh and blood cannot inherit the kingdom of God, nor does the perishable inherit the imperishable.
>
> Lo! I tell you a mystery. We shall not all sleep, but we shall all be changed,[10] in a moment, in the twinkling of an eye, at the last trumpet. For the trumpet will sound, and the dead will be raised imperishable, and we shall be changed. For this perishable nature *must* put on the imperishable, and this mortal nature *must* put on immortality. (15.47–53, my italics)

In this passage Paul continues his effort to clarify the "logic" of ultimate victory. How could heaven not triumph over dust? The same "natural" process that causes plants to be "born" after seeds have been buried in the ground will overcome our physical bodies and make them spiritual, so that humankind may conquer death. The repetition of "must" in verse 53 illustrates the force Paul gives to his parallel with both natural science and the progression of history: as the plant is to the seed and Christ is to Adam, so are the resurrected bodies of human beings to their dead, physical bodies. The immortal *must* prevail. It is a law of nature.

> When the perishable puts on the imperishable, and the mortal puts on immortality, then shall come to pass the saying that is written:
> "Death is swallowed up in victory."
> "O death, where is thy victory?
> O death, where is thy sting?"
> (15.54–55)

There is only one hint in this long discussion that the resurrection will not apply to all. Verse 48 states that some are "of the dust." Depending on the force one gives this phrase, it may be necessary to consider it as operating

10. The Vulgate text on this is very different. It says "Omnes quidem resurgemus, sed non omnes immutabimur," that is, "We shall all rise, but we shall not all be changed." The Vulgate reading was the one known to the Latin Middle Ages.

like the expression "those who belong to Christ" in verse 23 and therefore limiting the number of those who share in the victory of life. If one reads verse 48 as a contrast between those who retain a loyalty to dust, or to the inheritance of Adam, and those who are loyal to heaven and Christ, then Paul implies a separation here and an exclusion of some from the resurrection. In fact, I do not think that is Paul's intention. The theme here is metamorphosis, renewal. As the seed is transformed into the plant, so are Adam and those of the dust transformed into Christ and those of heaven. The process is irresistible; "this mortal nature *must* put on immortality" (verse 53).

This survey of 1 Corinthians reveals two tendencies in Paul's mind. At 6.9 and 15.23 he suggests that there are some who do not "belong to Christ" and will not "inherit the kingdom of God," but at 15.42–55 he suggests an irresistible law by which all must *necessarily* be transformed into higher, spiritual, immortal beings. Perhaps this apparent contradiction may be resolved by naming one of these tendencies Paul's ethical view and the other his anthropological view. In his ethical thought, the more Paul considers the evil actions of specific persons or groups (persecutors of the church, libertines, and others named in 1 Corinthians 6.9, 10), the more strongly he feels that some will be excluded from the kingdom of God. By contrast, in his anthropological thinking, the more he considers humankind in general as the race whose existence is defined by the tripartite history, the more he sees humanity in its potential relationship to God, where redemption is irresistible, and so he sees less or, indeed, no possibility of exclusion.[11]

Certainly the notion of exclusion is what appears in 2 Corinthians. Paul opens chapter 5 with a consideration of resurrection. He compares the resurrected body to an eternal (*aiōnion*) dwelling or a garment awaiting the soul in heaven, in contrast to which the body in which the soul now resides offers nothing and indeed makes it feel naked. But at verse 10 it becomes clear that not all will receive this heavenly reward.[12] First one must pass

11. See Udo Schnelle, "Der erste Thessalonicherbrief und die Entstehung der paulinischen Anthropologie," *New Testament Studies* 32 (1986): 207–24; Brendan Byrne, S.J., "Lining Out the Righteousness of God: The Contribution of Rom. 6:11–8:13 to an Understanding of Paul's Ethical Presuppositions," *Catholic Biblical Quarterly* 43 (1981): 557–81.

12. See T. Francis Glasson, "2 Corinthians 5:1–10 versus Platonism," *Scottish Journal of Theology* 43 (1990): 145–55; R.D. Zorn, "II Corinthians 5:1–10: Individual Eschatology or Corporate Solidarity, Which?" *Reformed Theological Review* 48 (1989): 93–104; and Joseph Onei-Bonsu, "Does 2 Cor. 5:1–10 Teach the Reception of the Resurrection Body at the Moment of Death?" *Journal for the Study of the New Testament* 28 (1986): 81–101.

divine scrutiny: "For we must all appear before the judgment seat of Christ, so that each one may receive good or evil, according to what he has done in the body" (5.10). Christ himself will separate the damned from the saved, according to the actions performed by individuals during their lives. Those who have done good will receive good, those who have done evil will receive evil. "Evil" functions here as "wrath" did earlier (e.g., 1 Thessalonians 2.16 or 5.9). The deeds done in the body for which reckoning must be given pertain to the ethical theme and elicit an evil fate. Sentencing the wicked to an evil fate is also different from Paul's anthropological notion of an irresistible renewal of the earthly made spiritual.

At the same time, although the opportunity exists in this passage, Paul refrains from saying that the wicked receive eternal evil, even though he does say that the good receive eternal good (2 Corinthians 5.1). Paul's reluctance to specify that the evil fate awaiting the wicked is eternal, even though he has just proclaimed the "eternal" good awaiting the good is remarkable. It defines the positive tradition.

Further on, Paul speaks differently of the Judge. "In Christ, God was reconciling the world to himself, not counting their trespasses against them"; he was charging Paul and his fellow preachers with "the message of reconciliation" (2 Corinthians 5.19). This reconciliation is not irresistible or automatic, however, for Paul next urges his readers: "We beseech you on behalf of Christ to be reconciled to God" (5.20). This sentence introduces a new theme. As compared to judging according to deeds done in the body (5.10), this sentence suggests that some individual initiative must be taken. Through some seeking, some sign, it seems, either of assenting to faith or improving one's life there must be some individual commitment that answers the mercy and justification Christ offers. This provision is vitally important, because it provides a futher rationale for excluding those who did not make the request, did not give that indication, did not show that receptivity to grace. That is why, earlier in this passage, Paul specifies "those who live" (verse 15), implicitly excluding those who do not live, and in proclaiming the "new man," he adds the qualification "if anyone is in Christ" (17). Progressively, it seems, Paul is adding more and more grounds for exclusion.

Again and again the conditions of his apostolate remind Paul that there are wicked people, such as his opponents and detractors, whose allegiance to Christ is only feigned and who, in reality, serve the Devil: "For such men are false apostles, deceitful workmen, disguising themselves as apostles of Christ. And no wonder, for even Satan disguises himself as an angel of light. So it is not strange if his servants also disguise themselves as servants of righteousness. Their end [*telos*] will correspond to their deeds" (2 Corinthians 11.13–15). By now the theme of judgment according to one's deeds is clear. It is also mentioned in Romans 2.6, 5.18, and Ephesians 5.6, 6.8.

The Epistle to the Galatians provides another criterion for distinguishing those who will inherit the kingdom of God from those who will not. Inheritance depends on whether one "crucifies" the flesh in order to be "led by the Spirit".

> But I say, walk by the Spirit, and do not gratify the desires of the flesh. For the desires of the flesh are against the Spirit, and the desires of the Spirit are against the flesh; for these are opposed to each other, to prevent you from doing what you would. But if you are led by the Spirit you are not under the law. Now the works of the flesh are plain: fornication, impurity, licentiousness, idolatry, sorcery, enmity, strife, jealousy, anger, selfishness, dissension, party spirit, envy, drunkenness, carousing, and the like. I warn you, as I warned you before, that *those who do such things shall not inherit the kingdom of God*. But the fruit of the Spirit is love, joy, peace, patience, kindness, goodness, faithfulness, gentleness, self-control; against such there is no law. And those who belong to Christ Jesus have crucified the flesh with its passions and desires. (5.16–24, my italics)

In this famous passage, Paul asserts the implacable opposition of spirit and flesh. Naming the works of the flesh, he warns that "those who do such things shall not inherit the kingdom of God." The discipline required to control the desires of the flesh Paul likens to a personal crucifixion, and he makes this conformity to the sacrifice of Christ the criterion of true loyalty.

Here, judgment is also by one's deeds, but those deeds are classified as pertaining either to the spirit or the flesh. Note, however, that these quotations from letters whose order is not certain but which are held to be close together in time (that is, 2 Corinthians and Galatians) raise very important themes: the opposition of Satan to Christ, angels of darkness to angels of light, and the flesh to the spirit. In both passages, the ethical choices of humans are described as belonging to one of two categories, with one's fate depending upon one's choice. All he tells of the fate of those who chose wrongly, however, is that they will not inherit the kingdom of God. This fate is not said to be either unpleasant or eternal. Simple exclusion is all that is mentioned.

From the division of deeds in Galatians, Paul turns, in the opening pages of his Epistle to the Romans, to the Day of Judgment, the time when people will be separated according to those deeds. Just as there are two types of deeds, those done according to the spirit and those done according to the flesh, so there are two outcomes resulting from judgment.

> Do you not know that God's kindness is meant to lead you to repentance? But by your hard and impenitent heart you are storing up wrath for yourself on the day of wrath when God's righteous judgment [*dikaiokrisias*, avenging judgment] will be revealed. For he will render to every man according to his works: to those who by patience in well-doing seek for glory and honor and immortality, he will give eternal life [*zōēn aiōnion*]; but for those who are factious and do not obey the truth, but obey wickedness, there will be wrath and fury [*thymos kai orgē*]. There will be tribulation and distress [*thlipsis kai stenochōria*] for every human being who does evil, the Jew first and also the Greek, but glory and honor and peace for every one who does good, the Jew first and also the Greek. For God shows no partiality. (Romans 2.4–11)

Two themes are clear in this passage. First is the greater insistence on the inner disposition toward receiving divine mercy, the assent to faith. Here, it is stated that one must melt one's hard heart and turn from impenitence to penitence or else experience God's wrath (verse 5).[13] By implication, penitence will be met with forgiveness. Second is the notion that, like those who repent, those who seek glory through "patience in well-doing" will be given eternal life (7).

Equally remarkable in this passage, however, is the contrast between the fates of those who persevere in goodness and the wicked who obey evil. The good, Paul says, will receive "glory and honor and peace, . . . immortality, eternal life." The evildoers will receive "wrath and fury, . . . tribulation and distress." Again Paul shows restraint in characterizing the fate of the wicked. He could have paired eternal life with eternal death or stated that the wrath, fury, tribulation, or distress would be eternal, but he did not. The remarkable aspect of this passage is Paul's reluctance to characterize

13. Stephen H. Travis, *Christ and the Judgment of God: Divine Retribution in the New Testament* (Basingstoke, England: Marshall, Morgan, and Scott, 1986), 36–39, uses Romans 1.18–32 to develop a line of reasoning different from the one pursued here. Using Paul's ideas in this passage he sketches a nonretributive, intrinsic justice, whereby sin is its own punishment and the sinner suffers according as he or she moves away from God. In this sense divine justice is "not retributive" but "relational." He says: " 'Wrath' is a word for the destiny of those who persist as God's 'enemies.' . . . It is the culmination of a present condition." Cf. his restatement, p. 77. Travis's idea is similar to what I have called "reflexive justice.

postmortem punishment as eternal. The same reticence appears at Romans 6.20–22 and, as we have already seen, at 2 Corinthians 5.10.[14]

Paul now returns to the theory of history that he described in 1 Corinthians 15.24, the sequence that runs from Adam to Christ to the Last Judgment.

> Since all have sinned and fall short of the glory of God, they are justified by his grace as a gift, through the redemption which is in Christ Jesus, whom God put forward as an expiation by his blood, to be received by faith. This was to show God's righteousness, because *in his divine forbearance he had passed over former sins;* it was to prove at the present time that he himself is righteous and that he justifies him who has faith in Jesus. (Romans 3.23–26, my italics)

This passage shifts from Paul's ethical theory to his anthropological theory. Here he is dealing with the quality of human history as a whole. Adam's story shows that all creatures fall short of God's goodness; yet this difference can be made up, humanity can be "justified," through a divine gift called "grace," bestowed specifically as an expiation of Adam's sin accomplished through the redemptive action of Christ. Again Paul asserts God's willingness to overlook former sins (cf. 2 Corinthians 5.14–21). Yet there is a condition repeated twice (verses 25 and 26). In order to benefit from this mercy, this divine forbearance, one must accept by faith the truth of Paul's statement. Except for the possibility that one might lack faith (only implicit here), no one would seem to be exluded from this dispensation.

This theme is reiterated at Romans 5.8–9: "But God shows his love for us in that while we were yet sinners Christ died for us. Since, therefore, we are now justified by his blood, much more shall we be saved by him from the *wrath* [*orgēs*] of God" (my italics). This passage must be seen in the light of a later one:

> If, because of one man's trespass, death reigned through that one man, much more will those who receive the abundance of grace and the free gift of righteousness reign in life through the one man Jesus Christ. Then as one man's trespass led to condemnation [*katakrima*] for all [*pantas*] men, so one man's act of righteousness leads to acquittal and life for all [*pantas*] men. For as by one man's disobedience many [*polloi*] were made

14. Travis, *Christ and the Judgment*, 71–72, notes how "remarkable" Paul's "reticence" is but questions whether Paul followed his own logic so far as to accept "the annihilation of the wicked." See also C. Clifton Black, "Pauline Perspectives on Death in Romans 5–8," *Journal of Biblical Literature* 103 (1984): 413–33.

sinners, so by one man's obedience many [*polloi*] will be made righteous. (Romans 5.17–19)

Paul reiterates the theme of Christ's redemptive action canceling the effects of Adam's fall. Yet verses 18 and 19 differ in describing how many will benefit from it. In the light of Romans 3.26 ("[God] justifies him who has faith in Jesus"), it would be reasonable to interpret this discrepancy to mean that Christ's sacrifice made it potentially possible for all to be justified. Yet justification depends upon the individual's faith in, or assent to, the efficacy of redemption. The beneficiaries of redemption are *only* "those who receive the abundance of grace and the free gift of righteousness" (17). Some, therefore, will be excluded: "many" are not "all." Exclusion here depends on whether or not one accepts God's gift of grace.

Now this proposition raises a question: If humans cannot initiate their own salvation but are dependent on grace, a divine gift, how can God justly exclude those who were never given a chance, that is, were never favored with grace? Paul was certainly aware of this issue and in one famous passage dealt with the question simply by referring to the absoluteness of God's will, which cannot be understood by human reason.[15] It is not so much a solution as an imposition of divine superiority over the human mind.

> But who are you, a man, to answer back to God? Will what is molded say to its molder, "Why have you made me thus?" Has the potter no right over the clay, to make out of the same lump one vessel for beauty and another for menial use? What if God, desiring to show his wrath [*orgēn*] and to make known his power, has endured with much patience the vessels of wrath [*orgēs*] made for destruction [*apōleian*], in order to make known the riches of his glory for the vessels of mercy, which he has prepared beforehand for glory, even us whom he has called, not from the Jews only but also from the Gentiles? (Romans 9.20–24)

Again Paul distinguishes between members and nonmembers of the community. In this passage, central to the belief in predestination, membership is not determined by any human act or choice. Rather, the fate of the creature is known to the Creator from the very act of creation and it is only when it conforms to the purpose of the maker that a vessel will be destined for glory. Therefore, in contrast to the theme of the individual's seeking, Paul now declares the need for him or her to be called (verse 24). Paul implies, then, an arrangement of reciprocal acceptance: to be saved one must be called; if called, one must answer positively. Those not called and those called who

15. For an introduction to the issue of Jewish and Greek influences on Paul, see Black, "Pauline Perspectives."

fail to answer will know the wrath or exclusion that, among other things, Paul was seeking to define.

At the meeting point between divine choice and human acceptance stand the Jews. Their continued adherence to the "old" law would seem to be a negative example for the Gentiles whom Paul seeks to convert, whereas their having been chosen earlier by God is a positive example—indeed, he thought, a historical precedent for salvation itself. Thus, Paul must set out the relationship between the Jews and the Gentiles. To do so he fits the Jews into his historical schema, running from Adam to Christ to the Last Judgment, and ends with a statement cited by advocates of universal reconciliation.

> As regards the Gospel they are enemies of God, for your sake [you Gentiles, who should learn from their negative example]; but as regards election they are beloved for the sake of their forefathers [i.e., because of earlier covenants]. For the gifts and the call of God are irrevocable [the chosen people are always a chosen people]. Just as you [Gentiles now or about to become Christians] were once disobedient to God [while the Jews lived under the covenant] but now have received mercy because of their disobedience, so they have now been disobedient in order that by the mercy shown to you they also may receive mercy. (Romans 11.28–31)

According to this history, everyone at one time suffered in disobedience. Whereas the Jews do so now (that is, in Paul's time) while they are temporarily hardened, as Paul put it just previously (11.25), the Gentiles, who are now Christians, did so until they accepted Christ. Believing that this fault affects all humanity at one time or another, Paul concludes: "For God has consigned all men to disobedience, that he may have mercy upon all" (11.32). Have mercy upon all! Clearly Paul retains his hope for universal reconciliation. On the one hand, he demands a response to God's call as a prerequisite to justification, and, on the other hand, he remains committed to the notion of a historical imperative that almost necessitates universal salvation through the irresistible efficacy of divine action.

Yet the idea that eventual mercy cancels the effects of disobedience may lead some to exalt themselves above the laws of the constituted order, that is, the Roman state. Thus, Paul warns that the governing officials exercise authority from God and that the prince "is the servant of God to execute his wrath on the wrongdoer" (Romans 13.4). Here is a vital link between the authority of the earthly and heavenly ruler. Does God also legitimate the tyrant or other human oppressors? Christian citizens are not to take the law into their own hands:

> Bless those who persecute you. . . . Repay no evil for evil [cf. Matthew 5.39]. . . . Beloved, never avenge yourselves, but leave it to the wrath

[*orgēi*] of God; for it is written "Vengeance [*ekdikēsis*] is mine, I will repay, says the Lord" [cf. Deuteronomy 32.35]. No, "if your enemy is hungry, feed him; if he is thirsty give him drink; for by so doing you will heap burning coals upon his head" [cf. Proverbs 25.21–22]. Do not be overcome by evil, but overcome evil with good. (Romans 12.14, 17, 19–21)

Paul stated in 1 Thessalonians 2.16 that the wrath of God will discipline those who persecute believers. Speaking more broadly here, of all earthly justice, Paul enjoins human passivity before injustice with the promise of divine correction later. How long one must wait for divine vengeance remains an open question here, as it does in the passages he quotes from the Hebrew Bible.[16] Until that vengeance comes, the ability to punish and to administer order is conferred on the secular government.

Let every person be subject to the governing authorities. For there is no authority except from God, and those that exist have been instituted by God. Therefore he who resists the authorities resists what God has appointed, and those who resist will incur judgment [*krima*]. For rulers are not a terror to good conduct, but to bad. Would you have no fear of him who is in authority? Then do what is good, and you will receive his approval, for he is God's servant for your good. But if you do wrong, be afraid, for he does not bear the sword in vain, he is the servant of God to execute his wrath on the wrongdoer. Therefore one must be subject, not only to avoid God's wrath but also for the sake of conscience. (Romans 13.1–5)

The laws of the state are instituted by divine authority. To resist them is to resist God and to end in judgment. The world's judge is a delegate of the divine Judge. No promise of future reward can weaken one's earthly obligations.

But these promises impose obligations, and Paul knew that many fail to meet them. This chapter has reviewed the options Paul explored when he considered those who conduct themselves evilly or spurn God's offer of justification. Speaking anthropologically of the whole human race, Paul believed God has the power and the design to save all, for all have been disobedient and all, then, may receive mercy. Nonetheless, obstacles arise in two areas. The individual cannot presume upon the efficacy of divine action; when grace is granted one must, through faith, actively acknowledge, accept, develop its benefits. Further, the evil actions of specific persons or groups warrant exclusion from the kingdom of God.

16. Prov. 25.22, with an echo from Ps. 140.10. See also 2 Sam. 22.9 and Job 41.21 for fiery coals as image of divine wrath.

Paul's statements about those who fail under either or both of these headings vary according to whether he is speaking within an ethical or an anthropological context. In his ethical statements there appear to be two possible solutions. In one group of texts, Paul says that the wicked will experience God's wrath, judgment, or an evil end. These passages suggest punishment after death, though not eternally, for Paul never envisions that. The second option within the ethical context threatens the wicked with destruction, the annulment of their being. These two suggestions are mutually exclusive: what is destroyed cannot be punished.

Considering Paul's anthropological discussion helps to resolve this contradiction, for in the context of the whole human race, Paul advances the hope of a universal return to God, a reconciliation, in which God will be all in all and a perfect unity or harmony will be attained. Now, if we assume that "wrath" and its related terms mean postmortem punishment, that solution seems inconsistent with reconciliation, because the continued existence of wicked people being punished is inconsistent with a cosmos in perfect harmony with God, who is to be all in all. Fulfillment of the prophecy that God will be everything for everyone depends on the destruction of those for whom God will not be everything. In Paul, then, wrath must function like destruction or else God will never be all in all. Those who separate themselves through unbelief or evil actions must be destroyed so that nothing may diminish the beauty of participation in the kingdom.

We may test this hypothesis by considering one final passage, which might, at first glance, appear to contradict the notion that wrath, evil, and judgment are synonymous with destruction: "None of us lives to himself, and none of us dies to himself. If we live, we live to the Lord, and if we die, we die to the Lord; so then, whether we live or whether we die, we are the Lord's. For to this end Christ died and lived again, that he might be Lord both of the dead and of the living" (Romans 14.7–9). In the light of Paul's frequent references to the kingdom that will come for those who believe, there is no difficulty in seeing how Christ might be the lord of the living. To understand how Christ might be lord of the dead, it is necessary to distinguish the wicked dead from the blessed. Clearly, Christ is king of the saved, who reign with him. But how can Christ also be lord of the wicked dead if they have been destroyed? If one were to look only at this line, it would be possible to make a mistake, that is, to assume anachronistically that, for Paul, Christ's rule over the dead involves his ability to punish them in a kind of kingdom of the damned like the hell that would later be developed. If that were the case, this would be Paul's only reference to it. Further, Paul consistently refuses to posit a parallel between the saved and the not-saved. It is safer to assume that this lordship of the dead was not an ongoing sovereignty but another expression for an idea presented in parallel fashion elsewhere. The formula in 1 Corinthians 15.25—"for he must reign until he has put all his enemies under his feet" and the time comes when "all things are subjected to him"—also posits a lordship of the sort that has the power to dispose and yet whose continuous rule is not implied. Indeed, 1 Corinthians 15.24, 26, explicitly states that the rival powers are destroyed. And in the letter to the Romans (at 2.8–9), Paul refrains from positing any future for those failing at the judgment. Again at Romans 9.22 the vessels of wrath intentionally designed for the purpose are said to be made for "destruction" not eternal punishment. Christ's lordship of the living and the dead, therefore, suggests that at the Last Judgment the living and the dead will be raised, and before the tribunal of their lord they will be judged (cf. "We will all stand before the judgment seat of Christ" [2 Corinthians 5.10]). And although later authors in the New Testament will speak of this lordship, in Paul it probably does not mean that just as Christ will rule the living (that is, the resurrected) in the kingdom of God, so he will also rule the dead, those sentenced to the second death and a separate kingdom where they are punished. In Paul there seems to be no evidence of that kind of symmetry but indeed an avoidance of it.

It seems clear, then, that Paul had no desire to describe the condition of those not rewarded with the kingdom. Even in marginal texts, where it is only just conceivable that he envisaged something other than annihilation (here I am referring to 2 Thessalonians 1.9 and Ephesians 2.2–3, where the sons of disobedience are linked with the children of wrath), the need to qualify my characterization of Paul is tempered by the extreme ambiguity of the passage or—in the case of the last two passages mentioned—by the questionable attribution to Paul. It should nonetheless already be clear that there is a definable cluster of texts associated almost unanimously with Paul and dating from the fifth decade of the first century which analyze the criteria for entry into the kingdom and refuse to speculate on the fate of those found lacking.[17]

JOHN

Although the furthest removed from Paul in time (written probably

17. For a similar conclusion, see J. Gwynn Griffiths, *The Divine Verdict: A Study of Divine Judgement in the Ancient Religions*, Studies in the History of Religions, Supplements to *Numen*, 52 (Leiden: Brill, 1991), 275: "Eschatologically, however, death or annihilation, though not eternal torment, is the fate of those who reject God's proffered grace." Griffith cites concurring opinions in note 263.

around 90 or 95), the Gospel according to John is the closest to him in spirit.[18] That affinity is certainly borne out in the passages in which John discusses the fate of nonbelievers. Like Paul, John holds that the judgment probes for faith and that those lacking faith when examined suffer exclusion, wrath, and destruction as consequences of failing the test. Like Paul, John examines the puzzle of how God's plan for human redemption could be foiled, "for God so loved the world that he gave his only Son, that whoever believes in him should not perish [apōletai] but have eternal life. For God sent the Son into the world, not to condemn [krinēi] the world, but that the world might be saved through him" (John 3.16–17). Only through human failure to believe can the mission be blocked. Yet the consequences are dire: "He who believes in him is not condemned; he who does not believe is condemned already, because he has not believed in the name of the only Son of God" (3.18). Thus belief is the key to eternal life. Judgment will test for that faith, whose lack brings "perishing" (3.16) or "condemnation" (3.17) or "wrath" (3.36). The dead will be resurrected for this inspection, which will be conducted by the Son. At that time, some will enter into eternal life, others into judgment, which is equated with death: "He who hears my word and believes him who sent me, has eternal life [zōēn aiōnion]; he does not come into judgment [krisin], but has passéd from death [thanaton] to life [zōēn] (5.24). In addition to being examined for whether they loved the light (3.19) or heard the word (5.24), the resurrected will be assessed for their virtue: "Those who have done good [will be sent] to the resurrection of life [anastasin zōēs], and those who have done evil, to the resurrection of judgment [anastasin kriseōs]" (5.29).

The structure of this system is very similar to Paul's, although the terminology is somewhat different. John uses "judgment" where Paul tended to use "wrath," though "wrath" is not foreign to John. The biggest contrast is that John is free of Paul's earlier hesitation about any mention of those who fail in the divine scrutiny. John's position is the solution that Paul arrived at only gradually. John's formula can be stripped to the barest essentials. The judgment by the Son on the authority of the Father will yield eternal life for those who believe but judgment, wrath, death for those who do not.

This is not a theory of eternal punishment. The wrath of God is expressed as a denial of eternal life. As in Paul, there is no reference to what the content

18. For recent scholarship on John, see D. A. Carson, "Selected Recent Studies of the Fourth Gospel," *Themelios* 14 (1989): 57–64; M. M. Thompson, "Eternal Life in the Gospel of John," *Ex auditu* 5 (1989): 35–55; Christian D. Von Dehsen, "Believers and Non-believers in Paul'and John," *Lutheran Forum* 23 (1989): 10–14; Friedmar Kemper, "Zur literarischen Gestalt des Johannesevangeliums," *Theologische Zeitschrift* 43 (1987): 247–64.

of that death may be. It is "mere" death. This is actually a "middle" position for John, for advocates of a fiery hell advance some passages of John on behalf of their view, and other passages are brought forward on behalf of universalism. Let us examine these possibilities in turn.

When Jesus contemplates the events he must undergo at the end of his life on earth, he prays. A voice from heaven answers him. The crowd in Jerusalem hears the voice and Jesus explains "I, when I am lifted up from the earth, will draw all men to myself" (John 12.32). As with similar Pauline passages, subsequent sentences qualify this apparently self-evident statement. Jesus continues by referring to the possibility that some will not benefit from the light he sheds: "The light is with you for a little longer. Walk while you have the light, lest the darkness overtake you; he who walks in the darkness does not know where he goes" (12.35, repeated in different terms at verse 36). This statement leaves the very real possibility that some will remain in darkness and, as stated before, be liable to judgment.

A more extended prayer of Jesus gives an even stronger impression of a mystical unity by which he and humankind might be joined in the same fusion that he shares with his Father, "that they may be one, even as we are one" (John 17.11). Only Satan seems to be excluded: "None of them is lost but the son of perdition" (17.12). Again, Jesus in his prayer seems to remind his Father that this unity had been arranged from all eternity: "Father, I desire that they also, whom thou hast given me, may be with me where I am, to behold my glory which thou has given me in the love for me before the foundation of the world" (17.24). There are, nonetheless, conditions present in this prayer. The "son of perdition" may refer not only to Satan as chief of the sons of perdition but to any and all adherents of Satan, whom John sometimes considers those who love the darkness. More serious is the frequent use of the possessive, so that Jesus refers to those who are "mine," whom he says "thou hast given me" (17.9). One senses that he is referring to the apostles and, through them, the church and consequently only to believers: "I do not pray for these only, but also for those who believe in me through their word" (17.20). There is still the suggestion that the whole world might be won over through this unity, "so that the world may know that thou hast sent me" (17.23); yet "the world has not known thee" (17.25). The world's acknowledgment of the mission of Jesus is not complete; thus, he distinguishes those "whom thou hast given me [17.9, 11, 24] . . . before the foundation of the world" (17.24). Throughout this prayer, the pronouns "they" and "them" seem to refer to this restricted group to whom Jesus conveyed God's glory and the truth of his mission, so that the world might know. The unity for which Jesus here prays, modeled on his own with the Father, is essential for spreading word of his mission; yet "the world has not known thee" (17.25). Jesus requested unity not for the world but only "for those whom thou hast given me" (John 17.9). Thus there are restrictions, and this unity applies only to believers.

On the other side of John's "middle position" is the parable of the vine and the vinedresser, with its references to the fruitless branches that are pruned away and burned (John 15.1–8). Similarly constructed images are far more numerous in the synoptic Gospels, the subject of Chapter 9. Still, when John quotes Jesus pointing to the viticultural example—"If a man does not abide in me, he is cast forth as a branch and withers; and the branches are gathered, thrown into the fire and burned" (15.6)—this is the fire of daily life on the farm and not that of Gehenna, except by extension from other texts. For a clear example of that use of symbolism, one must look at the synoptic Gospels.

I take these texts from Paul's letters and John's Gospel to represent that strand within the New Testament which emphasizes the positive force of the divine intention, the aspiration for a perfect unity in which all might be saved. This tradition recognizes the need of assent from fortunate human beings who have been given the opportunity of redemption, and it states with varying degrees of clarity the possibility that not all will respond positively. Failure to respond earns the wrath of God expressed as a denial of eternal life, exclusion from the kingdom. Although they deny the reward of the blessed to those who are excluded, these positive texts do not actually describe the consequence of exclusion or the nature of any further existence. The excluded die, are destroyed or annihilated. Very different is the fate of the excluded in the symmetrical texts, where both fates are described in full.

Damnation

Paul and John clearly voice their aspiration for universal salvation and almost audibly avoid mentioning eternal damnation, but other New Testament authors, particularly in the synoptic Gospels, explicitly evoked eternal punishment as the fate of those who persecute the church, behave immorally, or fail to accept the faith. Some passages explicitly refer to Gehenna. They describe it as fire, call it eternal, and declare it to be the fate of those found wanting at the Last Judgment. Three crucial passages in the synoptic Gospels helped form the concept of hell. Mark 9.43–48 and Matthew 25.31–46 call the place of punishment Gehenna. Luke 16.19–31 refers to Hades, but the suffering of the sinner described there puts this passage at the punitive extreme of the classical Hades or the Hebrew Sheol. In actual practice, because of the fire, suffering, and the denial of the sinner's two requests, Luke 16 served to support advocates of eternal punishment. Gehenna is again mentioned explicitly in Revelation, which will be discussed in the next chapter.

The passage in Mark, considered to be the earliest Gospel, was the first to identify the fire and the worm of Isaiah 66.24 with Gehenna:

> If your hand causes you to sin, cut it off; it is better for you to enter life maimed than with two hands to go to hell [Gehenna], to the unquenchable fire. And if your foot causes you to sin, cut it off; it is better for you to enter life lame than with two feet to be thrown into hell [Gehenna]. And if your eye causes you to sin, pluck it out; it is better for you to enter the

kingdom of God with one eye than with two eyes to be thrown into hell [Gehenna], where their worm does not die, and the fire is not quenched. (Mark 9.43–48)

There can be no question about the threat of hellfire here. Since Gehenna is the Greek rendering of Ge-Hinnom, Mark quotes Jesus referring to the accursed valley, the permanent prison for the worst offenders, not Hades or Sheol, the neutral grave for all the dead. Mark's reference to the endless torments of Isaiah 66.24 is clear.[1] Here Mark identifies Isaiah's undying fire and worm with Jeremiah's Ge-Hinnom. Yet, by calling it Gehenna, he avoids the limited duration of rot and corrosiveness in the heap of carrion alluded to in Isaiah .[2] In Mark's use, the torments of the fire and the worm are meant to be sacred to the Lord and unending. This appears to be the earliest New Testament reference to an eternal hell.[3] Here Mark agrees with Paul that the body can lead one away from the eternal kingdom, but unlike Paul, he indicates the consequences: not lasting separation, denial of the kingdom, but a fate that he affirms in specific terms.

The context of this important passage clarifies its meaning. Prior to introducing the threat of Gehenna, Mark quotes Jesus' teaching that any who offend against the innocence of children is to be severely punished: "Whoever causes one of these little ones who believe in me to sin, it would be better for him if a great millstone were hung round his neck and he were thrown into the sea" (9.42). Moreover, an offense against a child or an innocent believer is equated with an offense against Jesus and his Father, for "whoever receives one such child in my name receives me, and whoever receives me, receives not me but him who sent me" (9.37). Mark, therefore, shows Jesus establishing a severe sanction against violating the innocence of a person Jesus says is like him.[4]

1. Some deny that the words "where their worm does not die, and the fire is not quenched" (verse 46) are in the original text. See Urban C. Von Wahlde, "Mark 9:33–50: Discipleship, the Authority That Serves," *Biblische Zeitschrift* 29 (1985): 58 and n. 28. The references to Gehenna would remain.

2. As we have seen, the term "Gehenna" was rooted in the original mass grave for victims of sacrifice and executed criminals in Ge-Hinnom, but it had since been given a figurative sense in Jer. 19:2–13, where the prophet reveals that the Lord would convert the valley into his own place of punishment, clarified in Jer. 31:40, and promoted to cosmic status in the *Book of Enoch*.

3. Matthew also took up this passage at 18.8–10.

4. There is some question as to whether only children as such or any innocent follower of Jesus is meant. See Will Deming, "Mark 9:42, Matthew 5:27–32, and B. Nid. 13b: A First-Century Discussion of Male Sexuality," *New Testament Studies* 39 (1990): 130–41, for the first view; and Walter W. Wessel, in *The Expositor's Bible*

In Matthew that sanction will become more severe, and the classes of protected persons will be further itemized. The sanction for an offense against persons with whom Jesus identifies himself is already clear in Mark. According to this principle, injury to an innocent person is injury to Christ and will be avenged as such.[5] Matthew carries this idea further.

Matthew announces the subject of eternal subjection to fire by reporting the prophecy of John the Baptist warning the Pharisees and Sadducees that Jesus will come to separate good from evil: "His winnowing fork is in his hand and he will clear his threshing floor and gather his wheat into the granary, but the chaff he will burn with unquenchable fire" (3.12). Thus, even before narrating the teaching of Jesus, Matthew uses the unquenchable fire from Isaiah 66.24 to foretell the fate of those discarded by the one who is coming.[6]

Reporting the Sermon on the Mount, Matthew changes slightly the context in which Mark referred to the fire and the worm. Here Jesus proposes not children as such as the model of innocence but rather the poor in spirit, the meek, the merciful, the pure in heart, the peacemakers, the persecuted. Their qualities are the measures of righteousness, without which "you will never enter the kingdom of heaven" (5.3–20).

After these positive recommendations essential for entrance to the kingdom of heaven, Matthew's report shows Jesus turning to examples of misdeeds that can bring punishment.[7] "Whoever says 'you fool!' shall be liable to the hell [Gehenna] of fire" (5.22), apparently the same that Mark referred to. Also like Mark, Matthew reports that Jesus recommended harsh measures against threats to innocence, whether from a person who brings temptation or from a physical longing that weakens one's resolve: "Woe to the man by whom the temptation comes!" (18.7b). Not even the limbs that taint one's innocence are to be spared: "If your right eye causes you to sin, pluck it out and throw it away; it is better that you lose one of your members than

---

Commentary, ed. Frank E. Gaebelein (Grand Rapids, Mich: Zondervan, 1984), 8:707 for the second.

5. See J. D. M. Derrett, "Two 'Harsh' Sayings of Christ Explained," Downside Review 103 (1985): 218–29.

6. For recent scholarship on Matthew, see Mark McVann, ed., "The Gospel of Matthew: Current Discussions," Listening 24 (1989): 223–309; G. E. Okeke, "The After-life in Matthew as an Aspect of the Matthean Ethic," Communio viatorum 31 (1988): 159–68; Doris Donnelly, "Preaching the Hard Word," Princeton Seminary Bulletin 6 (1985): 135–37.

7. Craig S. Keener, "Matthew 5:22 and the Heavenly Court," Expository Times 99 (1987): 46.

that your whole body be thrown into hell [Gehenna]. And if your right hand causes you to sin, cut it off and throw it away; it is better that you lose one of your members than that your whole body go into hell [Gehenna]" (5.29–30).

In this passage famous for the spiritual interpretation of the Judaic law, by which the ban against adultery becomes a prohibition against looking lustfully (5.27–28) and the ban against murder becomes a prohibition against anger (5.21–22), even against calling one's brother a fool, the sanction, too, is escalated. Instead of "judgment," a threat common in both testaments, the punishment is explicitly called the hell into which one's "whole body" will be thrown.

But just as Matthew shows how Jesus warned against adultery not merely by recalling the law but even by demanding excision of the inner disposition that might violate it, so Matthew quotes his teaching that judgment will depend on how well one transfers the quality of charity into deeds. In what is perhaps the single most important biblical passage for the history of hell, Matthew relates the reply of Jesus on the Mount of Olives to the disciples' question about his return. Jesus precedes this account of his return with parables that explain the unexpectedness of the Second Coming. The Son of man will come like a thief in the night, and so salvation will be possible only for those who have lived well, in expectation of a final reckoning. He illustrates the lesson with the parables of the good and wicked servants, the wise and foolish virgins, and the talents. Servants who do not prepare for the return of their master will be punished with banishment to "the outer darkness; there men will weep and gnash their teeth" (25.30; cf. 24.51).

Then comes the account of the judgment itself: "When the Son of man comes in his glory, and all the angels with him, then he will sit on his glorious throne. Before him will be gathered all the nations [*ethnē*], and he will separate them one from another as a shepherd separates the sheep from the goats, and he will place the sheep at his right hand, but the goats at the left" (25.31–33).[8] With the angels in attendance and the nations gathered before him, the Son of man will separate the sheep, who were obedient, from the goats, who were independent and rebellious.[9] "Then the King will say to

---

8. See J. M. Court, "Right and Left: The Implications for Matthew 25:31–46," *New Testament Studies* 31 (1985): 223–33; J. A. T. Robinson, "The 'Parable' of the Sheep and the Goats," *New Testament Studies* 2 (1956): 225–37. Robinson discusses the composition of the whole passage.

9. The term "nations" is a surprise here. Given the preceding parables, one expects a judgment of individuals. In fact, what follows relates individual deeds of charity. One can, of course, conceive of nations that feed, clothe, and shelter, but to insist on

those at his right hand, 'Come, O blessed of my Father, inherit the kingdom prepared for you from the foundation of the world'" (25.34).

Jesus next explains how the reward is earned: "For I was hungry and you gave me food, I was thirsty and you gave me drink, I was a stranger and you welcomed me, I was naked and you clothed me, I was sick and you visited me, I was in prison and you came to me" (25.35–36). These are the outward manifestations of internal qualities, particularly charity.

> Then the righteous will answer him, "Lord, when did we see thee hungry and feed thee, or thirsty and give thee drink? And when did we see thee a stranger and welcome thee, or naked and clothe thee? And when did we see thee sick or in prison and visit thee?" And the King will answer them, "Truly, I say to you, as you did it to one of the least of these my brethren, you did it to me." (25.37–40)

Those about to receive the reward will be surprised; apparently they did not perform these charitable actions with any thought of personal benefit. Yet, whereas in Mark 9.37, Jesus identifies himself with children in their innocence, here he identifies himself with the poor in their need. "Then he will say to those at his left hand, 'Depart from me, you cursed [ones], into the eternal fire [*pyr aiōnion*] prepared for the devil and his angels" (25.41). The punishment will be like the reward—preexisting from the beginning of time.

The fire is here called eternal. Moreover, it is a fire from that past prior to the fall of Satan and his angels. It encloses all evil, intelligent beings, whether angels or humans. This prophecy declares damnation to have been known to God from the beginning. The fall of the angels, and subsequently that of men, must have been anticipated when God prepared the fire.

The reason for damnation is omission of what is required for salvation: "For I was hungry and you gave me no food, I was thirsty and you gave me no drink, I was a stranger and you did not welcome me, naked and you did not clothe me, sick and in prison and you did not visit me" (25.42–43). These actions are a denial of charity. The damned will object: "'Lord, when did we see thee hungry or thirsty or a stranger or naked or sick or in prison, and did not minister to thee?' Then he will answer them, 'Truly, I say to you, as you did it not to one of the least of these, you did it not to me'" (25.44–45). Those about to receive punishment will be surprised, as apparently they

---

a judgment of nations rather than of persons runs counter to the emphasis noted before on the inner, spiritual qualities of individuals. This prophecy reverses the contrast put forward in the Sermon on the Mount between an external act and its corresponding internal disposition (e.g., adultery and lust) and becomes a test for those inner qualities as manifested in action.

were not so foolish as to deny charity to their judge. Those failing in charity could not see the divinity in the "children" of the world, could see no potential benefit in aiding the hungry, thirsty, and needy and so did not sacrifice, indeed could not, even for their own advantage, have sacrificed for these with whom Christ identified himself. A final verse encapsulates the symmetry of the vision:[10] "And they will go away into eternal punishment [*kolasin aiōnion*], but the righteous into eternal life [*zōēn aiōnion*]" (25.46).

This passage, Matthew 25.31–46, is remarkable for its balance and its clearly articulated sense of justice. As a description of the end of time and a universal reckoning (of all "nations"), it unites a number of mythic elements. Both the kingdom for the blessed and the fire for the reprobate derive from the beginning of the cosmos. Both fates are said to be eternal. The Devil is named the leader of the first group consigned to the eternal fire (the fallen angels), and Christ sends the human damned to the same place. In this action he avenges the wrong committed by those who denied charity to the needy. Both the saved and the damned were faced with the same challenge, the need of the poor. Their fates differ as their responses differed. As Christ reveals that he is to be identified with each poor person, he returns as representative and avenger of the humble to reward their benefactors and punish their oppressors. Since Mark 9.48 identified the undying fire of Isaiah 66.24 with Gehenna, it must also be what Matthew calls "the eternal fire prepared for Satan and his angels."[11]

Surely John the Baptist was preaching this same vision metaphorically when he threatened the Pharisees and Sadducees. The burning of chaff is a typical metaphor in Matthew. The same message is carried in other images and sayings, for example, "Every tree that does not bear good fruit is cut down and thrown into the fire" (Matthew 3.10; cf. 7.19). Jesus is quoted citing examples from the Hebrew Bible, where the wicked are identified and

10. David R. Catchpole, "The Poor on Earth and the Son of Man in Heaven: A Reappraisal of Matthew 25:31–46," *Bulletin of the John Rylands University Library of Manchester* 61 (1979): 355–97, takes "the least of my brethren" to be the poor. Lamar Cope, "Matthew XXV:31–46: The Sheep and the Goats Reinterpreted," *Novum Testamentum* 11 (1969): 32–44, takes them to be the disciples or all followers of Christ. Dan O. Via, "Ethical Responsibility and Human Wholeness in Matthew 25:31–46," *Harvard Theological Review* 80 (1987): 91–94, considers the difference in standards of ethical judgment for those who have and have not heard the teachings of Jesus.

11. Travis, *Christ and the Judgment*, 137–39, concedes the irreversibility of the punishments threatened in Mark 9.42–48 (with its reference to Isa. 66.24) and Matt. 25.31–46, but irreversibility does not imply, he says, "that their victims endure conscious pain for ever."

destroyed. "As were the days of Noah, so will be the coming of the Son of man" (Matthew 24.37). Sodom and Gomorrah add the elements of fire and brimstone. Jesus compared his disciples to children and expected them to exemplify the virtues named in the Sermon on the Mount. He could therefore judge the communities to which they preached according to the reception given his "little ones": "And if anyone will not receive you or listen to your words, shake off the dust from your feet as you leave that house or town. Truly, I say to you, it shall be more tolerable on the day of judgment for the land of Sodom and Gomorrah than for that town" (10.15).

Yet we must have caution. Not every fire is eternal. Sodom and Gomorrah were destroyed by a fire that ended. Thus when Jesus recalls the fire that annihilated these cities, he refers not to Gehenna but to Hades, which (as we shall see in the Book of Revelation) will end: "And you, Capernaum, will you be exalted to heaven? You shall be *brought down to Hades*. For if the mighty works done in you had been done in Sodom, it would have remained until this day. But I tell you that it shall be more tolerable on the day of judgment for the land of Sodom than for you" (11.23–24, my italics). Here, as in Paul and in the Hebrew Bible (where it is called Sheol), Hades symbolizes death, an end to life on earth, for Jesus is alluding to the absolute end of Sodom and not the eternal suffering of Gehenna. At the same time, comparison with Sodom gives this reference to Hades (as to the one in Luke 16.19–31) a more distinctive color than the deathly pall of Sheol.

In preparation for the vision of judgment, Matthew relates two parables that mention weeping and gnashing of teeth as the fate of those who do not measure up (the wicked servants 24.51 and the parable of the talents 25.30, cf. the marriage feast 22.13). These miseries anticipate and parallel the eternal fire of Matthew 25. Although not all fires can be compared to Gehenna, it seems clear that the parable of the wheat and the tares can be linked to Matthew 25 through the weeping and gnashing of teeth.

In that parable, an enemy has sowed weeds in a man's wheat field, the servants ask what should be done, and the master answers: "Let both grow together until the harvest; and at harvest time I will tell the reapers, Gather the weeds first and bind them in bundles to be burned, but gather the wheat into my barn" (13.30). Questioned by the disciples about the meaning of the parable, Jesus replies:

> He who sows the good seed is the Son of man; the field is the world, and the good seed means the sons of the kingdom; the weeds are the sons of the evil one, and the enemy who sowed them is the devil; the harvest is the close of the age, and the reapers are angels. Just as the weeds are gathered and burned with fire, so will it be at the close of the age. The Son of man

will send his angels, and they will gather out of his kingdom all causes of sin and all evildoers, and throw them into the furnace of fire; there men will weep and gnash their teeth. Then the righteous will shine like the sun in the kingdom of their Father. (13.37–43)

This is a clear reference to a judgment with a fate for the rejected which includes a furnacelike fire that induces pain. Although the fire is not said here to be eternal, two aspects of this explanation, besides the fire itself, link it with the eternal fire of Matthew 25. First, this fire begins at the close of the age; so it cannot be confused with Hades. Second, since the weeds are identified with the Devil, as his sons, they have an affinity for evil comparable to that of those who denied charity and will be damned according to Matthew 25. Thus, these weeds do not stand generically for things that are useless or threatening to a good crop. Jesus himself says they signify those loyal to the Devil. Hence their torment can be assimilated to "the eternal fire prepared for Satan and his angels" (25.41).[12] This parallel to the great vision of judgment, introduces a new factor: criteria for judgment other than works of charity.

Even in teaching this fearful punishment, Matthew explicitly states the criteria for judgment and sets forth the justice of damnation. Here loyalty to the Son of man is opposed to affinity with the Devil. Judgment is sometimes said to be by conformity of wills: "Whoever does the will of my Father in heaven is my brother, and sister, and mother" (12.50). Again: "He who is not with me is against me" (12.30). Sometimes receiving the disciples on their preaching missions is enough: "He who receives you receives me, and he who receives me receives him who sent me. . . . And whoever gives to one of these little ones even a cup of cold water because he is a disciple, truly, I say to you, he shall not lose his reward (10.40–42; cf. Mark 9.37–41). This passage manifests a pattern. There is a reward for treating little ones well. As you behave to the little ones, you behave to Christ, and so you will be judged. Matthew 25.31–46 makes eternal fire the punishment for offending them. Whether a disciple or not, any humble person is "the least of my brethren," and Christ can avenge any wrong done or charity denied to himself in their guise.[13]

12. Matt. 13.47–50 may be considered parallel.

13. For a similar tendency to expand "the little ones" from a restricted sense of Christ's disciples to the broader sense of "anyone who was in distress," see Griffiths, *Divine Verdict*, 279. Travis too (*Christ and the Judgment*, 133) sees the deeds for which people (particularly the Gentiles) are judged as indicative of an inchoate relationship with Jesus expressed "by their acts of love toward 'the least' with whom he has identified himself," quoting with approval D. R. A. Hare and D. J. Harrington, "'Make Disciples of All the Gentiles' (Mt. 28.19)," *Catholic Biblical Quarterly* 37 (1975): 365.

What emerges is reflexive punishment similar to the pattern in the Hebrew Bible. It involves these stages: a sinner harms or declines to help another; Christ has identified himself with victims (the hungry, thirsty, naked, abandoned, imprisoned) whom one has declined to help; thus, harming another offends the one who will judge the offender; therefore, harming another harms oneself.

When Christ declared himself the surrogate for and the avenger of all victims, he made it inevitable that a person's evil behavior would reflect back on himself. I believe that this is more than retribution. Retribution explains punishment by saying that one who inflicts harm should suffer injury. Society intervenes and the punisher is not the one who was offended. In the system implied in the Sermon on the Mount, by divine intervention, punishment for any wrong becomes inevitable. The misdeed entails the punishment. Thus, like the action of a reflexive verb, the evildoer punishes himself by his own sin. Therefore any injury one does to another, one also does to oneself:[14] "What man of you, if his son asks him for bread, will give him a stone? Or if he asks for a fish, will give him a serpent? If you then, who are evil, know how to give good gifts to your children, how much more will your Father who is in heaven give good things to those who ask him!" (7.9–11). As you would treat a request from your son, so will God treat one from you, but you must ask. By the same token, you must grant what is asked of you: "So whatever you wish that men would do to you, do so to them; for this is the law and the prophets" (7.12). This provision is particularly important where mercy or forgiveness is concerned, for "if you forgive men their trespasses, your heavenly Father also will forgive you; but if you do not forgive men their trespasses, neither will your Father forgive your trespasses" (6.14–15). If you do not forgive, you will not be forgiven.

In the Sermon on the Mount Jesus teaches: "Judge not that you be not judged. For with the judgment you pronounce you will be judged, and the measure you give will be the measure you get" (7.1–2). Any falseness in the judgment you give will be measured back to you, and judgment will follow directly from one's own words: "I tell you on the day of judgment men will render account for every careless word they utter; for by your words you will be justified, and by your words you will be condemned" (12.36–37).

14. This is similar to Travis's "intrinsic" judgment (*Christ and the Judgment*, 39), which he wishes to distinguish from retribution. Yet, because such judgment would not operate unless God had set up the world that way, it cannot be considered intrinsic to the individual. God is necessary as stand-in for the victim, and he is necessary as the punishing agent without which the system would not work. This is equally true whether the offender suffers in his or her own life (as Travis says Paul intends) or at the end of time, or both.

Clearly, there is a pattern of reflexivity. Let us recapitulate. You will be forgiven as you have forgiven (Matthew 6.14–15) and judged as you have judged (7.2). You will be judged according to your own words (12.37). Further, actions done to others are done also to Christ. "He who receives you receives me" (10.40), and "as you did it to one of the least of these my brethren, you did it to me" (25.40), and as you neglected the least of my brethren you neglected me (cf. verse 45).

Christ's identification with the "little ones" (Mark 9.42; Matthew 25.40, 44) ensures, by divine provision, that anyone who harms the "little ones" will thereby harm oneself. The point here is not simply that one should do to others as one would have others do to oneself because it is right. Rather, in addition, it is also because Christ has identified himself with those others. This is therefore a new, more powerfully sanctioned arrangement. The "other" person is Christ. He has declared himself both stand-in for the victim and avenger of the offense. Thus a wrong against the least person is no longer merely that, a minor incident, like a brusque word to a beggar, but a personal offense to Christ. According to this system, when one offends him, one offends divine majesty and one becomes liable to a commensurate punishment. In this passage, therefore, Christ simultaneously identifies himself with the least of his brethren and announces that he will judge for eternity according as "he" has been treated.

Our treatment of one another can no longer be assessed in purely human terms. Christ is involved. For injustice, punishment will always come: "Do not fear those who kill the body but cannot kill the soul; rather fear him who can destroy both soul and body in hell [Gehenna] (Matthew 10.28). Those who persecute "the least of these my brethren" (Matthew 25.40, 45) will be punished body and soul in Gehenna.

The great judgment scene of Matthew 25.31–46 enhances the absoluteness of the sanction and its administration. The judgment of the nations makes the assize universal in competence. That the peoples of all the world are divided into two groups, distinguished by their treatment of "the least," who will be sent to two corresponding and absolutely opposed fates, each prepared from the beginning of the world, gives cosmic force to the alternatives. The ability of Jesus to prophesy about the actual sentence, the blessing or condemnation to be pronounced by the Son of man in terms of the universe as established by his Father also reinforces his position as "prophet."

The uniqueness of this conception appears more forcefully from a brief review of some of the other judgments of the dead available in the ancient world. The judgments that Plato proposed were approximations by one who purported to understand the cosmos but claimed no mastery over it. His belief in reincarnation undercut the uniqueness of a person's life as a unit. In his judgments, some souls were recycled into new lives, while the good (such as philosophers) were retained in eternal blessedness and the incurably wicked were retained eternally in Tartarus. In ancient Egypt, remember, because magical texts and amulets might ease souls through the judgments, the criteria for successful passage were not based entirely on one's life. The judgment in Daniel's vision did not comprise all (only "many"), though the sentences awarded were to be eternal. The books attributed to Enoch reported what he had seen and learned, but ascribed to him no direct role in either creation or judgment. Compared with these alternatives, the perspective of Matthew 25.31–46 conveys an unmatched absoluteness.[15]

Now that the absolute character of the judgment is clear, it is important to analyze the criteria for sentencing. Who are the "little ones" or "the least" of the brethren of Jesus? The passages considered thus far indicate a range of possibilities. The first sense is that of Mark 9.37 and 42, where they are children or like children, and can be interpreted as any helpless person who has never done harm. Matthew 25.35–36 and 42–43 create a second category by giving further examples of those in need: the hungry, the thirsty, strangers, the naked, the sick, and prisoners. As long as the "little ones" are in these categories, the use of postmortem sanctions against oppression is a universal ethic encouraging support of the helpless or needy. A third sense is narrower. It limits the "little ones" to those who, like the actual disciples of Jesus, accept his message, avow their discipleship, and actively proclaim it to others. If one focuses on this third sense of "little ones," the evangelists would appear to portray Jesus as threatening with Gehenna those who impede the spread of his teachings. When applied in that fashion, the threat of hell takes on a far more sectarian tone, a supernatural sanction for one particular outlook. Further, the third sense can bend the range of meanings into a circle and merge with the first and second.

The identity of the "little ones" or "the least" cannot be settled textually. Like the positive and the symmetrical views, both have ample scriptural authority. The difference between them is a matter of emphasis. Should hell threaten wrongdoers because they violate a universal ethic or should wrongdoing be identified with opposition to a particular inspiration and its advocates? In the latter case, absolute authority stigmatizes opposition as evil and consigns its opponents to a punishment of cosmic proportions.

Yet, for all the clarity of Matthew's Gehenna, there remains one escape—forgiveness. The Sermon on the Mount declares that we will be forgiven as

15. Griffiths, *Divine Verdict*, is a magisterial review of judgments of the dead in the ancient world.

we forgive (Matthew 6.14–15). But does this rule not apply to the One who pronounces it? Should there be no forgiveness of the damned? Ever? Apparently, this option was considered long enough to be rejected. There is one offense that can never be forgiven: "Therefore I tell you, every sin and blasphemy will be forgiven men, but the blasphemy against the Spirit will not be forgiven. And whoever says a word against the Son of man will be forgiven; but whoever speaks against the Holy Spirit will not be forgiven, either in this age or in the age to come" (Matthew 12.31–32). What is this possibility of forgiveness in the age to come? Can it take place in Gehenna? What other places are there? In the New Testament, Gehenna was not the only place for punishment of the dead.

In recounting a parable of Jesus, Luke calls the area Hades, using the term familiar throughout the Greek-speaking world, the term used by Greek-speaking Jews to translate the Hebrew Sheol. The territory is only sketched, but the parable's spare details match the geography of Sheol to the character of its protagonists: "There was a rich man, who was clothed in purple and fine linen and who feasted sumptuously every day. And at his gate lay a poor man named Lazarus, full of sores, who desired to be fed with what fell from the rich man's table; moreover the dogs came and licked his sores" (Luke 16.19–21). The tale does not state that Dives (another name for the rich man, based on the Latin for "rich") denied Lazarus the surplus from his table; yet the implication is that the dogs were quicker to show him compassion than his wealthy neighbor. The situation soon changed: "The poor man died and was carried by the angels to Abraham's bosom. The rich man also died and was buried; and in Hades, being in torment, he lifted up his eyes, and saw Abraham far off and Lazarus in his bosom" (Luke 16.22–23). The contrast in their physical conditions after death reverses their situations in life. Lazarus (who should not be confused with the Lazarus of John, chapters 11 and 12, whom Jesus resurrected from the dead) is safely elevated above the fire of Hades and comforted by Abraham.[16] The rich man suffers beyond endurance. In his desperation, seeing Abraham, the patriarch of his people, and Lazarus, a former dependent, he makes two requests. Abraham denies them both. It is important to see how and why.

> And [the rich man] called out, "Father Abraham, have mercy upon me, and send Lazarus to dip the end of his finger in water and cool my tongue; for I am in anguish in this flame." But Abraham said, "Son, remember

16. On the matter of rest in the period between death and the Resurrection, see Alfred Stuiber, *Refrigerium interim: Die Vorstellungen vom Zwischenzustand und die frühchristliche Grabeskunst*, Theophaneia: Beiträge zur Religions- und Kirchengeschichte des Altertums, 11 (Bonn: Hanstein, 1957).

that you in your lifetime received your good things, and Lazarus in like manner evil things; but now he is comforted here, and you are in anguish. And besides all this, between us and you a great chasm has been fixed, in order that those who would pass from here to you may not be able, and none may cross from there to us." (16.24–26)

In answer to the request for a drop of water, Abraham invokes the chasm. An impenetrable barrier prevents Lazarus from helping the rich man, for the geography of the netherworld supports the moral order. The selfish are divided from the innocent and their fates are different. Sufferers are refreshed; the complacent are tormented. Help is as removed from Dives as it had been from Lazarus.

As if presiding over the lower world, Abraham explains these inversions as conforming to a principle of justice. Dives received good things in life and Lazarus evil. Combining the ministrations of the dogs (verse 21) with Abraham's explanation (verse 25), we infer that the parable assigns responsibility for the unfortunate to the rich. The implication is that a refusal to share bounty in life brings just deprivation in death.

When his request for a drop of water has been denied, Dives makes his second petition: "And he said, 'Then I beg you, father, to send [Lazarus] to my father's house, for I have five brothers, so that he may warn them, lest they also come into this place of torment'" (16.27–28). In one impulse of apparent generosity, albeit restricted to his own kin, Dives asks Abraham to send Lazarus to warn his brothers about how painful Hades is. (Despite the reversals of their fortunes, Dives continues to regard Lazarus as a potential servant.) Abraham denies the request partly because Dives and Lazarus are dead. The temporal barrier of death, which prevents any return to the living, matches the physical chasm between Hades and the bosom of Abraham (or between these two parts of the otherworld). Death limits the selfish enjoyment of wealth. Death also constitutes the deadline for amending one's life and instructing one's associates: "But Abraham said, 'They have Moses and the prophets; let them hear them.' And he said, 'No, father Abraham, but if some one goes to them from the dead, they will repent.' He said to him, 'If they do not hear Moses and the prophets, neither will they be convinced if some one should rise from the dead'" (16.29–31).

Abraham's answer situates the story temporally. The otherworld experience of Dives and Lazarus concerns the time between the death of individuals, Abraham, Dives, and Lazarus, but before the Second Coming, the Resurrection of the dead, the Last Judgment, and the final separation of good from evil prophesied in Matthew 25.31–46. In fact, Dives is survived by his five brothers and the story takes place while they are still alive. The errand of

Lazarus would be possible from a chronological point of view. Further, because the General Resurrection has not taken place, the protagonists exist only as souls, without their bodies; so Lazarus could emerge as a shade to carry out the rich man's bidding. Dives' brothers' disdain for Jewish law, however, indicates to Abraham that not even someone returning from the dead would make a difference in their conduct. What is the ghost of the beggar from their brother's gate compared to Moses and the prophets? By showing how Abraham prohibited the return of Lazarus at the rich man's request, Luke portrays Jesus as emphasizing the individual life as a temporal unit, the deadline for charity and instruction. He shows how leniency will be denied after the original sentence has been passed at death and why. He uses the parable's account of death to teach right conduct in life.

The links of this New Testament parable with the Jewish tradition are obvious. The rich man's appeal to "father" Abraham and the idea that Abraham should be an important figure in the underworld are clearly Jewish. He seems to preside over this divided land, he comforts the righteous and admonishes the victims of the flames. In Luke's account of the parable, Abraham's reference to the law and the prophets identifies its legal and moral frame of reference. Deuteronomy calls upon Jews to remember that they themselves had been "slave[s] in the land of Egypt" (15.15), therefore they should concern themselves with the poor and needy among them (e.g., Deuteronomy 15.7–11). Starting with Amos, the prophets identify mistreatment of the poor with wickedness and dramatize the confrontation of rich and poor at the gate: "For I know how many are your transgressions, and how great are your sins—you who afflict the righteous, who take a bribe, and turn aside the needy in the gate" (5.12). Ezekiel itemizes the reasons for God's anger with Israel and includes this charge: "The people of the land have . . . oppressed the poor and needy" (22.29). Conversely, helping the poor is counted as good. As Job reflects on how his past life might have earned him God's favor, he says, "I delivered the poor who cried. . . . I was a father to the poor" (29.12, 16). Moreover, to recapitulate some of the themes already mentioned in Jewish sources, the strand of Jewish writing known as the Wisdom literature considers the opposition between malefactors and the righteous, oppressors and their victims. Psalms 49 and 73 contrast the righteous to the scoffers who appear to benefit from flouting the law, accumulating wealth and wielding their baneful influence.

Indeed, some sayings in Proverbs seem to anticipate the story of Dives and Lazarus. "He who closes his ear to the cry of the poor will himself cry out and not be heard" (21.13). "He who oppresses the poor to increase his own wealth, or gives to the rich, will only come to want" (22.16). "Do not rob the poor, because he is poor, or crush the afflicted at the gate; for the Lord will plead their cause and despoil of life those who despoil them" (22.22–23). Yet none of these statements implies that requital comes after death.

To find specifically postmortem retribution it is necessary to review how Jewish apocalyptic speculation predicted a reversal of fortunes. Isaiah 26.14–27.1 prophesies a resurrection that would permit a defeated and oppressed Israel to rise from death as its conquerors and persecutors are destroyed. For all the clarity of its vision, Daniel 12.2 does not specify the criteria of judgment except to say that those inscribed in the book (12.1), the pure (12.10), will awake to "everlasting life" and the wicked to "everlasting contempt" (12.2). Whereas apocalyptic passages in the Hebrew Bible transfer retribution to the next world, they do not make charity, treatment of the poor, a special concern. Conversely, those passages that discuss one's obligation to the needy, make no reference to punishment after death. The apocryphal *Book of Enoch* connects these two elements. Angels will gather the abetters of sin into one place in preparation for judgment. Those who oppressed the righteous will be requited according to their deeds, and no one will help them (100.4–8). "Woe unto you, sinners, because of the works of your hands [and the words of your mouths]. On account of the deeds of your wicked ones, in blazing flames worse than fire, [the conflagration] shall burn" (100.9). "Woe unto you sinners who are dead" (103.5). It makes no difference that your heirs will envy your "prosperity and wealth" and the ease with which you escaped judgment (103.6). "You yourselves know that they [the angels; cf. 100.4] will bring your souls down to Sheol; and they [your souls] shall experience evil and great tribulation—in darkness, nets, and burning flame" (103.7). As in Luke 16, it is the soul that suffers, and the punishment is for complacency in wealth.

It is hardly surprising to see continuity in the teachings of Jesus with themes in the Hebrew Bible. By stressing the finality of death, Abraham (or Luke in his recounting of the parable told by Jesus) emphasizes the authority and regularity of the Jewish tradition as compared to the more haphazard appearances of the dead in the larger Mediterranean culture.[17] Yet the story of Dives and Lazarus has a certain resonance (though not in every particular) within that broader context.

One example is Egyptian. The story is recorded on the back of a discarded Roman administrative papyrus bearing the date 46–47 C.E., though it is impossible to know when that scrap was actually used or how old the story

17. The illicit necromancy by which Saul had Samuel raised (1 Sam. 28:3–19) is an exception condemned in the narrative that relates it.

itself might be.[18] Given the moral concerns of the protestation of innocence and the judgment of one's deeds against *maat* under the jurisdiction of Osiris, it is fair to state that the concerns of this story probably antedate the time of its actual recording.[19] The son of Pharaoh Usimares, Satni-Khamois, was the most gifted scribe in his court, well versed in mathematics and magic. Yet he and his wife Mahituaskit were unable to conceive a child. When Mahituaskit sought aid in the Temple of Imuthes, the god Horus became the seed from which their child Senosiris would be born. An avatar of the god, the young Senosiris matured more quickly than other children and attained greater wisdom while still a child than most men in their maturity. One story told of his precocity bears directly on the moral of the parable of Dives and Lazarus.

One day Satni-Khamois and his still-young son Senosiris were looking out over the city from the roof of their house, when the lamentations rising from the gorgeous funeral procession of a rich man attracted their attention. Soon thereafter, they saw the miserable obsequies of a poor man, wrapped only in a mat, lacking any of the trappings of the earlier train. The father sighed and prayed aloud that he should have the fate in the underworld of the elaborately lamented wealthy man rather than of the pauper. His son immediately contradicted him. Chastised for this apparent insubordination, Senosiris guided his father through a tour of the seven halls of Amentit (the underworld), where he demonstrated how one's fate after death depends on the balance of good versus evil deeds done in life rather than in the splendor of one's funeral. The man buried only in his floor mat they saw clothed in fine linen and seated in a place of honor near Osiris in the very room where merits are weighed. The recipient of the sumptuous funeral procession, who had been found wanting in the balance, they found immured in the floor face up, the pivot of a great door rotating in the socket of his right eye while his

18. The story is in Gaston Maspero, *Popular Stories of Ancient Egypt*, translated by A. S. Johns from the 4th French ed. and rev. by Gaston Maspero (New Hyde Park, N.Y.: University Books, 1967), 144–70. It is summarized at length in Lévy, *La légende de Pythagore*, 185–86. S. G. F. Brandon, *The Judgment of the Dead* (New York: Scribner's, 1967), 43–45, analyzes it and provides a reference to Luke 16. See also Francis Bar, *Les routes de l'autre monde* (Paris: PUF, 1946), 22–23.

19. Uncertainty about the date abounds. The consensus favors the second century C.E. Griffiths, *Divine Verdict*, 229–30 and n. 113, quotes Eric Hornung, *Altägyptische Höllenvorstellungen* (Berlin: Akademie, 1968), 10 n. 1, who gives a range of dates from the first century B.C.E. to the second century C.E. Jan Zandee, *Death as an Enemy*, 298–302, avoids dating the work, but stresses the continuity in its nomenclature with the *Book of Gates* and the *Book Am-Duat*.

mouth uttered loud cries. Moreover, Osiris had ordered the clothing of the splendidly buried man stripped from him and given to the unlamented man now in a place of honor. Summing up the lesson for his father, Senosiris declared: "He who does good on earth, good is done to him in Amentit, but he who does evil, evil is done to him."[20]

The differences in detail between this tale and the parable of Dives and Lazarus are many. The most important is that despite the reversal of fortunes in the Egyptian story, it is not said that the rich man had specifically wronged the poor man to whom the gods awarded his funerary attire and with whom the tale contrasts his fate. Nonetheless, this difference hardly conceals the underlying similarity that they share: station in life and the symbols that proclaim it, whether banquets or funerals, are extraneous to moral excellence, which alone determines status after death. Beyond illustrating the irrelevance of wealth and the contrast between the two men's conditions, however, the parable adds this specific, personal element: the complacent and the neglected or, put more strongly, the offender and the victim will confront each other directly, personally, and will know each other's fate in the hereafter.

Ancient Greece knew this lesson too. In the *Phaedo* (113e–114b), Plato allowed victims comfort on the banks of the Acherusian Lake and the authority to forgive or not to forgive their offenders. He also taught that one should live not in pursuit of pleasure or wealth but with a concern for the long-term good of the soul (*Republic* 618–19). The second-century C.E. travel writer Pausanias (10.28.4) describes a fifth-century B.C.E. painting at Delphi by Polygnotus depicting the underworld, as he said, according to Homer. But if Pausanias's account of the now-lost illustration is faithful, Polygnotus portrayed a direct reversal of offense and suffering on a personal basis. The painting represents, says Pausanias, "a man who had been undutiful to his father . . . being throttled by him" on the shores of the Acheron, where Plato said forgiveness might take place.

In his own derisive way, Lucian echoes these ideas when he imitates the judgment scene of Plato's *Gorgias* in the *The Downward Journey*. He also

20. Maspero, *Popular Stories of Ancient Egypt*, 144–70, esp. 144–52, 169. The association of this Egyptian story with the parable of Dives and Lazarus is credited to Hugo Gressmann, *Vom reichen Mann und armen Lazarus: Eine literargeschichtliche Studie*, Abhandlungen der königlich preussichen Akademie der Wissenschaften, philosophisch-historische Klasse, 7 (Berlin: Königliche Akademie der Wissenschaften, 1918). For an account of the success of this argument, see Ronald F. Hock, "Lazarus and Micyllus: Greco-Roman Background to Luke 16:19–31," *Journal of Biblical Literature* 106 (1987): 449 n. 7. Hock finds a closer parallel in certain characters of Lucian, a hypothesis to be considered shortly.

praises wisdom, frankness, and truth over wealth. He frequently ridicules those who die lamenting the wealth in which they wrongly placed their hopes. Although Lucian's dates (120–200 C.E.) make him more a candidate for receiving the influence of Christian Scripture than the other way around, the point is not that Lucian might be a direct source of the parable or a direct recipient of Christian influence, but that Lucian's late date illustrates in a Greek context the longevity of pagan views of moral death and the continuity of Greek philosophical traditions, such as Neoplatonism, Cynicism, and Stoicism, which emphasized the contrast between physical objects and truth, between possessions and moral goodness.[21]

This tendency may be encapsulated in some of Lucian's dramatic themes, where, as we have seen, he juxtaposes the postmortem fates of victims and their offenders. He shows rich men ignoring the poor at their gates, heedless of the contrast between their excessive trappings and the miserable condition of the others from whom they demand deference. He also shows the reversal of fortunes between rich and poor as classes and provides dramatic contrasts between individuals.[22]

Readers or hearers in the Greek-speaking world, Palestine, and Egypt, therefore, would recognize the moral teaching conveyed by Luke's parable of Lazarus and the rich man. Its correspondence with themes already found around the Mediterranean, however, hardly diminishes its importance for the developing notion of moral death in the Christian tradition. In the underworld of Luke's parable, the good and the wicked are separated into areas of refreshment and torment. There is no return to life, since death limits one's opportunities for acting on altruistic impulses. Although Luke considers the bosom of Abraham a separate place, his idea of Hades is conceptually closer to the Gehenna of *1 Enoch*, Mark, or Matthew than to the Sheol of the Hebrew Bible or Paul's one reference to Hades, where it is equated with death in general. It is certainly not a neutral place where the undifferentiated dead reside in a gray half existence.[23] It is not possible to

21. For the relationship between Lucian and Christianity, see Hans Dieter Betz, *Lukian von Samosata und das Neue Testament: Religionsgeschichtliche und Paräne-tische Parallelen*, Texte und Untersuchungen zur Geschichte der altchristlichen Literatur, 76 (Berlin: Akademie, 1961).

22. For a careful study of these parallels, drawing particularly on the *The Cock (Gallus)* and *The Downward Jourrney (Cataplus)*, see Hock, "Lazarus and Micyllus," 455–62. Hock (459) notices the bargaining between Megapenthes and Clotho (*The Downward Journey* 8–13) and compares it to the dialogue of the rich man with Abraham (Luke 16: 24–31). It is not wealth itself but its abuse that Lucian condemns, according to Hock (460).

23. Milikowsky, "Which Gehenna?" Citing parallels in Rabbinic literature, Mili-

say whether the fire that burns the rich man is the same as the eternal fire prepared for Satan and his angels mentioned in Matthew 25. The fire of Hades in Luke 16 is a temporary place of torment for the wicked from the time of their death to the Resurrection. The eternal fire is called Gehenna; it will receive the wicked after their condemnation in the Last Judgment.

Despite the possible contrast in fires, the parable of Dives and Lazarus could easily illustrate the theory of justice in Matthew 25. Lazarus could be any of those not fed by the "cursed" ones mentioned there (verse 41). The rich man's neglect of Lazarus is a sin of omission so great as to determine his postmortem destiny. It would be easy to regard the explanation in Matthew 25 as the rationale for the fate of Dives. Implicit is the idea that the rich man has offended not only the suffering Lazarus but also the Son of man, who will return to judge the world according to each person's acts of charity. Hades is part of God's plan for the world: it exists, it is painful, and it punishes the souls of the wicked from the time of their deaths.[24]

One advantage of the immediate punishment of the wicked in Hades, before the Last Judgment, is that it permits news of the consequences of sin to reach the living—not, to be sure, by the return of Lazarus at the rich man's behest but by the teaching of Jesus. Jesus' account of the Last Judgment in Matthew 25 is prophecy. His tale of the rich man is recent history, perhaps even current events. If the witch of Endor could overhear the conversation between the living Saul and the raised Samuel, certainly Jesus could report Dives' negotiations with Abraham, which may indeed have still been continuing. If Jesus was to resurrect the dead, he certainly had the power to report their conversations while he awaited the correct moment. In this way he could use his knowledge of the present state and future function of the other world to warn the living against delayed repentance.

---

kowsky argues that for Luke, postmortem punishment takes effect immediately at death and affects souls only (not bodies). The dead await no universal judgment or general resurrection, since only the just would be resurrected to life. This arrangement would affect Luke's position within the symmetrical tradition, because the symmetry he conceives would end with the resurrection of the just (Luke 14.14).

24. Hock, "Lazarus and Micyllus," argues against the notion that an Egyptian folktale concerning the contrast in otherworldly fate between a man buried splendidly and another buried simply is the source of the parable of Dives and Lazarus. Instead, he cites the *topos* of the Greco-Roman rhetorical tradition of fortune reversal after death. We have already seen this in the satires of Lucian, whose *Gallus* (*The Cock*) and *Cataplus* (*The Downward Journey*) Hock cites. Hock concludes: "The parable of Lazarus has an unmistakable Cynic coloring" (462). For the assignment of influence to the Egyptian folktale, see Joachim Jeremias, *The Parables of Jesus*, rev. ed. (New York: Scribner's, 1963).

The Hades of Luke 16, therefore, is a punishing realm for the wicked dead, who, as Job and the Preacher of Ecclesiastes would have appreciated, are separated from the good by a great chasm. However distant they are, the rich man can see Lazarus and imagine an errand of mercy for him. Nonetheless, Luke 16 clearly fits within a symmetrical system that proposes separate fates for the good and the wicked. The good receive the succor of their moral exemplars, relief from worldly cares, and immunity from the torments of the underworld. The wicked receive physical discomfort, the shame of having their punishment visible to those they persecuted earlier, and the anguish of having the nature of divine justice explained to them when it is too late either to repent oneself or to warn one's kin.

This symmetry is enhanced even further in the vision of Matthew 25.31–46, where both fates are said to be eternal. Mark 9.43–48 specifies more precisely what that fate will be and names the fire as Gehenna, identifying it with the inextinguishable fire and the undying worm of Isaiah 66.24. Between the writings of Paul and the composition of the synoptic Gospels, therefore, Christian thought varied considerably on the subject of the fate of the wicked after death. Paul and John believed them subject to annihilation, Luke to long-lasting torment, Mark and Matthew to eternal suffering.

The reflection I offered at the end of the discussion of *1 Enoch* concerning the latitude to be granted rival exponents of a single religious tradition applies here too. No one should expect unanimity or the coherence of philosophy. Part IV will provide an occasion to trace the tensions between the different tendencies already visible in the New Testament.

Grouping allusions to judgments, to fire, and to places of punishment accentuates the underlying coherence between these scattered references. Yet to reconcile them with one another, to eliminate "accidental" discrepancies between these passages, would be to write theology. By contrast, looking "in the other direction," at the underlying perception, the existential aspiration for justice which these texts seek to articulate, shows how they reflect different aspects of a broader vision that informs them all.

The Myth behind Hell

Behind the New Testament lies some background knowledge in the form of a time line or a narrative upon which its writers drew freely but usually silently. An analogy from their use of historical events will illustrate their practice. References to the destruction of Sodom and Gomorrah, for instance, serve to exemplify divine punishment. Invoking the Flood could also remind listeners of destruction. Korah, Dathan, and Abiram were other frightening precedents. The story of Noah and that of Jonah and the conversion of Nineveh functioned similarly, but to opposite effect, as an invitation to consider the effectiveness of repentance and the benefits of hearing the word of God.

In the Hebrew Bible too, these events (and others, particularly the Exodus and the establishment of the covenant) exercised potent force as precedents, foundations of a tradition, and examples of divine power to be regarded respectfully if not fearfully. New Testament authors developed a different emphasis; they strove to set these historical moments within a single time frame, a history of the world moving from Creation to a never-ending eternity after the end of time. They identified this history as a providential plan, which could be revealed to humans or discovered through active reflection on the givens of the oral and written traditions that conveyed it. Distinct from the actual biblical text, yet undergirding and in a certain way explaining it, the antecedent background story must be called the myth.

I use the word "myth" here not because of any putative falsity but because the narrative to which I am referring, and whose composition I shall examine, functions like a myth. That is, it is a powerful narrative that guides, structures, and even scripts the imagination, thinking, and perception of a people as they work out their place in the world, their collective identity, and their relationship to time, eternity, and God. Nor do I mean "myth" in the sense of Rudolf Bultmann, for whom it was the residue of the ancient world's primitive mind set. More than "narrative," the term "myth" conveys the driving force exercised by the constellation of images, emotions, precepts, and behavioral models conveyed by the New Testament. Crucial to understanding how the myth behind the New Testament works, though, is recognizing the degree to which New Testament authors organized their ideas around this dynamic central core, a narrative with a specific beginning, middle, and end.

Drawing significantly upon key elements of Jewish belief, some aspects of which were added only in the intertestamentary period, it runs from the mythic past in the Creation, the Fall of the Angels, expulsion from Eden, through the virgin birth, the temptation, the Crucifixion, the descent into Hades (which is only hinted at in the New Testament), the Resurrection, and into the mythical future, the Parousia, the General Resurrection, and Last Judgment, to name only the most salient points.

If the chronology of the composition of the New Testament is correctly understood in the scholarly consensus I have used to guide my analysis in Part III, it is possible to trace the evolution of conscious reflection upon and articulation of the elements of this myth. We have already considered some of these. Paul was quite knowingly explaining a key element of the myth when, in Romans 5.17–19 and 11.32 and 1 Corinthians 15.22–26 and 45, he traced a chronology of world history from Adam, through Christ, to the end of time. Other allusions point to critical moments related by the myth. John 17.24 refers to what happened "before the foundation of the world" and Matthew 25 to "the eternal fire prepared for the Devil and his angels" (41) as well as "the kingdom prepared for you from the foundation of the world" (34).

These are examples of how the myth manifests itself in the New Testament. Statements that can be explained in terms of prior events, a mythic past, show that some story about a prior relationship between God and Adam, between Adam and Christ, Satan and Adam, Jesus and Satan, lies in the background. That background is the myth.

An excellent example occurs in the sending of the disciples. Luke 10 relates how Jesus named the seventy disciples and instructed them to go from town to town preaching and healing (verses 1–11). He threatens towns with the fate of Sodom if they do not receive his envoys (12). "The seventy returned with joy, saying, 'Lord, even the demons are subject to us in your name!'" (17). The explanation Jesus gives refers to events long past in the early history of heaven: "And he said to them, 'I saw Satan fall like lightning from heaven. Behold, I have given you authority to tread upon serpents and scorpions, and over all the power of the enemy; and nothing shall hurt you. . . . The spirits are subject to you'" (Luke 10.18–20). The statement "I saw Satan fall like lightning from Heaven," seems like a surprise in a narrative of the sending of the disciples. It assumes the identity of Satan with Lucifer, the fallen star of morning, referred to in Isaiah 14.12, and it recalls Paul's observation about false apostles, "even Satan disguises himself as an angel of light" (2 Corinthians 11.14). The implication is that the disciples of Jesus have authority to cast out demons because Jesus is himself associated with the divine power that cast Satan out of heaven—the very event that brought demons into being. Thus the reference to Satan connects the narrative of Luke to a broader, antecedent myth.[1] The two narratives reflect a generic relationship: the disciples' authority over demons is one manifestation of Christ's authority over all spirits. His words are an assertion, using the logic of myth, of who he is.

Though Luke 10 alludes to the fall of Satan and implicitly to that of the other angels who became demons, it suggests that they fell to earth and remain active here, though subject to greater spiritual authorities such as Jesus and his disciples. Other passages ascribe a more grievous fate to them. The letter of Jude warns of false teachers loose in the church and stigmatizes them as followers of a long series of defeated rebels. The Israelites who did not believe despite their salvation out of Egypt were destroyed (1.5). They are followers of Cain and resemble those who perished with Korah (1.11). By linking them with these figures Jude also suggests their fate. This strategy recalls the allusion to Sodom and Gomorrah, which Jude explicitly says "serve as an example by undergoing a punishment of eternal fire" (1.7). Eternal punishment is the fate of the rebellious, as is known not only from the case of these wicked men but even from that of more exalted rebels: "And the angels that did not keep their own position but left their proper dwelling have been kept by him in eternal chains in the nether gloom until the judgment of the great day" (1.6). Like the fallen angels, these false

1. John Knox agrees with this perspective: "I saw Satan fall like lightning from Heaven" is "another reference to the myth of Lucifer (cf. Rev 12:9–10)," quoted in *The Interpreter's Bible*, 12 vols. (New York: Abingdon-Cokesbury, 1951–57), 8:189. See also Samuel Vollenweider, "Ich sah den Satan wie einen Blitz vom Himmel fallen (Lk. 10:18)," *Zeitschrift für neutestamentliche Wissenschaft und die Kunde der älteren Kirche* 79 (1988): 187–203.

teachers resemble "wandering stars for whom the nether gloom of darkness has been reserved for ever" (1.13). Whether the punishment is the fire that rained on Sodom and Gomorrah or the chains and gloom that bind the angels (stars), we see here the use of myth (taken as history) as precedent to establish a sanction against nonconformists within the church.[2] That sanction is the threat of eternal punishment. As if to legitimate this literary (one should almost say legal) technique, Jude cites Enoch, one of his predecessors in encouraging the blessed by foretelling the dire fate that awaits their enemies. For Enoch prophesied, Jude reminds his readers, that the Lord would come with his "holy myriads, to . . . convict all the ungodly" (1.14–15; cf. *1 Enoch* 1.9).

Similarly, 2 Peter assures the church that just as God can separate Noah from the Flood and Lot from the rest of Sodom and Gomorrah, so the church can be cleansed of false teachers and destructive heresies. What are false prophets to God, if he "did not spare the angels when they sinned, but *cast them into hell* and committed them to pits of nether gloom to be kept until the judgment" (2.4, my italics)?[3] "Cast them into hell" translates a Greek coinage *tartarōsas* (from *tartaroō*), which is used only this once in the New Testament, a verb built on the noun Tartarus. The rebellious angels had been "Tartared" or "Tartarized" or "Entartered." Peter, therefore, is drawing on the Greek tales of the overthrown Titans to explain the divine power to imprison the rebellious angels. Translators of the Septuagint made a similar analogy when they referred to the rebellious angels and their offspring as giants or Titans. The term "nether gloom" (*zophos*) carries similar echos of Greek thought. Although this text refers back to the primal fall, it alludes not to an indefinite punishment in the future but to one that lasts only until the Last Judgment.

The device is Jude's. This strategy is less a case of pious plagiarism than the beginning of a policy of invoking eternal punishment to promote discipline within the church. This escalation in the appeal to sanctions was provoked by doctrinal dissent, and it presupposes the church's greater institutionalization and an attendant ability to identify heresy. Some must have held that the fate of nonbelievers should no longer be passed over in silence and that the eternity of their torment should be proclaimed. The clarity of that negative vision would increase with a more careful balancing of the mythic material. The fallen angels referred to in Isaiah, *1 Enoch*, and Luke

2. Edwin A. Blum, "Jude," in *Expositor's Bible Commentary* 12:389–90. Blum sees in Jude's angels the angels of *1 Enoch*, though he neglects the element of *eternal* punishment that is so important a part of that text.

3. See Blum's commentary on 2 Peter in *Expositor's Bible Commentary* 12:277–78.

could be made to foreshadow the fates of Noah's contemporaries, of Korah, Dathan, and Abiram, of Sodom and Gomorrah, which in turn could presage the end of all human rebels and unbelievers. The symmetry used to shape and interpret the mythical past could also be used to extrapolate a mythical future, to forecast human destiny: judgment, eternal life, eternal damnation.

This technique was not always used to threaten. Another area in which New Testament hints point to an antecedent myth, also alluded to, some would say, in the Hebrew Bible, is Christ's descent into Hades, often misleadingly called the Harrowing of Hell. In brief, the descent is the narrative of how, while his body lay in the grave, Christ descended in spirit into Hades, overcame the forces of death (remember that Hades/Sheol was sometimes a synonym for death), and resurrected the major figures of the Hebrew Bible, including Adam and Eve, Noah and Moses, the patriarchs, David, Solomon, the prophets, and other righteous persons who died before his coming. In fact, the descent literature portrays these figures as having prophesied his redemptive action.

Some early accounts of the descent will be analyzed later. For now it is sufficient to illustrate how scattered references show that biblical authors took for granted a widespread familiarity with this story, circulating in the oral tradition. Romans 10.7 refers to a descent "into the abyss" by which Christ may be brought "up from the dead." Similarly, Acts 2.24 says, "But God raised him up, having loosed the pangs of death, because it was not possible for him to be held by it." These texts, like Luke (11.30) and Matthew (12.39–40, 16.4), which refer to Jonah as a precedent for resurrection, may refer only to Christ's *own* resurrection; yet they imply a divine power over death. The parallel with Jonah may be extended to the redemption of others if one considers the eventual repentance of Nineveh and how the city evaded destruction.

Awareness of this tradition helps align two passages in 1 Peter. The first refers to Christ's "being put to death in the flesh but made alive in the spirit; in which he went and preached to the spirits in prison" (3.18–19). The second clarifies: "For this is why the Gospel was preached even to the dead that though judged in the flesh like men, they might live in the spirit like God (4.6)." From allusions to the resurrection of others, some texts get much closer to the idea of an escape from the clutches of death, a prison break. In Matthew 27.52 after Jesus gave up the spirit, "the tombs also were opened, and many bodies of the saints who had fallen asleep were raised." Ephesians 4.8 goes even further, specifying that "When he ascended on high he led a host of captives." (Another version: "When he ascended up on high, he led captivity captive.") Thus, in the light of these passages, when Hebrews 13.20 refers to a shepherd who is raised from the dead ("the God of peace who brought again from the dead our Lord Jesus, the great shepherd of the sheep"), one expects him to lead his flock out of death.[4]

Evidence in the New Testament for an antecedent belief in the fall of the angels or the descent of Christ is more fragmentary than the references to Hades and Gehenna. In the case of the fall of the angels, the Jewish tradition, particularly the intertestamentary literature such as *1 Enoch*, strengthens the hypothesis. While it would be a mistake to interpret every reference to resurrection as applying to the descent into Hades, it would be equally wrong to demand an actual retelling of the myth, where a simple reference was adequate. Allusions of this sort functioned to establish parallels between heroic actions and turning points in the history of creation. Even when recounted with all its dramatic detail, the descent must be seen as allegorically illustrating the conquest of death and the benefits of redemption. Thus it contrasts neatly with the overthrow and imprisonment of the fallen angels.

Sodom and Nineveh, the fall of the angels, the descent into Hades, these references remind us of the construction, through reflection and commentary, in the early Christian textual community, of a system of beliefs and myths which came to represent the Christian faith. Perhaps the clearest example of how this was done occurs in the Book of Revelation.

Revelation is a very difficult text. A word is needed about the framework of its message. John relates a vision in which he saw a person "like a son of man" who revealed a prophecy to him and directed him to write his words to the seven churches of Asia (1.4–1). The Book of Revelation has the form of that letter, and it therefore presents a special difficulty in reading. John writes, "and then I saw . . . and then I saw." The "seeing" he is narrating is in his recent past, the vision he has witnessed, but since it is prophecy, it depicts future time for us. Thus, his text relates in the past tense ("I saw" or "I heard") things that the world will experience in the future. The order of events will remain unchanged.

The speaker seems to be the resurrected Christ. He defines himself as one who has personally overcome death, and he claims the ability to do so for others because he has "the keys of Death and Hades" (1.18). Linking death

4. For a sample of the scholarship on the rich interrelationship between the Hebrew tradition and the New Testament, see Hermann Strack and Paul Billerbeck, *Kommentar zum Neuen Testament aus Talmud und Midrasch*, 6 vols. (Munich: Beck, 1926), 3:596, cited by Francis W. Beare in *The Interpreter's Bible* 10:688–89; Richard Rubinkiewicz, "Ps. LXVIII.18 (= Eph. IV.8) Another Textual Tradition or Targum?" *Novum Testamentum* 17 (1975): 219–24; Gary V. Smith, "Paul's Use of Psalm 68:18 in Ephesians 4:8," *Journal of the Evangelical Theological Society* 18 (1975): 181–89; and Richard A. Taylor, "The Use of Psalm 68:18 in Ephesians 4:8 in Light of the Ancient Versions," *Bibliotheca sacra* 148 (1991): 319–36.

and Hades is significant because Revelation distinguishes them from "the lake of fire," a subsequent receptacle for the wicked dead, equivalent (as we shall see) to Gehenna.

John's vision advances with the orderliness of a procession. The sights presented to him are arranged in groups of seven. The speaker dictates letters (letters within the letter) to the angel of each of the seven churches of Asia. The Lamb opens seven seals. Four horsemen appear with the opening of the first four seals. Seven angels sound their trumpets as signals for incidents within the vision. Within this series of sequences there is a progression of symbolic references: first to the earliest history of the world, then to the present conflict between the church and its enemies, and finally a prophecy of the last days. This time line moving from past to present to future is full of anticipations and recollections that foreshadow and recapitulate related symbols.

Dictating his letter to the first church of Asia, the speaker warns of tribulation to come and offers those who persevere the crown of life and immunity from the second death (2.10–11). What is the meaning of the second death? In a church led and motivated by martyrs from the very beginning, the reward for steadfastness would be not long life but rather the life that conquers death, of which the speaker is himself an example. Freedom from the second death is eternal life, but it implies a contrary fate, which is a denial of the resurrection to life: a resurrection to death, the second death. "The second death" is a coinage of the symmetrical tradition to contrast the distress of unbelievers to the happiness of the faithful.

After messages are dictated to each of the seven churches John sees a scroll with seven seals, which no one is worthy of opening until there appears "a Lamb, standing as though it had been slain" (5.6). Those in attendance proclaim the Lamb worthy to open the seals, "for," they say in adoration, "thou wast slain and by thy blood didst ransom men for God" (5.9). The Lamb, then, is a victim, who by his sacrifice obtained liberation for humankind. The theme of sacrifice is by no means absent from other books in the New Testament, but here its redemptive function is balanced against its function as a legitimation of vengeance.[5] As each seal is opened a rider appears. After the fourth seal comes "a pale horse, and its rider's name was

5. Some examples of scriptural passages on sacrifice: "We were reconciled to God by the death of his Son" (Romans 5.10); "The Son of man came . . . to give his life as a ransom for many" (Matt. 20.28); "For God so loved the world that he gave his only Son" (John 3.16); "The bread which I shall give for the life of the world is my flesh" (John 6.51); "I am the good shepherd . . . and I lay down my life for the sheep" (John 10.11–15).

Death, and Hades followed him" (6.7). Again (cf. 1.18) this pair is closely associated, and here both are personified. But more important in this passage is the vision that follows the opening of the fifth seal, for then the martyrs buried beneath an altar cry out to the Lamb: "How long before thou wilt judge and avenge our blood on those who dwell upon the earth" (6.10). This is the appeal for vengeance from other victims to the foremost Victim. The Lamb, by virtue of his sacrifice, is not only a redeemer but also an avenger. Would the events foretold in Matthew 25.31–46 satisfy this appeal?

After the seventh seal is opened, seven angels blow their trumpets in turn. As the fifth angel blows his trumpet, John sees a star fall from heaven to earth and the angel is given "the key of the shaft of the bottomless pit" (9.1), which he opens, letting out a cloud of smoke as from a furnace, which cloud nonetheless is a maze of locusts the size of horses with tails like those of scorpions, whose sting will hurt men for five months (9.10). These monstrous insects will attack "those of mankind who have not the seal of God upon their foreheads" (9.4) and will torment them so that "men will seek death and will not find it; they will long to die, and death will fly from them" (9.6). This longing for death, the result of a sting from locusts who rise from the bottomless pit, describes the damned, and it occurs in the context of the second death. The meaning is clarified by naming the angel who is king of the locusts: "His name in Hebrew is Abaddon, and in Greek he is called Apollyon" (9.11). Abaddon, meaning "destruction" (Psalms 88.11; Job 26.6), is a term from the Hebrew Bible synonymous with Sheol. Here then is a new description of death, a death so miserable that those not resurrected from it long to die. Yet this is the second death; so it is not in Sheol. It is the fate of those who suffer the second death.

The second death, the appearance of the Lamb sacrificed to ransom humanity, the call for vengeance, the pale horse with death and Hades, the opening of the pit—these symbols foreshadow the fate prepared for enemies of the Lamb. But if reference to the benefit of the sacrifice (5.9) establishes the right of the avenger, it is necessary to know who these enemies were or are or will be. As if in reply, the visionary is now allowed to see the genealogy of the persecutors. A woman ready to bear a child appears in heaven, and she is challenged by a dragon, whose "tail swept down a third of the stars of heaven, and cast them to the earth" (12.4). The dragon attempts to devour the child, a male, "one who is to rule all the nations with a rod of iron" (12.5), but the child is given to God on his throne and the woman escapes. A war in heaven ensues. The dragon is defeated by Michael and his angels: "And the great dragon was thrown down, that ancient serpent, who is called the Devil and Satan, the deceiver of the whole world—he was thrown down to the earth, and his angels were thrown down with him" (12.9). The identification of the dragon with the Eden serpent, the Devil, and Satan powerfully consolidates mythic time. Linking the serpent with Satan connects the fall of the angels to the deception of Adam and Eve. The dragon's attack on the childbearing woman symbolizes Satan's temptation of Christ and the Devil's opposition to the church. The expulsion of the dragon has been accomplished (it is stated again) "by the blood of the Lamb" (12.11a) and by the steadfastness of the testimony of the martyrs (12.11b). Heaven can now rejoice, for the Devil has been cast down to the earth and sea, whose woe will now begin (12.12). And the dragon goes off to make war on the woman and her "offspring, on those who keep the commandments of God and bear testimony to Jesus" (12.17). The scene is now set for the struggle between the church and the lord of the world. The scene has shifted from the mythical past to the historical present. "Here is a call for the endurance and faith of the saints" (13.10).

Then John sees two beasts. The first beast, which rises out of the sea, has power delegated by the dragon (13.2) This beast will be worshiped by all those not inscribed in the book of life, which was written *before* the foundation of the world to be used at the Last Judgment (13.8). The second beast, the false prophet (see 19.20), rises out of the earth (13.11). It produces great signs in the presence of the first beast and causes humans who will not worship the image of the first to be slain. The second beast will cause the worshipers of the first beast to be branded with his mark on the right hand or on the forehead (13.16–17), a sign opposed to the seal on the foreheads of the servants of the Lamb (7.3, 9.4). Thus, all will bear the brands of their lords.

But those bearing the mark of the beast

> shall drink the wine of God's wrath, poured unmixed into the cup of his anger, and he shall be tormented with fire and sulphur in the presence of the holy angels and in the presence of the lamb. And the smoke of their torment goes up for ever and ever [*aiōnas aiōnōn*]; and they have no rest, day or night, these worshipers of the beast and its image, and whoever receives the mark of its name. Here is a call for the endurance of the saints, those who keep the commandments of God and the faith of Jesus. (14.10–12)

In contrast to Paul's references to the Lord's anger and wrath, this description specifies that they consist of the fire and brimstone associated with Sodom and Gomorrah and that these torments will endure forever, as Revelation 20.10 will confirm. This passage also reinforces the idea present in

Luke 16 that the good will see the torments of the wicked, although here it is the angels and the Lamb who will witness them, not the redeemed humans. These sufferings are not in oblivion (at least before the Last Judgment) but are supervised by the highest authorities.

The damned are guilty not only of misplaced allegiance but of specific acts against the church, for which they suffer a matching, though not equal, punishment:

> For men have shed the blood of saints and prophets,
> and thou has given them blood to drink.
> It is their due!
>
> (16.6)

Further, when God's angels sent plagues, darkness, heat, and sores to chasten men with signs of his power, they did not repent (16.8–11). As the requisition against the wicked grows longer, the rationale for their punishment grows more explicit. Beyond the evil that derives from worshiping an evil master and persecuting the church, is what comes from immoral living, personified here in a great genetic symbol, the origin of luxury and vice, Babylon (an earthly counterpart to the dragon in heaven), "mother of the earth's abominations" (17.5), which bore in its cup a brew of wickedness. A voice from heaven explains the justice due Babylon:

> Render to her as she herself has rendered,
> and repay her double for her deeds;
> mix a double draught for her in the cup she mixed.
> As she glorified herself and played the wanton,
> so give her a like measure of torment and mourning.
>
> (18.6–7)

Later commentators will observe the contradiction between a "double" dose and a "like measure" of retribution for Babylon's misdeeds. Whatever the formula, John the visionary now hears the voice of a heavenly multitude celebrating the judgment of God, for "the smoke from her goes up for ever and ever" (19.3). However it is calculated, Babylon's punishment will be eternal.

From the present opposition between the church and its persecutors and tempters, the vision focuses now on the end of time. Again the vision proceeds in a sequence of related events. Perhaps in conformity with Paul's statement about the defeat of the rules and authorities and powers in 1 Corinthians 15.24, we see here a series of conquests of enemy forces. Appearing on a white horse, the Lord of Lords overthrows the kings of the earth (19.11–19). In the fray, the first and second beasts are captured: "The beast . . . and with it the false prophet [the second beast of 13.11] . . . were thrown alive into the lake of fire that burns with sulphur" (19.20). Then the angel of the bottomless pit "seized the dragon, that ancient serpent, who is the Devil and Satan, and bound him for a thousand years, and threw him into the pit, and shut it and sealed it over him" (20.2–3). The dragon's confinement will last till the end of a thousand years, when he will be freed briefly.

Then John sees the martyrs and those "who had not worshiped the beast or its image" or "received its mark" (20.4): "They came to life, and reigned with Christ a thousand years. The rest of the dead did not come to life until the thousand years were ended. This is the first resurrection. Blessed and holy is he who shares in the first resurrection! Over such the second death has no power, but they shall be priests of God and of Christ, and they shall reign with him a thousand years" (20.4–6). The first resurrection protects from the second death the martyrs and those not marked by the beast, that is, those who bear the name of the Father on their forehead, as stated in 2.11, 7.3, 9.4, and 14.1. These martyrs and the unmarked will reign alongside God for the thousand years during which, as we saw (20.2), the dragon/Satan is imprisoned. These martyrs and the unmarked have been entrusted with the judgment (20.4). The theme of vengeance is enhanced by investing with the power of judgment those who suffered at the hands of the wicked or were able to resist the temptations to which those marked by the beast fell prey. Here is simple retribution.

With the thousand years ended, Satan is freed from prison, gathers his innumerable confederates, and they besiege the camp of the saints, but fire from heaven consumes them (20.7–9). "And the devil who had deceived them was thrown into the lake of fire and sulphur where the beast and the false prophet were, and they will be tormented day and night for ever and ever [eis tous aiōnas tōn aiōnōn, for the ages of the ages]" (20.10). The lake of fire now contains the Devil (previously identified with Satan and the Eden serpent), the beast (delegate of the dragon, worshiped as an idol by those who accept his mark), and the false prophet (who is the deceiver who works great signs in the presence of the first beast and induces people to receive the mark). In their receptacle these figures of cosmic evil will be tormented forever.

That the formula translated as "for ever and ever" denotes eternity is hardly open to question. What other purpose would be served by "squaring" the word depicting the longest unit of time available, the aiōn? The fire lasts not for ages but for ages of ages—or, as Jerome will translate it, not for centuries but for centuries of centuries (saecula saeculorum). Also, in other references God is characterized similarly. Thus any fire that is long lasting, on a scale somehow conceived as comparable in duration to God, should also be eternal like God, though, strictly, nothing can be compared to him. The torments of the lake of fire, therefore, will last as long as the second death that follows the Last Judgment.[6]

After the confinement of the Devil and the beast and the false prophet, the books are opened and the judgment proceeds: "And I saw the dead, great and small, standing before the throne, and books were opened. Also another book was opened, which is the book of life. And the dead were judged by what was written in the books, by what they had done" (20.12). Here the books are of two types. First are those that contain all the deeds done by a person in life. Second is the book of life mentioned at Revelation 13.8, in which the names of the predestined had been inscribed from before the foundation of the world. As in Matthew 25, judgment is according to one's deeds.

Who goes into the lake of fire and sulfur? The Devil (20.10) has joined the beast and the false prophet, who were put there at Revelation 19.20. Death and Hades, now deprived of all their prey, are consigned there: "And the sea gave up the dead in it, Death and Hades gave up the dead in them, and all were judged by what they had done. Then Death and Hades were thrown into the lake of fire. This is the second death, the lake of fire; and if any one's name was not found written in the book of life, he was thrown into the lake of fire" (20.13–15).

The second death, therefore, is the lake of fire, which by now contains all the authors of evil. It is the unique repository of any evil remaining in the universe. This is a model of centralization that even the Roman beast would admire. Moreover, the lake of fire seems to resemble Gehenna. It is eternal, fiery, and contains all whose robes were not made "white in the blood of the Lamb" (7.14). Even though it is not explicitly stated that Babylon is in the lake of fire (and perhaps this is the one exception to the centralized scheme), its torment is also everlasting (19.3). Into the lake of fire, along with the Devil, the beast, and the false prophet, go death and Hades, and anyone whose name was not found written in the book of life, whose contents were known from the foundation of the world—another reference to the origin of time. There they will be tormented day and night for ever and ever—a reference to an endless time in the future.

As the account of the disposition of the wicked comes to an end, signs indicate clearly that the cosmos is being transformed. Earth and sky have fled (20.11). The sea has been emptied of the dead (20.13) and then "was no more" (21.1). There is a similar disposition of the blessed. As the first death

6. For the use of the same phrase as here (Rev. 20.10) applied to the divinity, see Rev. 1.6, 4.9–10, 5.13, 7.12, 10.6, 11.15.

has yielded to the second death, so "the first heaven and the first earth [have] passed away" (21.1). Down from the new heaven descends the new Jerusalem. As John sees a new heaven and a new earth, a voice from heaven narrates and an angel guides him through the purged world. A voice cries, "Death shall be no more" (21.4), that is, the first death, since the second death is tormenting the wicked for ever and ever. Here the full symmetry of this tradition emerges: even as the vision begins to focus on the new Jerusalem, "He who sat on the throne" promises in balanced terms "the water of life" (21.6) for the thirsty, but for the wicked, who could not conquer the temptations of the deceivers, "their lot shall be in the lake that burns with fire and sulphur, which is the second death" (21.8). The angel explains that nothing unclean shall enter the heavenly Jerusalem but "only those who are written in the Lamb's book of life" (21.27). These enjoy the tree of life, whose fruit is for the healing of the nations (22.2). One senses a promising theme, the idea that healing could proceed from the new Jerusalem all over the world, but a final description contrasts the city and its gates through which the blessed may enter to those still outside, "the dogs and sorcerers and fornicators and murderers and idolaters, and every one who loves and practices falsehood" (22.15). For whatever reason, evil remains to the very end of the tour of the new Jerusalem. The symmetrical tradition conceives of bliss in contrast to suffering, the city and its garden in contrast to the surrounding plane, the new heaven in contrast to the lake of fire. Evil is not annihilated but contained, and those in its thrall will suffer forever.

This survey of the concept of punishment after death in the New Testament has necessarily been selective. I have attempted to balance the most important texts on either side, both those that establish hell (Gehenna) and those that have been cited against it. I feel that both the logic and the textual basis for eternal damnation are explicitly presented. In connection with Paul and the positive tradition, there remains one text that I omitted. Whether or not it is genuinely written by Paul, it is certainly biblical and should be treated here as unfinished business. The passage, 2 Thessalonians 1.5–10, comes from an epistle whose authorship is still unresolved.[7]

7. Robert M. Grant, *The Formation of the New Testament* (London: Hutchinson University Library, 1965). See also Grant, *A Historical Introduction to the New Testament* (New York: Harper and Row, 1967). J. A. T. Robinson, *Redating the New Testament* (London: SCM Press, 1976), and Joseph Rhymer, *The Bible in Order* (Garden City, N.Y.: Doubleday, 1975), assign it to Paul and date it to 50 or 51. Perrin and Duling, *The New Testament, an Introduction*; and Krister Stendahl and Emilie T. Sander, "Biblical Literature: New Testament Literature, the Pauline Letters," in *The New Encyclopaedia Britannica, Macropaedia* (Chicago: Encyclopaedia Britannica, 1980), 2.958 and 965–66, deny Paul's authorship. Samuel Sandmel, *Judaism*

The letter writer (perhaps Paul), seeks to encourage the Christians of Thessalonica in the persecutions they endure. These sufferings will help make the members of the community worthy of the kingdom of God (2 Thessalonians 1.5), and they will bring suffering to those who oppress them: "God deems it just to repay with affliction those who afflict you, and to grant rest with us to you who are afflicted" (1.6–7). This formulation recalls 1 Thessalonians 5.9 and 2 Corinthians 5.10, where the fates of the saved and the wicked are also juxtaposed. Here too the afflicted receive "rest with us" and the oppressors receive "affliction." Considering that in those other passages the benefits of the righteous are called eternal but the sufferings of the wicked are unspecified, it would be a surprise were Paul to call the punishment of the wicked eternal when he has not also applied that word to the saved. Yet this author reverses the procedure Paul applied twice before: "They shall suffer the punishment [*tisousin*] of eternal destruction [*olethron aiōnion*] and exclusion from the presence of the Lord and from the glory of his might" (1.9). If these words are Paul's they contain his only reference to the fate of the excluded as "eternal" and "punishment," an especially anomalous reference in a text supposedly written in 50 or 51. Paul's thought has been traced from 1 Thessalonians, generally considered his first letter, to Romans, one of his last letters, perhaps of 57, without seeing any such specificity. This expression, otherwise lacking in Paul's writing and apparently so foreign to his thinking on the matter, could come only through the influence of another Christian source (since symmetry in the Jewish tradition, as in Daniel 12.2, had been available to Paul all along). This passage would therefore have to date after Mark, if not after Matthew, where the symmetry of the fates of the saved and the damned is expressed even more clearly.[8]

This survey of the New Testament has presented two themes that develop over time. The first occurred within the positive tradition, which proposed destruction for the wicked. Although he never lost faith in the potential of

---

and Christian Beginnings (New York: Oxford University Press, 1978), 309, considers the question unresolved. More recently, Wanamaker (37) supports its authenticity but dates it prior to First Thessalonians.

8. To avoid confusion later when I consider theologians discussing this passage, it would be wise to observe that there is no term for "exclusion" in either Greek or Latin. Its function is carried by adverbs meaning "away from" or "without." The Revised Standard Version has made a noun do the work of an adverb. A more literal translation would be: "And they will give eternal punishment in destruction away from or (outside of) the face of the Lord and the glory of his power."

the human race, Paul's missionary experience reminded him that only certain kinds of people really seemed to be fitted for eternal life. In his letters he seems to uncover more and more profound reasons why people are excluded from the kingdom. In 1 Thessalonians he is concerned with moral behavior. In 2 Corinthians he urges his fellow Christians to reconcile themselves to Christ; mere conformity to a code is not sufficient. In Romans he focuses on the condition of one's heart. Eternal life awaits only those who are disposed to interact with the grace that may be offered. Paul seems always to be sharpening his focus on internal disposition. At the same time, he refrains from qualifying the fate of those not saved as eternal punishment. Although he refers to wrath and evil in contrast to eternal life in the kingdom, he does not describe them fully enough to make them distinguishable from annulment and destruction. An indeterminate wrath or evil fate, when compared to eternal life can only become destruction.

The symmetrical tradition leaves no such ambiguity, and here is the second theme. Mark applied the unquenchable fire and undying worm from Isaiah 66.24 to the wicked dead and called it Gehenna. Matthew attributed to Jesus a formula whose symmetry could hardly be matched: "And [the cursed] will go away into eternal punishment, but the righteous into eternal life" (25.46). Revelation contrasts the people of the Lamb to the people of the beast. It promotes the former to a heavenly company in a new Jerusalem and consigns the latter to a lake of fire and sulfur.

Paul's own experience is the key to this development. Even as he increasingly narrowed his definition of the qualities of the blessed, so, in the fifty or sixty years separating Romans from Revelation the church changed from a small community of isolated cells, where reminders of personal contact and the thrill of conversion were sharp enough rebukes, to a more cosmopolitan community, whose members no longer experienced direct contact with the evangelists. Among these members severe differences had arisen. Paul had to warn of false prophets. Second Thessalonians alludes to doctrinal differences, and Acts recounts the debate over adherence to Jewish law. Matthew 18.15 sets down a procedure for resolving disputes. It could only be a matter of time until readers of Daniel or Enoch or Mark or Matthew would "balance" Paul's reticence with symmetrical formulations and insist that eternal punishment was the only alternative to salvation. My hypothesis is that postmortem sanctions became more dire as internal sanctions became more necessary. Between 1 Thessalonians and Revelation, the church came to be in need of an avenger, whether against wayward members or outside oppressors.

Moreover, it is clear in Latin literature from Lucretius to Virgil that the administrative machinery, judicial institutions, and expansionist propaganda of the Roman state provided copious examples of judicial uniformity. Thus Christian notions of avenging judgment could, like the administration of the worldly beast they abhorred, be centralized and supranational in its jurisdiction. As opposed to the Jewish judicial system of the New Temple, which was destroyed in 70 C.E., and whose law Paul had disputed, the Roman model was more immediate and relevant for Gentile converts.

I am speaking here not of a pope or a Christian emperor but of a perfect justice that can right all the wrongs suffered by the just. This judge must be perfect. Although the church taught forgiveness and opposed the evils of the Roman world, in the climate I have described we should not be surprised to see influence from the outside world. In Matthew's vision the Son of man is compared to a king who sits on a throne, like the emperor, before all the gathered nations. His jurisdiction is universal and, like the emperor's, is rendered before attendant advisers, in this case the angels, martyrs, and saints. Each soul gets one verdict, irreversible, eternal. The scheme is centripetal: all evil, whether Satan's initial fall or that of the impenitent sinners who follow Satan, leads to one place only. In a cosmopolitan, centralized empire, the rejects of a universal religion can be confined to a single, centralized hell.

Despite these structural correspondences, it would be wrong to exaggerate the external influences on the Christian concept of hell. The logic that undergirds the development of sublimated vengeance in the Hebrew Bible also led to the supernatural retribution envisioned in the Christian Scriptures. As anticipated in Matthew 25.46 and reiterated in Revelation, the Christian notion of punishment after death derived from two psychological starting points.

First is the need for the desired vengeance to be just. Vengeance is sublimated only because it is humanly impossible to bring it about; thus, God must do it. If God is to carry out the human wish for vengeance, that desire must be just or God's action will not be just. At this stage, God's action is simply punishment of wrongdoers and not vengeance, for God was not wronged directly. If the notion is extended, however, a wrong by one human against another may be considered a wrong against God or his law, which God can then avenge. Mark 9.37 and Matthew 25.40 and 25.45 accomplish this extension, for in these passages Jesus is reported as declaring himself a substitute for all innocent victims. As one behaves to the innocent child or to the helpless, one behaves to Jesus. Thus, any wrong against the innocent is an affront to Christ. Correction of that wrong is no longer punishment but vengeance. If vengeance is delayed, a surplus of wrongs to be avenged accumulates.

Second, one must be willing to subject oneself to the same standards that one wants God to enforce over others. The scruple that longed-for retribution be just is one manifestation of the urge to cleanse one's whole inner life, all one's desires. Yet as one sees in oneself the need for discipline, to curb oneself, one also desires the same curbs for others. This sense of justice assumes an ideal system in which misdeeds will be punished and good deeds (such as the purification of one's desires) rewarded. It is clear, however, that evil flourishes, injustice goes unpunished. The good are suffering undeserved hardships, and the wicked are getting less punishment than they deserve. How can this imbalance be rectified?

Psalm 73 also asked this question. Christianity proposed a different solution. One possibility would be for some good person voluntarily to accept more suffering than he deserves, to make himself a willing victim, and thereby to absorb some of the excess affliction that is being endured. Such a sacrifice would have no effect unless wrong actions signify suffering for both the doers and the sufferers of wrong. They reflect suffering for evildoers because they indicate an inner disorientation. Satan, Adam, and Eve suffered from such a lack of inner order. Paul suggests in Romans 1.28 that baseness of mind is a punishment for sin: "And since they did not see fit to acknowledge God, God gave them up to a base mind and to improper conduct." For Paul, this lack of rectitude is both a result and a cause of sin. Obviously, the actions of such people also cause suffering to innocent victims.

All these actions, whether internal vices or external wrongs, through the history of the human race would constitute the sum of evil in the world. They are what the New Testament calls "the sins of the world," and a voluntary acceptance of these wrongs by an innocent victim would release some or all of them, or as John records John the Baptist saying of Jesus (John 1.29), it would "take away the sins of the world." In an extreme situation, the victim would not merely suffer but actually die for these sins. The case would be more extreme if the victim were divine and more extreme yet if the victim were simultaneously divine and human.

The sacrifice of this victim would remove pressure from the present. Evil could be tolerated better for the time being, indeed until the end of the world. At the end, however, the same divine victim would have to punish all those evils or else they would remain unpunished. Under this system, sublimated vengeance is deferred to the end of time. The cost of this new understanding of evil is faith in the efficacy of the sacrifice. Indeed, the victim would be entitled to punish those who reject the efficacy of his sacrifice. This system, then, requires not only performance of good deeds and abstention from bad deeds but also *acknowledgment of the fact and efficacy of the sacrifice.*

Second Thessalonians 1.5–10 combines many elements of this abstract model. The system is referred to as a "righteous judgment of God" (5); it involves affliction that is paid for with affliction (6), rest is given to the afflicted (7). When Jesus returns, he inflicts "vengeance upon those who do not know God and upon those who do not obey the gospel" (8), who will suffer "eternal destruction and exclusion" (9), which is here called punishment and is therefore consciously endured (cf. affliction, [6]), while he will "be glorified in his saints," and "marveled at in all who have believed" (10). Only steadfast faith will avert the delusion that will ensnare nonbelievers, "so that all may be condemned who did not believe the truth but had pleasure in unrighteousness" (2 Thessalonians 2.12). Here, then, is a community defined by faith in the sacrificial victim who, in order that good may finally triumph over evil, takes up the excess of unpunished sin and will later punish both those who sin and those who deny the effectiveness of the action.

Tensions in Early Christianity

You who were damned by the tree and the devil
and death now see the devil and death damned by
the tree.

—*Gospel of Nicodemus* 24.1.3–5

On the very day on which I rose from the dead I
grant to you all who are being punished a day and
a night of ease for ever.

—*Apocalypse of Paul* 44

The more enjoyment man found in God, the greater
was his wickedness in abandoning him; and he who
destroyed in himself a good which might have
been eternal, became worthy of eternal evil.

—Augustine, *City of God*, 21.12

Divine Sovereignty

Part III has shown how the New Testament expresses different views of punishment after death reflecting different religious sensibilities. This variation continued into subsequent ages and informed the treatment of hell ever after.

Diversity within Scripture was matched by cultural division in the declining Roman political fabric. Christianity was a persecuted sect within the Roman Empire until Constantine's Edict of Milan in 313 prescribed toleration for the new religion. Even when Theodosius I abolished the Roman state religion in 392 and his successors legislated against Christian heresies, thus making Nicene Christianity the official religion of the Roman Empire, differences in Christian teaching continued.[1]

Beyond Christian efforts to suppress the paganisms of the Mediterranean world and the early Christian heresies, there was still competition with Judaism, whose rabbis were composing the Babylonian and Jerusalem Talmuds during this period.[2] Further, Christian rulers could not prevent the

---

1. Ramsay MacMullen, *Christianizing the Roman Empire (A.D. 100–400)* (New Haven: Yale University Press, 1984); J. N. Hillgarth, *Christianity and Paganism, 350–700*, rev. ed. (Philadelphia: University of Pennsylvania Press, 1986).

2. Sandmel, *Judaism and Christian Beginnings*; Paula Fredriksen, *From Jesus to Christ: The Origins of the New Testament Images of Jesus* (New Haven: Yale University Press, 1988); Morna D. Hooker, *Continuity and Discontinuity: Early Christianity in Its Jewish Setting* (London: Epworth, 1986); Pieter Willem van der Horst, *Essays on the Jewish World of Early Christianity*, Novum Testamentum et orbis

migration of Germanic peoples across the empire. Whether the new arrivals came from Central Asia, like the Goths, or from the south shores of the Baltic Sea, like the Franks, they imported their own, vastly different myths and religious practices, particularly to northern Europe.[3] During the seventh century, Mediterranean Europe confronted Islam, whose view of punishment after death has obvious affinities with Christian doctrine, and whose Scripture it shares by reference in the Qur'an, yet which nonetheless regulates daily life and locates religious authority in a manner sharply different from Christianity.

The authority of the pope was embryonic. Christians of Greek-speaking lands, commonly called Byzantine, who formed the root of the Greek Orthodox church (officially, the Holy Eastern Orthodox Catholic and Apostolic church) did not recognize, or only sporadically recognized, papal authority, preferring that the emperor and his patriarch in Constantinople and the councils (called with papal approval, it is true) should define matters of faith.[4]

antiquus, 14 (Freiburg, Switzerland: Universitätsverlag; Göttingen: Vandenhoeck und Ruprecht, 1990); James D. G. Dunn, *The Partings of the Ways between Christianity and Judaism and Their Significance for the Character of Christianity* (London: SCM; Philadelphia: Trinity International, 1991); Marcel Simon, *Verus Israel: A Study of the Relations between Christians and Jews in the Roman Empire, 135–425*, trans. Henry McKeating, Littman Library of Jewish Civilization (Oxford: Oxford University Press, 1986).

3. See Hans Joachim Diesner, *The Great Migration: The Movement of Peoples across Europe, A.D. 300–700*, trans. C. S. V. Salt (London: Orbis, 1982); Lucien Musset, *The Germanic Invasions: The Making of Europe, A.D. 400–600*, trans. Edward James and Columba James (University Park: Pennsylvania State University Press, 1975); Fritz M. Heichelheim, *An Ancient Economic History, from the Palaeolithic Age to the Migrations of the Germanic, Slavic, and Arabic Nations.* Rev. and complete English ed. (Leiden: Sijthoff, 1968–70).

4. Robert B. Eno, *The Rise of the Papacy*, Theology and Life Series, 32 (Wilmington, Del.: Glazier, 1990); Robert Markus, *The End of Ancient Christianity* (Cambridge: Cambridge University Press, 1990); James Stevenson, ed., *A New Eusebius: Documents Illustrative of the History of the Church to A.D. 337* (London: S. P. C. K., 1968); idem, *Creeds, Councils, and Controversies: Documents Illustrative of the History of the Church A.D. 337–461* (London: S. P. C. K., 1966); Beresford James Kidd, *The Roman Primacy to A.D. 461* (London: Society for Promoting Christian Knowledge, 1936). Bernard Schimmelpfennig, *Das Papsttum: Grundzüge seiner Geschichte von der Antike bis zur Renaissance* (Darmstadt: Wissenschaftliche Buchgesellschaft, 1984); Arnold Angenendt and Rudolf Schieffer, *Roma—Caput et Fons: Zwei Vorträge über das päpstliche Rom zwischen Altertum und Mittelalter* (Opladen: Westdeutscher Verlag, 1989); Alfonso Carrasco Rouco, *Le primat de l'évêque de Rome: Etude sur la cohérence ecclésiologique et canonique du primat de juridiction*, Studia Friburgensia, Sectio canonica, 7 (Freiburg, Switzer-

These difficulties of the officially Christian empire do not annul the very real victories won over Gnosticism, Manicheanism, Donatism, Pelagianism, Adoptionism, and other threats to Roman Catholicism.[5] Yet they indicate the scope of an insurmountable problem. Aided by the official support of the Roman Empire, late ancient and early medieval Christianity could not attain a greater uniformity than Roman political power itself.[6] Since that authority was severely curtailed after the first century and then declined further, it is hardly surprising to see a proliferation of views about hell, which is a very important aspect of a religion whose other doctrines also engendered divergent interpretations.

Of course these different treatments provoked debate. Some views were condemned by ecclesiastical authority. Yet in the early Middle Ages the church itself had not yet attained the institutional articulation or the political power that would permit it to suppress heresy as effectively as it did after 1200. Thus, during the early Middle Ages, among authors who considered themselves Christian, there was a remarkable variety of interpretations of hell. A brief sketch of the sources to be treated in Part IV will support the point. The story of Christ's descent, as told in the *Gospel of Nicodemus*, affirms Christ's sovereignty over the underworld. The *Apocalypse of Peter* vividly recounts a harsh system of retribution to establish precise links between the punishment and the crime. The *Apocalypse of Paul* begins from this premise, but then asks why, if Christ is in charge and is full of mercy, he would not display that mercy to the damned.[7] Origen takes that idea to its

---

land: Editions universitaires, 1990); Michele Maccarrone, *Romana ecclesia: Cathedra Petri*, Italia Sacra, 47–48 (Rome: Herder, 1991); Giovanni Falbo, *Il primato della Chiesa di Roma alla luce dei primi quattro secoli* (Rome: Coletti, 1989).

5. For a recent bibliography, see Henry Chadwick, *Heresy and Orthodoxy in the Early Church*, Collected Studies, 342 (Aldershot, Hampshire, Great Britain: Variorum, 1991); Manfred Jacobs, *Die Reichskirche und ihre Dogmen: Von der Zeit Konstantins bis zum Niedergang des weströmischen Reiches*, Zugänge zur Kirchengeschichte, 3, Kleine Vandenhoeck-Reihe, 1525 (Göttingen: Vandenhoeck und Ruprecht, 1987); Hans-Georg Beck, *Actus fidei: Wege zum Autodafé*, Sitzungsberichte der bayerischen Akademie der Wissenschaften, Philosophisch-historische Klasse, 3 (Munich: Bayerische Akademie der Wissenschaften, in Kommission bei C. H. Beck, 1987).

6. Jean Gaudemet, *L'église dans l'empire romain: IVe–Ve siècles*, Histoire du droit et des institutions de l'église en occident, 3 (Paris: Sirey, 1989).

7. For a bibliography on these texts, see James H. Charlesworth, *The New Testament Apocrypha and Pseudepigrapha: A Guide to Publications, with Excursuses on Apocalypses* (Chicago: American Theological Library Association; Metuchen, N.J.: Scarecrow, 1987).

logical conclusion by asserting that divine punishment must purify and, consequently, cannot be eternal. Defending its justice, Augustine reasserts the eternal hell.

These texts show that debate continued over the questions of divine power, justice, and mercy. If God is omnipotent, how can any refuse to do his will? Can his ability to save be resisted? If humans should be punished for freely rejecting Christian teachings about right conduct or belief, how should that discipline be applied? Should it occur in this life or the next? Should it torment the body or the soul? If suffering from punishment after death provokes repentance, can postmortem penance be effective? Can divine mercy in any way avail the damned? These and related questions circulated within the Christian community of the Latin West in the first centuries C.E. Because these questions concern the power and justice of God as much as they do hell itself, it is necessary to begin by considering a text whose primary purpose is to celebrate the divine victory over death, the *Gospel of Nicodemus*.

CHRIST'S DESCENT INTO HADES

By resurrecting Lazarus and himself rising from the dead, Christ asserted his dominion over the underworld. The theme is an ancient one. The psalmist, too, proclaimed divine rule over the dead: "If I make my bed in Sheol, thou art there!" (139.8). In his challenge to Job, speaking from the whirlwind, God asserted the rule of Providence over Leviathan, a monster of the deep, and, quoting Isaiah's and Hosea's taunts of death and Hades, Paul extolled its extension to the grave. The classical tradition of Greece and Rome, too, asserted the power of its heroes over the land of Hades. The account of Christ's descending to the underworld in the time between his burial and resurrection, to rescue from death the prophets who anticipated his coming, powerfully dramatizes these biblical passages and the idea of divine sovereignty over death.

This power, however, carries with it great responsibility. From Job on, many asked how so mighty a lord could rule the way he does. If his power extends to the pit, then retribution for the dead may be questioned. Christianity was not very old before differences arose concerning the implications of divine mercy and divine justice for the dead. There was a wide variety of views on that matter, but before considering them, it is well to look at a dramatic expression of that sovereignty itself. For unless divine control of the dead is explicitly claimed, challenges to God over the fate of the dead may be misdirected.

Although the Bible did not put the question in precisely these terms, it did not take long for subsequent Christian legend to assert that the benefits of the Resurrection were not reserved for the future but also ran back to the very beginning of humankind. Paul's parallels of Christ and Adam were too powerful for anything less. Besides, Daniel and Revelation prophesy the resurrection of the dead. Adam, Eve, Abraham, Isaac, Jacob, David the psalmist, the prophets of the Messiah—these protagonists of the Hebrew Bible were to benefit retroactively from their relation to the new era. Although clearly suggesting that Christianity superseded Judaism, this belief also engendered respect for a religious vision Christians considered (and still consider) akin to their own. This ambivalence is also manifest in the story of Christ's descent into Hades.

Although fully narrated only in apocryphal texts preserved in comparatively late manuscripts, the story of Christ's Harrowing of Hades develops motifs expressed in biblical allusions considered in connection with the myth behind hell. These themes had begun to be combined into narrative form during the second century.[8] The *Homily* of Melito of Sardis contains what might be an older hymn in which Christ identifies himself as the doer of heroic deeds in the underworld: "I am he who put down death, and triumphed over the enemy, and trod upon Hades, and bound the Strong One and brought man safely home to the heights of the heavens."[9] The earliest creeds are silent on the subject of Christ's descent to the netherworld until

8. In the *Shepherd of Hermas*, 9.16.5–7, it is "the Apostles and preachers" who went down with the water of baptism and the "knowledge of the name of the Son of God" and brought the dead up alive. See *The Apostolic Fathers*, trans. Kirsopp Lake, 2 vols. (Cambridge: Harvard University Press, 1924), 2:262–63. The *Epistola apostolorum*, written in the mid-second century, reflects knowledge of the *Shepherd of Hermas*. The *Odes of Solomon* present (albeit in a different order) these key elements of the story: the breaking of a door, the penetration of the utmost depth, the essential freedom of the righteous, the irony that former captives of death are now alive and free, the grief of Hades, and the liberation of "many" whom Christ resurrects along with himself. Johannes Quasten, *Patrology*, 3 vols. (Westminster, Md.: Newman, 1953–62), 1:101, 150–52, 162, 166–67.

9. Quasten, *Patrology*, 1:242–45. Jerome knew an apocryphal *Gospel of Bartholomew*, which, in the much later redaction that has survived, tells the story in abbreviated form. M. R. James, *The Apocryphal New Testament* (1924; rpt. Oxford: Oxford University Press, 1966), 166–70; Edgar Hennecke and Wilhelm Schneemelcher, eds., *New Testament Apocrypha*, trans. R. McL. Wilson, 2 vols. (Philadelphia: Westminster, 1963), 1:484–92. This work will hereafter be abbreviated HSW. A revised edition by Wilhelm Schneemelcher, English trans. edited by R. McL. Wilson, 2 vols. (Louisville, Ky.: Westminster/John Knox, 1991), appeared after these chapters were written. References are to the 1963 edition.

the Apostles' Creed of circa 390 mentioned by Ambrose.[10] The most influential accounts of the descent are contained in two versions of an apocryphal *Gospel of Nicodemus*, which Constantin von Tischendorf, their first editor, labeled Latin A and Latin B.[11] These have been dated from "about 395" to "after 554."[12]

The legend narrated in the *Gospel of Nicodemus* cannot be understood without considering the textual tradition that frames it. The Gospel of John refers to a Jewish scholar named Nicodemus, who became sympathetic to the teachings of Jesus, went to him at night with questions (3.1–15), and with Joseph of Arimathea, helped arrange for his burial (19.39). The apocryphal gospel attributed to this Nicodemus relates that after the Resurrection of Christ, rumors circulated in the Jewish community that others had been resurrected too. Temple authorities delegated Nicodemus, Joseph, and other rabbis to inquire specifically about Karinus and Leucius, the twin sons of Simeon, who were said to have returned from the dead. The brothers' account of what they saw in Hades after they died, when Jesus broke down the gates of Hades and resurrected them along with other righteous men, forms the basis for the descent narrative, which circulated as the *Gospel of Nicode-*

10. Henricus Denzinger and Adolfus Schönmetzer, *Enchiridion symbolorum definitionum et declarationum de rebus fidei et morum*, 24th ed. (Barcelona: Herder, 1967), no. 16, introduction at p. 20.

11. In my analysis of the *Gospel of Nicodemus*, the text that narrates the descent, I cite the version called Latin A in the edition of H. C. Kim, *The Gospel of Nicodemus* (Toronto: Pontifical Institute of Mediaeval Studies, 1973). I sometimes make comparisons from the version called Latin B in the edition of Constantin von Tischendorf, *Evangelia apocrypha*, rev. ed. (Leipzig: Mendelssohn, 1876), 417–32. Tischendorf also edited a Greek version. Though I have translated the passages quoted here myself, those wishing to read the entire text in English are advised that M. R. James's translation in *The Apocryphal New Testament*, 117–46, juxtaposes Latin A and B and the Greek versions in toto, whereas Felix Scheidweiler's in HSW 1:470–84 does not. For example, it omits the crucial variants in chap. 8 of Latin B.

12. For the early date, see Scheidweiler in HSW 1:447; for the late date, see G. C. O'Ceallaigh, "Dating the Commentaries of Nicodemus," *Harvard Theological Review* 56 (1963): 57. Note that O'Ceallaigh's date refers to what he considers a core text, the "Commentaries of Nicodemus," from which he says Tischendorf's Latin A and B derive. They would thus be even later. It is nonetheless clear from material already presented that a legend of Christ's descent had been forming since the time of the composition of the New Testament. Kevin Roddy of the University of California at Davis has analyzed complementary liturgical and homiletic witnesses to the emergence of this narrative in the paper he delivered to the Medieval Academy of America on April 1, 1993: "Encompassing an Apocryphon: Establishing a Complete Narrative for the Descensus Christi ad Inferos."

mus. A later tradition has it that Joseph and Nicodemus then relayed to Pontius Pilate their account of how they gathered the testimony of Karinus and Leucius. Pilate included that statement in a report of his own to the emperor Claudius. Woven together over the course of centuries, the final document, the *Acts of Pilate*, containing the *Gospel of Nicodemus*, which in turn contains the "affidavits" of Karinus and Leucius, is thus a fiction three levels deep.

Even without any reference to Pilate, it is clear that the *Gospel of Nicodemus* "invented"[13] Karinus and Leucius so as to fabricate reports of evidence from resurrected Jewish witnesses about the power of Jesus over death and to put the affirmation of key Christian beliefs into the mouths of Jews contemporary with his Passion. This polemical purpose cannot be separated from the *Gospel of Nicodemus*.[14] Further, in chapter 20, the *Gospel of Nicodemus* is defamatory, portraying Jews as tools of Satan. Nonetheless, the anti-Jewish elements do not make up the whole story. The *Gospel of Nicodemus* is a key text in the history of hell.

In the narrative, Hades and Death appear as allegorical personifications.[15] Satan is himself, portrayed as an exile from heaven who has attempted to associate himself with Hades' rule of the underworld. Because he has meddled in the affairs of the host kingdom, however, he is considered a nuisance. The relationship between Hades and Satan typifies that between Satan and humankind, though in this text Hades acts correctly and expels the evil influence. The dead who have lived in the shadows of the underworld's gates also participate. Sometimes they act as a chorus taunting Satan and Hades; sometimes they speak individually, quoting to the infernal authorities their earlier prophecies that a savior would come to put an end to death. Constructing the drama around Psalm 24 and using its verses 7–10 for dialogue heighten the effect of having ancient Jewish authors invoke their own texts. In addition to these Jews in the underworld, the story prominently features Jews who were associated with Jesus during his lifetime and who, in the present tense of the *Gospel of Nicodemus*, react to the Resurrection.

13. The term is O'Ceallaigh's, "Dating the Commentaries," 24.

14. O'Ceallaigh, ibid., 44–45, makes an analogous assertion for the testimony of Phineës, Addas, and Haggai, who in chapter 14 are said to have been eyewitnesses to Jesus' Ascension. This attribution to Jewish witnesses of matters central to the Christian creed, he considered the "raison d'être for the writing of this whole work of 'Nicodemus.'"

15. Both the place and the person are called *Inferus* in Latin A and *Hades* in the Greek version. Latin B calls the place *inferus* and the person *Infernus*. I call them both Hades.

Joseph of Arimathea, who had obtained the body of Jesus and buried it, speaks to the priests Annas and Caiaphas and remarks that Jesus had not only risen himself but resurrected many others as well. He suggests going to see the open tombs of Karinas and Leucius, the twin sons of Simeon, the then-deceased rabbi who had earlier received the young Jesus at the Temple. Thus Joseph leads the high priests Annas, Caiaphas, Nicodemus, and Gamaliel to Arimathea to question the two brothers, whose death had been witnessed by all. Karinas and Leucius refuse to speak but go into separate rooms to write down the deeds they had witnessed when Christ visited the underworld and raised them together with many others. In the end it turns out that the twins have written identical accounts—a terrific embarrassment for the Jews, to whom this kind of unanimity recalls the legend of the translation of the Septuagint, which is said to have emerged in seventy-two identical versions from the pens of seventy-two translators working independently.

In their own identical accounts, Karinus and Leucius describe how, immediately after they had died and descended into the netherworld of darkness, a bright light illumined the gloom. Simeon, being dead and living below, recognized the light as Jesus and called him "the Lord Jesus Christ, the Son of God," whom he had acknowledged even while living. John the Baptist said this is the one he had declared the Lamb of God and baptized in the Jordan before hearing a voice proclaiming, "This is my beloved Son in whom I am well pleased" (2.18.2–3).[16] Adam asked his son Seth to tell how archangel Michael had revealed to him that relief for Adam would be available only in 5,500 years, through baptism (3.19.1).

Recognizing Christ as the source of the light, Satan assumed command of the underworld and ordered Hades, whom he treated as a lieutenant, to prepare for the assault against the gates. He reassured Hades that Jesus, though he claimed to be the Son of God, was in fact merely a death-fearing man. Hades seemed to have an inkling of the divinity of Jesus, and the more imminent Satan's defeat appeared, the more outspoken Hades became. Satan tried to spur Hades into a more spirited defense by listing the "wrongs" Jesus had done: curing the blind, the lame, and the dumb and even resurrecting the dead (4.20.1). Can these be the deeds of a man? Hades asked. Satan urged Hades not to fear Jesus, for he had aroused "my ancient Jewish people with envy and anger against him" (4.20.2, lines 13–14) and prepared for his crucifixion "that I may bring him to you, to be subject to you and me" (4.20.2, lines 18–19). Understanding that this was indeed that same Jesus who resurrected Lazarus, Hades acknowledged that this was the savior of

16. Cf. James, *Apocryphal New Testament*, 124–25.

the human race. He foresaw that if Jesus gained entry, all their prisoners would be released (4.20.3).

As Jesus approached the gates of Hades, the script for his words and the answers from inside came directly from Psalm 24. Biblical text doubled as a responsive reading and a dramatic script. Christ challenged: "Lift up your gates, princes, and be lifted up, eternal doors, and the king of glory will come in" (verse 9) (5.21.3, lines 4–5). Hearing these words, Hades ordered the gates barred, sent Satan to do battle with Jesus, and then expelled Satan from his jurisdiction. The prisoners in the underworld began to mock Hades, repeating their prophecies. [Hosea] taunted, "Did I not say, 'O Death [*Infere*], where is thy victory'?" Then Jesus repeated the cry from Psalm 24. Hades exclaimed in puzzlement, "Who is this king of glory?" (verse 8a). David (considered in the Middle Ages to be the author of Psalms) recognized the words from his psalm and answered Hades' question by saying, "The Lord strong and mighty, the Lord mighty in battle, he is the King of Glory" (verse 8b; cf. verse 10).[17]

Karinas continued: "As David was saying this to Hades, the King of Glory arrived in the form of a man. The Lord of Majesty illuminated the eternal gloom and burst the unbroken bonds. The aid of his unconquered virtue visited us sitting in the gloom of transgressions and the shadow of the death of sinners" (5.21.3, lines 16–20). As Hades and Death and their ministers took flight, they acknowledged their defeat and wondered aloud about the identity of the aggressor, whom they had just seen dead and buried. "Who are you who absolves [the captives] bound by original sin and detained here and recalls them to their pristine liberty?" (6.22.1, lines 16–18). "Then the King of Glory, the Lord, trampled upon Death, apprehended prince Satan, delivered him to the power of Hades, and drew Adam to his own brightness" (6.22.2, lines 1–4). The world was turned upside down. The groans of the captives would no longer be heard; their tears would no longer flow. The narrator reflects this new condition by the frequent use of antithesis. Those who formerly sighed in torments beneath the rule of Hades and Satan now ridiculed them (7.23.1, lines 10–11).

This reversal, Hades scolded, was all because Satan caused Jesus to be crucified. What Satan had gained by the tree of transgression he had now lost by the tree of the cross. By bringing the innnocent in, he lost the guilty. Consequently, Satan was to suffer eternal punishment under Hades' supervision (7.23.1, lines 28–30). The King of Glory confirmed this sentence. Speaking to Hades, he said, "Prince Satan will be under your power forever in the place of my just ones, Adam and his sons" (7.23.2).

17. Part of David's speech is a paraphrase of Ps. 102.18–22.

In its most important divergence from Latin A, Latin B is far more explicit about events at this point. Christ's entry shattered the hardware that had barred the doors. Jesus wrapped Satan in chains, placed his foot on his neck, and as he forced him into Tartarus ("eum elisit in Tartarum" [Latin B 8.24]), declared, "Through all the ages you have done great evil, nor have you ever been at rest. Today I deliver you to eternal fire." Then he commanded Hades: "Take this most evil and wicked one and keep him in your custody until the day which I shall command you." Then both Satan and Hades were plunged "into the depth of the abyss" (8.24). Clearly, then, Latin B departs from Latin A by identifying hell proper as Tartarus, filled with eternal fire, and ready to receive Hades and Satan.

The saints threw themselves on their knees, Latin A continues, acknowledging the identity of Jesus in terms taken from Psalm 29. Jesus explained the new situation: "You who were damned by the tree and the devil and death now see the devil and death damned by the tree" (8.24.1, lines 3–5). The saints urged him to set up his cross to end the dominion of death (8.24.1, line 26). Jesus made the sign of the cross over Adam and the others. "And taking the right hand of Adam he ascended from the underworld [*inferis*] and all the saints followed the Lord" as David quoted Psalms 98 and 118 and prophets recited their prophecies (8.24.2).

Again Latin B is more explicit. After Jesus received the thanks first of Adam and Eve, then of all the saints, "the Savior, searching everywhere, stung [*momordidit (sic)*] Hades. Then he threw part into Tartarus, part he led back with him on high" (9.25).[18] Thus Jesus made a clean sweep. After individual examination (*perscrutans de omnibus*), everyone in Hades was divided, either cast into Tartarus or taken to heaven. The history of Sheol would start again at this point. This action simultaneously sealed the conquest of death and anticipated the Last Judgment. All involved went either with Christ to paradise or with Satan (and Hades) into Tartarus (9.25). Though only Latin B divides the netherworld by referring to Tartarus, both texts make it clear that Satan will suffer more in the future, and forever.

Leading Adam by the hand in the account of Latin A, Jesus delivered the saints to archangel Michael. Before dwelling definitively in paradise, the

---

18. *Mordeo* is the verbal counterpart of *morsus*, which appears in the taunt from Hosea 13.14: "Ero mors tua, o mors; morsus tuus ero, inferne." ("O Sheol, where is your destruction?" [Revised Standard Version]; "O grave, I will be thy destruction" [King James]) At 1 Cor. 15.55 *morsus* is changed to *stimulus* ("Death where is thy sting?") The meaning is that Christ has here come to fulfill the prophecy and deliver the "bite" or the "sting" that the grave has hitherto claimed from humankind.

risen Jews were granted three days to spend Passover alive with their families. Then they were baptized in the River Jordan, given white robes, and caught up in the clouds. But Karinus and Leucius were to live in Arimathea (9.25–10.26).

Karinus and Leucius concluded their written accounts. Karinus gave what he had written to Annas, Caiaphas, and Gamaliel. Leucius gave his report to Nicodemus and Joseph. When the Jewish authorities compared the documents, they were found to agree letter for letter. When this was announced in the synagogue, the Jews were confused and beat their breasts.

According to the later, starkly anti-Jewish text of the *Acts of Pilate*, which resumes here, where the *Gospel of Nicodemus* leaves off, Joseph and Nicodemus reported these things to Pilate, who in turn wrote them in his records (11.27). His curiosity aroused, Pilate went to the Temple to determine whether or not the Jews crucified Jesus knowing who he was. Annas and Caiaphas cleared the Temple and privately told Pilate that they crucified Jesus not knowing who he was, but that many of their nation had seen him alive after his Passion and they saw two witnesses whom Jesus raised from the dead and what marvelous things he did among the dead, "which things we have in writing in our hands."[19] Ignorance over the identity of Jesus was made to appear unlikely, since Annas and Caiaphas explained to Pilate that biblical prophecies indicated his coming in the 5,500th year of creation, as, they said, Jesus did (12.28).

Pilate included these words of Annas and Caiaphas in his report to Emperor Claudius, which is appended to the *Acts of Pilate*. In fact the purported text of this letter says that (although the people considered him the Son of God) the chief priests of the Jews framed Jesus before Pilate and crucified him. When he rose from the dead, they bribed the Roman soldiers guarding the tomb to say his disciples had stolen his body. Thus the account of Christ's descent is embedded in a series of "official" documents whose correct relationship to one another can be seen by looking backward from Pilate's letter.[20]

In the descent, then, Hades is both a protagonist in, and the site of, a drama of cosmic proportions. This area resembles not the Hades of Luke 16, with its chasm and fire, but Sheol. The prophets hail Christ as he subjugates the enemy and establishes divine sovereignty over territory claimed in the psalms but now subjected personally by the appearance of the conqueror and maintained symbolically by his banner.

19. For this section, see James, *Apocryphal New Testament*, 144–45.

20. Inclusion of Pilate's investigation gives the later text an even harsher anti-Jewish tinge, since it involves "evidence" of knowing participation in the Crucifixion.

Christ's action removes the torpor that afflicts the fallen human race. Adam recounts how he had sent his son Seth to heaven in search of a cure for the sickness that had come over him (3.19.1, lines 8–9). The archangel Michael tells Seth that Adam must wait 5,500 years before his grief will be salved (3.19.1, lines 15–18). The balm will come when death is abolished, with the coming of Christ. By extension, all humankind shares this affliction and awaits the same cure. What is this disease but the consequence of Adam's sin, death itself? (6.22.1, lines 16–18).

Similarly, when Karinus describes his own death, he speaks (in terms borrowed from the Hebrew Bible) of being "set together with all our fathers in the deep, in [the] obscurity of darkness" (2.18.1, lines 5–7). This is Sheol. Christ's arrival, in sharp contrast, is represented as "a light as brilliant as the sun, but purple and royal, [that] came and shone upon those who were sitting in death" (2.18.1, lines 7–9). The dead can be portrayed confined in never-broken bonds, enclosed in prison (4.20.3, lines 23–26). The earth holds their inert bodies, but Hades, personified, holds them in captivity, as he held Lazarus for four days, stinking and rotting (4.20.3, lines 8–9). This land is very much the grave. The conditions Christ abolished for the saved are described as the "eternal shadows," "the never-broken chains," and— the only reference here to darkness as the result of error or misdeeds rather than "mere" death—"the gloom of transgressions and the shadow of the death of sinners" (5.21.3, lines 18–20). Here is a mostly static storehouse where angels of death stash "the tribute of the living" (6.22.1, lines 24–26); yet there are sufficient torments to provoke sighs (7.23.1, lines 10–11), moans, groans, and tears (7.23.1, lines 23–24). It is clear, however, that in the *Gospel of Nicodemus* the righteous ancients suffer far less from the physical aspects of the place than from longing for the fulfillment of prophecy.

A fascinating conjunction of textual variants permits a glimpse into the variety of early medieval views of what the condition of the virtuous ancient Hebrews might have been. The manuscripts give three different readings to describe the nature of Hades' prison. The first editor, Tischendorf, chose a phrase that translates as "all [who are] enclosed in the cruelty of the prison" ("in crudelitate carceris clausi").[21] Yet he reports a variant in a manuscript in Einsiedeln, which substitutes "credulity" for "cruelty." H. C. Kim, a recent editor of the Einsiedeln manuscript, contradicts Tischendorf and, drawing support from another codex, in the Laud collection of the Bodleian

21. Tischendorf, *Evangelia apocrypha*, 397.

Library in Oxford, reads: "in the incredulity of the prison" ("in incredulitate carceris clausi" [20.3.23–24]).[22] The confusion comes from the similarity between the two Latin words *credulitas* (credulity) and *crudelitas* (cruelty). Tischendorf's reading, "in the cruelty of the prison," emphasizes the literal level, the physical condition of the underworld, which causes the dead sighs, moans, groans, and tears. Tischendorf's reading of the Einsiedeln variant ("in the credulity of the prison") suggests that "credulity" can have a positive connotation and derives from the notion that Jewish prophecy anticipated Christian faith. Kim's reading of the Laud manuscript ("in the incredulity of the prison") emphasizes the differences between Judaism and Christianity.

Although the grip of this underworld need no longer be considered eternal, as the cross planted at the gates forever proclaims, Hades himself describes for Satan and, implicitly, for those who ignore these events, a future of "great eternal torments and infinite tortures . . . in my everlasting custody" (7.23.1, lines 28–30). A worse condition for future dead, who do not escape death by their faith, is foreshadowed by the sentence Christ pronounces against Satan: in the place of Adam and the righteous, Satan will be placed in the eternal custody of Hades (6.22.2, 7.23.1, lines 28–30, 7.23.2), and as Latin B specifies (8.24), both will be consigned to eternal fire, deep in the abyss.

The fiery abyss, a part of the underworld not mentioned in connection with the suffering of the prophets awaiting deliverance, reveals how much the story of the descent builds upon the fall of the angels. Latin A makes it clear that Satan is no longer in heaven. Moreover Hades' staff of adjutants, "all my despicable officers," he calls them (4.20.3, lines 15–16), seem to be fallen angels. "Cruel servants" aid them (6.22.1, lines 1–2). The troop is composed of "all the legions of demons" (6.22.1, line 20). The source of their power seems to be the same as Satan's, for Hades says to Satan: "All the powerful of the earth, whom you have led subject by your potency [*potentia*], are held subject by my power [*potestas*]" (4.20.2, lines 3–5). Thus the guardians of Hades are those who followed Satan in his fall. And Tartartus, to which Hades himself, Satan, and these guardians were consigned by Christ at the moment of the descent fits "the eternal fire prepared for the devil and his angels" of Matthew 25.41 and the lake of fire and brimstone to which the beast, the false prophet, the Devil, Death, and Hades are sentenced in Revelation 19.20, 20.10, and 20.14. Therefore, the descent does more than liberate the righteous ancients from the pangs of death.

22. Kim, *Gospel of Nicodemus*, 40.

It also inaugurates the fiery abyss that had been awaiting the wicked from the beginning. Christ's action during his descent reaffirms the relationship between what the Hebrew Bible called Sheol and Ge-Hinnom, the Greeks called Hades and Tartarus, the Greek New Testament called Hades and Gehenna, and Jerome, in his Latin New Testament, called Infernus and Gehenna.

The central message of the Gospel of Nicodemus is that, for followers of Christ, Hades is nullified. The abolition of Hades for the saved, however, raises the stakes for the damned. In contrast to the righteous ancients, who endured only the psychological pain of anticipation, the sufferings of Satan's followers will henceforth be actively applied and far more severe than those of the grave. It remains to consider what might have been in store for them. Whereas the first text celebrates the conquering Christ's lordship over Hades, the second proclaims him as the overseer of hell.

VENGEANCE: THE APOCALYPSE OF PETER

Although even the strictest New Testament references to eternal damnation remain symmetrical in that they keep the possibility of eternal life clearly in view, it was not long before a heightened emphasis on damnation provided a pronounced zeal for vengeance. Written before the middle of the second century, the *Apocalypse of Peter* was the first major Christian account of postmortem punishment outside the New Testament.[23]

The scene is set at the Mount of Olives and recalls the opening of Matthew 24. Under the leadership of Peter, the apostles question Jesus about his return and the signs that will precede it. Almost immediately a great drama occurs. Jesus opens his palm and looking there, as if at a screen, Peter and

23. M. R. James, *Apocryphal New Testament*, 504, dates it "early second century." Ch. Maurer, trans. *The Apocalypse of Peter*, in HSW 2:664, says, "around 135," interpreting the parable of the fig tree as a reference to Bar Cochba. Dennis D. Buchholz, *Your Eyes Will Be Opened: A Study of the Greek (Ethiopic) "Apocalypse of Peter"* (Atlanta: Scholars, 1988), 408–10, concurs with the connection to the Bar Cochba war. Martha Himmelfarb, *Tours of Hell: An Apocalyptic Form in Jewish and Christian Literature* (Philadelphia: University of Pennsylvania Press, 1983), 8, calls it "no later than the middle of 2nd c." Bernard Teyssèdre, *Le diable et l'enfer*, 222, reviews evidence for the date "around 150 and perhaps . . . a few years earlier." Teyssèdre uses the *Apocalypse of Peter* to close his history of hell in the time of Jesus, which he considers to have begun with *1 Enoch* (222–41).

the others see the future separation of the righteous and the sinners (3).[24] He says of the blessed that "they will come to me" and further specifies their fate in negative terms: they "will not see death by devouring fire." This expression seems designed to emphasize the predicament of the damned. In contrast to those who escape are "the evil creatures, the sinners and the hypocrites [who] will stand in the depths of the darkness that passes not away, and their punishment is the fire" (6).

Despite this emphasis on the lost, the *Apocalypse of Peter* takes care in the beginning to defend the justice of damnation. Jesus declares that he will appear to judge "with my cross going before my face" (1). This is the first reference I know to the cross at the Last Judgment. It is an allusion to the sacrifice and how Jesus "earned" the "right" to judge (cf. Romans 3.24–25; Hebrews 12.2–3). Further, the very palm through which the torments are viewed will soon be pierced in the Passion that liberates from hell. The people they are seeing punished will therefore have rejected redemption and, in that sense, will deserve to be abandoned to their fates. Even the damned, who will be tormented forever and will call out for mercy, will nonetheless acknowledge the rightness of their fate, "since we are punished according to our deeds" (13).

Nonetheless, all who see their suffering, including Jesus, are moved to tears (3). When Peter remarks that these sufferers would be better off if they had never been born,[25] Jesus rebukes him, as if Peter were claiming to have "more compassion" for humans than God for his own image (3). In fact, Jesus reassures his followers, the judgment will be carried out with the same care for each person as the creation that made them and the resurrection that will remake them (4). When the judgment is concluded, the elect will receive eternal life and all its blessings, one of which is the ability to "see (their desire [effectuated]) on those who hated them, when [God] punishes them" (13).[26] Justice, in the sense of vengeance, will be accomplished.

24. For the setting, see Buchholz, *Your Eyes*, 267 and 289, where he also refers to a screen. Buchholz gives another perspective on the significance of Jesus' behavior and the condition of his body at 428. There are two different versions of the apocalypse (both given by Maurer), one complete text in Ethiopic and a more fragmentary but still extensive Greek text discovered in Akhmim (Egypt). Buchholz (426) concludes that the Ethiopic version is a close translation from an earlier Greek original. The Akhmim version, though in Greek, differs, he finds, from the consensus of these two. Other fragments are known, of which the one in the Bodleian is the most significant. Unless otherwise noted, I cite the Ethiopic text, by paragraph. Where comparison with the Akhmim text enhances our understanding, I cite it as well.

25. Thus paraphrasing Mark 14.21 and parallel passages. Cf. Mark 9.42.

26. For this important theme see Ps. 58.11, 54.7, 59.10.

It is important to realize that the torments about to be reviewed are those that take place after the General Resurrection and the Last Judgment. Thus, these bodies have flesh, and the punishments depicted will endure eternally.[27]

Before describing the punishments, it would be a good idea to review the moral, differentiated tradition I have traced from the beginning of this volume. From ancient Egypt on, it has been possible to discern a tendency to subdivide the underworld and arrange within it different torments for different violations of divine authority. Homer separated the rebellious demigods for individual punishment. Plato distinguished between the curable and incurable wicked and in the *Phaedrus* distributed them around the innards of a spongelike earth. Virgil suggested a variety of torments in Tartarus which would wear out a throat of iron in the telling. The Jewish netherworld acquired distinguishable zones only late in the biblical tradition, and only in a branch of apocryphal literature was the idea developed so that different valleys could confine different offenders. Perhaps the most detailed analysis of postmortem punishment encountered so far is Plutarch's, and it is worth noting that the last trace of his career (120 C.E.) is just prior to the composition of the *Apocalypse of Peter*. Yet his spinning and disoriented, scarred and bleeding souls, which could be flayed, turned inside out, set upon by vipers and hordes of resentful descendants, immersed in ponds of molten metal, and finally forged by blacksmithlike demons into new bodies—these belong to no fixed place but will return to earth. These different punishments do not correspond to particular crimes; they vary only the techniques of uprooting vice, not individual vices. In the *Apocalypse of Peter*, although the locations are distributed no more systematically, the punishments, in most cases, are very clearly linked to the sins.

Before they can distinguish individual scenes, the gaze of Peter and the other apostles must penetrate the infernal environment as it will be in the last days. In an atmosphere of flame and darkness, all the elements conspire to torment the damned. The air, the water, and the earth have become cataracts, rivers, and a sea of fire, whose waves seethe in "a stream of unquenchable fire which flows, flaming with fire" (5). The stars melt; the heavens pass away; the spirits of the dead themselves become fire (5). Within this murky conflagration, flaming gorges divide cliffs that plunge into pits and lakes. The landscape is relieved only by trees, which serve as gibbets, another symbol of justice, and one that recalls Lucretius's allusions to earthly judicial institutions. Punishing angels wear dark clothing to match the air of the place (21).[28]

27. Buchholz, *Your Eyes*, 398, 428, correctly emphasizes this point.

28. The theme of tormenting angels is mentioned frequently here, as it is in the Book of Similitudes in *1 Enoch*, esp. at chap 56. In the thirteenth century, Caesarius, a tutor of novices in the Cistercian house of Heisterbach in the Rhineland, re-

The apostles' vision shifts its focus from torment to torment. Although the physical clearly dominates this hell, the complementary psychological factors are powerful. The most basic psychological punishment is the relationship, sometimes only implicit, between the fates and the offenses, the punishments and the crimes. For example, blasphemers hang by their tongues, suspended over a lake of burning mire (E 7, Ak 22). Thus they are punished in the organ through which they offended (cf. Wisdom 11.16) and they are punished together. Idolaters are burned with their idols in the fire (6). In addition to being punished together, the idolaters are victims of reflexive justice, for the idols made by these sinners become their own chains (10), and so, in making false gods, they have made bonds for themselves. In doing wrong, they have prepared their own punishment.

Another psychological torment comes from the principle of juxtaposition, as when sinners are placed with others guilty of similar deeds (as we have seen), or with their partners in sin, or with their victims. The adulterers illustrate this principle well. Women who plaited their hair to attract men for this purpose hang by their hair over a pool of boiling mire (E 7, Ak 24). The men who lay with them are suspended by their thighs (E) or feet (Ak) with their heads in the sewage as they call out "We did not believe we would come to this place!" (Ak 24).

Although possibly independent of this group, murderers are included here, presumably because murder and adultery are sometimes associated. The two sources differ on whether they are punished in the same place as the previous sinners. The murderers are cast into a gorge (Ak) or into the fire (E) in a place full of venomous beasts and tormented without rest by worms so numerous as to form a dark cloud. The angel Ezrael will bring the murderers' victims to see their torments and they will declare: "Righteousness and justice is the judgment of God!"[29]

Juxtaposition links abortion to adultery and murder. Those who obtained abortions are confined up to their throats in pits of bodily excretions. The Akhmim fragment specifies that they are sitting. The women who had abortions (men are not mentioned) see their premature children, that is, the fetuses, sitting around the pits "and lightnings [or rays of fire (Ak)] go forth from those children, which pierce the eyes of those who, by fornication, have brought

_____

garded as axiomatic the notion that angels punish in purgatory but demons in hell. *Dialogus miraculorum*, ed. Josef Strange, 2 vols. (Cologne: Lempertz, 1851), 1:32, 38.

29. It remains ambiguous whether those who praise justice are the murder victims or the murderers being punished. The Ethiopic manuscript (7) seems to make it the criminals, the Akhmim (25), the victims.

about their destruction [and smote the women on the eyes (Ak)]." The aborted fetuses cry out to God (Ak 26).

Similarly, men and women who exposed their children to the elements, thus causing their early death are just above, and opposite these are their infant victims. The children sigh and cry to God because of their parents. "And the milk of the mothers flows from their breasts and congeals and smells foul, and from it come forth [tiny] beasts that devour flesh, which turn and torture them forever, with their husbands" (E 8). This is reflexive justice too, in that the guilty parents (this time the men are included) are attacked by the substance they should have provided. The children will be entrusted to the angel Temlakos.

Another series of groups is formed by those who offended Christ's "righteous ones."[30] These can be either children or martyrs, but they are clearly in a different place. Ezrael, angel of wrath, chastises their persecutors and betrayers, men and women. He casts them, with half their bodies burning, into darkness, tormented with all manner of chastisement, and afflicted in their entrails by a worm that never sleeps (E 9). Near the betrayers are people who slandered and cast doubt upon Christ's righteousness and those who follow it. These men and women chew their tongues (E 9) or bite through their lips (Ak 28) and are tormented with red-hot irons in their eyes. Opposite these are false witnesses, who slew the martyrs by lying. They have their lips cut off (E 9) or bite through their tongues (Ak 29), so that "flaming fire" enters their mouths and descends into their entrails.

From those who wronged Christians, the author turns to those guilty of commercial crimes against a more general population. The misers, the greedy, those who despised widows and orphans, are dressed in rags and filthy garments and cast upon a pillar of fire (E 9) or glowing pebbles (Ak 30) sharper than swords. Male and female usurers are immersed to their knees in a boiling lake of discharge, blood, and mire (E 10; Ak 31).

No explicit reason is given for listing usurers and homosexuals in succession (though Dante will stipulate that usury and homosexuality are both sins against nature.) The *Apocalypse of Peter* simply refers to "others" punished in a different place for a different sin. Homosexuals "and the women who were with them" throw themselves down from a precipice but are driven back up by demons, so that the torment is endlessly repeated. The offenders are described as men who defiled their bodies, behaving like women, and who behaved with one another as men do with a woman (E 10; Ak 32).

Hot metal figures, as it did for the idol makers, in the torments of other men and women of unspecified sins who smite each other with glowing rods (Ak

30. See Mark 9.42 and parallels, and the *Apocalypse of Peter*, chap. 3.

33). If one can imagine a cook's spit as the instrument that makes the next torture possible, there are "men and women who were burned and turned and were baked" (Ak 34). These are those who forsook the commandments. The spit keeps them more rigidly in line.

Now the focus moves to those punished for offenses against the authority of parents and slave owners. The disobedient walk along the edge of a steep cliff or over a narrow bridge above a gorge through which fire flows. At a false step, one goes rolling down to "where the fear is." The angel Ezrael brings children and maidens to see the torment of the disobedient children (runaways?) who withdrew from their parents. Flesh-eating birds peck at sinners hung up along the sides of the precipice. These are those who showed disrespect for their elders. Disobedient slaves will ceaselessly chew their tongues and be tormented with eternal fire (11).

Maidens who did not keep their virginity until marriage are clad in dark raiment, their flesh torn to pieces. These presumably acted in secret since they are punished in dark clothes (or in darkness), whereas the next group, the hypocrites, who publicly proclaimed virtues they lacked, are punished in white. Hypocritical almsgivers, who declared, "We are righteous before God," as they gave alms, yet never strived for righteousness, are packed closely together, struck blind and dumb, and made to fall on coals of unquenchable fire. Ezrael allows them to move from there to a stream of fire (11–12). By this stream are whirling wheels of fire from which sorcerers and sorceresses are spun about (12).

The catalog of torment ended, the account emphasizes the justice of the punishments. As noted, Jesus informs the apostles that the blessed will be able to witness them, so that they may "see (their desire [effectuated]) on those who hated them" (13). The damned will recognize that they should have believed. They will call out for mercy, declaring their willingness now to believe the prophecies that told of this place. But the angel Tatirokos (whose name is also given as Tartarouchos, thus revealing his relation to Tartarus) will chide them for repenting too late, at a time when no repentence is permitted (13).[31] Death is the deadline. Compelled by the clarity with which they finally see the nature

31. For the name Tatirokos and his companion in the *Apocalypse of Peter*, the angel Temlakos, see Jean-Marc Rosenstiehl, "Tartarouchos-Temelouchos: Contribution à l'étude de l'Apocalypse apocryphe de Paul," in *Cahiers de la bibliothèque copte* 3, Deuxième journée d'études coptes, Strasbourg, 25 mai 1984 (Louvain: Peeters, 1985), 29–56, where he shows that Temlakos (Temelouchos) derives from the Greek Poseidon and the Hebrew Behemoth, and Tatirokos (Tartarouchos) derives from Pluto and Leviathan, powers of the submarine and subterranean underworlds respectively.

of God's world, the damned acknowledge its justice and admit that they are punished according to their deeds (13).

Jesus enjoins Peter to make these things known to the world. Baptism and salvation are said to gain admission for the righteous to the field of Acherusia, which is called Elysium (14).[32] After Jesus goes with his disciples to pray, they ask to see "one of our righteous brethren" who had been saved. Moses and Elijah appear and take them to see the place of all the righteous (E 15–16; Ak 5–20).

Does the *Apocalypse of Peter* depart from the biblical model in more than its lurid details? The words of Tatirokos at the end recall the situation of the rich man in Luke 16, who wishes to go warn his family about the torment he suffers, but Abraham answers that "Moses and the prophets" should have been warning enough. Believe the Scriptures and change your ways, is the message of the *Apocalypse of Peter*. But what ways do people practice, and what are the consequences of continuing unchanged? Here is where this vision innovates, for its analysis of sins by type and with appropriate punishment for each is pursued more analytically than in any other account we have considered.

The *Apocalypse of Peter* emphasizes the consequences of sin far more than those of faith. Further, torments that are summed up in one word in the New Testament are elaborated here in dramatic detail. The fire of Gehenna mentioned by Jesus in Mark 9.48 is expanded far beyond Revelation's lake of fire, into burning coals, fire poured down throats, chains of fire, and rays of fire that go forth from aborted fetuses to smite their mothers' eyes. The worm from the same passage in Mark is here applied to entrails and female breasts. Also varying the biblical idea of fiery punishment with a new specificity come the molten idols, the heated pebbles, the glowing rods and pokers. The *Apocalypse of Peter* interprets the generic fire of the Bible and applies it to individual uses, making it more concrete.

The notion in Revelation that the victims should witness the punishment, is here developed with dramatic force. By sending fiery beams into their eyes, aborted fetuses punish their mothers. Murderers are confronted by their victims, whose revenge is thus manifest for eternity. Unlike Plato's *Phaedrus*, which allowed an end to confrontation (and to punishment) when victims pardoned their offenders, here accusing stares form part of the hellscape forever.

The only biblical instance of words spoken by one in Hades is in Luke 16. The *Apocalypse of Peter* makes hell much noisier. The taunts of the tormenting angels, the cries of the damned for mercy, the hymns of their victims in praise of

32. The transferral of this name from the Greek netherworld to the Christian heaven is clear evidence of transcultural influence. The *Apocalypse of Paul* took over this usage.

divine justice echo forth. The biblical gnashing of teeth would hardly be audible.

The geography of the place does not in general reinforce the moral situation, as it does in Luke 16. There is only one example of a feature of the hellscape specifically said to enhance the terror of the inmates, when sinners above a precipice must contemplate falling into the place "where the fear is." No other emotion is named. More usually, the cliffs, not mentioned in the New Testament, are barriers and props in the work of demons. Similarly, the pools and rivers of fire serve only to transport or contain the damned; though sporadic reference is made to depth of immersion, it is no systematic measure of guilt. Darkness is pervasive, but its potential as a symbol is not developed.[33]

The punishment for adultery uses juxtaposition to represent guilt as seducers are hung by the hair alongside their lovers. Partners in sin become companions in punishment. The anguish of sinners who call out that they did not believe such a place really existed is also psychological, but inspired only by the pain and disgust they feel. There is no evidence that they recognize the symbolism of their being lowered into mire as a reflection on the baseness of their deeds. (Dante would have them gurgle these words.) Hanging as a punishment after death is not biblical, though Judas hanged himself to end his life.

The use of bodily discharges in all their forms sometimes fits the crime (abortion, exposure) and sometimes seems simply a generic form of unpleasantness. Terms such as "filth," "slime," "mire" must be taken, I think, as sewage, and may be extensions of such stinking heaps or pools as were known in the ancient world: the privy, the slaughterhouse, the bathhouse, the farmyard, the gutter, the cloaca maxima and its more modest parallels in smaller towns. It is indicative of the author's rhetoric that these concrete images should be preferred to the more generic, and biblical, source of stench, namely brimstone. This slime surely resembles the mud to which Aristophanes condemned the frogs.

Economic crimes attract relatively little attention. Only the market for idols is condemned by the text. Greater emphasis is given to martyrs and their betrayers than to a priesthood or standardized doctrine within the community addressed by the *Apocalypse of Peter*. These observations support the dating of this text in the first half of the second century, before the new religion could develop extensive formal institutions.

Yet the psychology of a community united in discipline is clearly present. As part of the vision he was enjoined to relate, Peter sees the angel Ezrael bring live children down to see how the disobedient are punished. The apostle's efforts

33. Both fire and darkness have moral overtones, but they are left undeveloped by this author.

will be supplemented by these youngsters, who will no doubt also warn their playmates about what awaits unruly children. The punishment they see is particularly pertinent: birds peck at the sides of the disobedient hanging alongside cliffs. We have come a long way from Hesiod! The punishment reserved for the superhuman Prometheus or Tityos is now applied even to the humblest, to slaves and children. Similarly, the repetitive torment associated with Sisyphus and Tantalus is now the fate not of rebellious demigods but of simple individuals. The Greek idea of apotheosis has also changed. Formerly the privilege was reserved to heroes such as Herakles. In Christianity, the Resurrection achieved by Christ became available to "the least." The converse, however, is also true: abandonment in death no longer leads merely to a dim future in the land of Hades; it brings eternal torment providentially fitted to the vagaries of the individual soul.

The range of postmortem conditions is as broad as the difference between good and evil. Yet the difference is heightened by the addition of vengeance and shame. Not only do the elect obtain eternal life, they also see the punishment of the damned: it is a final victory over those who hated them. Moreover, in some cases, the victims (of murder, exposure, and abortion) participate in punishing the guilty. This combination—matching the punishment to the sin, the victim to the offender, and placing like offenders together—demonstrates even to hardened sinners that God's design is equitable. They sing praise of his plan, acknowledge his justice, and beg for mercy, but the attendant angel only taunts them for not mending their ways in life, while there was still time. Penance in this text does not mean any particular ceremony but simply repudiating one's evil life.

That this hell was considered excessive is clear from the later transmission of this very text. In a fragment of the *Apocalypse of Peter* in the Rainer Collection in Vienna, the cries for mercy are heard by the saved, to whom God grants this boon: "Then will I grant to my called and chosen whomsoever they shall ask me for out of torment."[34] Although the gist of this line is not certain, it is much clearer in a text of about 150.

The Second Prophecy of the Christian Sybil includes a description of the underworld which is clearly derived from the *Apocalypse of Peter*. Thus, other views expressed in it may also be related to the same textual tradition or they may form an early gloss on it. In that oracle we read:

> And for them will almighty, eternal God provide yet more.
> To the pious, when they ask eternal God,
> He will grant them to save men out of the devouring fire
> And from everlasting torments. This also he will do.

34. HSW 2: 679 n. 3.

For having gathered them again from the unwearying flame
And set them elsewhere, he will send them for his people's sake
Into another life and eternal with the immortals,
In the Elysian plain, where are the long waves
Of the ever-flowing deep-bosomed Acherusian lake.[35]

This quotation suggests that not all the damned are definitively condemned at death. Intercession by a saint could reverse the fate of named beneficiaries. Presumably any of the saved, remembering any boon performed by a sufferer in eternal fire or simply feeling compassion, could, through prayer, obtain the salvation of the prisoner. Since the *Apocalypse of Peter* portrays the damned calling for mercy and many victims watching their persecutors, conceivably one witness could eventually intercede and obtain clemency. This would be a variant and a distortion of the dialogue between the rich man and Abraham in Luke 16, but it is easy to see how some authors would modify this arrangement, especially on behalf of a person who had done some good deeds (unlike the rich man in Luke 16). It is even easier to see how saints might be considered likely to intercede for petitioners who had previously been devoted to them. This tendency, when maintained and carefully refined, developed into the doctrine of purgatory.

The idea of mitigating damnation generated one of the richest strands in all the literature concerning hell. The result was anything but unanimity. Late antiquity and the Middle Ages saw a full spectrum of variations of biblical eschatology. If even the author of the *Apocalypse of Peter* could show Jesus weeping and the apostles cringing at the fate of the damned, what changes would more lenient writers make? With the words of Paul and the Gospel of John enshrined in the Bible for a foundation, what objection would there be to an effort to construct a more forgiving theology? One option would be to make the punishments either less horrible in themselves or finite in duration. The remainder of Part IV will consider the tension between these different approaches. In the apocryphal *Apocalypse of Paul*, the torments are as severe as in the *Apocalypse of Peter*, but the text innovates by proposing intermittent relief from torment.

---

35. "Christian Sybillines," 2.330–38, trans. A. Kurfess, in HSW 2:718 and 708 for the date.

Divine Mercy

The setting for the *Apocalypse of Paul* comes from Scripture and legend. In 2 Corinthians 12.2–4 Paul tells of a man who was caught up into paradise (or the third heaven) and heard unutterable things. That person was assumed to be Paul. Then, in 380 or 388, a resident of Tarsus, who lived in the house tradition said had once belonged to Saint Paul, claimed he saw a vision commanding him to dig up the foundation and to publish whatever he found there.[1] He discovered a box, which he sent to Emperor Theodosius, who opened it.

Although this story of discovery is fabricated to give allure to the text, the date is approximately correct, for Augustine and Prudentius (348–c. 410) knew this work.[2] Augustine treats it as an object of scorn. He celebrates the church's rejection of its authenticity and refers to it as "full of I know not what fables." Then he ridicules its author for telling what is "unutterable."[3] Sozomen, the early fifth-century continuator of Eusebius, calls it a late work

1. For the dating see Theodore Silverstein, *Visio Sancti Pauli: The History of the Apocalypse in Latin together with Nine Texts*, Studies and Documents, 4 (London: Christopher's, 1935), 91 n. 2, 103 n. 7. Hugo Duensing, trans., *Apocalypse of Paul*, in HSW 2:755, denies the identity of the text published by M. R. James with the apocryphal work known to Origen.

2. Duensing, *Apocalypse of Paul*, 755; James, *Apocryphal New Testament*, 525.

3. Augustine, *In Iohannis Evangelium* 98.8.13–23, Corpus Christianorum, Series Latina, 36 (Turnhout: Brepols, 1954), 581.

unknown to ancients; yet its dependence on the *Apocalypse of Peter* for some of the torments clearly reflects knowledge of earlier sources.[4] Also known as the *Vision of Paul*, this text was best preserved in its Latin versions, which remained a powerful influence on the Western European imagination throughout the Middle Ages. It was translated into virtually every vernacular and, until Dante, it was the most widely known of all narrative tours of hell. Similarly, the image of guardian angels, the deathbed scenes, the conversations with the blessed remained a part of European folklore. Dante had only to add conversations with the damned to adapt this structure for the *Divine Comedy*. Of course Virgil helped with that.

Paul's tour is not simply of heaven and hell. Rather, he is shown the whole administration of justice beyond the grave. Before seeing "the place of the righteous" and "the abyss" that receives sinners after their judgment, Paul witnesses the divine court to which souls are brought by the angels who watched over them or tempted them in life (11–12).[5] Each soul has an angel and a spirit of his or her own, which advises the soul in life, reports to God on its behavior, and at death defends it in the heavenly court. Opposed to these are "princes of wickedness" (11), "evil powers" and the "spirit of error" (14). As souls arrive in heaven they are instructed to look back at their physical remains, for they will reinhabit them at the Resurrection: those of the good man are called his body (*corpus* [14]), the bad man, his flesh (*caro* [15]). Teams of good and evil angels await the arrival of a soul before the divine throne and seek whatever of their own nature they find in it. When a

4. Further evidence for dependence on the *Apocalypse of Peter*, such as the recurrence of Greek terms, names of angels, Lake Acherusia, etc., is listed in HSW 2:757. Noteworthy in this connection is the Coptic ending, which returns Paul to earth on the Mount of Olives, where Christ then appears and exempts from the underworld anyone (and his children for two generations) who "takes care of" and copies this apocalypse. He commends the text as one in which "I have revealed the whole mystery of my deity" (797). It is hard to imagine that a text given out only in 380 could have met with the extensive popular acceptance evidenced by Augustine's reaction in *Enchiridion* 112–13. Silverstein's hints of a third-century date deserve serious consideration. *Visio Sancti Pauli*, 91 n. 2.

5. In my analysis I follow the translation of Duensing in HSW (cited by paragraph number), because he follows variants in Greek, Coptic, Syriac, and Armenian. When indicated, I prefer variants from the text James gives in *Apocrypha Anecdota: A Collection of Thirteen Apocryphal Books and Fragments*, Texts and Studies, Contributions to Biblical and Patristic Literature, 2.3 (Cambridge: Cambridge University Press, 1893), 1–57. Duensing records the variants preserved by Silverstein's *Visio Sancti Pauli*, to which Silverstein himself added a supplement: "The *Vision of Saint Paul*: New Links and Patterns in the Western Tradition," *Archives d'Histoire doctrinale et littéraire du moyen âge* 26 (1959): 199–248.

good soul reaches God, announced by its angel and spirit, God explains that he will treat the soul as the soul has treated him: "As this soul has not grieved me, so I shall not grieve it; as it has had compassion, so I shall have compassion on it." The soul is saved. "Let it therefore be handed over to Michael, the angel of the covenant" (14). The Judge clarifies his principle of justice when confronted with a wicked soul: "For whoever has shown mercy, to him will mercy be shown, and whoever has not been merciful, God will not have mercy on him."[6] If a soul does not measure up, "let him therefore be handed over to the angel Tartaruchus, who is appointed over punishments, and let him send him into outer darkness where there is wailing and gnashing of teeth and let him remain there until the great day of judgment" (16). Tartaruchus is the angel of Tartarus, who gets his name from the prison he guards.[7] In another sentence, pronounced over another sinner, the Judge declares: "Let that soul be handed over into the hands of Tartarus [variants read: Tartaruchos and Temeluchos], and it must be led down to the underworld. Let it be led into the prison of the underworld and be cast into torments and be left there until the great day of judgment" (18). In this text, then, Tartarus is the name of the holding place for the wicked before the Second Coming. The judgments Paul has just witnessed are of individuals at the time of their death. They dispose souls prior to the Last Judgment.

In one case, the Judge is not at all quick in deciding and allows the angel extra time to represent the sinner. This soul has been dead for seven days before he is brought before the Judge. Angels have shown him the places of punishment and the soul wishes to appeal. God explains damnation: the soul has been handed over to angels who have no mercy because in his life he showed no mercy. Then God gives him several extra chances to pass the judgment. First he is invited to confess his sins, but the soul denies having any (17). The familiar angel produces a list of all that soul's sins. Negotiating for the soul, the angel proposes considering only those wrongs committed since the sinner was fifteen years old. God asks for all the sins of the last five years. Finally, it is clear that had there been "a conversion one year old, the evils which [the soul] had formerly done would now be forgotten and it would have remission and pardon of sins. Now however let it perish" (17).

The souls of those whom he victimized are now brought in to testify against the defendant soul. God explains that victims who die before their persecutors are kept "in this place" until both can stand before the judge

6. The symmetry of these statements recalls that of Matthew 25.31–46.

7. See the exhaustive treatment accorded the name of this angel and those mentioned in the *Apocalypse of Peter* in Rosenstiehl, "Tartarouchos-Temelouchos," 29–56.

simultaneously, so that each may "receive according to what he did" (18). This detail (which is presented out of order in the narrative, since we would expect testimony to come before the judgment), recalls two themes we have encountered before: the accusing glances of the victims in the *Apocalypse of Peter* and the evildoers' supplications of the people they wronged on the banks of the Acherusian Lake in Plato's *Phaedo* (113e–114b). God's willingness to settle for any sign of repentance or awareness of sin in even the recent past (up to one year before death) is an example to bear in mind when we read the claims of later theologians that God judges less harshly than he might. The Talmud, too, reports the attempts of rabbis to figure out where God's mercy gives way to the need to condemn.

After they witness the heavenly review and see how hard God works to find some way to save even the soul who has admitted no sins, the angel takes Paul to the third heaven. On golden pillars he sees the names of the blessed inscribed even before their death. As they journey, the angel shows Paul sights that "cannot be told" (2 Corinthians 12.4). They come to a land of milk and honey, where trees produce abundant fruit. Yet even this region pales before another part of heaven where the promises are seven times greater. The sevenfold difference corresponds to that between, for example, fidelity in marriage and lifelong virginity. This division of heaven will be matched by a similar partition in hell, below which the torments are seven times worse. These divisions in the third heaven and in hell are matched by a division in an intermediate region for the repentant. Paul encounters it on the way between the land of milk and honey and the city of Christ.

Before seeing the most exalted sights, which this text calls "promises" (*terra repromissionis* [21] and *promissa* [22]) the angel takes Paul across Lake Acherusia, where the repentant are baptized by angel Michael. This baptism cleanses them so that they may join those who have not sinned. Soon, however, Paul and his guide meet penitents who must wait. At the gates to the city of Christ, Paul and the angel encounter souls weeping amid fruitless trees that alternately bow down and rise up. These are those who performed forced penance only when compelled by human circumstances. They will enter the city only at the end, when Christ does. These two classes of penitents are of vital importance. They indicate a division about which Augustine will have much to say. The first group, washed in the Acherusian Lake, is promoted by its penance into the city. The second, although not in torment, is conscious of not being in the city, and these souls weep in expectation of a promise withheld.

Thus the *Apocalypse of Paul* presents a tripartite afterlife, each division of which is in two parts. The blessed are in two major ranks that differ in quality by a factor of seven, mirrored by the damned, who are also separated by a factor of seven. In the middle but closer to the blessed (and in fact physically in heaven) are the repentant, divided into those worthy of joining the elect before the Last Judgment and those who must await the end of time. The wood before the gate of the city of Christ is not as clearly defined a place as purgatory would become, but those who reside there are clearly intermediate in virtue, and they live there in the interim period between their death and the Last Judgment.[8]

Paul now sees four rivers.[9] Each flows through a land bearing blessings for people distinguished by particular virtues. The River of Honey irrigates the land of the twelve prophets, where those live who on earth renounce their own will. The River of Milk nourishes the innocents and those who preserve their chastity. On the banks of the River of Wine, Paul meets Abraham, Isaac, Jacob, Lot, Job, and other holy men, and learns that that river rewards those who freely offered hospitality. The River of Oil traverses the country of those who praise God (25–28). This plenty compensates the blessed "above number or measure" for the sacrifices they made in the name of God (23). Their blessings may be beyond proportion to anything known in life, but the principle of enumeration—naming four virtues, grouping their adherents into lands where each virtue is pursued—is a fundamental structural element that will figure prominently in my history.

Paul continues to the middle of the city, where he learns of the ranks of the blessed and encounters those who obeyed the law even though they were unlettered (29). There the mystery of "Halleluja" is explained. In Hebrew, the language of God and the angels, it means "Let us bless him all together."

The tour of heaven is finished. As the angel takes Paul to see the souls of the godless and the sinners, the character of the text changes slightly. Although some of these characteristics were present before, in the tour of hell the imagery becomes more wooden, prosaic, and the structure of the narrative seems forced and artificial. Gone are the longer dramas as at the heavenly court. More than before we are conscious of the question-and-answer

---

8. On purgatory, see Jacques Le Goff, *The Birth of Purgatory*, trans. Arthur Goldhammer (Chicago: University of Chicago Press, 1984; orig. 1981); "Fegfeuer," in *Theologische Realenzyklopädie*, vol. 11 (Berlin: de Gruyter, 1983), 69–78; Karl Bauer, "Zu Augustins Anschauung von Fegfeuer und Teufel," *Zeitschrift für Kirchengeschichte* 43 (1924): 351–55; Marcus Landau, *Hölle und Fegfeuer in Volksglaube: Dichtung und Kirchenlehre* (Heidelberg: Winter, 1909); Joseph Ntedika, "La pénitence des mourants et l'eschatologie des pères latins," *Message et mission* (1968): 109–27; Erich Fleischhack, *Fegfeuer: Die christlichen Vorstellungen vom Geschick der Verstorbenen geschichtlich dargestellt* (Tübingen: Katzmann, 1969); Stuiber, *Refrigerium interim*.

9. For the four rivers of paradise, see Gen. 2.10–14.

form as Paul asks, "Sir, who are these?" and the angel answers, "They are those who . . . ." Episodes are divided by repetitious phrases "And I saw another" or "And after this I saw." Each view of punishment ends with a refrain that is only slightly varied: "Therefore they pay their own penalty unceasingly." In only one place does the grouping of sinners have more apparent coherence than in the *Apocalypse of Peter*. In other places, Paul sees punishments that lack the pungent irony and poignant sense of self-confrontation—the individual facing his or her own guilt—which are so dramatic in the *Apocalypse of Peter*. We shall see why the author of the *Apocalypse of Paul* is comparatively less interested in the infernal torments for their own sake.

As in Homer, the way to hell is beyond the ocean that encircles the earth, in a region with no light but full of darkness, sorrow, and distress. Paul sighs (31), "And there I saw a river boiling with fire." Punished here are those who were neither hot nor cold, who were found neither among the godless nor among the righteous. They mixed their lives with prayers and sin. For the first time, hell includes offenders against a specific ecclesiastical discipline. These sinners of mixed life attended church, received the Eucharist, but failed to change their lives.

Among them, however, there were different degrees of offense, and so, people are immersed in the fiery river to different levels, measured against points of reference on their bodies. Those in the fire up to their knees are those who used to leave church and resume idle talk. Those wading up to the navel used to receive Communion, but did not cease their sins. Those immersed up to their lips would meet in church but slander one another. Covered with fire up to their eyebrows "are those who give the nod to one another and (in that way) secretly prepare evil against their neighbour" (31b). Although no reason is given why one sin is more serious than another, by using the body as a standard of measure, the author distinguishes differences in guilt and punishment with great clarity. The technique of progressive immersion constitutes a major refinement in categorization as compared to the *Apocalypse of Peter*: gradations within the same environment reflect degrees of guilt in the same sin.

Thus Paul brings to the banks of the river of boiling fire the images of a new world, for offenses against ritual and improved techniques of categorization are signs of the church's institutionalization. Paul's hell will also include hypocritical clergy.

But before proceeding further, Paul looks to the north and sees a river of fire cascading over very deep pits containing many souls. Inmates sigh and weep and ask for mercy. "These are those who did not hope in the Lord that they would be able to have him for a helper" (32). Thus a very general form of unbelief is punished here, with much the same kind of retribution as is practiced on the faithless by the evil angels (11). Paul estimates the depth of the pits and asks if they will ever be filled. The angel says the souls do not hit bottom after five hundred years (32).[10]

The resultant sigh from Paul recalls the *Apocalypse of Peter*. "Are you more compassionate than God?" the angel chides Paul. Yet in explaining himself, the angel creates a surprise: "for since God is good and *knows that there are punishments*, he bears patiently the race of men, permitting each one to do his own will for the time that he lives on earth" (33). There is a hint here that God did not set up the punishments; he only knows that they exist. If indeed the punishments were established independently of God, that would be a hint of Manichean influence. More consistent with the trial scenes that open the *Apocalypse of Paul*, is the idea that God uses the existence of hell to allow humans a lifetime to reform themselves and does not take them away at the first sin.

Paul is able to distinguish four individuals in the river of fire, all of them church officials whose lives did not suit their calling. The first is being strangled and attacked by guardians of Tartarus, who use a three-pronged iron fork to pierce his intestines. This was a presbyter who did not execute his ministry properly but ate and drank and fornicated while "serving" the altar (34). "Not far away I saw" one who is being pursued and beaten by four angels, who do not allow him to call for mercy. He had been a bishop but his justice was crooked and he had no compassion for widows and orphans. "But now he is being requited according to his iniquity and his deeds." (35) The third is a deacon up to his knees in the river of fire. He has bloody hands, worms come out of his mouth and nose, and he asks for mercy (36a). At his side angels with a blazing razor lacerate the lips and tongue of another man, a reader who read the commandments to the people but did not himself keep them. "Now he also pays his own penalty" (36b). The pairing of punishments and crimes of the bishop and the reader is evident.

In the next section the technique of matching sins to torments takes priority over the relationship of the punishments to the landscape or the sinners to each other. A multitude of male and female usurers is attacked by worms (37a). In another, narrow place a fire is confined against a wall, and inside it men and women are chewing their tongues. These had reviled the word of God in church (37b). Paul had learned in heaven that not to sing "Hallelujah" is itself a form of reviling the word of God (30); so these

10. It is even deeper than Hesiod's Tartarus, whose depth could not be reached in ten days by a falling anvil of bronze (*Theogony* 722–25).

offenders may have refrained from participating in chants and responses in church. Paul sees magicians who dispense charms submerged to their lips in blood (37b). Adulterers and fornicators "pay their own penalty unceasingly" in a pit of fire (38). Angels lay blazing chains on the shoulders of girls committed by their parents to virginity, who nevertheless gave up their maidenhood before marriage (39a). This is an offense from the *Apocalypse of Peter*, but separated from its context. In a place of ice and snow, Paul sees men and women with lacerated or severed hands and feet consumed by worms. These had harmed orphans, widows, and the poor (39b). A cleric, however, who committed the same offense, is punished separately. Those who broke their fasts are hung over a channel of water with fruit close by but (like Tantalus) are not allowed to consume any of it. Another offense related to those in the *Apocalypse of Peter*, but lacking the rationale given there, is adultery. Here men and women who committed adultery are suspended by their eyebrows and their hair presumbably in the river, whose current stretches them out, because, the text specifies, "a fiery stream drew them along" ("igneum flumen traebat eos" [39d]). Male homosexuals are found in a pit of tar and sulphur running in a river of fire covered in dust, with faces the color of blood (39e). The blind men and women in bright clothing in a pit of fire are the heathen who gave alms but did not know the Lord God (40a).

These punishments lack coherence; they do not fit the crimes (or if they do, the reasoning is not explained, and it would be inappropriate to speculate on what the author might have intended). Frequently the mixture of setting and experience becomes so complicated that it loses its force. For example, severed and lacerated limbs might bleed onto the snow creating a powerful visual impression, but the introduction of worms seems gratuitous. Similarly, the homosexuals seem to have been set apart in the tar and brimstone, since these elements have not been mentioned before, yet they run in a river of fire, like so many others.

The account of abortion and exposure is weakened as compared to the *Apocalypse of Peter*, because the two offenses are fused. Moreover, the victims no longer witness the punishments. Thus the logic of the scene is radically changed. The *Apocalypse of Paul* regards men and women as equally guilty, for they are heaped together on a fiery pyramid harried by wild animals so that they cannot plead for mercy. The angel of punishments, Aftemelouchos, reminds them that Scripture warned of this fate. Instead of accusing their parents, the children appeal for help: "Defend us from our parents, for they have defiled what is fashioned by God" by exposing us to dogs and pigs and throwing us into the river. "But those children were handed over to the angels of Tartarus, who were over the punishments, so that they should lead them into a spacious place of mercy. However, their fathers and mothers were strangled in an everlasting punishment" (40b). These punishments are radically changed from a pair of striking encounters of almost visual immediacy between the persecutors and their victims into a narrative that relegates the children's appeal to the past. Although it makes for a less dramatic account of these two sins, the *Apocalypse of Paul* moves the confrontation of victim and offender from the fiery pits of Tartarus up to the heavenly court, where the victims serve as witnesses as they do in the judgment scene that opens this apocalypse. This shift from an emphasis on drama to a refinement in legal techniques is another indication of more clearly defined procedures within the church as an institution by the fourth century.

Beyond the appearance of a ministering clergy, which is one of the important differences already noted between this text and its predecessor, is the introduction of a new punishment for a new class of offenders: the false monastics. "And after this I saw men and women clothed in rags full of tar and sulphurous fire" (40c). Dragons were wound around their necks, shoulders, and feet. Angels with fiery horns guarded them, struck them, closed up their nostrils, and taunted them: "Why did you not know the time in which it was right for you to repent and to serve God, and [why did you] not do it?" (40c).[11] These are those who assumed the monastic habit without accepting the responsibility. An angel parades them past the other places of torment, from which inmates call out to them that in life they had regarded them as happy because they had found their calling, but they were false. "Therefore these, too, pay their particular penalties" (40c).[12]

Within the hell Paul has reported so far, there is a depression in the floor which runs to a blood-colored hole "below in the pit." This is the lowest point in this level of hell, for Paul is told, "all (the) punishments flow together into this pit" (38). Although Paul and the angel passed that point just after seeing the revilers of God's word (37b), it is only now that its significance becomes clear.

Having taken all this in, Paul sighs again. The angel again asks if he is more compassionate than God. It is not only that God conferred a great boon on these souls by making them free but these are not even the "greater punishments." Now Paul will see torments that are "seven times greater than these" (40d). These most severe punishments are not for evil deeds but for the denial of specific tenets of Christianity. As in the *Apocalypse of Peter*

---

11. The double negative is also in the original: "Quare non cognouistis tempus in quo iustum erat uos penitere et deseruire deo, et non fecistis?" (James, *Apocrypha anecdota*, 33, lines 11–12).

12. Ibid., 33, line 27: "Propter quod et ipsi soluunt proprias penas."

(13), the damned learn the truth of Christianity only in hell, for their unbelief caused them to scorn its sanctions.

The angel leads Paul to the north, back to "the place of all punishments" where there is a well sealed with seven seals and guarded by an angel. Paul's angel tells the other to open it up because Paul is authorized to see "all the punishments of the underworld [*inferni*]." The angel of the well warns them to stand back on account of the stench, which by itself surpasses all the punishments encountered so far (41).

The well permits passage of only one at a time, but once anyone goes inside, says the angel of the well, "reference is never made to him before the Father and the Son and the Holy Spirit and the holy angels" (41). Inside the well, Paul sees fiery masses burning on all sides. These are those who denied the incarnation, the virgin birth, and the miracle of the Eucharist.

To the west, Paul sees men and women in snow, where it is so cold that even if the sun's rays ever penetrated there, they would not warm that space. He hears the biblical gnashing of teeth, which is here imagined to come from cold. There is a two-headed worm "a cubit in size." Frozen here are those who deny the resurrection of Christ and the resurrection of the flesh (42a).

At this sight, Paul again sighs, "It would be better for us if we who are all sinners had not been born." Instead of a rebuke, this time Paul's exclamation produces different results. Hearing him, the damned themselves sense his sympathy, lament, and call for mercy. Then, from the enclosed, reeking cavern of this cisternlike chamber which is the lower hell, Paul and all the company of the damned see the heavens open. Paul sees the twenty-four elders and the four beasts of Revelation 4.9 adoring God (44). From that opening the archangel Michael and his host of angels descend.

Greeting Michael as the one whose prayers ensure the continuance of the human race (because his intercessions delay the Last Judgment), the damned in the lowest pit now acknowledge the judgment of the Son of God, although, as the angels in the *Apocalypse of Peter* proclaimed, it is now too late. They had heard, they say, of such a judgment, "but all our wordly preoccupations did not allow us to repent" (43).[13]

Michael replies that not one hour goes by in which he does not pray for the human race; yet people continue to sin, and you, in particular, he addresses the damned, "wasted the time, in which you should have repented, on frivolities" (42).[14] He formally declares that he would strive to protect

13. Ibid., 5, lines 6–7: "Inpedimenta et uita saecularis nos penitere non sinuerunt."

14. Ibid., 35, lines 14–15: "Vos consumpsistis tempus in uanitate in quo debuistis penitere."

any soul who has done even a little good from "the judgment of punishments." Finally, as if penitence were possible in hell, as if prayers could be heard from the pit, he challenges the damned: "Where are your prayers, where is your repentance?" He leads the inmates of the pit in weeping and imploring God for mercy. Paul joins in and prays, "Have mercy on what thou hast fashioned, have mercy on the children of men, have mercy on thine own image" (43). Like a preacher, the archangel has moved the mass of the damned[15] to regret their former stubbornness and to implore the Lord for pardon. The response is as thunderous as the descent itself, as compelling as the view through the hand of Jesus. Christ hears!

The heavens open farther, and Paul sees the throne of the Lord. The petitioners remind Christ of his "great goodness to the human race" (44). After this, Paul sees the Son of God descend. The damned call out for mercy, saying that just this sight of him gives them some ease (*refrigerium*). Almost disdainfully, he reproaches them. By each of the pains of my passion, he says, enumerating them one by one, "I gave you the opportunity for repentance, and you were not willing" (44). Thus the damned are in their present condition for refusing to acknowledge the efficacy of Christ's sacrifice and spurning his call to a new life. Yet, however deserved their damnation, Christ deigns to hear their plea for mercy.

He agrees, first, because of his love for Michael, the angels, and Paul. These, however, are not the only ones who have prayed on the sinners' behalf. Second, Christ shows magnanimity "for the sake . . . of your brethren who are in the world and [who] present offerings" (44). The *Apocalypse of Paul* encourages the custom of praying for the dead by attributing to Christ this reference to the practice. In addition to entreaties from the saints, Christ has heard and is responding to the prayers of the living for the dead, which, as is clear from this context, includes the damned. Future writers will have much to say about prayers for the damned.

The third reason for agreeing to show mercy amounts to conceding a certain failure in the redemption of humankind. Since his sacrifice and the knowledge he revealed of the future judgment and its consequences did not bring these damned souls to amend their lives, Christ is merciful "for the sake of your children, because my commandments are in them"—as if a new gracious act were needed to give further evidence of his love for humanity. A variant text in two other manuscripts reads: "and for the sake of your

15. 1 Peter 3:18–19 suggests Christ preached "to those in prison" in hell. This text's practice of increasing the specificity of Scripture and reattributing deeds from the divinity to others associated with his cult is typical of apocryphal literature.

friends who do my commandments."[16] This suggests that too harsh a hell might discredit the authority that established it and promulgated the law and so discourage even the obedient.

This implication leads to the fourth reason Christ grants mercy: more especially (*magis*) "for my own goodness—on the very day on which I rose from the dead I grant to you all who are being punished a day and a night of ease for ever." It later becomes clear that he means the Lord's day, Sunday, not Easter only. On Sundays, then, and the following (or preceding) night, the punishment of the damned will be suspended! (44).

Now the damned call out in thanks that each day of repose in hell will be more to them than their whole lifetimes on earth. They repeat that if they had known about the torments of hell they would have lived differently. Yet the expression they give this sentiment is a surprise. One might expect them to say they would have committed no evil, but they precede that statement with a declaration of total inaction. I think the text must be emended as follows: "We would have done absolutely no other work [but virtue], we would have conducted no other business [but prayer], and have committed no evil." This emendation accords with the earlier emphasis on monastic life. It also fits with the next sentence, a rhetorical question whose meaning is clearer if one assumes a propagandistic endorsement of monastic discipline.

Yet the next sentence also pivots to raise yet another challenge: "What need was there for us to be born into the world?" (44). With this question, the author of the *Apocalypse of Paul* encapsulates the behavioral recommendation of his text and glosses the biblical teaching on hell to do it. How could God have created humanity for damnation? He could not have. Then what were we created for? To obey God and to praise him (to practice virtue and refrain from evil). How is this done? Within the ranks of the Christian clergy. What if we refuse? Then hell is our end.

Still, the *Apocalypse of Paul* does not define damnation as oblivion.[17] Its model for damnation is closer to the tantalizing punishment given those who break their fasts. The damned have learned about Christ the hard way. They call to him for mercy because he is a benefactor of the human race. In the critical mythical moment presented in the *Apocalypse of Paul*, he even moderates the punishments of hell—indeed, of the lowest hell. Their punish-

---

16. The variant is reported in HSW 2:788 n. 8, citing the Coptic text and St. Gall, Stadtbibliothek MS 317, edited by Silverstein, *Visio Sancti Pauli*, 147.

17. True, the angel of the well says that no mention of those in the lowest region is made before the Trinity.

ment, then, is not to be excluded from God's goodness forever but to enjoy it only sporadically and negatively—that is, as a cessation of punishment. The rich man in Luke 16 received even less. Any permanent, conscious exclusion from God is stricter. Yet here is a suggested solution that balances goodness and evil in one fate. The cycle of punishment and relief matches God's attributes of justice and mercy.

Finally, the wicked angels, clearly not beneficiaries of boons granted the human race, refer back to the letter of the law: "You have shown no mercy" (44)—a reference to Scripture and to the trial scene at the beginning, which says that those who showed no mercy are handed over to pitiless angels (16). These torturers resent being idled "merely" to commemorate the Resurrection—surely not a sufficient reason for them. But they acknowledge: "You have received this great grace—ease for the day and night of the Lord's day for the sake of Paul, the dearly beloved of God, who has come down to you" (44).

Paul's tour of hell ends abruptly as the angel takes him again to paradise. There, instead of focusing on the distribution of persons in the heavenly space, Paul is presented to the blessed. First is the Virgin Mary and two hundred angels, who explain Paul's experience by saying that he is so ardently desired in heaven that the blessed have implored Christ to bring him there even before he dies (46). The conversations have a pronounced polemical tone. Major figures of the Hebrew Bible are introduced as residents in a Christian heaven. They each stress three themes: Paul is to be praised for spreading the message of Christ; the people to whom he spreads it (the Gentiles) are blessed; heavenly rewards are out of all proportion to earthly suffering. Job's words are typical: "I know that the trials of this world are nothing in comparison to the consolation that comes afterwards. Therefore Paul you are blessed, and blessed is the race which has believed through your agency" (49). Moses appears, weeping because he tended trees that bore no fruit and the flock he pastured is now scattered. He expresses amazement that Paul could do better with aliens, the uncircumcised, and idol worshipers than Moses could do with Israel. This is simply the most dramatic of the anti-Jewish sayings in the closing part of the *Apocalypse of Paul*, one of whose purposes seems to be to compare Judaism unfavorably to Christianity or, to put it more positively, to portray Judaism as superseded by Christianity. Adam himself paraphrases 1 Corinthians 15.22 and 45 as he concludes the heavenly procession, saying: "I myself have repented and received my praise from the Compassionate and Merciful One" (51).

This echo of Paul's letter is a fitting end to an apocalypse recounting "his" vision. Although the earliest testimonies of this text date only from the late fourth century, as has been said, they preserve a certain fidelity to the Pauline view of otherworldly sanctions in the tempering of infernal punishments through weekly mitigation and in the theological suggestion that Christ's rule over "all," even if it does not cause everyone to be saved, can extend his mercy to the damned. At the risk of exaggerating the significance of the hint that he "*knows* that there are punishments" (33), as opposed to creating or administering them, this extension of Christ's rule to the underworld becomes even more impressive. Thus, his ability to relieve punishments would be accomplished on "foreign territory" and the *Apocalypse of Paul* would be connected to the tradition of Christ's descent. Knowing that the tour of the places of punishment would be interrupted by an epiphany, the author of the *Apocalypse of Paul* routinized his account of the torments, marking time, as it were, until the moment for the mythic appearance that would parallel the descent and extend a weekly commemoration of the Resurrection even to hell.

So far the texts considered in Part IV share a conviction that, whatever the character of hell, the divinity can accept full responsibility for it. In the *Gospel of Nicodemus*, Christ rescued the last righteous of an earlier age. In the *Apocalypse of Peter*, although no fates were changed, Christ's challenge to Peter, asking whether he is more compassionate than the judge who will resurrect all flesh as carefully as he created it (and in his own image) and his showing hell's justice through the very palm that achieved redemption for the willing constitute an absolute basis for reaffirming that justice. Looking over the shoulder of Peter and the other apostles, the reader is made to feel that hell was, at last review, just. Even if the *Apocalypse of Paul* shows a later correction, the grace bestowed there demonstrates God's willingness to amplify his mercies and reaffirms his control of the underworld. At his word the raging fire, the roaring wind, the devouring beasts, the crushing dragons, and the taunting demons all are still. So powerful a God creates the universe as he wants it. How, then, could anyone be damned at all? How could torments so justly measured out, so specifically aimed at each individual and each vice, fail to eradicate the targeted evil? Why, in fact, can the damned not be saved? This is the line of questioning developed by Origen of Alexandria.

Origen (c. 185–c. 254) ran the school of catechumens in Alexandria from 203 to 231. At the beginning of his teaching career, he castrated himself, having taken literally Jesus' statement about those "who have made themselves eunuchs for the sake of the kingdom of heaven" (Matthew 19.12). In about 231 he moved to Caesarea in Palestine, where he was imprisoned and tortured in a persecution ordered by Emperor Decius. He died at Tyre in

254, his life shortened by the torture. His own bishop, Demetrius of Alexandria, pursued him legally, first for teaching theology while still a layman and then, after he had been ordained, for violating canon law by receiving orders even though castrated.[18]

Origen's concept of hell owed much to his philosophical training in Neoplatonism, which requires a brief description in order to appreciate the structure of his thought. Ammonius Saccas influenced both Origen and Plotinus (204 or 5–270), whose ideas were compiled in the *Enneads*, a classic statement of Neoplatonism. According to this sytem the world can be seen as a cycle comprising two basic motions: emanation and return. The source of everything and the goal of return is the One, which religious readers consider analogous or identical to God. This One, the supreme being, has a knowledge of itself which is distinguishable from the One, and so, decadence and plurality begin with the One's knowledge of itself. This knowledge consists of the Ideas, which seem to circulate under the One. From this source there emanate, in creative but regressive cascades, other levels of existing beings that form the world. No level of being exists as fully as the One, and each successive lower level exists less excellently than the one above it.

Beneath the Ideas is the World Soul, an agent that allows the Ideas to become reality. Through the World Soul the ideas function as the forms of all things. In combination with these forms, matter emanates from the World Soul to produce corporeal and sensible things, that is, things perceptible through the senses. Yet matter alone, apart from the idea-forms that give it shape, approaches nothingness. All these inferior beings conceive a longing for reunion with their source, and all intelligent beings (including humans) strive, through the intellect, to regain the One. Return, therefore, is possible and, indeed, almost necessary, since every existing being bears the stamp of its origin and, through the use of mind, longs to return to its pristine state.[19]

18. See the sketch of Origen's life in Quasten, *Patrology* 2:37–40. See also Charles Kannengiesser and William L. Petersen, *Origen of Alexandria: His World and His Legacy*, Papers from the Origen Colloquy held at Notre Dame University, April 11–13, 1986 (Notre Dame, Ind.: Notre Dame University Press, 1988); Antonia Tripolitis, *Origen: A Critical Reading* (New York: Lang, 1985); Joseph Wilson Tigg, *Origen: The Bible and Philosophy in the Third-Century Church* (Atlanta: John Knox, 1983); Henri Crouzel, *Bibliographie critique d'Origène*, Instrumenta patristica, 8 and supplement (The Hague: Nijhoff, 1971).

19. There is an excellent account of Neoplatonism in Eduard Zeller, *Outlines of the History of Greek Philosophy*, 13th ed., rev. by Wilhelm Nestle (1931), and trans. L. R. Palmer (Cleveland: World, 1964), 311–36.

Now Origen saw affinities between the One and the Christian God. For him, God, as a source of grace, could effectively help every rational being accomplish this return. When this cycle is supervised by a loving God, who could fail to return?

Origen's view of punishment after death may be summed up by the Greek word *apokatastasis*, which means "restoration." He believed that all would eventually be restored to God. He used the axiom of Neoplatonic philosophy that the end should resemble the beginning and the Christian principle that God's action is always good and always effective to argue that punishment must correct and that once sinners are corrected, there is no further need to punish them. Consequently, all who are punished are cured and restored to divine favor. On this basis he denied eternal punishment.[20]

This process, he thought, takes ages and involves transmigrations to rise to angelic status or fall to human or demonic status according as individual souls, exercising their free will, seek or neglect God. Since goodness inheres essentially only in the Godhead, it is accidental in all others, who can fall away. By the end of the last cycle, however, Origen expected a complete restoration of all souls to their original image-likeness to God, a time when God would be all in all.[21]

Origen's works were translated into Latin by Rufinus (c. 345–410), who was sympathetic to the Alexandrian's views. Jerome (c. 342–420), the great biblical scholar, opposed Origen's theories and accused his former friend Rufinus of covering up Origen's heresy in the translation. As a result of the condemnations of Origen under Justinian in 543 and 553, the Greek text was destroyed. That text, therefore, must be reconstructed from Rufinus's Latin translation, Jerome's quotations, sentences of condemnation which quote from it, and more isolated quotations or fragments.

Origen's application of the cycle of emanation and return to Christian theology builds on certain key notions, which it is best to articulate from the beginning. At stake in the cycle of emanation and return is the fate of all the rational creatures ever created, which are finite in number. Rational creatures, which are also endowed with free will, may be either angelic or human, and these identities are interchangeable according to merit, that is, perseverence in the cultivation of God. Depending on merit, then, a single soul may transmigrate from an angel (in which case it inhabits an immaterial

20. Constantine N. Tsirpanlis, "Origen on Free Will, Grace, Predestination, Apocatastasis, and Their Ecclesiological Implications," *Patristic and Byzantine Review* 9 (1990): 95–121.

21. For the importance of the idea of image-likeness to God in early Christian thought, see Gerhart Ladner, *The Idea of Reform: Its Impact on Christian Thought and Action in the Age of the Fathers*, rev. ed. (New York: Harper and Row, 1967).

body of light) to a human (in which case it inhabits a body of flesh), to a demon (in which case it inhabits an immaterial body of darkness), when it is also called an opposed power. Because of transmigration, these statuses can be corrected after death, in the otherworld, during endless cycles or until one final consummation, when the end of the universe will resemble its beginning.

Through all these cycles, there is no moment when the power of God is not at work; thus, the ultimate end is total subjection to God. Each demotion from greater to lesser adherence to God is perceived as suffering by the rational creature. Thus, as the suffering increases, the reason is more capable of discovering fault in the conscience, which, ultimately is the seat of punishment. Therefore the fire of suffering strengthens the conscience and gradually leads to its correction. This process cures the ailing soul, redirects its will, and leads to renewed happiness.

With this anticipatory sketch completed, it is possible to consider Origen's views in more detail. According to Origen, the human condition, like that of the fallen angels, reflects the loss of a prior perfection in which all were blessed and enjoyed a perfect knowledge of God. But that loss could have taken place only gradually. In contrast to the persons of the Trinity, in whom goodness exists essentially, rational creatures, who are capable of exercising the freedom of their wills, may begin to neglect the cultivation of God and so begin to fall (1.5.5).[22] Thus, as a skilled craftsman never loses his art all at once, but only little by little and through neglect, so the fall from perfect blessedness can never be sudden or total but only gradual (1.3.8). From the knowledge of God, which constitutes perfect happiness, all rational creatures who are incorporeal and invisible fall by degrees from the ethereal to the aerial and then to grosser bodies and finally to human flesh and then to the darkness of demons (1.4.1). Since there is no moment when the powers of God are not at work (1.4.3), however, and the rational creature is always capable of exercising free will, that fall can always be arrested and reversed. These successive steps of degeneration and regeneration may continue in endless cycles from the angelic to the human to the demonic and back (1.4.4).

22. Origen, *De principiis*, ed. Paul Koetschau, vol. 5 of *Origenes Werke*, Die griechischen christlichen Schriftsteller der ersten drei Jahrhunderte, 22 (Leipzig: Hinrichs, 1913). G. W. Butterworth has translated Koetschau's edition as Origen, *On First Principles* (New York: Harper and Row, 1966), with an introduction by Henri de Lubac, from his *Histoire et esprit: L'intelligence de l'Ecriture d'après Origène* (Paris: Aubier, 1950), chaps. 1 and 2. For information on the textual background, see Lubac's introduction. When I have made my own translation, I cite the text as K, referring to the Latin in Koetschau; when I use Butterworth's translation (usually from Greek) I cite the text as B.

As each rational creature either adheres to or rejects what is just and right, it deserves either praise and advancement to better things or blame and subjection to pains and penalties (1.5.3). The expression "rational creatures" includes the human soul, which Origen places in an intermediate position between holy and wicked powers, between the angels (thrones, dominions, principalities, powers, and sees) and the demons. Considering its intermediate status in Origen's system, a human soul cannot be distinguished from either an angel falling or a demon rising (1.5.2), for any rational creature "may descend to such a state . . . as to be changed into what is called an opposing power" (1.5.5 B).

That blessed beings do not always cleave to the good, Origen infers from Ezechiel 28.11–19, which tells of the "prince of Tyre" who had been in Heaven but sinned and was cast down. Isaiah 14.12–22 describes Lucifer the same way. Luke 10.18 is related: "I saw Satan fall like lightning from heaven." Further, Ephesians 6.12 refers to "those principalities 'against whom our wrestling is'" (1.5.2 B). The fallen nature of these opposing powers comes not from their creation, but from their sin.

Just as angels can fall, so demons can rise. If degeneration is at once a choice (because of neglect) and a punishment, then eventually the punishment (since it is divinely inflicted, and God's power never ceases to be effective) will correct the fault, and neglect will turn back into devotion. This potential for conversion belongs to the Devil and his angels too. Thus, according to their merits, some sooner and some later, in some cases only after centuries, rational beings will be "repaired and restored" by their very punishments. They will be gradually educated, first by angels and then by higher powers, until they have been trained in every type of heavenly instruction. Thus, every individual rational creature can potentially advance or regress through each order of being (angelic, human, demonic) by means of its own free will (1.6.3 K).

What Jerome made clear in his paraphrase of this passage is that the progress is not constant. There is a question whether these ups and downs continue eternally or whether there will be an end, at which time, or by which time, all will have become corrected. This ambiguity may not be in Origen, although Rufinus's translation leaves it unresolved. According to Rufinus, Origen used not the the future perfect tense but the future. The consummation comes not at the time when everyone *will have been purged* of all evil but at a time known only to God, when payment for all sin *will be exacted*. "The end and consummation of the world will come when everyone will be subjected [*subicietur*] to the punishments according to the merit of their sins, . . . when everyone will pay [*expendet*] what is owed" (1.6.1 K).

Origen sees the spiritual progress that comes even from decline and increased punishment as eventually leading to a greater perfection and to restoration. Thus, it would seem that there will be a time when all debts *will have been paid*. One should not base that conclusion on Rufinus's translation, but it follows from the nature of Origen's argument in this way. In Origen's system, no debt can be infinite, because that would imply that God's healing powers could not redeem it. Since no debt is infinite, any debt can be paid, and once it has been paid, no further punishment is deserved unless the soul begins to neglect God again, in which case a new cycle is initiated. It appears nonetheless that eventually and by the end of the world, "the goodness of God through Christ will recall into one end His entire creation, even the enemies, once they have been overcome and subjected" (1.6.1 K). At the end of the world every soul will pay for its sins and even the opposing powers will have been changed into conformity with Christ.

In support of this "recall" or restoration, Origen quotes the biblical passages favoring universal restoration examined in the study of Paul in Chapter 8 (1 Corinthians 15.24–28; John 17.20–23). This is "the goal of that blessedness . . . to which even God's enemies are said to be subjected, in which end God is said to be 'all things' and 'in all things'" (1.6.4 K; cf. 1 Corinthians 15.24, 25, 28). With all creation back under the dominion of God, history will have returned to its original condition according to the Neoplatonic axiom: "The end is always similar to the beginning" (1.6.2 K).

What is remarkable in this system is that it offers Christianity a philosophy of punishment different from the one in the symmetrical tradition of the New Testament. Origen's theory of punishment is reflexive without being retributive. Unlike the belief that punishment after death is eternal, which applies the philosophy of retribution and must answer challenges as to why any sin requires eternal punishment, Origen's belief considers punishment corrective. Corrective punishment eventually eliminates the condition that brought it into action. The neglectful soul is punished by demotion into demonic status, the pains of which eventually move it to begin its return. It recovers its cultivation of God, progresses to human and then angelic status, and is eventually liberated from suffering, because nothing remains in it which warrants punishment. When that process has been completed for everyone, God will be all in all.

The ability of souls to change position does not diminish the difference between one status and another. The difference between statuses for angels and demons is the difference between light and darkness, heat and cold (2.8.3). Human souls occupy an intermediate status for which "God made the present world and bound the soul to the body as a punishment" (1.8.1 B). Nor does the soul die when these bodily punishments die, for there is evidence that souls existed prior to their enclosure in bodies. Why should some be born blind unless they are being punished for a previous sin? Origen asks. The same soul, therefore, is the subject of these promotions and demotions from status to status. Metempsychosis, the transmigration of souls, is required to allow these souls sufficient time to complete their cycles of lives (8.1.1).

Demons have their rank because of their own motives and pursuit of evil. They have "so precipitately given themselves over to wickedness that they are unwilling, rather than unable, to be recalled, as long as the eagerness for evil deeds is a passion and a delight" (1.8.4 K). By contrast, angels occupy their position through the proper reception of the Holy Spirit (1.8.3 K). Humans, being intermediate in the scheme, can turn from "darkness" and mortify their members to transcend their bodily nature. In this way, they can become "entirely spirit" (1.8.4 K).

The freedom Origen assigns to rational creatures: the freedom to turn, to rise, to become wholly spirit, ascribes responsibility to the individual soul for its own level of existence. Although God is clearly the author of the cosmos that functions in the way Origen describes, the rational creature plays a crucial role in its own punishment; its punishment is reflexive.

The importance of this reflexivity emerges dramatically in Origen's discussion of the eternal life after the General Resurrection. Incidentally, his belief in the final resurrection reinforces the impression that Origen believed the cycle of transmigration, promotion and demotion, would finally come to an end. According to Origen, at the Resurrection, the soul is joined to a body immune from death but still fitted to the dignity of each one's life and the purity of each soul. The incorruptible resurrected body, he says, is such that, even for those sentenced to supposedly eternal fire, the body cannot be harmed by those punishments (2.10.3 K). What is the nature of that fire?

Origen's fire comes from Isaiah 50.11: "Walk by the light of your fire and by the brands which you have kindled." Here is reflexive punishment. This is not the eternal fire prepared for Satan and his angels. It is one's own internal fire. "The fire by which each person is punished is proper to oneself" (2.10.4 K).[23] So strongly does Origen feel about the inner, personal nature of this fire, that he contradicts Matthew 25.41 by insisting: "And one is not sunk into some preexisting fire or one that has been kindled before by another" (2.10.4 K). Our own sins fuel this fire, which burns in our conscience. "Of this fire the food and material are our sins, which are called by the apostle Paul wood and hay and stubble [1 Corinthians 3.12]" (2.10.4). The fire is

23. The reflexivity of the punishment stands out in the original: "Unusquisque peccatorum flammam sibi ipse proprii ignis accendat."

fueled by the accumulated sins of a lifetime, which, as in the case of indigestion, boil up inside and provoke a fever whose intensity and duration depend upon the frequency and seriousness of overindulgence. Put another way, Origen compares this mass to the passions familiarly expressed as the "flames" of love, the "fires" of envy, the "torments" of jealousy, being "consumed" with sadness.

While the memory contains this mass of rotting matter, the conscience focuses the soul on its own faculties and reviews the series of evil deeds and all the memories of sin. "Then the conscience is spurred by its own goads and driven to remorse. It becomes its own accuser and witness against itself" (2.10.4 K). This, Origen says, is what Paul meant when he explained, "Their conflicting thoughts accuse or perhaps excuse them on that day when . . . God judges the secrets of men" (Romans 2.15–16). Indeed, the soul's very essence is reflexive, Origen concludes, for "certain torments are generated from precisely those harmful passions that lead to sin" (2.10.4 K).

This being the case, Origen is moved to wonder whether a person who has found no cure for these passions in life but suffers a very long time for them in death can exhaust and change them and so be freed from both the source and the fact of suffering, or whether such a person will still be liable to a general punishment (2.10.5 K). To answer his own question Origen posits a corollary to his maxim that the power of God is always effective: all suffering is beneficial. When the soul endures the fires imposed upon it by its own disordered passions, the resultant discord is at once a punishment and a remedy. Punishment cures. If God's power is always and everywhere effective, it is also effective in "hell." If hellfire exists in the conscience of the soul after death, then divine power is at work; no other definition of Providence is possible. Suffering can never be undeserved, nor can it ever be detrimental, and certainly it can never be contrary to the goodness and efficacy of God. Thus if punishment after death accords with the divine system, and God gave freedom to all rational creatures, then their suffering must contribute to the final goal, which is the restoration of the end to conformity with the beginning. Punishment, then, must heal; passions must be corrected; all must eventually move from neglect to cultivation of God; and punishment must end.

But how, precisely, can that happen? In addition to the torments provoked by the noxious passions themselves, Origen explains, there is another type of punishment. Just as excruciating pain results from the dismemberment of the physical body, the same occurs when the proper order, coherence, and harmony of the soul is disrupted. "But a soul that has experienced this breakdown and distortion, once it has been probed by reason of the fire applied to it, will, without a doubt, be prepared for its more solid coherence and foundation" (2.10.5 K). Disorder in the soul causes intense suffering, which in turn leads to amendment.

These pains after death resemble the bitterness of some medicine, the pains of an operation. God is a physician. Origen observes that Jeremiah says, "If anyone refuses to drink [the cup of God's fury] he shall not be cleansed" (25.28–29, as quoted in Koetschau). From this statement Origen concludes that "the fury of God's vengeance advances the purification of souls" (2.10.6 K). Under a providential healer, the universe becomes self-correcting. Thus, the agony of a disordered soul will eventually strengthen that soul and bring about the reversal that makes restoration possible.

A fragment omitted by Rufinus but included by Paul Koetschau and trans-lated by G. W. Butterworth sums up this idea: "There is a resurrection of the dead, and there is punishment, but not everlasting. For when the body is punished the soul is gradually purified, and so is restored to its ancient rank. . . . For all wicked men, and for daemons, too, punishment has an end, and both wicked men and daemons shall be restored to their former rank" (2.10.8 B; fragment 25 K).

The system Origen developed was not only a philosophy supported by quotations from (mostly) Paul. For all his intimate connection to the Alex-andrian school, Origen regarded Christ as the archetypal illustration of his view of the world. It was, in his view, the world's gradual divergence from the good that called forth a divine response in the form of a savior. "By fulfilling in himself what he wished to be fulfilled in others" (3.5.6 K), Jesus reestablished the right relationship between (divine) ruler and ruled. The Son came to "teach obedience," to those "who could obtain salvation only through obedience" (3.5.6 K). In Origen's view Christ's exemplary obe-dience made possible the final restoration and the subjection of all things to the Father as foretold in 1 Corinthians 15.28, where Paul says God will be all in all.

Similarly, the return of the end to the beginning is not just a metaphysical principle but the recovery of humankind's original image-likeness to God. The more closely the human species comes to resemble God, the closer he is to being all in all, the less power is retained by evil and death. As conformity approaches, death, the last enemy, will be destroyed, not so much by its elimination as by its conformity to the source of all goodness. It will then lose its hostile character, its "bite." Nor will this happen quickly, but "over the course of immense and infinite ages," for the changes will be realized at different times in different people through the "many and innumerable de-grees of those advancing" until even the last enemy, death, shall have been reconciled (3.6.6 K).

Eternity Defended

It would be hard to exaggerate the effect that Augustine, bishop of Hippo (354–430), has had on Christianity.[1] In his *Confessions*, an extraordinary autobiographical account of his conversion to Christianity, Augustine established a standard for the explanation of religious faith in rational terms, especially drawing on Neoplatonism.[2] Even before he was

1. See Peter Brown, *Augustine of Hippo: A Biography* (Berkeley: University of California Press, 1967). For bibliography, see Terry L. Miethe, *Augustinian Bibliography, 1970–1980, with Essays on the Fundamentals of Augustinian Scholarship* (Westport, Conn.: Greenwood, 1982); and Etienne Gilson, *Introduction à l'étude de saint Augustin*, 2d ed. (Paris: Vrin, 1982), which includes extensive bibliography on Augustine's philosophical thought to 1943. For an introductory overview in English, see Henry Chadwick, *Augustine*, Past Masters (Oxford: Oxford University Press, 1986).

2. For some perspectives on this central work, see Colin Starnes, *Augustine's Conversion: A Guide to the Argument of "Confessions" I–IX* (Waterloo, Ont.: Wilfrid Laurier University Press, 1990); Pierre Paul Courcelle, *Recherches sur les "Confessions" de saint Augustin*, 2d ed. (Paris: de Bɔccard, 1968); Courcelle, *Les "Confessions" dans la tradition littéraire: Antécédents et postérité* (Paris: Etudes augustiniennes, 1963); Emmet T. Flood, "The Narrative Structure of Augustine's *Confessions*: Time's Quest for Eternity," *International Philosophical Quarterly* 28 (1988): 141–62; Donald E. Capp, ed., "Symposium on Augustine's *Confessions*," five articles in the *Journal for the Scientific Study of Religion* 25 (1986): 56–115 (each article, whether theological, literary, or psychoanalytic, ends with a useful

made bishop of Hippo in 396, Augustine exercised a vital influence on the church. He replied to the major challengers of Christianity in a series of polemical treatises against the Manicheans, the Donatists, and the Pelagians.

Augustine exemplifies the philosophical or rational approach to faith. Though he always allowed for the suprarational elements of faith, he nonetheless distributed these elements over a framework whose parts fit together as a philosophical synthesis, that is, theology. Once the emperor Theodosius I (379–95) had made Christianity the official religion of the empire, the backing of the Roman state reinforced the universalizing nature of Christianity itself. The need for systematic expositions of its tenets to serve, as it were, as the law of the land, elicited efforts such as Augustine's to expound the whole faith systematically. That stance would come, later in the Middle Ages, to represent an almost judicial role for theology, which, when backed up by legal authority almost gave it the force of law.

In contrast, then, to the dialogue and difference represented by the conflict between justice and mercy, eternity and temporality considered so far in Part IV, it is now necessary to examine Augustine in his function as theologian, systematizer, one who seeks the coherence of all the parts of faith. In that faith, hell had a vital role. This chapter, then, will consider Augustine's view of punishment after death from two points of view. First, it will investigate his position. Second, it will consider how he functioned as a theologian, that is, how he used his confidence in his overall system, the coherence he claimed for his outlook, to monitor competing beliefs.

In the *City of God*, Augustine replied to pagan assertions that the sack of Rome by Alaric in 410 was punishment for desertion of the ancient gods. Augustine argued that Rome's had been a false prosperity, and that life should be seen as a struggle between good and evil, which are mixed in the present life but will be separated at the end of time. He traces the conflict of good and evil from Cain and Abel to the Last Judgment and closes his magisterial review of all history with a discussion of the two final destinations: hell and heaven, the city of the Devil and the city of God.[3]

---

bibliography of works in the field); Janet Varner Gunn, "The Religious Hermeneutic of Autobiography: Augustine's *Confessions* and the *Credo ut Intellegam*," *Journal of the American Academy of Religion: Thematic Studies* 49 (1983): 61–70 (with bibliography).

3. See Etienne Gilson, *Les métamorphoses de la "Cité de Dieu"* (Louvain: Publications universitaires de Louvain, 1952); John Joseph O'Meara, *Charter of Christendom: The Significance of the "City of God"* (New York: Macmillan, 1961); Ernst Troeltsch, *Augustin, die christliche Antike und das Mittelmeer: Im Anschluß an die Schrift "De Civitate Dei"* (1915; rpt. Aalen, Germany: Scientia, 1963).

In the *Enchiridion*, Augustine expounded the whole of Christian doctrine under the headings "Faith," "Hope," and "Charity."[4] The section on faith (chapters 9–113) follows the elements of the Apostles' Creed, which, by recounting the deeds of Christ, may itself be viewed as a history of the world from Creation to the Second Coming. Thus, book 21 of the *City of God* and chapters 54–113 of the *Enchiridion* give systematic expositions of the Resurrection of the flesh, the Last Judgment, hell, and heaven. These will form the basis for discussion.

It is hard to imagine a more severe contrast than that between Origen's view of punishment after death and Augustine's. Origen's view of time is cyclical, like Plato's. Augustine's is teleological, like Matthew's or John's in Revelation. The consequences are astounding. Augustine agrees with Origen that the rational creature is free to choose between a higher and lower good, to cultivate or neglect God. That is how he describes the fall of Satan in the *City of God*.[5] Yet, building on a linear view of history, at the human level, Augustine imposes a deadline for each one's choice, after which the consequences are irreversible. The sinner must repent before death. All fates are pronounced in the Last Judgment. From then on there will be no change.

For Augustine, evil originated when Satan and his followers among the angels chose mutable rather than immutable good and, in desiring a lesser good, fell from the pinnacle of creation, the enjoyment of ineffable beauty which had been their original station (CD 11.9–15, 29–32; 12.1, 6–9; 20.6–7). Augustine regarded the fall of the angels as an anticipation of the fall of Adam. Fallen angels and damned humans will, according to Matthew 25.41, be damned to eternity in the same fire, and saved humans will join the angels in heaven. Therefore, Augustine frequently considers the fates of angels and humans together. That first occurrence of evil, the fall of Satan, created the source of temptation, the serpent, by which the first parents were led astray: "But from then on, in [Adam] human nature was vitiated and changed in such a way that its members were laid open to the restless appeals of lust and bound to the necessity of death. Furthermore, he transmitted to his offspring what he himself suffered through vice and punishment, making them also liable to sin and death" (13.3.41–45).

The death to which Adam subjected humans, however, is twofold: the first death separates the body from the soul; the second death must in turn be regarded from two points of view. As regards God, the second death is a death because it separates the soul from God, its life, and without its life, it

4. Augustine, *Enchiridion* 1.3.21–28. Corpus Christianorum, Series Latina, 46 (Turnhout: Brepols, 1969).

5. Augustine, *De civitate Dei, libri XXII*, 12.6–9, Corpus Christianorum, Series Latina, 48 (Turnhout: Brepols, 1955), hereafter abbreviated CD.

cannot be said to live. As regards the body, the second death is a death because, at its separation from the body, the soul is made subject to eternal pains. Augustine says the first death terminates punishment because he views life in the world (as opposed to Paradise) as punishment. It is penal because of Adam's fall (CD 21.14–15). Yet, whereas life in the world is ended by the first death, the second death, also a punishment, is more severe because no (subsequent) death will terminate it (19.28).

This punishment may be either purgatorial or not and may take place either in this world or the next. Punishments are purgatorial if they correct the fault that elicited them. The good suffer heaven-sent adversity on earth, receive their hardships as correction, and change their ways. In this case, punishment is purgatorial in life. Those cleansed by suffering either in life or after death will know an end to punishment and finally achieve eternal bliss.[6] Those not chastened by hardship in life will suffer unending adversity in death (CD 21.13, 41–47).[7]

If the two deaths differ in that the second one is endless, they share a common aspect of suffering. As in life, the pains experienced by the body after death affect the soul too. Whereas the first death results from great pain that drives the soul *from* the body against its will, the second death holds the soul *in* the body against its will. In both deaths, the soul suffers from its body against its will (CD 21.3.30–33).

That suffering Augustine calls *passio*, which cannot be translated simply by the English "passion." "Suffering" is a better translation, because, like the passive voice in grammar which derives from the same root, it takes its force from the subject's receiving an action from outside. The *passio* that punishes the damned soul is a form of grief (*dolor*) imposed by unwanted impulses from its body. Augustine calls the resultant conflict a war with no victory (CD 19.28.13–16). Such is the evil end the wicked soul attains.

The first death occurs when the individual dies. The second death occurs at the Second Coming, with the General Resurrection and the Last Judgment, after which no one's fate can change. During the two deaths, souls that suffer are in two different places. Here the distinction comes into play between Hades and Gehenna established in the Greek New Testament and translated as Infernus and Gehenna in the Vulgate. Augustine uses the Vul-

6. The possibility of being cleansed by postmortem suffering is an anticipation of the doctrine of purgatory, but Augustine develops it no further here.

7. Cf. Augustine, *Enarrationes in Psalmos* 9 n. 1, Corpus Christianorum, Series Latina, 38 (Turnhout: Brepols, 1956), 58: "The hidden judgment is a punishment by which everyone is either tried, resulting in purgation; warned, resulting in conversion; or if one scorns the summons and chastening of God, one is blinded, resulting in damnation."

gate's terms. The *Enchiridion* specifies the time but does not name the place: "The time that comes between the death of a man and the last Resurrection encloses the souls in hidden receptacles providing either the rest or tribulation allotted to each person while alive in the flesh" (29.109.1–4). The receptacle for tribulation was the fate of the rich man who denied charity to Lazarus in Luke 16, which Augustine says was located in the underworld (*apud inferos*), that is, in Hades (CD 21.10.29). "But," Augustine says in the *Enchiridion*, "after the Resurrection, when the full and universal judgment is completed, the two cities, both Christ's and the Devil's will have their entire complement, the one with the good, the other with the wicked, though both will comprise angels and humans" (29.111.33–35). This, he specifies in the *City of God*, is "that Gehenna which is called a lake of fire and sulfur" (21.10.40). Calling it Gehenna brings in the New Testament references to the place where the worm does not die and the fire is not extinguished (Mark 9.43–48, referring to Isaiah 66.24), and identifying it as "the lake of fire and sulfur," brings in Revelation 19.20, 20.10, and 20.14, which name the lake as the final destination of the beast, the false prophet, the Devil, death, and Hades. It will be the same fire, Augustine further stipulates in the *City of God*, that receives both the demons and the wicked humans (21.10.46). This allusion brings in Matthew 25.41.

Here, then, is one of the principal functions of theology: to combine scattered scriptural references according to meaning and function. Augustine has defined Gehenna by virtue of a tripod of texts whose accord he establishes by association. In this grouping, differences from the original context are lost. Combined thus in theology it does not matter that Matthew 25.41 refers simply to fire, Revelation refers to a lake of fire and sulfur, and Mark/Isaiah to a heap of carrion outside Jerusalem. This way Augustine reinforces the concept.

One principal consequence of combining Matthew 25.41, Revelation 20.10, and Mark 9.43–48 (quoting Isaiah 66.24) is to insist on Gehenna's eternity. In book 21 of the *City of God*, Augustine discusses one by one a series of objections to the notion of eternal punishment. This, then is another function of theology: to refute objections raised against the contentions of one's faith.

Augustine attacks the most literal objection first: If resurrected bodies are subject to the fire of hell, they could not last for eternity without being consumed. The error here, Augustine contends, is to assume that resurrected bodies are like the ones we know. In fact, the fire of hell will affect resurrected bodies in the same way bodies now affect souls (CD 21.3.39–41). Hellfire will cause suffering without causing death (21.3.76–80).

Some contend, he says, that eternity is too long a sentence for a sin that may have been performed in only a moment or may have brought only a brief pleasure. Augustine replies that human punishments, such as exile or enslavement, are often unending; they stop only because the criminal dies, not because the legislator shortens the sentence. And when civil courts pass a sentence with unending consequences, they judge not by the duration of the crime but by its seriousness (CD 21.11.29–33). By that standard, damnation must surely be eternal, for what could be more serious than the sin of Adam "who destroyed in himself a good which might have been eternal" and so "became worthy of eternal evil" (21.12.6–8). Moreover the exile and the sentence of death imposed by the civil courts are perpetual separations, at least until the first death. Eternal damnation is likewise an exile, which cuts men off from that future city (of God), but because the good from which the sinner is excluded is eternal, so the punishment is eternal (21.11.36–39; cf. 21.23, 27).

Another challenge to the eternity of hell came from Origen's theory of *apokatastasis*, or the general restoration of all souls to their original company with God. On this subject, Augustine's invective is unrestrained. Disregarding that Origen posits decline only for souls that fail to cultivate God, he attacks the possibility of alternating advance and regression over ages as an affront to the blessed. He assumes that the cycle is involuntary and accuses Origen of imposing a sporadic "false happiness" on the saints and angels. Moreover, Augustine leaps immediately to the final result. Ignoring Origen's view that advances are always preceded by purification, he bitingly dares the proponents of Origen's theory to profess the final salvation of the Devil (CD 21.17).

A very technical version of this discussion takes place in a letter Augustine wrote to Orosius. He defines *apokatastasis*, or restoration, as "the correction and restoration of the Devil and his angels to their pristine condition."[8] Although so happy a return could justly be denied to them simply because they tried to impede the path of the righteous to that destination, one should refrain from seeking to perfect the divine sentence already pronounced in Matthew 25.41 and 46: "Go into the eternal fire prepared for the devil and his angels." Augustine admits that the Greek word for "eternal" is based on the noun *aiōn*, an age, and thus an adjective derived from it might sometimes mean "centuries long" and sometimes "eternal," that is, "with a very far-off end" or "with no end." Eager not to lose his case on technicalities of translation, Augustine avers that the adjective *aiōnion*, although it derives from a noun of some ambiguity, has none itself and always

---

8. Augustine, *Ad Orosium contra Priscillianistas et Origenistas* 5.5.106–7, Corpus Christianorum, Series Latina, 49 (Turnhout: Brepols, 1985).

means "endless" (5.5.130). He suggests that the eternity of God is denoted by the same term and that therefore the fires of hell are equally long when called *aeternum* or *aiōnion* (6.7.152–53). Further, if eternity does not describe the punishment of the damned, it also does not apply to the blessedness of the saved. "Let us not, when we grieve over the sufferings of the Devil, come to doubt the kingdom of Christ" (6.7.163–64). Or again, in the *City of God* he remarks, "To say in one and the same sense that 'Eternal life will be without end, but eternal punishment will end' is entirely absurd" (21.23.48–50). How could "eternal" mean one thing when applied to the bliss of the saints and another for the torments of the damned?[9]

In another letter Augustine rejects the contention that Matthew 7.2— "The measure you give will be the measure you get"—shows that punishment after death cannot be eternal but must be measured. This is a variant on the objection to eternal punishment from lack of proportion. Augustine answers that one should not confuse the measure with the quantity. Eternity is an immeasurable quantity of time, and all the damned are punished equally in that they are punished eternally. An eternal duration, however, can vary in intensity. The intensity of punishments will vary according to a fixed measure, which Augustine identifies as the perversion of the will. Thus all damnation is eternal, but the intensity of the punishment varies or is measured according to the degree of deviation from the divine will. Thus, he concludes, these two scriptural ideas are not contradictory.[10]

Augustine has been organizing his discussion by refuting contentions that he has read or heard argued in his day. This approach reveals another function of theology, that of supervising the discussion of religious topics. Of those we have just considered the unfairness of eternal punishment comes from philosophy, the need of damnation to correct God's failure to save comes from what Augustine would call exaggeratedly merciful Christians. If the theologian seeks to divert false ideas from his community, he must also refine pious notions that are nonetheless not understood rigorously enough. One example of these would be misunderstanding the descent of Christ into hell, so much more vivid in popular apocryphal literature than Scripture authorizes. His procedure illustrates well the function of the theologian. Whereas Augustine combines three key biblical passages to establish the

9. For Augustine's view of time and eternity, see Gottlieb Locker, "Die Beziehung der Zeit zur Ewigkeit bei Augustin," *Theologische Zeitschrift* 44 (1988): 147–67; and Jaroslav Pelikan, *The Mystery of Continuity: Time and History, Memory and Eternity in the Thought of Saint Augustine* (Charlottesville: University Press of Virginia, 1986).

10. Augustine, Epistola 102, "Sex Quaestiones contra Paganos," 4.26, Corpus scriptorum ecclesiasticorum Latinorum (Prague: Tempsky, 1895), 34:544–78.

eternity of Gehenna, in defending the descent into Hades he casts aside one verse that he feels should not be connected with it.

It is wrong, Augustine argues in a letter to Evodius, to believe that the statement that Christ, in his spirit, "went and preached to the spirits in prison" (1 Peter 3.19) applies to the descent. If that prison were Hades, it would raise the question how such divine preaching could fail to be entirely efficacious. Augustine affirms Christ's descent and cites Acts 2.31, quoting Psalms 16.10—"Thou wilt not leave my soul in Sheol [*infernus*]"— and Acts 2.24—"It was not possible for him to be held by it [*infernus*]"—in its favor.[11] But whom did he set free? Perhaps only himself? Perhaps it was the virtuous pagans, the philosophers, Adam, Abel, Seth, Noah and his household, Abraham, Isaac, Jacob, and other patriarchs and prophets. Lazarus, who was in the bosom of Abraham while Jesus was teaching, was not in those sorrows. Nor was the believing thief crucified with Jesus to be found in that prison (Luke 23.43). Thus some righteous were never there. Still it would be wrong to believe either that his descent was fruitless or that he emptied Hades of everyone (2.5).

All this may be true, said Augustine, but if the prison of 1 Peter 3.19 were Hades, it would be possible to infer that "men who did not believe during their lifetime can believe in Christ in Hades" (Epistola 164, 4.13). Then there would be no reason to acknowledge one's faith during one's lifetime, to mend one's ways while still alive. Everything could be postponed until after death. If this deadline is not firmly maintained, he reasons, it would follow "that the Gospel ought not to be preached *here*," since one could always hear the divine word *there* and convert later (4.13). Thus the "prison" of 1 Peter 3.18–21 is not Hades but must be understood figuratively. "Let us not maintain that the Gospel was preached in Hades to convert and liberate believers, or that it is still preached there as if the church were set up there too" (5.15). Instead, the spirits in prison to whom Christ preached are the souls imprisoned in bodies alive in this life and "in the darkness of ignorance as in a prison" (5.16).

The possibility of converting in Hades is similar to another idea that Augustine combated, namely, that the saints, through their constant intercession, would eventually be able to empty hell by their prayers. Although this is its most extreme form, it is apparent from the *Apocalypse of Paul* that some believed the saints could affect the conditions of those in hell. Could they not, therefore, liberate its inmates? Origen's "restoration" would empty hell, but on an individual basis, not through the saints. Yet Augustine denied

11. Augustine, Epistola 164, "Ad Evodium," 2.3, Corpus scriptorum ecclesiasticorum Latinorum (Vienna: Tempsky, 1904), 44:521–41.

that even Christ had emptied Hades. In the face of such a threat, Augustine took pains to define precisely the relationship between the saved and the damned, between the living and the dead. This discussion fits with a section of the *City of God* in which Augustine rules out a number of acts that lukewarm believers advance as adequate to keep themselves out of hell. Just being baptized is not enough if one strays from the true faith (21.19), just professing the true faith is not enough if one does not live rightly (21.20–21); just giving alms occasionally is not enough (21.22). Furthermore, the actions by which one will be judged must be completed in this life. Nothing done in the next life can add, retroactively, to one's merits from this life. Death is the deadline.

Though one's merits cannot change after death, it is nonetheless possible to benefit after death from the prayers of others. To see how, it is necessary to understand the condition of souls between their individual deaths and the General Resurrection. As mentioned before, the *Enchiridion* gives a systematic outline of the possibilities. First, between death and the Last Judgment, souls are in hidden places called "receptacles," where they experience refreshment or pain in proportion to the merit earned during life on earth (29.109.1–4). Conditions for some of the dead in these receptacles, however, do not remain constant. Rather, the living can benefit the dead by performing certain deeds in their memory, saying Mass or giving alms, for example. One's ability to benefit after death from these aids (or, as they will later be called, suffrages), however, depends upon how well one lived one's life. Augustine's discussion of the rules concerning suffrages is so important and had such profound consequences later as purgatory came to be seen as separate from hell, that it is worth devoting considerable attention to the matter now.[12]

Augustine insisted that only some people can benefit after death from the

---

12. On suffrages, see Konde Ntedika, *L'évocation de l'au-delà dans la prière pour les morts: Etude de patristique et de liturgie latines, IVe–VIIIe siècles*, Recherches africaines de théologie, 2, Université lovanium de Kinshasa publications (Louvain: Nauwelaerts, 1971); idem, *L'évolution de la doctrine du purgatoire chez saint Augustin*, Université lovanium de Léopoldville, Faculté de théologie publications, 4, Université lovanium de Léopoldville publications, 20 (Paris: Etudes augustiniennes, 1966); Salomon Reinach, "De l'origine des prières pour les morts," *Revue des études juives* 41 (1900): 161–73, cited by Le Goff, *Birth of Purgatory*, 45–46, and see 380 n. 57, and Le Goff's discussion of Augustine, 61–85. See also R. R. Atwell, "From Augustine to Gregory the Great: An Evaluation of the Emergence of the Doctrine of Purgatory," *Journal of Ecclesiastical History* 38 (1987): 173–86. This is the belief encountered first in Plato's *Republic*, where Adimantus attributes it (albeit scornfully) to the Orphics. Virgil had the Sybil deny it outright.

suffrages dedicated to them by the living. Those whose lives were wicked beyond a certain point cannot benefit. The extremely holy have no need of them. A middle group, however, lived neither so well as not to have need of them nor so ill as to be beyond benefiting from them.[13] Suffrages have a different significance according as they are offered for individuals in each of these groups. "For the very good, they are a way of giving thanks."[14] In the intermediate group he mentions only those tending toward the good: "For the not very good, they are *propitiationes*."[15] That is, they are propitiatory offerings seeking to lighten God's disciplinary action toward those who receive purgatorial punishments after death. Augustine delays explaining what suffrages achieve for the not very wicked. "For the very wicked, even if they provide no help to the dead, they constitute a certain consolation for the living."[16] It would be tempting to consider this division equivalent to a tripartite schema comprising the saved, the damned, and a middle group of souls experiencing purgatorial punishment from which they will eventually be released. Augustine did not go that far, however. True, it is only the middle group that can be affected by suffrages. Yet Augustine refrains from saying that the whole middle group will eventually escape suffering. "For those whom [the suffrages] benefit," he says, "either they will benefit in a full remission, or, at least, in their *damnatio* becoming more tolerable."[17] "Full remission" must mean the final extinction of any remaining responsibility for sin, so that the purgatorial process is completed and the soul may proceed to heaven.

Thus Augustine presents a four-part division overlaid on a three-part division. The dead are divided into three groups as far as benefiting from suffrages is concerned. There are those whose situation does not change because they were so good; there are those whose situation does not change because they were so wicked, and there are those in between, whose situation *does* change. In the middle group, though, according as they resembled the good or the wicked more, they merited different fates. Those who were

13. In my analysis, I have changed the order of these groups. Augustine lists the middle group first, 29.110.9–13: "Est enim quidam uiuendi modus, nec tam bonus ut non requirat ista post mortem, nec tam malus ut ei non prosint ista post mortem; est uero talis in bono ut ista non requirat, et est rursus talis in malo ut nec his ualeat cum ex hac uita transierit adiuuari."

14. "Pro ualde bonis gratiarum actiones sunt" (29.110.26).

15. "Pro non valde bonis propitiationes sunt" (29.110.27).

16. "Pro ualde malis, etiam si nulla sunt adiumenta mortuorum, qualescumque uiuorum consolationes sunt" (29.110.27–29).

17. "Quibus autem prosunt, aut ad hoc prosunt ut sit plena remissio, aut certe ut tolerabilior fiat ipsa damnatio" (29.110.29–31).

relatively good would eventually escape suffering. Those who were relatively evil were still not good, and so, although their punishment might be lightened, it would continue forever and must be called damnation. The Latin phrase *tolerabilior damnatio* means "a more tolerable damnation."[18] Therefore, although Augustine conceived of a middle group that could benefit from suffrages, the territory these souls occupy between their individual deaths and the Resurrection was divided by a ridge whose slopes ran either to heaven or to hell.[19]

This division of souls changes at the Last Judgment, after which there will be only two groups, one of the good angels and humans with Christ in eternal happiness, the other of the wicked humans with the wicked angels in eternal misery. Both groups will live without end (29.111.32–39). These, then, are the types of fates possible after death, both before and after the Last Judgment.

"And so it is in vain," Augustine continues, "that some people, nay, indeed, very many," who do not exactly disbelieve, but rather consider the Scriptures "more frightening than true," imagine that there must be some way of softening these terrible judgments (29.112.41, 46–47). Although he contends that they hold this belief in vain, so strong are these views and so widespread that, even as he expounds theology dogmatically, he must refer to what he knows many people believe. It is clear why the bishop of Hippo could not compromise on the eternity of punishment for the damned. Not even so formally trained a thinker as Origen could sway him on that issue. Is it necessary, however, to maintain his own categories in the face of widespread insistence on the biblical references to divine mercy? What concession can be made to the views of other believers? "They may suppose, if they wish, that the punishments of the damned are periodically lightened to some extent, . . . not putting an end to the eternal punishment, but providing or introducing an alleviation of the torments" (29.112.56–63). If this were the case, this leniency (*levamen*) would extend to the "more tolerable damnation," that Augustine said applied only to the not very wicked and only as suffrages regulated by the church and only until the Last Judgment.

18. The phrase also occurs at *Ench.* 23.93.136–37, where the possibility of interpreting *damnatio* as "punishment" is slightly greater, but is offset by the slightly preceding use of *sempiterna damnatio* at 23.92.123.

19. How difficult this subject is may be seen in the discussion by Le Goff, in *Birth of Purgatory*, where he neglects the overlay of the threefold division on the fourfold division. Le Goff believes that it was not until Peter Lombard in the mid twelfth century that the division became tripartite; it is that moment which serves as the starting point for the "birth" of purgatory a generation later. See Le Goff, 73–74 for Augustine, 149 and 222–23 for Peter Lombard.

But these periodic reductions of torment would exist even after the Last Judgment, since that is where Augustine introduced them into the text. Thus, if they exist, they would relieve, though not end, the punishments of even the very worst of the damned. Still, Augustine regards this only as a possibility he will allow the many to believe, however vainly. He does not himself profess it.[20] Indeed, in the next paragraph he refers scornfully to "whatever people may conjecture about the variety of punishments, the mitigation or suspension of the pains, for their own human motives" (29.113.74–76). Therefore, it would be wrong to attribute Augustine's concession directly to the impact of a popular text such as the *Apocalypse of Paul*. Yet it would be equally wrong not to see a persistent current of popular belief lying behind both the apocryphal text and Augustine's concession. In this most schematic of theological treatments, Augustine devotes a paragraph to define and limit a popular idea that his political instinct warns him it would be imprudent to ignore or to deny altogether. Even as it is the task of the theologian to establish boundaries between ideas that sustain and contradict the system being considered, it is the historian's task to see when those boundaries are modified to accommodate the lay of the land. This particular border, around the permissible influence of the living on the fate of the dead, and particularly the damned, was to be highly contested. However grudging, Augustine's concession proved ripe with significance in future debates.[21]

To sum up, Augustine has set down two rules concerning suffrages. The first is that suffrages benefit not all the dead but only those who qualify. The second is that one may qualify for suffrages only in life. "It is here that one obtains all the merit by which one may be relieved or burdened after death" (29.110.13–15). So vital is this rule that Augustine warns (with an emphasis remarkable in a summary as condensed as the *Enchiridion*): "Let no one hope that after he dies, he will be able to obtain from the Lord what he neglected to merit here" (29.110.15–16).

These two rules came to guide the church in regulating the devotion of the

---

20. It is as a reaction against this popular pressure for a more merciful hell, Le Goff thinks (*Birth of Purgatory*, 62, 68–69), that Augustine began to insist precisely on its harshness.

21. For the general issue of communication or rhetoric, see Alan Brinton, "Saint Augustine and the Problem of Deception in Religious Persuasion," *Religious Studies* 19 (1983): 437–50; G. Wright Doyle, "Augustine's Sermonic Method," *Westminster Theological Journal* 39 (1977): 213–38; and Balthasar Fischer, "Nicht wie die Gelehrten reden, eher wie die Ungelehrten: Eine Mahnung Augustins an den christlichen Prediger (*De doctrina Christiana* 4.65)." *Internationale katholische Zeitschrift "Communio"* 11 (1982): 123–29.

living for the dead. As time went on they were taken to endorse the practice of dedicating certain good works in memory of the deceased. Thus believers endowed charitable practices and funded houses where the clergy would pray or lead prayers for the souls of the dead. It was on this basis that the concept of indulgences arose.[22]

Before leaving the subject of those who may gradually receive full remission, it is necessary to consider an earlier chapter of the *Enchiridion* to see how that may come about. Remission obtained gradually after death would be classified, as in the *City of God*, as a temporary, purgatorial punishment after death. Augustine believed he saw a scriptural basis for this punishment in the fire that tests each person's life's work, mentioned in 1 Corinthians 3.13. In chapter 68 of the *Enchiridion*, he interprets this passage to suggest three criteria for an individual's salvation: (1) faith in Christ, that is, in the terms of 1 Corinthians 3.11, whether Christ is one's "foundation"; (2) the works one builds upon that foundation, which may be likened to "gold, silver, and precious stones" or to "wood, hay, and straw"; and (3) one's relative loyalty under pressure, to either the works or the foundation. Some will become so devoted to their own works that they forget the foundation and are more willing to lose Christ than their own earthly achievements. Such people do not survive the trial by fire. Others may be tempted by the loss of their life's works, but prefer to retain their foundation in Christ. These, though they are tried by the fire and do suffer loss, are saved because they retain their foundation, "but only as through fire" (1 Corinthians 3.15).

We know from the *City of God* 21.13 that God sends punishments to try the human race in this world and, sometimes, in the next. Thus in *Enchiridion* 69, Augustine extends the testing fire of 1 Corinthians 3.13 into the next world. If that purgatorial fire exists in the next world, "in proportion as they have loved with more or less devotion the goods that perish, [the faithful will] be more or less quickly delivered from it" (18.69.76–78). Thus this purgatorial fire might exist after death to burn away any remaining loyalty to human works which once distracted one from the foundation of Christ. Here is a fire in the afterlife which is at once punitive and purifying, enduring only to the extent that the individual's misplaced loyalty kindles it. It would seem that this fire might be the punishment described in *Enchiridion* 110 through which the not very bad can be aided by the prayers and almsgiving of the living. If so, this *purification*, which punishes in propor-

22. See Gustav Adolf Benrath's article "Ablaß," in the *Theologische Realenzyklopädie* (Berlin: de Gruyter, 1977), 1:347–64, with bibliography, and the exhaustive article by Etienne Magnin, "Indulgences," in the *Dictionnaire de théologie catholique*, 16 vols. in 28 (Paris: Librairie Letouzey et Ané, 1903–72), vol. 7, pt. 2, cols. 1594–1636.

tion to the degree of wavering but fundamentally rooted loyalty, would parallel the *punishment* in hell, which punishes (as is clear in Augustine's Epistola 102) in proportion to the degree of deviation from the divine will.[23]

Whether the fire torments or purifies during the interim period, it must be such that it can affect immaterial substances, such as human souls, whose bodies are in the grave, or the fallen angels (the demons), who have no bodies. To understand how fire can affect these spiritual substances, Augustine uses the example of the rich man of Luke 16.19–31, who refused hospitality to Lazarus, died, and suffered in fire. Luke 16.22–23 locates the place "in Hades" (*in inferno*); Augustine "in the netherworld" (*apud inferos*) (CD 21.10.29). Both, therefore, are referring the receptacle of suffering which receives the wicked (as Augustine put it in *Enchiridion* 109–10), prior to their final disposition. It is not Gehenna, which, for Augustine, does not come into play until the Last Judgment. It will become clear that the distinction is not only temporal, for the fire in both places is quite different.

In the *City of God*, Augustine considers how it is that the soul of the rich man could burn and be thirsty at a time before the Resurrection, when it is separated from the body. He concludes that in the place to which he was consigned before the Last Judgment, the fire is not material: "Both the fire in which he was burning and the drop for which he pleaded were incorporeal, for such are the visions of dreamers or of those transported in ecstasy that, although they are incorporeal things, they nonetheless have a similarity to bodies" (21.10.34–37). Thus, Augustine bases the soul's ability to suffer apparently corporeal torments (the rich man's fire and thirst) on his hypothesis that the soul contains within itself an image of the body it animates or animated: "This very man, although he is in the spirit, not in the body, in visions of this sort, sees himself in a form so similar to his body that he is entirely unable to tell the difference" (21.10.37–40). Thus, although without a body or a physical basis for sense perceptions, the soul, through the image of the body that it contains within itself, will experience the same suffering in visions or when separated from the body after death as if sensations from a physical body were afflicting it.

In book 12 of his work *On the Literal Interpretation of Genesis*, Augustine posits not only an image of the body in the soul, but even an image of that body's surroundings. He says, "If [the soul] bears this likeness [of the

23. Here I am connecting *Ench.* 110 to Epistola 102. The connection suggested here differs from the view that would become widespread among the scholastics of the thirteenth century, because here the intensity of punishment is regulated according to the deviation of loyalty from the foundation, not progress through penance. In this passage of Augustine, penance is not really taken into account, though it is mentioned in a slightly different context at *Ench.* 69.

body] into the lower regions, that likeness will not be corporeal, but analogous thereto, and it will be seen in the same way in places which are not corporeal but analogous thereto, whether it is in repose or in affliction."[24] From this it follows that in the interim period between death and the Last Judgment, those receptacles, whether of refreshment or of bitterness, need *not* be real places in the physical sense, for the soul's knowledge of what is happening to it comes from no place but from the perceptions of the likeness of the body that the soul contains.[25] These perceptions themselves come from the sensory equipment in the soul's inner body. For people who experience the otherworld without their bodies, such as visionaries, "bear in themselves a certain likeness to their own bodies, through which they are able to be borne to those places and to experience such things through the likenesses of the senses" (12.32). Nor is there any reason why the perceptions of visionaries, who "see" the other world without the senses of their physical bodies, should be any different from the experiences of souls whose bodies lie in the grave (12.32).

After the Last Judgment and the final damnation of the wicked, however, souls will be reunited with their resurrected bodies.[26] How will the addition of their bodies affect the suffering of the damned, especially inasmuch as Paul in 1 Corinthians 15.44 called the resurrected bodies "spiritual"? Does the spiritual nature of the resurrected body mean that the fire of hell, even after the Last Judgment, will remain incorporeal? Or if the fire is material, how can the resurrected spiritual bodies be affected by material fires?

Perhaps the problem can be resolved through analogy with the saved. In the *City of God*, Augustine declares that the resurrected bodies of the blessed will have "a spiritual flesh, which is still flesh even though it is joined to a spirit, just as now, in life, the spirit, might be considered 'corporeal,' but is still spirit even though it is joined to a body" (22.21.10–12; cf. *Enchiridion* 23.91). By the same token, therefore, in hell this resurrected "spiritual body" would remain "a body" and so be subject to the pain inflicted by corporeal fire, while not being weakened by it (21.9.62–63).

But the term "spiritual" does not apply equally to the bodies of the saved and the damned. There is a warning in the *City of God* 21.10, where Augustine refers to the bodies of resurrected damned humans as "solid"

24. Augustine, *De Genesi ad litteram* 12.33, Corpus scriptorum ecclesiasticorum Latinorum 28. 1 (Prague: Tempsky, 1894), 428, lines 16–19.

25. *Ench.* 29.109.2–3 calls them "hidden receptacles"—"animas abditis receptaculis continet."

26. On the Resurrection of the flesh, see John G. Gager, "Body-Symbols and Social Reality: Resurrection, Incarnation, and Asceticism in Early Christianity," *Religion: Journal of Religion and Religions* 12 (1982): 345–63.

contrasting them to the bodies of demons, which are "aerial." If the resurrected bodies of the saints, and only the saints are spiritual, what of the bodies of the damned? In *Enchiridion* 91 Augustine says precisely that the bodies of the *saints* are spiritual, but in chapter 92 he considers speculation about the bodies of the damned to be beneath serious concern, as long as they are susceptible to pain and unable to die.

The answer, then, cannot be derived from any knowledge about the nature of the resurrected bodies of the damned, because speculation on that matter is beneath pious occupation. Further, two different places are involved. Whereas the spirit of the rich man was in Hades (*apud inferos*) before the Last Judgment, where the fire is incorporeal and afflicts the image of the body in the soul; after the Last Judgment, the damned are sent to "that Gehenna, which has been called 'a lake of fire and brimstone' [Revelation 20.9], where the fire will be corporeal and will torture the bodies of the damned . . . or at least the bodies of men with their spirits" (*CD* 21.10.40–42).

Although the distinction between Hades and Gehenna is not new, there is a shift in the time when souls are moved from one to the other. In the *Gospel of Nicodemus* souls were cast into hell (Tartarus) by Christ at the time of his descent. Augustine says that Hades torments the wicked from their deaths until the end of time, when, pursuant to the results of the Last Judgment, the damned will be cast from the Hades of Luke 16 into Gehenna, the lake of fire and sulfur, in accordance with Revelation 20.9–10 and Matthew 25.41.

Thus Augustine proposes these differences. Between death and the Last Judgment, the souls of the wicked are punished in Hades (*apud inferos*) by an immaterial fire that they perceive through the models of the body that the soul bears with it to the underworld. After the Resurrection of the flesh and the Last Judgment, the wicked will be sent to Gehenna, where eternal, material fire will punish the soul together with the resurrected body.

The comparison with the demons evokes Matthew 25.41, where the damned are said to go to the fire prepared for the Devil and his angels. Thus, Augustine devotes a chapter of the City of God to explaining how resurrected human bodies can be punished in the same fire as demons, who have no bodies.[27] Thus he considers Isaiah's prophecy (66.24) concerning the

27. Though the demons have no bodies, Augustine is concerned that the corporeal fire which torments them in Gehenna not give them a substance that might bring them to life. "That Gehenna, which has been called a lake of fire and sulfur," he writes, "will be a corporeal fire, and it will torment both humans and demons: whether the solid bodies of the humans or the aerial bodies of the demons; whether the bodies of the humans together with their spirits or, in the case of the demons, unattached to bodies, these corporeal fires will be able to inflict punishment without imparting life" (21.10.40–44).

bodies of God's enemies: "Their worm shall not die, neither shall their fire be quenched." The evangelist Mark says that Jesus applied this description of the carnage outside Jerusalem to eternal punishment (Mark 9.43–48). Augustine asks whether the fire and the worm are applied primarily to the body or the soul. Some believe, he says, that the fire and the worm both apply to the soul. Others imagine the worm attacking the soul and the fire the body. Augustine states that speculation on this question should be open as long as no one imagines that "grief will be lacking from either the body or the soul in that place, which would be absurd" (*CD* 21.9.30–31). Augustine believes the relationship of hellfire to the resurrected body in the next world will be like the relationship of the mortal body to the soul in this world. Hence, he prefers to say that "it is easier to believe that both [the fire and the worm] apply to the body than to suppose that neither does" (21.9.32). He concedes that "Scripture is silent regarding the spiritual pain of the damned" (21.9.33–34), but uses that very silence to reinforce positions he stated in 21.3 that the fire affects the body, which in turn torments the soul. Thus, although Scripture names no specific torment for the soul, "it is understood to follow, even if not stated, that in a body thus tormented, the soul too is tortured with a sterile repentance" (21.9.34–36).

It is worth observing, with Augustine's letter to Evodius in mind, that it is in this way that the spirits in the "prison" come to believe in Christ—not because, as some interpreted 1 Peter 3.19, he came and preached to them in Hades but because, having seen him at the Last Judgment and suffering now under his sentence, they have no choice but to believe and, believing, to regret their earlier scorn. That regret is the sterile repentance.

This consideration completes a full cycle, because it also answers the question of how the demons, who have no bodies, can suffer in the eternal fire to which they will be consigned in the Last Judgment. If sterile repentance in the will of human spirits in resurrected bodies in the fire is what causes that *passio* that is the essence of the second death, then the same applies to the fallen angels who freely chose to depart from God and so, too, are brought to a condition in which they regret their choice. If the spirits of humans, which are also incorporeal, can suffer as a result of these fires, then surely the incorporeal demons can too (21.10.14–19). This will be their fate in that Gehenna where one fire will be the lot of both damned humans and fallen angels (21.10.46).

The ability of these incorporeal substances to suffer from corporeal fire (21.10.20–21) is only one part of their punishment. The other is the death that consists of separation from God, the source of life.

If one were to experience [the anger of God], even the slightest aspect of it that can be imagined, taken by itself: to perish from the kingdom of

God, to be an exile from the City of God, to be alienated from the life of God, to lack the immensity of God's sweetness, which he reserved for those who fear him and perfected for those hoping in him, that fate, if it were eternal, would nonetheless be so great a punishment that no torment which we know here, were it to last for as many ages as we can conceive, may be compared with it. (*Enchiridion* 29.112.65–71)

Augustine's contrast between the physical pain we know in this world and eternal separation from God would seem to place them entirely on different planes. Yet this difference should not be exaggerated, since the pains of the damned are not entirely absent even from the saints in heaven. Indeed, Augustine teaches that knowledge of the punishment of the damned constitutes part of heavenly bliss.

To understand Augustine's belief, it is necessary to see how he introduced his account of heaven by adverting again, eloquently and vehemently, to the fallen human condition. In the *City of God* 22.22–23 he lists natural disasters, sickness, accidents, human crimes, and even, for the righteous, the war of spirit against flesh. And these, as we have seen, are not "natural," "chance," or "human" phenomena but part of the penal regime applied by Providence since the Fall. Who can recount, he asks, "how heavy and how numerous are the punishments that agitate the whole human race, and which pertain not to the malice and iniquity of the wicked, but to the misery of our common condition?" (22.22.49–52). This life is so miserable as to be "almost a kind of hell."[28] Escape is possible only by means of divine grace, without which "one incurs, after this, a more miserable and eternal not life but death" (22.22.114–15).

For those who accept Christ's way, Augustine says, waits a heaven filled with every joy and free from every evil. Yet if the saints were to be entirely free of evil they would lose sight of the liberation from which they benefit. In order to give thanks properly, therefore, they must have some knowledge of evil. The blessed will obviously no longer experience any evil directly. Intellectually, however, "neither their own past misery, nor even the eternal misery of the damned will be concealed from them" (22.30.94–95).

Later writers will expand more on this point, but it is not new. In the *Apocalypse of Peter* the saved witness the torments of the damned. In the *Gospel of Nicodemus*, those about to be rescued watch Christ throw the wicked into Tartarus. Augustine explains his statement only with reference to the past sufferings of the saved during their penitential life on earth. For if they did not remember those sufferings, "if they were not to know that they had

28. "Ab . . . quasi quibusdam inferis" (22.22.11). Literally, "almost a kind of underworld existence."

been miserable, how, as the psalm says, 'will they sing the mercies of the Lord forever'?" (22.30.95–97; cf. Psalm 89.1). Yet when Augustine says "the eternal misery of the damned" will not be concealed from them, they must also know the miseries of "that Gehenna, which . . . is called the lake of fire and sulfur," which he defined by combining three scriptural passages (21.10.40). Thus it is not only by knowing their own past miseries as human beings living in the world but also by knowing the condition of the damned that the saved can fully appreciate the action of their liberator. In this sense the pleasure of the saved will be enhanced by knowing the condition of the damned.

In conclusion, despite the wide range of his treatment of punishment after death, for Augustine the essence of damnation boils down to three things. One is the exclusion from God, the source of life, absence from whom causes the second death. Second is the fate of the resurrected bodies of the damned: preserved from consumption but liable to pain from the fire. And third, with these torments upon the body, and conscious of its separation from God, the soul is tortured with a fruitless repentance.

Part IV has reviewed a broad range of views concerning punishment after death. These views have varied on matters of vengeance as compared to mercy, eternity as compared to temporality, the possibility of mitigating hell's torments, and the essence of its punishments. Yet these subjects are pursued in sources that differ greatly in character. This review has illustrated how dialogue shaped the formation of doctrine, how an Augustine knew and was concerned about the opinions of the many, even though he sometimes derided these views and, less frequently, classified them as heresy. There is no denying the influence of an Augustine or an Origen. Yet if one considers only writers with philosophical training who learned to present their ideas with the appearance of systematic exposition, much of what occurred would escape.

What is loosely called popular religion addresses the beliefs and behavior of the community at large. Granted that those in authority and possessed of great learning sought to shape the broader population, it is still crucial to understand the interactions among all parties, the give and take that produced the resultant beliefs that constituted consensus.

Augustine excluded one biblical quotation from among those that might apply to the descent of Christ. He celebrated the exclusion of the *Apocalypse of Paul* from the list of legitimate teachings. He denounced Origen. He ridiculed the variety of "merely human" speculation on the length and nature of hell's punishments. This is a theologian at work.

Not every believer, however, is a theologian. The variety that Augustine deigned to mention made up the fabric of his religious community, as it does of any community. Augustine need have considered only his own life as recounted in the *Confessions* to know that others would have unresolved doubts about God's incorporeality and many other things, some of which, including his justice, his mercy, and his system of punishing sinners after death, are dealt with in book 21 of the *City of God*. It is from this point of view that the other sources are vital: they represent other levels of discourse.

In the *Gospel of Nicodemus*, the patriarchs sigh, Christ carries a banner, the demons bicker, Satan is bound in chains, Hades has a door. In the *Apocalypse of Peter* the punishments are so numerous and so vivid that it would be distasteful and certainly impractical to review them here. One need remember only the birds who eat from the sides of victims hung alongside precipices, guilty of disrespect for their elders—Tityos made Everyman. And who could forget in the *Apocalypse of Paul* the stench that emerges from the well within which all the punishments are seven times more severe than the tortures already encountered? Are these details necessary? Not to an Augustine. He thinks symbolically, abstractly. He greatly stresses the importance of "mere" separation from God. The only physical torments he mentions are fire, sulfur, and the worm. Specifically biblical, they stand by synecdoche for any other punishment one wishes to imagine.

The others think symbolically too. Surely the author of the *Apocalypse of Peter* used the "screen" in the palm of Jesus to attribute the vision to divine authority. Yet he also needed to prove the justice of hell's punishments by listing them serially. The *Apocalypse of Paul* uses a physical tour, with the visionary following a guide, to order the narrative. These are the techniques of different literary genres, and they operate at a level different from theology. Although they reflect popular religion, they are not primitive. A contemporary witness, Augustine of Hippo, attributed the curiosity they betray to "the many." They are "fables" of broad diffusion. Yet without knowledge of these widespread ideas and the scholars' concern to review, shape, and sometimes oppose them it would be impossible to write satisfactorily about the formation of doctrine. Both sides contributed to this exchange of reciprocal influence. Augustine's high theology, then, must be viewed in the context of a whole community's beliefs.

Conclusion

Just as Augustine's theological expositions form only a part of the great debate over hell in the first centuries of Christianity, so too early Christianity, with all its variety and tensions, formed only part of antiquity's concern with postmortem morality. To see Christianity in context, it is necessary to group loosely together themes whose differences have been carefully noted. One extreme position was the banishment of the dead in the ancient Near East, Israel, and archaic Greece, but even in these cases the division between the living and the dead was to some extent porous. Gods could descend; spirits could be raised; ghosts could return of their own accord. In Lucian's writings philosophers, lovers, and chthonic gods went back and forth across the Styx to compare the worlds of the living and the dead. An assembly of impoverished shades, mindful, like Homer's dead, of the lives they had lived, legislated about the transmigration of souls on earth. They sentenced the wealthy to live for generations as beasts of burden goaded by country bumpkins. From their new home after death, the poor thus acquired more clout than they ever had in life. Yet this porosity had its limits. Ishtar's threat to release the dead brought instant compliance to her will. In monotheistic Judaism and Christianity, whether one refers to Sheol, Hades, Ge-Hinnom, or Gehenna, entrance and exit are regulated by one Authority.

Divine mastery of death emerges clearly in Psalm 139, which reports God's presence throughout all nature, from the peaks of the mountains to the depths of Sheol. In Luke 16 permission to send a dead messenger to the living is denied. In John 11 Jesus prays effectively that another Lazarus be raised from the dead. In the *Enchiridion* (chapters 109–12), Augustine analyzes the "hidden receptacles" that hold the dead until the General Resurrection. How interesting it is that Augustine's purpose in that passage is to analyze the effectiveness of prayers by the living for the souls of the dead! The living can affect the dead, or at least those who lived well enough to deserve it. Thus the theme of porosity continues. Yet Augustine's receptacles are categories like those against which, in pagan antiquity at least, the imagination rebelled. The Christian imagination does too, for by its very nature Christianity proclaims the porosity of death. If Christ can break the barriers of Hades, so can his followers. Augustine knew that, but he also knew and respected the stories of ghosts revealing their unburied bodies to friends who would carry out their obsequies. He related sympathetically how a dead man in Milan had appeared to reveal the location of a receipt to his son, who was thereby able to ward off a dishonest creditor.

Even when banishing the dead was effective, imagining them as a vaguely uniform horde confined to a single land had its costs. Neutral death had to be viewed as an evil (Cicero's opponents), a misfortune (Homer), or—if it came too early—a punishment (the Deuteronomic view). Moreover, the experience of life showed too much variety for a homogeneous death. Although the simplicity of a single grave or underworld fortress offered the living safety from the dead, it minimized moral difference. Even when Sheol looked like a release to Job, he balked at the thought of sharing his tomb with the slick and the wicked. Saul and Samuel should not be neighbors in death.

When Socrates interpreted death as an opportunity to converse with Homer, when Psalm 73 imagined a different end, "near God," or the poet of Psalm 49 that God would "receive" him, death began to bifurcate. It would separate the righteous from the scornful, the exploited from the exploiter; it would distribute like with like. The oldest subdivision of the underworld identified here occurred in ancient Egypt. Districting laws applied. Osiris or Re allotted land according to one's choice of divine patron, possession of magic formulas, and to some extent, guiltlessness. Though the idea was based on very different premises, sectioning the otherworld overcame Job's objection to uniform death. The shame of lying unburied which drove the warriors of Homer and Virgil took on a moral dimension in Ezechiel 32. A similar dividing line became part of the hellscape and thus attained cosmic proportion in Luke 16, where a physical chasm that reflects a moral opposition finally divided Lazarus from his selfish neighbor immediately after their deaths. The symmetry of the judgment of Matthew 25.31–46 matched that contrast. To this separation of sheep from goats can be added the satisfaction that the victims derived from seeing the disgrace of their persecutors, a dramatic feature of the Book of Revelation and the *Apocalypse of Peter*. The *Apocalypse of Paul* moderated the harshness of these confrontations, but Augustine insisted on it.

The bifurcation of death occurred in both the Greco-Roman and Jewish cultures, which informed the Christian idea of hell. Though in different ways, ancient Greece and ancient Israel moved from an undifferentiated, morally neutral view of death to one that considered postmortem fates a consequence of how one lived. The biggest difference between them was that the older, Deuteronomic view never yielded ground and is still fundamental to Judaism, whereas the differentiated or moral view was a late and relatively minor current. The differentiated view was crucial to the legend of *1 Enoch* and gained momentum in the intertestamentary period, becoming a powerful force in Jewish life at the time when Christianity arose. By contrast, the neutral conception of death in ancient Greece did not have the staying power it demonstrated in Jewish thought. Philosophical trends gained more ground. Certainly it was the philosophical strain, particularly in the Neoplatonists of whom Augustine was so fond, that Greek thought most influenced Christian eschatology. Even without philosophy, however, the Greek stamp on Christianity is apparent in the terminology in which its ideas about death are expressed. Gehenna, Hades, and Tartarus are technical terms in the Greek New Testament. Jerusalem may have turned its back on Athens, but it always knew where it was.

When distinctions between a good and an evil life determine the shape of one's death, however, finer and finer distinctions need to be made. Plutarch's whirling souls suffered various degrees of disorientation. How many vices are there, and should they all be punished equally? In partial reply, the *Apocalypse of Peter* delineated precise connections between particular sins and their punishments. Differing levels of immersion reflected differing degrees of guilt. In the *Apocalypse of Paul*, lower hell was seven times worse than upper hell; and heaven was similarly divided. Nuance overlies dichotomy.

Similar analogy with heavenly reward renders the punishments of Mark 9, Matthew 25, Revelation, and the *Apocalypse of Peter* unchangeable. For the saved, the end of time restores an imbalance or satisfies a yearning. It is perfection, and perfection must be eternally immutable. Ups and downs can be no part of this ideal state. Correspondingly, as Augustine (for example) reasons in his refutation of Origen, damnation too must be unchanging. Since the damned willed something other than God, their satisfaction, the consummation of their desires, will remain what they freely chose. To the extent that the damned can regret the distortion of their wills because of its consequences, theirs will be a sterile repentance that only augments their suffering. The static resolution, the perfect ending, provides bliss for the blessed, but for the damned, it instills a constant sense of loss and pain. For the damned it does no good. Advocates of the static afterlife see it as an emanation of divine justice, perfect by definition—for believers, who will not endure it and who emphasize the price paid to overcome death. Guilty of denying the efficacy of a sacrifice that achieved infinite good, the damned must suffer infinite evil.

An opposing view is not static but dynamic. Plato, Plutarch, and Origen, basing themselves on the transmigration of souls, conceived in different ways of postmortem punishment with curative effects. Plato's curable souls undergo their century-long torments ten times to achieve purification, after which they choose a new life. His uncurably wicked, it is true, remain in Tartarus as a warning to all. Plutarch dispatches the very wicked into oblivion, where, appropriately, we hear no more about them. Others he reforms by means of alchemical, mechanical, and psychological treatments before sending them back to a new life. Origen's spirits, whether human or angelic, neglecting God, fall, suffering, farther and farther from God until they conceive a new desire for return. Then conversion begins, and they ascend gradually toward their source. This cycle might be repeated often or it might end with a restoration of all to a state of original perfection.

Though Catholicism would develop its own theory of purgatorial punishments, initial Christian reserve on that subject came not, as Part IV shows, from a lack of advocates of divine mercy but rather from the singular linearity of the Christian conception of time. If time itself, existing as an instantaneous exception to eternity, runs from Creation to the Last Judgment in a straight line, there is no room for epicycles permitting individuals to circle around improving their lives, learning, forgetting, and relearning what has already been divinely revealed once and for all. Perhaps that is what one should make of Paul's reticence on the subject. Christian teleology, like monotheism itself, is absolute. There is only one point at the end of the line, the kingdom of heaven. Little can be known about any other place. Only further revelation could supply the missing information. Are the wicked destroyed or do they suffer punishment?

The punishments themselves migrate from culture to culture. The dead are surely thirsty. From the descent of Inanna to the suffering rich man, who declined to share a crumb, water is a valued commodity. Fire fills lakes in the Egyptian underworld, *1 Enoch*, and the Book of Revelation. It lubricates all the earth's innards in Plato's *Phaedrus* and channels sinners to their destinations in the *Apocalypse of Peter*, where it fulfills more specific uses too. Tar, brimstone, ice, snow, and horrific stench figure in the *Apocalypse of Paul*.

Beyond the extremes of climate, the netherworld hosts the most disagreeable fauna. Serpents figure prominently in the Egyptian works, worms in the *Apocalypse of Peter* and the *Apocalypse of Paul*. The serpents of ancient Egypt are so fantastic that they could be the ancestors of the dragons that torment the false monastics in the *Apocalypse of Paul*, where, it says, in lower hell, the worms have two heads. In the *Apocalypse of Peter*, flesh-eating beasts attack parents who exposed their children. Worms figure prominently in Jewish and Christian sources also because of the Jewish conception of the otherworld as a grave and because of the powerful image in Isaiah 66.24 of the carrion attacked by fire and worm, taken up again in Mark 9.43–48.

Human contrivances such as chains appear in Jude 1.6 in the New Testament, and according to 2 Peter 2.4, fallen angels are "en-Tartared" (a term that betrays cross-cultural influence). Attending the three ponds, Plutarch's ethereal demons work transmuting souls from iron to gold to lead.[1] Later, Plutarch employs demons in a workshop that reshapes souls, molding them for reincarnation. The *Apocalypse of Peter* employs trees as gibbets. Angels apply pitchforks and flaming razors to the deserving sinners in the *Apocalypse of Paul*. Virgil's Tartarus creaks and clanks with the sounds of machines inflicting who knows what tortures.

Although it drew on this vast stock of folkloric motifs common to the whole Mediterranean, hell as it emerged in this variety of early Christian sources preserved certain characteristics that were uniquely its own. In this, it owed much to Judaism. These two monotheistic religions presented justice as an expression of the Creator. The "judge of all the earth" must "do right" (cf. Genesis 18.25). The contrast with polytheism, obvious in any event, is crucial here. Whereas Greek and Roman thinkers considered the social utility of ideas about death a crucial test of their coherence, Christian writers did not. For them, the existence and nature of hell was an outflowing of the Providence that created the world. It reflected their ideas of God's attributes: justice and mercy. Seeing the afterlife as a divine creation rather than a human construction, they reversed the perspectives of men such as Critias, Polybius, Cicero, Livy, and Lucian. Even Plato and Plutarch, who, more than the others, considered the otherworld an expression of a certain providential intelligence, bolstered their arguments with reference to social utility. This dimension of analysis was absent in ancient Judaism and early Christianity.

That is not to say that Jews and Christians were not concerned with the justice of their God. Even if their adherents' ideas, like Job's, could not change God and were woefully inadequate to understanding him, within their own community they could share the assumption that he would be self-consistent. His justice, however harsh, would be comprehensible! For this reason it would be a distortion to examine the formation of hell simply from the perspective of the punishments. Even the direst of torments must be seen as part of a whole system, the system sketched at the conclusion of the discussion of the Book of Revelation. At least by the time Revelation was written, that judge was a self-sacrifing victim, and his punishments were inflicted on his tormentors.

What is unique about the formation of the Christian hell is its location within a universe whose judge, being divine, will, by definition, judge justly and, beyond that, being an innocent victim, will judge with supreme com-

---

1. Transmutation of souls also occurs in the late Book of Similitudes (*1 Enoch* 67.9), though the identity of the laborers (good angels?) is not given.

passion. Receiving the mark of the Lamb, however, implies accepting the efficacy of his sacrifice. The inclusion of faith as a component of justice carries with it a difficult corollary. In contrast to deeds that can be observed from the outside, faith is harder to define. At the time of Paul's writing, faith was seen as an invisible bond complementing or complemented by the Spirit which united a church composed more of personal than institutional ties. With the rise of a more institutionalized church, already visible during the later years of the New Testament's composition, possession of faith might come to be measured in verbal formulations, and authority could define heresy, forcing possibly well-intentioned members of the community into splinter groups and putting them under the threat of damnation. It is also clear in Paul's letters that even if one focused on deeds alone, new Christians such as those referred to in 1 Thessalonians 4 and 5, believing their new status placed them above morality, posed a problem. Paul threatened them with God's wrath. Within the positive tradition, the threat of exclusion from the kingdom was severe in the extreme. As later Christian writers in the symmetrical tradition filled in perceived gaps in the accounts of what happens to the wicked, they described dire fates: eternal fire, sulfur, chains, darkness, and gnashing of teeth. If these conditions could threaten misguided members of the Christian community, how much more certainly would they imperil others who had rejected the Gospel, spurned baptism, or for other reasons remained independent of the new revelation?

Surely these questions also apply to the Jewish believers in the apocalyptic tradition, who endorsed judgment and damnation. These issues are also implicit in the mysteries of the ancient world. Yet a monotheistic system is absolute. With one God there is one truth, and nonconformity is correspondingly abhorred.

The more vivid the images of hell, the more drastic are the fates one imagines for one's enemies. The emphasis on faith and the implications of positing a universal jurisdiction for a divine victim/avenger seriously heightened the consequences of deviance. There is a wide spectrum in the range of threats an individual or a community perceives, from active persecution to disregard for authority to doctrinal difference. I believe that despite all the prehistory of the concept reviewed in this volume, hell as portrayed in the symmetrical tradition was qualitatively different from any sanction imagined before. The Orphics' mire, Plato's philosophical categories—even in the guise of a geological model as in the *Phaedrus*—and the accursed valley of *1 Enoch* never attained the unity of conception and the economy of formulation of Matthew 25 or Revelation. Here the coherence of the mythic time line, the formality of the proceedings, the gathered witnesses, the strict record keeping, and the presence of the Roman state as a model (how ironic that the

Great Beast should have had this influence!) made the practical consequences of potential intolerance very severe. The symmetrical tradition of justice threatens more than the wayward within its own community. It menaces all who deny the belief system that erected it. For that reason, the horror lies less in hell's torments than in the damning dismissal of its detractors.

Bibliography

The parts of this bibliography correspond to the parts of the text.

PART I. *The Netherworlds of Greece and Rome*

Alderink, Larry J. "Mythical and Cosmological Structure in the Homeric *Hymn to Demeter.*" *Numen: International Review for the History of Religions* 29 (1982): 1–16.

Apollonius Rhodius. *The Argonautica.* Trans. R. C. Seaton. Loeb Classical Library. Cambridge: Harvard University Press, 1988.

The Ardai Viraf Nameh; or, The Revelations of Ardai Viraf. Trans. J. A. Pope. London: printed for Black, Parbury, and Allen, 1816.

Arda Wiraz Namag: The Iranian "Divina Commedia." Trans. Fereydun Vahman. Scandinavian Institute of Asian Studies Monograph Series, 53. London: Curzon Press, 1986.

Aristophanes. *The Frogs.* Trans. Benjamin Bickley Rogers. Loeb Classical Library. London: Heinemann, 1924.

Austin, R. G. *P. Vergili Maronis Aeneidos Liber Sextus: Commentary.* Oxford: Clarendon Press, 1977.

Bar, Francis. *Les routes de l'autre monde.* Paris: Presses Universitaires de France, 1946.

Bleeker, Claas Jouco, and Geo Widengren, eds. *Historia Religionum: Handbook for the History of Religions.* 2 vols. Leiden: Brill, 1969.

Boer, Charles, trans. *The Homeric Hymns.* Dallas: Spring, 1970.

Boyancé, Pierre. *Etudes sur le "Songe de Scipion."* Bordeaux: Feret 1936. Rpt. New York: Garland, 1987.

Brandon, S. G. F. *The Judgment of the Dead.* New York: Scribner's, 1967.

Büchner, Karl. *Somnium Scipionis: Quellen-Gestalt-Sinn.* Wiesbaden: Steiner, 1976.

Budge, E. A. Wallis. *The Egyptian Heaven and Hell.* Books on Egypt and Chaldaea. 3 vols. 1905. Rpt. New York: AMS, 1976.

———. *The Egyptian Heaven and Hell.* 1925. Rpt. La Salle, Ill.: Open Court, 1974.

Burkert, Walter. *Greek Religion: Archaic and Classical.* London: Basil Blackwell; Cambridge: Harvard University Press, 1985.

Caster, Marcel. *Lucien et la pensée religieuse de son temps.* 1937. Rpt. New York: Garland, 1987.

Cicero. *De natura deorum.* Trans. Harris Rackham. Loeb Classical Library. Cambridge: Harvard University Press, 1967.

Clay, Diskin. *Lucretius and Epicurus*. Ithaca: Cornell University Press, 1983.

Colish, Marcia L. *The Stoic Tradition from Antiquity to the Early Middle Ages*. Studies in the History of Christian Thought, 34–35. Leiden: Brill, 1985.

Collison-Morley, Lacy. *Greek and Roman Ghost Stories*. 1912. Rpt. Chicago: Argonaut, 1968.

Conte, Gian Biagio "Il trionfo della morte e la galleria dei grandi trapassati in Lucrezio III, 1024–1053." *Studi italiani di filologia classica* 37 (1965): 114–32.

Critias. *Sisyphus*. Trans. Kathleen Freeman. In *Ancilla to the Pre-Socratic Philosophers*, 157–58. Cambridge: Harvard University Press, 1948.

Cumont, Franz. *Lux perpetua*. Paris: Geuthner, 1949.

Curotto, Ernesto. *Dizionario della mitologia universale*. Torino: Internazionale, 1958.

Dalley, Stephanie. *Myths from Mesopotamia: Creation, the Flood, Gilgamesh, and Others*. Oxford: Oxford University Press, 1989.

De Ruyt, Franz. *Charun, démon étrusque de la mort*. Etudes de philologie, d'archéologie, et d'histoire anciennes, 1. Rome: Institut historique belge, 1934.

Desmouliez, André. "Cupidité, ambition, et crainte de la mort chez Lucrèce (*De R.N.* III, 59–93)." *Latomus* 17 (1958): 317–23.

Dieterich, Albrecht. *Nekyia: Beiträge zur Erklärung der neuentdeckten Petrusapokalypse*. Leipzig: Teubner, 1893.

Diogenes Laertius, *Lives of Eminent Philosophers*. Trans. Robert D. Hicks. 2 vols. Loeb Classical Library. Cambridge: Harvard University Press, 1966.

Dowden, Ken. "Grades in the Eleusinian Mysteries." *Revue de l'histoire des religions* 197 (1980): 409–27.

Edwards, M. J. "Treading the Aether: Lucretius, *De Rerum Natura* 1.62–79." *Classical Quarterly* 40 (1990): 465–69.

Eliade, Mircea. *A History of Religious Ideas*. Trans. Willard R. Trask. Vol. 1: *From the Stone Age to the Eleusinian Mysteries*. Chicago: University of Chicago Press, 1978.

Festus, Sextus Pompeius. Ed. W. M. Lindsay, in *Glossaria Latina*, 4.93–467. Paris: Belles Lettres, 1930.

Finazzo, Giancarlo. *La realtà di mondo nella visione cosmogonica esiodea*. Rome: Atenea, 1971.

Finucane, R. C. *Appearances of the Dead: A Cultural History of Ghosts*. London: Junction Books, 1982.

Foucart, Paul. *Les mystères d'Eleusis*. Paris: A. Picard, 1914. Rpt. New York: Arno, 1975.

Garland, Robert. *The Greek Way of Death*. Ithaca: Cornell University Press, 1985.

Gerould, Gordon Hall. *The Grateful Dead: The History of a Folk Story*. Publications of the Folk-lore Society, 60. Nendeln, Liechtenstein: Kraus Rpt., 1967.

Gigon, Olof. "Die Erneuerung der Philosophie in der Zeit Ciceros." *Entretiens Fondation Hardt* 3 (1955): 25–59.

Goar, R. J. *Cicero and the State Religion*. Amsterdam: Hakkert, 1972.

Görler, Woldemar. *Untersuchungen zu Ciceros Philosophie.* Bibliothek der klassischen Altertumswissenschaften. 2d ser. Vol. 50. Heidelberg: Winter, 1974.

Graves, Robert. *The Greek Myths.* 2 vols. Baltimore: Penguin, 1955.

Griffiths, J. Gwyn. *The Divine Verdict: A Study of Divine Judgement in the Ancient Religions.* Studies in the History of Religions. Supplements to *Numen,* 52. Leiden: Brill, 1991.

Guthrie, W. K. C. *The Greeks and Their Gods.* Boston: Beacon, 1950.

Handwörterbuch des deutschen Aberglaubens. 10 vols. Ed. Eduard Hoffmann-Krayer and Hanns Bächtold-Stäubli. Berlin: de Gruyter, 1930–31.

Hani, Jean. *La religion égyptienne dans la pensée de Plutarque.* Paris: Belles Lettres, 1976.

Hastings, James, ed. *Encyclopaedia of Religion and Ethics.* 13 vols. Edinburgh: T. and T. Clark; New York: Scribner's, 1908–27.

Heitsch, Ernst. *Hesiod.* Wege der Forschung, 44. Darmstadt: Wissenschaftliche Buchgesellschaft, 1966.

Helm, Rudolf. *Lucian und Menipp.* Leipzig, 1906. Rpt. Hildesheim: Olms, 1967.

Herodotus. *The Histories.* Trans. Aubrey de Selincourt. Harmondsworth: Penguin, 1954.

———. [Works]. Trans. A. D. Godley. 4 vols. Rev. ed. Loeb Classical Library. Cambridge: Harvard University Press, 1922–81.

Hesiod. *Hesiod, the Homeric Hymns, and Homerica.* Trans. H. G. Evelyn-White. Loeb Classical Library. Cambridge: Harvard University Press, 1982.

———. *Theogony.* Trans. Norman O. Brown. New York: Bobbs-Merrill, 1953.

Hock, Ronald F. "Lazarus and Micyllus: Greco-Roman Backgrounds to Luke 16:19–31." *Journal of Biblical Literature* 106 (1987): 447–63.

Homer. *The Iliad.* Trans. Richmond Lattimore. Chicago: University of Chicago Press, 1951.

———. *The Odyssey.* Trans. Richmond Lattimore. New York: Harper and Row, 1967.

Hornung, Erik. *Aegyptische Unterweltsbücher.* 2d ed. Zurich: Artemis, 1984.

———. *Altägyptische Höllenvorstellungen.* Abhandlungen der Sächsischen Akademie der Wissenschaften zu Leipzig, Philologisch-Historische Klasse, 59. 3. Berlin, Akademie, 1968.

———. *Das Grab Sethos' I.* Zurich: Artemis, 1991.

———. ed. *Das Amduat.* Die Schrift des verborgenen Raumes, Ägyptologische Abhandlungen, 7. Wiesbaden: Harrassowitz, 1963–67.

Hornung, Erik, Andreas Brodbeck, and Elisabeth Staehelin, eds. *Das Buch von den Pforten des Jenseits: Nach den Versionen des Neuen Reiches.* Aegyptiaca helvetica, 7–8. Geneva: Belles-Lettres, 1979–80.

Hutter, Manfred. *Altorientalische Vorstellungen von der Unterwelt.* Orbis biblicus et orientalis, 63. Freiburg, Switzerland: Universitätsverlag; Göttingen: Vandenhoeck und Ruprecht, 1985.

Janko, Richard. *Homer, Hesiod, and the Hymns: Diachronic Development in Epic Diction.* Cambridge: Cambridge University Press, 1982.

Jones, Roger Miller. *The Platonism of Plutarch and Selected Papers.* Menasha, Wis.: Banta, 1916. Rpt. New York: Garland, 1980.

Kajanto, Iiro. *Classical and Christian: Studies in the Latin Epitaphs of Medieval and Renaissance Rome.* Annales Academiae Scientiarum Fennicae, ser. B, vol. 203. Helsinki: Suomalainen Tiedeakatemia, 1980.

Keller, Mara Lynn. "The Eleusinian Mysteries of Demeter and Persephone: Fertility, Sexuality, and Rebirth." *Journal of Feminist Studies in Religion* 4 (1988): 27–54.

Kerényi, Karl. *Eleusis: Archetypal Image of Mother and Daughter.* Trans. Ralph Manheim. New York: Pantheon Books, 1967.

Kleijwegt, A. J. "Philosophischer Gehalt und persönliche Stellungnahme in Tusc. I, 9–81." *Mnemosyne* 4th ser., 19 (1966): 359–88.

Lamberton, Robert. *Hesiod.* New Haven: Yale University Press, 1988.

Lemke, Dietrich. *Die Theologie Epikurs.* Munich: Beck, 1973.

Lévy, Isidore. *La légende de Pythagore de Grèce en Palestine.* Bibliothèque de l'Ecole des hautes études . . . sciences historiques et philologiques, 250. Paris: Champion, 1927.

Lewis, Charleton T., and Charles Short, eds. *A Latin Dictionary.* Rev. ed. Oxford: Clarendon Press, 1958.

Liljeblad, Sven. *Die Tobiasgeschichte und andere Märchen mit toten Helfern.* Diss. Lund: P. Lindstedts Univ.-Bokhandel, 1927.

Limón, José E. "*La Llorona*, the Third Legend of Greater Mexico: Cultural Symbols, Women, and the Political Unconscious." *Renato Rosaldo Lecture Series* 2 (1984–85): 59–93.

Lortie, Paul Eugène. "Crainte anxieuse des enfers chez Lucrèce: Prologomènes." *Phoenix* 8 (1954): 47–63.

Luce, T. J. *Livy: The Composition of His History.* Princeton: Princeton University Press, 1977.

Lucian. [Works]. Trans. A. M. Harmon, K. Kilburn, and M. D. MacLeod. 8 vols. Loeb Classical Library. London: Heinemann; New York: Putnam's, 1913–67.

MacKendrick, Paul. *The Philosophical Books of Cicero.* New York: St. Martin's, 1989.

Macrobius, Ambrosius Aurelius Theodosius. *Saturnalia.* Ed. Jacob Willis. Bibliotheca teubneriana. Leipzig: Teubner, 1963.

Mitsis, Phillip. *Epicurus' Ethical Theory: The Pleasures of Invulnerability.* Cornell Studies in Classical Philology, 48. Ithaca: Cornell University Press, 1988.

Morris, Ian. "Attitudes toward Death in Archaic Greece." *Classical Antiquity* 8 (1989): 296–320.

——. *Burial and Ancient Society. The Rise of the Greek City-State.* New Studies in Archaeology. Cambridge: Cambridge University Press, 1987.

Mylonas, George Emmanuel. *Eleusis and the Eleusinian Mysteries.* Princeton: Princeton University Press, 1961.

Norden, Eduard. *P. Vergilius Maro "Aeneis" Buch VI.* 4th ed. Stuttgart: Teubner, 1957.

Oberhuber, Karl, ed. *Das Gilgamesch-Epos.* Wege der Forschung, 215. Darmstadt: Wissenschaftliche Buchgesellschaft, 1977.

Oxford Classical Dictionary. 2d ed., by N. G. L. Hammond and H. H. Scullard. Oxford: Clarendon Press, 1970.

Panagiotou, Konstantinos St. *Die ideale Form der Polis bei Homer und Hesiod.*
Bochum, Germany: Studienverlag Dr. N. Brockmeyer, 1983.

Pauly, August Friedrich von. *Der kleine Pauly: Lexikon der Antike*, based on
Pauly's Realencyclopädie der classischen Alterumswissenschaft, ed. Konrat
Ziegler with the participation of many expert scholars. Stuttgart: A.
Druckenmüller, 1964–75.

———. *Paulys Real-encyclopädie der classischen Altertumswissenschaft.*
New revision begun by Georg Wissowa, Wilhelm Kroll, and Karl Mittelhaus.
34 vols. plus 15 vols. of supplements. Stuttgart: Metzler, 1893–1980.

Pausanias. *Description of Greece.* Trans. William H. S. Jones. 5 vols. Loeb
Classical Library. Cambridge: Harvard University Press, 1954.

Phlegon of Tralles. *De mirabilibus and longaeuis libellus.* Trans. Guilielmus
Xylandrus. In Antoninus Liberalis, *Transformationum congeries.* Basel: Thomas
Guarinus, 1568.

Pindar. *The Odes.* Trans. Sir John Sandys. Loeb Classical Library. London:
Heinemann, 1915.

Plato. *The Collected Dialogues.* Ed. Edith Hamilton and Huntington Cairns.
Bollingen Series, 71. Princeton: Princeton University Press, 1961.

Plischke, Hans. *Die Sage vom wilden Heere im deutschen Volke.* Diss. Leipzig:
Offenhauer, 1914.

Plutarch. *De Iside et Osiride.* Ed. J. Gwyn Griffiths. Cardiff: University of Wales
Press, 1970.

———. *Lives.* 11 vols. Trans. Bernadotte Perrin. Loeb Classical Library. Cambridge:
Harvard University Press, 1958–62.

———. *Moralia.* 15 vols. Trans. Phillip H. de Lacy and Benedict Einarson. Loeb
Classical Library. London: Heinemann, 1959.

———. "Sur les délais de la justice divine." Trans. Robert Klaerr and Yvonne
Vernière, 89–225. In *Oeuvres morales*, vol. 7, pt. 2. Collection des universités
de France. Paris: Belles Lettres, 1974.

Price-Wallach, Barbara. *Lucretius and the Diatribe against the Fear of Death: "De
Rerum Natura" III 830–1094.* Supplement to *Mnemosyne*, 40. Leiden: Brill,
1976.

Pritchard, James B. *Ancient Near Eastern Texts Relating to the Old Testament.*
3d ed. Princeton: Princeton University Press, 1969.

Rohde, Erwin. *Psyche: The Cult of Souls and Belief in Immortality among the
Greeks.* London: Routledge and Kegan Paul, 1925.

———. "Zu den Mirabilia des Phlegon," *Rheinisches Museum für Philologie* 32
(1877): 329–39.

Roscher, Wilhelm Heinrich. *Ausführliches Lexikon der griechischen und
römischen Mythologie.* 6 vols. and 4 supplements. Leipzig: Teubner, 1884–
1937.

Rose, Herbert Jennings. *A Handbook of Greek Mythology.* New York: Dutton,
1959.

Rumpf, Ewald. *Das Muttertrauma in der griechischen Mythologie: Eine
psychologische Interpretation der "Theogonia" von Hesiod.* Frankfurt am
Main: Peter Lang, 1985.

Sabbatucci, Dario. *La religione di Roma antica, dal calendario festivo all'ordine cosmico.* Milan: Mondadori, 1988.

Salem, Jean. *La mort n'est rien pour nous: Lucrèce et l'éthique.* Bibliothèque d'histoire de la philosophie. Paris: Vrin, 1990.

Schneider, Vera. *Gilgamesch.* Zurich: Origo, 1967.

Segal, Charles. *Lucretius on Death and Anxiety: Poetry and Philosophy in "De Rerum Natura."* Princeton: Princeton University Press, 1990.

Sladek, William. "Inanna's Descent to the Netherworld." Ph.D. diss., Johns Hopkins University, 1974. Ann Arbor, Mich.: University Microfilms International, 1974.

Spronk, Klaas. *Beatific Afterlife in Ancient Israel and in the Ancient Near East.* Alter Orient und Altes Testament. Kevelaer: Butzon und Bercker; Neukirchen-Vluyn: Neukirchener Verlag, 1986.

Tarrant, R. J. "Aeneas and the Gates of Sleep," *Classical Philology* 77 (1982): 51–55.

Terpening, Ronnie H. *Charon and the Crossing: Ancient, Medieval, and Renaissance Transformations of a Myth.* Lewisburg, Pa.: Bucknell University Press, 1985.

Tigay, Jeffrey H. *The Evolution of the Gilgamesh Epic.* Philadelphia: University of Pennsylvania Press, 1982.

Van den Bruwaene, Martin. *La théologie de Cicéron.* Louvain: Bureaux de recueil, Bibliothèque de l'université, 1937.

Vermeule, Emily. *Aspects of Death in Early Greek Art and Poetry.* Berkeley: University of California Press, 1979.

Virgil. *Aeneid.* Trans. W. F. Jackson Knight. Baltimore: Penguin, 1956.

——. *Aeneid.* Trans. Allen Mandelbaum. Berkeley: University of California Press. 1971.

Weniger, Ludwig. "A. Feralis exercitus," *Archiv für Religionswissenschaft* 9 (1906): 201–47; "B. Der Weisse Heer der Phöker," ibid., 223–47; 10 (1907): 61–81 and 229–56.

West, Martin L. *The Orphic Poems.* Oxford: Clarendon, 1983.

Zandee, Jan. *Death as an Enemy according to Ancient Egyptian Conceptions.* New York: Arno Press, 1977.

Zeller, Eduard. *Outlines of the History of Greek Philosophy.* 13th ed. Rev. by Wilhelm Nestle (1931). Trans. L. R. Palmer. Cleveland: World, 1964.

Zuntz, Günther. *Persephone: Three Essays on Religion and Thought in Magna Graecia.* Oxford: Clarendon Press, 1971.

PART II. *The Afterlife in Ancient Judaism*

Systematic Commentaries on the Bible

(Commentaries covering both the Hebrew Bible and the New Testament are listed here.)

The Anchor Bible. 44 vols. Garden City, N.Y.: Doubleday, 1964–91.

Dictionary of the Bible. Ed. James Hastings. 5 vols. New York: Charles Scribner's Sons, 1900.

The *Expositor's Bible Commentary*. Ed. Frank E. Gaebelein. Grand Rapids,
Mich.: Zondervan, 1976–91.
Harper's Bible Commentary. Ed. James L. Mays. San Francisco: Harper and Row,
1988.
The International Bible Commentary. Ed. F. F. Bruce. Rev. ed. London: M.
Pickering; Grand Rapids, Mich.: Zondervan, 1986.
*The International Critical Commentary on the Holy Scriptures of the Old and
New Testaments*. Ed. Samuel Rolles Driver, Alfred Plummer, and Charles
Augustus Briggs. 48 vols. to date. Edinburgh: T. and T. Clark, 1895–.
The Interpreter's Bible. 12 vols. New York: Abingdon-Cokesbury, 1951–57.
The Interpreter's Dictionary of the Bible. 4 vols. Nashville: Abingdon, 1976.
The Jerome Biblical Commentary. Ed. Raymond E. Brown, Joseph A. Fitzmyer,
and Roland E. Murphy. Englewood Cliffs, N.J.: Prentice-Hall, 1968.
A New Catholic Commentary on Holy Scripture. Ed. Reginald C. Fuller. Old
Testament ed. Leonard Johnston. New Testament ed. Conleth Kearns. New and
fully revised ed. London: Nelson, 1969.
The New Jerome Biblical Commentary. Ed. Raymond E. Brown, Joseph A.
Fitzmyer, Roland E. Murphy. Englewood Cliffs, N.J.: Prentice-Hall, 1990.
The New Oxford Annotated Bible, Revised Standard Version. Ed. Herbert G.
May and Bruce M. Metzger. New York: Oxford University Press, 1973.
Peake's Commentary on the Bible. General ed. and New Testament ed.: Matthew
Black. Old Testament ed.: H. H. Rowley. London: T. Nelson, 1962.
Theological Dictionary of the Old Testament. Ed. G. Johannes Botterweck and
Helmer Ringgren. Rev. ed. 5 vols. Grand Rapids, Mich.: Eerdmans, 1977.
Torch Bible Commentaries. 24 Vols. London: SCM, 1949–73.

Books and Articles

Bailey, L. R. "Gehenna: The Topography of Hell." *Biblical Archeologist* 49
(1986): 187–91.
Bampfylde, Gillian. "The Similitudes of Enoch: Historical Allusions." *Journal for
the Study of Judaism in the Persian, Hellenistic, and Roman Periods* 15 (1984):
9–31.
Barth, Christoph F. *Die Errettung vom Tode in den individuellen klage- und
Dankliedern des Alten Testaments*. Zollikon, Switzerland: Evangelischer Verlag,
1947.
Bauckham, Richard J. "Early Jewish Visions of Hell." *Journal of Theological
Studies* 41 (1990): 355–85.
Beckwith, Roger T. "The Pre-history and Relationships of the Pharisees,
Sadducees, and Essenes: A Tentative Reconstruction." *Revue de Qumrân*,
no. 41 (1982): 3–46.
Beer, Georg. "Der biblische Hades." *Festschrift Holtzmann*, 1–29. Tübingen:
J. C. B. Mohr, 1902.
Bewer, J. A. *The Literature of the Old Testament*. 3d ed. rev. by E. G. Kraeling.
New York: Columbia University Press, 1962.

Black, Matthew, ed. *The Book of Enoch or I Enoch: A New English Edition.* Studia in Veteris Testamenti pseudepigrapha, 7. Leiden: Brill, 1985.

Bogaert, P.-M. "Les trois rédactions conservées et la forme originale de l'envoi du Cantique de Moïse, Deut. 32.43." In *Das Deuteronomium: Entstehung, Gestalt, und Botschaft,* ed. Norbert Lohfink, 329–40. Bibliotheca ephemeridum theologicarum lovaniensium, 68. Leuven: University Press, 1985.

Bowker, John. *The Targums and Rabbinic Literature: An Introduction to Jewish Interpretations of Scripture.* London: Cambridge University Press, 1969.

Braulik, Georg. "Zur Abfolge der Gesetze in Deuteronomium 16.18–21.23: Weitere Beobachtungen." *Biblica* 69 (1988): 63–92.

Brooks, Roger, and John J. Collins, eds. *Hebrew Bible or Old Testament? Studying the Bible in Judaism and Christianity.* Christianity and Judaism in Antiquity, 5. Notre Dame, Ind.: University of Notre Dame Press, 1990.

Cazelles, H. "Le jugement des morts en Israël." In *Le jugement des morts,* 103–142. Sources Orientales, 4. Paris: Seuil, 1961.

Charles, R. H. *Eschatology, the Doctrine of a Future Life in Israel, Judaism, and Christianity: A Critical History.* New York: Schocken Books, 1963.

——, ed. *The Apocrypha and Pseudepigrapha of the Old Testament in English.* 2 vols. Oxford: Clarendon Press, 1968.

——, ed. and trans. *The Book of Enoch or 1 Enoch.* 2d ed. Oxford: Clarendon Press, 1912.

Charlesworth, James H., ed. *Old Testament Pseudepigrapha.* 2 vols. Garden City, N.Y.: Doubleday, 1983–85.

Childs, Bernard S. *Introduction to the Old Testament as Scripture.* Philadelphia: Fortress Press, 1979.

Coggins, R. J. *Introducing the Old Testament.* Oxford: Oxford University Press, 1989.

Coppens, Joseph. "L'élu et les élus dans les Ecritures saintes et les écrits de Qumrân." *Ephemerides theologicae lovanienses* 57 (1981): 120–24.

Dahood, Mitchell. *Psalms: Introduction, Translation, and Notes.* In *The Anchor Bible.* Vols. 16–17A. Garden City, N.Y.: Doubleday, 1966–70.

Day, John. *Molech: A God of Human Sacrifice in the Old Testament.* Cambridge: Cambridge University Press, 1989.

De Jonge, Marinus, comp. *Outside the Old Testament.* Cambridge Commentaries on Writings of the Jewish and Christian World, 200 B.C. to A.D. 200. Cambridge: Cambridge University Press, 1985.

DiLella, A. A. "The Problem of Retribution in the Wisdom Literature." In *Rediscovery of Scripture: Biblical Theology Today,* 109–28. Report of the 46th Annual Meeting of the Franciscan Educational Conference, August 8–11, 1965. Burlington, Wis.: Franciscan Educational Conference, 1967.

Dion, Paul E. "Deutéronome 21:1–9: Miroir du développement légal et religieux d'Israël." *Studies in Religion/Sciences Religieuses* 11 (1988): 13–22.

Eichrodt, Walther. *Ezekiel: A Commentary.* Philadelphia: Westminster, 1970.

——. *Theology of the Old Testament.* 2 vols. Philadelphia: Westminster, 1967.

Eissfeldt, Otto. *The Old Testament, an Introduction: The History of the Formation of the Old Testament.* Oxford: Blackwell, 1962.

Encyclopaedia judaica. 16 vols. Jerusalem: Encyclopaedia judaica, 1978.

Evans, Carl. D., et al., eds. *Scripture in Context: Essays on the Comparative Method.* Pittsburgh: Pickwick Press, 1980.

Fackenheim, Emil L. *The Jewish Bible after the Holocaust: A Rereading.* Manchester: Manchester University Press, 1990.

Finkel, Avraham Yakov. *The Great Torah Commentators.* Northvale, N.J.: J. Aronson, 1990.

Fishbane, Michael. *Biblical Interpretation in Ancient Israel.* Oxford: Clarendon Press; New York, Oxford University Press, 1985.

Fohrer, Georg, and Kurt Galling. *Ezechiel.* Handbuch zum Alten Testament, 13. Tübingen: Mohr, 1955.

Forsyth, Neil. "Rebellion and Lust: The Watcher Angels in the Aramaic Enoch Books." In Forsyth, *The Old Enemy: Satan and the Combat Myth,* 160–181. Princeton: Princeton University Press, 1987.

Fox, Samuel J. *Hell in Jewish Literature.* Northbrook, Ill.: Whitehall, 1972.

Friedman, Richard Elliott. *The Exile and Biblical Narrative: The Formation of the Deuteronomistic and Priestly Works.* Harvard Semitic Monographs, 22. Chico, Calif.: Scholars Press, 1981.

Friedman, R. Z. "Evil and Moral Agency." *International Journal for the Philosophy of Religion* 24 (1989): 3–30.

Fröhlich, Ida. "Les enseignements des Veilleurs dans la tradition de Qumrân." *Revue de Qumrân* 13 (1988): 177–87.

Gaster, Moses. "Hebrew Visions of Hell and Paradise." *Journal of the Royal Asiatic Society of Great Britain and Ireland* (1893): 571–611.

Gaster, Theodor H., trans. *The Dead Sea Scriptures.* Garden City, N.Y.: Doubleday, 1976.

Geyer, John B. "Mythology and Culture in the Oracles against the Nations." *Vetus testamentum* 36 (1986): 129–45.

Gowan, Donald E. *Eschatology in the Old Testament.* Philadelphia: Fortress Press, 1986.

Grabbe, L. L. "The Scapegoat Tradition: A Study in Early Jewish Interpretation." *Journal for the Study of Judaism in the Persian, Hellenistic, and Roman Periods* 18 (1987): 152–67.

Gunneweg, Antonius H. J. *Vom Verstehen des Alten Testaments: Eine Hermeneutik.* Göttingen: Vandenhoek und Ruprecht, 1977.

Hanson, Paul D. "Rebellion in Heaven, Azazel, and Euhemeristic Heroes in I Enoch 6–11." *Journal of Biblical Literature* 96 (1977): 195–233.

Hartley, John E. *The Book of Job.* The New International Commentary on the Old Testament, ed. R. K. Harrison. Grand Rapids, Mich.: Eerdmans, 1988.

Hartman, Louis F., and A. A. DiLella. *The Book of Daniel.* Vol. 23 of *The Anchor Bible.* Garden City, N.Y.: Doubleday, 1978.

Hayes, John H. *An Introduction to Old Testament Study.* Nashville: Abingdon, 1979.

Heider, George C. *The Cult of Molek: A Reassessment.* Supplement to *Journal for the Study of the Old Testament,* 43; Sheffield, England: JSOT, 1985.

Himmelfarb, Martha. *Tours of Hell*. Philadelphia: University of Pennsylvania Press, 1983.

Hubbard, Robert L. "Dynamistic and Legal Processes in Psalm 7." *Zeitschrift für alttestamentliche Wissenschaft* 94 (1982): 267–79.

The Jewish Encyclopedia. Ed. Cyrus Adler. 12 vols. New York: Funk and Wagnalls, 1903–6.

Knight, Douglas A., and Gene M. Tucker, eds. *The Hebrew Bible and Its Modern Interpreters*. Chico, Calif.: Scholars Press, 1985.

Krasovec, Joze. *La justice (Sdq) de Dieu dans la Bible hébraïque et l'interprétation juive et chrétienne*. Orbis biblicus et orientalis, 76. Freiburg, Switzerland: Univerversitätsverlag, 1989.

Krenzer, Siegfried. *Die Frühgeschichte Israels in Bekenntnis und Verkündigung das Alten Testaments*. Beiheft zur Zeitschrift für die alttestamentliche Wissenschaft, 18. Berlin: de Gruyter, 1989.

Laffey, Alice L. *An Introduction to the Old Testament: A Feminist Perspective*. Philadelphia: Fortress Press, 1988.

Levine, Baruch A., and Jean-Michel de Tarragon. "Dead Kings and Rephaim: The Patrons of the Ugaritic Dynasty, with Text and English Translation of KTU 1.161." *Journal of the American Oriental Society* 104 (1984): 649–59.

Lewis, Theodore J. *Cults of the Dead in Ancient Israel and Ugarit*. Harvard Semitic Monographs, 39. Atlanta, Ga.: Scholars Press, 1989.

L'Heureux, Conrad. "The Ugaritic and Biblical Rephaim." *Harvard Theological Review* 67 (1974): 265–74.

Lods, Adolphe. *La croyance à la vie future et le culte des morts dans l'antiquité israélite*. Paris: Fischbacher, 1906.

Loretz, O. "Vom kanaanitischen Totenkult zur judäischen Patriarchen- und Elternehrung." *Jahrbuch für Anthropologie und Religionsgeschichte* 3 (1978): 149–204.

Luyten, J. "Primeval and Eschatological Overtones in the Song of Moses, Deut. 32.1–43." In *Das Deuteronomium: Entstehung, Gestalt, und Botschaft*, ed. Norbert Lohfink, 341–47. Bibliotheca ephemeridum theologicarum lovaniensium, 68. Leuven: University Press, 1985.

Maag, Victor. "Tod und Jenseits nach dem Alten Testament." *Schweizerische theologische Umschau* 34 (1964): 17–37.

Mannati, Marina. "Le Psaume XI." *Vetus testamentum* 29 (1979): 222–27.

Martínez, Florentino García, and E. J. C. Tigchelaar. "The *Books of Enoch* (*I Enoch*) and the Aramaic Fragments from Qumran." *Revue de Qumrân* 14 (1989): 131–46, 149–74.

Mason, Steve. *Flavius Josephus on the Pharisees*. Studia post-Biblica, 39. Leiden: Brill, 1991.

Milik, J. T., ed., with the collaboration of Matthew Black. *The Books of Enoch: Aramaic Fragments of Qumran Cave 4*. Oxford: Clarendon Press, 1976.

Molenberg, Corrie. "A Study of the Roles of Shemihaza and Asael in *I Enoch* 6–11." *Journal of Jewish Studies* 35 (1984): 136–46.

Mulder, Martin Jan, ed. *Mikra: Text, Translation, Reading, and Interpretation of the Hebrew Bible in Ancient Judaism and Early Christianity*. Section 1: The

Literature of the Jewish People in the Period of the Second Temple and the Talmud; section 2: Compendia rerum Iudaicarum ad Novum Testamentum. Assen: Van Gorcum, 1990.

Neusner, Jacob. *Formative Judaism: Religious, Historical, and Literary Studies.* 5th series: Revisioning the Written Records of a Nascent Religion. Brown Judaic Studies, 91. Chico, Calif.: Scholars Press, 1985.

——. *Foundations of Judaism.* Philadelphia: Fortress Press, 1989.

Newsom, Carol A. "The Development of *1 Enoch* 6–19: Cosmology and Judgment." *Catholic Biblical Quarterly* 42 (1980): 310–29.

Nickelsburg, George W. E. "Apocalyptic and Myth in *1 Enoch* 6–11." *Journal of Biblical Literature* 96 (1977): 383–405.

——. "*1 Enoch* and Qumran Origins: The State of the Question and Some Prospects for Answers." *Society of Biblical Literature Seminar Papers* 25 (1986): 341–60.

——. *Resurrection, Immortality, and Eternal Life in Intertestamental Judaism.* Harvard Theological Studies, 26. Cambridge: Harvard University Press, 1972.

Niehr, Herbert. *Der höchste Gott: Alttestamentlicher JHWH-Glaube im Kontext syrisch-kanaanäischer Religion des 1. Jahrhunderts vor Christi.* Beiheft zur Zeitschrift für die alttestamentliche Wissenschaft, 190. Berlin: de Gruyter, 1990.

Nötscher, Friedrich. *Altorientalischer und alttestamentlicher Auferstehungsglauben.* 1926. Rpt. Darmstadt: Wissenschaftliche Buchgesellschaft, 1980.

Oesterley, W. O. E., and Theodore H. Robinson. *Hebrew Religion: Its Origins and Development.* 2d ed. London: Society for Promoting Christian Knowledge; New York: Macmillan, 1961.

Ogden, Graham S. "Qoheleth IX 1–16" *Vetus testamentum* 32 (1982): 158–69.

Propp, William, Baruch Halpern, and David Noel Friedman, eds. *The Hebrew Bible and Its Interpreters.* Winona Lake, Ind.: Eisenbrauns, 1990.

Rankin, O. S. *Israel's Wisdom Literature.* 1936. Rpt. New York: Schocken, 1969.

Redditt, Paul L. "Once Again, the City in Isaiah 24–27." *Hebrew Annual Review* 10 (1986): 317–35.

Reid, Stephen B. "The Structure of the Ten-Week Apocalypse and the Book of Dream Visions." *Journal for the Study of Judaism in the Persian, Hellenistic, and Roman Periods* 16 (1985): 189–201.

Rodd, Cyril S. *The Book of Job.* Philadelphia: Trinity Press International, 1990.

Rost, Leonhard. *Judaism outside the Hebrew Canon: An Introduction to the Documents.* Nashville: Abingdon, 1976.

Rowley, H. H. *The Faith of Israel: Aspects of Old Testament Thought.* Philadelphia: Westminster, 1956.

Russel, David Syme. *The Old Testament Pseudepigrapha: Patriarchs and Prophets in Early Judaism.* London: SCM, 1987.

Scharbert, Josef. *Nachtrag zum Neudruck.* In Friedrich Nötscher, *Altorientalischer und alttestamentlicher Auferstehungsglauben,* 349–97. Darmstadt: Wissenschaftliche Buchgesellschaft, 1980.

Schmidt, Werner H. *Einführung in das Alte Testament.* Berlin: de Gruyter, 1979.

Schoors, Anton. "Koheleth: A Perspective of Life after Death?" *Ephemerides theologicae Lovanienses* 61 (1985): 295–303.

Segal, Moses Hirsch. *The Pentateuch: Its Composition and Its Authorship and Other Biblical Studies.* Jerusalem: Magnes Press, Hebrew University, 1967.

Silver, Daniel Jeremy. *The Story of Scripture: From Oral Tradition to the Written Word.* New York: Basic Books, 1990.

Smith, Mark S. *The Early History of God: Yahweh and the Other Deities in Ancient Israel.* San Francisco: Harper and Row, 1990.

Smith, Morton. " A Note on Burning Babies." *Journal of the American Oriental Society* 95 (1975): 477–79.

Snaith, Norman H. "Isaiah 40–66: A Study of the Teaching of the Second Isaiah and Its Consequences." In *Studies on the Second Part of the Book of Isaiah.* Supplements to *Vetus testamentum*, 14, 135–264. Leiden: Brill, 1967.

Soggin, J. Alberto. *Introduction to the Old Testament: From Its Origins to the Closing of the Alexandrian Canon.* 3d ed. Louisville, Ky.: Westminster, John Knox Press, 1989.

Spronk, Klaas. *Beatific Afterlife in Ancient Israel and in the Ancient Near East.* Alter Orient und Altes Testament, 219. Kevelaer, Germany: Butzon und Bercker, 1986.

Starobinski-Safran, Esther. *Le buisson et la voix: Exégèse et pensée juives.* Paris: A. Michel, 1987.

Stone, Michael E. "The *Book of Enoch* and Judaism in the Third Century B.C.E." *Catholic Biblical Quarterly* 40 (1978): 479–92.

Suelzer, Alexa, and John S. Kselman. "Modern Old Testament Criticism." In *The New Jerome Biblical Commentary*, 1113–29. Englewood Cliffs, N.J.: Prentice-Hall, 1990.

Suter, David W. "Weighed in the Balance: The Similitudes of Enoch in Recent Discussion." *Religious Studies Review* 7 (1981): 217–21.

Tromp, Nicholas J. *Primitive Conceptions of Death and the Nether World in the Old Testament.* Biblica et orientalia, 21. Rome: Pontifical Biblical Institute, 1969.

Tsevat, Matitiahu. *The Meaning of the Book of Job and Other Biblical Studies: An Essay on the Literature and Religion of the Hebrew Bible.* New York: Ktav, 1980.

Vanderkam, James C. "Studies in the Apocalypse of Weeks: *1 Enoch* 93:1–10, 91:11–17." *Catholic Biblical Quarterly* 46 (1984): 511–23.

Von Rad, Gerhard. *Old Testament Theology.* 2 vols. New York: Harper and Row, 1962.

Walton, John H. *Ancient Israelite Literature in Its Cultural Context: A Survey of Parallels between Biblical and Ancient Near Eastern Texts.* Grand Rapids, Mich.: Regency Reference Library, 1989.

Walton, Robert, ed. *A Basic Introduction to the Old Testament.* London: SCM, 1980.

Weinfeld, Mosche. "The Worship of Molech and of the Queen of Heaven and Its Background." *Ugarit-Forshungen* 4 (1972): 133–54.

Weingreen, Jacob. *Introduction to the Critical Study of the Text of the Hebrew Bible.* Oxford: Oxford University Press, 1982.

Wright, David P. "Deuteronomy 21:1–9 as a Rite of Elimination." *Catholic Biblical Quarterly* 49 (1987): 387–403.

Zeitlin, Irving M. *Ancient Judaism: Biblical Criticism from Max Weber to the present.* New York: Polity, 1984.

Zimmerli, Walther. *Ezekiel: A Commentary on the Book of the Prophet Ezekiel.* 2 vols. Hermeneia. Philadelphia: Fortress Press, 1979–83.

PART III. *Hell in the New Testament*

Systematic Commentaries on the New Testament

Augsburg Commentary on the New Testament. 12 vols. to date. Minneapolis, Minn.: Augsburg, 1980–.

Dictionnaire de théologie catholique. 16 vols. in 28. Paris: Librairie Letouzey et Ané, 1903–72.

Exegetical Dictionary of the New Testament. Ed. Horst Balz and Gerhard Schneider. Grand Rapids, Mich.: Eerdmans, 1990.

New International Greek Commentary. Exeter: Paternoster Press; Grand Rapids, Mich.: Eerdmans, 1978.

Theological Dictionary of the New Testament. Ed. Gerhard Kittel and Geoffrey W. Bromiley. 10 vols. Grand Rapids, Mich.: Eerdmans, 1964–76.

Books and Articles

Agbanou, V. K. "Le discours eschatologique de Matthieu 24–25: Tradition et rédaction." In *Etudes bibliques*, new series, no. 2.; Paris: Lecoffre, 1983.

Betz, Hans Dieter. *Lukian von Samosata und das Neue Testament: Religionsgeschichtliche und paränetische Parallelen.* Texte und Untersuchungen zur Geschichte der altchristlichen Literatur, 76. Berlin: Akademie, 1961.

Black, C. Clifton. "Pauline Perspectives on Death in Romans 5–8." *Journal of Biblical Literature* 103 (1984): 413–33.

Brandenburger, El. *Das Recht des Weltenrichters.* Stuttgarter Bibelstudien, 99. Stuttgart: Katholisches Bibelwerk, 1980.

Brown, Schuyler. *The Origins of Christianity: A Historical Introduction to the New Testament.* Oxford: Oxford University Press, 1984.

Byrne, Brendan, S.J. "Lining Out the Righteousness of God: The Contribution of Rom. 6:11–8:13 to an Understanding of Paul's Ethical Presuppositions." *Catholic Biblical Quarterly* 43 (1981): 557–81.

Carson, D. A. "Selected Recent Studies of the Fourth Gospel." *Themelios* 14 (1989): 57–64.

Catchpole, David R. "The Poor on Earth and the Son of Man in Heaven: A Reappraisal of Matthew 25:31–46." *Bulletin of the John Rylands University Library of Manchester* 61 (1979): 355–97.

Chilton, Bruce. *Targumic Approaches to the Gospels: Essays in the Mutual Definition of Judaism and Christianity*. Lanham, Md.: University Press of America, 1986.

Cope, Lamar. "Matthew XXV:31–46: The Sheep and the Goats Reinterpreted." *Novum Testamentum* 11 (1969): 32–44.

Court, J. M. "Right and Left: The Implications for Matthew 25:31–46." *New Testament Studies* 31 (1985): 223–33.

Davies, W. D. *Jewish and Pauline Studies*. Philadelphia: Fortress Press, 1984.

———. *Paul and Rabbinic Judaism*. New ed. Philadelphia: Fortress Press, 1980.

Deming, Will. "Mark 9:42, Matthew 5:27–32, and B. Nid. 13b: A First-Century Discussion of Male Sexuality." *New Testament Studies* 39 (1990): 130–41.

Derrett, J. D. M. "Two 'Harsh' Sayings of Christ Explained." *Downside Review* 103 (1985): 218–29.

Donahue, J. R. "The Parable of the Sheep and Goats." *Theological Studies* 47 (1986): 3–31.

Donnelly, Doris. "Preaching the Hard Word." *Princeton Seminary Bulletin* 6 (1985): 135–37.

Dupont, J. *Les trois apocalypses synoptiques: Marc 13, Matthieu 24–25, Luc 21.* Lectio divina, 121. Paris: Cerf, 1985.

Ernst, Josef. *Die eschatologischen Gegenspieler in den Schriften des Neuen Testaments*. Regensburg, Germany: Friedrich Pustet, 1967.

Flusser, David. *Jewish Sources in Early Christianity*. New York: Adama Books, 1987.

Freed, Edwin D. *The New Testament: A Critical Introduction*, Belmont, Calif.: Wadsworth, 1991.

Glasson, T. Francis. "2 Corinthians 5:1–10 versus Platonism." *Scottish Journal of Theology* 43 (1990): 145–55.

Grant, Robert M. *The Formation of the New Testament* London: Hutchinson University Library, 1965.

———. *A Historical Introduction to the New Testament*. New York: Harper and Row, 1967.

Gressmann, Hugo. *Vom reichen Mann und armen Lazarus: Eine literargeschichtliche Studie*. Abhandlungen der königlich preussichen Akademie der Wissenschaften, philosophisch-historische Klasse, 7. Berlin: Königliche Akademie der Wissenschaften, 1918.

Griffiths, J. Gwynn. *The Divine Verdict: A Study of Divine Judgement in the Ancient Religions*. Studies in the History of Religions, Supplement to *Numen*, 52. Leiden: Brill, 1991.

Gundry, Robert H. "The Hellenization of Dominical Tradition and Christianization of Jewish Tradition in the Eschatology of 1–2 Thessalonians." *New Testament Studies* 33 (1987): 161–87.

Hare, D. R. A., and D. J. Harrington. "'Make Disciples of All the Gentiles' (Mt. 28.19)." *Catholic Biblical Quarterly* 37 (1975): 359–69.

Harris, Murray J. *From Grave to Glory: Resurrection in the New Testament*. Grand Rapids, Mich.: Zondervan, 1990.

Hill, C. E. "Paul's Understanding of Christ's Kingdom in I Corinthians 15:20–28." *Novum Testamentum* 30 (1988): 297–330.

Hilton, Michael. *The Gospels and Rabbinic Judaism: A Study Guide*. Hoboken, N.J.: KTAV, 1988.

Hock, Ronald F. "Lazarus and Micyllus: Greco-Roman Background to Luke 16:19–31." *Journal of Biblical Literature* 106 (1987): 447–63.

Hooker, Morna Dorothy. *Continuity and Discontinuity: Early Christianity in Its Jewish Setting*. London: Epworth Press, 1986.

Horn, Friedrich W. *Glaube und Handeln in der Theologie Lukas*. 2d ed. Göttinger theologische Arbeiten, 26. Göttingen: Vandenhoeck und Ruprecht, 1986.

Jeremias, Joachim. "Gehenna." In *Theological Dictionary of the New Testament* 1:657–58. Grand Rapids, Mich.: Eerdmans, 1964.

———. "Hades." In *Theological Dictionary of the New Testament* 1:146–49. Grand Rapids, Mich.: Eerdmans, 1964.

———. *The Parables of Jesus*. Rev. ed. New York: Scribner's, 1963.

Keener, Craig S. "Matthew 5:22 and the Heavenly Court." *Expository Times* 99 (1987): 46.

Kemper, Friedmar. "Zur literarischen Gestalt des Johannesevangeliums." *Theologische Zeitschrift* 43 (1987): 247–64.

Knox, Wilfred L. *Some Hellenistic Elements in Primitive Christianity*. London: Published for the British Academy by H. Milford, 1944.

———. *The Sources of the Synoptic Gospels*. Ed. H. Chadwick. Cambridge: Cambridge University Press, 1953–57.

Kreitzer, L. Joseph. *Jesus and God in Paul's Eschatology*. Supplement to *Journal for the Study of the New Testament*, 19. Sheffield: Sheffield Academic Press, 1987.

Lachs, Samuel Tobias. *A Rabbinic Commentary on the New Testament: The Gospels of Matthew, Mark, and Luke*. Hoboken, N.J.: KTAV, 1987.

Lambrecht, Jan. "Paul's Christological Use of Scripture in 1 Cor. 15:20–28." *New Testament Studies* 28 (1982): 502–27.

McGhee, Michael. "A Rejoinder to Two Recent Studies Dealing with 1 Thess. 4:4." *Catholic Biblical Quarterly* 51 (1989): 82–89.

McVann, Mark, ed. "The Gospel of Matthew: Current Discussions." *Listening* 24 (1989): 223–309.

Marguerat, D. *Le jugement dans l'évangile de Matthieu*. Diss. Le Monde de la Bible. Geneva: Labor et Fides, 1981.

Maspero, Gaston. *Popular Stories of Ancient Egypt*. Trans. A. S. Johns from the fourth French edition and revised by Gaston Maspero. New Hyde Park, N.Y.: University Books, 1967.

Meade, David G. *Pseudonymity and the Canon: An Investigation into the Relationship of Authorship and Authority in Jewish and Earliest Christian Tradition*. Grand Rapids, Mich.: Eerdmans, 1987.

Mearns, Christopher L. "Early Eschatological Development in Paul: The Evidence of I and II Thessalonians." *New Testament Studies* 27 (1981): 137–57.

Metzger, Bruce Manning. *The Early Versions of the New Testament: Their Origin, Transmission, and Limitations*. Oxford: Clarendon Press, 1977.

——. *New Testament Studies: Philological, Versional, and Patristic*. Leiden: Brill, 1980.

Milikowsky, Chaim. "Which Gehenna? Retribution and Eschatology in the Synoptic-Gospels and in Early Jewish Texts." *New Testament Studies* 34 (1988): 238–49.

Mulholland, M. Robert. *Revelation: Holy Living in an Unholy World*. Grand Rapids, Mich.: F. Asbury Press, 1990.

Okeke, G. E. "The After-life in Matthew as an Aspect of the Matthean Ethic." *Communio viatorum* 31 (1988): 159–68.

Onei-Bonsu, Joseph. "Does 2 Cor. 5:1–10 Teach the Reception of the Resurrection Body at the Moment of Death?" *Journal for the Study of the New Testament* 28 (1986): 81–101.

Perrin, Norman, and Dennis C. Duling. *The New Testament, an Introduction: Proclamation and Paranesis, Myth and History*. 2d ed. New York: Harcourt Brace Jovanovich, 1982.

Reicke, Bo Ivar. *The Roots of the Synoptic Gospels*. Philadelphia: Fortress Press, 1986.

Rhymer, Joseph, ed. *The Bible in Order*. Garden City, N.Y.: Doubleday, 1975.

Robinson, J. A. T. "The 'Parable' of the Sheep and the Goats." *New Testament Studies* 2 (1956): 225–37.

——. *Redating the New Testament*. London: SCM Press, 1976.

Rowland, Christopher. *Christian Origins: An Account of the Setting and Character of the Most Important Messianic Sect of Judaism*. London: SPCK, 1985.

Rubinkiewicz, Richard. "Ps. LXVIII.18 (= Eph. IV.8): Another Textual Tradition or Targum?" *Novum Testamentum* 17 (1975): 219–24.

Russell, Jeffrey Burton. *The Devil: Perceptions of Evil from Antiquity to Primitive Christianity*. Ithaca: Cornell University Press, 1977.

Schnelle, Udo. "Der erste Thessalonicherbrief und die Entstehung der paulinischen Anthropologie." *New Testament Studies* 32 (1986): 207–24.

Schoeps, H. J. *Paul: The Theology of the Apostle in the Light of Jewish Religious History*. Trans. Harold Knight. Philadelphia: Westminster, 1961.

Seccombe, D. P. *Possessions and the Poor in Luke-Acts*. Diss. Studien zum Neuen Testament und seiner Umwelt, B/6. Linz, Austria: Studien zum Neuen Testament und seiner Umwelt, 1982.

Segbroeck, Frans van. The Gospel of Luke: A Cumulative Bibliography, 1973–1988. Leuven: University Press, 1989.

Shorter, Aylward. *Revelation and Its Interpretation*. Introducing Catholic Theology, 1. London: Geoffrey Chapman, 1983.

Smith, Gary V. "Paul's Use of Psalm 68:18 in Ephesians 4:8." *Journal of the Evangelical Theological Society* 18 (1975): 181–89.

Strack, Hermann, and Paul Billerbeck. *Kommentar zum neuen Testament aus Talmud und Midrasch*. 6 vols. Munich: Beck, 1922–61.

Stuhlmann, Rainer. *Das eschatologische Maß im Neuen Testament*, Göttingen: Vandenhoeck und Ruprecht, 1983.

Stuiber, Alfred. *Refrigerium interim: Die Vorstellungen vom Zwischenzustand und die frühchristliche Grabeskunst*. Theophaneia: Beiträge zur Religions- und Kirchengeschichte des Altertums, 11. Bonn: P. Hanstein, 1957.

Sullivan, Clayton. *Rethinking Realized Eschatology*. Macon, Ga.: Mercer University Press, 1988.

Talbert, Charles H. *Reading Corinthians*. New York: Crossroads Press, 1987.

Taylor, Richard A. "The Use of Psalm 68:18 in Ephesians 4:8 in Light of the Ancient Versions." *Bibliotheca Sacra* 148 (1991): 319–36.

Teyssèdre, Bernard. *Le diable et l'enfer au temps de Jésus*. Paris: Albin Michel, 1985.

Thompson, Leonard L. *The Book of Revelation: Apocalypse and Empire*. Oxford: Oxford University Press, 1990.

Thompson, M. M. "Eternal Life in the Gospel of John." *Ex auditu* 5 (1989): 35–55.

Travis, Stephen H. *Christ and the Judgment of God: Divine Retribution in the New Testament*. Basingstoke, England: Marshall, Morgan, and Scott, 1986.

Via, Dan O. "Ethical Responsibility and Human Wholeness in Matthew 25:31–46." *Harvard Theological Review* 80 (1987): 79–100.

Vielhauer, Philipp. *Geschichte der urchristlichen Literatur: Einleitung in das Neue Testament, die Apokryphen, und die Apostolischen Väter*. Berlin: de Gruyter, 1975.

Vollenweider, Samuel. "Ich sah den Satan wie einen Blitz vom Himmel fallen (Lk. 10:18)." *Zeitschrift für neutestamentliche Wissenschaft und die Kunde der älteren Kirche* 79 (1988): 187–203.

Von Dehsen, Christian D. "Believers and Non-believers in Paul and John." *Lutheran Forum* 23 (1989): 10–14.

Von Wahlde, Urban C. "Mark 9:33–50: Discipleship, the Authority That Serves." *Biblische Zeitschrift* 29 (1985): 49–67.

Wagner, Günter, ed. *An Exegetical Bibliography of the New Testament: Matthew and Mark*. Macon, Ga.: Mercer University Press, 1983.

Wanamaker, Charles A. *The Epistles to the Thessalonians: A Commentary on the Greek Text*, New International Greek Testament Commentary. Grand Rapids, Mich.: Eerdmans, 1990.

Zorn, R. D. "II Corinthians 5:1–10: Individual Eschatology or Corporate Solidarity, Which?" *Reformed Theological Review* 48 (1989): 93–104.

PART IV. *Tensions in Early Christianity*

Althaner, Berthold. *Patrology*. New York: Herder and Herder, 1960.

Angenendt, Arnold, and Rudolf Schieffer. *Roma—Caput et Fons: Zwei Vorträge über das päpstliche Rom zwischen Altertum und Mittelalter*. Opladen: Westdeutscher Verlag, 1989.

Apocalypse of Paul. Trans. Hugo Duensing. In Edgar Hennecke and Wilhelm Schneemelcher, eds., *New Testament Apocrypha* 2:755–97. Trans. R. McL. Wilson. 2 vols. Philadelphia: Westminster, 1963.

Apocalypse of Peter. Trans. Ch. Maurer. In Edgar Hennecke and Wilhelm Schneemelcher, eds., *New Testament Apocrypha* 2:663–83. Trans. R. McL. Wilson. 2 vols. Philadelphia: Westminster, 1963.

Atwell, R. R. "From Augustine to Gregory the Great: An Evaluation of the Emergence of the Doctrine of Purgatory." *Journal of Ecclesiastical History* 38 (1987): 173–86.

Augustine. *Ad Orosium contra Priscillianistas et Origenistas.* Corpus
Christianorum, Series Latina, 49. Turnhout: Brepols, 1985.

———. "The Care to be Taken for the Dead." Trans. John A. Lacy. In *Saint Augustine: Treatises on Marriage and Other Subjects,* 349–84. Ed. Roy J. Deferrari.
The Fathers of the Church, 27. New York: Fathers of the Church, 1955.

———. *De civitate Dei, libri XXII.* Corpus Christianorum, Series Latina, 48.
Turnhout: Brepols, 1955.

———. *De Genesi ad litteram.* Corpus scriptorum ecclesiasticorum Latinorum 28.1.
Prague: Tempsky, 1894.

———. *Enarrationes in Psalmos.* Corpus Christianorum, Series Latina, 38.
Turnhout: Brepols, 1956.

———. *Enchiridion.* Corpus Christianorum, Series Latina, 46. Turnhout: Brepols,
1969.

———. Epistola 102, "Sex quaestiones contra Paganos." Corpus scriptorum
ecclesiasticorum Latinorum 34:544–78. Prague: Tempsky, 1895.

———. Epistola 164, "Ad Evodium." Corpus scriptorum ecclesiasticorum
Latinorum 44:521–41. Vienna: Tempsky, 1904.

———. *In Iohannis Evangelium.* Corpus Christianorum, Series Latina, 36.
Turnhout: Brepols, 1954.

Bardenhewer, Otto. *Geschichte der altkirchlichen Literatur.* Vol. 1. 2d ed. 1913.
Rpt. Darmstadt: Wissenschaftliche Buchgesellschaft, 1962.

Bauer, Karl. "Zu Augustins Anschauung von Fegfeuer und Teufel." *Zeitschrift für
Kirchengeschichte* 43 (1924): 351–55.

Beck, Hans-Georg. *Actus fidei: Wege zum Autodafé.* Sitzungsberichte der
bayerischen Akademie der Wissenschaften, Philosophisch-historische Klasse, 3.
Munich: Bayerische Akademie der Wissenschaften, in Kommission bei C. H.
Beck, 1987.

Benrath, Gustav Adolf. "Ablaß." In *Theologische Realenzyklopädie* 1:347–64.
Berlin: de Gruyter, 1977.

Billerbeck, Paul, and H. L. Strack. *Kommentar zum Neuen Testament aus Talmud
und Midrasch.* 6 vols. Munich: Beck, 1922–61.

Brinton, Alan. "Saint Augustine and the Problem of Deception in Religious
Persuasion." *Religious Studies* 19 (1983): 437–50.

Brown, Peter. *Augustine of Hippo: A Biography.* Berkeley: University of
California Press, 1967.

Buchholz, Dennis D. *Your Eyes Will Be Opened: A Study of the Greek (Ethiopic)
"Apocalypse of Peter."* Atlanta: Scholars, 1988.

Capp, Donald E., ed. "Symposium on Augustine's *Confessions.*" Five articles in
the *Journal for the Scientific Study of Religion* 25 (1986): 56–115.

Caesarius of Heisterbach. *Dialogus Miraculorum.* Ed. Josef Strange. 2 vols.
Cologne: Lempertz, 1851.

Chadwick, Henry. *Augustine.* Past Masters. Oxford: Oxford University Press,
1986.

———. *Heresy and Orthodoxy in the Early Church.* Collected Studies, 342.
Aldershot, Hampshire, Great Britain: Variorum, 1991.

Charlesworth, James H. *The New Testament Apocrypha and Pseudepigrapha: A Guide to Publications, with Excursuses on Apocalypses.* Chicago: American Theological Library Association; Metuchen, N.J.: Scarecrow, 1987.

——. *The Old Testament Pseudepigrapha and the New Testament: Prolegomena for the Study of Christian Origins.* Cambridge: Cambridge University Press, 1985.

"Christian Sybillines." Trans. A. Kurfess. In Edgar Hennecke and Wilhelm Schneemelcher, eds., *New Testament Apocrypha* 2:703–45. Trans. R. McL. Wilson. 2 vols. Philadelphia: Westminster, 1963.

Courcelle, Pierre Paul. *Les "Confessions" dans la tradition littéraire: Antécédents et postérité.* Paris: Etudes augustiniennes, 1963.

——. *Recherches sur les "Confessions" de Saint Augustin.* 2d ed. Paris: de Boccard, 1968.

Crouzel, Henri. *Bibliographie critique d'Origène.* Instrumenta patristica, 8 and supplement. The Hague: Nijhoff, 1971.

Denzinger, Henricus, and Adolfus Schönmetzer. *Enchiridion symbolorum definitionum et declarationum de rebus fidei et morum.* 24th ed. Barcelona: Herder, 1967.

Diesner, Hans Joachim. *The Great Migration: The Movement of Peoples across Europe,* A.D. 300–700. Trans. C. S. V. Salt. London: Orbis, 1982.

Dieterich, Albrecht. *Nekyia: Beiträge zur Erklärung der neuentdeckten Petrusapokalypse.* 2d ed. Leipzig: B. G. Teubner, 1913.

Doyle, G. Wright. "Augustine's Sermonic Method." *Westminster Theological Journal* 39 (1977): 213–38.

Dunn, James D. G. *The Partings of the Ways between Christianity and Judaism and Their Significance for the Character of Christianity.* London: SCM; Philadelphia: Trinity International, 1991.

Eno, Robert B. *The Rise of the Papacy.* Theology and Life Series, 32. Wilmington, Del.: Glazier, 1990.

Falbo, Giovanni. *Il primato della Chiesa di Roma alla luce dei primi quattro secoli.* Rome: Coletti, 1989.

Fischer, Balthasar. "Nicht wie die Gelehrten reden, eher wie die Ungelehrten: Eine Mahnung Augustins an den christlichen Prediger (*De doctrina christiana* 4,65)." *Internationale katholische Zeitschrift "Communio"* 11 (1982): 123–29.

Fleischhack, Erich. *Fegfeuer: Die christlichen Vorstellungen vom Geschick der Verstorbenen geschichtlich dargestellt.* Tübingen: Katzmann, 1969.

Flood, Emmet T. "The Narrative Structure of Augustine's *Confessions*: Time's Quest for Eternity." *International Philosophical Quarterly* 28 (1988): 141–62.

Fredriksen, Paula. *From Jesus to Christ: The Origins of the New Testament Images of Jesus.* New Haven: Yale University Press, 1988.

Gager, John G. "Body-Symbols and Social Reality: Resurrection, Incarnation, and Asceticism in Early Christianity." *Religion: Journal of Religion and Religions* 12 (1982): 345–63.

Gardiner, Eileen. *Visions of Heaven and Hell before Dante.* New York: Italica Press, 1989.

Gaudemet, Jean. *L'église dans l'empire romain: IVe–Ve siècles.* Histoire du droit et des institutions de l'église en occident, 3. Paris: Sirey, 1989.

Gilson, Etienne. *Introduction à l'étude de saint Augustin*. 2d ed. Paris: Vrin, 1982.

———. *Les métamorphoses de la "Cité de Dieu."* Louvain: Publications universitaires de Louvain, 1952.

The Gospel of Nicodemus. Ed. H. C. Kim. Toronto: Pontifical Institute of Mediaeval Studies, 1973.

The Gospel of Nicodemus, Acts of Pilate, and Christ's Descent into Hell. Trans. F. Scheidweiler. In Edgar Hennecke and Wilhelm Schneemelcher, eds., *New Testament Apocrypha* 1:444–84. Trans. R. McL. Wilson. 2 vols. Philadelphia: Westminster, 1963.

Gunn, Janet Varner. "The Religious Hermeneutic of Autobiography: Augustine's *Confessions* and the *Credo ut Intellegam*." *Journal of the American Academy of Religion: Thematic Studies* 49 (1983): 61–70.

Heichelheim, Fritz M. *An Ancient Economic History, from the Palaeolithic Age to the Migrations of the Germanic, Slavic, and Arabic Nations*. Rev. and complete English ed. Leiden: Sijthoff, 1968–70.

Heist, W. W., ed. *Vitae sanctorum Hiberniae*. Subsidia hagiographica, 28. Brussels: Société des bollandistes, 1965.

Hennecke, Edgar, and Wilhelm Schneemelcher, eds. *New Testament Apocrypha*. Trans. R. McL. Wilson. 2 vols. Philadelphia: Westminster, 1963.

Hillgarth, J. N. *Christianity and Paganism, 350–700*. Rev. ed. Philadelphia: University of Pennsylvania Press, 1986.

Himmelfarb, Martha. *Tours of Hell: An Apocalyptic Form in Jewish and Christian Literature*. Philadelphia: University of Pennsylvania Press, 1983.

Hooker, Morna Dorothy. *Continuity and Discontinuity: Early Christianity in Its Jewish Setting*. London: Epworth, 1986.

Horst, Pieter Willem van der. *Essays on the Jewish World of Early Christianity*. Novum Testamentum et orbis antiquus, 14. Freiburg, Switzerland: Universitätsverlag; Göttingen: Vandenhoeck und Ruprecht, 1990.

Jacobs, Manfred. *Die Reichskirche und ihre Dogmen: Von der Zeit Konstantins bis zum Niedergang des weströmischen Reiches*. Zugänge zur Kirchengeschichte, 3. Kleine Vandenhoeck-Reihe, 1525. Göttingen: Vandenhoeck und Ruprecht, 1987.

Jaeger, Werner. *Early Christianity and Greek Paideia*. Oxford: Oxford University Press, 1969.

James, M. R. *Apocrypha Anecdota: A Collection of Thirteen Apocryphal Books and Fragments*. Texts and Studies. Contributions to Biblical and Patristic Literature, 2.3. Cambridge: Cambridge University Press, 1893.

———. *The Apocryphal New Testament*. 1924. Rpt. Oxford: Oxford University Press, 1966.

Kannengiesser, Charles, and William L. Petersen. *Origen of Alexandria: His World and His Legacy*. Papers from the Origen Colloquy held at Notre Dame University, April 11–13, 1986. Notre Dame, Ind.: Notre Dame University Press, 1988.

Kidd, Beresford James. *The Roman Primacy to A.D. 461*. London: Society for Promoting Christian Knowledge, 1936.

Kroll, Josef. *Gott und Hölle: Der Mythos vom Descensuskampfe.* London: Warburg Institute, Studien der Bibliothek Warburg, 20. 1932. Rpt. Darmstadt: Wissenschaftliche Buchgesellschaft, 1963.

Ladner, Gerhart. *The Idea of Reform: Its Impact on Christian Thought and Action in the Age of the Fathers.* Rev. ed. New York: Harper and Row, 1967.

Lake, Kirsopp, trans. *The Shepherd of Hermas.* In *The Apostolic Fathers* 2:262–63. 2 vols. Cambridge: Harvard University Press, 1924.

Landau, Marcus. *Hölle und Fegfeuer in Volksglaube: Dichtung und Kirchenlehre.* Heidelberg: Winter, 1909.

Le Goff, Jacques. *The Birth of Purgatory.* Trans. Arthur Goldhammer. Chicago: University of Chicago Press, 1984. (*La naissance du purgatoire.* Paris: Gallimard, 1981.)

Locker, Gottlieb. "Die Beziehung der Zeit zur Ewigkeit bei Augustin." *Theologische Zeitschrift* 44 (1988): 147–67.

Lubac, Henri de. *Histoire et esprit: L'intelligence de l'Ecriture d'après Origène.* Paris: Aubier, 1950.

Maccarrone, Michele. *Romana ecclesia: Cathedra Petri.* Italia Sacra, 47–48. Rome: Herder, 1991.

MacCulloch, John Arnott. *The Harrowing of Hell: A Comparative Study of an Early Christian Doctrine.* Edinburgh: T. and T. Clark, 1930.

———. *Early Christian Visions of the Other-world.* Edinburgh: St. Giles, 1912.

McGinn, Bernard, ed. and trans. *Apocalyptic Spirituality.* New York: Paulist Press, 1979.

MacMullen, Ramsay. *Christianizing the Roman Empire (A.D. 100–400).* New Haven: Yale University Press, 1984.

Magnin, Etienne. "Indulgences." In *Dictionnaire de théologie catholique* 7.2, cols. 1594–1636. Paris: Librairie Letouzey et Ané.

Maier, Franz Georg. *Augustin und das antike Rom.* Tübinger Beiträge zur Altertumswissenschaft, 39. Stuttgart: W. Kohlhammer, 1955.

Markus, Robert. *The End of Ancient Christianity.* Cambridge: Cambridge University Press, 1990.

Miethe, Terry L. *Augustinian Bibliography, 1970–1980, with Essays on the Fundamentals of Augustinian Scholarship,* Westport, Conn.: Greenwood, 1982.

Musset, Lucien. *The Germanic Invasions: The Making of Europe, A.D. 400–600.* Trans. Edward James and Columba James. University Park: Pennsylvania State University Press, 1975.

Ntedika, Joseph. "La pénitence des mourants et l'eschatologie des pères latins," *Message et Mission* (1968): 109–27.

Ntedika, Konde. *L'évocation de l'au-delà dans la prière pour les morts: Etude de patristique et de liturgie latines, IVe–VIIIe siècles.* Recherches africaines de théologie, 2. Université Lovanium de Kinshasa publications. Louvain: Nauwelaerts, 1971.

———. *L'évolution de la doctrine du purgatoire chez saint Augustin.* Université Lovanium de Léopoldville, Faculté de théologie publications, 4. Université Lovanium de Léopoldville publications, 20. Paris: Etudes augustiniennes, 1966.

O'Ceallaigh, G. C. "Dating the Commentaries of Nicodemus." *Harvard Theological Review* 56 (1963): 21–58.

O'Meara, John Joseph. *Charter of Christendom: The Significance of the "City of God."* New York: Macmillan, 1961.

Origen. *On First Principles.* Trans. G. W. Butterworth. New York: Harper and Row, 1966.

———. *De principiis.* Ed. Paul Koetschau. Vol. 5 of *Origines Werke.* Die griechischen christlichen Schriftsteller der ersten drei Jahrhunderte, 22. Leipzig: Hinrichs, 1913.

Pelikan, Jaroslav. *The Mystery of Continuity: Time and History, Memory and Eternity in the Thought of Saint Augustine.* Charlottesville: University Press of Virginia, 1986.

Quasten, Johannes. *Patrology.* 3 vols. Westminster, Md.: Newman, 1953–62.

Reinach, Salomon. "De l'origine des prières pour les morts." *Revue des études juives* 41 (1900): 161–73.

Rosenstiehl, Jean-Marc. "Tartarouchos-Temelouchos: Contribution à l'étude de l'Apocalypse apocryphe de Paul." In *Deuxième journée d'études coptes* (Strasbourg, May 25, 1984), 29–56. *Cahiers de la bibliothèque copte* 3. Louvain: Peeters, 1985.

Rouco, Alfonso Carrasco. *Le primat de l'évêque de Rome: Etude sur la cohérence ecclésiologique et canonique du primat de juridiction.* Studia Friburgensia, Sectio canonica, 7. Freiburg, Switzerland: Editions universitaires, 1990.

Rouët de Journel, M. J. *Enchiridion patristicum.* 25th ed. Barcelona: Herder, 1981.

Russell, Jeffrey Burton. *Satan: The Early Christian Tradition.* Ithaca: Cornell University Press, 1981.

Sandmel, Samuel. *Judaism and Christian Beginnings.* New York: Oxford University Press, 1978.

Schimmelpfennig, Bernard. *Das Papsttum: Grundzüge seiner Geschichte von der Antike bis zur Renaissance.* Darmstadt: Wissenschaftliche Buchgesellschaft, 1984.

Schneemelcher, Wilhelm, ed. *New Testament Apocrypha.* English translation edited by R. McL. Wilson. 2 vols. Louisville, Ky.: Westminster/John Knox, 1991.

Silverstein, Theodore. "The Vision of Saint Paul: New Links and Patterns in the Western Tradition." *Archives d'histoire doctrinale et littéraire du moyen âge* 26 (1959): 199–248.

———. *Visio Sancti Pauli: The History of the Apocalypse in Latin together with Nine Texts.* Studies and Documents, 4. London: Christopher's, 1935.

Simon, Marcel. *Verus Israel: A Study of the Relations between Christians and Jews in the Roman Empire, 135–425.* Trans. Henry McKeating. Littman Library of Jewish Civilization. New York: Oxford University Press, 1986.

Starnes, Colin. *Augustine's Conversion: A Guide to the Argument of "Confessions" I–IX.* Waterloo, Ont.: Wilfrid Laurier University Press, 1990.

Stevenson, James, ed. *A New Eusebius: Documents Illustrative of the History of the Church to A.D. 337.* London: S. P. C. K., 1968.

——, ed. *Creeds, Councils, and Controversies: Documents Illustrative of the History of the Church, A.D. 337–461.* London: S. P. C. K., 1966.

Stuiber, Alfred. *Refrigerium interim: Die Vorstellungen vom Zwischenzustand und die frühchristliche Grabeskunst.* Theophaneia; Beiträge zur Religions- und Kirchengeschichte des Altertums, 11. Bonn: Hanstein, 1957.

Theologische Realenzyklopädie. Ed. Horst Robert Baltz. 21 vols. to date. Berlin: de Gruyter, 1976–.

Tigg, Joseph Wilson. *Origen: The Bible and Philosophy in the Third-Century Church.* Atlanta: John Knox, 1983.

Tischendorf, Konstantin von. *Evangelia apocrypha.* Rev. ed. Leipzig: Mendelssohn, 1876.

Tripolitis, Antonia. *Origen: A Critical Reading.* New York: Lang, 1985.

Troeltsch, Ernst. *Augustin, die christliche Antike und das Mittelmeer: Im Anschluß an die Schrift "De Civitate Dei."* 1915. Rpt. Aalen, Germany: Scientia, 1963.

Tsirpanlis, Constantine N. "Origen on Free Will, Grace, Predestination, Apocatastasis, and Their Ecclesiological Implications." *Patristic and Byzantine Review* 9 (1990): 95–121.

Young, Frances M. *From Nicaea to Chalcedon: A Guide to the Literature and Its Background.* Philadelphia: Fortress Press, 1983.

General Index

Athena, 44, 103

Atlas, 35, 37, 38

Atonement, Day of, 148

Auguries, 104

Augustine: on the body after death, 318–19, 327–30; on the Book of Genesis, 327–28; Christian timeline in, 316, 317, 318, 329; defends eternal damnation, 267, 318–20, 321–22; on the descent of Christ into Hades, 320–21; divisions of dead in, 323–24; on ghosts, 95, 335–36; Last Judgment in, 324–25, 328; life of, 314–15; on purgatory, 296n8, 317, 318, 322–23, 326; on receptacles for souls awaiting judgment, 185, 318, 322, 335; Second Coming in, 317; on separation from God, 330–31, 332; on suffrages for the dead, 322–23, 325–26

Augustine (texts): *City of God*, 267, 315, 316, 318, 319, 320, 322, 327, 328–29, 333; *Confessions*, 314, 333; *Enchiridion*, 316, 318, 325, 330–31, 335; *On the Care to be Taken for the Dead*, 95; *On the Literal Interpretation of Genesis*, 327–28

Avernus. *See* Orcus

Azaz'el, angel, 183–84, 192

Babel, Tower of, 136

Babylon, 165–66

Babylonian Exile, 154

Babylonian land of the dead: descent of Inanna (Ishtar) into, 5–10; Gilgamesh in, 4–5, 8, 9; as neutral storehouse, 1, 3–11, 172

Bacchus, cult of, 44

Balbus, 90–91, 104, 118

Baptism, postmortem, 295

Beast(s): the four, 301; the Great, 203, 341; mark of the, 256; the two, 256, 257–58. *See also* Monsters; Satan

Behemoth, 193

Belides, 45–46. *See also* Danaides

Bible. *See* Hebrew Bible; New Testament; Septuagint

Blessed, Land (or Isle) of the, 15, 56, 70–72

Blessedness and virtue, 293, 295; in Christianity, 232, 234, 235, 237, 241;

faith as, 218, 256, 340; in Judaism, 148–49, 162, 170, 190; in Lucian, 125–26, 244–45; martyrdom as, 258, 286; in Plato, 55–56, 71, 244; rewards for, 15, 41, 42, 44–45, 46, 47, 48, 71; salvation as reward for, 259–69, 283; witnessing torments of damned, 300, 331–32. *See also* Forgiveness; Grace; Heaven

Blood, 13, 31, 173, 257, 286, 298, 300; of the Lamb, 254; river of, 48; of sacrificed animals, 24, 43–44, 148; thirst of shades for, 26–27, 30

Boats and boatmen, 10, 11, 14, 15; *See also* Charon

Body: mutilation of, 16–17, 59, 82, 83, 217, 299, 312–13; resurrection of, 211, 318–19; resurrection of, in Origen, 311–13. *See also* Soul-body relation

Book of Gates, 15–17, 83

Book of life, 256, 259

Book of the Dead, 13

Brimstone, 170, 256, 299

Bultmann, Rudolf, 249

Burial, 26, 138; funeral rites, 26n, 62, 109–10, 162n9; tombs opened, 252. *See also* Cremation; Grave(s); Unburied

Burning, 152, 170; of chaff and weeds, 230, 233, 234–35

Cain, 135–36n, 200, 250

Categories of the dead. *See* Division of the dead

Caves, 62, 63, 72, 89, 138

Cerberus: guard dog of Hades, 38, 68, 87, 90, 91, 113, 115, 119; theft of, 32, 64, 88–89

Chaos, 33

Charon, boatman to Hades, 11, 64, 68, 85, 87, 92, 93

Charon (Lucian), 87

Chasms between worlds, 79, 240, 247, 336

Children and infants, 65, 160, 168n17, 229n4, 232–33, 235, 300. *See also* Offspring

Christ. *See* Jesus of Nazareth

Christianity, 2, 264–65, 315; the Eucharist, 301; Greco-Roman influence on,

Damnation (*cont.*)
ened emphasis and refinement of, 263,
282, 300; religious discipline and, 251,
262, 303, 340. *See also* Eternal fire;
Punishment, postmortem

Damned. *See* Wicked (the)

Danaides, 113. *See also* Belides

Daniel, Book of, 175, 178, 179, 261;
raising and judging dead in, 174–75,
242

Dante, *Divine Comedy*, 30, 64, 293

Darkness, 30, 40, 45, 160, 257, 340;
Land of, 4, 8; nethergloom, 30, 34, 35,
40, 41, 45, 46, 251; night and, 37,
258; the outer, 231

Dark One, 14

Dathan, 145, 248, 252

Dead (the): banishment of, 25, 92, 105,
107, 335; communication with, prohibited, 138; desire to communicate with,
105, 106, 107; honoring, 95, 101–4,
110, 136, 139, 326; offerings or ceremonies to, 3, 23–24, 43–44, 101–4, 105.
See also Ancestors; Burial; Community
of the dead; Ghosts; Shades

Dead, Book of the, 13

Dead Sea Scrolls, 183, 190

Death, 2, 8n10, 23n6, 68, 91, 200; as be-
nevolent or peaceful, 85, 115, 117,
128, 159, 160; continuation of life in,
32, 49, 65, 71, 128, 160, 172; as
deadline for virtue and repentance,
205, 240, 241, 242, 301, 316, 330;
emphasis on means or moment of, 30,
42, 64; as an enemy or fearsome, 113–
14; guiding life, 45, 128; as punishment, 28, 147, 169, 336; reconciliation
to, 85, 210, 223, 262; the Second,
254, 255, 316. *See also* Democratic
model of death; Moral death; Neutral
death; Oblivion

Death, divine power over, 252, 259–60;
God (Yahweh) reaches into Sheol, 144–
45, 157, 158, 272, 335; Jesus conquers, 205, 214, 253, 259; penetration
of life-death boundary, 12, 15, 39, 40,
272–73

Demeter, 39, 41, 91, 112. *See also* Hymn
to Demeter

Democratic model of death, 166, 190;

equality in, 4, 12–13, 86, 126, 127;
immortality for all in, 12–13, 127;
Tityos made everyman, 333; uniformity
in, 26, 32, 336

Demons, 8, 13, 71, 329; salvation for (in
Origen), 309; as tormentors, 13–14,
59, 81; as transformers, 81, 82, 83,
339

Descent of Christ into Hades, 249, 252,
253, 272–82, 302–4, 305; Augustine
on, 320–21; emphasized in apocryphal
texts, 320; empties Hades, 259, 278;
the "Harrowing of Hell," 252; raises
biblical prophets and figures, 252, 273,
277, 278, 304

Descents into the netherworld: of Aeneas,
61–70; of Amon-Re, 12, 14, 16; of
Gilgamesh, 4–5, 8, 9, 25; of Inanna
(Ishtar), 5–10; of Michael the Archan-
gel, 301–2; of Odysseus, 23–33, 61; of
Orpheus, 42–50; of Persephone, 11,
19, 22, 39, 40; of Theseus, 62, 70, 88.
See also Death, divine power over;
Life-death boundary

Destiny. *See* Fate; Providence

Destruction. *See* Exclusion from the
Kingdom; Oblivion

Deutero-Isaiah, 165–66

Deuteronomic system of justice, 336;
destruction of wicked in, 171, 189,
196, 197; Job criticizes, 157–59,
160–72, 336; punishment of wicked
in, 146–51, 152, 169, 336; stresses
on, 143, 152–56. *See also* Jewish law;
Job

Deuteronomy, Book of, 131, 137, 147–
48, 149–52, 166

Deviancy. *See* Nonconformists

Devil. *See* Satan

Dike, 35, 74, 77–78, 82, 153. *See also*
Justice

Diodorus of Sicily, 88

Diogenes of Sinope, 41n30, 85

Dionysus (citizen), 46–49

Dionysus (god), 43–44, 48, 88

Dis, or Dispater, 63, 90, 100. *See also*
Hades (god)

Dis, Lady, 63, 90

Disease, 149, 257

Dives, 63, 90. *See also* Hades (god)

Dives and Lazarus, parable of (Luke), 239–40, 243, 272, 276, 327

Dividing of the Road, Meadow of, 56

Divine authority: cosmic and social order, 128; God's will, 220, 222, 235, 272; Olympian world order, 22, 33, 35, 36, 39, 88. *See also* Revelation, Book of

Divine justice. *See* Community of the dead; Judgment; Justice: divine

Divine mercy, 271, 302

Divine sovereignty, 12, 15, 39, 40, 144–45. *See also* Death, divine power over

Divine substance, 15

Divine wrath, 339; biblical flood, 135, 136, 181, 182, 183–84, 187, 188, 196; in Hebrew Bible, 135, 147, 149, 150, 165, 200; hiding from, 141; of Osiris, 14–18

Divinity and gods: chthonic, 11, 12, 18, 44, 122; devotion to, 11–12, 14–18; shedding of, 5–6; soul's reminiscence of, 53, 55–56, 60, 71, 112. *See also* Pagan cults and mysteries; Rulers of the dead

Division of the dead: in Egyptian netherworld, 11–13, 15–18, 165, 336; increasing refinement of, 297; in Jewish afterlife, 164–67, 172, 185–87; moral categories, 12–13, 68–69, 70–71; moral categories in Christian afterlife, 231–32, 240, 283, 295, 323–24; moral categories in Greco-Roman netherworld, 49, 50, 55–59, 73–76, 82–83, 105, 336, 340; in Plato, 56–57, 60, 61; in Plutarch, 79–81; in Virgil, 68–71, 73. *See also* Judgment; Moral death; Netherworld geography

Donatism, 271

Dragons, 255–56

Dreams and visions, 92, 112; Book of Dream Visions, 188–89; of netherworld, 10–11, 72, 76, 182–83, 184. *See also* Apocalyptic tradition

Drunkenness, 211, 217, 298

Dualism. *See* Body; Soul; Soul-body relation

Dust, 5, 8, 131, 160, 215

Dying, remembrance of, 28–29, 33

Dynamic concepts of afterlife: in Origen, 338; in Plato, 55–60, 337–38; in Plu-tarch, 76, 77–83, 337. *See also* Cycles; Reincarnation

Earth: end of, 189, 257–58, 259–60; Gaia, 33, 34; Plato's anatomy of, 54–55, 59, 61–62. *See also* Fertility; Meadows; Openings to the nether-world

Edict of Milan, 269

Egypt, 135, 162, 196, 200

Egyptian Book of the Dead, 13

Egyptian netherworld, 3, 11, 243; divine punishment in, 14–18; divisions of, 11–13, 15–18, 165, 336; fauna of, 14, 15–16, 17; folklore of, 242–44; geography of, 11–13, 15–18, 336; immersion in, 16. *See also* Judgment; Moral death

Eidōlon, 27, 31, 45, 83

Elders, twenty-four, 301

Elect One, 191, 192

Eleusinian Mysteries, 40, 41, 44, 51n5, 112

Elohim, 138, 139

Elysian Fields (Elysium), 65, 68, 71, 73, 127

Enoch, Book of, 180, 193–94, 251; accursed valley in, 186–87; antiquity of, 179–82, 190–91, 195; Apocalypse of Weeks, 187–88, 189, 190, 196; Book of Dream Visions, 188–89; Enoch as narrator, 180, 181, 184, 190, 195; mountain tomb in, 182–83, 184; Nephilim (giants) in, 182, 183, 187, 197–98; Sheol in, 185–86. *See also* Simili-tudes, Book of; Watcher angels

"Enthusiasts," 209, 211

Enumeration principle, 296

Epic of Gilgamesh, 4–5, 8, 9, 25

Epithemeus, 35, 38

Equality. *See* Democratic model of death

Er, myth of, 52, 58–60, 73, 84

Erebos, 25, 30, 35, 63. *See also* Hades

Ereshkigal, 5–8, 9

Erinyes (Furies), 28, 77, 78

Essenes, 179

Eternal fire, 194, 203, 228, 257, 281, 340; denied by Origen, 311; in Isaiah, 171, 200, 230, 233, 238, 247, 262,

Eternal fire *(cont.)*
338; in Matthew, 203, 229, 230, 232, 233, 246, 262, 263, 311, 318
Eternal punishment, 250, 258–59, 319–20; in *Hymn to Demeter*, 19, 42; in Matthew, 262, 263, 319; in Plato, 55, 59, 61. *See also* Damnation; Eternal fire
Eternity, nomenclature of, 60–61, 319–20, 327
Ethical theory of Paul, 215, 223
Ethics and myth, 117–18, 123
Ethiopic Enoch, 180. *See also* Enoch, Book of
Eucharist, 301
Evil. *See* Satan; Sin and evil
Evocation, 102–4
Exclusion from the Kingdom, 211–12, 215–16, 220–21, 222, 261n8, 265; as mere death (John), 225, 227; torment of, 330–31, 332
Exodus, 248
Expiation, 11, 55
Exposure of infants, 286, 299
Ezekiel, 241; resurrection of the dead in, 173–74

Faith, 218, 256, 340; in Christ's sacrifice, 225, 226, 264
Fall: of man, 135, 316; of Satan and angels, 253, 258, 278, 281, 309, 316, 333, 339; of stars, 187, 189, 198, 250, 251, 255; of Titans, 22, 33, 38, 41–42, 69–70; of Watcher angels, 180, 185, 187, 189, 194
Fallen angels, 250, 251
Falling: as punishment, 285, 286, 287; souls in Plato, 53
False prophets, 258, 262
Famine, 8, 9, 22, 35, 40
Fate: differences in, 23, 43, 46–49, 51; Greco-Roman concept of destiny, 32–33; Plato's four fates, 55–60, 61
Fate, reversal of, 125, 126, 165, 243, 246n24, 335; Egyptian story of rich and poor man, 242–44; in Hebrew Bible, 124–25; in Lucian, 125, 126, 245; parable of Dives and Lazarus, 239–40, 304, 318
Fertility: life-death boundary and, 9, 21,

22, 40; netherworld as granary, 22, 39, 41; seeds, 40, 41, 90–91, 214. *See also Hymn to Demeter*
Fire, 35, 45, 55, 146, 192; and brimstone, 170, 256; burning and, 152, 170, 233; divinities of, 13, 16; of Gehenna, 168, 189, 192, 194; internal, 311–12, 328–30; lakes of, 1, 14, 15, 258, 338; purgatorial, 326; rivers of, 297; sea of, 284; serpents of, 15–16; smoke and, 203. *See also* Eternal fire; Pit(s); Sulphur
Fire and the worm, 1, 194, 229, 330, 338; in Gehenna, 171, 228, 229
Flesh. *See* Body; Soul-body relation
Flood: Babylonian, 4; biblical, 135, 136, 181, 182, 183–84, 187, 188, 196
Forgetfulness of past lives, 71, 86, 126
Forgiveness, 218, 236, 238–39; post-mortem, 55, 244. *See also* Repentance
Four Beasts, 301
Four heavenly rivers, 296
Four horses of Revelation, 254–55
Four Hundred, 49
Freedom, 60, 71, 311; between lives, 60; sin and will, 307–9, 316
Funeral rites, 26n, 62, 109–10, 162n9. *See also* Burial
Furies (Erinyes), 28, 77, 78

Gabriel, angel, 183
Gaia. *See* Earth
Gamaliel, Pharisee, 208
Ganzir. *See* Babylonian land of the dead
Gates: to Babylonian land of the dead, 5, 7, 9, 11; to Gehenna, 167; of Hades, 24, 25, 61, 69, 72; of hell, 276, 277, 281; of Tartarus, 11, 37, 38–39, 42; of Tuat, 15
Gates, Book of, 15–17, 83
Gehenna: abominations at, 168–69, 171, 172; the accursed valley (in Enoch), 186, 192, 340; cited in Gospels, 1, 207n2, 228–29, 230–31, 246; distinguished from Sheol or Hades, 167–68, 197, 282, 317–18, 329; fire and the worm in, 171, 228, 229; the historical place, 167–69; imprisonment of angels in (hinted), 185, 194; juxtaposition with Sheol, 197, 199; as place for the

Gehenna (*cont.*)
wicked, 168, 185–86; punishment for
the wicked in, 168, 187, 198. *See also*
Hell; Tartarus; Topheth
Ge-Hinnom. *See* Gehenna
Gender, 28, 35–36, 257; dead separated
by, 26, 27, 33; eunuchs' role, 7–10;
male and female forces, 192, 193; male
homosexuality, 285; mother and child
pairs, 12, 15, 40, 255–56; sex between
angels and women, 181–85, 187;
women as source of evil or sin, 28, 35–
36, 184, 257
General Resurrection, 211, 213, 241,
249, 284, 317, 335
Genesis, Book of, 180, 327–28
Ghosts, 94–95, 185; belief and fear of,
92, 93, 96–97, 107, 110, 335; bodies
of, 98–99, 116; groups of, 99,
104n44; *lemures*, 101–2, 102n38;
manes, 100–104; prophesying, 99;
vengeance of, 95–96; visiting relatives,
97–98. *See also* Shades
Giants: *Nephilim,* 182, 183, 187, 197–
98; *Rephaim,* 144n21, 197. *See also*
Titans
Gilgamesh, 4–5, 8, 9, 25
Gnosticism, 271
God: the Father, 211, 330–31, 332; the
Holy Spirit, 209, 239; as the One,
306–7; Yahweh (in Hebrew Bible),
138, 139n13, 189, 193; Yahweh raises
the dead, 146; Yahweh reaches into
Sheol, 144–45, 158, 272, 335. *See also*
Divinity and gods; Jesus of Nazareth;
Providence
Gold, 62, 81, 112, 326, 339
Golden bough, 62, 71
Golden staff of Minos, 31
Goliath, 197
Good deeds. *See* Blessedness and
virtue
Gorgons, 32, 48, 63
Gospel of Nicodemus, 267, 271, 272,
275–79; commentary on, 279–82,
331, 333; Hades personified in, 275,
276, 277–79; history of and versions,
274–75, 280–81
Gospels. *See* New Testament
Grace, 220–21

Grave(s), 39, 98; Hades as, 39, 86; Sheol
as, 135, 140, 142, 143–44, 161, 338
Great Beast (Satan, Rome), 203, 341
Greco-Roman mythology, 21, 22n4. *See
also* Hesiod; Homeric age; Pagan cults
and mysteries; Pindar; Virgil
Greco-Roman philosophy, 2; contempla-
tion of divinity in, 55–56, 71, 112;
discourses on death in, 85, 111, 116;
Neoplatonism, 306, 314, 337. *See also*
Lucian; Lucretius; Plato; Plutarch; Re-
ligion: reflection on utility of
Greed, 70, 81, 286
Greek Bible, 2, 167, 197–98, 251, 317
Greek city-state, 49, 57–58
Greek language, 2, 139
Greek Orthodox Church, 270
Guardian angels, 293
Guardian spirits, 54
Guides and helpers, 6, 10, 76–77; Eu-
nuch of Babylon, 9–10; heavenly or
angelic, 183, 186, 189, 295, 301; from
Sheol (denied), 335; Zoroastrian
magus, 87, 124. *See also* Seers
Guilt, 74, 113

Hades: Charon (boatman to), 11, 64, 68,
85, 87, 92, 93; divisions of, 55, 70,
71–72; gates to, 24, 25, 61, 69, 72;
geography of, 54–55, 58, 68–69, 70–
71, 105, 340; as granary, 22, 39, 41;
as grave, 39; the meadow Asphodel
and, 24, 26–31; as negative force, 39,
41n29; openings from earth to, 54, 89;
palace in, 38, 48; passage to, 21, 25–
26, 47; personified, 275–79; shades in,
26–27, 29, 31–32, 38, 64; social status in, 26, 27, 33. *See also* Cerberus;
Erebos; Orcus; Tartarus
Hades, Christian, 249; in Augustine, 317,
321, 327, 329; Christ empties Hades,
259, 278; Christ's descent into, 249,
252–54, 272–82, 321; in *Gospel of
Nicodemus,* 272–82; in Luke, 228,
239–40, 245–57; in Matthew, 234; in
Paul, 205, 207–8; in Revelation, 253,
255, 259
Hades (god), 39, 40–41, 42, 62, 89, 90,
100, 102; abducts Persephone, 11, 19,
22, 39; as Dis (Dispater) or Dives, 63,

Hydra, 69
Hymn to Demeter, 22, 39–42, 43, 44, 50

Iacchus, 48. *See also* Dionysus (god)
Ideology in religious texts, 35, 262, 275, 304, 315
Idolatry, 211, 217, 260
Iliad, 23, 25, 27, 37, 57
Images. *See* Netherworld imagery
Immersion, 16, 285, 297
Immortality, 34, 214; ambition for, 4–5, 6; democratized, 12–13, 127; false sense of, 85–86; in Hebrew Bible, 136, 179, 188, 194; Plato on, 60–61. *See also* Afterlife; Reincarnation; Soul
Imprisonment in netherworld: of angels, 180, 185, 187, 189, 194, 316; of the dead, 8, 11, 53, 69, 78, 252, 277, 280; escape alarm, 59; host of captives, 252; of Titans, 34, 39; of Watcher angels, 185, 187, 189, 194
Inanna (Ishtar): descends into underworld, 5–8; threatens to raise the dead, 6, 7, 8–10, 335
Incarnation, 301
Incense, 45
Incurable souls: in Plato, 55, 57, 59; in Plutarch, 77, 78
Infants and children, 65, 160, 168n17, 232–33, 235, 300
Infernus, inferus, or *inferi*, 139, 275n15, 282, 301, 317, 321, 327. *See also* Hades
Internal fire, 311–12, 328–30
Intertestamentary period, 253, 282, 337; nomenclature in texts of, 191, 192
Isaiah, 2, 171–72, 277; apocalypse of, 144, 173–74, 175, 198, 242, 251, 329; on the eternal fire, 171, 200, 233, 238, 247, 338; on the fire and the worm, 1, 194, 229, 330, 338; internal fire in, 311
Isaiah, Deutero-, 165–66
Isaiah, Trito-, 171
Ishtar. *See* Inanna (Ishtar)
Isis and Osiris, 12, 15
Isle of the Blessed, 15, 56, 70–72
Ixion, 20, 70

Jacob, 138, 140
Jeremiah, 168, 172–73
Jerome, 258, 307, 309
Jesus of Nazareth, 191, 254, 257, 276, 277; ascension of, 167, 252; as avenger, 255, 258; empties Hades, 259, 278; as judge and victim, 254, 255, 264, 283, 339; life-giving, 213, 224; as Lord of the underworld, 223, 224, 272, 305; as the Other, 232, 237–38, 263; power over death, 205, 214, 253, 259; raises Adam, 252, 273, 277, 278; raises Hebrew prophets, 252, 273, 304; raises Lazarus, 335; the redeemer, 276–77; Resurrection of, 1, 205, 211, 252, 258, 305. *See also* Descent of Christ into Hades; Redemption; Resurrection
Jewish Covenant, 135, 150–51, 169, 294; breach of, 200–201; establishing Jewish law, 146–47, 248
Jewish law, 146–49, 154; cited in Gospels, 222, 231, 241, 242; of obedience, 148, 222. *See also* Deuteronomic system of justice; Justice
Jewish model of afterlife, 199–201; division of the dead in, 164–67, 172, 185–87; geography of underworld, 165, 185–87; moral death in, 174, 185–86, 191, 192–94, 200–203; moral division of the dead in, 162–67; punishment in, 162–67, 185–86, 208, 242; rewards of righteous in, 148–49, 162, 170, 190; shades (*rephaim*), 142, 144, 158, 160, 198–99; shame in, 163, 165, 167, 168; sublimated vengeance in, 152–53, 190, 202; three views of, 178–79
Jewish Scriptures. *See* Hebrew Bible
Jewish Temple, 139, 145, 263
Jews, 248; Paul on, 218, 221; Qumran community, 183, 190; Sadducees, 179, 230, 233. *See also* Judaism
Job, 2, 156, 272; in heaven, 304; on injustice of Deuteronomic system, 143, 157–59, 160–72, 336
Job, Book of, 74, 156–57, 159, 176
John (apostle), 1; breadth of positions on afterlife, 225–26; positive tradition of

John (apostle) (*cont.*)
afterlife in, 224–27. *See also* Revelation, Book of
John the Baptist, 230, 233, 276
Jonah, 248, 252
Jonah, Book of, 135
Joseph, 140
Joseph of Arimathea. *See Gospel of Nicodemus*
Josephus, Flavius: *Jewish Antiquities*, 178–79; *Jewish War*, 178
Jove, 69. *See also* Zeus
Jove, Stygian, 63. *See also* Hades (god)
Judaism, 148, 154, 269, 278–79; anti-, 274–75, 279, 304; Essenes, 179; minority traditions in, 136, 167, 175–77, 178, 196–97, 200; monarchy and, 139. *See also* Hebrew Bible; *and by individual prophet*
Judas Iscariot, apostle, 82
Jude, Book of, 250, 251
Judges: the Anunnaki, 6, 8; court of Minos, 31, 66–68; Jesus as victim and judge, 254, 255, 264, 283, 339; Rhadamanthus, 56, 68, 73, 77, 92, 126, 127; role of "the silent, " 65, 66, 67; victims as, 67–68, 258
Judgment, 13, 15, 45, 54, 235; in Book of Daniel, 174–75, 242; in Daniel, 174–75, 242; by the dead, 56–57; in Hebrew Bible, 103, 180, 188, 189, 193, 194; in Plato, 55–57; souls awaiting, 185–86, 190, 240–41, 335; souls on trial, 293- 94. *See also* Division of the dead; Justice; Last Judgment
Juno, infernal, 62. *See also* Proserpine
Jupiter, 69. *See also* Zeus
Justice, 2, 200; Dike as divine retribution, 35, 74, 77–78, 82, 153; divine, 131, 135, 159, 186, 202; divine in Christianity, 209, 214, 263–65, 283, 339; of eternal punishment, 267, 283, 318–20, 321–22; ethical theory of Paul, 215, 223; faith as a component of, 218, 256, 340; in Matthew, 1, 232–33, 237, 336; in Plutarch, 77–78, 87; refinement of postmortem, 263, 300; reversal of fate as, 241–42; scale of (*maat*), 12–13, 14, 15, 243–44; secular, 113, 222, 319; secular in Lu-

cretius, 114, 262, 284. *See also* Deuteronomic system of justice; Judgment; Moral death; Poine; Positive tradition of afterlife; Punishment; Symmetrical tradition of afterlife
Justice, reflexive: in Christian afterlife, 218n, 236–37, 285, 286; in Jewish tradition, 151, 152, 192; in Origen, 310, 311–12
Justice, utility of postmortem, 52, 73–76, 82, 107–8, 338; Cicero on, 115–22; Critias on, 108–9; Livy on, 122–23; Lucian on, 123–28; Plato on, 52, 56, 108; Plutarch on, 73–76, 82; Polybius on, 109–11; religious discipline and, 251, 262, 303, 340
Juxtaposition principle, 245, 285–86

Khet, 15–16
Kim, H.C., 280
Kingdom of God. *See* Exclusion from the Kingdom; Heaven
King of Glory, 277
Knowledge of What is in the Other World, Book of, 14
Koheleth, 155, 156n2
Korah's rebellion, 145–46, 248, 250
Kronos (Saturn), 22, 34, 56, 88
Kumma, 10–11
Kurnugi. *See* Babylonian land of the dead

Lakes: Acherusia, 55, 295; of fire, 1, 14, 15, 258, 338; Serser, 15; Stygian, 55
Lamb: Blood of the, 254; Mark of the, 211, 214, 258, 340. *See also* Sacrifice
Lambrecht, Jan, 213n
Land of the Blessed, 15, 56, 70–72
Last Judgment, 1, 217, 224, 251, 256, 259, 294; in Augustine, 324–25, 328; Day of Atonement, 148; in Matthew, 230, 237–38, 316; nations at, 231, 237; raising the dead in, 224; vengeance in, 255, 258. *See also* Christian timeline; Second Coming
Lazarus (in John), 335
Lazarus and Dives, parable of (Luke), 239–40, 243, 272, 276, 327
"Least" or "little ones," Jesus' identification with, 127, 232, 235n13, 237
Legislation. *See* Community of the dead

Netherworld imagery (*cont.*)
131, 160, 169, 215; dirt or clay, 5, 6, 7, 35; fortresses, 5, 8, 68, 69, 336; furnaces, 192; grave(s) and gravestones, 39, 86, 98; halls and palaces, 15, 38, 48; mire (waste), 47, 48, 172, 286; music, 45; sieves, 37, 46, 113; skeletons and skulls, 86, 125, 174; smithy, 82, 83; stench, 301; valleys and abysses, 191, 252; vessels for souls, 55. *See also* Blood; Darkness; Fire; Gates
Netherworlds, Christian. *See* Hell
Netherworlds, Greek. *See* Erebos; Hades; Tartarus
Netherworlds, Jewish. *See* Gehenna; Sheol
Netherworlds, pagan. *See* Babylonian land of the dead; Egyptian netherworld; Hades
Netherworlds, Roman. *See* Orcus
Neutral death, 2, 18, 26, 55, 68; defined, 3; equality of, 4, 26, 32, 86, 126; impatience with, 43, 48, 115, 131, 135, 143, 159–62, 172, 336; Jewish concept of, 336–37; obliterated by Christ, 259, 278; suffering in (blameless), 28, 29- 30, 32–33, 280; *thanatos* in Gospels, 207; uniformity in, 26, 32, 336. *See also* Oblivion
Neutral underworld: categories of dead in, 26, 27, 65; immortality for all in, 12–13, 127; Sheol as, 139–41, 196, 198; as storehouse, 1, 3–11, 172. *See also* Babylonian land of the dead; Community of the dead; Dead (the): banishment of
New Testament: chronology and history of, 205–6, 224–25, 249, 260–61; Gehenna cited in Gospels, 1, 228- 29, 230–31, 246; nomenclature in, 205, 207, 234, 327; the Septuagint, 2, 139, 167–68, 197–98; Synoptic gospels, 206, 207n. 245–46n23. *See also* Intertestamentary period; John (apostle); Luke; Mark; Matthew; Paul; Revelation, Book of
New Testament, nomenclature in, 205, 327; Gehenna, 228, 230–31, 234; Hades, 207, 228, 234, 239, 245–47, 253–55, 259, 305

Nicodemus. *See Gospel of Nicodemus*
Night, 37, 258
Ninevah, 248, 253
Ninshubur, 6
Noah, 135, 187, 234, 248, 252. *See also* Flood; Utnapishtim
Nonbelievers. *See* Unbelievers
Nonconformists, 251, 340, 341; doctrinal differences, 262; "enthusiasts," 209, 211; false prophets, 258, 262; heretics and heresies, 251, 269, 332; malcontents, 169. *See also* Origen; Rebels; Unbelievers
Nothingness in death, 78, 112, 117, 338
Numa, tale of, 122

Oaths, 12, 13, 37–38
Objects in netherworld. *See* Netherworld imagery; Punishment, objects for
Oblivion: death as nothingness, 78, 112, 117, 338; destruction and (Christian), 206–7; destruction and (Jewish), 131, 135, 189, 197. *See also* Death
Oceans, 23n7, 32, 55, 259; of fire, 284
Odysseus, 32, 103; in Hades, 25–31, 61; journey to Hades, 23–24, 25–31, 61; makes offerings to dead, 23- 24; views Tartarus, 31–33
Odyssey, Book 11, 21, 24n8, 32n6; compared with *Aeneid*, 72–73; compared with *Theogony*, 38–39
Offenses. *See* Sins
Offspring: ancestors and, 77, 92; attaining glory through, 30, 32–33, 71; curses related to, 149–50, 152; punishment through, 74–76, 77, 81
Old Testament. *See* Hebrew Bible
Olympian rebels, 22, 33, 38, 41–42, 69–70
Olympian world order, 22, 33, 35, 36, 39, 88
One, God as the, 239, 306–7
Openings to the netherworld, 54, 90, 105; mouthlike or cavelike, 59, 62, 63, 72, 83, 89, 138, 145; the *mundus*, 100, 106; *ploutōnia* and *psychopompeia*, 90. *See also* Life-death boundary
Oral tradition, 89, 133, 206. *See also* Myth; Popular religion
Orcus: administration of, 66–68, 262;

Orcus (*cont.*)

Aeneas's journey through, 62–63, 69-70, 72–73; categories of dead in, 65–69; as a god (Hades), 63. *See also* Hades; Pluto

Origen: on curative punishment, 271- 72, 305, 310–13; *De principiis*, 308n; dynamic view of afterlife, 311, 338; on General Resurrection, 311–12; internal fire in, 311–12; on Jesus, 306–7; life of, 305–6; Neoplatonism of, 306–7; reflexive justice in, 310, 311–12; on resurrection of the body, 311–13; on the soul and will, 307–11, 312; theory of restoration (*apokatastasis*), 307–10, 319, 321; timeline of, 309, 310–11, 313

Orion, 30n, 31, 33

Orpheus, 44

Orphism, 42–44, 50, 340; body-soul dualism of, 43–44, 51; Pindar on, 44–46; Plato on, 50–51

Osiris, 12, 14–17

Other, Jesus as the, 232, 237–38, 263

Ovid, 89, 99, 102, 122

Pagan cults and mysteries, 51n3, 52; of ancient Egypt, 11–12, 14–18; Bacchic cult, 44; Eleusinian Mysteries, 40, 41, 44, 51n5; eternal punishment in, 19, 42, 55, 59, 61; increasing heterogeneity of, 90–92; local differences in myths, 88–89, 91; Orphism, 42–44

Paradise, Four Rivers of, 296

Parentalia, 101

Parousia. *See* Second Coming

Passio, 317

Patriots, 119–20, 121–22

Patroklos, 24, 27, 94

Paul, 214, 222, 313, 338, 340; Christian timeline in, 205, 211–13, 215, 220, 224, 249; on divine wrath, 209, 218–19, 222; epistles of, 206, 209; ethical vs. anthropological views of, 215, 222, 223; on fate of the wicked, 74n21, 211–12, 215–16, 217, 222, 223–24; on grace, 220–21; on the Jews, 218, 221; on the Last Judgment, 209–10, 217–19, 224; life of, 207–8; moral

death in, 214, 305; positive tradition of afterlife in, 207, 209, 210, 216, 218–19, 224, 238; on reconciliation, 210, 223, 262; soul-body relation in, 213–14. *See also* Exclusion from the Kingdom

Paul, Apocalypse of. *See* Apocalypse of Paul

Pausanius, 89, 96

Pelagianism, 271

Penitence. *See* Repentance

Periander, 94–95

Perithous, 20, 70, 88, 89

Persephone, 10, 64, 89; abduction by Hades, 11, 19, 22, 39; cyclical return of, 40; as queen of underworld, 19, 27, 28, 32, 45, 86. *See also* Proserpine

Peter, Apocalypse of. *See* Apocalypse of Peter

Pharisees, 179, 230, 233

Pherecydes, 116

Philosophy. *See* Greco-Roman philosophy

Phlegethon, river, 55

Physicality, desire of souls for, 78, 79

Pilate. *See* Acts of Pilate

Pindar: *Fragments*, 45–46; Orphism and, 44–46 "Second Olympian Ode," 45

Pit(s): of blood, 31, 32; bottomless, 255, 298; of fire, 16–18; lords and dwellers of, 13, 15–16; Sheol as, 141, 146, 163–64, 166, 167, 272. *See also* Gehenna; Tartarus

Plague, 149, 257

Plato, 2, 50n, 116; curative punishment in, 54, 55–57, 337–38; division of the dead in, 55–60, 61, 91–92; earth's geography in, 54–55, 340; eternal punishment in, 55, 59, 61; four fates of, 55–60; on immortality, 60–61; judgment in, 54, 57; on nature of the soul, 52–54, 56–57, 60–61; Orphism and, 50–51; reincarnation in, 59–61, 99, 238; on utility of postmortem justice, 52, 108; on virtue and perfectibility, 55–56, 244

Plato (texts): *Cratylus*, 50, 51n2; *Gorgias*, 56–57, 58, 65, 108, 126, 208; *Laws*, 50, 59n10; *Letters*, 52; *Phaedo*, 19, 53–55, 56, 91–92, 108, 244; *Phaedrus*, 52–53, 54, 56, 75, 76,

Plato (texts) (*cont.*)
116; *Republic*, 51, 52, 58–61, 73, 75, 84, 116, 244
Pliny the Younger, 94
Plotinus, *Enneads*, 306
Plutarch, 74; aerial otherworld in, 76, 78–80, 81, 82–83; categories of the dead in, 79–81; justice in, 77–78, 83; life of, 73, 79; reincarnation in, 76, 81, 83; transformation by punishment in, 77, 78, 80–83; on utility of postmortem punishment, 73–76, 82; whirling souls in, 76, 78, 83, 337; whirlpools and juxtaposed ponds in, 71, 81, 83, 193, 284
Plutarch (texts): *Moralia (Ethical Works)*, 73; *On the Delays of the Divine Vengeance*, 73
Pluto, 41, 42, 63, 86, 90–91, 101, 117, 287n31. *See also* Hades (god)
Poine, 77, 80, 82. *See also* Dike
Polemical functions in religious text, 35, 262, 275, 304, 315
Pollux, 62
Polybius, *Histories*, 109–11
Polytheism, 339. *See also* Pagan cults and mysteries
Poor and needy or "little ones," Jesus' identification with, 127, 232, 235n13, 237
Popular religion: folklore, 293; theology and, 320–21, 325, 332
Porous death. *See* Life-death boundary
Porphyrion, Pomponius, 102
Poseidon, 22, 37, 287n31
Positive tradition of afterlife, 227, 260, 261–62; destruction of or oblivion for wicked in, 207, 239, 254–55, 279, 282; in John, 224–27; in Paul, 207, 209, 210, 216, 218–19, 224, 238. *See also* Exclusion from the Kingdom; Heaven
Postmortem justice. *See* Justice; Punishment
Power: abuse of, 57; of death, 8n10; "words of," 16, 17. *See also* Death, divine power over; Royalty and earthly power
Preacher (the), 155
Priestess. *See* Sybil (priestess)

Priests. *See* Clergy
Progressive immersion, 297
Prometheus, 35–36, 38, 41
Propaganda. *See* Polemical functions in religious text
Prophesies, 72, 79; auguries, 104; of ghosts, 99; as propaganda, 31; from the underworld, 21, 26, 29
Prophets: false, 258, 262; of Hebrew Bible raised by Christ, 252, 273, 304; the twelve, 296. *See also by individual name*
Proportion, principle of, objection based on, 319, 320
Proserpine, or Proserpina, 62, 90–91, 100. *See also* Persephone
Protesilaus, 86–87
Proverbs, 241–42
Providence: biblical, 108, 128, 248, 272; in pagan antiquity, 51, 60, 83, 339
Psychē. *See* Soul
Psychological torment, 77–78, 81, 82, 285
Psychopomp, 183
Punishment: based on offense, 31, 236; cyclical, 55, 303–4; death as, 28, 135, 147, 169, 336; fitting the offense, 70, 283–87, 299; in life, 35, 74, 77, 114, 135–36, 272; long-term, 135–36, 171, 197; retroactive, 172–73; victims or blessed witnessing, 74, 300, 331–32. *See also* Deuteronomic system of justice; Dike; Poine; Purification; Reflexive justice; Suffering
Punishment, curative, 59–60; in Origen, 271–72, 305, 310–13, 317; in Plato, 54, 55–57, 337–38; in Plutarch, 77, 78, 80–82. *See also* Purgatory; Transmutation of souls
Punishment, objects for: anvils, 37; chains, 124, 192, 285, 338; clubs, 31; cook's spit, 287; gibbets, 339; heavy metal nets, 192; irons or rods, 286; pitchforks, 298, 339; razors, 298, 339; sieves, 37, 45–46, 113; tongs, 81; wheels, 70, 287
Punishment, postmortem, 19, 46n42, 52, 61, 68–70, 77–82, 83, 121, 202; in Gospels, 236–39; as superstition, 113–14, 120–21. *See also* Justice, utility of

Punishment, postmortem (cont.)
postmortem; Mitigation of conditions
in death
Punishment, types of: falling, 285, 286,
287; hanging, 285, 289; immersion,
16, 285, 297; lashing and beating, 69;
through offspring, 74–76, 77, 81, 83;
psychological torment, 77–78, 81, 82,
285; repetitive labor, 31, 33, 37, 45–
46, 59, 70, 113; reversal of fate, 125,
126, 165, 246n24, 335; torment and
torture, 82–83, 284, 285
Purgatory, 296n8, 317, 318, 322–23,
326; suffrages and, 322–23, 325- 26.
See also Punishment, curative
Purification: Christian, 264, 326–27;
Jewish sacrifice and, 148; in pagan antiquity, 51, 57, 71, 83, 326
Pyramid Texts, 12
Pythagoras, 3, 44, 116, 127

Qoheleth (Koheleth), 155, 156n2
Qumran community, 183, 190

Raising the dead: in Daniel, 174–75;
Ezekiel prophesying, 173–74; Inan-
na/Ishtar's threats re, 6, 7, 8–10, 335;
Isis revives Osiris, 12, 15; Jesus raises
Lazarus, 335; Saul summoning Samuel,
138–39, 242n; tombs opened in Resurrection, 252; Yahweh (God) from
Sheol, 146
Re (Amon-), 12, 14, 16
Rebels: defeated, 250–51; Korah's rebellion, 145, 248, 250; Prometheus, 35–
36, 38, 41; Salmoneus, 70; superhuman, 20, 69–70; Titans, 22, 33, 38,
41–42, 69–70; Tityos, 31, 33, 38, 70,
113, 333. See also Nonconformists; Satan; Watcher angels
Receptacles for souls, 185, 318, 322,
335; vessels, 55
Reconciliation to death, 85, 210, 223,
262
Redemption, 203, 220, 276, 326; Christ
as redeemer, 276–77; efficacy of
Christ's sacrifice, 210, 225, 264, 337;
legitimating vengeance, 254; retroactive, 273. See also Expiation; Forgiveness; Sacrifice

Reflexive justice: in Christian afterlife,
218n, 236–37, 285, 286; in Jewish
tradition, 151, 152, 192; in Origen,
310, 311–12
Reincarnation, 205; cycles of life and
death, 27, 37, 59–60, 127, 316;
forgetfulness of past lives, 71–72, 86,
126; freedom between lives, 60; Orphic
concepts of, 44; in Plato, 59–61, 98–
99, 238; in Plutarch, 76, 81, 83; revenants, 92. See also Transmigration of
souls
Religion, 135, 146–47, 150–51, 169,
197, 200, 263; authority of, 145; authority of, and postmortem punishment, 251, 262, 303, 340; competing
religions of Roman state, 269–70; false
teachers and bad clergy, 251, 297, 298,
300; functions of theology, 315, 318,
320, 325, 332; Lucretius on, 112, 115;
polemical functions in religious text,
35, 262, 275, 304, 315; reflection on
utility of, 49, 108, 109, 111–18, 121–
22, 123, 128, 339; self-reflexive texts
and, 42. See also Christianity; Divine
authority; Jewish Covenant; Jewish
Temple; Pagan cults and mysteries;
Popular religion; Theology
Remembrance: of the divine, 53, 60; of
dying, 28–29, 33; of the netherworld,
82
Repentance, 218; death as deadline, 205,
240, 241, 242, 316; too late, 301, 330,
332. See also Expiation; Forgiveness
Repetition, 33, 59
Rephaim: giants, 144n21, 197; shades in
Jewish afterlife, 142, 144, 158, 160,
198–99
Reproduction. See Fertility
Restoration principle (apokatastasis),
307–10, 319, 321
Resurrection: Christ's, 1, 205, 211, 252,
258, 305; the General, 211, 213, 241,
249, 284, 317, 335; in Hebrew Bible,
173–75, 192; of Hebrew prophets and
figures, 252, 273, 277, 278, 304; for
the just only, 245–46n23; in Origen,
311–12; in pagan antiquity, 6, 12, 15,
40, 41; timeline from Creation to, 205,
211–13, 214, 220; timeline from, to

Resurrection (*cont.*)
Second Coming, 205, 211–12; tombs
opened in, 252. *See also* Ascension of
Christ; Raising the dead; Universalism
Retribution. *See* Justice; Punishment
Retroactive punishment, 172–73
Retroactive salvation, 273
Revelation, Book of, 1, 191, 192, 228,
234, 259–60, 338; angel Abaddon as
second death, 255; angel Michael slays
dragon, 255–56; blood of the Lamb,
254; book of life, 256, 259; bottomless
pit, 255; Christian timeline in, 316;
earthly power overthrown, 257–58; fire
and brimstone, 256, 281; first Resurrection, 258; four horses, 254–55;
mark of the beast, 256; mother and
child, 255–56; mythic background of,
253; Satan cast into hell, 158–59;
seven angels, 255; seven seals, 254. *See
also* John (apostle)
Reversal of fate. *See* Fate, reversal of
Reversal of offenses, 31
Rhadamanthus, 56, 68, 73, 77, 92, 126,
127
Rich man–poor man story: Egyptian,
242–44; in Hebrew Bible, 124–25; in
Luke and variations, 239–40, 304, 318
Righteousness. *See* Blessedness and virtue
Ritual(s): of cleansing, 148; festivals in
Roman state, 101–4; funeral rites,
26n, 62, 109–10; honoring ancestors,
110, 139, 142, 326; offenses against,
297; rites of Dionysus, 48
Rivers, four heavenly, 296
Rivers of the netherworld, 11, 14, 24, 25,
54–55; Acheron, 23, 48, 55, 89; Co-
cytus, 23, 48, 55; Lethe, 71, 86, 126;
Phlegethon, 55; Styx, 23, 37–38, 48,
89
Roman Catholic Church, 270–71
Roman state, 73, 101–4, 122, 269;
Christianity and, 315; cultural and religious divisions in, 269–70; legitimation of, 2, 71, 73, 109–11, 118–19,
121–23; as model for hell, 259, 262–
63, 340–41
Romulus, 102, 105, 122
Royalty and earthly power, 4, 12, 27,
57–58, 165–66, 198–99; overthrown,

257; unending punishment for, 193–
94. *See also* Social status
Rufinus, 307, 310, 313
Rule of the dead. *See* Community of the
dead; Dead (the): banishment of; Rulers of the dead
Rulers of the dead, 10, 15, 17, 48;
Abraham, 239, 240–41; the Anunnaki,
6, 8; Christ as Lord of death, 223,
224, 272, 305; chthonic gods, 11, 12,
13, 18, 44, 122; the court of Minos,
31, 66–68; Dis or Dispater, 63, 90;
Ereshkigal, 5–8, 9; Hades, 10, 22, 24,
36–37, 39, 86; King Minos, 31, 77,
92, 127; Osiris, 12, 15–17; Persephone, 19, 27, 28, 32, 45, 86; Pluto,
41, 42, 63; Proserpine or Proserpina,
63, 90–91, 100; Rhadamanthus, 68,
73, 77, 92, 126, 127; the *Tchatcha*,
15. *See also* Satan; Titans

Saccas, Ammonius, 306
Sacrifice, 43, 51, 148, 168; animals used
in, 24, 43–44, 148; Christ as Lamb,
254; efficacy of Christ's, 210, 225, 264,
337; offerings to the dead, 3, 23–24,
43–44, 137; offerings to gods, 3, 15,
19, 41n29, 42, 63. *See also* Blood; Redemption; Victims
Sadducees, 179, 230, 233
Salmoneus, 20
Salvation. *See* Redemption
Samuel, 138–39, 242n
Satan: in Book of Job, 156; in Book of
Similitudes, 192; fall and imprisonment
of, 250, 253, 258, 278, 309, 333, 339;
false light of, 217, 250; followers of,
203, 216, 235; in *Gospel of
Nicodemus*, 275–79; the Great Beast,
203, 341; as Lord of underworld, 276;
opposing Christ, 216, 217; thrown into
hell, 258
Satni-Khamois, 243–44
Saturn. *See* Kronos (Saturn)
Saul, King, 138–39, 242n
Scale of justice (*Maat*), 12–13, 14, 15,
243–44
Scapegoat, 148n29. *See also* Redemption;
Sacrifice
Scipio the Elder, 120

Scorpions, 250, 255

Scriptures. *See* Hebrew Bible; New Testament; Septuagint; Theology

Seals, seven, 254

Seas, 23n6, 32, 259; of fire, 284

Second Coming, 1, 211–12, 240, 249, 294, 318; in Augustine, 317; from Resurrection to (timeline), 205, 211–12; suddenness of, 231

Second death, 254, 255, 259–60, 316

Sectarianism, 238

Secular justice, 114, 222, 319; in Lucretius, 114, 262, 284

Seeds, 40, 41, 90–91, 214

Seers, 44, 71; Hecate, 39; oracle at Delphi, 73, 79; Teiresias, 21, 26, 27; witch of Endor, 138–39. *See also* Sybil (priestess)

Segregation of the dead. *See* Dead (the): banishment of

Self-reflexive texts, 42

Semyaz, angel, 183–84, 186

Senosiris, 243–44

Septuagint, 2, 167, 197–98, 251, 317

Sermon on the Mount, 230, 231–33, 234, 236

Serpents: Babylonian, 5; dead in shapes of, 81; Egyptian, 14, 15–16, 17; in Hades, 47; in hell, 250

Serser lake, 15

Set-Heh, 16–17

Seven angels, 255

Seven seals, 254–55

Sexuality, 9–10, 41n29, 189; between angels and women, 181–82, 183–85, 187; crimes of, 70, 211, 217, 260, 286, 298; homo-, 285. *See also* Fertility; Gender

Shades: in pagan antiquity, 26–27, 29, 31–32, 38, 64; *rephaim*, 142, 144, 158, 160, 198–99. *See also* Ghosts

Shadows, 13, 102, 124

Shame, 77–78, 81, 82; in Jewish afterlife, 163, 165, 167, 168

Sheol, 10, 172; distinguished from Ge-Hinnom in Hebrew Bible, 167–68; divisions of dead in, 164–67, 172; as fiery, 146, 242; God reaches into, 144–45, 157, 158, 272, 335; as grave, 135, 140, 142, 143–44, 161, 338; juxta-

position with Gehenna, 197, 199; as neutral death, 139–41, 159–60, 196, 198, 207; pit imagery, 141, 146, 163–64, 166, 167; as place hidden from God, 141, 142–44; tomb imagery, 185, 186, 187; translated as Hades in Septuagint, 139, 167–68, 239. *See also* Abaddon

Sieves, 37, 45–46, 113

"Silent, the," 65, 66, 67

Similitudes, Book of, 181; chronology of, 190–91; parallels with Revelation, 191, 192; punishment and eternal fire in, 192–94. *See also* Enoch, Book of

Sin and evil, 55–56, 127, 217, 309; affecting divinity, 229, 232; community polluted by, 147–48, 151, 201–2, 219–20; existing even to the end, 260, 331–32; expiation and, 11, 55; and free will, 307–9, 316; origin of, 191, 256, 277, 316; as its own punishment, 74, 113; staining the soul, 57, 65, 126, 208. *See also* Punishment; Purification; Satan

Sinners. *See* Repentance; Wicked (the)

Sins: abortion or exposure, 285–86, 299; abuse of power, 57; of angels, 194–95; anger or strife, 217; betrayal, 58; blasphemy, 187, 239, 285; cupidity or greed, 70, 81, 286; drunkenness, 211, 217, 298; envy, 217; failure to honor gods, 19, 41n29, 42, 52; honoring false gods, 211, 217, 260; honoring wrong gods, 11–12, 14–18; hubris or pride, 35, 57, 74, 81; hypocrisy or sycophancy, 124, 211, 297, 298; incest, 70; murder, 55, 260; offenses against ritual, 297; sexual crimes, 70, 211, 217, 260, 285–86, 298; slander, 170; sorcery and magic, 217, 299; thievery, 45, 211; usury, 286, 298

Sisyphus, 31, 33, 45, 113, 115

Sky: fleeing, 259; Uranus, 33

Sleep, 37

Social order, 52, 104n41, 109, 112; centralization and, 139; the community polluted by sin, 147–48, 151, 201–2, 219–20; cosmic order and, 128; derived from God, 221–22; Greek city-state, 49, 57–58; Jewish monarchy,

Tartarus (*cont.*)
55, 68–69; gates to, 11, 37, 38–39,
42; in *Gospel of Nicodemus*, 278,
281–82; Homeric, 22, 31–33; location
of, 11, 22, 34, 37, 38, 298n; mapping
of, 37, 54–55, 68–69; in New Testament, 251; openings from earth to, 59,
72, 83, 90, 105; in Plato, 55–56, 57;
superhuman rebels cast into, 34, 37,
38, 39, 69–70; translated as hell, 251;
in Virgil, 68–70; wicked sent to, 55–
56, 59, 68–69, 281–82, 294
Tchatcha, 15
Teeth, gnashing of, 231, 234, 340. *See
also* Suffering
Teiresias, 21, 26, 27, 124
Temple. *See* Jewish Temple
Temptation, 156
Ten Commandments, 146
Theologizing, 198, 247
Theology: functions of, 315, 318, 320,
325, 332; social order and, 119–20,
128–29
Theseus, 62, 70, 88
Thespesius: crossing life-death boundary,
76–77, 79; vision of otherworld, 76–
82
Three ponds of Plutarch, 81
Time. *See* Christian timeline; Cycles
Time, Antecedent of, 191
Tischendorf, Constantin von, 274, 280
Titanes. See Giants; Titans
Titanic nature, 44, 45n39, 50, 71
Titans, 22, 38, 43–44; fall of, 34, 37, 39.
See also Tartarus
Tityos, 20, 31, 33, 38, 70, 113, 333
Tombs, 14; opened, 252
Topheth, 168, 171, 172. *See also* Gehen-
na
Torah. *See* Hebrew Bible
Tower of Babel, 136
Transmigration of souls, 307–8, 311. *See
also* Reincarnation
Transmutation of souls: by punishment
(Plutarch), 77, 78, 80–83; whirlpools
and ponds for, 71, 81, 83, 193; work-
shop for, 82, 83
Trees: of the cross, 277, 281; fruitless,
295; as gibbets, 284, 339
Trito-Isaiah, 171

Tuat. *See* Egyptian netherworld
Twenty-Four Rhapsodies, 43
Typhoeus, 36–37, 38, 42, 69n
Tyre, destruction of, 146

Unbelievers, 1, 225, 337, 340, 341;
damned, 265, 283, 297–98, 337, 340,
341; as enemies of the Jews, 137, 164,
169, 340; as followers of Satan, 203,
216, 235; gaining faith too late, 283;
John on, 225; severest punishment for,
300–301, 333. *See also* Nonconfor-
mists
Unburied, 335–36; in pagan antiquity,
24–25, 63–64, 93, 94; in Sheol, 164–
67, 172. *See also* Burial; Ghosts
Uncircumcised, 163–64, 165, 166
Underworld. *See* Hell; Netherworld
Unfortunates, 107, 232, 237
Universalism, 207, 222, 226, 310
Unjustly executed, 67
Uranus, 33
Uriel, angel, 183, 186
Usury, 286, 298
Utility. *See* Justice, utility of postmortem;
Religion, reflection on utility of
Utnapishtim, 4–5, 9. *See also* Noah
Utukku, 10

Valley, accursed, 186, 192
Valley of Hinnom. *See* Gehenna
Valley of the Rephaim, 197
Vengeance, 27–28; in the Last Judgment,
255, 258; legitimation of, 254, 263–
65, 282, 300; sublimation of, 152–53,
190, 202
Vessels for souls, 55
Victims, 52, 66, 173, 230; Jesus as victim, 255, 264; as judges, 67–68, 258;
martyrs, 258, 286; scapegoat, 148n29;
witnessing punishment, 74, 300. *See
also* Job; Redemption; Sacrifice
Virgil, 2, 108, 122; on administration of
Orcus, 66–68, 262
Aeneid, 61–70, 73; Aeneas's journey
through Orcus, 62–63; categories of
the dead in, 64–72; compared with
Odyssey, 72–73; land of the blessed
in, 72–73; on reincarnation, 71–72;

Virgil (*cont.*)
superhuman rebels in Tartarus, 69–70
Virgin birth, 301
Virgin Mary, 301, 304
Virtue. *See* Blessedness and virtue
Vision of Paul. See Apocalypse of Paul
Visions. *See* Dreams and visions
Void (Chaos), 33
Voyage of St. Brendan (Heist), 82n
Vultures and flesh-eating birds, 31, 36, 69, 113, 149, 333

Warriors, 27, 29, 65; enemy, 164
Watcher angels, 180–86, 194, 195; whether destroyed or punished, 187, 189, 192–93. *See also* Giants; Satan
Watchers, Book of, 181, 183–87. *See also* Enoch, Book of
Waters of death, 4, 32; drying up or emptying, 31, 46, 113, 259; of judgment, 194; ponds and whirlpools, 71, 81, 83, 193, 284; of Sheol, 146, 158. *See also* Flood; Lakes; Oceans; Rivers of the netherworld
Waters of life, 6, 7, 8, 9, 260, 338; Lake Acherusia, 55, 295
Wells, 300
Wheat and chaff, 230, 233
Wheat and the tares, parable of the, 234–35
Whirling souls, 76, 78, 83, 337
Whirlpools and juxtaposed ponds, 71, 81, 83, 193, 284
Whirlwind, 272
Whore of Babylon, 257
Wicked (the), 211, 234, 255; cast into hell (Matthew), 203, 230, 231, 232–33, 235, 239; as complete criminals, 186; death (oblivion) as fate of (John), 225, 227; destroyed by God (Deuteronomic system), 171, 189, 196, 197;

as enemies of Judah, 137, 164, 169, 340; as enemies of the Lamb and Church, 210, 216, 255, 257, 286; excluded from the Kingdom (Paul), 211–12, 215–16, 217, 222, 223–24; as false teachers and bad clergy, 251, 297, 298, 300; fate of, 220–21, 225, 227, 261, 262, 265; as the incurables, 55, 57, 59; punished in life (Deuteronomic system), 135–36, 147–51, 152, 169, 191, 336; repenting too late, 301, 330, 332; serving Satan, 203, 216, 235; three Christian views on fate of, 206–10; three Jewish views on fate of, 178–79. *See also* Rebels; Unbelievers
Wicked angels. *See* Satan; Watcher angels
Will, 58n; divine, 220, 222, 235, 272; sin and, 307–9, 316
Wind, 170
Wisdom, 46n41; Lord of, 6, 9. *See also* Seers
Wisdom literature, 241
Wisdom of Solomon, 285
Witch of Endor, 138
Witnesses, 74, 285–86, 300, 340; the blessed as, 300, 331–32
Women. *See* Gender; Sexuality
"Words of power," 16, 17
World Soul, 306
Worms, 298, 301, 330. *See also* Fire and the worm
Wrath of God. *See* Divine wrath

Xanthias, 47, 48

Yom Kippur, 148

Zagreus. *See* Dionysus (god)
Zeus, 22, 34, 35, 36, 40, 42, 43, 56, 69, 88; in *Theogony*, 34, 35, 36
Zoroastrian magus, 87, 124

Index of Biblical References